FOR CHRIST
and the
UNIVERSITY

The Story of
InterVarsity Christian Fellowship
of the U.S.A./1 9 4 0 - 1 9 9 0

Keith Hunt & Gladys Hunt

foreword by
John R. W. Stott

INTERVARSITY PRESS
DOWNERS GROVE, ILLINOIS 60515

InterVarsity Press is the book-publishing division of InterVarsity Christian Fellowship, a student movement active on campus at hundreds of universities, colleges and schools of nursing in the United States of America, and a member movement of the International Fellowship of Evangelical Students. For information about local and regional activities, write Public Relations Dept., InterVarsity Christian Fellowship, 6400 Schroeder Rd., P.O. Box 7895, Madison, WI 53707-7895.

ISBN 0-8308-4996-3

Printed in the United States of America ∞

Library of Congress Cataloging-in-Publication Data.

Hunt, Keith.

For Christ and the University: the story of Intervarsity
Chrisitan Fellowship—USA, 1940-1990/Keith Hunt & Gladys Hunt.
    p. cm.
Includes bibliographical references and index.
ISBN 0-8308-4996-3
    1. Inter-Varsity Christian Fellowship—History.   2. College
students—United States—Religious life—History.   I. Hunt, Gladys
M. II. Title.
BV970.I6H83   1992
267'.13—dc20   91-39666
                                                                              CIP

15   14   13   12   11   10   9   8   7   6   5   4   3   2   1
02   01   00   99   98   97   96   95   94   93   92   91

Dedicated to the staff of InterVarsity Christian Fellowship
who, over the past fifty years,
sacrificially served generations of students,
inspiring their vision
for effective university witness,
and the development of a Christian world view.

Foreword

I have been gratefully involved in the worldwide InterVarsity movement since my own student days at Cambridge University in the 1940s. For twenty-five years (from 1952-1977) I had the privilege of leading university missions on five continents, and during the four months of October 1956 to January 1957 I was engaged in student evangelism in seven North American universities at the invitation of the IVCF organizations of Canada and the United States.

Why am I committed to the InterVarsity vision?

First, because it encourages *thoughtful evangelism*. I have always been impressed by Luke's description in Acts of how the apostles "reasoned" with people out of the Scriptures and of how many people in consequence were "persuaded." Of course, God made us emotional as well as intellectual creatures. Nevertheless, our mind is the controlling citadel of our personality, and true evangelism never bypasses the mind. What the Holy Spirit does in conversion is to bring people to Christ, not in spite of the evidence, but because of the evidence when he opens their minds to attend to it. In the New Testament, conversion is not infrequently portrayed as a response not only to Christ but to "the truth," even to a "form of teaching" (Rom 6:17). InterVarsity encourages the kind of evangelism which expects a total commitment to the total Christ.

Second, InterVarsity goes beyond conversion to *discipleship*. It does not win people in order to abandon them. On the contrary, it is concerned to nurture converts, especially through disciplined habits of prayer, Bible study and church membership, into maturity in Christ. In this connection Colossians 1:28-30 have always been important verses for me. Here the apostle Paul summarizes his goal, which is not just to preach Christ and win converts, but rather so to proclaim Christ in his fullness as to present each convert "mature in Christ." To this end, he adds, he bends all his God-inspired energies. Moreover, Christian maturity includes Christlikeness of character and conduct, indeed the integration of our whole human personality under the lordship of Christ.

Third, the International Fellowship of Evangelical Students, of which IVCF-USA is a member, has from the beginning been committed to *indigenous principles,* that is, to developing a worldwide fellowship of autonomous, national, evangelical student movements. There has never been any attempt to control the movement from a distant headquarters in Europe or America. Instead, each national movement has been free (within a commonly accepted doctrine and ethos) to develop its own identity and its own program. Moreover, each national movement has itself encouraged student leadership. It is this principle, I believe, which explains why so many of today's Third World evangelical leaders have had an IFES background and upbringing.

John R. W. Stott, rector emeritus
All Souls Church—London

Preface

> "Look to the LORD and his strength; seek his face always. Remember the wonders he has done, his miracles, and the judgments he pronounced. . . . He remembers his covenant forever, the word he commanded, for a thousand generations." 1 Chronicles 16:11-12, 15 (NIV)

One of the most frequent direct commands of the entire Bible is that God's people should "remember" their past and what God has done for them. They are to establish memorials (1 Samuel 7:12), they are to hold feasts of remembrance (Exodus 13:14-16), they are to sing of his mighty acts (Psalm 105; Hebrews 11). Although we seldom reflect on it, every time we set aside a day to worship or share communion together, we do so because God has told us to remember. Why?

First, we remember because it is in the nature of God himself to remember, and we want to be like him. He is the God who has remembered his covenant with his people and will do so for a thousand generations. In Hebrew the word *remember* means "to imprint." Except in the area of our sins, about which there are a number of prayers asking that God might forget, it is comforting to know that we serve a God of utter consistency and faithfulness. He will not forget his promises.

Second, we are to remember because it is a sure way for us to get in touch with the reality of what God has done. Sometimes it is hard to see

God in the present moment or to trust him with the future. He can seem silent or distant, and we can wonder whether he will be faithful to us this time. Looking at and celebrating what God has done in the past, and how he has worked in the lives of others, reminds us of his character—his faithfulness, his love, his timing and his power which have been so evident and real. Remembering helps us to trust him in the present. It encourages our perseverance and our endurance. And it stimulates our hope as we look to the future.

As an organization, we are pleased to celebrate fifty years of commitment to students with a purpose that has not changed, a vision that has not diminished and a dedication to Scripture that has not been diluted. But even more so, it is a privilege to reflect on the part which InterVarsity has played in Christ's kingdom, "so that people may see and know, may consider and understand, that the hand of the LORD has done this, that the Holy One of Israel has created it" (Isaiah 41:20).

Steve Hayner, president
InterVarsity Christian Fellowship—USA

Acknowledgments

Many people were eager to help us in the adventure of history writing. In the course of researching material we moved most of the scattered archival materials of InterVarsity Christian Fellowship into the archives of the Billy Graham Center in Wheaton, Illinois. Our gratitude goes to the board of InterVarsity for the decision to place these valuable documents in proper archival space. This not only saved the collection, but saved us from working in dusty attic space and made available the comfortable and convenient facilities of the archival research center. Our thanks to archivist Paul Erickson of the Billy Graham Center for his help in this project.

Our research led us to interview about two hundred people who have played a significant role in InterVarsity's past and present. Most of these interviews were transcribed by Ruth Shaw, who volunteered herself and her friends for this awesome task. When she agreed to do this, she had no idea of the extent of the undertaking. Her work made the information readily available to us.

Those interviewed shared their own experiences and gave us pertinent facts, additional documents, insights and dates that helped frame the larger picture of our history. We are grateful for their time and fellowship, and were especially impressed with the loyalty and affection of graduates and past staff members. In almost every case there was a healthy nostalgia in their remembering and a feeling of deep gratitude for the values received from their involvement with InterVarsity. We felt a great loss at the death of Joseph T. Bayly. He died in 1986 just before this project began, and we are the poorer without his contributions to this manuscript.

A manuscript advisory group met with us regularly to go over our manuscript drafts. It was composed of Robert Frykenberg, professor, department of history at University of Wisconsin (Madison); Pete Hammond, director of IVCF's Marketplace ministry; Andy Le Peau, IVP editorial director; James Nyquist, former IVCF staff, now IFES consultant; Dawn Pickard, former IVCF staff, now faculty member at Oakland University (Michigan); James Reapsome, former IV staff member, board member and editor of Missionary Information News Service; and Tom Trevethan, IVCF area director. They were not only a source of encouragement, but an inspiration to us. They helped us catch mistakes of fact and nuance. We are deeply indebted to them for the time they gave from their busy lives. Each of them has a long history with InterVarsity. Yvonne Vinkemulder, IVCF legal counsel, produced materials. John Alexander, president emeritus, and Steve Hayner, IVCF president, also made valuable manuscript contributions.

Our association with Andy Le Peau, editorial director of InterVarsity Press, and Jim Hoover, managing and academic books editor at IVP, has been a pleasure. Kathy Lay Burrows's creative work on the layout of the book brings joy to a writer's heart.

More people than we can mention sent us documents, stories and encouragement. The friendship and inspiration of Douglas Johnson, the first general secretary of the British Inter-Varsity and author of its history, *Contending for the Faith,* is a gift we treasure. How can anyone understand the roots of InterVarsity without knowing this great champion of student work?

C. Stacey Woods, who pursued with relentless perseverance his vision for student work around the world, left few papers behind, considering his prolific output. He died in Switzerland on April 10, 1983, after a brief illness, at the age of seventy-three. Copies of some of his letters are in the archives, but he had already thrown out far more than he saved. We are grateful for the two books he wrote as memoirs of his time with the Fellowship. Stories about him were fresh in the minds of many of the people we interviewed. He left a deep impression on anyone who knew him, and we, too, remember him with thankfulness and affection. "Remember your leaders, those who spoke the word of God; consider the outcome of their life, and imitate their faith" (Hebrews 13:7). The friendship of his wife, Yvonne K. Woods, has meant much to us. We have found her insights and support valuable and uplifting.

Charles H. Troutman, who died on November 18, 1990, at the age of seventy-six, was tireless in helping us find important documents. Charles was a natural archivist and historian himself, and he gave us free access to his unpublished papers. We sought his advice on many occasions. He was pleased when we decided to begin with an historical overview of how students had influenced the expansion of Christian faith over the centuries. He had long wanted someone to do this and gave us research that he had already done on this subject. We owe him a great debt, not just for his help in this project, but for his godly influence in our lives.

Large numbers of people, including our children, realized the enormity of the task we were undertaking and prayed for us. We probably owe the completion of this project to them. It is difficult to adequately thank people for this kind of loyalty. We have known the excitement of the Holy Spirit's help and inspiration as we attempted to be accurate word-smiths in recording what has happened in this important work of God. Our own lives have been enriched as we have worked together. While we give gratitude to many, the responsibility for the end product of this history is ours.

Keith and Gladys Hunt

Introduction

C. Stacey Woods came running down the hill and onto the dock just as the barge was pulling away from the island, headed for the mainland. The 1948 staff training had ended at Campus-in-the-Woods, and along with it the heavy decisions of dividing student work for the whole country among twenty staff members. In their last meeting they had been throwing states around like ping-pong balls. Anne Childs (Hummel), a recent graduate of Wellesley College and newly appointed staff member, was assigned to pioneer student work in North and South Carolina and Georgia. Now, over the din of laughter and conversation on the moving barge, Stacey Woods, with a sheaf of papers in his hand, was gesticulating wildly to catch the attention of the departing staff and calling out, "Anne, Anne. Take Florida too!"

It's a favorite Inter-Varsity story because it tells so much about the spirit of the early days. (It is entirely believable, even though somewhat apocryphal since it was Regional Director Joe Bayly, rather than Stacey Woods, who called out to Anne, and the state was Virginia.) We were pioneering a student movement in a vast country, with small resources except for the expectation and the vision given by the Holy Spirit. Inter-Varsity Christian Fellowship was eight years old then, begun officially in 1940, but four of these years had felt the stress of war with all its limitations and surprises.

The phenomenal growth of the student movement was directly related to the principle of student initiative. A folder published in the 1942-43 school year, while World War 2 was still in progress, showed work on over one hundred twenty campuses with only eight staffworkers, plus Stacey Woods, general secretary. (See Timeline beginning page 385.) The work was a merging of two strands of evangelical student witness: the first, the alive and growing movement of students in Britain called the Inter-Varsity Fellowship, and the second, the frayed threads of a long history of evangelical student witness in the United States.

Initiating the work of "the Fellowship," as it was called, was a matter of *kairos*: it was the right time. The religious climate within America in the 1930s was a clarion call for action. The method and philosophy of the student movement grew out of the effectiveness of student witness over the centuries. In writing about Cambridge students, John Pollock began, "This is the story of *ordinary* men and this may be *repeated.*" John R. Mott, speaking in Rochester, New York, in 1943 had said, "My work the world over and across the many years has shown me that young men and women can be trusted with great loads and great responsibilities. Youth have never disappointed me when I have put heavy burdens on them." He believed that "heroic appeal makes possible heroic action."

What happened on the campus during World War 2 was evidence that student witness was the best principle. So convinced were the early leaders of Inter-Varsity about the strength of indigenous witness that Charles Troutman, who did the first Inter-Varsity staff work in the States, later commented, "Student initiative is so natural and necessary in the university world that, if any organization abandons it, God will raise up another movement which will place student leadership as its operating principle."

While both C. Stacey Woods and Charles H. Troutman, Jr., are rightly called "founders" of the Inter-Varsity movement in the United States, it is important to note that evangelical Christian student groups existed independently on a number of campuses across the country. Many of these were struggling groups without a clear focus and, when they heard of the Inter-Varsity movement, they gladly became part of it, eager to link up with a national movement among students. Yet it is one of the myths that grow up around organizational principles that student initiative alone brought about the work of Inter-Varsity. Where the work has flourished, it has always been the result of initiative on all fronts. The prodigious energy of men like Stacey Woods and Charles Troutman—indeed, of all the early staff—changed not only the thinking of a segment of the evangelical Christian world, but its shape.

1/On Writing History

Writing the history of this significant organization has been a challenge. Someone said that to be a good historian you must love your subject. In that sense we qualify. Following active involvement as undergraduates in an Inter-Varsity chapter, we have spent forty years of our lives on the staff of Inter-Varsity, champions of students and their ministry on campus.

We are not writing this history primarily to instruct, but to tell a story. Our task is not to make Inter-Varsity look good or to make it look bad. It is to tell what happened. After telling the story, we see in retrospect that many threads are woven into the events we recounted. The threads have not been placed there by design; they came out of the story and are the "stuff of human organizations."

We have lived through much of Inter-Varsity's history, which brings its own strengths and disadvantages. We have been inside the events we write about. On the other hand, we have tried to be objective. We discovered a surprising benefit in our research: the more research we did, the more detached we became from the events. However, there is no such thing as a neutral or purely objective historian. "Without an opinion a historian would be like a metronome . . . and his work would be unreadable," writes historian Barbara Tuchman. The historian has to choose what to include and what to leave out. That very fact brings a subjectivity to the task.

History is not just dates and places, important as these are; it is primarily people, real people with daring and vision. History is people who laugh and cry, who are exhilarated and frustrated, who are sometimes caught in the trap of events and the actions of others. History is people who know both triumph and failure. History is life.

The study of history is not a nostalgia trip or an enslavement to the past, but an exercise liberating us from both the past and the present. It is not the remembered past but the forgotten past that enslaves us. The study of history also frees us from our enslavement to recent events, from what C. S. Lewis calls "the idols of our own marketplace." It pushes us to take a long look. Henry Ford once said that "the farther you look back, the farther you can look ahead."

We learn from history when we see the issues of the past are essentially the issues of today. While the past can't provide us with neat formulas, it can establish a context, emphasize a pattern and point in a direction. Mark Twain is reputed to have quipped, "History doesn't repeat itself, but sometimes it rhymes." The whole of history is bound up in what God is doing among people, and it involves ordinary and extraordinary men and women, known and unknown.

One of the hazards of writing history is a preconceived notion of what history should tell us. Such a history ends up stronger in ideology than in historical understanding. Our intent has been to tell the story of Inter-Varsity as it was when it happened, not from the perspective of hindsight. We sought out primary sources in order that what has happened not be edited by present understanding. We have used chronological narrative, roughly by decades, to recount what happened with some of the coexisting crosscurrents and countercurrents of that day. Readers can draw their own conclusions. We have tried to tell what happened within the disciplined framework of our research. Distilling the facts is the hardest job. We had to decide what to leave out and when to stop. The search for truth is never done. Research has its own beguiling effects. We have been seduced down some trails that led to the inconsequential. Research can go on forever.

2/The Historical Context of Student Witness
We began our history a long way in the past. We became intrigued with the role students have played in spreading the Christian message in the years since the founding of the modern university in A.D. 1090. This "pre-history" proved an exciting detour on the way to understanding our own history and helped us put the story of Inter-Varsity in context. Although we do not claim to have ferreted out all the evidence, what we found was enough to lead us to the conclusion that students have played a significant role in building the kingdom of God. The Inter-Varsity movement is an extension of student initiative that has existed since the earliest days.

Readers may observe that the weight of historical details for Inter-Varsity's history rests on the earlier years. (This is especially true in the use of photographs.) This choice was made with some deliberation, since the past is harder for contemporary readers to discover. Weighting the past years will disappoint some of the very fine cadre of men and women now leading the movement who deserve their own place in history. It is also easier to chronicle the past than the present. Contemporary events lack perspective; "everything is in the foreground and appears the same size," to quote Tuchman, who questions whether history can or should be written while it is still smoking.

3/Some Further Notes
We truly regret that the complexity and size of the story we have written required us to keep details lean. It is disappointing that we could not

include a comprehensive listing of all the people who have given years of their lives to InterVarsity work. Therefore, readers of this book may look and not find the name of a favorite staffworker whose influence marked their personal lives. We acknowledge with thankfulness the rich contribution made to InterVarsity by those many people not mentioned in this book simply because of space limitations. These include hundreds of effective campus staffworkers and office staff; spouses who played a crucial part while receiving little thanks and no money for their involvement; valuable board members who gave energy and wisdom; volunteers and praying friends without whom the movement would not exist. Their being omitted from this book in no way diminishes their contribution.

The notes in the book are extensive and contain many wonderful stories, as well as illuminating details, that would have been distracting in the text. We suggest you *read with a marker in the notes and follow them carefully.*

This is no bloodless, faceless story. We did not skip over our troubles, as some suggested we should. That would not be history. All the players in this history are good people, intent on doing their best in the situations in which they found themselves. That they experienced pain or made poor decisions or did glorious deeds is all part of the human story. But there is more. It can't all be told. No history is ever quite finished. As you read, we invite you to add your insights and come to your own conclusions.

1
A Long Look at Student Witness

There is no place like the university for the sharpening and expansion of the Christian faith.[1]
Charles H. Troutman, *general director, Inter-Varsity Christian Fellowship*

Universities are centers for ideas and action. That is why tyrants want them closed down. The climate of the university provides a unique environment for inquiry and, at its best, inspires an idealism that changes the world. Student leadership has introduced reforms, led to powerful freedom movements and brought down kings and rulers.

What is often unknown and unsung is the role university students and professors have played in Christian witness and in the preservation of truth over the centuries.[2] Student initiative in religious matters was seldom, if ever, encouraged by the power structure. Instead it was viewed as a kind of dangerous radicalism. Student initiative in matters of faith existed then and now because of a dynamic within human beings. An "inconsolable longing," a wistfulness about eternity has marked the lives of thoughtful men and women. C. S. Lewis described it as a "lifelong nostalgia, our longing to be reunited with something in the universe from which we now feel cut off"[3]—a conviction that we are not a product of a materialistic universe. It drives men and women to pursue Truth.

Charles Troutman's statement: "There is no place like the university for the sharpening and expansion of Christian faith," stops the reader cold. Hardly any one today thinks of the university as a place where the Christian faith is honed and expanded. Rather they believe the reverse is true. The university has become a place that gives credentials for a career, a profession. Few enter its doors who seek only to be educated and to discover truth. Yet it remains uniquely a place where questions are asked and answers sought. The complexity of life insists that those who are listening ask the right questions.

What has the university offered, during the thousand years of its existence, that has contributed to the extension of Christian faith and sharpened individual understanding of it? It is a study worth pursuing. What students have dared to do through the centuries, and the significance of their actions, are an important part of the history of the church of Jesus Christ and provides the setting for Inter-Varsity Christian Fellowship (IVCF). The story goes back a long way. The few historical references given here in no way encompass all that has happened since the founding of the university at Bologna, Italy, about A.D. 1090.

1/Pre-Reformation Student Heroes

Before universities existed, even in the most rudimentary form, Pierre Abelard (1079-1142) was content to be disinherited rather than abandon the life of a student. In his search for meaning, he wandered from one cathedral school in France to another, sharpening his reason and questioning the presuppositions of his teachers. In his pursuit of truth, Abelard became the originator of the method of inquiry that eventually brought the university into being. While scholars today name him the greatest intellect of the Middle Ages, Rome twice condemned him. When he was exiled by the church in Paris to a crude thatched hut in the country, three thousand students paid little heed to the ban on his teaching. They unwittingly formed an unofficial university, pitching their tents in the fields to study with this great scholar. Although it took sixty years for the establishment of an official university in Paris, these students made a beginning with their insistence on the right to free inquiry. This was the intellectual movement out of which the university came into being.[4]

A century and a half later, while still a student, John Wycliffe (1329-1384) became a popular lecturer at Oxford University. Lecturing as an undergraduate was not uncommon for outstanding students. It was Wycliffe's reputation of scholarship that gave weight to his theological teaching and made his influence long-lasting, later called Wyclifism. The classes he taught were crowded and his ideas had the support of fellow students and part of the faculty. He reasoned that some of the practices of the Church did not conform to Scripture. He initiated biblical reform, not by appealing to bishops or the pope, but by translating the Bible from Latin into English so the common people could understand. Then he organized students into preaching bands, sending them into the countryside to explain the gospel.

Wycliffe contended that Scripture was the supreme authority in matters of salvation. This threatened the ecclesiastical power structure. Severe persecution followed and while Wycliffe survived, some of his student preachers did not. The Bible groups went underground, and some secretly perpetuated themselves until the English Reformation nearly two centuries later. Wycliffe was condemned as a heretic some thirty years after his death, but well before then his teaching had spread across the English Channel to Europe.

Students from the Continent who were studying at Oxford took their notes of John Wycliffe's brilliant lectures back to their home countries. John Hus (1372-1415) was a student in Prague when he first read Wycliffe's notes and was so greatly influenced by them that he became a prominent exponent of Wycliffe's writings. As a student who also lectured at the university, Hus spoke powerfully about the sufficiency of Scripture in matters of life and faith. When he became a member of the faculty of liberal arts and later dean of faculty, his influential position gave weight to his teaching, which, in turn, also became more controversial. In 1415 he was tried for heresy by the Council of Constance, found guilty and burned at the stake. His numerous followers carried on his teaching, igniting ideas of freedom for religious thought and biblical truth that remained alive in the Bohemian Brethren, or Hussites, as they were called. Persecution over the next three hundred years caused them to flee to various parts of Europe where their ideas enlightened others, spreading the influence of Hus far beyond the borders of Bohemia.

Sometimes it was a professor who led the way to Truth. Desiderius Erasmus (c. 1469-1536), probably the greatest of the Renaissance scholars, did more to bring about pre-Reformation thinking than any other person. He was at heart a literary man, not a philosopher or a theologian, but his own experience of monastic life and the self-aggrandizement of religious leaders led him to advocate a return to the Bible and the simplicity of the early church. During his first visit to Cambridge, Erasmus completed his editing of the New Testament in Greek, with his own Latin translation in parallel columns. This was published in 1516 and its impact was devastating to the Church because of the errors it revealed in the Vulgate.

During the time that Erasmus was translating the New Testament, his lectures at Cambridge University attracted increasing numbers of students. In the late afternoon or by candlelight, students would gather in his private rooms to listen as Erasmus went through the text of the New Testament, line upon line, explaining and teaching, never realizing that many of them would later be burned at the stake for the faith they were finding under his exposition. He allowed the Scripture to speak with authority and this gave students a deep hunger to study the Bible. In his rooms at Cambridge, Erasmus restored the Bible to the church.

Erasmus's Greek New Testament was widely read, along with the writings of his younger contemporary, Martin Luther, in Cambridge and other universities of northern Europe. King Henry VIII banned Luther's writings from entering England, but ships from Holland and Germany had no difficulty in dumping contraband cargo along the East Anglia coast. Stories tell that local farmers retrieved the cargo and, in the case of the small "Lutheran" books, they knew who wanted them. They hollowed out large cabbage heads to hide the books and then proceeded upstream to the first bridge over the Cam River. Students would hurl stones—and among them the appropriate coins—in a mock prank, and the farmers would hurl cabbages back in "self-defense." Students have always found a way to avoid censorship!

2/Reformation Leaders

Martin Luther (1483-1546) became a student at the university at Erfurt, Germany, in 1501. There he found a copy of the Latin Bible in the university library. Although almost twenty years old, he had never seen a Bible nor held one in his hands. He opened it at random and followed the story of Samuel and his mother on the first pages that met his eyes. Though the words he read offered little to ease the burden of guilt he felt, he saw for the first time that the Bible contained more than the few verses read and explained in the church. He was a brilliant student, but he was not at peace with God and desperately afraid of dying. Though he took Communion daily and put himself under disciplines, these did not help, and he was often in a deep depression.

On one occasion a lightning bolt struck nearby and the frightened Luther resolved to become a monk, as if to appease God. While a student at the

Augustinian monastery he rigorously studied Scripture on his own. Eventually he came to understand the gospel truth that "the just shall live by faith," an enlightenment that changed his whole life and the witness of the Christian church. *Kairos.* It was the right time. When we picture Luther writing his Ninety-five Theses and taking his courageous stand against the corruption and power of the Church of Rome, it is important to remember that he was thirty-two years old and had wrestled with these truths since his student days.

The winds of student unrest were blowing elsewhere across the Continent. In Switzerland, a student named Huldreich Zwingli (1484-1531) developed a hunger to read the New Testament in Greek and to learn "of the teachings of Christ from the original sources." He came to personal faith in Christ during his student days. Later, when he had matured in his understanding of the Bible, he used his position to initiate a radical program of reform, which included the use of Scripture as the guide for faith and practice and a rejection of the papacy.

Some years later he came into conflict with his own youthful disciples when they believed that, under pressure from the Zurich city council, Zwingli had compromised his beliefs about the conduct of the Lord's Supper. Students have always had the freedom to ask questions, to resist institutional rigidity and to take risks. These took the risk of meeting for home Bible study, which the law forbade. They began re-baptizing each other, and later were called Anabaptists.

When John Calvin (1509-1564) became a law student at Orleans, France, among his fellow students were those who had found a new faith in Christ. One of his younger lecturers was privately "a Lutheran." These new beliefs were the subject of many student discussions in the cafes of Orleans. In only two places in his later writings does Calvin refer to his student days. In the preface of his *Commentary on the Psalms* he states that in the course of his law studies "by a sudden conversion, He tamed my heart and made it teachable." In his great apology for the Reformation, his *Letter to Sadolet,* Calvin reveals that as a student he felt overwhelmed by his sinfulness, and had a hunger for something of which he was not sure. His experience was repeated many times in the lives of students during this half century and led some to a martyr's death.

News of new-found faith among the Orleans law students brought action from the Inquisition. Calvin fled to Geneva. During Calvin's lifetime, Geneva became the great Christian city and the center of the Reformation as no other city in Europe. Calvin became the leader of the French Protestants or Huguenots from whom the English Puritans received their theology.

The Spirit of God seemed to be stirring students everywhere. While Zwingli was finding faith and sharing it in Geneva, another student in England began his spiritual journey. Thomas Bilney (1494-1531) came to Cambridge just after Erasmus's visit while the excitement of his lectures and translation work was still strong. Bilney heard some of his student friends "speak of Jesus" in such a personal way that he was led to purchase a Latin Bible and begin reading. The words of 1 Timothy 1:15, "It is a true saying and worthy of all men to be embraced that Christ Jesus came into the world to save sinners," brought him to personal faith. Later he became a lecturer in order to continue his studies. In his enthusiasm for Scripture he rented facilities in the White Horse Inn so that he could share his Bible studies with all who cared to come. As news leaked out about these studies, people associated Bilney with Martin Luther and some began to refer to the inn as "Little Germany." Bilney became the first of the Cambridge students to take a strong stand for the reformation of the church.

This irregular activity of a junior lecturer leading studies from the Bible aroused the indignation of Hugh Latimer (1485-1555), one of the prestigious "Twelve Preachers" at Cambridge. Listening to his tirades against "these new ideas," Bilney recognized in Latimer a man who had a troubled heart. Taking an unusual step, Bilney went to Latimer and asked him to hear his confession. When Latimer agreed, Bilney poured out his own experience of finding peace and confidence in the work of Jesus Christ.

Latimer was later to tell how Bilney's words had caught his heart, evoking a familiar echo of his own search. He heard the Holy Spirit speaking to him. For Cambridge University, the conversion of Latimer was as cataclysmic as that of the apostle Paul. Because of his prominent position in the university Latimer's declaration of personal faith had great impact at both Cambridge and Oxford, and many in academia became believers. One of these was Thomas Cranmer (1489-1555) who later became archbishop of Canterbury. All three of these men—Bilney, Latimer and Cranmer—eventually were martyred. The words of Bishop Hugh Latimer, who was burned at the stake with Bishop Ridley, are prophetic as well as a reminder of the cost of personal faith: "Be of good comfort, Master Ridley, and play the man; we shall this day light such a candle, by God's grace, in England, as I trust shall never be put out."[5]

One of the students who came to Bilney's Bible studies at the White Horse Inn was William Tyndale (1492-1536) whose faith was greatly enhanced by his association with these earnest Christians. Tyndale exemplified a growing belief that the reform of the church and the salvation of men and women depended upon dispelling spiritual ignorance through a knowledge of Scripture, the sure word of God. He dedicated himself to translating the New Testament and parts of the Old Testament into the common language, something that had not been done since the days of Wycliffe. His work laid the foundation for later English versions. When the conflagration excited by Luther began to reach English shores, it found flames already kindled by the Bible readings of Tyndale in Magdalen Hall at Cambridge.[6] Later he, too, was martyred.

It is hardly too much to say that the existence of universities made the Reformation a possibility. The use of Latin as the language of academic life threw open the lecture room of a university to every part of Europe.[7] The Reformation did not begin with the nailing of the Ninety-five Theses to the door of the Wittenburg Church, significant as that was. It had been coming for hundreds of years as thoughtful, courageous students and professors made inquiry into truth and propagated their convictions. The Reformation was born in the university.

3/Truth Kept Alive in Music

Luther gave another spiritual gift to the church. His love of music and the hymns he wrote set a precedent for the Reformation church to become a singing church. Out of their personal dealings with God and the challenge of this chaotic period in the 1600s, believers wrote many of the hymns students have been singing ever since that time. Some are found in Inter-Varsity Press's *Hymns II:*

"O Sacred Head Now Wounded," attributed to Bernard of Clairvaux (1150), translated by Paul Gerhardt (1607-1676)

"Now Thank We All Our God," Martin Rinkart (1586-1649)

"The God of Love My Shepherd Is," George Herbert (1593-1632)

"Let Us with a Gladsome Mind," John Milton (1608-1674)

"Jesus, Priceless Treasure," Johann Franck (1618-1677)

"If Thou but Suffer God to Guide Thee," Georg Neumark (1621-1681)

"Thee Will I Love, My Strength," Johann Scheffler (1624-1677)

"My Song Is Love Unknown," Samuel Crossman (1624-1683)

"Glory to Thee, My God," and "Awake My Soul," Thomas Ken (1637-1711)

"The Lord's My Shepherd," Scottish Psalter (1650)

"Praise to the Lord, the Almighty," Joachim Neander (1650-1680)

"Fairest Lord Jesus," *Gesangbuch* Münster (1677)
The events that culminated in the Protestant Reformation were more than philosophical and religious. Power structures were challenged and political alignments changed. Persecution came from all sides according to religious conviction. Violation of perceived orthodoxy was both a civil and religious offense. Thousands met death.

Moreover, out of the conflict and suffering of these religious wars came a second Reformation: Spiritual revival broke out in the "believing" church. In Germany Jacob Spener (1635-1705) led a movement called Pietism and founded a university in Halle that became a center of Christian outreach. Here, under the leadership of A. H. Francke (1663-1727) the first Protestant students responded to the call of missions and the evangelization of the world. It has been said that the first Reformation rescued believers within the Church; the second Reformation gave the believers a missionary vision. Subsequent student groups have been deeply affected by the pietistic movement, including the Inter-Varsity Christian Fellowship 250 years later.

4/The Organization of Student Groups
The earliest record of a formally organized, student-initiated Christian student group in Great Britain is at Aberdeen, Scotland. In 1665, fifteen-year-old Henry Scougal entered the university and there brought the more serious of his fellow students together, organizing a "Religious Society" for prayer, Bible study and fellowship. A few years later he was made professor of divinity at Aberdeen. Although he died at the age of twenty-seven, he left a valuable legacy in what was to become a most influential devotional book in the subsequent century, *The Life of God in the Soul of Man.* Appended to this book were the rules for his student religious society.[8] These rules and this small student group later served as a prototype for the formation of the Holy Club at Oxford as well as the Praying Societies of eighteenth-century Scotland.

Susannah Wesley so valued this devotional book that she lent "this excellent good book" to her sons, John and Charles, when they went to Oxford University. John and Charles Wesley were repulsed by the immoral life they found at the university and decided to protect themselves from backsliding by strict spiritual disciplines. They gathered around them others of similar convictions. Scougal's rules for the student society became the basis of "the Holy Club"[9] founded in 1729 by the Wesleys, with about twenty-seven members. (Later John Wesley (1703-1791)[10] was to borrow freely from Scougal in instructing his lay preachers.)

Meanwhile Charles Wesley (1707-1788) lent this same small volume to the spiritually restless George Whitefield (1714-1770), who was converted through reading it. He was the first member of the Holy Club to see salvation as a gift of God, not the result of good works. His conversion started the evangelical revival in Britain. Only a few years later his preaching marked the beginning of the Great Awakening in the thirteen colonies of British America, profoundly affecting the vitality of student witness in the colonies. The ever-widening ripples from the faithfulness and initiative of one student after another continues to this day; it is essentially the theme of this book.

On the Continent, Count Nikolaus Ludwig von Zinzendorf (1700-1760) studied in the *paedagogium* (high school) in Halle, Germany, in the early 1700s. With five other boys he formed the Order of the Grain of Mustard Seed, a secret spiritual society whose members were bound together in prayer. Their purpose was to witness to the power of Jesus Christ, to draw other serious students into fellowship and to carry the gospel of Christ overseas. Zinzendorf took this same vision to his university days at Wittenburg and Utrecht. It is not surprising that he later became the leader of the Moravians, one of the great missionary movements of the eighteenth century.[11]

Many years later, in 1825, another student at the University of Halle, a leader in the mad pranks of a hard-drinking, profane crowd of students, had his life changed by an encounter with a small group of eight Christian students. These students, whose names remain unknown to the world, met daily to pray on campus. "Along toward the close of my university course," he said, "something seemed to go wrong with me. I was not sick, and I had no misfortune, but I was unhappy." His unhappiness only increased, despite his efforts to study harder and be more sociable. He goes on,

Then I remembered the eight Christian students who had a prayer meeting. I was promptly on hand at the hour. A chapter in the Bible was read, a few prayers offered, some remarks were made, and the prayer meeting was over. But I detained the young men and told them my case. I said, "I don't know if it is what you have that I need, but tell me what it is." One and another told me of Christ. At last I saw Christ as my Savior and a great love for Christ filled my soul.

That man was George Mueller (1805-1898), who established a work among orphans which ministered to as many as 2,000 children, depending on God for their sustenance. His practical faith has inspired thousands.[12]

5/The Legacy of Charles Simeon

Prejudice against "religious enthusiasm" was strong at both Cambridge and Oxford Universities. By this time both were strongholds of the formal Church of England and students suspected of definite evangelical sympathies were usually censured. In 1661 when William Penn, the Quaker founder of Pennsylvania, was a student at Oxford, he was "sent down" for non-conformity. From boyhood he had a strong bent toward pietism and while at Oxford he corresponded with John Owen and listened to the discourses of the Quaker Thomas Loe. This was unacceptable.[13]

In 1778 six students were expelled from Oxford on trumped-up charges when it was discovered that they met for Bible study. Evangelical piety was virtually unrepresented in the university scene in the late 1700s; Methodist or other Free Church influences were greatly feared. The Wesley brothers, Whitefield and other members of the Holy Club had not endeared themselves to the university community or to the Church of England with their "vulgar" expressions of faith and open-air preaching.

Two men were particularly used by God to break the stranglehold of formal religion at Cambridge. The first was Charles Simeon and the second Isaac Milner, who became a staunch friend and supporter of Simeon.

Charles Simeon (1759-1836) became a Christian while a student at Cambridge in 1779. Wealthy, robust and totally irreligious, he intended to sow his wild oats along with many other students on his arrival at Cambridge. When his tutor informed him that under college rules he was expected to attend the Holy Communion service in three weeks time, he was aghast. He later wrote, "The thought rushed into my head that Satan himself was as fit to attend as I; and if I must attend, I must prepare." He at once purchased several books that did not seem of much help. His reading was arrested, however, by references to the Old Testament sacrifices and the transferring of personal guilt to the head of the offering. This concept and its application to the death of Christ amazed him.

> What? Can I transfer all my guilt to another? . . . Accordingly, I sought to lay my sins upon the sacred head of Jesus. . . . From that hour peace flowed in rich abundance into my soul, and at the Lord's Table in our Chapel I had the sweetest access to God through my blessed Savior.[14]

He did not meet nor did he know of another Christian throughout his undergraduate days, but he continued to systematically study Scripture on his own.

In 1782 following his ordination at the age of twenty-three, Simeon began a remarkable pastoral ministry, spanning fifty-four years, as vicar of

Holy Trinity Church at Cambridge. He began to preach in a way unknown in his times, attracting students to his teaching and bringing upon himself considerable opposition and scorn from the Establishment. Sermons at that time were supposed to entertain. Bible-oriented messages were considered an intrusion on the congregation's privacy. Simeon was locked out of his church by the vestry on one occasion, and later they locked the pews so that students had to stand in the aisles to hear him preach. He was jeered as he went about town. But he persevered. He created a new tradition of Bible preaching and influenced scores of young men to follow his example when they took pulpits all over the country.

He gathered students in his home for Bible study and prayer, bringing many of them to faith in Christ and nurturing the biblical understanding of scores of others. As the years went on he preached a series of University Sermons, taking his turn in rotation, and many who came to mock him went away impressed. When he died the shops were closed in Cambridge and half the university came to pay their last respects. Meanwhile from his influence hundreds of young men had gone out as missionaries or ministers.[15] When he began his ministry the Church of England had only a handful of evangelicals; when he died it was estimated that a third of the pulpits were in evangelical hands.

In 1827, following a discussion of a fiery sermon by Simeon, a group of Cambridge undergraduates formed the Jesus Lane Sunday School in an attempt to reach boys and girls of a poor, neglected neighborhood. While the students had little vision for reaching their peers, this outreach gave them opportunity to learn and share the gospel. It was a practical training ground as well as a useful ministry. Many who later became influential Christian leaders taught in this Sunday school, following in the train of the Simeonites.

In 1848 one of the first-year students who joined the "Jesus Lane lot," as they were called, suggested that they form a Cambridge Prayer Union, agreeing to pray for each other one hour a month. Within a year's time the group had grown to one hundred members, never meeting but praying privately for one another. Following the visit to the university of the missionary-explorer David Livingstone in the autumn of 1857, an undergraduate student brought together all those he could contact who were especially interested in missions. By 1858 the members of this group had formed the Cambridge University Church Missionary Union. Its purpose was to meet regularly to pray for missionaries. This was a significant first: an organized meeting of Christian students for missions.

In 1862 the Daily Prayer Meeting (DPM) was begun at the initiative of
two freshmen who had the experience of such a meeting before coming
to the university. It met with strong opposition from "many of the most
esteemed men in our university." What could undergraduates know about
prayer? There were never more than thirty present at first and it lasted only
half an hour. As time went on the DPM began to invite noted Christian men
to address the group. Eventually they began inviting well-known evange-
lists to address the whole university, taking the risk of renting a hall for
the meetings.[16]

At last came the crucial step of merging all of these groups into a comprehensive Christian society which would effectively continue their purposes. In 1877 the Cambridge Inter-Collegiate Christian Union (CICCU)
was formed, again as the result of student initiative. CICCU (pronounced
Kick-U) has the longest continuous history of student witness of any
known student group, encompassing more than a hundred years of effective evangelistic outreach and discipleship and continuing strong to this
day. Its beginning was a natural spill-over of spiritual life, culminating forty
years after the death of Charles Simeon.

Oxford's OICCU (pronounced Oik-U) followed two years later. Student
initiative led other universities to form Christian Unions throughout Britain. In 1928, after a struggle with the theology of the Student Christian
Movement (SCM), which was related to the World's Student Christian Federation (WSCF), these groups were organized as the British Inter-Varsity
Fellowship (IVF), now known as University and Colleges Christian Fellowship (UCCF).

6/Historical Roots in North America

At the same time and in much the same way, God was at work in the
colleges in North America. The earliest record of a voluntary student religious society in North America dates back to January 10, 1723, at Harvard.[17] Twenty-six students signed a statement outlining the purposes of
the society. Fifteen of this group later became clergy. Their objectives
required that the members meet twice a week for worship, that they take
turns in leadership, that they watch over one another with love and behave
so that none should speak evil of them.

It is clear that these societies had a friend and counselor in Cotton
Mather (1662-1728) and may have begun several years before 1723. During
a funeral sermon Mather spoke of "some of the students who formed a
society in 1706 . . . to speak to one another in . . . brotherly love, and watch

over one another and carry on some suitable exercises of devotions together." In 1716 he recorded in his diary a note about a "society of pious and praying youths at the colledge."[18] His diaries reveal his distress at the low moral standards of New England colleges. He began gathering some of the more serious students to meet with him on Sunday evenings.

This was the beginning of many religious societies in the colleges of New England, such groups often called Mather Societies. American evangelical student groups communicated with each other (and thus were intercollegiate) from the beginning, in contrast to those in Europe and Britain, where isolated groups of students existed on the various campuses. Well before 1800, secret religious groups were found in sixteen of the twenty-two American colleges. Such a group existed at Yale during the student days of David Brainerd (1718-1747), and he was later expelled from Yale partly on account of his religious convictions. Yale was one of several colleges opposing the irregular behavior and religious enthusiasm of the revivals. This is likely the major reason so many of the societies were secret in the early 1700s.

The Great Awakening, the revival which swept America from 1725 to approximately 1770, increased both the size and number of these student religious groups. The powerful, Spirit-filled preaching of George Whitefield, Jonathan Edwards and others provided a climate that swept students, along with others across the country, into the kingdom of God. The influence of Jonathan Edwards (1703-1758) on students, as well as his passion for renewal and the life of the mind, has had a long-lasting effect on American Christianity. He founded Dartmouth College, had a powerful pulpit ministry and later served as the president of the fledgling Princeton College just before his death. As a primary American literary and philosophical figure, Edwards was mentor to a large company of students and insisted on intellectual integrity in matters of faith.

The aim of these early religious societies was the promotion of practical ethics and religious life. Strict Christian conduct was required of their members. The existence of these groups is recorded in the minute books still found in the libraries of their respective universities. Their names reveal their mission: The Private Meeting (Harvard), Adelphi Theologia (Harvard), The Moral Society (Yale), The Religious Society (Dartmouth), The College Praying Society (Brown), The Rising Sun (Williams), The Society for Inquiry Concerning Missions (Andover), Philadelphia Society (Princeton) and the Society for Religious Inquiry (Vermont).

During the stresses and rising climate of secularism surrounding the events of the American Revolutionary War, the revival movement almost died out; but toward the close of the 1700s the movement reappeared in what has been called the Second Great Awakening. By 1800 evangelistic revivals swept across the country, taking away some of the intellectual opposition to spiritual life at the colleges. Timothy Dwight (1752-1817),[19] appointed president of Yale in 1795, became the spokesman for the revival in academic circles. When students challenged him to debate on the authority of Scripture, Dwight accepted and began a series on Christian apologetics in defense of the faith. In 1802 under his strong preaching a third of the students at Yale were converted. Life at Yale changed with the revivals that marked these years.

During the revival years several young men became Christians in Fitchburg, Massachusetts. Entering Williams College as freshmen, they decided to protest the prevailing infidelity on campus and held a weekly prayer meeting in a student's room. The next year four more students came from the revival area and joined the prayer meetings. These students decided to challenge personally every student in the college with the claims of Christ. (Williams then had an enrollment of less than a hundred.) It is not surprising that a revival soon broke out that affected a large part of that student body.

As a freshman, Samuel J. Mills, Jr. (1783-1818), became part of that group and one of its key leaders, bringing with him the strong concern for "heathen peoples" he had felt ever since his conversion. Meeting on Wednesday and Saturday afternoons, the group called itself The Rising Sun because of its commitment that every morning at sunrise members would "address the Throne of Grace in behalf of the object of this Society."

One sultry August afternoon in 1806, five of the group were out walking and took shelter from a rainstorm under a haystack. Praying through the storm, they focused their concern on Asia, the largest continent. Mills proposed that some means be found to send the gospel there, saying, "We can do it if we will." Bowed in prayer, these student volunteers for foreign missions covenanted together to see this happen. And it did. This event later became known as the Haystack Prayer Meeting.

The missionary vision of this group of students, under the leadership of Mills, is the more remarkable since no missionary societies existed in America at that time. So concerned was this student group about world missions that in 1810 their vision and zeal brought about the formation of the first church-sponsored sending agency in America, the Board of Commissioners for Foreign Missions. Within four years of the prayer meeting, the first volunteers for missionary work were on their way to Asia. Adoniram Judson was one of these. Within the next fifty years, 125 men from Williams College went to foreign fields, and many more took the gospel west to Native Americans.

A monument was erected in 1867 to commemorate the significance of the Haystack Prayer Meeting for the cause of world missions. "For once in the history of the world a prayer meeting is commemorated by a monument," said Mark Hopkins, then president of the American Board of Commissioners for Foreign Missions, in his dedicatory address.[20] In 1981, 175 years later, as part of the missions thrust of Inter-Varsity Christian Fellowship, students again gathered at Williams College to commemorate that Haystack Prayer Meeting.

While still students, Mills and his colleagues also pioneered Christian student groups by transferring to other colleges and beginning Societies for Missionary Inquiry in each. Despite difficulties in travel and communication (the postal system was not yet begun), these zealous young men established contact with most of the twenty-five colleges in the young nation, urging them to form such a society. Within three years the societies had 527 members and more than fifty per cent of these eventually went to foreign fields.

Although Mills himself never went to the mission field, he clearly gave the impetus to many who did go. He played a part in the formation of the American Bible Society and worked in the slums of New York and among Native Americans. He later helped form the American Colonization Society for the evangelism of slaves and their repatriation in what is now Liberia. In 1817 he was sent on a survey trip to West Africa, where he purchased land for the founding of Liberia. He died of a tropical disease on the way home and was buried at sea.

7/The Genesis of the YMCA
In 1858 an extraordinary revival swept through the country, adding a million converts to the churches and doing much good through charitable and rescue societies. With it came a new urgency for prayer. In Middlebury, Dartmouth, Yale and elsewhere daily prayer meetings began to thrive, and in some colleges almost the entire student body was converted. Revival moved into the cities and later swept through the armies in both the North and the South during the desperate years of the Civil War. All of this coincided with and aided the rapid growth of the Young Men's Christian Association (YMCA) in the United States.

In June 1844, George Williams, a London dry-goods clerk, and eleven of his fellow clerks formed the first Young Men's Christian Association. They felt young men in the trades needed a Christian witness and the churches of England were not reaching them. They insisted that "the supreme aim of your daily life should be to bring glory to your Redeemer, and that the most appropriate sphere for the attainment of this is in your daily calling." It is nothing less than astonishing that a movement started by a dozen clerks spread so rapidly that within less than a decade it had reproduced itself throughout Great Britain, Europe and America.

This was to become a powerful evangelizing and discipling movement. By 1851 the YMCA had come to the North American continent in Montreal and Boston. A New York University student visited the London YMCA on vacation and on his return spread the spark that began the YMCA in New York. In three years almost every city had its YMCA, springing up independently as the news of the idea spread. By 1856 there were 205 associations with 25,000 members, a spontaneous development without a national organization, centered principally in large cities where young men were seeking the jobs emerging from the Industrial Revolution. Two years later it was infused by the 1858 Revival with new interest in evangelism, Bible study and discipleship.

The wide range of YMCA activities—Sunday schools, soup kitchens, lectures, tract distribution, Bible studies, open-air evangelism and a host of other projects—attracted the attention of a young shoe salesman named Dwight Moody (1837-1899). Its goals were his goals, and he became one of its chief enthusiasts. Moody is primarily remembered as the leading evangelist of the late 1800s, but his contemporaries would have described him as the real leader of the YMCA movement.

The reputation and effectiveness of the YMCA soon became appealing to university students. Between 1857 and 1858 students at the University of Virginia had formed the YMCA's first collegiate chapter. Within a year two hundred students attended daily prayer meetings and fifty were engaged in evangelism in the community and at other universities. For many years this collegiate YMCA was the largest student organization at Virginia, with a membership comprising over eighty-five per cent of the student body.

A Christian group already in existence at the University of Michigan decided to become a YMCA chapter about that same time. Students met twice a day to pray for the cause of Christ at Michigan. The records give their agonizing prayer, "O God, give us this university." In the years that followed, two-thirds of the five hundred students on campus and half of the faculty became members of this chapter. In a public speech in 1868 Erastus Otis Haven, president of the university, said, "We have a flourishing Christian Association at the university and more than a hundred have been brought to Christ during this past year."[21]

Spontaneous student leadership spread the YMCA movement across American campuses, something that would have awed Williams and his clerks. It is significant that these first student YMCAs were formed at state universities, where there was an atmosphere of religious freedom and where students felt a responsibility to propagate their faith. This was fertile soil for the growth of indigenous, student-initiated interdenominational fellowships.

Christian students already meeting on campuses joined their organizations to the YMCA. Their program was basic: prayer, Bible study, discipleship and student leadership. Students in the Y movement evangelized their peers without apology. The membership committee at the Cornell YMCA chapter in 1885 assigned every unconverted student to some Christian who should "pray for him, invite him to meetings, and at the right time . . . kindly and firmly press upon him the claims of Christ."

In 1876 the president of Princeton invited Moody to speak at the college's Annual Day of Prayer. Moody had to cancel out, but the students went ahead with their plans and revival broke out on the campus. Later, when Moody spoke at Princeton, a wave of conversions resulted, declared to be "the most remarkable event in Princeton's history." Moody forgot his limited education; he became interested in students.

The collegiate YMCAs were a thoroughly indigenous, evangelical[22] student movement, with students taking the initiative to begin and maintain the work. The leadership within the YMCA was unprepared for this; they were hardly organized to care for the city YMCAs. For nearly twenty years the students petitioned the YMCA to recognize their college chapters. Finally in response to the strength of this student initiative, in 1877 (the same year that CCICU was formed at Cambridge) a collegiate division of the YMCA was formally organized.

Luther Wishard was appointed the first American secretary, followed by John R. Mott in 1888. They were the first two professional full-time workers ever appointed outside the university world to help a student religious group. Prior to this all the workers were volunteers within the official university community. Full-time staff workers allowed intercollegiate continuity in a way never possible before. In the years that followed these two men, along with Robert Wilder, ignited an evangelical student witness around the world.

8/The Character of Student Christian Movements

In tracing the history of early student movements in America, Clarence Shedd, in *Two Centuries of Student Christian Movements*,[23] calls attention to ten chief features of these early societies. Writing in 1934, his acute observations throw light on the rise of the Inter-Varsity Christian Fellowship (IVCF) in the United States.

1. Student societies are indigenous to the religious and educational life of American colleges. They are neither a "flash in the pan" nor something outside the life of these institutions. . . . If we were to wipe out entirely the present local and national Christian Student Society organization, an organization of that same general characteristic would in a short time reappear, possibly under a different name.

2. There is a strong urge within these student groups for inter-collegiate fellowship.

3. The societies are interdenominational in outlook and composition.

4. Christian societies consistently have emphasized devotional, academic, missionary and life-transforming involvement.

5. From the beginning, Christian student societies have expressed themselves internationally, both through foreign missionary service and through international student organizations.

6. These theologically conservative students had a clear sense of the social issues of their day.

7. In these movements the fundamental decisions were made by the students, undergraduate and graduate. Mature leadership also played a part in the life of the movements, but these leaders have been content to let responsibility be given to student leadership.

8. While there is an independent history of women's Christian student societies, as colleges became co-educational the student societies did also.

9. Loyalty was to intercollegiate interests. The most vigorous of the student societies separated their campus witness and their concern for the Christian message from denominational concerns.

10. Student societies have a prophetic dimension and are activist in their approach to problems.

These ten characteristics spell out the dynamics of healthy student witness in the first two centuries of American university life, and continue to be the touchstone in evaluating student work today.

2
The Rise and Fall of the Student Christian Movement

In light of its past history, the biggest single danger to the Evangelical Movement comes not from its declared opponents, but from some of those who claim to be its friends. Many of those who have been nurtured and developed in evangelicalism . . . have ceased to act in its best interests when they relax their vigilance and maybe from good motives begin to advocate dangerous departures from the beaten pathway. The point of departure from the true course . . . comes at the moment that Holy Scripture ceases to be the completely reliable record of the Divine Revelation. . . . It is not easy to notice that fatal step from the firm ground of objective truth, once given by God. . . . After that step, it is only a matter of degree and how far one plunges on into the quicksands.[1]
Douglas Johnson, *general secretary (1924-64), Inter-Varsity Fellowship, England*

Seven years after his great London evangelistic campaign, Dwight L. Moody received an invitation to speak at a week of meetings for the CICCU at Cambridge University in 1882. Kynaston Studd, captain of the university cricket team and president of CICCU, took the initiative to invite him because his father had been converted from a totally worldly life through Moody's Mission in London. Three of the Studd sons had also become Christians, through someone associated with Moody.

From one point of view Moody was a poor choice for a student mission because he was neither British, middle class nor a university man. It was a rash decision, but it was also of God.

Seventeen hundred men entered the building, laughing and talking with the intent of making a joke out of the meeting. Although they tried their best to drown out Moody's preaching with noise and escapades, the meetings continued on, supported by prayerful students. At the end about two hundred men stood to indicate a decision for Christ during the week.

Moody is reported to have whispered under his breath, "My God, this is enough to live for." From this zealous student group came the Cambridge Seven and a great outpouring of missionary concern.[2]

In 1885 Moody, eager to see a similar work of the Spirit of God in his own land, invited Kynaston Studd to come to the United States and share what God was doing in CICCU. He arranged with Luther Wishard, general secretary of the YMCA, for Studd to tour twenty American colleges telling the story of the Cambridge Seven and challenging students about the world's needs.

Whatever else he accomplished, Studd's visit to Cornell was used by God to deepen the spiritual life of a freshman student named John R. Mott. Probably no single name had greater drawing power for Mott than that of the famous English cricketer, J. F. K. Studd. Torn between his desire to hear Studd and his fear of overly emotional religious meetings, Mott paced the hall before he finally resolved to go in. As he opened the door to the meeting hall Studd was thundering out the Scripture passages for his talk, "Young man, seekest thou great things for thyself? Seek them not. Seek ye first the kingdom of God."

Mott later said: "I have forgotten everything else, but these two passages fastened themselves into my memory like barbs. I could not rid my mind of them." Early the next day he got up his courage to seek an interview with Studd. The commitment Mott made that day never faded. Studd was later to say to Wishard, "You had better keep your eyes on that young man."[3] Mott would later promote student work around the world and found the World's Student Christian Federation.

1/Mount Hermon, Mott and the Intercollegiate Missions
During the summer of 1886 Luther Wishard cautiously proposed to Moody that they hold a month-long national Bible conference for students at Moody's Mount Hermon School grounds in Northfield, Massachusetts. (The one-month model that was later to be so important in training students in the early days of Inter-Varsity Christian Fellowship!) Like many IVCF staff members since, Moody found it hard to believe that college men would give up a month of time in the summer vacation. Wishard prayed and did his part as a salesman for the idea. It seemed crucial for the future of the work.

After Moody agreed, only three months remained to recruit students. Wishard met the next day with C. K. Ober and Richard Morse, two YMCA college secretaries, and drafted a circular inviting students to come to

Mount Hermon. Ober left immediately for Cornell University. On arrival in Ithaca he met with the newly elected vice president, John R. Mott, and after clinching the matter with him they went out together and got nine other men, so that Cornell had a delegation of ten picked men at the Mount Hermon Conference. These ten students, with Mott as their leader, went back to Cornell and revolutionized the religious life of the university in the next college year.

Wishard went to recruit at Princeton University and prevailed upon Robert Wilder, a senior, to come to the Mount Hermon conference. Wilder was reluctant because he was a senior and would not be able to return to Princeton to spread the results of this conference. Wishard saw Wilder's past experience as key for what he hoped would happen at Mount Hermon. In 1883, as an undergraduate, Wilder had attended a conference sponsored by a group of seminary students who had formed the Inter-Seminary Alliance for the promotion of missions. (This group later became the theological section of the intercollegiate YMCA-YWCA.)

Wilder later wrote about this Inter-Seminary conference, "We three college students returned to Princeton inspired with the desire to accomplish two things: First, to pray and work for a revival in our college, and second, to stir up missionary interest." They arranged for Dr. A. J. Gordon, Baptist missionary pioneer and educator, to come to Princeton, and a significant stirring by God's Spirit led to the formation of the Princeton Foreign Missionary Society. Robert Wilder and his sister Grace Wilder began praying together for a widespread missionary movement among university students, asking God that ultimately one thousand volunteers would go to the foreign fields from other colleges and universities, and what had begun at Princeton would become an intercollegiate movement.[4]

Wishard had also been deeply moved by the emphasis of the Inter-Seminary group. He had made a trip to Williams College and knelt in the snow at the Haystack Monument and made "an unreserved surrender to the great Leader of these earlier volunteers. I am willing to go anywhere at anytime to do anything for Jesus," he later wrote.[5] Wishard and Wilder shared a common heart for missions. Wishard wanted him at the Mount Hermon Conference. At last he overruled Wilder's objection and he agreed to come. As Wilder left for Mount Hermon, his sister Grace said she believed God would call a hundred students from that conference to serve overseas. Clarence Shedd reflects,

It staggers one's imagination to picture the significance to the religious and missionary life of the world of the persistence of both Wishard and

Ober in securing the attendance of these two students from Cornell and Princeton to this first summer student conference.[6]

Two hundred and fifty students came to Mount Hermon from ninety colleges, representing twenty-six states and every section of the country. Most of the recruiting had been done by mail. Ober met Wishard at the station of Mount Hermon on July 3, 1886, and told him that "such an avalanche of students had come that we would probably have to overflow the haymows."

The program was not finally shaped until the beginning of the conference. In the opening meeting of the conference Mr. Moody said,

I have been asked for programs . . . I don't have any. If you want to know what is ahead, we don't know except that we will have a good time. We want to stir you up and get you in love with the Bible, and those of you who have a voice, in love with music. . . . Our talks are going to be conversational. If you want to ask a question, speak out; that's what we are here for, to get all the cobwebs swept away and go back to your college mates inspired with the truth.[7]

Mott was later to remark that nobody had thought of this meeting as being a missionary conference but rather, as Moody said, a place "to stir you up and get you in love with the Bible." However, Wilder and twenty-one other students met regularly to pray for the needs of the world during the conference. Mott recalls,

The students had the spirit of propagation. Probably Wilder himself did not secure more than eight or ten. They got one another. They multiplied. I suppose the most sacred ground here is that grove back of this hall. I never went into that grove but that there were men praying there in groups or alone. Men talked missions everywhere—running, tramping, eating.[8]

Students began to commit themselves to go to the mission field and by the closing night, ninety-nine had done so. The next morning those ninety-nine met for a farewell meeting, and as they were kneeling in prayer, the hundredth student volunteer joined them. Though not present at the conference, Grace Wilder had known what God would do.

The enthusiasm and vision of these students could not be contained. Wilder and another Princeton student, John Forman, were sent to tour the universities of North America for a year. More than once Wilder woke in the night to hear Forman pouring out his heart to God in the next room. They seemed aware of the enormous significance of what they were doing. Together these two students visited 162 institutions during 1886-87.

Wilder's health broke from the demanding schedule, but they kept at the task. Often they traveled separately to reach as many campuses as possible, keeping in touch by almost daily post cards and hourly prayer for each other. Wilder wrote that time and again they need only "to strike a match, and the whole college blazed up." In all, 2,106 students—about 1,600 men and 500 women—signed a volunteer declaration. Among these was Samuel Zwemer, who became the great apostle to the Muslim world, and Robert Speer, destined to be one of the outstanding missionary statesmen of the next generation.[9]

At the completion of the year of recruiting, Forman sailed for India and Wilder pursued a seminary education. Wilder continued to give his attention to the missionary volunteers and by visiting nearby colleges and churches recruited another 600 students to become foreign missionaries.

The missionary movement within the YMCA was a spontaneous movement without national leadership. In 1888 fifty of the volunteers met again at Mount Hermon and formed the Student Volunteer Movement for Foreign Missions (SVM). John Mott was chosen as chairman; Robert Wilder became traveling secretary; Nettie Dunn was to represent the intercollegiate YWCA. Their watchword became "the evangelization of the world in this generation."

The growth of the SVM in the next three decades was nothing short of phenomenal. The first of their quadrennial international student missionary convention was held in Cleveland, Ohio, in 1891. By this time there were 6,200 student volunteers. Already 321 volunteers had sailed for overseas service, only five years after the first student conference at Mount Hermon. Five missionary movements among students began during the years 1883-84 in Norway, Sweden, Denmark, Great Britain and North America. Robert Wilder later said of this,

> It seems clear that the source of the modern missionary uprising among students must have been in Heaven, appearing as it did on earth at the same time in lands so remote as Scandinavia, Great Britain and North America. This source was clearly in the great power of God.[10]

In the space of a generation, 175,000 students signed the SVM pledge and 21,000 went overseas from North American colleges. The pledge stated, "It is my purpose, if God permit, to become a foreign missionary." It was understood that a student signing the pledge was responding to a call from God. David Howard, IVCF missions director 1968-1976, was later to describe the SVM as "igniting a roaring flame of missionary vision among America's youth."[11]

2/The World's Student Christian Federation

Luther Wishard had a dream of a worldwide alliance of student movements affiliated with the YMCA. He spent much of his time traveling throughout the world laying foundations for what would later become the World's Student Christian Federation (WSCF). By 1895 such an organization was in place and John Mott was made its general secretary. The SVM was only one part of the WSCF, but it is notable that its leaders were also the leaders of the worldwide student movement. Mott's plan was that each country would develop its own national student movement, adopt its own name, plan its own outreach and be linked together in a federation. Such an approach would build on student initiative and the work of the Holy Spirit. This is the same pattern the International Fellowship of Evangelical Students[12] follows today.

Thoroughly committed to Scripture, both Mott and Wishard urged students to have a daily Quiet Time and to consider the world's need to hear the gospel. The time was right for a movement like this, and nothing since has touched the religious life of the total student body in the universities of America with the same impact as that of the intercollegiate YMCA movement and the SVM. (Later the combined movement was called the Student Christian Movement or the SCM.)

Charles Troutman writes about this movement:

The story of the Intercollegiate YMCA until World War I is a thrilling one of deep Christian commitment among students, amazing evangelistic outreach in and beyond the universities and a great outpouring from the student world to the mission field. In enthusiasm and quantity and in spiritual confidence it was a unique time, not equalled since the days of the German Reformation. The Christian church was in the process of becoming literally a world religion for the first time, and much of the initiative was in the hands of undergraduates. Kenneth S. Latourette described to me how before World War I he had met with 160 leaders of Bible classes at Yale early each Sunday morning in preparation for their own Bible classes among fellow students later in the day. About 75% of the student body were in those study groups.[13]

The roster of those who went to the mission field under the impetus of the Student Volunteer Movement is impressive and records the history of missions from the late 1880s until the 1930s, a period of about fifty years.

William Borden of the Yale class of 1909 was one of these leaders. The son of wealthy Chicago parents, he had decided to be all out for Christ when he went to Yale. He kept a card file on every student with whom he spoke about Christ, with notes about the person, their openness and the subject of the conversations, using these as prayer reminders. He volunteered for the mission field through the China Inland Mission, a "waste of talent and wealth" in the eyes of many of his friends. He died of meningitis in Egypt on his way to China. His biography has since influenced many generations of students and is still in print.

Writing later, Robert Wilder reflected on the keen sense of blessing he felt in those years of recruitment. He quotes from a letter written in 1926 by Raymond B. Buker, a former track star at Bates College and member of the U.S. Olympic track team:

Do you remember the winter of 1918-1919 on a visit to Bates College that one evening you walked along College Street talking with a student by the name of Buker? You did your best to persuade him to become a foreign missionary. Though he did not decide at the end of the conversation, my twin brother, a doctor, and myself will sail next Sunday from Boston to Burma under the Baptist Board.[14]

Raymond Buker later became the field secretary of the Conservative Baptist Foreign Mission Society and a missionary statesman in the church at large. He left his mark on Inter-Varsity as a member of the corporation and the missions committee. He spent many summers in upper Michigan at Cedar Campus, an Inter-Varsity training center, influencing students in the cause of missions. He, like many others from the early days of the SVM, later gave leadership and vision to IVCF's burgeoning missions program. Another one of these was Margaret Haines, who went out to India as a student volunteer, and later became a key supporter and board member, helping to form the early student work of Inter-Varsity.

3/The Decline of the Student Volunteer Movement

The Des Moines SVM convention in 1920 marked the peak of the movement. At the end of the convention 2,783 students signed the pledge for foreign missionary service. After that high point in 1920, the SVM experienced a steady decline. Statistics tell part of the story. Twenty-five volunteers enrolled in SVM in 1938, compared to 2,738 in 1920. By 1940 a limited quadrennial convention was held in Toronto attended by 465 delegates, compared to 6,890 in 1920.

What was happening in the SVM reflected what had already happened in the collegiate YMCA-YWCA (the Associations). Increasing pressure for the Student Christian Movement to become part of a more "inclusive" religious group was eating at the core of the movement. By 1940—and earlier in some sections of the country—the Y movement had ceased to be an influence in student religious life. Most theologically conservative chapters had removed themselves from their allegiance to the Y Associations as early as 1925.

In the last twenty years of its organizational life, policies of inclusivism led to many mergers. In 1944 the intercollegiate YMCA-YWCA joined with the denominational student work under the framework of the United Student Christian Council (USCC). In 1956 the USCC and the Interseminary Movement merged to form the National Student Christian Federation (NSCF). In 1959 the Student Volunteer Movement (SVM) merged with the NSCF. By 1966 the NSCF had merged with the Roman Catholic National Newman Student Federation and other groups to form the University Christian Movement (UCM). This led the leaders of the WSCF to feel "a tremendous sense of excitement" over this "ecumenical breakthrough."[15] However, three years later in 1969, the UCM voted itself out of existence. One perceptive student explained his vote, "We have refused to be self-consciously Christian."

What had happened? It would be simplistic to state a single cause. Nor is it possible to list reasons in order of importance. World events and new philosophies gained momentum and met to form a formidable vortex of change and confusion. What looked so harmless and interesting became unbalanced and gradually the real substance of the movement leaked away. Shedd lists the historical realities which affected this great movement over a period of time. Some are more dramatically obvious than others, but all give insights into a movement under pressure.

1. *The conflict between religion and science.* In 1859 Charles Darwin published his *Origin of Species.* The idea of progressive development was not new, but with this publication the rationalists forced the issue that scientific evidence "proved" that God did not exist and that religion was irrational. The problem for the church was the misuse the rationalists made of the data. This led to a slow but certain erosion of biblical authority. Christians were unprepared for this attack. Prior to this time theologians argued effectively in the realm of philosophy; now they faced the argument of science, which was often unfamiliar territory.

The conflict between science and religion over the theory of evolution was never as bitter in Europe as it became in North America. A young graduate of the University of Edinburgh named Henry Drummond had published his series of lectures on the subject of evolution in book form, *Natural Law in the Spiritual World.* Drummond posited that the God of revelation was the same as the God of creation, and we could expect a corresponding harmony in His two manifestations—in nature and in Scripture. He became known as the great prophetic reconciler of science and religion. Dwight Moody brought Professor Drummond from Edinburgh in 1887 to speak to student groups about this controversy.

Shedd, in writing about the relationship of Moody and Drummond, remarks that "the great friendship between Moody and Drummond was all the more remarkable because Drummond was extremely liberal theologically, whereas Moody . . . tended toward a conservative theology." Whether Shedd is right about Drummond's theology may be questionable. It may be closer to the truth to say that neither Moody nor Drummond were astute theologians. Drummond, however, was disarming and spoke powerfully on the point that was at issue. As the author of the classic book on 1 Corinthians 13, *The Greatest Thing in the World,* his own transparent religious life and genuine comeliness gave him an open door. When Moody was criticized for his use of Drummond he said, "I have never heard or read anything by Drummond with which I did not heartily agree—though I wish he would often speak of the Atonement." When he promised to question Drummond about some of his beliefs, Moody said, "Before he had been downstairs ten minutes he showed himself in various ways to be so much better a Christian than I am that I simply hadn't the nerve to tackle him and I cannot do it."[16] Drummond's dynamic personality and Christian graces may well have masked the weak points of his theology.

While interesting, Moody's use of Drummond is not a cause of the demise of this great student movement. In fact, Drummond undoubtedly helped many Christians in the science/religion controversy. We mention it in this context to point up a weakness within the structure of the SCM and the worldwide student movement it became. This great and effective movement had no well-defined theological statement against which to measure truth or personal orthodoxy. When the movement began, theology was not an issue. From the great revivals of the past everyone knew that vital Christianity meant biblical Christianity. It didn't need to be defined; it needed to be preached. The absence of a clear statement of faith regarding biblical truth put the whole movement in a slippery place in light of what ensued. Men of good will tended to give too much room for differences of opinion or interpretations because there was no specific statement which served as a plumb line for the organization.

2. *Scientific historical criticism.* About this same time theologians in Germany were applying the methods of historical criticism to the text of

Scripture. Many of these men were devout Christians, but the effect on those they taught was to eliminate the supernatural from the Bible. By altering the traditional authorship and dates of many books in the Bible, the overall effect was to undermine confidence in the Scripture. The scientific method had an intellectual appeal and applying this to the Bible gave a feel of mastery of the text. Soon miracles were eliminated or explained away. People stood in judgment on the Bible, instead of the other way around. Human beings were not as sinful as first thought; they were getting better and better all the time. Human effort could bring in the kingdom of God. Good works made more sense than grace.

By the early 1900s, these teachings began to affect American seminaries and the church. It caught evangelical scholars unaware; concern with apologetics[17] was not a contemporary issue. Between 1910 and 1915 thoughtful evangelical scholars responded by producing papers called *The Fundamentals*[18] on subjects that affirmed the trustworthiness of Scripture and all it proclaims. Others thought higher criticism offered new horizons for scholarship and were attracted to it. It tickled the fancy and mentality of some preachers, but in the pews of many mainline denominations parishioners wondered how this kind of theorizing met the spiritual needs they felt.

3. *Growth of student population.* Prior to 1900 most campus work was interdenominational and Protestant. The successful spiritual work on campus was being done by the Young Men and Women's Christian Associations with student leadership and traveling Association secretaries. Students sought to translate personal faith into the larger life of the campus and the world. Church denominations were relatively unimportant to most students.

In the early 1900s the steady growth of student population, particularly in the state universities, brought denominational student foundations to the campus. Most of the mainline churches had their own schools, but now more and more of their students were coming to the state universities and leaders felt concern for denominational loyalty. Denominational leaders feared that an interdenominational work would not produce strong loyalty to denominations at state institutions.

In 1913 the Methodist Church built a student center, Wesley Foundation, at the University of Illinois and soon other denominations followed suit on the major campuses across the country: Westminster Foundation (Presbyterian), Canterbury House (Episcopal), Roger Williams Foundation (American Baptist), Lutheran Campus Ministry and others. The chaplain's goal was to minister to "our" students while they were at the university. (Roman Catholics had begun the Newman Clubs in 1885. The first full-time rabbi for Jewish student work was not appointed until 1923 at the University of Illinois.)

Because the work of the Associations (as the Y chapters were called) had such vibrant student leadership, the denominations suggested cooperation, lest they duplicate efforts. The Association secretaries itinerated, serving a large number of colleges; the denominational foundations had resident ministers or chaplains who were always on hand.

Ever so subtly and over a period of time, ideas of ecumenicity meant giving ground to the more liberal theologies. Leadership in the World's Student Christian Federation (Mott and Wilder among them) had hoped the vitality of their work would help the biblical integrity of more liberal student work. But cooperation had a domino effect. Liberal seminaries produced liberal ministers who influenced churches, and usually the ministers with the broadest theology became denominational campus pastors. The church undercut its students who were active in Christian work on the campus. Two essentially different belief systems began confronting each other. The issues centered on the Scripture and the deity of Christ. In reality, the demise of the movement grew out of the soil of the church.

College administrators welcomed the building of beautiful college chapels. Chairs of religion were generously funded through denominations, giving religion a new dignity in administrative eyes. University deans took over more and more of the voluntary activities of the Y chapters. Religion in Life or Religious Emphasis Week was held on campus as a way for the university to "tip its hat" to religious groups.

By 1944 a federation of denominational student ministries and all other Protestant agencies (notably the YMCA and YWCA) was formed, called the United Student Christian Council (USCC), but by that time the Y was hardly recognizable to those who had known its former effectiveness.

As colleges and universities expanded they became more impersonal. Students had a growing interest in science and technology, which meant that liberal arts no longer had the ascendancy. A growing plurality in religious convictions and cultural backgrounds among students made it increasingly difficult to emphasize the centrality of Christ. Up until this time the colleges had been controlled largely by white Protestant males. The climate on campus was changing.

4. *World War 1.* Tremendous optimism marked the beginning of the twentieth century. Some even went so far as to predict it would be the

Christian century. World War 1 (1914-18) brought alarming disillusionment to every level of society. Almost a whole generation of young people had been wiped out. The observable facts were that the world was not getting better and better, as many had said. Human beings were incapable of ushering in the kingdom of God; post-millennialism (the arrival of the kingdom of God on earth by a process of human effort) was obviously a farce. Where was a theology that fit what was happening in the world?

At the onset of the war, enrollment in colleges dropped off as much as sixty-five per cent. Student members of the Y chapters, as well as their traveling secretaries, left in rapid succession for the armed forces or for YMCA work among the military overseas. The government, to prevent the emptying of colleges as well as to protect future educational needs, put the colleges under the control of the War Department. Essentially the government organized the work of the Y chapters, putting people who had little experience in the student movement into leadership roles. They were enlisted to do big social-service projects; spiritual commitment was not as important as action. It was hard for the Y leadership to sort out the completeness of the break with the past made during these war years.

5. *The democratization of the movement.* The Y collegiate chapters had always prided themselves on being a movement of students. The secretaries and professors who were counted most successful knew how to share their insights without dominating the students. However, in intercollegiate affairs or formation of policies for the movement, national leaders would seek counsel with student leaders, but the larger vision was the responsibility of the leaders who directed the movement.

In 1913 the first radical proposals were made for regional control of the movement, and by 1927 the movement was democratized to the extent that the students became a movement within a movement. This decentralization meant that student work risked losing its values. Shedd writes approvingly of this decision, "This does not mean that a movement values prophets less but rather that it attempts to create a better setting for the multiplying of the word and influences of the prophet." However, this move opened organizational doors to others who were not part of the Y movement. The students could do what they wanted and some student groups were replaced by societies of other names. This meant that there could be as many purposes as there were groups. When "What do the students want?" becomes the first question, it is easy for groups to lose their way unless some standard holds them to their original commitment.

Attempting to interpret this move in the best possible light, Shedd writes,
This policy of trusting students and secretaries (campus staff members)
to lead in the intercollegiate life of the Movement as they were trusted
in their local Christian Associations, was wholly new. It gave the U.S. an
intercollegiate Movement really rooted in the religious life of the universities, responsibly connected with the great issues of the day, *seeking
and finding a more adequate Christian message* and willing to change
or lose its organizational forms if by so doing it could help to prepare
the way for a Student Christian Movement better fitted to make a distinctive contribution to the Christian Student Societies to the life of our
times (italics ours).[19]

Practically, this often meant that student groups were carried in the direction of the interests of the students or the secretaries who wearied of the
basic discipleship needs of each freshmen class (the "unending kindergarten"). Bible study, evangelism, daily prayer meetings could be considered irrelevant in light of the social and international problems of war,
peace and colonial injustice. It depended largely on the secretaries' commitment to orthodoxy and the vitality of their own spiritual lives. The
secretaryship (staff members) had become a developed and self-conscious
profession, writes Shedd. The majority had advanced degrees or the equivalent in professional training. Volunteers were used less and less in helping
the campus ministry.[20]

6. *Shift to the social gospel.* It was called a new realism about the nature
of the world and the Christian message. Associations were urged to place
"special emphasis on the present world situation, with an effort to discuss
in the spirit of Christ the lessons our students should learn from the vast
tragedy of Europe." Leaders said the student movement must become
more intellectually competent and this world-mindedness must break
beyond the traditional religious channels for the development of world
consciousness.

New policies came into place after World War 1. Membership was broadened to include those interested, but not necessarily committed to Christ.
Only one national discussion of membership basis took place after the war.
Students and secretaries alike began asking how relevant it was to take the
gospel to other lands when our own country was so needy. Wasn't that just
a form of imperialism or colonialism? Could any message be significant
except as related to the urgent needs of the world? Does Christ offer an
adequate answer for the burning social and international questions of the
day?

According to Shedd, a new kind of evangelism for social concerns came into place:

> Students feel that it is not a time to merely talk about religion; it is a day to act courageously, to practice generous brotherhood; to denounce old alliances between Christianity and imperialism; and to grapple with the industrial exploitation of backward peoples. They match Bible study with a study of the world conditions.[21]

With the exception of the first few years after the war, Personal Evangelism Institutes, once a vital part of the movement, were not promoted. The development of psychology and the personal counseling movement may well have been responsible for this change. Large meetings for the proclamation of biblical truth ended and small group discussions took their place. Attendance at summer training camps, once thought so vital for the health of the movement, plummeted.

While campus programs in the past had reflected the needs of the local situation, guides and manuals gave standardized help, which not only gave consistency to the movement, but also kept it on the official track. Writing in 1934, Shedd says, "The break with any conception of standardized programs has become so great that it is no longer possible to say what are the characteristic features of any association."[22] By allowing this to happen, the leadership gave away the focus and vision that had once been central.

4/ Erosion among the Leaders

At the 1920 SVM convention in Des Moines, John Mott gave a brief keynote address called "The World Opportunity," in which he contrasted the optimism of 1914 with the exhaustion and confusion of 1920 and challenged his hearers to become active participants in building a new world by a thrust of fresh leadership that would apply the principles of Jesus Christ to industry, finance, national and international politics. The watchword, "The evangelization of the world in this generation," so important in the earlier days of the SVM, was not mentioned. Many of the students were in no mood to accept what they called "this piffle, these old shibboleths, these outworn phrases."[23]

The disillusionment of World War 1 was followed by the Roaring Twenties and a great disregard for tradition. By the thirties the country was deep into a depression which further devastated the SVM. Without a strong theological position the weakening movement was prey to cultural pressures. In 1932 the SVM published *A Philosophy That Works,* a pamphlet with the basic tenet that "all peoples are essentially alike, that we all stand or fall together, that the only solution of the problem lies in persons, and that it is the way of love that works." This was a world away from the heart of the movement that began at Mount Hermon forty-six years earlier.

Culling the minutes and correspondence of the Student Volunteer Movement, some observations have been made about what was happening to this once vital movement:[24]

dependence on numbers rather than upon the Holy Spirit's power;

vocabulary changes—phrases like "The Spirit fell upon us" or "God has done a wondrous thing" were used less often. Instead, letters contained phrases like "careful supervision," "cautious, balanced approach," "approved by every leading denomination." Letters once signed, "Yours for God's greater glory," now simply ended, "Sincerely yours";

organization was promoted more than the movement and mission God had given—top-heavy programs and staffing;

changes of leadership broke up the continuity of its life;

difficulty in financing, closely related to the Depression;

emphasis on social concerns rather than "the simplicity of the gospel";

feeble prayer life of the movement.

It is both important and instructive to emphasize that those who were taken in by the new liberalism all had biblical backgrounds. Many continued to emphasize prayer, Bible study and missions. Gradually, however, truth was prefaced with, "It seems to me," "I believe," and "I suppose we would all agree." The element of clear authority expressed in the words, "Thus saith the Lord" became inappropriate. It did not happen all at once, but the seeds of destruction were growing. Some of the men in leadership "appreciated the great movement of the Spirit manifested in the work of Biblical scholarship, technically known as Higher Criticism," and felt that this approach to the Bible kept many thoughtful men from putting the Bible on the shelf.[25]

The original vision of the leaders of this great movement of God cannot be overestimated. Wishard urged young American professors to take teaching posts overseas with the goal of establishing Christian strongholds by forming a Student YMCA. This happened in Sri Lanka (then Ceylon), Turkey, Syria, India, Japan and China. Wishard visited Japan and held remarkably successful evangelistic meetings and by the time he left twelve Student YMCAs existed. The Japanese students decided to hold a national conference, under the theme, "Christian Students United for World Conquest." They cabled a greeting to the American students conference, "Kyoto, July 5, 1889. Make Jesus King. (Signed) Five hundred students." Indeed all over

Europe and Asia, Wishard and Wilder and Mott were used by God to win thousands to Christ and ignite students to begin their own evangelizing Y chapters.

Mott wrote pamphlets on *Bible Study for Personal Spiritual Growth, Secret Prayer, The Morning Watch* and *Personal Work.* In 1911 he spoke of the necessity to have absolute faith in the authority of Christian scriptures. "It is back, back to Christ and His redeeming blood," he affirmed, "or it is on, onward to despair." But Mott chose the inclusivist path and later became one of the key people in the formation of what later became the World Council of Churches.

Robert Wilder resigned in 1927, singling out the problems of universalism and syncretism, the lack of time given to prayer and Bible study and destructive higher criticism, which led "many students to doubt the trustworthiness of the sacred Scriptures." He was later to play a role in events leading to the formation of the International Fellowship of Evangelical Students.

The division began early in Britain. The CICCU, after internal struggles regarding the basic tenets of faith, withdrew from any association from the Student Christian Movement in 1910. Only the London medical schools joined CICCU in its withdrawal from the SCM. These two groups stood virtually alone against the other British groups who remained in the SCM.

In America the division was already clear in the SVM conference of 1920. Remarks like, "We used to speak of folk being saved and unsaved; now we are starting to wonder whether the state of the heathen is really as serious as we thought it was," could only lead the movement one way. By 1925 many American evangelical groups had already disaffiliated with the SVM and the Student Christian Movement.

5/The Evangelical Decline in University Life

As a result of what they saw happening in the early 1900s many evangelicals began to react against all higher education and all intellectual activity. Learning was becoming a dangerous thing. Opposition to the theory of evolution became the touchstone of biblical fidelity. The Scopes Trial in 1925 between the leading criminal lawyer, Clarence Darrow, and William Jennings Bryan, a Christian and former Secretary of State, was a tragic fiasco and biblical Christianity lost much public credibility in the United States.

The campus was increasingly deserted by Bible-believing Christians. Very little strong biblical scholarship existed. More time was spent defending the faith than proclaiming it. Arguments over words and what they meant absorbed energy that in another era could have been spent advancing the kingdom. The evangelical church was on the defensive. And a great movement, so influential in advancing the kingdom of God, died.

In 1975 a group of former Student Christian Movement staffworkers met at the YMCA Blue Ridge Assembly in North Carolina to assess the dissolution of the SCM. Writing about this meeting in the *Christian Century,* Andrew T. Roy makes this telling remark: "The institutions enveloped the (student) revolution and quieted it."[26]

The tragedy related in this chapter is more than history. It serves as a reminder to all the member movements of today's International Fellowship of Evangelical Students, of which the IVCF in the United States is but one, that "fire has a tendency to go out." Unswerving loyalty to an unambiguous biblical theology is crucial. Otherwise it could be said of us that "The reason we do not learn from history is because we are not the people who learned the last time."[27]

3
The Resurgence of Evangelical Student Witness

The times call for more rather than fewer Christian students who can act on their own initiative as the "bellringers" to make contact and awaken interest of fellow students. The typical student-led Christian group is more important than ever. On it may largely depend how far the Christian "presence" can survive in the colleges.[1]
Douglas Johnson, *general secretary, Inter-Varsity Fellowship, England*

The students who formed the first Christian groups in the nineteenth century were spiritual heirs of Jonathan Edwards, Charles Simeon and other men of the Great Awakenings. The Spirit-empowered student movement that came from their proclamation of Jesus Christ lasted nearly fifty years and sent thousands of proclaimers of Christ around the world. It was scarcely believable that a movement of such strength should peter out as it did.

John R. Mott, so greatly used by God in the Student Volunteer Movement and in spreading the Student Christian Movement around the world, began a deliberate policy of throwing the net as widely as possible. In non-Christian lands he enlisted men of "good will" from other religions. He was obsessed with interfaith ecumenicity. Emphasis upon the uniqueness of Christ, mankind's need for a divine Redeemer, the work of the Holy Spirit in conversion, programs of prayer and Bible study were gradually displaced. It was not a massive hemorrhage; it was a slow leak. It was a gradual downward decline, "a gentle slope, soft underfoot, without sudden turnings, without milestones, without signposts."[2]

1/Passing the Test in Great Britain

In Britain the CICCU experienced tensions and divisions over growing liberalism both prior to World War 1 and immediately after the war. The British SCM insisted that CICCU should broaden its membership. The evangelical CICUU could become the devotional section of the SCM, or as one don put it, "a commando unit" attached to the larger and more varied forces of the SCM. When they resisted, the CICCU was accused of being divisive. This was heavy-going for undergraduates.

Eventually it was arranged that some of the CICCU's officers meet with the SCM committee in their president's rooms in Trinity College towards the end of the summer term of 1919. Two CICCU men—Norman Grubb and R. P. Dick—went to the meeting. Grubb tells the story:

> There were ten of them and two of us. After an hour's talk we appeared to be getting nowhere, so I asked their president point blank—"Does the SCM put the atoning blood of Jesus Christ *central* in its beliefs?" He hesitated and then answered, "Well, we acknowledge it, but not necessarily as central." The CICCU president [R. P. Dick] . . . and I then said that this really settled the matter for us in the CICCU. This set the CICCU going again on its old foundations and from which it has not moved.[3]"

The CICCU General Committee returned to Keswick the following summer to pray and plan. One evening as they prayed together, a new sense of God and his power transformed the students, and the meeting lasted until the early hours of the morning. Grubb later said, "With the decision against union (with the SCM) came *faithfulness;* at Keswick came *fire.*" It is significant that it was *students* who handled the pressures of the SCM. The test was met by undergraduates, none of whom were over the age of twenty-two. Many of these became outstanding Christian leaders in the years that followed.

The Oxford Inter-Collegiate Christian Union (OICCU) had been absorbed by the SCM before the outbreak of World War 1. The CICCU students thought the situation of OICCU almost beyond hope. Then in 1919, after recovery from war wounds in the emergency tent hospital near Cambridge, Noel "Tiny" Palmer was notified of acceptance at Oxford University. While still in Cambridge a former school friend invited him to tea and a CICCU Bible reading. He later graduated to a daily prayer meeting. He later wrote, "I had never before in my life met anything like it! R. P. Dick, when we were walking home one night, suddenly asked me if I knew my sins were forgiven! I said—in a hollow way—I thought that they were." The CICCU men kept after him until Palmer was firmly converted.

> When it was reported in Cambridge that I had been accepted in Oxford . . . they [the CICCU men] gathered round me with fervent prayer before I left, so that I had the feeling that I was being commissioned by them to start something new in a benighted place.[4]

At Oxford word soon spread that Tiny Palmer (he was 6'8") had got religious mania. His immediate attempts to get something going at his college met with many obstacles. Nevertheless he persisted, giving the testimony of what the Lord had done for him to those who cared to listen in the Junior Common Room. Within four weeks after that about forty men were meeting for Bible study and a daily prayer meeting began.[5] The SCM would not give permission for them to use the Oxford Inter-Collegiate Christian Union (OICCU) title because it was considered the Oxford branch of the SCM, so the new group was called the Oxford University Bible Union (OUBU). Not until 1928 was the appellation OICCU restored to a strong witnessing Christian Union at Oxford as part of the Inter-Varsity Fellowship.

Meanwhile Christian Unions (CUs) began to spring up at other universities and colleges. At Norman Grubb's suggestion an Inter-Varsity (between universities) Convention was held December 8-11, 1919, for spiritual fellowship and encouragement of the existing CUs. These conferences, continued year by year, gave the growing movement a sense of unity, and talk began of a federation of Christian Unions. CICCU took the initiative to plan and execute these conferences for the first several years, but by 1923 a general committee, with representatives from each of the CUs, took over the responsibility, with an executive committee to oversee the agenda. A new national student witness was under way.

This fledgling movement was almost scuttled before it was born. When the general committee met in 1924 the Oxford delegation proposed the forming of a federation, and the appointment of Dr. Frank Buchman as general secretary. Buchman was the popular head of the Oxford Movement (later called Moral Rearmament) and had financial backing which was important to the students who wondered how they would fund what they were beginning. The majority at the meeting seemed in favor. Douglas Johnson, a medical student and substitute delegate from the London CU (LIFCU), hoped someone else would torpedo the idea, but finally stood to voice an objection. He expressed uncertainty about the proposal and that the LIFCU thought the timing was wrong.

With Buchman sitting in the meeting and expecting to be appointed it was difficult to elaborate the objection. Johnson considered the Oxford Movement too subjective and not sufficiently Bible-based. P. K. Dixon from Dublin rose to support Johnson, saying that it had never been discussed in his CU committee and he would "find it difficult to go back and tell our chaps that what I've done is help make an organization with a full-time person when we've heard nothing about it until now." He moved for deferment. The deferment won by two votes.[6]

Two insightful students saved this student witness from what would surely have been a serious defeat, since not many years later Buchman had led the Oxford Movement into increasing pluralism and away from biblical Christianity. The birth date of the fellowship was postponed until the next year when Douglas Johnson, just finishing up at medical college in London, was asked to be the general secretary, a post he held for the next forty years. Why did he take the job when he was just about to begin a medical career? Much later he would say part of the reason was "fear of the Devil catching the movement for something else."[7] *The right student in the right place at the right time is a critical factor in student witness.* By 1928 the Inter-Varsity Fellowship of Evangelical Unions (IVFEU) became an official national entity. Within ten years it included all but one university with groups in technical and teacher's training colleges as well.

2/A Slow Start in the United States

About this same time in America, evangelical students were also reorganizing student witness. Within the theological section of the intercollegiate YMCA, called the Inter-Seminary Alliance, increasing conflict between liberal and evangelical theology came to a head at a conference in 1924. The delegation from Princeton Seminary found themselves in disagreement with liberal doctrinal formulations on almost every point. The admission of a Unitarian seminary into membership was passed by a majority. In a discussion about the doctrinal platform for recruiting men for the ministry, delegates argued over words and meanings formerly taken for granted. It became apparent that they couldn't even agree on the meaning of John 3:16 and the reference to Jesus as the only begotten Son of God.

As a necessary response, on April 4, 1925, and under the leadership of J. Gresham Machen, representatives from six conservative theological institutions met and formed the League of Evangelical Students (LES). The intent of this new organization was to "raise up a student protest against modern unbelief and to take a stand for the defense and propagation of the gospel of everlasting salvation through the sacrificial death of God's only begotten Son."[8]

Initiated and staffed by seminary students, the LES committed itself to work hard on theology in the face of the overwhelming liberal consensus. They had no full-time staff and a small budget. They purposed to do whatever they could to demonstrate the respectability of biblical scholarship, holding frequent conferences primarily for seminary students.

The ministry of the League was carried on principally by students from Princeton and Westminister seminaries, both schools with strong Reformed theological convictions. Student teams traveled to other seminaries, usually at their own expense, establishing chapters and searching for fellow evangelicals. They produced a magazine, *The Evangelical Student,* and with committed volunteers held both national and regional conferences each year. In the course of their activities they attracted and encouraged some undergraduates in secular universities to begin chapters, since by then many student groups had disaffiliated with the SCM. When in 1929 Princeton Seminary reorganized to include liberal faculty members, the responsibility and leadership for LES shifted to newly founded Westminster Theological Seminary.

In reality, these courageous seminary students were fighting a battle on several levels. It was a rescue operation for students in liberal seminaries by providing scholarship and spiritual fellowship. It meant fresh effort at a carefully reasoned theology. In addition, they stirred up students on secular campuses to be thoroughly biblical in their thinking. The weakness of the LES was the lack of natural, enthusiastic evangelism and sufficient staff to encourage campus groups. They were in a strongly defensive mode—a fortress mentality. In that stance, they reflected the evangelical church of that time. At the peak of their history in 1937 the League had sixty-one chapters, most of these east of the Mississippi River.

Across the country, disillusioned students on many campuses withdrew from the SCM or the Y Associations. Small independent clusters of evangelical Christian students formed new groups.[9] Most often these were for self-defense rather than outreach. Christian students, then as now, needed each other, but viewed those outside their group as the enemy. The onslaught of liberal theology had left American Christians paralyzed in face of the need for a natural, vital expression of faith.

3/Solid Foundations for Canada

Norman Grubb, who had been traveling in Canada on deputation for the Worldwide Evangelization Crusade, returned to England with news of the spiritual decay in the universities of Canada in early April 1928. He arrived on the day that the annual Inter-Varsity Conference began at High Leigh and headed there almost immediately. He insisted on addressing the executive committee, and a special meeting was called for 9:30 P.M. With fire in his eye Grubb made an impassioned plea that the general committee appoint someone and send him to Canada to begin an evangelical student work there. This was an opportunity that could not be missed, he said. He related conversations with R. V. Bingham, founder of the Sudan Interior Mission, and entreaties from other Canadians, with promises of support, making it a formal invitation which demanded a response.

Douglas Johnson describes what followed:

We were forming a constitution for our own student work at this meeting. We hadn't got a real society going yet, but we were working on it. OICCU rejoined us at this meeting. And now we were being challenged to become a missionary society more or less. Everyone seemed stunned at the idea. We had never sent an emissary abroad.

At the end of Norman's "tour de force" more or less ordering the youthful committee to send out an Apostle to the Canadian campuses, there was a dead hush. Then somebody said, "I think we ought to do it, in faith."

"But who?" said Hugh Gough from the Chair.

"You," said several.[10]

The general committee heartily endorsed the proposal the next day. Johnson remembers thinking that perhaps Gough would be another Kynaston Studd who would ignite another John Mott for work in North America.

Hugh Gough had completed two years as president of the CICCU and had already postponed his entry to a theological college in order to serve as a traveling secretary for the CUs. Now they were asking him to delay his studies for another year and to leave for Canada in September. He needed permission from the Bishop of London for another delay. To the great disappointment of the executive committee, the Bishop said no. Johnson notes that the youthful committee was inclined to doubt the Bishop's "Christianity," but in view of Hugh Gough's subsequent career as Archbishop of Sydney, its members have come to admit the Bishop may have been right![11]

The executive committee immediately turned to their vice chairman,

Howard Guinness, whose leadership of the London Union (LIFCU) had been so dynamic. He would finish his medical finals in October. Johnson writes that Guinness had the unquenchable optimism of a pioneer. "I went into his room and deflected his mind from the textbooks and said, 'Howard, if you get through in October, would you go to Canada, for the Bishop has turned down Hugh's request?' He paused for several moments and then said, 'Yes, I will. But whatever happens, I must be back by Easter ready to take a house-job at Hospital.' "[12]

Howard Guinness had a passion to see people won for Christ. He was enthusiastic, an extrovert and highly motivated. He inspired others to a powerful sense of dependence on the Holy Spirit to do a job that was impossible. He writes about his student days:

Life was exuberant in those days and every day brought its overflow of joy. I formed the habit of choosing a chorus for each day and whistling it wherever I went. I also formed the habit of speaking to fellow travelers on the morning bus to work and the evening one home. Later, I bought a motor bike and so my travelling opportunities of witness to Christ ceased. As I rode into hospital each day I had to pass through the Smithfield Meat Market, so I fixed to my bike two notice boards, one on each side of my rear wheel, to hold messages which I could change week by week.[13]

Geraint Fielder writes of him,

Guinness had the approach . . . of a cavalry charge officer. He rode, not a horse, but a big motorbike with sandwich boards tied to the carrier. Doubtless this was one of his wilder student ideas, but few will forget the sight of his bike . . . festooned with the text "Prepare to meet thy God." His life was all risk, attack, venture, daring. But he loved people, and his warm-heartedness came through.[14]

The sending committee, made up largely of second- and third-year students, sent word to Canada that Guinness was coming. Professor A. Rendle Short provided him with a one-way ticket and Norman Grubb gave him the enormous, fur-lined coat he himself had used the winter he had toured Canada. At the last minute the student committee realized that their missionary would need some expense money and scraped together the modest sum of fourteen pounds (about seventy dollars) from the sale of hockey sticks, books and the like.

On Friday, October 26, 1928, the night before departure, a small group gathered in his mother's flat to commission Howard Guinness, thanking God for the good things He was going to do. Guinness later wrote, "Then they laid their hands on my head, as the Antioch elders had done to Paul, and sent me out in the Name of Jesus and in the power of the Holy Spirit." Only Howard's widowed mother demurred, "Knowing Howard, I fear he will never return to Medicine." And he never did. Howard exchanged medicine for a lifetime of preaching Christ.

The stormy November 1928 Atlantic crossing kept Howard mostly below deck, desperately seasick. Each morning he would struggle up on deck for a couple of hours to make friends with the children and teach them some choruses. On the day before disembarking he wrote in his diary. "My cabin-mate, Runciman, an engineer emigrating to Canada, received Christ. To Him be all the glory. Allelujah."

The executive committee in England had sent word of Guinness's arrival, but he soon found out he was on his own in making contacts in the universities and whatever else he hoped to accomplish. None of the people whom Grubb had mentioned had set up any contacts or were anywhere around in those first weeks. The invitation given was not taken as seriously as the invitation received.

On his second day in Montreal he wrote in his journal:

I realize that my first duty to the student of Canada is to lead him into the *fullness of the Holy Spirit's power*. This must come before any attempt to get the lukewarm man to form a Union of any sort. Unions [student groups] of man-made energy, however true to God's Word, would be a disaster to Canada. However, the Holy Spirit has been brooding over these Varsities and preparing certain hearts to receive this message and power through me and then to do something! Allelujah!

By his third day he had seen only one student (and that for a half hour) from McGill University where he had hoped to see a group formed. His journal entry, "I am not going to hurry on from here D. V. [God willing] until something deep is done."[15] He had an unshakable confidence that God was in this journey he was taking.

When Guinness reached Toronto about three weeks later he found the encouragement he had hoped for earlier. It was Noel "Tiny" Palmer of Oxford who made the difference. Palmer, by now a Toronto pastor, and his wife, Josephine (daughter of Catherine Booth), had the same heart for student work as Guinness, and together they prayed and sought out contacts. So much began to happen among the students in Toronto colleges that Noel Palmer began praying about taking up "Varsity work" full-time and the executive committee back in London worried about Guinness's "hugging" Toronto rather than getting on to the West.

Reading *Journey Among Students,* Guinness's published account of his Canadian adventures, is like reading a modern version of the book of *The Acts of the Apostles.* He traveled across Canada to British Columbia, then back to the maritime provinces, then revisiting his student contacts, he returned to the West Coast. His tremendous enthusiasm for knowing Jesus Christ as Lord left behind a trail of men and women who had given themselves unreservedly to Christ. He gave a simple organizational structure as a model students could build on: daily prayer meetings and a weekly Bible study, plus a huge vision to small groups of students in almost every university. His six-month stay in Canada stretched out to fourteen months. Dr. Arthur Hill, general secretary of the Canadian IVCF, 1933-34, said of Guinness, "He went across our country just like a flame of fire; wherever he touched down there came life."[16]

From the first Guinness saw the need to train leaders in the high schools to get them ready for varsity witness. He was a strong promoter of camps for boys and girls as a way to win and train future leaders, and held several of these during his time in Canada. His vision was behind what is now the Inter-School Christian Fellowship and the impressive Pioneer Camps spread across the provinces.

On his first arrival in Vancouver, Guinness discovered an already existing Christian student group at the University of British Columbia (UBC). In 1925 evangelical students at the university found it increasingly difficult to express their faith within the SCM. Some of these posted a notice on the bulletin board, "Everyone wishing to defend the faith once and for all delivered to the saints, please meet in Lecture Room 202, Thursday noon, and bring your lunch." They called themselves the Student Christian Fundamentalist Society, known on campus as the SCFS as distinct from the SCM.

Across the border in Seattle, Washington, a vital group of about a hundred students met at the University of Washington (UW), calling themselves the Evangelical Union (EU). The EU was in affiliation with the League of Evangelical Students and held periodic conferences at The Firs, a conference center in Bellingham, near the Canadian border. UBC students soon found encouragement from attending these conferences and, influenced by students at UW, in 1927 joined the American LES, the only Canadian group to do so, changing its name to Varsity Christian Union. Guinness was excited to find this organized CU and he set it afire with his enthusiasm. He gave them a new vision for outreach to their non-Christian friends and, to their surprise, several were converted at the first meeting.

At their invitation Guinness spoke to the Evangelical Union at the University of Washington. He made no other university visits in the United States, even though he had invitations to do so. Dr. Howard Kelly, a prominent gynecologist from Johns Hopkins University, offered Guinness an office, a secretary and a salary if he would pioneer a student work in the States. Kelly had a summer home near IVCF's Pioneer Camp, and he began hearing more and more about what was happening in Canada. He mourned the demise of the once-effective intercollegiate Y movement and wanted an evangelical student work in the U.S. But Howard Guinness had been sent to Canada, and he declined the invitation.

Guinness wanted to know more about The League of Evangelical Students work in America. He accompanied Noel Palmer to the Chicago convention of the LES in early December that first year in Canada to investigate firsthand the nature of their ministry. He noted in his diary that practically all of the League chapters were in theological seminaries and that their only aim seemed to be apologetics, "appealing to the mind alone and dealing with such subjects as Christ's Deity, Theism, etc. . . . Dead theology is stifling the League," he concluded.

One gets the impression of an indomitable force stirring up students in Canada in reading about Guinness's influence. But Howard Guinness had his share of defeats like any other staff member since. His strength was in his optimism which kept him honest and yet full of expectancy about the future. In the fall of 1929, with his usual verve, he sent out announcement flyers for

the First Evangelical Students Conference to be held at a lovely Tourist Camp just outside Kingston, Ontario, September 13-20, rates $2 a day. All students who have been born again are urged to be present at all cost—especially Freshmen. Representatives expected from Saskatchewan, Manitoba, Western, Varsity, Queen's and McGill.[17]

Guinness had turned down an offer of good conference facilities in the Muskoka area, hoping that his chosen location would bring a good number of students from McGill and Queens. He was wrong. Three students came, plus the speaker and two helpers. The facilities proved to be so dirty that within two and a half hours they packed up and left for the city where they used a large church hall. Here is Guinness's description:

It was really another fiasco. I can never remember it without my hair standing on end. It was terribly difficult. The Anglican church near the University opened its doors to us and let us use the Sunday School hall. Seven people in a church hall, feeling that—I, at least, feeling reluctant to be there, wishing I were somewhere else. . . . As a matter of fact, we closed it down a day early and went back to Toronto.[18]

Three students at the first annual national student conference that Howard had planned! In his diary Guinness wrote: "September 1929, First IVF Conference, Kingston, Ont. 6 present. A failure!" However, Arthur Hill, one of the students and later general secretary, says of this meeting,

> We prayed about the whole work, and then we finally decided to organize. One of the girls nominated me to be president, the other girl seconded the nomination, they both voted in favor. It was unanimous. I was president of the newly formed students' Inter-Varsity Christian Fellowship of Canada. And by the way, I chose that name, too.[19]

Great ministries sometimes have humble beginnings.

On reaching Vancouver for the second time in late 1929, Guinness responded to an invitation to visit the universities and camps of Australia and New Zealand, sailing in early January 1930. Within hours of his arrival in Australia he was taken to a Scripture Union boys' camp where he would be chaplain for the next ten days. The two young men running the camp were C. Stacey Woods, who would later play such a large role in the Inter-Varsity movement around the world, and Vincent Craven, whose ministry at Ontario Pioneer Camp would be notable.

Guinness later returned to Britain from Australia by way of Vancouver, visiting the Christian Unions in Pauline fashion as he crossed the continent, reaching British shores in early January 1931. For the next ten years Guinness continued to extend the kingdom among university students with travels to India, South Africa, Spain, Norway, Sweden, Finland, Hungary, Switzerland and Belgium. He seemed never to waste opportunities, often engaging people on trains or buses in conversations that, in the end, made significant contributions to God's work.

Howard Guinness had left his mark on Canada, spreading a vision from coast to coast. As he made preparations to go on to Australia, the Christian leaders concerned for consolidating what he had begun, wrote to Douglas Johnson of the British IVF, "Guinness is leaving us for Australia. Can you send us another leader who is an organizer as much as evangelist?" Kenneth Hooker agreed to a four-month visit, arriving in Montreal as Guinness was making preparations to sail from Vancouver in late 1929. In his diary he records that he traveled 13,686 miles building on the work Guinness had begun.

The Inter-Varsity Christian Fellowship of Canada had been officially organized since that fateful conference in September 1929. One year later in

1930 Noel Palmer left his pastorate to become the first IVCF general secretary, taking a three-year leave of absence from the Anglican church. In
fact, the letterhead contained both the names of Noel and Josie Palmer as
general secretaries. That God would give leaders of this caliber to a young
movement at this critical moment in their history was a tremendous boon.
The Palmers took on the arduous task of crisscrossing the continent, building up existing CUs and encouraging other students to begin an organized
witness.

When the Palmers' three-year leave was past, Arthur Hill, who had just
finished his medical training, became general secretary for one year to
keep the momentum going. Since he could delay his medical practice no
longer, finding a successor was crucial. In September 1934, C. Stacey
Woods became general secretary of the Canadian Inter-Varsity Christian
Fellowship.[20]

4/The Spread of the Work in North America

Stacey Woods, born and raised in Australia, had not intended to come to
Canada. In 1934 after he had finished his training at Wheaton College and
Dallas Theological Seminary, he planned to join Howard Guinness in India
to do a work among English-speaking schoolboys. Stacey had already
booked a ticket to India. His long-range plans were to work with Guinness
for a few years and then return to Australia for ordination in the Church
of England diocese of Sydney.

When a letter came from Arthur Hill inviting him to become his successor at a salary of fifty dollars a month,[21] he never stopped to pray. He
assumed he knew what God wanted him to do and turned down the offer.
Stacey writes,

The days following the dispatch of this letter were filled with depression. God seemed to be saying to me, 'You have made your decision
without consulting me, yet you claim to be yielded to my will.' In an
agony of repentance I told the Lord I would go to Canada for one year,
providing he would make this unequivocally clear.[22]

Within the next three days letters from his parents came expressing their
doubts about his plans for India. A cable from Howard Guinness said that
he was being recalled to England and the plan to work with him was
canceled. When the second letter came from Canada asking him to recon-
sider and come immediately, Stacey Woods felt the clear call of God to take
the offer.

He was twenty-five years old when he became the general secretary of the Canadian movement. One student, Yvonne Ritchie who later became his wife, couldn't imagine that he could be the general secretary when she first saw him because he looked "like a young boy." When he and staff-worker Cathie Nicoll went in to meet a school principal to get permission for the Inter-School Christian Fellowship work, the principal gave the permission to Cathy and suggested Stacey go on to his class, figuring he was one of the high-school students.[23] But as J. Edwin Orr later wrote, "In 1934 a director of normal height but abnormal energy, C. Stacey Woods, took up the task."

Noel Palmer's work as general secretary had been foundational and his travels across the provinces had stabilized the pioneering work of Howard Guinness, Dr. Arthur Hill had kept up this ministry of encouragement, often at great cost to himself. It had been pretty much a hand-to-mouth existence for both men. Money was scarce; the movement was new. The Great Depression had affected the wealthy business men who had given funds to establish this student witness. Stacey's task was to put structure to the work, to develop an effective staff, and to get support from Christians and churches concerned about the university. The great distances and meager finances at first did not permit staff visits outside Ontario and Quebec. Some of the provinces had not been visited since the Palmers' tour in 1932. By the time Woods arrived on the Canadian scene in 1934, the students who had been influenced by Howard Guinness had graduated. Some of the Christian Unions in the east were thriving, but across the country many places had only scattered contacts.

By 1935 a new constitution for the Canadian IVCF was in place with a governing body—a board of directors—with women among its members. These by-laws (slightly amended) were later adopted in the U.S. IVCF constitution:

1. The Fellowship shall guard against incurring indebtedness of any kind.

2. It shall guarantee no income to its secretaries (staff members), but will seek to provide them their maintenance as funds permit.

3. The staff members shall depend on God alone for the supply of their temporal needs, but the Board of Directors shall assume an attitude of responsibility and honest endeavour before God to support them.

4. All financial obligations shall be met in the following order: (a) Overhead current expenses of the office and the travelling expenses of the staff; (b) Any remaining moneys shall be divided among the staff members in the proportions fixed by the Board of Directors in its An-

nual Budget establishing their stipends; provided, however, that the amount paid to the staff members shall not in any event exceed the stipends established by the Board of Directors.

5. No indebtedness to any staff member on account of salary shall extend beyond the termination of the fiscal year of appointment.

The Basis of Faith was carefully spelled out as evangelical and interdenominational. In 1936 Stacey Woods made his first visit to student groups across the country, and the movement began solid growth. Soon the Inter-Varsity Christian Fellowship in Canada began to receive inquiries from students in the United States who had heard the good news of what God was doing in Canadian universities. They asked for help. Stacey was cautious about responding since the League of Evangelical Students was functioning in the U.S., but he began to make inquiries.

In February 1935, Calvin Cummings, general secretary for the LES, wrote to Stacey,

> You are right about the League's emphasis being apologetic. We believe that this approach is not only Biblical but the only alternative in view of what the student hears on every hand: namely, that Christianity is not true. We find that students are indifferent to the Savior because they do not believe that Christianity is true. They are not reading the Bible because they are not convinced it is true. True faith involves among other things conviction that a thing is true. To put it tersely, we believe that without a healthy apologetic there can be no healthy evangelism.[24]

It was a good summary of the League's philosophy.

Yet it was increasingly obvious that the theological weightiness of the LES did not have a wide appeal to undergraduates. Charles Troutman, League president at Wheaton College in 1936, traveled with the college debate team and visited forty other colleges while on tour. He found many students seeking Christian associations, but none of them interested in joining the LES. Students who went to LES functions spoke of the content "being over my head," and "I couldn't understand what they were saying." Cornelius Van Til of Westminster Theological Seminary, who was brilliant in teaching students later when Inter-Varsity established a training center known as Campus-in-the-Woods, was described as "deadly dull" when speaking at LES conferences. This eminent scholar and others in the LES doubtless assumed college students were as interested in the theological issues of the fundamentalist/modernist controversy as they were.

As general secretary of the Canadian Inter-Varsity, Stacey Woods was invited to be a fraternal observer at the 1936 convention of the League.

After earnest prayer, five undergraduates under the leadership of Charles H. Troutman, Jr., dared to ask the leadership of the League to demonstrate a more realistic concern for the needs of the average undergraduate student and to place a greater emphasis on a student's personal devotional life and evangelism. Immediately a number of professors jumped to their feet to defend their emphasis on theology, and the conference by-passed Troutman's petition for the second time. This reaction highlighted the problem of trying to make an effective theological seminary movement into an undergraduate one. It also signaled to both Woods and Troutman the need for an undergraduate student work in the United States.

Clearly the LES stood in the gap, proclaiming biblical Christianity at a critical moment in history, reinforcing the evangelical theology of many seminary and college students. Its strength was the statement it made about biblical scholarship and truth. The weakness of the League as a student movement was that it was seminary-dominated. It was "monastery-based." Its tone did not match the college students' mindset nor their more basic needs.

It was at this LES meeting that Stacey Woods invited his good friend from Wheaton College, Charles Troutman, to join the Canadian IVCF staff after his graduation. Charles had already been accepted at three medical colleges and had planned to pursue studies at one of these. He agreed to come to Canada for one year. Little did he know then that student work can become like a virus in your bloodstream, making you forget you ever wanted to do anything else. Stacey Woods wrote,

> There was not a better loved American who came to Canada than Charles Troutman. For the first academic year he worked largely in the high schools of Ontario. Then from the autumn of 1937 until 1939 he concentrated on Quebec, particularly at McGill University. Men like Dr. Gordon Thomas, who later blazed a trail to become director of the Grenfell Mission in Labrador, were nurtured under his leadership.[25]

In the next three years the Canadian work experienced growth on three levels—Christian Unions (IVCF chapters) in universities, the Inter-School Christian Fellowship in high schools and the establishment of the outstanding Pioneer Camps. Stacey had a gift for choosing pioneer staff members whose sense of sacrifice matched his own, a willingness to give to build a student movement in a vast country. The Christian church became increasingly aware of what was happening among university students.

By this time both Stacey and Charles had come to know many Christian students in the United States and scarcely a month passed without letters from struggling groups asking for help. It was an awkward situation, but files contain hundreds of letters in return, suggesting the basic format of daily prayer meetings and weekly Bible study as foundational for anything else they might do on their campus.

During the school year 1937-38 Stacey Woods inquired of the LES leadership whether Inter-Varsity would be welcome in the United States. According to Robert E. Nicholas, then general secretary of the LES, most of those in leadership recognized that Inter-Varsity had resources and a program that fit the secular campus and undergraduate students. The wise thing to do would be to cooperate. Charles and Stacey began to make forays into the States to visit student contacts who had requested help.

Others more protective of the League's ministry saw the advent of IVCF in the States as competition or "sheep-stealing." Some were concerned that IVCF did not have a sufficiently well-developed theology. This objection largely disappeared when T.C. Hammond's *In Understanding Be Men* (published by the British IVF) was adopted as a teaching tool in student chapters.[26] As a Westminster seminary student participating in the LES, Edmund Clowney was hesitant about Inter-Varsity's policy of student leadership. He argued that staff leadership would be necessary to guard student chapters from falling into theological error. Now, as a president emeritus of Westminster Theological Seminary, Dr. Clowney says, "I was wrong. Students do need instruction and counsel, but leadership develops where students have a real responsibility for witness."[27] He has since become a strong supporter of IVCF in the States and a favorite speaker at Inter-Varsity training events.

More and more requests came from students and from Christian leaders who saw the great need of undergraduate students. Gifts were received, banked and held in reserve until the time when IVCF would come to the United States. Stacey Woods made it a policy that Inter-Varsity would not make contacts on any campus that had a LES chapter, and later that any chapter requesting affiliation must first withdraw from the League and state that their new affiliation was not initiated by IVCF. That proved difficult since the LES still counted chapters who did not think they were LES chapters. Since by 1940 there were only twenty-two LES chapters left and almost all of these at seminaries, supporters of Inter-Varsity urged IVCF to begin a campus witness more suited to undergraduates.

The League gradually disappeared from the scene. In 1943 it merged with the Inter-Collegiate Gospel Fellowship (IGF) and disappeared from the campus scene. Supported by funds from L. G. LeTourneau, the leader of the the IGF, L. Craig Long, proved hostile to the advance of Inter-Varsity. He used *Christian Opinion,* the IGF magazine, as a platform for his attacks for the next four years. Calling personal evangelism a "spiritual scurvy," Long maintained that only ordained pastors are authorized by God to do that work. By 1948 the IGF had slipped into oblivion.

Canadian board minutes for 1938 show Troutman and Woods both spending two months of the year in the United States making contacts with students and interested supporters. James Forrester, Canadian staffworker responsible for work in British Columbia and Alberta, also visited students in adjacent states. The schedule of examinations in Montreal colleges enabled Troutman to cross the border without missing a beat on the campuses for which he was responsible. Troutman's letters to praying friends read like this:

9/23/38—"Without opposing or running competition with the LES as God leads we shall enter where there is a door open."

10/17/38—"In two weeks I am going down to Union College where there is a small group of Christian men. Beyond that I have no contacts at present. As the Lord opens up different schools I shall do what I can personally to help students in their witness for Christ. Will you be much in prayer that this trip may be used of God? I feel very much like a pioneer missionary without the dignity of such status."

Spring, 1939, to a student—"It would seem in a student body the size of Rensselaer that there would be at least one student who is interested in spiritual things. I hope you will make some attempt in locating such a one. We shall be praying for you. When you find this fellow, the two of you could come to the Conference together. It will be a small conference of Christians to pass on the vision."

12/13/39—"I had a good trip into the U.S. I was able to meet with Christian students at Union College, Russell Sage, Rensselaer Tech and Hunter College in New York City."

In the fall of 1938 Stacey Woods accepted an invitation to the University of Michigan where a cadre of students were ready to begin a student group associated with Inter-Varsity Christian Fellowship. Michigan Christian Fellowship resulted from that visit. By the end of the 1938 school year, chapters were identified at five colleges—University of Michigan, University of Washington,[28] Wayne University, Michigan State College and Drexel University. Woods and Troutman had their hands full of requests for counsel and help as a result of their brief visits into the States. Troutman noted that whenever he found an existing evangelical student group he also found a dedicated Christian in the community or on campus who served as a rallying point. Some of these were people who had come out of the student Y movement in its evangelical heyday and had been praying that God would raise up a new student witness.

The magnanimous spirit of the Canadian IVCF Board, undoubtedly spurred on by the visionary Woods, became evident. On their doorstep, but across the border, was potential for student work that staggered the imagination. They rose to the occasion. By the 1939-40 school year they had appointed three Americans to the Canadian board—H. J. Taylor, J. F. Strombeck and C. H. Troutman, Sr., father of Charles Troutman, as a first step in initiating a movement in the United States.

In September 1939, as World War 2 began in Europe, three Americans were appointed to pioneer student work in the United States under the Canadian board. Charles Troutman was sent to Michigan, Grace Koch[29] to work in Pennsylvania and Herbert Butt[30] to the Northwest. Those same board minutes list only four staff members for all of Canada. Once again, a new movement (not a decade old) began unselfishly to pioneer student work in another country to the glory of God.

4

The Making of an Ethos*

Leadership is an interpersonal matter. People do not follow programs, but leaders who inspire them. They act when a vision stirs in them a reckless hope of something greater than themselves, hope of fulfillment they never before dared to aspire to. And hope is passed from person to person. God-given visions of hope are shared, shared by leaders who see the vision with people who don't. But sharing is more than talking. Hope bursts into flame when leaders begin to act. As they follow their vision, clearly and openly facing the difficulties, God mobilizes the many by the challenging actions of the few.[1]
John White, *author*

S tacey Woods was a restless man. He was never content with present boundaries, always pushing on to new frontiers. His favorite verse became a fitting epitaph, "Let us press on . . ." Reaching out and making things happen became a lifelong habit. He continued even in retirement—seeking ways to help students establish a Christian witness in the Soviet Union, inviting college students in for Bible study, sharing a vision of what one person yielded to God could do. One could not help being impressed with his single-minded drive.

Whether the committee who urged Stacey Woods to come to Canada as the general secretary of the fledgling Inter-Varsity Christian Fellowship had insight to see what kind of person this promising twenty-five-year-old man was may not be important at this juncture. He seemed destined for the task at hand. Stacey bore the influence of his maternal grandfather, an authoritarian English gentleman with whom the family lived while his father

---

* *Ethos: the characteristic spirit, prevalent tone of sentiment, of a people or community; the 'genius' of an institution or system. (Oxford English Dictionary)*

served as a chaplain during World War 1. An old-world sense of what makes for proper manners never left him, although he managed to combine this with unusual personal freedom and whimsy in a way that was sometimes unsettling.

Although their home was in Sydney, his father, Fred Woods, followed the pattern of the apostle Paul, as an evangelist with the Brethren. He went to villages that had no evangelical church, pitched his tent, visited in the homes of the people, invited them to meetings, brought them to conversion, instructed them in the Scripture, established a church and then moved on to the next place. His zeal, his sacrificial spirit and his consistent godliness influenced Stacey profoundly, as well as providing a model for the way pioneering work is done. "Trusting God for everything," Stacey said, "was a way of life for our family. My parents lived a life of faith in quiet simplicity without making much of it before others."

His Plymouth Brethren roots gave Stacey not only a strong background in the Bible, but an emphasis on the importance of Scripture as a guide for daily life. It was to be read and obeyed. As he became more seasoned in his leadership he would thunder out his disdain for shallow, superficial Christianity. He had a keen sense of awe and reverence before God and an earnestness about worship that became a standard of IVCF. Charles Troutman speaks of his genius in refusing to be enmeshed in the conservative/liberal debate that consumed the energy of the church in the thirties and forties, "and Stacey did that by exalting Jesus Christ."

Evangelism was not an extra to either Woods or Troutman, but a natural part of being a Christian. While students at Wheaton College they got a taste of student evangelism through the rather bold projects of the Scripture Distribution Society sparked by Paul Guinness, a relative of Howard Guinness. Armed with 5,000 copies of John's Gospel called *His Triumph,* a team of students went to the University of Chicago football game to hand out the booklets. Later they organized a rally at Thorne Hall on Northwestern's downtown campus attended by 2,000 students. Ten students gave their testimony—no singing, no praying—just an opening statement by Paul Guinness as he introduced each person. Charles writes of this,

> We were all spellbound. I think most Evangelicals in the 1930s had written off the universities as possibilities for the Gospel. I believe Stacey would say the same thing—that the football distribution and the Thorne Hall meeting opened our eyes to the opportunity of witness in the university world.[2]

They learned equally helpful lessons through further distribution projects.

One year Wheaton students raised $8,500 (in 1934-35 that was a handsome sum!) to send 14,000 copies of *His Triumph* to students at the University of Minnesota. They prayed as the envelopes were addressed, stuffed and stamped; enthusiasm ran high. They gave the Minnesota chapter of the League of Evangelical Students (LES) as a return address. After a dedication service the bundles were sent off. But there was not a single response; the booklets were tossed on the floor of the university post office. LES students gathered them up and gave them to the city mission. Direct mail distribution was a questionable way to reach students. Whenever early IVCF groups contemplated a direct mail project for student evangelism, Woods and Troutman had some words of wisdom.

During his student days at Dallas and Wheaton, Stacey Woods spent the summers doing evangelism with the Children's Special Services Missions at Victoria Beach on Lake Winnipeg. Ruth Oliver, a Canadian whose family summered at Victoria Beach, comments, "Stacey was very attractive. We kids loved him; he and the other young leaders were so much fun. At that time in my life, it was an important spiritual input." Stacey already had a good deal of experience in his work in the Scripture Union Boy's Camps in Australia in reaching young people for Christ.

And Stacey Woods was fun to be with. Mel Donald, who was his associate general secretary in Canada in the early years, called him a natural raconteur. He saw and described happenings in technicolor, a talent that sometimes led him astray, but which often made for great hilarity. With all the pressure of directing two national movements he managed to see the funny side of his own behavior and the situations he got himself into.

Returning to his desk after campus visits, he would take the office by storm. He went at his correspondence with verve, dictating letters at a mad pace, punctuating the sentences with "period," "paragraph" or whatever was required as he raced along. One evening, after voluminous output, he attended a staff prayer meeting and unwittingly put the punctuation marks verbally into his prayer: "Dear Lord comma . . ." Later he laughed as heartily as anyone else at what he had done. He was charming and entertaining. At other times he was a bit of a prankster and took delight in shocking people. As time went on it was as if he was aware that he was becoming a legend and maybe even subtly promoted it.[3] Being in his company was a high-energy experience.

Stacey put his pre-seminary business experience to work in organizing the Canadian and American Inter-Varsitys. He allowed himself to be greatly influenced by people whom he respected spiritually and practically. He sought advice without losing leadership. He would not be bought and could hardly be reined in by any board, but so compelling was his outlook that he was set free to carry out his plans. When he spoke about what he believed God could do on the campus, people sensed the hand of God on him and began praying regularly for him, some for as many as forty years.

He also set others free. He had an uncanny gift for choosing strong people to help him in the work. He didn't want followers; he wanted leaders who knew their own minds and even felt free to disagree with him. He gave people impossible tasks, confident that God could help them do it. His fast pace usually meant that he didn't check back very often to see if they were surviving. A few didn't, but most did more than survive. They helped blaze the trail. As one board member put it many years later, "The Lord surrounded Stacey with people who put legs on his vision."

The friendship and camaraderie between Charles Troutman, Jr., and Stacey Woods in IVCF's early years was of great importance in setting the tone of the work. Charles grew up in Butler, Pennsylvania, in a godly Lutheran home. His father was a successful business man and a well-known Christian leader, serving on the board of Wheaton College and active in other organizations. His close and stable family life, the model of his parents and the opportunities he enjoyed contributed to the secure and trustworthy person he became.

Charles was as thoughtful as Stacey was impulsive. He was a good listener, a question-asker, a philosopher. Staff and students thought of him as a friend and mentor. He modeled a practical kind of wisdom and godliness.

"They were perfect for their jobs," Howard Larsen, a former staff member who became the secretary and treasurer of the International Legal Center in the United Nations, recalls. "For a field general you couldn't beat Charles Troutman. He was marvelous. No matter what you wrote to Charles, within forty-eight hours you had an answer on a penny postcard. You just knew you could depend on him—he was always reliable, never got excited and was so understanding. There is no way Stacey could have done what Charles did, and Charles could not do what Stacey did. They were two different men who beautifully supported each other and worked together on different jobs. Stacey was one of the most remarkable men I have ever worked for. He was a dynamic, exciting man who would drive you to exhaustion but make you glad to do it again the next day. I was inspired by Stacey, but I looked to Charles for guidance. Both were complex; both were in the right place at the right time."

Together these two men—Stacey Woods and Charles Troutman—hammered out the philosophy and methods that marked the future of IVCF's student work. Building on the British heritage of the Inter-Varsity Fellowship, they forged a student work that combined what they considered the biblical essentials with the needs of American university students.

Of first importance, they wanted to establish an "evangelizing fellowship." In addition, they believed the student work should not be paternalistic. The biblical teaching of the priesthood of the believer had practical implications. Students who knew Christ were responsible for the gospel and their own witness on campus. Inter-Varsity would be a student movement, rather than a movement to students. When asked by a group of businessmen, who were rather skeptical of this philosophy, what justification he had for insisting upon a student movement rather than a mission to students, Stacey Woods replied, "The Word of God."

He went on to say that

the concept of a student movement is only the unavoidable outworking of the principle of responsibility given in the Great Commission, applied to the undergraduate student world. From the early days of the Christian church it was the ordinary Christian who was scattered abroad preaching the Word. In addition to this Biblical reason, unquestionably this is, in the long run, the most effective method of insuring campus evangelism. Someone may come in from outside for a special campaign and leave again. The university population is not static; perhaps a third of a student body changes each year. The only way this constantly changing student body can be evangelized is by a continuing work of evangelism carried on within the university itself. Furthermore, the greatest apologetic for the Gospel is a Christian student living in the power of the Holy Spirit, demonstrating the reality of the Christian faith.[4]

It was critical that they find staff members who could inspire and coach without usurping the unique opportunities of the students. Witness must come from within the university.

Sometime later Stacey attended a conference on religion at a state university. Inter-Varsity was only one of quite a number of religious associations meeting with faculty members from across the nation. A faculty member approached him and said,

I do not agree with Inter-Varsity in its theology. It is old-fashioned, obscurantist and reactionary. But there is one thing that does appeal. This movement is not working from the outside like a propaganda agency trying to tell students what they should believe or what they should do. Rather, this is a genuine grass-roots student movement, a genuine expression of undergraduate feeling and conviction. We may not agree with your viewpoint, but we will defend your right to carry on a work when it is on this basis.[5]

In the years that followed, staff members often heard remarks like this from university officials. Woods once commented:

If undergraduate days are a preparation for that larger life beyond the microcosm called university, could there be a better training for Christian service in later life than that of the undergraduate taking an open stand for the Lord Jesus, assuming the spiritual burden for the ministry in daily prayer, himself engaged in studying the Bible and teaching the Bible to his classmates, and individually and corporately with his fellow Christian students endeavoring to lead others to the Lord Jesus Christ? Admittedly, such a program will have all the weaknesses of the immature undergraduate. But it has all the strength of personal conviction and God-given initiative and responsibility. And it has the great advantage of fulfilling the Biblical principle of Christian witness and of being a genuinely grass-roots student movement.[6]

This philosophy of student work was distinctively Inter-Varsity. In the late 1930s the conservative Christian church was largely in a protective mode, frightened by the onslaught of liberalism. Much of the church was uncertain about the ability of young people to withstand intellectual pressures, least of all to expect them to be aggressive in sharing and living out their faith.[7]

The daily prayer meeting (DPM) was the touchstone for a chapter. The strategy was to win people for Christ through prayer and Bible study. It happened over and over. Whenever a student inquired about having a chapter on their campus the staff asked, "Are you meeting regularly to pray for people on your campus?" If a campus group did not have a vital DPM, they probably weren't ready to become a chapter. Stacey wrote:

Without wishing to be pious or presumptuous, in those beginning days all of us felt we were under the direction of the Holy Spirit. Ours was no spirit of expansion and empire. We loved students, longed for their spiritual well-being . . . but always with the sense that we were behind the living God, following him, entering through doors he opened.[8]

Charles Troutman writes of this time,

For various reasons, we thought we were pioneering a new thing. . . .
It came as a complete surprise when we discovered the Holy Club of

Oxford, the early history of the intercollegiate YMCA, and especially our own background in the CICCU, only sixty years before. It does not speak well for our upbringing that we didn't know this, but it speaks volumes concerning the change in religious climate. As a result we began ransacking every second-hand bookstore we could find. In the Midwest, rural funeral parlors were a fruitful source of material since clergy burial expenses were often paid for by the deceased's library. The books may have gathered dust for decades. Some undertakers gladly gave us whole shelves of books just for a dollar. My first reading of Brainerd's *Journals* was in a beat-up, leather volume published in 1831. What we discovered was that there was a long line of Christian students who had faced very similar situations as we were facing at that time. The more we dug into the past, the further back the student struggle to witness went. . . . These discoveries gave us a new confidence in the Lord, in the universities and in students.[9]

Both men took the university seriously. It was not a fishing pond where staff would be sent to catch fish. It was a society that God wanted to invade. Inter-Varsity was to be integral to campus life because of its student witness and thus influence the university with the message of God. Men and women must confront their classmates, professors and, indeed, the system itself with the glorious gospel of our God.

This could not happen apart from quality spiritual life in believers on campus. The lordship of Christ was central. Students across the country were to hear Stacey Woods say,

Two persons are not presented to us, on the one hand Jesus the Savior and on the other hand Christ the Lord. He is one, and God has declared him to be both Lord and Christ. There is something to be believed; there is Someone to be received. That One is Christ the Lord. Christ must become *your* Lord and King.[10]

Theology mattered to those early shapers of the movement. The Inter-Varsity Christian Fellowship must be absolutely true to the basic tenets of Scripture. The theological pressures of the 1930s, when the Basis of Faith for the Canadian IVCF was written, presented a challenge to Stacey Woods. Charles Troutman commented that a lesser person than Stacey would have capitulated to the special interest groups. Strong leaders, each certain their theology was the only right one, argued that their position be included in the Basis of Faith. At one point Stacey Woods was offered the assurance of an annual gift of $100,000 if he would include a premillennial statement in Inter-Varsity's theological statement. Stacey's response to that was, "Sir, that is bribery, not Christian giving." Other groups had different points important to their denomination. In the controversy, support for the movement was lost. But Inter-Varsity Christian Fellowship was to minister across denominational lines.

Thus the Basis of Faith was thoughtfully and carefully hammered out in this climate of theological tension. It was basic, not comprehensive, but easy to understand. It was simple; it was bedrock; it was fundamentalist. (The word *evangelical* was not commonly used in the 1940s.) It reflected a biblical response to contemporary issues:

1. The unique, divine inspiration, integrity and authority of the Bible.

2. The deity of our Lord Jesus Christ.

3. The necessity and efficacy of the substitutionary death of Jesus Christ for the redemption of the world, and the historic fact of his bodily resurrection.

4. The presence and power of the Holy Spirit in the work of regeneration.

5. The consummation of the kingdom in the "glorious appearing of the great God and our Savior Jesus Christ."

All staff members, student officers and speakers must subscribe to this statement. Stacey Woods and Charles Troutman never let it be a perfunctory statement: expansion of its significance was part of staff training, and, in particular, the first statement about the Scripture was reinforced again and again. "You have nothing to offer students if you weaken your position on the Scriptures," Stacey roared in his own convincing way. The five-point Basis of Faith was a serious matter. Inter-Varsity was interdenominational, but that did not mean theology was unimportant.

Stacey Woods later wrote in *HIS* magazine:

In preparing this Basis of Faith, leaders of the Fellowship have not tried to enunciate everything they believe about Christ and the Christian faith. . . . Instead, the Basis of Faith is an expression of the spiritual and doctrinal purpose of the organization. . . . A question sometimes arises for an Inter-Varsity chapter executive: just how should this Basis of Faith be used? It is not a flag to be waved aloft and saluted. Rather, it is an anchor that keeps the organization from drifting from its doctrinal and scriptural moorings. An anchor that is working is under water and thus invisible. . . . The real function of the Basis of Faith in chapter activities is in assuring that special speakers are truly evangelical. . . . Also, if a chapter is to cooperate with other organizations in holding a meeting, the Basis can properly be used as a yardstick to show whether the speaker in question is acceptable. . . . Perhaps the most important place for the functioning of the principles of faith is at elections within the chapter.[11]

The IVCF constitution also spelled out the purpose of Inter-Varsity:

The aim of the Fellowship shall be to establish and maintain groups of students whose aims are: a) to witness to the Lord Jesus Christ as God Incarnate, and to seek to lead others to a personal faith in Him as Savior, and b) to deepen and strengthen the spiritual life of members by the study of the Bible, by prayer and by Christian fellowship.

From the first, students were exposed to outstanding theologians, stretched beyond what they could understand so they would get a taste of how big God is and with what issues they needed to wrestle. Stacey would exhort the staff, "Get your students in touch with great men of God." He was always careful lest the Fellowship be heard talking to itself. In a letter to Joe Bayly in the late 1940s, Woods writes, "I am concerned to hear that the staff are speaking at weekend conferences instead of inviting someone from outside our Fellowship to expound the Word."

The vitality and strength of Stacey Woods's character left an indelible mark on Inter-Varsity Christian Fellowship. It went beyond the founding of a movement; he had a prophetic word from Scripture about contemporary culture and the disciplines of the Christian life. His deep respect for Scripture and the God of Scripture allowed him to say, "Thus says the Lord," with a quiet humility and spiritual authority. He had a way of cutting through fuzzy thinking about great truths to focus with prophetic clarity on the heart of an issue. He did not ask students what they *wanted;* he knew what they *needed* to become mature men and women of God. He was not a builder of a personal kingdom. He spoke his mind forcefully and cared little for what others thought of him, including students. His compelling vision for the glory of God was obvious and won him loyalty and respect. The basic values God led C. Stacey Woods to put in place are the heart of what Inter-Varsity work is all about as it prepares to enter the twenty-first century.

World War 2 seemed a terrible blow to an infant enterprise. Woods was able to maintain leadership of both the Canadian and American IVCF with a handful of staffworkers. Meanwhile Charles Troutman was shipped to Australia with the Army Corps of Engineers. His schedule allowed him to act as a staff member for the high-school groups in Brisbane and the IVF chapter at the university there. Night after night on his table in the supply room of his company he wrote his thoughts and observations about student work to Stacey until the letter was forty pages long. That letter no longer exists but, Charles says, "It required me to think through many of the things we were doing," and it gave impetus to planning and formed the basis for the development of IVCF in both Canada and the United States.

Some years later Troutman, on board the S. S. *Himalaya* returning from serving as the general secretary in Australia, distilled some of the principles of the way God led the Inter-Varsity movement in a paper called *Seven Pillars*. "Spiritual growth among university and college students seems to me," wrote Troutman, "to depend on seven great principles." They are given here in abbreviated form.

1. *By Faith Alone.* The trust and confidence we place in the living God is decisive. Faith brings us into relationship with God; it is the work of God in us; it brings us into maturity. We never outgrow our need to trust Him. Faith implies all-out confidence in God and his Word. It is a chief factor in student evangelism. For chapter members faith has two additional important aspects: first, an inward conviction that this student witness has been raised up by God for a specific purpose within his worldwide church and, second, a sense of personal call from God to participate in this witness.

2. *According to the Scriptures.* God speaks through the Scripture he has given us. We are under authority in matters of faith and conduct. The written Word is not separable from the Lord himself. The practical result of such an attitude toward the Bible is that its study becomes central in the program of reaching students for Christ. To make known what God says is the greatest evangelistic thrust possible. The attempt to know and apply the teaching of Scripture in daily life is the corollary of acknowledging the Lordship of Christ.

3. *The Necessity of the Second Birth.* No teaching of Scripture disappears from practice as quickly as the insistence of our Lord to Nicodemus, "You must be born from above." In the university setting there is a constant threat posed by a dilution of this principle of regeneration. People of intellectual and moral character are first to take exception to the idea of

man as a helpless sinner. Pluralism insists that we give ground on the exclusive claims of Christ. The very foundations of modern universities are challenged by this so-called "irrational intrusion." We are not at liberty to trim our position to make our message palatable. Through every means we seek to make Christ known. We ask men and women to decide for Christ. It is this act of will toward which the Holy Spirit moves. We exist at the university for this end.

4. *Indigenous Responsibility.* No principle is more firmly grounded in Scripture than this one. How very difficult this principle is and has been to maintain is seen by the shock of the early church fathers at the risks the apostle Paul was prepared to take. Paul was persuaded that God was able to keep his own, that the Scripture in their hands would guide them into truth, that in the fellowship of the Holy Spirit and one another would allow them to grow and to evangelize. The indigenous principle does not in itself provide spiritual vitality; it only provides a framework for developing maturity and growth. Outside stimulus and leadership is important to an indigenous group. The attitude of such leadership is key: are we trying to make followers or train leaders?

5. *The Principle of Remnant.* The dedicated few of God's choosing are prepared to spearhead God's cause at any cost. Few Christian student groups understand or willingly embrace this concept; it seems too restrictive. But an evangelical student group believes its members must speak for God in the context of their university. Their work is both prophetic and exemplary. To be a living illustration of God's presence requires a twofold openness—toward God and men. We must be on God's wavelength and on the wavelength of the people we are trying to reach. This places upon Christian students the double responsibility of serving God as his scholars and his spokesmen. It is a holy infiltration into the university itself.

6. *Our Missionary Purpose.* Our missionary purpose is defined not so much in terms of geography as of frontiers of faith, wherever they may be. We must face each believing student with the Lord's claim on his life in respect to his vocation and particularly to a call to take the message of God overseas.

7. *The Quiet Time.* It should not be necessary to press the case for the relation of this daily meeting with God to the spiritual vigor of student evangelism. Nothing must be allowed to displace or replace it. We cannot dispense with regular periods of communion with God, and we must impress this practice upon Christian students. These seven principles are inextricably entwined. We must never give priority to any one principle,

nor must we set one against another.[12]

Handing out booklets became an Inter-Varsity thing from the first. Students were urged to read *Quiet Time, Sacrifice* and *Henceforth,* a trilogy that undergirded the principles of the movement. Roland Allen's books *Missionary Methods: St. Paul's or Ours?* and *The Spontaneous Expansion of the Church* were required reading for staff and urged upon student leaders. *The Acts of the Apostles* was studied over and over again by leaders.

Troutman writes,

We did not differentiate then, as we did later, between the work of building up members of the group and that of reaching outside of our circle. Rightly, we held the biblical pattern that Christian witness involves every aspect of life: spiritual training, evangelism, vocational planning, family relationships, and academic life.[13]

These two men—the one mercurial, creative, always forging ahead, quick-witted, intuitively building the work; the other, often calming the waters and picking up the pieces, an encourager and counselor, philosophical by nature, willingly in a supportive role—were gifts to the formative days of a student movement that would change the lives of many. As one graduate commented, "The Inter-Varsity movement came as a new kind of Christianity, a deeper, a more life-encompassing relationship with God through Christ than we had ever known before."

5

A Whirlwind of New Beginnings: Decade of the 1940s

It was a case of staff following or trying to catch up with Christian students of faith and daring.
C. Stacey Woods, *general secretary (1940-1960), Inter-Varsity Christian Fellowship*

May 1938, report from J. Frank Cassel, Wheaton College: "The word went round the campus, 'Troutman is back. Troutman's back! Come to Ken Taylor's room.' Several of us met in Ken's room to hear Charlie tell of his work in Canada that year under Stacey Woods. I was impressed by his account of 'squashes,' of ski weekends and of the use of literature in witness. I remember how refreshing it was to hear of this approach after such emphasis on keeping the 'pure' faith and the critical concern about modernism."

November 1939, letter to donors: "After much thought, prayer and discussion with Christian leaders in the United States, it was agreed to launch the Inter-Varsity Fellowship in American colleges at the beginning of 1939. We have three full-time workers. . . . In their short experience they have made really splendid progress—report definite conversions, very genuine blessings and a constantly growing interest among university men and women. For the College year which has just started, our budget for the work in the U.S. is $6,000. This, you will agree, is a ridiculously small amount to support three full-time workers, pay travelling expenses, allow for the organizational work of the General Secretary. . . . We know of only a few hundred Christians in the U.S. to whom we have addressed this letter. . . . You would hearten us greatly if you could see your way clear to respond quickly . . . to the urgency of the financial need. . . . C. Stacey Woods."

March 1940, staff report: "The U. of Michigan sponsored a series of six lectures by Dr. Wilbur Smith. Attendance increased each meeting, with about 250 people at the last meeting. Dr. Smith was an inspiration with his fearless, inimitable manner—great for students to hear."

April 1940, board minutes: "At present twenty-two student groups formed. First IVCF student conference for eastern section of U.S. announced for April 27 in Philadelphia."

April 1940, executive committee minutes: "U.S. IVCF will accept Mr. H. J. Taylor's offer to share office and part-time secretary with Christian Worker's Foundation. Foundation will support work first year, $5,000; second year, $3,000; third year, $2,000. Muriel Clark, first office secretary."

September 1940: IVCF-USA set up as a separate movement with its own board, severing its organizational connection with the Canadian movement but maintaining an interlocking directorate.

November 1940, staff report: "The new group has only seven members, but already they have led three students to Christ as personal Savior."

February 1941, staff report: "A group of students from Adelphi College want to become part of IVCF, but it is a big step for them, since they have been part of the Association and the SCM leaders want to meet with them before they make a final decision. This is a touchy situation. I suggested they begin Daily Prayer Meetings."

March 1941, Radcliffe College student testimony: "This conference is just what I needed. I had gotten the idea that I was alone as a Christian on my campus, and it is strengthening to know that others are faced with similar problems. Every once in a while my courage sags. . . . It has been a real help and encouragement to talk with others who have the same problem."

Spring 1941, report to the board by Stacey Woods: "There is an immediate need for a university student magazine, edited by the staff, for both Canada and the U.S." (First issue slated for September 1941 in 5 1/2" x 8" size, called HIS, Robert Walker, editor.)

May 1941, letter from Stacey Woods: "Due to the rising cost of living I feel that we should endeavor to increase the minimum salary of staff from

$65 to $75 a month. Mr. Butt, on account of his marriage, will need in-creased support."

September 1941, board minutes: Canadian board frees C. S. Woods to assume responsibility as general secretary for the United States as well as Canada. The board adopts the constitution for IVCF-USA. An independent board formed, with two Canadian members, to care for U.S. work. Staff count doubles to eight members, plus three part-time staff. The Woods family prepares to move from Toronto to Wheaton, Illinois.

September 1941, report from Stacey Woods: "One hundred students have been converted during camps and conferences in this past year."

November 1941, memo from Stacey Woods: David Adeney released by China Inland Mission for staff work with IVCF for limited time with the hope of developing an effective missionary program within the Fellowship. The missionary thrust to be an integral part of chapter life, not just for the mission-minded.

> It is proposed that he (Adeney) spend three or four days with each chapter, speaking to the chapter two or three times, meeting informally with small groups, scheduled for personal interviews, etc. It may be arranged for him to meet with the chapter executive committee to discuss a possible missionary program. Prior to Mr. Adeney's visit there should be special preparatory prayer in the DPMs that this visit will revive students, fire them with soul-winning evangelistic zeal and call some to foreign service.

December 7, 1941: Pearl Harbor bombed by Japanese. The United States enters World War 2.

February 1942, Fellowship Day of Prayer bulletin: "Praise God for new centers of campus witness started since the Fall and for the approximately 90 campuses on which IVCF is now seeking to help Christian students. Pray for students who have asked for help, which we cannot YET give because of a limited staff."

April 1942: Charles Troutman called into the Army Corps of Engineers.

September 1942, staff reports: "The Inter-Varsity chapter at Duke University suddenly find themselves stripped of leadership and even interested members because of the war."

"At Lewis and Clark in Oregon every elected officer was missing this fall. Even the newly-elected president has since gone into service. Throughout the state we have, in the main, untried and inexperienced leaders."

"At Oregon College of Education in Monmouth approximately one out of every six students on campus are IVCF members. Four of these are missionary volunteers. God has honored this group with unusual spiritual understanding."

"A freshman girl, the only professing Christian in her large dorm, regularly brings ten of her friends to Bible study."

1942-43 staff listing for all of USA: Stacey Woods, Lois Troutman (who took her husband's place in the Midwest), Irene Webster-Smith (a seasoned Irish missionary to Japan assigned to California and the Southwest), Jane Hollingsworth (assigned to the Northwest) along with Herb Butt, Shockley Few (working in schools in the South), Bill Paul (Texas), Ann Chapman (Eastern U.S.), and David Adeney.

1943, Jane Hollingsworth's staff report: "The number of weak Christians who have places of leadership is appalling!"

1/The Shape of Inter-Varsity

The first ten years of American Inter-Varsity history is like a series of news bulletins; so much was happening. The few staffworkers felt like they had hold of the tail of a whirlwind. Wherever the staff went they created their own stir. On some campuses only a single contact became the stimulus for the beginning of a witnessing society. On other campuses small groups already existed who wanted to qualify for affiliation with IVCF. Other key campuses seemed to have only an occasional lethargic Christian without vision. In some colleges a vital group was already meeting. The staff were aggressive, each in his or her own way, and challenged every student they met about their relationship with Jesus Christ.

Stacey Woods urged the Christian public to send in names for student contacts. Grace Koch, staffing the Northeast, wrote to him, "Thanks for the names of the students. Our friends couldn't send enough of these to suit me. I hope there is a liberal sprinkling of non-Christians among them."

Reports of students becoming Christians, of new advances in faith within small groups, of vital daily prayer meetings seemed to feed the zeal of an overworked staff. In 1941 David Adeney, Ken Taylor, Neil Nellis and Bob Oerter joined the original four staff, with Paul Beckwith spreading news about IVCF in the churches. Staff enthusiasm heightened. Ken Taylor, working in the Southwest, wrote,

You know, Stacey, I don't see why there can't be student revivals again as there were a hundred years ago. Conditions on the campuses were often worse spiritually then than they are now. Yet the Spirit of the Living God was not hindered from a mighty sweeping work. And it seems that they always began with a little group of two or three Christian students

who had the vision of their campus for Christ and began to pray.[1]
Charles Troutman described revival as occuring when "the input is so little compared to the outflow." Was this what was happening on the campuses?

Letters between Troutman and Woods in 1940 discussed the minimum qualifications necessary for a group to become a chapter. A daily prayer meeting and a weekly Bible study were basic. The pros and cons of a signed membership were debated. Woods wondered if it would strengthen commitment to the group or whether it would limit outreach. Troutman thought they should adopt neither position: "the U. of Michigan will not allow it and the U. of Illinois must have it." Chapter officers must sign the Basis of Faith; that was agreed. A chapter must have an evangelizing outreach, a concern for unbelievers, instead of a club mentality.

Is campus work best carried on by single staffworkers rather than married ones? The question was especially relevant because Troutman's most recent report recorded a 1,250-mile tour. Troutman was concerned lest the work grow so rapidly that it would be too big to care for with the present staff and chapters would evolve without a deep work of God's Spirit. Woods expressed his hope for a greatly increased staff.

Meanwhile they needed a handbook to help both students and staff, but they questioned whether there was time or money to do a first-rate job. Stacey thought they should call it *Effective Witness,* do the best job possible, print 500 copies, and plan to upgrade it later. At Stacey's request, Charles sent an outline for a Fellowship Handbook consisting of four subdivisions:

I. Preface (including a brief history of Inter-Varsity worldwide)

II. Vision (perhaps the most important part of the book)

III. Organism (essentials of DPMs, Weekly Bible Study, Quiet Time)

IV. Organization (how to make it work)

While Troutman and other staff plowed new ground on the campus in the U.S., Stacey Woods was busy administering two national movements, making contacts with churches and interested donors, speaking on campus and writing long letters to keep in touch with his staff team. His ability to keep the movement growing on two fronts, initiate new ideas and shoulder financial responsibility was nothing short of remarkable.

2/Inter-Varsity's Progenitors

Behind the scenes in any new movement are "the believers," those who see what God can do, who are committed to the ethos, who pray and give with genuine interest. Margaret Haines, who had been active in the Student

Volunteer Movement and a missionary to India, was one of these and had a significant ministry in Inter-Varsity as a member of the first board of directors and as a personal counselor to many staff, including Stacey Woods. Together with her mother, Mrs. Robert Haines, Jr., she was not only financially generous, but she held regular prayer meetings in her Philadelphia home to intercede for the witness on various campuses. Staff members came away from her home deeply refreshed by her spiritual insights, her informed prayers and her concern for them as individuals.[2] If the Fellowship had a spiritual mother, she would be it.

Herbert J. Taylor decided early in life to use his business to build the kingdom of God. When he bought the Club Aluminum Company during the depression, he made a convenant that, if God would prosper his company, twenty-five per cent of its profit would go into The Christian Worker's Foundation. He used these funds to help get several parachurch organizations off the ground. His special interest in young people led him to help Child Evangelism, Pioneer Girls, Christian Service Brigade, Young Life and Youth for Christ. What he lacked was a ministry to university and college students. When he heard from Ted Benson, a Wheaton colleague of both Woods and Troutman, what Inter-Varsity Christian Fellowship was doing in Canada, Taylor agreed to meet Stacey Woods. The vision for university student work that Stacey outlined captured Herbert Taylor's imagination. His provision of the first office in the United States, a half-time secretary and a three-year support grant got university student work going across the border. He served as chairman of the board and a close counselor to Stacey Woods for the first twelve years of the American Inter-Varsity.[3]

The other members of the first board also had an investment in the work that warrants our gratitude. T. Edward Ross, Paul Westburg, J. F. Strombeck, C. Davis Weyerhaeuser and Charles H. Troutman, Sr., served in that capacity. Although never serving on the board, Dr. Howard Kelly[4] certainly must be mentioned as one whose example in witness and enthusiasm for Inter-Varsity significantly encouraged Stacey Woods. These people lent their names and gave support to an organization without reputation in a vast country, with a miniscule staff, in a conservative religious climate that was highly suspicious of anything having to do with secular education. And they believed God would do something with it.

3/Early Suspicions and Obstacles
While in one sense the university scene was ripe for a student movement like Inter-Varsity, in another sense the liberal/conservative debate made

both the campus and the Christian public wary. Troutman writes,

> We were most conscious in those first years of being opposed wherever
> we turned—not by the students, but by church and university author-
> ities. The denominational foundations felt we were competitive, al-
> though the small attendance at their functions did not speak highly of
> their effectiveness. On several occasions we were told that we had no
> place on a university campus since we held magical and superstitious
> views.[5]

Staff members also lived with negative feedback from fundamentalist writing, which bordered on yellow journalism. Dan Gilbert published a book
in 1940 called *Crucifying Christ in Our Colleges.* Using the most extreme
illustrations, he exposed "a concerted effort" to eliminate Christianity from
the universities. His case histories were not in doubt, but his accusation
that both faculty and administration were in a conspiracy was exaggerated.
It was sometimes difficult to prove that Inter-Varsity was not part of Gilbert's counterconspiracy. University administrators, wary of the modernist/
conservative controversy, were torn between their support for academic
freedom and their reluctance to get involved in a new conflict. Administrators in church-related colleges, except in the most secular, generally
refused permission for their evangelical students to organize.

The most surprising opposition came from pastors whom Inter-Varsity
expected would be supportive. Among conservative Christians there was
a general conviction, born out of sad experience, that a student could not
retain faith at a secular university. When a student did become a Christian,
some pastor would persuade him to transfer to a Christian college. One
year at the University of Michigan a dozen students became Christians and
all but one were persuaded to transfer to Wheaton or Taylor College.
Troutman said,

> It is not easy in the present student atmosphere to describe the sense
> of opposition under which the students worked. We were often tempted
> to go underground and the staff sometimes worked on a campus in spite
> of campus police prohibition. Yet it would be inaccurate to say we had
> no encouragement; a cadre of staunch friends on and off the campus
> made the work possible. Wherever we found a Christian group meeting,
> we found some professor or concerned Christian who served as a ral-
> lying point.[6]

Prior to World War 2 Troutman said that staff and students generally met
with massive indifference when trying to carry on conversations about
spiritual things with non-Christians in the student unions. But a growing

confidence infected the Christians on campus with the advent of visits from Inter-Varsity staff. In a December 1940 staff report Troutman tells of his visit to the University of Wisconsin:

> I found the group utterly discouraged. I went from one to another to try to show them that both the battle and the victory was theirs. When I talked with them separately it was OK, but when they got together they slunk back into their old position. Then prayers began to be answered. I was able to dig up about fifty names for them (from religious preference indicated in student records) and members of the group started out calling. By the time I left they had called on twenty and found most of them were Christians and five of them immediately came out to the DPMs. It was a joy to see the spirit of the group change within a few days time.[7]

When a group was formed at the University of Chicago by Edson Peck, the staff reported to students on other campuses what was happening. "If they can do it at the University of Chicago, we can do it here," was an almost immediate response. It was often hard going, but the intercollegiate thrust of the work helped in the contagion.

Another book published in 1940 gave some relief from the opposition the staff and students faced. William F. Buckley, Jr., a recent graduate of Yale and editor of its student paper, published *God and Man at Yale,*[8] in which he raised the question of why everything under the sun is permitted at Yale except conservative Christianity. This charge caused a flurry of denouncements, but it eventually created a more open atmosphere in the university world.

While the fundamentalist stance was to see a lurking heresy in practically every movement, even those that appeared healthy, the British heritage of Inter-Varsity served it to great advantage. Inter-Varsity student work was seen as an import, and as such it did not have ties to anything that was suspect to either the conservatives or the liberals. In a sense Stacey Woods and his staff had an enviable freedom to plow their own furrow. This did not entirely relieve them of suspicion from either side, but it enabled them to concentrate on exalting the person of Jesus Christ, rather than getting entangled in theological discussions.

4/A Network of Prayer

When the 1941-42 school year began, only six staff members and a few volunteers visited campus groups. They were kept scrambling. Their goals were to visit existing groups, to follow up on contacts, to find contacts on strategic campuses, to encourage volunteers and to give vision by their own involvement in life on that campus. Their mode was: "Get some of your friends together, and let's talk." Staff slept in the dormitories whenever possible, and although their visits were comparatively brief, they were round-the-clock and intense.

The staff wrote to Stacey about their dilemma: there was so much to do on the campus that they were not visiting people who might support the work. What should they do? Word came back to "Stay on the campus, but ask God to lead you to people who will pray for you and for these students when you have left for the next place."

Across the country a network of praying individuals developed, sometimes a couple, but most often older women who took that ministry seriously. It was a two-way partnership: lonely staff members had someone who cared about them and the students, and the "warriors in prayer" felt an involvement in what God was doing on campus. Who can know how this influenced what happened on campus. This emphasis on local "prayer warriors" continued during the years of Woods's leadership.

5/HIS Magazine

In those first years of pioneering a student movement in the United States, Stacey Woods made a number of decisions that had long-range effects. He went after the money and the personnel to begin a quarterly student magazine, with board approval. The first issue appeared in the fall of 1941. Robert Walker became the editor of the new periodical. Walker thought a one-word title for the magazine would be appropriate, after the style of the popular periodicals *LIFE* and *TIME*. Stacey suggested *HIS,* and subsequently found himself explaining to the Christian public that it was not presumptuous, that the magazine should be the Lord's and to his glory alone, and that all who read it should become His. Some Canadian board members wanted a dignified name like Inter-Varsity, reflecting the British tradition.

The magazine was not meant to be a public-relations piece. It was for students; it was to teach students the philosophy of Inter-Varsity and to act as a "staff member's visit." Bob Walker had the unorthodox idea that the magazine should reflect what God was doing through people rather than a devotional or polemic magazine, as most Christian periodicals were at that time.

For the most part it was an immediate success on campuses in the United States. The Canadians thought it was too American, a valid criticism that was taken care of in subsequent issues. Its detractors felt that the use of unnecessary colloquialisms was not appropriately Christian. Letters contained phrases like "an element of flippancy," "a lack of dignity," "speaking lightly of Holy things." Non-student readers exhorted the editor about pictures of girls wearing lipstick, articles that gave dating advice and anything else that appeared to be worldly. But the magazine did its job and helped many students learn to think "Christianly."

The picture on the first issue of *HIS* showed students streaming down a campus walk between classes. Since the caption read "Michigan State College" when the scene actually was on the campus of the University of Wisconsin, the editor commented in the second issue, "Take the average college student, assure him of decent room and board and a handy Coke shop, put him on any campus, and he can't tell the difference."[9]

The winter issue of *HIS* had a picture of L. G. Rothney of Michigan State College, wearing a suit with a handkerchief in his breast pocket, looking at recent additions to the Inter-Varsity book shelf maintained in the college library. An article inside made students aware that Christian books could be placed in campus libraries. The pictures in the magazine reveal that the dress code was suits and ties for men, skirts and sweaters for women students. The most popular feature was "News of the Campus" where students could find out what was happening at other colleges and put good ideas to work on their own campus.

The contents of the first issue of *HIS* reflect the magazine's purpose. An article entitled "Which College—and Why?" spoke to the Christian-versus-secular-college debate. It contains lines that Stacey Woods often used in speaking to this issue: "The safest place on earth is the un-Christian university, *if God sends you there.* Daniel in the lion's den was perfectly safe and for the simple reason that he was in the will of God." Woods also wrote on a favorite subject: "Faith—in the Bible or Christ?" in which he stated, "The living Christ is the object of our faith—not a system of truth," a good reminder for students not to lose their focus when facing attacks by rationalists against the Bible. A picture article demonstrating social gatherings and friendships as ways to evangelize broke new ground for many students used to a "holy huddle."[10]

HIS was never self-supporting, but "its enormous usefulness and influence did the work of two staff visits." The whole staff was unanimous in subsidizing it, even when it dug into staff salaries. Charles Troutman says, "I cannot imagine the first two decades of Inter-Varsity without *HIS* magazine." Alumni from the first three decades remark about its influence on their Christian lives with typical comments, "When it came I sat down and read it from cover to cover."

6/Commitment to Missions

A second strategic decision Woods made established the missions emphasis in Inter-Varsity. "Inter-Varsity is essentially a missionary movement to students, but every student needs to seriously consider the will of God for his life in terms of foreign missions," Woods said. In 1941 he invited David Adeney, a British graduate of Cambridge and a missionary to China, to join the staff of Inter-Varsity to promote interest in missions on campus in both the United States and Canada. Adeney, married to an American, had already considered living in America. As a staff member Adeney toured the campuses like other staff, giving students a vision for their witness on campus, but he also opened their eyes to a needy world with a challenge about the lordship of Christ.

Adeney's picture appeared in the first issue of *HIS* magazine, introducing him to students. He later appeared on the cover with the title "Missionary Secretary Adds Zip to Zeal" (to Adeney's great embarrassment). "I thought of my friends in England seeing this picture and wondering what I was up to," he said.[11] David Adeney served two years before going on to England to serve the China Inland Mission, but his influence on the American Inter-Varsity then and later is considerable and set both the place and the tone of the missions emphasis of the Fellowship.

7/Inductive Bible Study Enters the Fellowship

In the spring of 1942 Stacey Woods recruited Jane Hollingsworth for campus staff work. A Wheaton graduate, Jane had gone on to Biblical Seminary in New York where she was trained in inductive Bible study. As she approached graduation, her advisor presented her with numerous openings possible for women because men were rapidly being called into the military. She was considering the invitation from Stacey Woods, but knew very little of what was involved in the job. One day when one of her professors pressured her about her indecision, she heard herself announcing her choice, "I am going to work with students in Inter-Varsity Christian Fellowship."

Staff training turned out to be a meeting of the combined Canadian and United States boards and the staff in Guelph, Ontario. Eva McCarthy, a beloved China Inland Missionary and board member, gave devotional talks and national policies were discussed, but apart from praying for the campus no one told her what was expected of a staff member.

After the conference Jane asked Stacey what she was supposed to do when she met with students. He replied, "The Lord will lead you."

Jane said, "He can't lead a vacuum," to which Stacey replied, "Jane, you are no vacuum." Those words were her staff training.

Stacey arranged for Jane to go to Vancouver and observe staffworker Ann Carroll at work. She stayed with Mary Beaton, then a graduate student at University of British Columbia (UBC) and later to become an influential staff member in the U.S. movement. Ann took Jane to the UBC executive meeting. Wilber Sutherland was the chapter president and took charge of the meeting. (In 1952 Sutherland became the general secretary of the Canadian movement.) Ann made a few comments to the group that evening, and later Jane asked her, "What do you do?"

She replied, "I just did it." This was not much help to Jane. Ann put her to work speaking at one Inter-school Christian Fellowship (ISCF) meeting after another. Making speeches was not what Jane needed, so she decided to go on to the United States where her assignment was to staff the West Coast with Herbert Butt, a more experienced staffworker.

Jane made arrangements to visit students on the campus at Bellingham, Washington. She arrived on her birthday, nearly penniless, going first to the post office to pick up her mail, confident that she would find birthday cards with some money tucked in. There was nothing. She knew the students had reserved the guest room for her at the college, but it was still a lonely and desperate feeling.

Her father had been concerned that her salary would be only sixty-five dollars a month, and such a salary for a woman with a master's degree! He had fussed a bit and said that he didn't ever want her to go hungry, that money was as close as the nearest Western Union. His words echoed in her mind as Jane left the post office, and she was about to inquire the location of the Western Union office when another voice came to her, "Which father are you working for?" She felt the Lord was reminding her that he was trustworthy. She went on to the college guest room, and there found a birthday card from a friend who has never before nor since remembered her birthday. In it was three dollars, enough for the weekend until she met with the students on Monday.

Instead of eating, Jane decided to fast for the first time in her life. That weekend, sitting in that small guest room and thinking about the task before her, she was almost overwhelmed with the size and intelligent unbelief of the non-Christian college world and the small size of the

Christian community. Doubt and discouragement hung like doom over her until she asked God for an answer in "black and white." It came in Romans 3:4: "Let God be true and every man a liar."

When she met the students she still had no clear sense of the task, only a strong confidence in God. They greeted her with the startling news of an all-college convocation at which she was to present to the whole college the purpose and program of Inter-Varsity Christian Fellowship.

She stood to her feet having no idea of what to say, but claiming the promise to take no thought of what to say, expecting the Holy Spirit to give her the words at the time. She said,

> The Inter-Varsity Christian Fellowship exists for the purpose of giving to every college student a clear, intelligent explanation of the Christian Gospel. This then would give to each an opportunity to decide whether or not he wished to become a Christian. For those who make the choice, fellowship with others of like faith through Bible study, prayer and examination of channels for Christian vocation are made possible by your fellow students who ally themselves with the college Christian Fellowship.[12]

From her own mouth the purpose of evangelism was made clear and primary, and that first year was "a glorious year of witness in every college in Washington."

Jane brought inductive Bible study to the Fellowship. With her winsome personality and natural gift for teaching, she taught both the staff and students how to open Scripture. Stacey Woods and Charles Troutman had wanted this to be a Bible study movement, but Jane brought the skills and method into the movement. The American Inter-Varsity has been known for inductive Bible study ever since. The first Bible study guide Inter-Varsity produced was Jane Hollingsworth's *Discovering the Gospel of Mark*. Later, in 1945 Alice Reid, a missionary from India who also had studied at Biblical Seminary, co-authored the second study guide with Jane, *Look at Life with the Apostle Peter*.

Inter-Varsity is indebted to The Biblical Seminary of New York for training many of its staff in inductive study. During the 1940s and 1950s a number of staff members studied under a sizable faculty of godly and gifted teachers, including Robert Traina, and brought the riches of inductive study methods into the Fellowship. Barbara Boyd who later, with the help of many staff, developed the curriculum and training for Bible & Life, also studied there along with Gwen Wong, Anne Beguin (Horton) Dorothy Farmer, Rosalind Rinker, Anna Mary Williams (Ramer), Marilyn Kunz, Ruth

Stewart, Peter Northrup and others. The early Biblical Seminary identifies more closely with Inter-Varsity than the new seminary that emerged from it.[13] Barbara Boyd, in assessing Inter-Varsity's involvement in Bible study, said:

> One of the remarkable gifts of God to Inter-Varsity was the openness of Stacey Woods, coming as he did out of the British Empire and from a Plymouth Brethren background. For example, his openness to bring women right into the center of the ministry, his openness to reach into a seminary like Biblical, which might have been questionable to others because it had no written doctrinal statement. He set the tone for our movement to be open and not tight, to be open and ready for God to do anything God wanted to do. It was sort of like the Acts of the Apostles opened up to the Gentiles, and God has to have that kind of openness when he begins something new, doesn't he? Because if not, then leaders are tied in knots and all your questions are about minor points. Stacey wanted to major on the majors. He saw the big picture and his real consuming passion was the glory of God. He saw what this kind of Bible teaching could mean to Inter-Varsity.[14]

8/Explosive Growth during the War

The entry of the United States into World War 2 in 1941 brought enormous confusion to what Stacey Woods called "Inter-Varsity's kindergarten life." Already most of the men staff in Canada had been called into the armed services. By early 1942 many of the male staffworkers in the United States entered the armed services. A few gifted and loyal women took up the task of staffing huge areas in both Canada and the United States. It was hard to keep up with what was really happening. Staff members rotated in and out each year, filling empty staff positions sometimes for only part of a school year. Some of these were men who were between assignments; others in seminary stayed around longer (such as Christy Wilson and Al Newport). Most of them were women like Alice Reid, Catherine Alexander (both returned missionaries), Helen Martin, Ethel Smith, Connie Johnston, Pauline Barkhuff and others who covered the schools in vast territories.

College men called up from one campus were placed on another campus short-term to become officers in the Navy V-12 training or the Army Specialized Training Program (ASTP) programs. Men who were leaders in student witness either began chapters at their new locations or spurred on what already existed. These transplanted servicemen, looking for fellowship, bouyed the spirit of many groups which were sometimes all-women chapters.

Jane Hollingsworth tells of arriving late for an Inter-Varsity meeting on the campus at Central Michigan College in 1943. As she walked down the hall toward the room, she heard wonderful singing and opened the door to find a room full of V-12 men from Wheaton College who had been sent for training on this campus. A rather depleted chapter, mostly women, had a new look. An average of twenty-five attended the DPM. Sixty came to the first Bible study. A senior woman said to one of the V-12 men across a biology lab table, "I wish I had something to live for like you fellows do." Several students were won to Christ that year.

Glen W. Zumwalt was in the V-12 program at the University of Texas when Irene Webster-Smith, the venerable missionary to Japan, was the Inter-Varsity staff member. They saw her infrequently because her assignment included California and the Southwest, but the chapter was largely made up of V-12 men who carried the leadership. When they heard that Christy Wilson was coming through Texas and would be visiting their chapter, they decided to hold a weekend conference with Christy as the speaker. They rented a campground, bought the food, and eighty-five students attended. They got to the camp by riding to the end of the bus line and then walking a mile to the site. Several became Christians that weekend.[15]

Stacey Woods's move to Wheaton gave him easy contacts with students at Wheaton College. Through his frequent addresses at chapel and his personal contact with men going into military training programs in other universities, Stacey was able to inspire and "train" hundreds of students who were able to establish Christian groups on campuses where none existed, groups which included both military and regular campus students. It was not so much that Woods had a well thought-out strategy in doing this; rather it was typical of him to do everything he could to reach out. He was a great vision-giver.

Chapters began springing up across the country. The Inter-Varsity idea was widely sown. *HIS* magazine, February 1943, reported the formation of a new chapter at Ohio State University. The names of several Christian students had turned up at the Inter-Varsity office in Chicago. Lois Troutman, on staff during the war, got in touch with these students and more than twenty came to the first meeting. It was a time of excitement. Each of them had thought he or she was the lone Christian on campus until this meeting. The following night they came together again and brought other interested friends. They wasted no time to begin plans for a Christian witness on campus, working on a schedule for the rest of the semester. Then they wrote a constitution and applied for affiliation with IVCF with no delay.

A similar story could be told at campus after campus. The few staff could not keep up with what was happening. At the time of Pearl Harbor in 1941 there were approximately fifty official chapters, with contacts on many more campuses; by the time military men were discharged in 1946, about two hundred chapters existed, many of whom had never seen a staff-worker.[16] Like the dispersion in the book of Acts, transplanted Christian students from many campuses spread the student movement across the country.

The 1942 student-look of *HIS*—which became a monthly magazine, published nine times a year—changed to include military men on the cover and on the interior pages. Articles on evangelistic outreach to V-12 and ASTP men made students aware that these men were now part of the campus mission field. IV students in military service sent in articles about sharing their faith and trusting God in the stress of battle. News of campus leaders shot down over the Pacific, wounded or killed in battle in Europe, caused the close-knit Fellowship its own grief. The facts of war had a sobering effect on the whole campus, changing the atmosphere from the frivolities that had marked the 1930s. It was easier for students to talk about God. Prayer was high priority, and daily prayer meetings (DPMs) often had larger attendance than ever known before.

As an Australian, Stacey Woods was not subject to the United States draft. He volunteered to the Australian High Commissioner in Washington, D.C., and was offered a somewhat lucrative post with the Australian Purchasing Commission for the Australian Expeditionary Force. Stacey rejected that offer. It was clear that God wanted him to stay with Inter-Varsity. In 1944 Mel Donald, associate general secretary for Canada, was called into the armed forces along with the only other Canadian male staff member. That left a developed movement without leadership, and the Canadian board recalled Stacey Woods to Toronto. For the next three years, with the work rapidly expanding in the United States, Woods usually spent one week in the Toronto office, one week in the Chicago office and the other two weeks traversing across the two countries encouraging staff and students.

9/Expansion South of the Border

However that pace affected him, Stacey Woods was not content to leave it there. He became interested in developing student work in Latin America. Mel Donald, along with George Gay, who later served with the Latin America Mission, had been talking with students at the University of Toronto about extending student work to Latin countries. The students had responded with enthusiasm and began collecting money to help make this a reality after the war. Stacey learned about this and became enthusiastic about the idea.

In January 1944 he reported to the U.S. board of Inter-Varsity that "there has been an increasing awareness among many of our students as to the need of an evangelical witness among university students in Latin America" and proposed "that steps be taken immediately toward the opening of an evangelical student witness among Latin American students." He quoted Mel Donald saying, "that the board should either encourage or discourage this interest among students rather than to permit this interest to drift along without any guidance."

Stacey had by this time gleaned information from missionaries, made contacts with some Latin American students, and obtained a $300 grant from the Pioneer Missionary Agency to survey the possibility of student work there. He had also been selling U.S. Board President Herbert Taylor on the idea. Taylor accepted Stacey's report and proposed to the board that they send Woods for a survey of universities in Central America and the West Indies, going as far as Bogota, Colombia, and that the trip take four to five weeks and cost $600-800.

Taylor first made the proposal to the Canadian board, which had been reticent about the trip in view of the needs of Canada. In the end, they voted unanimously in favor of this tour. But the proposal floored the U.S. board. The country was in the middle of a terrible war on two fronts; the Inter-Varsity staff shortage and the growth of student work was of great concern, and now Stacey was suggesting a new pioneering venture! Stacey writes of this moment in *Growth of a Work of God,* "Yet with faith in God, the United States board and executive committee gave approval to this exploratory trip." He writes nothing of his own magnetism and strategy in getting the trip approved![17] United States citizens were forbidden to make such a journey in wartime, but Stacey held a British passport and was under no such restriction.

This was not an easy trip for Stacey Woods. He had an intense dislike for flying and became extremely nervous as the departure time drew near. He considered taking out a large insurance policy to protect his family. The insurance agent was an intimidating woman, small and stocky, who wore "fantastic big hats." When Stacey spotted her coming into the office one day, he suddenly disappeared. Mary Anne Klein went into his office to find him, and he was nowhere to be seen. Finally she heard Stacey's inimitable chortle coming from under the kneehole of the desk. "What on earth?" she asked.

He said, "I can't face her. Tell her to go away." In the end, he did talk with her, but the story of the general secretary hiding under his desk to avoid a saleswoman is part of the legend and has gathered some apocryphal details in the retelling.

The stories Stacey told upon his return kept interest in Latin America alive. His most hair-raising tale involved his flight home from Barranquilla, Colombia, in a lumbering, four-engine Pan American flying boat which, after three tries on a mirror-flat sea, was unable to become airborne. Finally the captain ordered everyone to sit in the rear of the plane on one another's knees so he could take one more try. Stacey had two people on top of him as once more they charged across the water. Finally with a great sucking sound the floats broke loose from the surface of the water and they were off. Landing in Jamaica was another tense moment, since the pontoons of the plane had been severely damaged and needed repairs.

During this unexpected layover in Jamaica, Stacey made contacts with Christian leaders that later resulted in the founding of student work in both high schools and universities throughout the British West Indies. In 1948 the Canadian IVCF sent veteran staffer Cathie Nicoll to Jamaica to pioneer the high-school student movement. Later work began in the new university there and spread throughout the English-speaking Caribbean. In 1945, shortly after Stacey's survey tour, Edward Pentecost was sent to Mexico, supported by North American students, to pioneer El Compañerismo Evangélico Estudiantil, the Mexican Inter-Varsity. That same year Leon and Ann Headington went to Costa Rica to begin student work.

10/Campus-in-the-Woods

About the time the Woods family moved back to Toronto, Stacey undertook another ambitious project. He and Charles Troutman had often discussed the need to train students to be effective leaders on campus. From his background Stacey was already convinced that camping was a way to minister to the whole person, especially to impart spiritual values. He began talking to the right people about finding an appropriate site for a camp as a training center. Cameron Peck, a member of the U.S. board and later its second chairman, offered the use of Fairview Island in Lake of Bays, Canada, about 150 miles north of Toronto. This island seemed ideal to Stacey: it was properly isolated; it had excellent recreational opportunities; the atmosphere encouraged serious study. An old house and a small dock came with the island. A kitchen, dining room, sleeping accommodations and a lecture room were needed to make proper facilities for a hundred students and staff. Building materials were virtually unavailable in the middle of the war and building permits were issued by the Canadian government only for "cinemas and bars," according to reports.

Stacey Woods was never one to look at the obstacles and be defeated. He believed that he would find a way if "the Lord was in it." Winning permission from local authorities took both faith and persistence. Vincent Craven, his cohort in camping in Australia and leader of Canadian IVCF Pioneer Camps, made several trips to the United States to find nails, which were unavailable in Canada. They scoured the country for lumber, paint and roofing. Stacey's brother-in-law somehow got a carload of plywood and plasterboard from British Columbia. Cameron Peck gave the camp an all-purpose boat to transfer people and supplies to the island. (Students christened her the Golden Sticky, and she became the subject of songs and poetry.) Stacey was hardly a carpenter, but he was a good recruiter. He got women from the Chicago and Toronto offices, local farmers and volunteers from everywhere to help.

When the building permit was canceled by a higher authority, they waited the legal limit to appeal, all the while building furiously. After some weeks, their appeal was refused. They appealed to a higher government authority and worked on. The Canadian IVCF Board took a dim view of all this, "fearing they might all go to prison." Finally the highest Canadian government office refused the permit and ordered Stacey to stop building or face prosecution. Stacey would not take the order over the phone, but insisted it be in writing, and while they waited for the letter they worked on the building. Writing about this, Woods said, "We installed an ancient diesel to provide electricity, a gift from a printing firm in Ontario. By this time some of the Canadian board members were distraught, promising to visit me in jail!"[18]

In late June Stacey saw a motor launch cut across the water from the mainland toward the island. It was a government official delivering the final order, just as nails were being hammered in the dining room flooring. When Stacey told him they were far enough in the project to hold their first camp in July, the messenger said, "We know all about it and held up your order to give you extra time. But this is the end." Telling the story later, Stacey would say, "It was all a glorious adventure."

In July 1945 the first session was held at Campus-in-the-Woods (CIW). Eighty-five students came from across the U.S. and Canada. The cutlery came only hours before the students arrived, and the dining room furniture came after they were asleep. The first meal was a stand-up buffet.

Many of the students at that first Campus-in-the-Woods session became key people in Inter-Varsity. Mary Beaton and Gwen Wong had come from California; George Ensworth came from Michigan; Anne Childs and Barbara Boyd were from the East Coast. Staff member Pauline "Polly" Barkhuff recruited Barbara Boyd, whose memories of that first camp still produce a glow.

> The dining room floor wasn't quite finished and you had to watch where you walked or you disappeared. I remember the first night walking into the lounge where Yvonne Woods was putting a framed Scripture text on the wall; it read, "He fed them according to the integrity of his heart and guided them by the skillfulness of His hand." Cornelius Van Til, Northcote Deck, J. F. Strombeck, Irene Webster-Smith, Jane Hollingsworth[19] and others were our teachers, but they were also just there *with* us—eating with us, doing dishes, swimming, working in the kitchen— letting us get to know them and influencing us profoundly. Some of what they said was over my head, but I remember Dr. Van Til really helped Anne Childs who was having a lot of questions thrown at her at Wellesley College.
>
> Jane Hollingsworth taught us inductive Bible study. I remember her taking us to Mark 1 and asking us what we knew about lepers. We began to tell her facts about lepers, and she said, "Suppose you were that man . . ." and I began to see how you could get right into the passage and feel Jesus' touch on your shoulder.
>
> And we had such fun. They decided our new dining room floor needed mopping, and so we made a pool out of the floor. I remember Jane riding on a mop and someone pushing it, and water and big mops going in every direction. I remember sitting out on a rock along the bluff, with the morning sun making the water sparkle, having an early morning Quiet Time (what a wonderful experience!) and while reading a Psalm I'd hear a lap of water and Northcote Deck, who swam around the island every morning, would glide past like a porpoise. That camp set my sails for life in many ways.[20]

That August the awesome news of the first atomic bomb reached CIW. The Japanese surrendered on August 14, 1945. The war was finally over, but with it came uncertainties about the discharge of soldiers, the potential of staff recruitment and the return of key leadership within the movement.

Charles Troutman was among the first to be discharged. He arrived on a ship in Tacoma, Washington, on the last day of 1945. After calling his wife, Lois, he took a bus to Bellingham because he knew a student conference was being held at The Firs over the holidays. Although he had been in Australia, his heart had been in student work in America. He arrived at the conference site at 2 A.M. and woke Grant Whipple, part-time staff and director of The Firs, by throwing pebbles at his window. The next morning while the group was kneeling in prayer, Charles went in and knelt besides Stacey Woods. Stacey writes, "It was Charles Troutman! I remember hugging him and all of us were filled with an emotion of Thanksgiving."[21]

After his discharge and a reunion with Lois and his family, Charles Troutman was appointed associate general secretary of the Inter-Varsity Christian Fellowship in the United States. While this added stability to the new movement, the whirlwind of new beginnings was not over yet.

6
Growing the Movement: Decade of the 1940s

The sign of an effective student group is not the appearance nor the claim of being "spiritually alive," but subjection to the Word of God. . . . To some it seems strange that an evangelistic group should base its life on Bible study. Yet a moment's reflection on the New Testament pattern of evangelism reveals the early church's use of and rootedness in the Old Testament, even in the absence of Jewish background and vocabulary. It is easy to divorce the gospel from the Scriptures and to produce an impassioned something that is less than the power of God. Particularly with students we need to go from our Bibles to the witness of life with the loving declaration of "Thus says the Lord."[1]
Charles H. Troutman, *general secretary, Inter-Varsity Christian Fellowship*

The Inter-Varsity Christian Fellowship grew in a myriad of ways in the 1940s, broadening its scope and its effect on university students in North America.

1/The Love of Hymns
Hymn singing was at a low ebb in evangelical circles in the United States in the 1940s. Youth workers built their ministry on bright, singable choruses, which either enabled the singers to "let off steam and have fun" or feel very sentimental. Students from conservative Christian backgrounds often brought the culture of their high-school "young people's society" to the early Inter-Varsity chapters. That was what they knew, and the new Christians on campus usually had nothing to compare it with. In the forties this meant singing was light, often frivolous, generally without much content and repetitive. To Stacey Woods this was an affront to God. Furthermore, such singing seemed incongruous with the university. It was neither

serious nor adult. He had a strong conviction that a big view of God produced a big hymnology. "We sing *to* God," he said, "and we sing *of* God."[2]

One student clearly remembers Woods's stand:

We were frightened to death of Stacey Woods. Wasn't everybody? Once he showed up at a Sunday afternoon meeting of the Michigan Christian Fellowship when some student zealot of the mid-1940s got us all singing "The Hallelujah Gospel Train" with gusto and choo-choos. Stacey came in and heard this stuff going on with almost unbelieving ears and eyes, and shouted out for us to stop the whole business, to the embarrassment of everyone. He then told us we should stop this childishness, grow up and begin singing adult Christian hymns of the faith. As I recall it, he then stomped out. I never heard another tooty-tooty chorus again in our IV group.

It was about that time that Paul Beckwith finished the first IVCF hymnal, *Hymns,* which I never thought I would understand, and which I came to love with a passion. Ah, the singing in MCF, long before I knew about the great singing at Urbana. We would sometimes sing hymns like "I Sought the Lord" all the way through and when the piano would stop, we would seem to begin again as one person, one heart, one harmony of voices to sing the hymn again in Lower Lane Hall, the low ceilings, the sounds intimate and tender, tears coming down our faces as we praised God as one person.[3]

As early as 1940 there was talk of a student hymnal. Charles Troutman prepared a list of hymns he thought students should be singing and sent it to Paul Beckwith. Before plans could be activated the war began, and the idea was put on hold. A few years later Stacey Woods put Paul Beckwith to work on the book. Paul began working with Inter-Varsity in public relations in 1941 and switched to working on campus when the war depleted the staff team. He had often accompanied song leader Homer Hammontree as pianist at evangelistic meetings, and had an excellent grasp of hymnology. He could be called Mr. Great Heart for he was guileless, loved students and in the decades ahead was tireless in teaching them how to sing thoughtfully.

He spent many, many hours at the Woods's home, going over the hymns that would be included in the book. Hymnals were scattered over the chairs and on the living room floor. Paul would say, "I like this tune because it fits the words better. Don't you think students will come to love it?" as he played the melody while Stacey and his wife, Yvonne, sang with him. Stacey said, "These were some of the happiest times of my life," and meant it. The sheer joy of singing great hymn tunes with great words— it is something we all remember about him, and his enthusiasm for good singing was carried into the Fellowship in ways that deepened the work of God. Inter-Varsity became a singing movement. Apart from inductive Bible study, our hymnology may well be one of the most binding element for graduates of IVCF, particularly those who have been involved in our camps.[4]

The publication of *Hymns* in 1947 was to a degree a landmark in American evangelical singing. It set a new standard and the hymnal was adopted by many Christian colleges. It also influenced the content of subsequent church hymnals and unquestionably raised the level of congregational singing. Many of the hymns now taken for granted in hymnals—"O the Deep, Deep Love of Jesus," "Like a River Glorious," "We Come, O Christ, to Thee," to name only a few out of *many*—were made familiar by *Hymns*. Burton Harding, regional director for the Southeast 1958-67, says about the contribution of IVCF's hymnology,

> Most of the hymns sung in the evangelical movement are songs of experience, and I think Inter-Varsity is unique in its emphasis on hymns that are theologically based, songs about God, who he is and what he has done.[5]

2/A Spurt of Christian Houses

On several campuses the solution to the hostility against Christianity in the early 1940s inspired the acquisition of Christian Houses. Horton Hall on Stanford's campus is perhaps the most famous of these. In 1942 Bethel Manor was incorporated as a men's Christian House at Michigan State College that would also serve as a base for the Inter-Varsity group. Next came Minnewa Lodge at the University of Illinois and Michigan House at the University of Michigan. Christian living units or co-ops began to dot the country's campuses.

In the beginning, reports lauded the effort. One staff wrote, "Already the Christian fellowship has been a strength to many and the spiritual help from one another resulted in more effectiveness in personal witness." But before many years had passed the validity of these houses was in question. At a board meeting in June 1942 Stacey Woods suggested that it might be wise for chapters to impose regulations for these houses, encouraging Christian students to live in regular dorms at least one or two years to win unconverted students to Christ. Otherwise he feared such student residences would become spiritual hothouses. Some fared better than others, given good leadership, but for the most part they became ways to hide from responsibility on the campus. Christian fellowship became careless living. For many it became a way to avoid taking the university seriously. Although some are still in operation, the idea never really took hold.

3/Important Staff Additions

In 1944 Joe and Mary Lou Bayly joined the staff of Inter-Varsity. During Joe's last year at Faith Theological Seminary, he and Mary Lou heard Stacey Woods speak in chapel about student work. Quite independently of each other, both of them began thinking about the possibilities of student work as God's call to them after seminary. The Baylys, like others of the early staff, were both Wheaton College graduates.[6]

When they went to visit Stacey to inquire about student work, Stacey hired them on the spot. They began with a summer assignment at Pioneer Camp and then became responsible for student work in all of New England and upper New York State. Mary Lou worked with Joe as a staff member until their first child was born. Joe was not subject to the draft because of his seminary status, and the gift of this mature couple to the work at this moment in history was surely of God. This began a sixteen-year ministry with Inter-Varsity, and Joe Bayly, with his quick wit and keen view of reality, became a major influence in the developing student work.

Pauline Barkhuff, a Wheaton graduate, began a decade of service with Inter-Varsity that same year, headquartering in Philadelphia and staffing the schools in Pennsylvania and Ohio. Harriette Sutherland, whose spirited witness and creativity brought about the birth of a flourishing chapter at Stanford, joined the staff just after graduation to work in central California.

Rosalind Rinker,[7] a returned missionary from China, was appointed to serve on staff in New York City, replacing Weips Rozelaar (who left to marry Howard Larson and teach in Afghanistan), and Mary Beaton,[8] an influential Canadian who was to have a long career on staff, began work on the campuses of Kansas, Nebraska and Iowa.

Bob Finley, a student from the University of Virginia and a member of the campus boxing team, was a convincing evangelist during his student days. After graduation in 1945 he came on the staff of Inter-Varsity and was itinerated as a campus evangelist, working with chapters for campus-wide evangelistic meetings for the next four years. The board minutes of September 1946 show twenty staff members, plus volunteers, approved by the board for campus work.

4/The Vitality of Personal Initiative

About this same time a student in Colorado named Gene Thomas picked up a *HIS* magazine in a dormitory lounge and read it while he waited for his date. He made no claim to being religious; his contact with the church had been spotty and largely negative. He had some interest in God, even prayed at times and read about the major religions of the world. He found *HIS* magazine attractive and relevant, and put subscription information in his address book, thinking, "I may send for that sometime." Weeks later he came across the information about *HIS* and sent in his subscription. In one of the issues he read something by C. S. Lewis that prompted him to go to the bookstore and order all the books Lewis had written. He was surprised when the order included books on medieval literature, but it also contained *A Case for Christianity,* which he found fascinating.

When *HIS* announced Jane Hollingsworth's study guide, *Discovering the Gospel of Mark,* Gene sent for it. It looked like a good way to get to know what the Bible was saying. It was written for small groups; he needed to get a group together. He was the president of the Colorado State College student body at the time; from his network of friends he found fifteen men who had never studied the Bible and invited them to come to a study. They bought a case of beer and met on Tuesday nights from 7 to 11 p.m. In the course of these studies, Gene became fascinated with Jesus. He found himself talking about Jesus to his partner on the dance floor. He even chided a local liberal minister saying, "I'm not a Christian, but I know what you are preaching is not Christianity."[9]

He became increasingly interested in Christianity and finally realized Inter-Varsity did more than publish *HIS.* He wrote to the address in the magazine and asked, "What do you guys do?" That next summer of 1946 Gene saw an article in *HIS* about the training being given at Campus-in-the-Woods. He made plans to attend, even though he had made no Christian commitment. It was an incredible month for him. He listened; he asked questions, and he found out how a person could become a Christian. He had a better grasp of the definitions than some of the Christian students, but wasn't sure he wanted to capitulate to God just yet.

After graduation he began teaching business courses in high school, but he missed the Bible study he had at college. He decided that every campus should have a Bible study and he could do something about that. So he spent his evenings making contacts and getting studies going at Colorado State, Denver University, Colorado University and the University of Wyoming.

By Thanksgiving time he was a committed Christian. The issue all along had been the lordship of Christ. Gene prayed, "Lord, you can have my life, but I'll be honest, I don't want to go to Bongo-Bongo land."

By Christmas time there were sixty students in a DPM at Colorado State University at Fort Collins. Quite on his own Gene had started a chapter at each of the schools he had been visiting. He had read about conferences in *HIS* magazine and thought a conference was what should come next.

In April 1947, 160 students came to a conference at Big Thompson Canyon. He wrote to Charles Troutman to tell him what was happening. Gene changed his employment to travel for an insurance company and for the next three years he visited campuses from Albuquerque to Salt Lake City, ferreting out Christians and getting groups started. It was not until the fall of 1949 that he joined the staff of Inter-Varsity as a regional director for the Rocky Mountain Region.

As a volunteer Gene Thomas built the student work in the Rocky Mountain states. His colorful story is only one example of how volunteers were used by God in place after place to get a vital student witness under way. With the limited staff team of Inter-Varsity, volunteers were not only essential, they were part of the strategy. Inter-Varsity was committed to the priesthood of the believer and individual responsibility.

It was only natural, for example, for Paul DeKoning, an engineering professor at Michigan State, to be the catalyst for student witness on that campus. He was indigenous to the university in a way that no staff member could ever be. Professors and graduates were involved with students across the country and account for much of the vitality of the witness.

Friendship evangelism became an important part of the ethos of Inter-Varsity because it was a natural way for believers to share their faith. It seemed so obvious, and yet IVCF's emphasis was a refreshing break-through. On the one hand a climate of heavy theological debate pressured participants to know all the answers before they could speak of Christ. On the other hand it broke with simplistic confrontations—"Are you saved?"—which became a kind of professionalized evangelism. Establishing a genuine and prayerful friendship with a non-Christian led to a natural sharing of personal faith.

5/The Early Phases of Publishing
In the 1943-44 school year Kenneth Taylor became the editor of *HIS* magazine, *Discovering the Gospel of Mark* was in print, and a monthly *Intercessor* was circulated to help people pray intelligently. Student response

to the Mark Bible study required that more Bible study helps be provided. *HIS* magazine began featuring *This Morning with God,* a Quiet Time guide written by Yvonne Woods, in January 1945. The guide used inductive questions to help students dig into the passage for themselves. *This Morning With God* was published continuously in *HIS* until June 1961, teaching many student generations how to study the Bible. The war was still in progress and staff members were few and often temporary volunteers, but one cannot help being impressed with the creative input and the unflagging zeal of the early staff families.

When Kenneth Taylor left *HIS* magazine in 1947, Virginia Lowell became editor, along with Wilbur Smith,[10] and the magazine changed to a 7 3/4 X 10 3/4 inch format. Subscription price was two dollars annually, and circulation ran at 6,250.

In February 1948 *HIS* published an article on the principles of student work by Dr. Ferenc Kiss, "How to Grow at College," a thoughtful article typical of the magazine, but one that must be read with the climate of the 1940s in mind, when there was fear that the gospel message might be lost in the intellectual climate of the university. Kiss had been involved in helping the Hungarian student movement and knew firsthand what had happened in the World's Student Christian Federation when it attempted to be more socially relevant:

In my sober judgment the single greatest danger . . . is the failure to preach the pure simple gospel week after week and month after month. University students have the peculiar temptation of trying to appeal to their fellow classmates who do not know the Lord by referring to their general interests—politics, philosophy, nationalism, historical research, or the current problems of the day. We seem to feel that if we can present the gospel in the framework of these current problems—suggesting a solution to economic, social or political ills—we shall be doing a two-fold task of interesting the students in the things of the Lord and making a constructive contribution to the problems of the present day.

This is the greatest of all fallacies. . . . Day by day politics, philosophy, history, science, psychology and sociology are taught in the classroom; the problems of today in relation to these points of view are discussed. Christ is seldom mentioned. The only excuse for a student group carrying on for God is their sense of responsibility to preach the gospel, to teach the Word of God to their classmates who otherwise will not hear it. This is the only justification of the student movement. There is

no more false concept than that the unconverted student can be interested in the things of God by an introduction in terms of politics,
philosophy, economics, etc. This sort of emphasis will produce the
complete degeneracy of the student movement and will actually weaken
spiritually the Christians themselves. I have observed this in a number
of countries.

Much of the heavier reading and study material for students came from
Inter-Varsity Press in England,[11] but gradually the American IVCF began
publishing to meet its own needs. Charles Miller joined the staff to work
in publications in 1946, handling books sent over from England, repub-
lishing booklets with an American imprint and arranging for the publication of small booklets written specifically for North American students—
often reprints of *HIS* magazine articles. In 1944 *The Man Who Lived Again,*
an apologetic on the resurrection by Wilbur M. Smith, was published as
an Inter-Varsity booklet. Mary Anne Klein edited a missionary booklet,
Called to Be Sent, and *Is Christianity Credible?* written by Kenneth Taylor
for *HIS,* was published in booklet form in 1948.

Stacey Woods wrote a *HIS* article, later published in 1949 as a small
booklet called *Taboo,* that had an influence all out of proportion to its size.
The subject was worldliness, and it powerfully delineated the biblical
teaching on the subject. In the 1940s conservative Christians had a long
list of cultural taboos; things that Christians didn't do included drinking,
smoking, dancing, movies, the theater and even wearing certain kinds of
bathing suits.[12] According to Woods such Christians had a "legality" in the
guise of a "spirituality."

He defined "worldliness as a self-indulgent attitude of the heart and
mind toward life—this material universe and all of life's relationships." In
that sense worldliness is what we are, not what we do. We are primarily
to be *separated to Jesus Christ,* not from worldly activities. "When our
hearts and lives are filled with the Lord Himself, He would crowd out the
world as He filled life with Himself." His words had a prophetic ring for
the culture in which he was writing. Stacey Woods wanted it to be clear
that IVCF believed the issue was Christ, not the taboos, that the Holy Spirit
would direct converts into truth.[13] This booklet put the Christian life in
focus for many students, and its teaching is fundamental for the world and
life view Inter-Varsity encourages its students to embrace.

In the 1940s Christian publishers in the U.S. were not producing the kind
of material staff members needed for student work. The British Inter-Varsity
published the serious reference works which served as the backbone of

the biblical libraries students were encouraged to establish. Staff members became book venders because this was the only way students had access to these books, except for Inter-Varsity conferences. Traveling from campus to campus by bus—and often state to state on clergy discount passes—staff members usually carried one suitcase full of literature and another with their clothes. (Barbara Boyd cites that as the reason her left shoulder is lower than her right.)

Most often staff were modeling what Stacey Woods and Charles Troutman had done for them by offering just the right book for the question at hand. Mary Anne Klein, who worked closely with Stacey in many capacities in the first years of Inter-Varsity, remarked,

> Stacey never batted an eye when I told him my doubts. He was always willing to listen without getting shocked or upset with me. His favorite reply was, "You know, I've got a book I think you would enjoy reading." He had a way of knowing the right thing for me to read and greatly expanded my spiritual horizons with books.[14]

The excellent flow of thoughtful materials from London made it unnecessary for the young movement in North America to divert its efforts immediately to publishing. However, in the academic year 1947-48 InterVarsity Press (IVP) became the official publishing arm of the Fellowship and the small beginnings made in this first decade met with such overwhelming approval that it was only a matter of time (and capital) before InterVarsity Press would become an important publisher in the evangelical world.

6/Racial Issues

Jane Hollingsworth had been a staff member first in Washington and then in the Midwest when Stacey Woods asked her to pray about going to New York City in the fall of 1945. The idea did not excite Jane, but she agreed to go if the Lord would give her a strong word from the Scripture that it was the right thing to do. She knew Stacey was sending her because of a problem in the area that he hoped she would solve. She said, "God did speak to me in the course of my regular Bible reading from Isaiah 58:12, 'You will be called the repairer of the breaches.' " Jane agreed to transfer to New York City.

For several years students in the New York City area gathered for monthly meetings in the home of Mrs. F. Cliffe Johnston who, as a member of the Inter-Varsity board of directors, demonstrated a genuine concern for students, particularly students from the Ivy League schools. Her beautiful home in the city was part of the drawing card. Students who knew fellowship with only two or three others on their campus took courage when they saw the large numbers involved in student witness at these monthly meetings. The singing was wonderful; they heard an outstanding speaker and went away uplifted. The meetings were always dress occasions, with Mrs. Johnston looking elegant in a gorgeous long gown as she greeted the students.

But now a problem had arisen. The members of the Inter-Varsity chapter at Hunter College were nearly all Black or blind people. Mrs. Johnston was a strong-minded and dedicated Christian woman, but her point of view reflected her culture and status in life. Today it would be unthinkable; in the late forties it was common. She "loved" Negroes but "in their place." Walter Liefeld, a mature freshman who helped begin the chapter at New York University (NYU), had a deep appreciation for the monthly gatherings at the Johnstons but sensed the latent racism clouding the fellowship at those wonderful meetings. He discussed his concerns with a strong letter to Connie Johnston, his staff member, and then wrote to Stacey Woods about the potential problem.

Jane had been sent to New York City by Stacey Woods partly because she was a southerner from Augusta, Georgia, but also because she was gracious and winsomely equal to the task.

In December of that year Jane was slated to speak at the Christmas monthly meeting at the Johnston home. When she received word that some Blacks might be at the Saturday night meeting, Mrs. Johnston phoned Jane, objecting vigorously. Jane held her ground. Mrs. Johnston threatened to report her to the board. Jane said,

> Please do. It is my understanding that our policy is that whatever the school does, that is what we do. There is no way that I can justify having everybody welcome except these Black students from these chapters. I will not come to the meeting [to speak]. I will meet the students at the front door and take them elsewhere.

Mrs. Johnston had met her match. Jane continues, "I don't know how it happened or how God did it, but sometime after that I was kneeling down by her bed with her and we were praying together."[15]

The race issue came up very early in Inter-Varsity's history. Jane tells of another time when she planned a student conference at the YWCA in Atlantic City and had the agreement canceled because Black students were coming. She said, "But you are a Christian organization!" The conference was held instead at a Black YMCA in the area. Inter-Varsity received the same treatment at Keswick Bible Conference. Stacey was furious. He determined that Inter-Varsity would not hold any national conference at a site where people of other colors and backgrounds were excluded. The IVCF Board passed the following statement at its June 5, 1948, meeting:

1. A Christian group in a Negro College which fulfills our regular affiliation requirements shall be accepted without distinction as an IVCF chapter.

2. All national IVCF or SFMF conferences shall be on a non-segregational basis.

3. Since colored people tend to relate segregation and the Christianity which we represent, we must demonstrate that in Christ there is neither black nor white.

It is recognized that the application of this policy could cause serious repercussions, particularly among our constituency in the south. Therefore it is the general feeling of the Board that this policy should not be the subject of propaganda, but as the Lord leads it should be put into effect on campuses and in student conferences.

Staff appointments for the academic year 1947-48 list Eugene Callendar as the first Black staffworker assigned to work in "Colored Colleges" in New York City. Hong Sit, who had been a staff member with the China IVCF as a missionary associated with the China Inland Mission, was assigned to work with Chinese students.[16] Both of these men continued with part-time assignments during 1948-49 while they did graduate studies. Their appointments made an early and necessary statement about concern for ethnic groups.

7/The Postwar Boom

By September 1947 over two million[17] war veterans enrolled in the colleges and universities of the U.S., bringing with them a maturity and experience in leadership the campus had not known before. The growth within the Inter-Varsity movement was staggering. Within a single year more than 150 new chapters had been formed. Stacey Woods appointed associate general secretaries—Herb Butt for the West Coast, Charles Troutman for the Midwest and Joe Bayly for the East—to help stabilize the growth.

On the staff level, men joined the IVCF staff whose input into the movement would be significant. Melvin Friesen came on staff almost as soon as he was released from the chaplaincy duties in the Philippines in 1947. Responsible for student work in all of central California, Mel[18] would arrive on campus, pulling a thirty-five-foot housetrailer, which was home for his family for that first year. Two other influential and mature leaders joined the ranks of IVCF in 1947 and left their mark on the Fellowship: Cleo Buxton[19] and Carl Thomas.[20] In 1949 James Nyquist, a former chapter leader from the University of Minnesota, accepted a one-year appointment that turned into a lifetime career with Inter-Varsity.

Inter-Varsity was working out its organizational structure throughout a decade of phenomenal activity. From 1939 to 1941 the U.S. student work was under the aegis of the Canadian IVCF Board, which included three U.S. members. The first official meeting of the U.S. Board of Inter-Varsity Christian Fellowship, operating under its own constitution, had taken place in Chicago on September 12, 1941. Those present were H. J. Taylor, Margaret Haines, T. Edward Ross, J. F. Strombeck, Paul Westburg, Robert Walker and C. Stacey Woods. The small size of this governing body enabled the whole board to act as an executive committee, even though the constitution called for an executive committee composed of chairman, vice chairman and treasurer plus two other members chosen from the board. The board maintained an interlocking arrangement proposed by the Canadian IVCF of two board members each. Two Canadians—Donald Fleming and John R. Howitt—served on the U.S. board, while Taylor and Ross attended Canadian board meetings. Each year others were added to the board, so that by 1946 it had twenty members.

The projected merger with Student Foreign Missions Fellowship required a revision of the original constitution and by-laws. By 1947 Stacey Woods had presented the names of ten business and professional men "for election to the membership of the Corporation."[21] This is the first occurrence of Inter-Varsity "corporation" membership, which was designed to bring in men and women whose interest and support could be the basis for selecting future board members. The Corporation met once a year, in conjunction with one of the semi-annual board meetings. Corporation members were invited to attend the board meeting for information purposes. The executive committee of the board met quarterly or as needed. By 1950, for the first time, the members of the corporation were more numerous than the elected board members, numbering twenty-two, making a corporate total of forty-two people. In 1960 that number had grown to ninety-one. As the board and corporation grew, the executive committee took over increasing responsibility, sometimes posing a problem of taking too much authority on behalf of an uninformed membership. Yet the very size of the corporation made it difficult to keep all informed.

A small cadre of strong staff had joined the Fellowship during the 1940s, all of them responsible to the general secretary. The January 1948 board minutes note the division of supervisory roles to better manage the work. The formation of the Senior Staff Council, consisting of regional secretaries, became responsible for the direction of the staff members in their areas and the student work. These regional secretaries reported to the general secretary through the associate general secretary, Charles Troutman. Four regional secretaries were appointed: East—Joe Bayly; Middle West— Charles Troutman (until a replacement could be appointed); North Central—Cleo W. Buxton; West Coast—Carl Thomas. Regional secretaries began to meet with their staff teams and attempt to give more instruction and pastoral care than had been known before. Business Manager Paul Hopkins[22] was given responsibility for public relations, promotion and publication as well as other business matters.

Until 1948 when William E. C. Petersen ("Pete" or the "Great Dane") became the secretary of stewardship, the funding of the movement had been largely the responsibility of Stacey Woods. Bob Walker, later the editor of *HIS* magazine, had joined the staff in 1940 to set up the office and launch a program for getting financial support. He recalls that Stacey brought a list of fifty potential supporters when IVCF came into the U.S. They had come a long way in eight years, but with new growth came drastic needs for greater funding.

Petersen had strong ideas about fund raising. His theory was to tell the story by letter and raise funds without staff involvement, and he did so with amazing effectiveness. Although attempts to form some kind of alumni association began as early as 1945, Petersen always managed to discourage that kind of outreach during his tenure. His letters were effective, and Stacey Woods had so many irons in the fire that he was content to defer to Petersen and let him do it his way. Between 1944 and 1950 the income grew 461 per cent, from $36,000 to $166,000 in 1950, but income still did not keep up with the pace of growth or the opportunities before this expanding movement. Although there were many fits and starts, the failure to establish a strong alumni program over the years may well be one of the tactical mistakes of the movement.

8/The Leader's Legacy

Stacey Woods would never have taken time to analyze his leadership style. He saw the task at hand and used all his resourcefulness to get the job done. His ability to accept and appreciate people of differing abilities and personalities was part of his genius. He looked for people who had "an excellent spirit in them" and who were faithful to the Word of God. In this and in other decisions he made, he had an enviable personal freedom in the religious climate of the 1940s. Ruth Paxson, a gifted Bible teacher, was one of his favorite speakers at Campus-in-the-Woods. He said of her, "Miss Paxson's ministry was a tremendous help and blessing. I cannot emphasize that too much."

Stacey invited Corrie ten Boom to speak at CIW in 1949,[23] and arranged for her to itinerate to speak to students of various campuses. His view of women in leadership was decades ahead of most other Christian leadership.[24] Throughout the country, women staffworkers were given the same assignments as men.

Stacey Woods also spoke with a prophetic voice in ferreting out error or recognizing potential problems. As early as 1949 he wrote to Dr. Edward Carnell about a book on television that Carnell was writing:

> I am very concerned about this whole problem [of the advent of television in every home] from the sociological point of view as well as from that which is Christian. One can't help but fear that unbelievable regimentation, mental atrophy, as well as general moral and volitional debility must result.[25]

In preparation for the November 15, 1949, Day of Prayer, Woods wrote to the staff,

> We must never give in to complacency or pride. We must take care not to feed our fleshly self instead of our spiritual self, to take care in the witness of our lives to students. We need to set the highest and best example Christward to the students among whom we work, and never contribute to any unfruitfulness in their lives. We are apt to fall into the sin of criticism. I know I have failed here.[26]

7

Two Important Mergers and Worldwide Fellowship

Inter-Varsity is universitywide and worldwide in scope. It thus contains within itself many strains of interest. Some of these are areas of specialization which remain motifs and themes within the Fellowship. Others are organizationally integral to the movement.[1]
C. Stacey Woods, *general secretary, Inter-Varsity Christian Fellowship*

The Student Volunteer Movement (SVM) had been slowly dying since their quadrennial in Des Moines in 1920. Christy Wilson, a Princeton student interested in missions, attended the 1944 SVM convention in Wooster, Ohio, and found little missionary interest among the delegates. The delegates themselves were a mission field. They seemed biblically illiterate when it came to understanding the missionary mandate. When a group of students gathered to pray, one of the leaders came in and stopped the prayer meeting, saying "We don't want anything emotional going on here."

Little of the glory of the past days remained, but John R. Mott was there, nearly eighty years old. Christy heard Mott give his testimony, of how he went to the meeting to hear Kynaston Studd and had his life changed. He spoke of what God had done in the student world and on the mission fields through the SVM. Mott concluded by saying, "Young people, to find Jesus Christ as your Savior and Lord is the most important thing you can do." But Christy could see the heart of this great man was broken because the spiritual life of the movement was gone. The consequences of the demise of the SVM were devastating for the historic missionary outreach of the church.

1/Student Foreign Missions Fellowship Merges with Inter-Varsity
However, in 1936 a revival at Wheaton College sparked the beginning of new missionary interest. During a week of special services in a brisk February, the Thursday chapel service turned into a period of confession of sin and prayer that lasted until the evening service began. Senior student Don Hillis had stood at the end of morning chapel and inquired what Christian students like himself should do to receive the fullness of the Holy Spirit's power. His earnest concern sparked a response in his fellow classmates and many of them experienced a new desire for clean and committed lives.

The next evening Robert C. McQuilkin, president of Columbia (South Carolina) Bible College (CBC), gave the closing address of the conference on a subject dear to his heart—the missionary mandate Christ gave to the church. At the end of his message he asked students who had committed themselves to the mission field to stand. Scores of students stood. He then invited those who were uncertain about God's will, but who would earnestly pray for God to reveal his will for them regarding foreign missions, to stand. In the revival atmosphere of that week, many students responded. It was clear that God was doing something new at Wheaton College. McQuilkin was already aware of student response at Columbia Bible College. He was convinced the time was ripe for the formation of a new student missionary society.

Concerned that evangelical seminaries and colleges had so little priority for missions, McQuilkin began corresponding with Calvin Knox Cummings, field secretary of the League of Evangelical Students (LES), about the possibility of the League expanding its purpose to include an aggressive student missionary movement. The correspondence was disappointing. Cummings was not enthusiastic and indicated that the LES had already amended its constitution to incorporate student missionary groups as part of the regular life of an LES chapter. While McQuilkin was concerned to "give liberty" to the Holy Spirit, Cummings was concerned about theological orthodoxy in a way that made McQuilkin somewhat impatient. Cummings's emphasis was the defense of the faith against the attacks of liberal theology while McQuilkin longed to see the advance of the gospel around the world. The extremely Calvinistic stance of the LES made Cummings concerned about how such a movement would be controlled. McQuilkin wanted it to be free and motivated by a central goal to reach the unreached millions with the good news of Jesus, the Lord. The LES was not only cautious, but negative about parts of the proposed program, calling it "dangerously unbalanced." The use of the Missionary Pledge Card was a major "red flag." How could they know whether God was really calling the people who signed pledge cards saying they would go to the mission field? McQuilkin, moved by the urgency and magnitude of the missionary task, concluded that the time was right to begin an independent organization with an updated strategy dedicated to missionary advance. He had already received word from Wheaton College students that they were forming a missionary committee.[2]

Student leaders from Wheaton, Columbia and other schools met at Keswick, New Jersey, in June of 1936 to discuss the organization of an evangelical student missionary society. Present at that meeting were people like Harvey Borton, a close friend of Robert Wilder, and Margaret Haines, a former SVM volunteer to India, who urged that a new movement be formed. A student steering committee chaired by CBC senior Joseph McCullough presented a constitution for discussion and before the conference ended the Student Foreign Mission Fellowship (SFMF) came into existence.[3] McCullough was appointed SFMF's first acting general secretary. "No monetary underwriting was promised, none was sought. The students were responding to what they understood God wanted them to do," writes Will Norton,one of the student founding members and second general secretary of the SFMF.[4]

The SFMF was a student movement from its inception. In the next two years teams of students traveled to other schools, visited churches and Bible conferences to advance the primary goal of the new organization: to stir the church to respond to the missionary mandate. The hallmark of the movement was getting the church to pray and to be informed about specific areas of need in the world. Many of the key leaders in the missionary enterprise from 1940 to 1990 were also leaders in the early days of SFMF. The leaders of SFMF modeled the commitment they espoused, leaving for the mission field as soon as their preparations were completed. At the five-year point in the history of the SFMF, four different general secretaries had served, resulting in groups established on thirty-six campuses.[5]

By 1941 both the Canadian and the U.S. Inter-Varsity movements were gaining momentum, and discussions about the future relationships of IVCF and SFMF took place. As noted earlier, Stacey Woods, out of concern for strengthening the missionary emphasis of the Fellowship, had invited David Adeney to the staff that same year. Both the U.S. and Canadian IVCF boards approved a proposal that a foreign missions program be established officially within IVCF. Woods was anxious to have the foreign missions thrust of student work on the secular campus be an integral part of the movement, not a separate organization.

Merger talks discussed whether SFMF should be the missionary arm of IVCF at all colleges and universities or whether SFMF would be the student missions arm at Christian campuses. IVCF staff tended to think the students at secular institutions would not fit into the SFMF program since students at Christian colleges were generally better informed about missions. The staff were also fearful that separate groups would begin meeting on the same campus in competition with each other. The SFMF, on the other hand, had its own fears of being swallowed up by the larger movement. In the end, among the stipulated agreements of the merger were (a) the missionary secretary of SFMF would serve as an associate general secretary of IVCF, (b) the SFMF senior committeemen would serve on the IVCF Board, and (c) IVCF would maintain a separate missions committee to assure that the goals of SFMF were kept in focus.

It took three years for merger plans to be worked out in a way that protected and enhanced the goals of each organization. In July 1945 the IVCF boards unanimously adopted the merger plans, subject to the approval of the SFMF groups. *HIS* magazine carried news of the merger, calling it "one of the most significant recent advances in the Christian student world of the U.S. and Canada." Christy Wilson, Jr., assumed duties as missionary secretary of the SFMF and associate general secretary of IVCF in January 1946[6] upon completion of his studies at Princeton Seminary.

2/Restoring a Heart for Missions
The impact of student missionary development in the early months of the merger set the mood for a student missionary convention similar to those of earlier SVM days. World War 2 was over, mission opportunities were exploding, and it was time to motivate students to consider the world. Christy Wilson had talked to Stacey Woods in 1944 about the importance of challenging young people for missions as soon as mission fields opened after the war. Now, as the missionary secretary, he was in a position to translate his vision into reality. Will Norton describes Christy's resolve as "a zeal bordering on desperation." It was nothing short of remarkable that,

within twelve months, Christy could pull off IVCF's first student missionary convention in Toronto at the end of 1946.

Christy Wilson first came in contact with Inter-Varsity in the fall of 1941 when David Adeney made a staff visit to see him while he was a student at Princeton University. The next summer he met Stacey Woods at a student conference at Keswick in New Jersey, and in classic Woods style, Stacey went to some lengths to share his vision of student evangelism with Christy. Stacey saw the potential and Christian maturity of Christy Wilson and had his eye on him for future involvement in the work of IVCF. Mrs. F. Cliffe Johnston, an influential New York board member, kept badgering Stacey about the need to get someone from an Ivy League School to serve on staff, and Christy Wilson fit the bill. In September 1943, just before Christy was to graduate from Princeton, Stacey convinced him to serve as part-time staff.

In the fall of 1943 Christy Wilson, still an undergraduate, began traveling on weekends for Inter-Varsity through all of New England and New York State. By December he had become a student at Princeton Seminary. This allowed him a clergy discount on the train. An upper berth in a Pullman car cost him three dollars, and on the weekends he often took an overnight train to Boston to stir things up at Harvard. Wilson says, "I remember trying to find a Christian at Harvard was like Diogenes going around with a lantern looking for an honest man." During those months of combining staff work and seminary, Christy began to feel a great burden for missions. He had grown up in Iran in a missionary family and from the time he was a little boy he felt called to serve overseas. It is not too surprising then that he should be invited to be the missionary secretary of Inter-Varsity following the merger of IVCF and SFMF in January 1945.

Christy Wilson found the old Student Volunteer Movement's quadrennial compendia in the library at the University of Chicago and began reading about the outstanding student missionary conventions of the past. The more he read in the compendia the more excited he became about planning Inter-Varsity's first missionary convention. Inter-Varsity was now in the flow of the biblical student missionary zeal he was reading about, and these books became the basis for the first convention.

Will Norton, just home from the rigors of five years of missionary work in the Belgian Congo during World War 2, came on staff as Christy's assistant. The first invitation for the speaker's rostrum for the convention was given to Dr. Samuel Zwemer, the legendary missionary pioneer to the Muslims. Zwemer made his commitment to missions during the first year of the SVM in 1888. He was a senior at Hope College when Robert Wilder visited and spoke of the needs of the world. Christy Wilson thought Zwemer's contribution would be a crucial link in the evangelical student missionary movement, giving biblical continuity with the SVM in its best days.

Will Norton traveled east to convince Harold J. Ockenga, the articulate pastor of Park Street Church, Boston, to speak at the convention. Margaret Haines, a staunch prayer warrior for this event, suggested Bakht Singh of India, a former Sikh with the passion of Christ for the people of India. L. E. Maxwell, president of Prairie Bible Institute, and Robert McQuilkin, president of Columbia Bible College, also agreed to address the convention. Mary Anne Klein, released from other responsibilities in the IVCF office, helped Norton and Wilson with the planning. Gradually the program came together.

Opposition came from every side. Norton and Wilson were ridiculed when they visited the mission leaders of the major denominations to invite them to send observers. Why should they be interested in this "fundamentalist" event? The SCM finally agreed to send three representatives, who later published and widely circulated a very negative report about the convention, among other things objecting to its emotionalism.[7] SCM leaders met with Stacey Woods after the convention and warned him that they would oppose Inter-Varsity in every possible way.

On the other side, the ultra-fundamentalists were upset because Zwemer had been invited to speak and Carl McIntire, an outspoken separatist and editor of *The Christian Beacon,* threatened to picket the convention unless Zwemer's invitation was withdrawn.[8] But problems only drove both leaders and students to pray more. Stacey Woods remarked that he had never seen as much prayer for any large gathering as this first IVCF missionary convention.

Christy Wilson traveled west across Canada to recruit students to attend the convention. By the time he reached California he ran out of money and was wondering how he would buy a ticket to the next place. He had talked with a woman on the train about Christ, and as they parted she gave him twenty dollars, which took care of his immediate needs. However, arriving in Chicago he found the IVCF office closed for the weekend, and he was again without money. One of the students at the International House at the University of Chicago, where Christy stayed when he was in the city, shared a chocolate bar with him, which was his food for the weekend. Someone with a lesser vision might have given up on the job. "It wasn't an easy time," Christy says, "but God was faithful."

3/The First SFMF/IVCF Missionary Convention

Despite the bitter Christmas cold and ice, 576 students reached the University of Toronto by train, car and bus from 151 colleges, universities and seminaries across North America. They were compelled by a new movement of the Spirit of God and concern for the world. With them came one hundred missionaries representing fifty-six mission boards. So many men had gone off to war that mission boards were concerned lest this be a gathering of women. Yet half of the delegates were men, a fact which added to the general amazement that so many would come for six days during the Christmas holidays in the chill of the present theological climate.[9]

An ice storm hit the day the convention began, making any kind of transportation dangerous. Bakht Singh, just arriving from the heat of India, slipped on the glassy sidewalk and suffered a compound fracture of his right arm. At the hospital the doctors looked at the X-rays and said, "You have so many breaks that we need to open up your whole arm to reset the bones." Bakht Singh asked if he could speak at the convention if they did that. When he was told that he would need to be hospitalized for some time, he asked them to put his arm in a sling; he would come for the surgery after he had given his address. Doctors warned him about the pain of delay, but they had a determined man.

With his arm in a sling, Bible in hand, Bakht Singh gave a stirring message on "counting the cost." He said, "Young people, don't follow Christ lightly. He gave his life for the world; he wants you to give your life. Be willing to pay the cost."[10]

Immediately after the meeting convention leaders took Singh to the hospital for surgery. When he found that the man in the second bed in his room did not know the Lord, he said,

> In India where I come from, we grow tea. For years we would export it to England, and they would put it in fancy boxes and sell it around the world. But we didn't drink tea. Finally we became curious and tried it ourselves. We've been drinking tea ever since. We didn't realize what a wonderful product we had been exporting. You Canadians have been doing the same thing. You've been sending missionaries around the world, exporting Jesus Christ. But you don't know what a wonderful product you are exporting. The Bible says, "Taste and see that the Lord is good. Blessed is the man who puts his trust in him."[11]

Bakht Singh led this man to faith in Christ, and he in turn asked Singh to tell all his family and friends about Jesus. Christy Wilson went to visit him each day and found his room an evangelistic center with doctors, nurses and patients from up and down the hall gathered in his room to listen to him. When a student asked Singh why God would let such an accident happen to a servant of the Lord, Bakht Singh said, "Well, I know one reason why. Since this happened I've been in such pain I haven't slept a wink and that has enabled me to keep awake and pray for you students."[12]

Christy Wilson had invited the president of the University of Toronto to give a word of greeting to the convention. Since he was going to be out of town, the president asked Burgon Bickersteth, Warden of Hart House, where meals were being served, to give the greeting. Hart House had a tradition of "men only," and Bickersteth was upset that the university had let this Inter-Varsity convention come to campus and, in addition, allowed *women* in Hart House! Instead of giving a gracious word of welcome to the university, he gave a polemic against separatism and an impassioned plea for ecumenicity, praising the Student Volunteer Movement.[13] His remarks left everyone stunned, and the students particularly confused. Harold J. Ockenga rose from his chair to give the opening address and began, "Since you asked, Mr. Bickersteth, these are the reasons why we are here and what we are doing." He proceeded through the objections with a brilliance and clarity that was convincing. He neatly "cleared the deck," gave his prepared message and shot the convention off to a rousing beginning.[14]

Subsequent missionary convention planners would get used to being hassled by unusual problems like these, as if the Enemy directed an extra barrage at attempts to spread the gospel, but this was a first, a groundbreaking in a climate far more hostile than any convention since. Yet staff members said the convention was successful by any measure. Three hundred of the delegates indicated their purpose to serve Christ overseas. Delegates sacrificially gave a $3,500 offering to help reach students, an astounding sum for the year 1946.[15] Students went back to their campuses to form mission study and prayer groups. At the University of Pennsylvania, for example, forty students began to attend the missionary prayer meeting. The missions department of IVCF issued a quarterly publication called *Missionary Advance,* which later became *Missionary Mandate.* Both the Canadian and U.S. offices began stocking missionary books for distribution on campus. A new era for evangelical missions began in Toronto.

4/The Second SFMF/IVCF Missionary Convention

In June 1947 Christy Wilson resigned his post as missionary secretary to pursue doctoral studies at the University of Edinburgh before going into Afghanistan as a teacher. He was succeeded by T. Norton Sterrett, a furloughing missionary from India who had played a significant role in establishing Inter-Varsity's counterpart, the Union of Evangelical Students of India.[16]

Under Sterrett's leadership new SFMF chapters were organized and regional conferences continued. In 1947 three student summer teams traveled through the U.S. and Canada, visiting churches and student missionary groups, telling what God was doing on the campuses. A Foreign Missions Fellowship Institute, directed by Sterrett, was held at Ben Lippen School (North Carolina) in July, 1948, and missions courses were offered for credit. Sterrett also proposed a prayer goal for 10,000 missionary volunteers by 1949. The impact of the Toronto convention continued to reverberate throughout the student world.

The IVCF movement in the U.S. had grown so rapidly that it surpassed the size of the Canadian movement. In light of the continuing relevance of the Toronto convention on the missionary movement, it seemed wise to plan a second missions convention and look for a site in the United States.

That proved more difficult than expected. One after another university refused to host such a convention. Finally Herbert J. Taylor, IVCF Board chairman in the U.S., forsook the normal channels and telephoned the president of the University of Illinois, on whose advisory council he served, and explained the purposes of Inter-Varsity and of this convention. As a result the University of Illinois at Urbana hosted the second SFMF/IVCF Missionary Convention, December 27 to January 1, 1948. The convention banner hanging above the rostrum read: "From Every Campus to Every Country."

Norton Sterrett and his committee had convened an impressive roster of missionaries to speak and lead workshops: Bishop Frank Houghton of the China Inland Mission, V. Raymond Edman of Wheaton College, G. Allen Fleece of Columbia Bible College, William "Billy" Graham, Northcote Deck of the South Seas Evangelical Mission, Wilbur Smith of the recently founded Fuller Theological Seminary, and others. Over 1,300 students from 154 campuses in Canada and the U.S. registered. Again, hundreds stood to affirm their purpose to serve Christ overseas. Students gave an offering of $6,000 for student work through the International Fellowship of Evangelical Students. Men and women who had come into new relationship with Christ while serving in the armed forces during the war began preparing to go back overseas, this time as heralds of the gospel. God clearly arranged the SFMF-IVCF merger to serve the explosion of missionary interest following World War 2.

Even on the campus of the University of Illinois the administration and staff felt the impact of the convention. They were amazed at the orderliness and discipline of the delegates. No cigarette butts, no vandalism or improper behavior. The personal belongings of the U. of I. students, whose rooms were used as housing, were untouched; only a single shower clog was reported missing. They had never seen anything like it. Since 1948 the university at Urbana has welcomed Inter-Varsity for succeeding student missionary conventions.

5/The Strengthening of IVCF's Missions Emphasis

James Kay, chairman of the board of Inter-Varsity in 1989, was one of many people influenced by the repercussions of the 1946 Toronto convention. In 1947 many specific interest missionary prayer groups were meeting on the Wheaton campus. Freshman Kay approached David Howard and Jim Elliot, two men who were then leaders of mission interest at Wheaton and who had signed the missionary pledge at Toronto, to ask if a missionary radio prayer group met on the campus. Elliot said, "Yes, a group is just being formed and you are the chairman. Get to work." He held Kay accountable to form a prayer group and he did. The next year, as a sophomore, Kay went to the 1948 missionary convention at Urbana where he manned a missionary radio display and talked to interested students about radio opportunities. He did not go overseas as a missionary, but he has had life-long mission involvements.

Norton Sterrett planned to return to India after the 1948 convention. At the last meeting of the convention, Wesley Gustafson was introduced as the new missionary secretary, effective August 1949. The Gustafson family had served as missionaries in China under the Evangelical Free Church of America. Wes had been president of his IVCF chapter as a student and active in the missionary band at Stanford's Horton Hall. David Howard was also introduced on that last evening at Urbana as a missionary staff member who would work with Gustafson serving the SFMF chapters in Canada and the U.S., following his graduation from Wheaton.[17]

That next summer Wes Gustafson attended the leadership camps at Campus-in-the-Woods and discovered he had access to strategic campus leaders from all over the country, as well as staff members. As a result of this experience the recommendation was made that twenty-five per cent of Inter-Varsity training hours at camps be devoted to foreign missions, and that personnel from the missionary department be present at such training, and that five of the camp sessions be devoted to missionary subjects.[18]

Sometime in 1948 Mary Anne Klein began to edit *Missionary Mandate.* Letters came almost daily from students asking for information about mission opportunities and in the same mail Mary Anne would be deluged with information from mission boards. She had to figure out a way to disseminate information, and so began a first-class student missionary publication that had a wide ministry and a long life. Briefs about what was happening in various countries of the world kept students (and church leaders) informed and helped them know how to pray. *Missionary Mandate* was a strategic publication, developing global interests and understanding just as a new wave of missionary interest was cresting. Clearly within the first decade of Inter-Varsity's life in the United States, the missions emphasis was firmly in place.

6/Christian Nurses Fellowship Joins Inter-Varsity

Back in March 1935 when some Wheaton College students held their stirring meeting at Thorne Hall on Chicago's Northwestern University campus,[19] some Christians saw new possibilities of what could happen in a city like Chicago. One of these was a concerned young minister named John Herman who formed The Christian Youth League (CYL) for the purpose of encouraging Christian witness in various high schools, colleges and professional schools in and around the city. Among these were the schools of nursing. The ministry of the CYL, although the organization was short-lived, can be credited with spinning off numerous other ministries because it helped people to see the city with fresh eyesight and boldness.

Three graduate nurses began meeting in late 1935 at Children's Memorial Hospital to pray and consider what they might do to help student nurses. Their prayers fueled their concern for those in the nursing profession, and in May 1936 they contacted all the Christian nurses they knew in Chicago, inviting them to meet at the Lawson YMCA to discuss forming an organization that would meet the spiritual needs of nurses. Nineteen nurses came to the meeting and Alvera Anderson, a graduate of Swedish Covenant Hospital School of Nursing, was appointed president of the newly organized group, called the Christian Nurses Fellowship (CNF). They purposed (a) to help nurses realize their need for a personal relationship with God through faith in Jesus Christ, (b) to aid in personal and small group Bible study, (c) to help nurses face personal and professional problems with a conscious Christian attitude, and (d) to present the worldwide need and opportunity of service for nurses.

The CNF monthly meetings proved a boon to those in the nursing profession in the Chicago area. Inspiring programs and speakers lifted the sights of the student nurses they invited to come. Some became Christians; others came to understand the lordship of Christ. Even when they moved the piano out into the hall, the room in the YMCA was soon too small to accommodate the 150 who sometimes attended the monthly meetings. They began praying for a new meeting place and finally got up courage to ask if they could meet in the First District Nurses Headquarters on South Michigan Avenue in the Professional Nurses Building. To their surprise, the request was granted and in the spring of 1937 the group shifted its meetings to an attractive lounge that lent a professional tone to the movement, encouraging more growth.

From the beginning CNF had a strong interest in missions. Whenever possible, a missionary spoke at the monthly meetings. As nurses from their fellowship left for the mission fields, CNF members contributed to their support and kept in touch with them through letters and prayer. Citywide rallies were cosponsored with other groups. At Easter sunrise services large numbers of nurses would parade in their uniforms as part of the Christian Youth League. A citywide Bible study taught by Edson Peck met regularly along with the monthly meeting.

Sometime in the 1930s guidelines for preparation of nurses were standardized and nursing became a licensed profession. Most hospitals established a school of nursing in order to have adequately trained staff for patient care. Christian nurses already working in the hospitals demonstrated consistent interest in these nursing students. Through the encouragement of the monthly meetings, they began to help Christian students pray together and begin Bible studies in their residences as a way to evangelize and grow together spiritually.

With the bombing of Pearl Harbor and onset of World War 2 the need for nurses resulted in burgeoning enrollments in nursing schools. Specialty standards were raised, and smaller nursing schools developed affiliations with schools of nursing in larger hospitals.

While on affiliation, students from smaller hospitals met other Christian nurses and joined Bible studies. Many affiliates became Christians. Back in their home schools, they started Bible study groups like the ones they had known while on affiliation. Hundreds of senior students were recruited into the Cadet Nurses Program, and many of them were able to introduce the ideas of the Christian Nurses Fellowship idea to their peers in military hospitals or schools where they were assigned.

The Chicago CNF purchased Cadet New Testaments from the Bible Society, contacted directors of nursing schools and received permission to distribute these to the entering classes. This gave CNF entry into all the Protestant hospitals in Chicago and the opportunity to explain their organization. Each time they ordered the New Testaments they wondered how they would pay for them, and each time exactly enough money was given at the monthly meetings.

The war also provided other opportunities for witness. When the fiance of one nursing student was killed in the invasion of Sicily, more than seventy other students approached her to ask for an explanation of her faith in Christ. A staff member said of her, "She is the most radiant example I have seen of the power of the triumphant Savior."

Nurses began to form groups in other parts of the country spontaneously and, hearing of CNF in Chicago, looked to it for leadership. Alvera Anderson was president of the organization, but there was no full-time staff. The possibility of giving help to those at a distance was limited to suggestions and encouragement through correspondence. By the end of World War 2 the Chicago CNF was known throughout the country.

In the meantime IVCF had begun on American university campuses. Nursing students were members of some of its groups because of the presence of large university hospitals on or near the campus. In 1944 a student at Wayne State University in Detroit told staff member Jane Hollingsworth, "If all of us were on our toes like the nurses in our university, we could have the largest organization in the school." This happened when a group from the Cadet Nurses Corps, taking three month's work at Wayne State University, had joined themselves to the local IV chapter.

Inter-Varsity leaders contacted CNF for help with requests received from nurses in Seattle and Portland. With increasing number of inquiries CNF began praying about becoming a national organization, not merely a Chicago fellowship. Stacey Woods took the initiative at this point and suggested the formation of a national movement that would affiliate with IVCF. The trend toward collegiate nursing was yet in its infancy, but increasingly nurses were part of IVCF chapters. Affiliation seemed to be a logical next step, although CNF also explored possible merger with Youth for Christ and the Christian Medical Society. Since its objectives were so similar to those of IVCF an agreement was worked out providing for mutual support and consultation on mutual problems.

In the fall of 1947 the Chicago headquarters of IVCF at 64 Lake Street were expanded to include the offices of CNF.

The decision to become a national organization brought representatives from across the country to form a national committee. At the first board meeting, held in June, nine committees were formed and officers elected to oversee the work. Three days later the U.S. Board of IVCF officially accepted CNF[20] as part of its organization. Alvera Anderson became the first CNF general secretary in April 1948, and Tressie Myers was appointed as the first staff member later that year.

Rapid growth came from a healthy grass-roots movement. Christian nurses motivated student nurses, and the expansion was all out of proportion to the size of the two-person national staff because of the effective mentoring of professional nurses. Student nurses and patients were becoming Christians through the concern and care of the members of CNF.

By the fall of 1949 organized groups were meeting in twenty-six states, and CNF had an active witness in 193 of the 1,300 existing nursing programs. Twelve cities had monthly citywide meetings. CNF continued the distribution of New Testaments to freshman nursing students after the war. In the summer of 1949 CNF gave out a thousand testaments at the International Council of Nurses meeting in Stockholm. They also had a visible witness as a recognized nursing organization at the conventions of the American Nurses Association and the National League for Nursing.

While the goals of CNF and IVCF are similar, from the first days of the merger CNF has had to keep explaining itself. The nurses' work included both student and professional nurses because the link is so natural. It is more than a student movement; it is also a professional Christian society, which has become more obvious over the years. Representation of nurses on the IVCF Board, begun in 1949, helped keep this distinctive clear.

In July 1945 a proposed merger or affiliation between the Christian Medical Society (CMS) and Inter-Varsity Christian Fellowship was discussed by the board in its summer meeting. General Secretary Stacey Woods was asked to discuss the matter further with a committee of the Christian Medical Society and submit a satisfactory basis prior to the fall board meeting. At the January board meeting Dr. John Hyde of CMS presented a proposed basis of cooperation, which was accepted by the board.[21] The matter of merging with professional societies came up again and again in the first decade. Whether wisely or not, both Woods and Troutman felt reluctant to expand when the work on the university campuses still lacked sufficient personnel and financing.

7/Looking beyond Our Borders

Stacey Woods's survey trip of Central America during the war had whetted his interest in the expansion of student work in other countries. Under his leadership Cathie Nicoll went to Jamaica to pioneer a high-school work. Ed Pentecost left for Mexico to begin student work in 1944. The Headingtons had gone to Costa Rica. As Stacey became involved in international fellowship, his vision grew. In 1948 he arranged for staff member Gwen Wong to pioneer student work in Hawaii. By 1952 Gwen Wong had gone on to the Philippines to work with students. Mary Beaton became her coworker there in 1956. This pioneering activity followed the pattern of the British Inter-Varsity whose members were taking positions in Africa to extend student witness on that continent. But we are getting ahead of the story.

Long before the IVCF-USA had begun, evangelical student groups in Europe, facing the strong liberal tendency to shift away from Scripture, had formed their own university groups of evangelical Christians. In Norway, Ole Hallesby, a young professor of systematic theology at the Menighetsfakultetet, the free evangelical seminary, saw the impossibility of continuing his active support of existing liberal Student Alliance, which was associated with the World's Student Christian Federation (WSCF). He began to speak to others about his concerns, and, in a crowded meeting held in the oratorium of the Menighetsfakultetet in April 1923, an evangelical student movement called Norges Kristelige Studentlog Skoleungdomslag (NKSS) was born.[22]

News of what was happening in Norway spread to other parts of Scandinavia. In 1923 the Swedes formed their own evangelical student work, and the following two years students from universities throughout Scandinavia met for student conferences in Sweden.

In 1934 Robert Wilder brought two recent graduates from the Norwegian movement with him when he went to England to speak at the British Inter-Varsity conference. One of these was Carl-Frederick Wisloff, who later became a noted Norwegian theologian.[23] When Wisloff saw that the British IVF was clearly caught up in the same task as the slightly older Norwegian movement, he suggested to the IVF General Secretary Douglas Johnson that more formal contacts be arranged with existing national student movements. Wisloff returned to Norway, consulted with the NKSS leaders, and an invitation was sent to the British IVF to attend a September 1934 conference in Oslo, the first International Conference of leaders from various kindred Christian student movements. Student groups from Finland, Denmark, Germany, Hungary, Latvia, Estonia and Sweden were also invited.

Ole Hallesby's address to the conference had a prophetic note. He called this meeting the "hour of God." He continued,

> When movements so alike suddenly and spontaneously spring up in so many countries at the same time, then we must see that God wishes to do something. It is God's hour. . . . Today we are here, representatives of our many nations, and we can each tell of a Christian student work based on the Bible as the Word of God. We can tell of a door which God Himself, in grace has opened unto us.[24]

No federation or formally organized fellowship emerged from the conference, only a commitment to meet again and a quiet sense that God was doing something new. A year later leaders from the various movements gathered in Johannelund, Sweden, where a conference constitution was adopted. Christian academics from one country made speaking tours in another; student teams visited campuses in other countries. In 1936 the Swiss hosted an international camp, which included the participation of the WSCF-affiliated, but largely evangelical, Pro Christo student movement in Hungary. The leader of that Hungarian movement, Ferenc Kiss, persuaded the gathering that the next (the third) International Conference should be held in Budapest.[25]

The Fourth International Conference of Evangelical Students was held in England, at Cambridge, from June 27 to July 3, 1939, just prior to the outbreak of World War 2. Over a thousand students from thirty-three nations attended. Delegates, observers and speakers came from Australia, Britain, Canada, Denmark, Finland, Holland, Hungary, Iceland, Norway, (Old) Russia, Scotland, South Africa, Sweden, The United States and Wales. The brochure advertising the conference provides details about the program and shows how developed the international movement had become:

> The Conference is being organized by an International Conference Executive Committee, which was elected—at a Conference in Budapest, September, 1937—by a General Committee, composed of delegates from those Evangelical Student Movements which are in agreement with the Doctrinal Basis of the Conference.[26]

All easy communication and future planning was interrupted with the outbreak of World War 2. Some of those who spoke at this last conference were later arrested by the Gestapo and died in concentration camps. For the Europeans it was six long years of misery and death. Shortly after the war was ended in Europe, members of the executive committee of the International Conference were invited by British student leaders to come to Oxford in April 1946 to lay plans for an international organization. This organization would encourage the formation of evangelical student groups in every country of the world.

The North American student work had been growing in spite of the war, and its enthusiasm for international fellowship was embodied in Stacey Woods, who was a delegate representing both Canada and the United States. A second American delegate was John Bolten, a German business-man who had fled Germany hours before he was to be apprehended by the Gestapo, and who had since moved his plastics business to America. He was a Plymouth Brethren who had become a friend of Stacey Woods and thus interested in student work. Bolten's heart was tender toward his German homeland. He longed to have German representation at the Oxford conference. His own deep feelings were matched by the deep feelings of those who, like the Norwegians, had suffered so greatly at the hands of Germany. At the Oxford conference, Bolten's impassioned plea that German students be included in future plans met with resistance. It was an emotional time for everyone, and the future of an international fellowship hung in the balance. The breakthrough finally came during a prayer meeting when God put his finger on the hatred and the pain, and the hostility melted with the tears that flowed.

Stacey Woods credits Douglas Johnson of the British Inter-Varsity Fellowship with the genius that brought about the International Fellowship of Evangelical Students. In return Johnson said that the American movement came to a weary Europe with the resources and the enthusiasm needed to make new advances in student work. It was as if "fresh forces had arrived." Stacey Woods needed no persuasion to throw his energies into the international work. He already had the vision and calling. Whether anyone else in America had the vision or not, Stacey did. A proposal was made that both Douglas Johnson and Stacey Woods share the general secretaryship. The group also resolved to send a draft constitution to the member movements that would change the International Conference into international fellowship. A meeting was called for Boston, Massachusetts, in 1947. As the last details were being spelled out for the provisional constitution, a cabelgram arrived from the new Chinese evangelical student fellowship calling for a worldwide movement. It seemed a strong confirmation to steps of faith.

The International Fellowship of Evangelical Students (IFES) came into being in the Phillips Brooks House at Harvard University in August 1947. The founding members of the new fellowship were Australia, Britain, Canada, China, France, Holland, New Zealand, Norway, Switzerland and the USA. It was not an easy meeting. The humidity and heat were at their summer's worst, and spirits were easily ruffled. British precision ("This is the way to do it") sometimes became a thorn in the flesh; at other times it saved the day. The Americans tended to act as if their way was God's way, and the Australians were out of step with everyone. A minor crisis developed when an American delegate took the British delegation on a tour of the battlefields of the War of Independence.

Martyn Lloyd-Jones, who chaired the meetings, bemoaned the lack of a "decent cup of tea which always makes a situation more civilized." The British wanted the Americans to have a national student committee as they did, and found it hard to think a genuine student movement could exist without one. The British, on the other hand, had no experience of American geography.

The determination of the delegates, however, was greater than their differences, and under the incisive leadership of Lloyd-Jones the group carefully hammered out a Basis of Faith and crafted the constitution to assure the autonomy of each national movement. The underlying belief that each country knew best how to do student work appropriate to their own culture contributed to the group's sense of unity.

The birth of this new indigenous international movement went largely unnoticed in the confusion after the war, but the genius of the idea and its timing were surely of God. Douglas Johnson turned over the minute books of the prior meetings[27] to C. Stacey Woods, who was made the general secretary of IFES. Martyn Lloyd-Jones became the first chairman, and Ole Hallesby the first president. With typical verve, *HIS* magazine announced in the October 1947 issue, "INTER-VARSITY GOES INTERNATIONAL,"[28] and carried a detailed article on the event.

Thus the opening decade of Inter-Varsity Christian Fellowship in the United States set the pace for future years. Before the movement was ten years old it had chapters on secular campuses, SFMF chapters on Christian campuses, CNF chapters in schools of nursing and international fellowship with other evangelical student movements. In the goodness of God, the Fellowship had gotten off to an excellent start.

8
Gains and Losses: Decade of the 1950s

The rare visits by staff were wonderful, life-changing times of training and encouragement. "Never did so many owe so much to so few."
John W. Alexander, *professor, University of Wisconsin*

The 1950s brought an aura of prosperity and hope that had not existed for over a generation. In spite of the Korean conflict optimism reigned. The technology of the war years turned toward producing consumer goods and improving the quality of life. The popular advertising slogan, "Better Living Through Chemistry," captured the smug mood of American science laboratories. It meant, among other things, new automobile designs, a flourishing plastics industry, along with the know-how to improve production of the land and provide consumers with an array of appliances. Increasing numbers of families arranged their living room furniture to face a new television set. The "good life" was suddenly available to masses of people, particularly white Anglo-Saxon Protestants. The GI Bill opened up a college education to people who had never dreamed of it before, and the expectation that one's children would go on for tertiary education became commonplace. Community colleges, organized to take care of burgeoning student populations, outwitted the predictions that only the exceptional student would find a place in the university.

On the campus, fraternity and sorority life reached its heyday, their members moving on the scene as the "insiders" of the system, the beautiful people whose success was assured by their connections. At the same time professors found encouragement in the rising number of "outsiders,"[1] who, intent on getting an education, made learning their reason for being in school. The campus became the place of opportunity for returning veterans, whose serious approach to higher education left little room for non-conformity. Conservatism and wealth returned to the campus. The McCarthy hearings made professors and students cautious about political opinions.

Colleges became universities. Without public notice, the campus began to change as numbers swelled. But whatever the student status, feelings of well-being tended to bring a complacency that made students want to blend, rather than to stand out. It was a comfortable time to be alive. In Inter-Varsity groups, this meant large chapters where members felt secure and happy to be with other Christians. It was respectable to be a Christian during these days when Dwight D. Eisenhower was president, and most families went to church.

The perception of teenagers as a major population group in our country—the youth culture—came into its own during the 1940s and 1950s. Being a teenager became more than a transitional period combining values of both childhood and adulthood. It had roles and values and ways of behaving that were distinctly its own. Christian parachurch organizations ministered to this growing youth culture during these decades. Inter-Varsity, as a continuation of a long tradition of university witness, has been perhaps less a response to the teenage phenomena than others. Collegians are young adults, not teenagers, in Inter-Varsity's view and thus able to bear responsibility. The amazing response of the youth culture to the gospel and to the mission field, along with the widespread evangelism within the country, during these postwar years cannot be overlooked. It revitalized the religious core of the nation.[2]

1/Campus Evangelism

The mature postwar students, many of them ex-servicemen whose life experiences had enriched Inter-Varsity chapters, graduated and left the campus by the early fifties. The immaturity and self-absorption of the fresh student generation frustrated the Inter-Varsity staff as they talked about vision and campus evangelism. Students were peer-oriented and other-directed, much less independent than the early leaders of Inter-Varsity chapters. In many places the courage to take a lone stand was not only missing; it seemed unnecessary. IV chapters had fewer non-Christians associating with their members, and Christian students were happy belonging to a safe club. In this they reflected what was happening in the local church. Again and again over the decade, Inter-Varsity leaders had to sound the trumpet for evangelism, so vital for chapter life.

"The Year of Evangelism," designated for the academic year 1950-51, came out of a meeting of the senior staff who had been struggling over the need for more forthright campus evangelism. Students at one college after another responded enthusiastically to the idea of having a campus mission and began making plans. Others were scared to death of the idea. A campus mission involved a series of campus-wide lectures presenting the gospel in a way that would engage the university community to consider the claims of Christ. The staff helped find gifted missioners, whose presentation would not only bring students back subsequent nights, but encourage them to invite their friends. A staff team was assigned to work with the missions, but the Christian students in the chapter bore the responsibility not just for arrangements, but for inviting their friends to come. It was an enormous undertaking, taxing both students and staff, but in the end sixty-five missions were conducted by thirty different missioners in the U.S. and Canada.

Students at the University of Minnesota held the first mission of the year in October, and the initiative for it came from students. One night in the summer of 1949 as Bonnie Anderson (now Addington) read her Bible, she had the overwhelming conviction that her IV chapter should invite Billy Graham to speak at a campus-wide evangelistic mission. Later when she shared the idea with her staffworker he only seemed embarrassed at the extravagance of the idea. But Bonnie was convinced that God had given her the inspiration, and when Charles Troutman came to campus, she told him about her plan. He gave her the encouragement she was looking for. Charles suggested she get students praying about the idea because group ownership was a necessity to carry off a meeting of this magnitude. He not only believed it could happen, but it was a good idea. And that was the encouragement Bonnie needed. Students in the DPMs spread across campus began to pray earnestly about the possibility. They became convinced that Bonnie and Lowell Johnson, the chapter president, should visit Billy Graham and ask if he would come.

Graham was quite taken with the idea, and very encouraging to the student delegation, who requested a date sometime in the fall of 1950. As he checked his calendar it didn't look hopeful, but he suggested they pray together and he would continue to seek direction on the matter. A short time later he contacted the students and agreed to come in October. University officials said they could use Northrup Memorial Auditorium but later reneged on that offer and gave them the armory instead. Was the university nervous about what they were going to do? That only intensified the student prayer and planning. Attendance at the meetings exceeded what they dared pray for: Records show an attendance of 8,500 for the four-day series of meetings. Bonnie Addington remembers that time:

> During that time on campus you could share with anyone and they would listen. Somehow all the barriers were down. God was really at work in the hearts of students. It was a very exciting time for us as a chapter as many of us saw our friends become Christians.[3]

Two other missions took place in the fall, at the University of Kansas and the University of Missouri, with James Forrester as missioner. Then in the spring of 1951 the momentum picked up, and more than sixty were held before the end of May. In November, *HIS* carried an article by Leith Samuel, one of the missioners, about "Preparing a University Mission," and Jane Hollingsworth wrote an editorial about "Spiritual Preparation for Evangelism," underscoring the importance of prayer and personal holiness. Staff members focused on preparing students for planning their mission.

Students enlisted prayer from graduates and local churches. They found creative ways to advertise. At several schools the students stamped all the dining hall napkins with "Hear Leyasmeyer." (Leyasmeyer was one of the missioners.) At Washington State College the first lecture was broadcast live over the college station, while taped lectures were played later over other college stations. The *McGill Daily* gave front-page coverage to the mission with a daily synopsis of the previous lecture. Every mission had its own story. But it was more than the story of an event; it was more than a story of conversions. What was happening in the lives of the students who extended themselves in planning, praying, trusting, inviting—who can tell that story?

Most of the thirty missioners did only one or two missions, but two gave substantial time. Karlis Leyasmeyer, a Latvian educator whose experiences under both the Nazis and the Russian Communists during World War 2 gave him a ready audience, did numerous effective missions. He had been in hard places during recent history, and he was convincing about the answer to man's dilemma. Leith Samuel, an engaging young British pastor who had conducted effective missions at Cambridge and Oxford, devoted the whole winter to this ministry as the chief missioner. He kept an incredible schedule, speaking at ten week-long missions in three months' time.

Samuel's training in the give-and-take of evangelistic encounters came partly from his experience as a youth as he stood on a box, proclaiming the gospel in London's Hyde Park. He spoke briefly and then opened up the meeting for questions. Samuel's presentations were so provocative that one young man, who fancied himself an "infidel," recorded them all on tape, and soon became a Christian.

Exceptionally gifted in answering questions from the audience, Samuel had an uncanny way of seeing the spiritual hunger at the core of each question or problem. When a student would quote a conflicting idea from some recent writing, Samuel would answer it with respect, but go on to point out that later in the book the author contradicted this statement— and he would sometimes give the page number! It became clear that Samuel knew what he was talking about. Students who heard him once made sure they came to hear him again and brought their friends. Staff felt that interest among non-Christians was nothing short of phenomenal, and in many cases the audience at his lectures was largely non-Christian. Leith Samuel was invited to come to the States with his family to continue a second year of campus evangelism, an invitation he was not free to accept.

Something wonderful happened among students who took the mission seriously. It was recognizable when it happened, and over thirty years later the experience still calls up glowing memories for many who participated. Students who felt helpless and insignificant in the milieu of the university dared to believe God wanted them to proclaim the good news about Jesus Christ. They met together and petitioned the living God with an earnestness new to them, and he answered. The unity and purpose they experienced brought a new maturity. Missions produced more than new converts.

Inquirers or new believers signed up for Bible studies, and discussion groups on basic Christianity followed the lectures. Students who had overextended themselves to pull off the mission now faced the task of followup on those who had become Christians. For some chapters, it was almost too much. It was not a problem-free venture. Mistakes were made in choosing missioners; weaknesses in planning showed up at some schools; in a few places no one responded to the gospel. Attendance at the missions varied from twenty to thirteen hundred, depending on the campus and the missioner. At a few colleges the Christian students did not feel the mission came from their initiative; it had been lowered on them by the Inter-Varsity staff. Yet on the whole the outreach went beyond the expectation of even the most optimistic.

Jane Hollingsworth, Gene Thomas, Paul Little and Alice Kitchen were assigned the preparation work for the Year of Evangelism. Jane had been in England the previous year where she participated in extensive evangelistic outreach. Gene Thomas was an obvious natural, at ease with non-Christians. It was his idea to get into as many dormitories, sororities and fraternities as possible. Gene had done enough of this kind of evangelism to field questions with comparative ease.[4] He gave rookie staff member Paul Little basic training in evangelism—training for a skill he later refined as his own.[5] "Don't give them a plan of salvation," Gene would say. "Tell them about Jesus."

The University of Michigan chapter negotiated to have Harold J. Ockenga invited as one of five speakers at the prestigious Rackham Lecture Series sponsored by the university. Ockenga spoke on "The Nature of Protestant Orthodoxy." At the end of a brilliant lecture he said, "It would be unfair to talk of orthodoxy and not to give you an opportunity to receive Christ." It was a year of great excitement for the students. But with typical Inter-Varsity conservatism, no numbers of converts were published. Students who did follow-up on each campus knew what had happened at their mission. The ensuing months would reveal how many really became Christians, and many of these would come from the Bible studies and follow-up. God would keep track of the numbers; Inter-Varsity students were to concern themselves with individuals. Charles Troutman estimates that between four and five hundred students became Christians.

Campus-wide missions did not end with the Year of Evangelism. In the 1952-53 school year Karlis Leyasmeyer spoke at half a dozen more evangelistic outreaches, and individual schools sponsored other missioners, who sometimes were staffworkers. Many chapters began off-campus evangelistic efforts. In 1954 forty students from Michigan Christian Fellowship called on every home in Milan, a nearby small town, inviting people to an evening at the high-school auditorium where students would be speaking on: "University Students Recommend Christianity." The publication of *Becoming a Christian* by John R. W. Stott in 1950 was timely and became a widely used booklet. Members of the Penn State chapter regularly visited nearby Rockview State Penitentiary to lead gospel services, attended by about two hundred men and resulting in a number of men coming to trust Christ. "News of the Campus," a regular feature in *HIS* magazine, carried stories like these throughout the decade.

Students began seizing opportunities offered by the university. An example of this took place at State University of Iowa when Iowa Christian Fellowship (ICF), under the leadership of student president Wesley Pippert,[6] participated in a campus-wide ecumenical mission. Pippert urged chapter members to participate in the Student Christian Council, the coordinating body for religious activities on campus. Some saw it as a risk; other saw it as an opportunity and got involved. When the council planned the 1954 Christian Emphasis Week,[7] the ICF chapter was able to invite Harold B. Kuhn, a professor of philosophy of religion at Asbury Theological Seminary, as one of the speakers.

It proved to have benefits beyond their wildest dreams. In cooperation with the university, the Council arranged for the faculty to examine the curricula vitae of the speakers and place them in classes accordingly. The ROTC unit noticed a single line in Dr. Kuhn's personal data stating that he had spent one year as an educational consultant to the U.S. Air Force in Germany. The ROTC requested Dr. Kuhn speak to all of the military science students on campus, and in that post-Korea period, that represented most of the male students. Uniform-clad officers checked off attendance at the doors of McBride Auditorium as hundreds of male Iowa students filed in under military orders to hear Kuhn speak. Pippert reports, "In one hour Kuhn reached more students for God than all the other speakers combined during the week." Because chapter members were willing to work on the Student Christian Council, two of the speakers invited to the campus were evangelicals, and Pippert became president of that council in 1955.

In 1959 news briefs like these peppered the pages of the *Inter-Varsity News:*

Five hundred students heard a clear presentation of the gospel through evangelistic discussions held in eighteen sororities and fraternities at Kansas State University. Five people indicated a commitment to Christ.

NCF staff member Joyce Hansen and IVCF staff member Barbara Boyd held evangelistic discussions in dormitories of four schools of nursing in San Francisco and Oakland.

Six hundred came out for two successive debates at UCLA. Fifty signed up for small discussion groups on Christianity.

Thirty students attended a dorm discussion at Southern Oregon and five are seriously considering becoming Christians.

At Queens College in New York City, Walter Liefeld conducted a five-day series on "The Impact of Jesus." Attendance averaged over one hundred, half of them Jewish. Several are seriously interested in Jesus.

Six evangelistic discussions were held in six fraternities at Columbia University.

Duke has begun plans for a campus mission in the fall of 1960.

2/Student Traveling Teams

John Paterson,[8] a British graduate student, did Inter-Varsity staff work in southern Wisconsin during 1949-50. His own university experience at Cambridge University made his influence on students particularly effective. Stacey believed in cross-pollination, and he got the idea of inviting other graduates from Oxford or Cambridge to come to the States. In the summer of 1950 at a student conference in Holland, Stacey met Peter Haile and asked if he would consider coming to the U.S. after he graduated from Oxford. That same fall Charles Troutman, visiting the university work in Britain, spoke to Peter again. Charles wanted to find a team of four men— two from Oxford and two from Cambridge—to come for a year with the hopes of building the work in Ivy League schools.

Eventually it was arranged with the British IVF General Secretary Douglas Johnson, who asked for help from Leith Samuel and Oliver Barclay in orienting these four men to a crosscultural experience in the United States. It was suggested that, among other things, they be wary of American women, who, the British thought, tended to be very aggressive! Leith Samuel warned them that American students liked to talk into the wee hours and they should be careful not to stay up too late at night. Time after midnight was the "devil's time." "Whatever you do," someone said, "when you give a talk, don't use the President of the U.S. in an illustration in the same way you would use the King or Queen of England."[9] And so they came in the midsummer of 1951: Peter Haile and John Weston from Oxford, Dane Gordon and John Holmes from Cambridge.

Campus-in-the-Woods was their first introduction to the American IVCF. They were tremendously impressed. The British IVF had no training that compared with what they found in this four-week camp. The exposure to theology by outstanding scholars proved first-rate. The inductive Bible study training[10] was new to them, since Bible studies on their campuses were usually taught by someone like Basil Atkinson, an evangelical scholar associated with the university. The team would use this training to good advantage in the months ahead. The American staff members demonstrated maturity and spiritual gifts. Peter Haile said, "It was a very exciting time of learning for us."[11] And they were especially impressed with the women staff. John Holmes said, "They were so attractive, and yet they could expound Romans in a way that made you sit up and take notice."

The prefect system in British high schools meant that students took on considerable responsibility as teenagers. In addition they spent an extra year in school. The team found the American freshman student inexperienced in running anything and quite immature. Those from a fundamentalist background seemed confused by the campus and tongue-tied in witness. However, they found students learned quickly and the training programs in IVCF helpful and effective, so that by the time a student was a senior their maturity fairly matched the British senior student at Cambridge or Oxford.

The British team were surprised to find the work in the Midwest schools much stronger than at Harvard and Yale. By Thanksgiving time they had slept in sixty-three different beds, most of them in dorms or student houses. Jim Nyquist, Jane Hollingsworth and Dorothy Farmer were their mentors. It was a rigorous schedule, traveling all over the Northeast, working in pairs (and making $50 a month). New student leadership emerged— Linden Cole and Joe Martin became pillars of Harvard Christian Fellowship—and students began to evangelize in a new way.

After Urbana 51, which they found impressively mind-boggling, the team split up to multiply their effectiveness. Dane Gordon worked in New York schools, Peter Haile took on Maine, Vermont and New Hampshire, John Weston went to Connecticut, and John Holmes stayed in the Boston area. Despite the cultural differences, the team made lasting contributions to the work in the States and the interchange benefitted both students and staff. The maturity of the team members and their leadership experience in their own British universities contributed to their effectiveness. When the year's commitment ended, only John Weston returned home. (He had left a fiancee back in England.) John Holmes[12] and Dane Gordon were engaged to be married to American women, and Peter Haile asked if he could stay on the staff for another year. Permission was granted, a visa obtained, and a year later Peter succeeded Jim Nyquist as the regional director for New

England in 1953. He also married Jane Hollingsworth in 1954, one of the most exciting pieces of in-house news that year.

Leaders in the Fellowship decided a traveling team approach to evangelistic ministry had benefits. In 1954 an American IVCF evangelistic team was formed with Bill Young (Indiana University), as team leader. Frank Van Aalst (Dartmouth), Austin "Swede" Christensen (Iowa State), and George "Bud" Murray (Kent State) were members of the team. They billed their ministry: "Man Alive! Who Is?" They began with a training session at Bear Trap Ranch, and then traveled east from region to region, spearheading evangelism with discussions in fraternities, sororities and dorms, working with local staff and students. They did fifteen major one-week stints on campus, plus shorter sessions at other schools, stirring up opportunities for chapter follow-up and leading some to Christ. Part way through the year, Bud Murray left for health reasons,[13] and the team continued without a replacement. They developed their own style of approach as they traveled east and had particularly effective meetings at Oberlin College, Duke University and the universities of New Hampshire and North Carolina.

The team members found their venture personally enriching and knew that their presence encouraged more aggressive student evangelism. It also gave lonely staff a lift, and the team became the confidants of many. "Swede" Christensen, who later became a campus staff member in Colorado, reflects:

> We were usually invited to dinner at the frat houses, sororities or dorms where we were introduced and gave a greeting, inviting those present to join us in the lounge after dinner. The politeness of the '50s insured that most of the students would come to the meeting. We gave a half-hour talk and then fielded questions for the next two hours or more. We always took members of the chapter with us, so they could do follow-up. Frank Van Aalst was the intellectual on the team and we referred philosophical questions to him.[14]

The concept of a traveling student team was not continued beyond that year, and Senior Staff Council (SSC) minutes give no reference to it. Perhaps, like other projects, it did not continue because no single person took responsibility for it. Increasingly the staff felt that effective campus evangelism required purposeful student friendships more than team forays onto a campus. The team idea, however, has continued with regional staff forming short-term teams for special evangelistic training and outreach on a given campus. In 1957 an Inter-Varsity team of staff, students and alumni did student follow-up after Billy Graham's New York Crusade, an enormous piece of work since hundreds of collegians had responded at the meetings.

According to the minutes, the SSC wrestled with the subject of evangelism repeatedly in the fifties. When he became national secretary, Charles Hummel prepared a paper based on an analysis of field staff, noting that the movement has drifted toward staff who counsel the wounded behind the lines at first aid stations. What Inter-Varsity needs is more staff like the early pioneers who were prepared to initiate and lead students in frontline evangelism, he said. The discussion of this paper at a crucial meeting of the SSC at Hudson House in the spring of 1957 marked a turning point in staff recruitment that exerted influence in the following years.

Known for his wry comments and wit, Paul Little commented, "Inter-Varsity staff are supposed to move in and out, but I think we have some staff who are better at moving out." Little by now had developed his own evangelistic skills. Out of concern that Christians were often found talking to themselves, in 1959 he wrote the useful booklet, *Lost Audience,* which was widely used in subsequent years to remind students of their calling. Looking at the history of the entire decade, however, the records show consistent evangelistic emphasis.

3/Expansion in Camping

Inter-Varsity training at Campus-in-the-Woods (CIW) flourished. Stacey Woods was so convinced of the strategic nature of this training that he said, "As goes CIW, so goes Inter-Varsity." Staff members found the four-week camp not only an effective way to impart information, but also sufficient exposure to influence a Christian world view in their students. Student training made a difference back on campus. Two one-month sessions were held each summer at CIW, sometimes with serious overcrowding and overextending the facilities on that small island. James Nyquist[15] had taken over the management of CIW in 1950, in addition to his other duties. It seemed obvious by then that something had to be done to take care of all the students who wanted training.

In January of 1950 Mel Friesen was instructed to begin looking for a camp on the West Coast to supplement the work of CIW. Inter-Varsity had used The Firs, a conference center in Bellingham, Washington, in the late forties to supplement training at CIW, but Woods thought IVCF should have its own site. Students had been coming from the West Coast since the opening of CIW in the mid-forties, but it was a long trip.

Mel scouted out the entire West Coast and found nothing suitable or available. However, on the way to look at a YMCA camp on Santa Catalina, a small desert island about twenty-five miles south of Los Angeles harbor, he noticed an empty cove named Gallagher Canyon and went to the Catalina Island Company to check on its availability. It had been used as a survival training camp during the war, and a few old gray buildings were on the site. The Company agreed to cooperate with Mel's plan to build a camp there, and even gave a gratuitous lease.

Mel spread the word among the alumni, who contributed about half of the money needed to build housing for campers. He shared his vision with architecture student Paul Byer, who came up with a design for simple cabins suited for the climate. Ten cabins were planned. Mel Friesen went ahead and bought the supplies, mortgaging his house to get the project started. His way of financing the project earned a rebuke from the IVCF Board when they learned of this.

During spring break Mel took a group of students from southern California colleges to the island for a work project. Somehow he talked the union out of unloading a barge carrying sixty-nine tons of material to the sandy cove at Gallagher Canyon. Instead, the students made makeshift gangplanks and a steady stream of fellows and girls carried lumber, cement, bedsprings, mattresses, stoves, a dismantled refrigerator and even a piano off the barge and away from the water. The steamship's captain remarked that he had "never seen the likes of it," and he had been in the shipping business a long time. The students finished the job in one day (to the captain's amazement) and their work saved the camp thousands of dollars. *HIS* magazine records somewhat awkwardly, "The God of real provision and strength proved Himself again to be a very present help in constant need by performing in mysterious ways to bring into existence the wonder of Campus by the Sea."

Two sessions of two weeks each were held during the summer of 1951, even though the campsite was not finished. Wild pigs and rattlesnakes made life exciting that summer. The next year the program at Campus by the Sea (CBS) was fashioned after the CIW training program, with one-month sessions.

From the first, CBS was a Friesen product, carried out with dogged determination and ingenuity. Although Stacey might not protect the person criticized for too much initiative, he liked leaders who could get things done like this. The Friesen family spent the summers on the island, with Mel leading the staff in training students from schools along the West Coast.

He had been made regional secretary for the entire West Coast in 1951, responsible for work from Washington State to Arizona, besides being a member of the Senior Staff Council. Four years later in 1955, exhausted from responsibility for so much student work plus the developing of CBS, Mel and Helen Friesen left the Fellowship to farm, teach school and spend more time as a family. It turned out to be a temporary leaving, because Mel and Helen returned to IV staff in the late 1960s.

Meanwhile CIW still faced an overflow situation. Herbert Taylor, who had served so many years as chairman of the IVCF Board, was convinced about camping, and purposed to give a camp to each of the organizations he had initially helped through the Christian Workers Foundation. He had been collecting pieces of property around Prentiss Bay, near Cedarville, in the upper peninsula of Michigan over a sixteen-year period. Eventually he had all the property around the bay, a magnificent site with about six miles of protected shoreline off of Lake Huron. He offered this to Inter-Varsity as a training center.

Midwest Regional Director Cleo Buxton had used the rather rustic lodge at the head of the bay as base for a work camp in 1949 and 1950, but no major improvements had been made to provide a site useful for camping. Some were hesitant about its development because it was relatively close to CIW.

In 1951 CIW had too many registrations. With no warning and little preparation, Inter-Varsity decided to hold a four-week overflow camp at the Prentiss Bay site. It was billed "CIW Overflow Camp," which gave the camp a negative flavor from the first. Paul Hanselman, staff member for Michigan, was assigned to hastily purchase beds and mattresses on an extremely limited budget and open up the buildings. Charles Troutman directed the camp.

Campers arrived in rainy, wet weather to find that they had not arrived at paradise. The wetness of the spring, plus inadequate buildings, made everyone a feast for the mosquitos. A mouse jumped out when Camp Secretary Polly Barkhuff (Davidson) opened her desk drawer. The kitchen was hardly adequate. Spirits were not high. Students called the camp "Rumpus in the Stumps."

In spite of all this, and maybe because of it, unusual blessing came out of that session. Dr. Francis Steele, a former staff member and then director of the North Africa Mission, and Northcote Deck, a former missionary doctor to the Solomon Islands, gave memorable plenary sessions. Several spontaneous all-night prayer meetings took place, and staff were later to comment on the unusually deep, lasting work that took place that summer.

4/Urbana 51

In late 1951 more than sixteen hundred collegians from more than three hundred colleges, seminaries and nursing schools in Canada and the U.S. attended the third Student Missionary Convention at the University of Illinois in Urbana, including students from seventeen different countries. West Coast students chartered buses for a three-day trip to Illinois. Wes Gustafson, missionary secretary, led the convention, and students heard from major speakers like John A. Subhan, Bishop of the Methodist Church in southern Asia, T. Stanley Soltau of Korea, Eugene Nida of the American Bible Society, Paul J. Lindell of the World Mission Prayer League, J. C. Macauley of Moody Bible Institute and W. Robert Smith of Bethel College. Northcote Deck, Wilbert Norton, David Adeney, Wilber Sutherland, Stacey Woods and Charles Troutman also spoke. Mrs. Ford L. Canfield of the China Inland Mission was the only woman speaker listed, labeled by her husband's given name in the publicity, a common practice at that time.

The number of missions sending representatives increased slightly, and conversations with students at mission booths created some excitement among mission leaders who had been slow to see the recruitment potential of the conventions. Stacey Woods, giving the opening plenary address, had an unexpected moment of levity when he made a special plea for students to interact with the missionaries, who were at that moment sitting behind him on the platform. Gesturing toward them, he said, "Now if you really are concerned to know the needs on the mission field you should interview some of these one-hundred odd missionaries sitting on the platform." A roar of laughter came from all corners of the auditorium at his use of the word *odd.* For a brief moment Stacey mentally backtracked to remember what he had said, and then remarked, "Well, some of them are odder than others." It was a classic Woods comment. The ensuing laughter broke down all reserve between missionaries and students.

The convention, heavy in plenary sessions, and with a theme: "By All Means—Proclaim Christ," found a responsive and enthusiastic audience, with about 500 more students in attendance than in the 1948 convention, a total of 1,646. Sixty per cent of the students indicated their purpose to proclaim Christ abroad, and thirty-five per cent indicated a willingness to go if God should call them. Charles Troutman sounded a strong note about the folly of promising to proclaim Christ in foreign lands if students were not willing to proclaim him on their campuses and in their homes.

By this time the purposes of the convention had been clarified: (1) to lay a foundation for the world mission of the Church through biblical exegesis, (2) to bring students into contact with the world situation by helping them face issues and interact with world Christian leaders, (3) to encourage each student to respond intelligently to God's claim on his/her life.[16] A convention format of early morning quiet times, small group Bible studies and evening prayer groups was in place. A compendium of major addresses was published after the convention.

Wes Gustafson had a special interest in SFMF and provided good leadership with David Howard and others who followed as SFMF staffworkers touring the country to encourage groups on Christian campuses. When Gustafson resigned in 1952, Lois Thiessen provided interim leadership in the Missions Department until the spring of 1953 when David Adeney became the missions secretary.

5/Great Strides in Publishing

Stacey Woods took over the editorship of *HIS* when Virginia Lowell resigned in 1950. He was at this point the general secretary of two national movements and the IFES. He also was responsible for whatever meager publishing was being done. *My Heart—Christ's Home* by Robert Boyd Munger, first printed as a *HIS* article in 1951, became one of the small booklets published by InterVarsity Press. While Stacey was listed as *HIS* editor, Lois Thiessen, who later edited *Missionary Mandate,* was a capable assistant editor, followed by Gertrud DeGroot. These women carried most of the responsibility for its production.

In 1951 Joseph T. Bayly left his regional secretary post to become the editorial secretary in charge of InterVarsity Press, a move which gave needed impetus to the press. His secretary and editorial assistant, Ruth Trumpfheller, represents many fine people who made quiet but major contributions to the work of the Fellowship.

In 1952 Joe took on the editorship of *HIS,* bringing his fresh creativity and insightful content to the magazine. Joe's leadership in *HIS* gave the magazine national acclaim among religious periodicals. Staff, students, alumni and church leaders all found inspiration in *HIS,* which began to reflect Joe Bayly's mature viewpoints. It was a "coming of age" for the magazine, but it also moved *HIS* beyond the basic vision for freshmen, away from the pioneering stages of the movement, into a strong emphasis on a Christian world view. Virginia Krauss (Hearn) worked with Joe as assistant editor beginning in 1957, with Lois Reid as art editor until 1959, when Gordon Stromberg joined the team. *HIS* was named Magazine of the Year by the Evangelical Press Association that year, the first of many accolades.

In later years Joe was described as a "prophet for our times" by the evangelical community, and it is clear that he developed his gifts as the editor of *HIS*. The right-wing separatists periodically wrote stormy letters of protest, one even calling Joe Bayly's basic loyalties into question because of the publication of an article by Ferenc Kiss, a Christian scholar from Hungary, who was labeled a communist.[17] Although his way of meeting editorial deadlines and answering mail often created a frenzy, the grace and certainty with which Joe kept on course made *HIS* magazine one of the most widely read of Christian periodicals. His large view of God and of student work gave him a strategic ministry through both *HIS* magazine and the books chosen for InterVarsity Press. His spiritual direction as a senior member of the SSC proved a source of stability to the growing movement.

6/Inter-Varsity Staff Additions
People did not apply for staff in these years; they were asked to join by leaders of the movement. Most often it was Stacey Woods, who had an intuitive sense about people. Charles Troutman and Joe Bayly also scouted out the kind of workers IVCF needed. Often students felt a reluctance about leaving campus and especially the fellowship that had meant so much to them. Applying for staff was a good way to stay with the glow of past experiences. So when a student asked about staff work, that person was told to find a job near the university and work on the campus to see if this ministry was God's calling.

Jim Ostle, student at the University of Arizona who later served IVCF as a local committee member, a board member, and an enthusiastic Urbana volunteer, tells of approaching Mel Friesen about student work. Mel's reply was, "What makes you think you can witness to students now. You didn't do much of it when you were a student." Ostle says, "I'm sure he said much more, but I don't remember any of it. The worst part of it was that he was right."

In the early 1950s a number of people whose names have become synonymous with Inter-Varsity were asked to join the staff. James Nyquist had already become a staff member in 1949. Paul Little, Barbara Boyd, George Ensworth, Charles Hummel, among others, became staff members in 1950. Keith Hunt joined Inter-Varsity in early 1951 as office manager, with a special assignment to organize a growing movement. He later transferred to campus staff work upon completion of the assignment. Paul Byer began working as staff in the Northwest that same year. James McLeish became the accountant in 1952, and Marie Huttenlock (Little) came to do international student work in New York City. Later in the decade people like Peter Northrup and Bill York joined the Fellowship.

Others—Bob Young, Warner Hutchinson, Bob Baylis, Ruth Stewart, John Hermanson, Alice Alter, James Reapsome, Paul Fromer, Burton Harding, Dorothy Farmer, George Norris, Harriet Marsh, Marilyn Kunz, Marge Ballard, Ruth Gordon, Fred Woodberry, Harry Burke, and many others—played important roles in the growing of the movement in the fifties and sixties, and later went on to the mission field or other professions.

In 1952 Stacey Woods invited Ivery Harvey to come on staff, the first Black to work full-time on Inter-Varsity staff. Ivery's first contact with Inter-Varsity came in 1947 through a student in one of his classes at Wayne University (Detroit) who had Matthew 16:26 on the side of his brief case: "What shall it profit a man if he shall gain the whole world and lose his own soul?" When Ivery asked him why he carried that message on his case, the student, Gordon Heimann, said that verse was very meaningful to him and he wanted to be reminded of its truth. Gordon mentioned a group of other students who also thought this important, and invited Ivery Harvey to come to their Inter-Varsity meeting.

Ivery accepted the invitation that day and heard a speaker he thought both interesting and convicting. Something about the quality of the fellowship of this group of students, their genuine spirituality and personal friendliness to him brought Ivery back again and again. He had never experienced anything like it—the praying together, sharing the reality of the Lord, discussing ideas. Sometime the next fall as they walked across campus, Gordon turned to Ivery and asked, "Have you ever made a real personal commitment to Christ?" Ivery couldn't recall that he had. He had been brought up in church but he had never been asked that question, even when he joined the church. At a chapter meeting soon afterward Ivery says,

> I accepted Christ as my *own* personal Savior. I continued in Inter-Varsity and took an active part in the chapter organization. The highlight of my college experience was the summer I spent at Campus in the Woods in 1949. It would be hard to relate all I learned there.
>
> The influence of Stacey Woods, Charles Troutman and Cleo Buxton were very evident in some of the decisions I made in life. I appreciate the stands they took and the courage they exemplified. Stacey's philosophy of service to Christ is still thought-provoking. Once during the fall of 1948 when the Wayne State University IVCF chapter went on a week-

end conference, the group was told by the proprietor that I, the only black student in the group, could not stay overnight. While I chose not to remain, the position that Cleo Buxton took on racial equality and the consequent dialogs with chapter officers pre-dated civil rights rhetoric by fifteen years.

Stacey assigned me to work in the south,[18] basically in Black Colleges in Georgia, Alabama, Tennessee, North and South Carolina and a bit of Virginia. I never regretted my decision to come on staff, but I regretted the fact that I wasn't as knowledgeable about the culture of the south or the Black church as I should have been. All the people in my home church were Blacks, but it was not a Black denomination. In the south the Black church was not acquainted with working with an independent organization like IVCF. IVCF was not related to a religious body and that made it difficult. I was warmly received on the campuses and had a good ministry with individual students. Black students saw college as a chance to change their lot in life—to get an education meant upward mobility. Their loyalty was to the church more than to the campus.[19]

Ivery Harvey served on staff for two years, and while he didn't see any groups organized at Black colleges, he was a forerunner of what was to come.[20] During his time in the South, Ivery came in contact with Martin Luther King and met Malcolm X. The first stirrings of the civil rights movement were taking place.

By 1955 Blacks in Montgomery were boycotting bus lines, and ever so reluctantly Christians began facing up to racial issues at home and abroad. *Missionary Mandate* took leadership in evangelical circles by publishing a strong article on race relations and apartheid in South Africa in a 1956 issue. The pain of the next two decades slowly changed the face of student work and appreciation of ethnic diversity.

7/Nurses Christian Fellowship

Tressie Myers became the Christian Nurses Fellowship secretary in 1951, and began planting a vision for the spiritual dimension of nursing that has made that Fellowship what it is today. In many ways she was a pioneer in total patient care, teaching and modeling its importance. Her first contact with CNF took place when she was teaching nursing at Michael Reese Hospital in Chicago. A small group of students asked her to become their faculty advisor. She got caught up in the vision of reaching nurses, and in 1948 left her job and joined the staff of CNF. After she became the second national director, Stacey and others on the Senior Staff Council affectionately called her St. Theresa. No one who has ever served under her leadership will forget her "Dear Girls" letters.

Under Tressie's leadership, CNF became a Christian professional society, building on the work with nursing students. CNF also changed its name to Nurses Christian Fellowship (NCF) in 1952 because it seemed less exclusive and more in line with their purposes. In doing so they made their name uniform with the name of similar organizations in other countries that had Christian nurses movements. Catherine Schell, Marjorie Davis, Virginia Sery, and Jeanne Axelson joined the staff early in the 1950s. Later Verna Nickelson, Mary Irwin Gordon, Jean Dickason, Joyce Hansen, Barbara Olin, Jean Stallwood and Ruth Stoll served on NCF staff during the decade.

A publication for nurses had been initiated in July 1951 as the *CNF Bulletin*. This was renamed *The Lamp* in October 1951, and the content changed from news items and prayer requests to include more articles on spiritual care. NCF also published *Standing Orders,* a Bible study guide prepared by NCF staff, and *On Call,* a devotional guide for students and nurses written by Lois Rowe.

During the fifties NCF developed a tradition of holding camping sessions, which proved helpful in building individuals and an esprit de corps among both professional nurses and students.

8/Organizational Growing Pains

On the campus scene, good things were happening in Inter-Varsity chapters. The basics that built strong chapters also built individual Christian lives. One graduate of the 1950s, speaking of her student years, captures the spirit of those interviewed across the country:

The quality of the fellowship within our IV chapter still warms my heart. I have never found anything like it since, and I think I will always be searching for it. I was a freshman in 1953, and three upperclassmen met with me regularly to pray. Sometimes we would learn a new IV hymn together and spend an hour praising God in song, or talking freely about what Christ meant to us. I learned how to share my faith with others. We saw God answer our prayers. The conferences, the speakers, the friendships all stretched my mind and my world. It was a life-directing experience for me.[21]

The phrase, "I've never found anything like it in all the years since then" was used repeatedly in interviews.

The impact of Inter-Varsity work was evident in other places. At one seminary more than sixty per cent of the students traced their conversion or their decision to serve God as a minister or missionary to Inter-Varsity's influence. *Youth for Christ Magazine* reported in its September, 1953, issue that one interdenominational mission board found that out of thirty-five missionary candidates, twenty-seven could trace their decision to serve on the mission field to some experience in an IVCF chapter during their college years.

But on the national organizational level, all was not well. Ever since his appointment as general secretary of IFES in 1947, Stacey Woods had been spending months at a time out of the country. He was carrying a staggering load but, while he sometimes complained about travel, seemed invigorated by it. In 1951 under Stacey's leadership the Senior Staff Council, made up of regional secretaries and department heads, was formed to help manage the work. That first group consisted of Troutman, Petersen, Bayly, Gustafson, Thomas, Nyquist, Adeney and Friesen, with Woods as chairman. The creation of this council officially recognized the responsibility these members felt for the work and gave the leaders access as a group to Stacey for future planning.

In 1952 the Canadian board made it clear that the Canadian IVCF needed a full-time person to lead the movement. Stacey resigned following that decision, and Wilber Sutherland became the general secretary for the Canadian IVCF.

Stacey Woods practiced a curious mixture of admirable delegation and end-runs. He wanted self-starters in the movement. He gives a rather extravagant and even chaotic picture in his own writing:

A general secretary may feel he is holding rein on a team of straining horses, often pulling in opposite directions, or driving a snow sled pulled by a team of savage independent huskies, but this sets the pace and wins the race and achieves. This allows for genuine creativity."[22]

He sincerely did not want to create a personality cult and would not have defined himself as an autocratic leader. In fact, he was almost frightened of the hero-cult in America. On the occasions when he was offered an honorary doctorate, he always refused. He delegated leadership easily and usually managed to find people who could "take the ball and run with it." He gave people huge tasks to do, and then expected them to do it. He was not interested in the details, unless he didn't like the way it was done. He had an amazing genius in "inspiring the troops" and a strong concept of "working together for God as a Fellowship." An exciting person to work with, he most often took seriously the ideas of the staff. But he also wanted people who worked *for* him as well as with him; he wanted to be the leader. As time went on it became obvious that he found it hard to be supplanted, the inevitable result of absentee leadership.

Over the years, in spite of all the gifted leadership Stacey accumulated around him, he never could find a worthy successor. He wanted someone to run the national movement, but always under him. In later years he mentioned one person whom he had hoped would succeed him in the U.S. movement, but some felt that it was safe to do that because the person had already died. He had a subtle way of discrediting others, often with brilliant humor, faint praise or a clever thumbnail sketch. Sometimes it was difficult to know whether a quip was intentional or just a habit borne out of keen observations. This began to cause a lack of confidence in the other senior leaders of the Fellowship, both among the leaders themselves and members of the official board.

Stacey Woods was not the first nor the last leader to have a certain insecurity set in while bearing too many responsibilities. Before leaving on one of his many tours overseas, he would delegate areas of authority. When he arrived home he would want to take up the reins he had let go. If he was not always happy with what was done while he was gone he expressed his criticism freely, but not necessarily to the responsible person and often to someone else. He began undercutting his team. The person who bore the brunt of most of this was probably his closest friend, Charles Troutman.

Charles, who felt called by God to be Stacey's right-hand man, had been the associate general secretary from the time of his arrival home after the war. Letters and memos record Stacey saying, "Let's divide the work. I want you to be in charge of the student work. I will do the rest." Charles would begin to operate on that basis, only to find that something as significant as staff training had been given to someone else or that some other conflict in responsibility would take place. He began keeping notes about what he was told to do as a necessary defense when he was accused of not doing it. He tried to give Stacey the benefit of the doubt. Charles realized his gifts were more relational than administrative, but he began to feel very unsupported.

As early as June of 1951, Troutman confronted Stacey with a memo of his interpretation of what was happening:

(1) You want people who will take your ideas and work out your general policy as you would do it, even though you have not told them how or what; (2) you want people who in working together are very dependent on you for the work; (3) you do not want any of them to

be too outstanding or dominant, so to keep balance you must give each slightly different information, take back responsibility, or refuse to give specific instructions; and (4) you require all decisions and initiative to come from you, but to do this you must be constantly available and issue more detailed and specific instructions.[23]

Memos in Troutman's personal papers reveal the inner anguish he was experiencing. He felt called by God to student work. He loved students. But friction was damaging the work. Charles Troutman was committed to the Fellowship; it had been his life. It is likely that no one knew then or now the deep sorrow he felt in tendering his resignation, effective for June 1953.

Concerned, and sensing that only one tension would be solved by Troutman's resignation, in April of 1953 the Senior Staff Council tried to indicate to the board the seriousness of the situation as they saw it.[24] They sent a recommendation to the IVCF Board—signed by David Adeney, Joseph Bayly, Melvin Friesen, James Nyquist, William E. C. Petersen and Eugene Thomas— essentially asking that they be given more authority. They asked: (1) that members of the Council be present at the board meetings with the privilege of speaking on matters of concern; (2) that no part of Inter-Varsity be excluded from the oversight of the senior staff council; (3) that the senior staff council act as the "field council" responsible directly to the board. The recommendation continued,

It is our conviction that (4) there is a need for a full-time General Secretary who would devote all his time to, and have his complete interest in student work in the United States. We believe that the initiation of appointment of the General Secretary or of any other staff member should rest with the senior staff council, subject to approval of the Board. . . . We believe that while the General Secretary should be a leader, he should not be a dictator in the Fellowship because of his appointment by the Board; rather, we believe that his authority should stem from his office as chairman of the senior council. We believe that his report to the Board should at all times reflect the thinking of the senior staff council."[25]

Another recommendation of the SSC affirmed the leadership of Stacey Woods as general secretary

subject to the following provisions: (1) that he give up the office and responsibilities as General Secretary of IFES, (2) that he not be in charge of IVCF overseas work or department, (3) that his complete interest shall be in IVCF, USA.[26]

It was a strong appeal for the board to act and solve the crisis the SSC felt the movement was facing. The board had been making administrative decisions since its inception. But Stacey Woods himself had always been their main source of information. With his long and frequent absences, the frustrated SSC wanted direct access to the board.

Some on the board believed that this recommendation from the SSC was an attempt to usurp the authority of the board, and so branded the SSC as power hungry and divisive. This label only served to separate persons of good will who were all "concerned about God's work through IVCF." This was the beginning of misunderstandings between the board and staff about how the movement should be run. Growth in size and complexity of the movement required new structures, but the leadership void caused a three-way tension between Woods, the SSC, and the board.

The members of the SSC understood and did not question that ultimate legal authority rested with the board, composed of Christian men and women who volunteered their services on a part-time basis. Their decisions directly affected the life and ministry of those who were full-time in the ministry. There was too little communication going to the board for an understanding of the concerns of the SSC and too little coming from the board to the staff to assure a sense of being cared for and appreciated.

The recommendations of the SSC were amended by the board. Access would be given to the SSC but only through the executive committee. Twice a year the SSC would meet with the board members. The board affirmed that the movement continue to operate as a fellowship,

> Divisions of responsibility and function are generally recognized, but at the same time there is also the recognition of the Scriptural principle that One is our Master, even Christ, and all we are brethren. It is the consensus of the board, the Executive Committee, and the Staff (as represented by the Senior Staff Council) that the over-all work of the Fellowship be conducted at all times in that spirit—as a fellowship — and that each and every phase of the work is and should continue to be the constant spiritual concern of all its members.[27]

No satisfactory action was taken about Stacey's divided loyalties. The board would not deal with this until seven years later.[28] The board itself was in a state of flux because of the sudden and unexpected resignation of its chairman, Cameron Peck.

The members of the Fellowship faced a confusing time. Both Charles's and Stacey's spiritual input into the lives of the staff had been significant. It was difficult for many on the staff to make sense out of what was happening. No one had all the answers or all the information, nor even knew the right questions to ask. The resignation of Charles Troutman[29] brought a time of sorrow and low morale for many of the leaders within the Fellowship, including Stacey Woods. The fall-out included others: Carl Thomas, Cleo Buxton and Mary Anne Klein had already left in 1951. Wesley Gustafson resigned from his post as missions secretary in 1952 to work with the Evangelical Free Church. Although he did not give this as his reason for leaving in 1955, Mel Friesen was also wearied by "the confusion" within the leadership.

9/Grassroots Strength

The organization and management of the movement were not unimportant. Top-level trauma always takes a heavy toll on middle management. It affected recruitment and training of field staff, and staff growth and budget expansion was slow. But student work on the campus and campus staff members were scarcely touched by management problems or most board decisions. What was to become increasingly evident as the years went by was that the fundamentals undergirding Inter-Varsity were not dependent on how smoothly the organization operated. It was the quality of the "idea behind the movement" that mattered. It was a grassroots movement in the best sense.

The philosophy of student leadership and student responsibility for witness kept Inter-Varsity campus work on track. The staff members were the key to the propagation of the fundamentals—the lordship of Christ, the authority of Scripture, the centrality of the Quiet Time. What mattered on the campus was not who was on the organizational chart but how much vision student leaders had and how much commitment they had to God and to each other. The individual histories of members of Inter-Varsity groups across the country—their Christian world and life view, their creative input into the kingdom of God, their steadfast application of the principles of discipleship over the years—this is the glory of a history of student work, a validation that this is "a movement of the Spirit of God."

9
The Expansion of Student Training: Decade of the 1950s

When IVCF started in the 1940s, we were told that students were too immature to be responsible for their own programs. In fact, many evangelical churches were horrified at the idea of campus inductive Bible studies where students didn't have a minister to teach them. Over the years we have had to resist the ever-present pressure and temptation to exert clergy-type control over our student groups. Recently I ran across an old African proverb, "Until the lions have their own historians, the histories will always glorify the hunters." That could be paraphrased, "Until the laity in our churches and universities are trained in leadership responsibility, the religious professionals will always find reasons why it can't be done."
Charles E. Hummel, *faculty specialist, Inter-Varsity Christian Fellowship*

I n the 1950s Inter-Varsity Christian Fellowship's commitment to the development of student leaders necessitated an investment in off-campus training centers to meet that goal. Each of the places that IVCF secured have an important place in the expansion of student training.

1/Bear Trap Ranch
The growth of student work in the thirteen-state area that comprised the Rocky Mountain region made it difficult to find camps to rent for conferences and retreats. Regional Secretary Gene Thomas felt a regional camp owned by IVCF would ease this pinch in student training. Late in 1952 a dude ranch, nestled in a small valley in the mountains about eighteen miles southwest of Colorado Springs, came on the market. The Antlers Hotel had put the ranch on the market and made George Krause, president of the Colorado Springs Company, responsible to sell it. Gene went into his office to inquire about Bear Trap Ranch. Krause, slouched down in his

chair, shot back, "What in hell do you want it for?" Gene replied, "Well, actually hell has quite a bit to do with it. We want to tell college students about Jesus and He had this thing about hell. He wanted to keep people out of it."[1] Krause was so disarmed that he became interested in helping keep college students out of hell. He offered to sell the ranch for $50,000. Gene knew that this was an incredibly good price, since the Antlers Hotel had just invested $75,000 in new plumbing and furnishings.

The board of Inter-Varsity refused to approve the purchase; other Fellowship causes needed funds. The board, however, agreed to give their approval if Gene Thomas raised the money himself without soliciting from already committed donors. When Gene went back to confirm his interest in the ranch, Krause told him that he had just been offered $150,000 cash for the ranch. Gene's heart sank. Then Krause continued, "I told him no, that I was going to sell to those people who were keeping students out of hell." The Christian realtor who had referred Gene to Krause contributed his $3,000 commission to the cause. Gene raised enough to make a downpayment of $5,000 and then made a commitment to pay the other $45,000 over a period of five years. Krause not only agreed to these unbelievable terms, but said he would charge no interest.

Gene challenged the regional staff team with the $45,000 goal, dividing the amount among them. At that time, a single staff member was making about $150 a month (married staff made about $300). None of them had ever raised $45,000 before. The staff, in turn, went to the students. Gene felt that the students should be the investors because they were the ones who would benefit from the camp. Students and staff took up the challenge. They sold everything from radios and rings to fur coats and cars. In addition to the cash they raised, they made pledges to meet the rest of the goal. For the next five years each $9,000 payment was made on time, and each year the fund contained no more than a dollar extra when payment came due.

Early the next summer, when Gene was in Canada for staff training at Campus in the Woods, his wife Gerry borrowed a truck and, with some friends in Colorado Springs, drove to the Antlers Hotel because Krause said he had some things for the ranch. "God must have moved his heart," Gerry says, "because he gave us thousands of dollars in sheets, blankets, beautiful Navajo Indian rugs, plates, flatware. We didn't need to buy a thing to operate that summer."

The camp opened at the end of June and was filled to capacity throughout the summer. Bear Trap Ranch held a one-month camp, a three-week camp and several one-week training camps. The region also sponsored camps at Thanksgiving and Christmas. Students developed a great sense of loyalty for Bear Trap Ranch as they came to view it as a spiritual home. Staff families were assigned to small rooms, but enduring this hardship meant more students could be accommodated. Two hundred and thirty students were packed into any livable space, including attics. The camp made a significant contribution to building up the regional student work during the following years.

2/Cedar Campus

Meanwhile the property at Prentiss Bay in the Upper Peninsula of Michigan lay idle, waiting for the decision to develop it. The 1951 overflow camp had given the site bad press, but Northcote Deck, a member of the IVCF Board, was an enthusiastic crusader. He had been at the 1951 camp and thought the site had great potential. Along with Stacey Woods, Deck felt that students needed to get away from life's distractions, to learn to be quiet, to enjoy the unspoiled world. He was no longer a young man, but he had often taken a morning swim from the north shore out to the point and back in the cold water of the bay. He urged Herbert Taylor not to give up, to keep the property for Inter-Varsity because the board would come around to see its value.

The site had an interesting history. In the late 1800s when lumber barons moved north to cut white pine, the town of Prentiss (pop. 500) developed on a point of land projecting into Prentiss Bay on the north shore of Lake Huron (about fifty miles south of Sault Ste. Marie, one of America's oldest cities, founded by French voyageurs). In the summer Prentiss Bay was jammed with logs, waiting to be put through the mill. Huge sailing vessels would dock along the point, load up with clear white pine boards sawn in the mill at Prentiss and transport them to Chicago. From there the lumber was shipped to the plains states, where a thousand feet of board sold for twelve dollars. When the timber was gone, people moved on. A fire took most of the buildings, and only a few evidences of the town remained. Cribs for log-lifting booms, rods for holding the steam-jenny and the sawmill chimney are reminders of what once took place on this site. Nine heirs of the land where the town stood were scattered all over the country.

Herbert Taylor, son of a lumberman, grew up in Pickford, a small town just north of Prentiss Bay. He had often visited the bay as a boy, and had dreams of a camp for young people along these shores. As he prospered in business, he began accumulating property around the bay. He first bought land at the head of the bay and brought his Sunday-school class from Chicago up for camping trips. They built a rustic lodge along Prentiss Creek and two cabins in the woods, complete with outhouses. Christian Service Brigade, a boys' club movement that interested Taylor, also used the camp for a brief time.

Taylor bought and traded until he finally came to own most of the land around inner Prentiss Bay. His next goal was to get the land out on the point. He delegated the initial contact with the nine heirs to one of his employees, offered a fair price, and the heirs began to sign for the sale of the property. The holdouts were two Hyde sisters who lived in Cheboygan, Michigan. They had built two primitive log cabins at Prentiss Bay for their occasional use and refused to sell, even after repeated contacts.

Finally, considering himself a successful salesman, Herbert Taylor went to see the sisters. Sitting on their porch on a summer day, he explained that he intended to give the property to a Christian organization working with college students, that he was particularly concerned that young people go out as missionaries to spread the gospel. The two sisters rocked their chairs and maintained their tight-lipped refusal; his sales pitch fell on deaf ears. He finally rose to go, thanked them for their time and went down the porch steps. Then he turned and said: "Ladies, I wouldn't want to be in your shoes on the day of judgment!" As he walked toward his car, one of the sisters called out, "Mr. Taylor, Mr. Taylor, come back. My sister and I want to talk this over." They did sign and that property is now part of Cedar Campus, the largest of Inter-Varsity's camps.

Early in the spring of 1954,[2] before the ice was off the bay, Stacey Woods asked Keith Hunt[3] and his wife, Gladys, to take a look at this 500-acre site in the north woods to see if they would be interested in developing it. The assignment would be "in addition to your other duties." Woods offered no promise of money to get the place operative, no vehicle to get supplies— just the opportunity to do it. How a campsite was carved out of the wilderness and the beautiful facilities developed is another story in which the members of the Hunt family are surely the major characters. Their conviction that camping programs are used by God to transform students accounts for their thirty-three-year involvement in the site.

That summer, after opening up the rustic facilities of what is now called Northshore, the first one-month missionary training camp (MTC) was held. David Adeney headed up the program. As part of their training, student teams adopted nearby towns as their week-end mission fields. Every inconvenience encountered was chalked up to GMT—good missionary training. MTC was held at Cedar Campus for the next fifteen years.

In 1954 the Christian Workers Foundation offered $45,000 for the construction of a new lodge out on Old Mill Point.[4] The next year Keith Hunt, in addition to staffing all the colleges in Michigan, took on the role of general contractor. He hired the construction crew, ordered the lumber, paid the workmen and conferred with the job supervisor to begin the building of the lodge. During the third summer of the camp, students recruited from universities in the region worked on completing the building. Even though the inside walls were rough studs, the Ralph Willoughby Lodge, containing kitchen, dining room, lounge, housing and office space, was dedicated during the missionary training camp in August 1956. For the next two years it was the primary facility at the new site.

The dedication was a gala celebration with an incongruous audience. As a result of their out-trips into the area, MTC Teams had met many local people and they were all invited. Stacey Woods, bursting with enthusiasm in his own inimitable fashion, came up from Chicago for the event. He and Herbert Taylor, who also traveled to the Upper Peninsula with his family from Chicago, had their own plans for the day. Notable guests came from far away. Among these was Stanley S. Kresge, a friend of Taylor's, who had given a gift through the Kresge Foundation to help furnish the new lodge. Harold J. Ockenga, then president of Fuller Seminary Board, was slated as the speaker. Fuller Seminary needed a new library, and Taylor, also on the board at Fuller along with Ockenga, hoped to influence Kresge's generosity toward that project. Ockenga's speech that afternoon was aimed at the Kresges and was almost incomprehensible to the five hundred local people gathered there. But they didn't seem to mind. The place was beautiful and the refreshments were good.

The five-state East Central region scheduled many regional student training programs in addition to MTC during the last years of the fifties. Students from this region still attended CIW for one-month training sessions. As other buildings were added to the Cedar Campus site, Stacey Woods wanted to try a training program for graduates which would better fit them for "marketplace witness." In 1957 a ten-week Summer Seminar for Biblical Studies began at Cedar Campus and, although each year it was shortened in length, it continued for the next three years. Many of the young graduates who attended eventually joined the staff of Inter-Varsity; others have been active Christians in business.

In the tradition of Inter-Varsity camps, exceptionally fine Christian leaders addressed the students and lived among them. For staff and students both, it was an opportunity to meet and learn from people they might never otherwise meet. Participants in these camps reflecting on their experience inevitably speak of the spiritual stimulus and exposure to outstanding Christians as significant factors in their lives. It was at one of these sessions that Joe Bayly read aloud by kerosene light in a small cabin his first draft of *The Gospel Blimp,* a clever parody on impersonal forms of Christian witness.

3/Hudson House

In 1952 Charles Hummel became the secretary of the Middle Atlantic region, an area that included New York City. He soon saw the need for some kind of conference center for student training within a reasonable radius of the city. Most of the students in the city commuted to their colleges and had little sense of community. Furthermore, many of them had never been outside the city. With encouragement from Stacey Woods, Charlie and his wife, Anne, began looking at properties in the vicinity of the city. A realtor took them to see an old, three-story mansion in Upper Nyack, along the Hudson River. The house had a gracious entrance, a library, an oversized living room, kitchen and dining room, plus two large screened porches and numerous large bedrooms. The north wing of the house contained two four-room apartments. The asking price was $45,000; the house seemed ideal.

General permission from the board was contingent on Charlie raising the funds to purchase the house. He began by making a offer for the house of $40,000 dollars, but that was still more money than he had ever raised in his life. An initial gift of $5,000 from Mrs. F. Cliffe Johnston gave some needed encouragement. The area staff and many students pitched in to help raise the required funds. One staff member gave a thousand dollars from a modest inheritance she had received. When they were within $5,000 of their goal, Charlie ran into what seemed an insuperable problem. The Village of Nyack trustees were not happy to have all the mansions along the Hudson become public buildings, and were especially reluctant to see the property go off the tax rolls. They refused a zoning variance. Charlie appeared before the zoning board and promised to pay the taxes, if that were the only problem. But the zoning board was adamant and responded to his offer with, "Yes, but what about the guy who follows you?" It seemed as if the project had been thwarted.

Sometime later Charlie met a Christian lawyer in New York City who gave him a glimmer of hope: an upstate New York college that had been refused permission to build a residence hall in the main part of their college town had taken the matter to court. The State Supreme Court ruled that since houseparents permanently lived in the house, it would be considered a residence with college students as guests of the houseparents. Charlie got the needed references and went back to the zoning board. Peter and Martha B. Northrup, Inter-Varsity staff members, would move into the house as permanent residents; the students would be their guests. Charlie said that he would abide by his original promise to pay property taxes even though he had no legal obligation to do so. Hummel reflects, "A disconsolate zoning board gave the variance."

In 1955, just as the contract was being prepared by the lawyer (the owner had waited in good faith for two years for clearance of the sale), Stacey Woods telephoned Charlie Hummel at Campus in the Woods, where Charlie was leading the student leadership camp. The executive committee of the board did not want to proceed with the purchase because only $35,000 had been raised. Charlie said, "I couldn't believe it. We had been working for two years to fund the project and we were so close. I found their decision impossible. I felt I couldn't take no for an answer." Stacey listened to Hummel's argument and agreed. He went back to the committee to get the purchase permission. Peter and Martha B. Northrup moved into what was dubbed Hudson House, and became both the residents and the spiritual directors of ministry there for the next five years. Their story includes remodeling, repairing the boiler, furnishing, creating more sleeping rooms and numerous repairs to a grand old house, plus hiring the cook and all the practical details of running a guesthouse. It proved a wonderful place of ministry and served the growing student movement in New York City for the next twenty-five years. Eventually the student work outgrew the accommodations, and Hudson House was sold in 1985.

4/Diverging Student Ministries
International student work in the Fellowship began in earnest after World War 2 when new doors were opened to students from other countries. International student conferences continued at The Firs conference center in Washington, along with other holiday conferences across the country. Houseparties were regularly held in Estes Park, Colorado. Marie Huttenlock (Little) was doing international student work in New York City by 1952, and other staff were combining concern for students from overseas with their regular campus work. Bob Finley, who had done campus evangelism

and work with foreign students during the late 1940s, undertook what turned out to be a very eventful evangelistic trip to Asia in 1951 under the auspices of IVCF. Shortly after his return, he left Inter-Varsity staff to work independently. In 1952 he organized a new work called International Students, Incorporated (ISI). There were discussions from the beginning of this work about the possibility of ISI becoming a division of Inter-Varsity, but it became immediately apparent that Finley expected to operate independently. Merger talks came up again in the 1960s, but did not materialize.

David Adeney had a keen interest in students from overseas, and during his tenure as missionary secretary, international students work was part of his department. In 1956 Paul Little took over the leadership of a special department for international students, a post he kept until he became the director of evangelism in 1965.

Bill Bright was a senior in 1951 at Fuller Theological Seminary when he became interested in student evangelism. Leading deputation teams of young people to local jails, hospitals and Skid Row missions to share their faith, he became increasingly aware that so many churches were doing this kind of evangelism that they frequently had to wait their turn. It occured to Bright that they wouldn't have to wait for a turn on the UCLA campus. Hundreds of students needed to hear about Jesus Christ. He began presenting the gospel to students there. The Inter-Varsity chapter at UCLA cooperated in several outreaches with Bright. When the Leith Samuel mission was held at the University of Southern California, Bright was appreciative of the outreach both at the public meeting and at the fraternity meeting afterwards. He commented to Charles Troutman, "If this is what IVCF is doing, I want to join you." It did not work out that way. As Bright tells in his book *Come Help Change the World* (1979), he believed God had given him a special vision to evangelize the student world in his own way.

In early 1952 Bright called on Stacey Woods at his home in Geneva, Illinois, to tell him that he was in the middle of a tour to collect teams of young men from some of the seminaries to come for training at Forest Home. He was beginning his own organization, but he also wanted officially to be in cooperation with Inter-Varsity. Bright had thought, in the beginning, to organize only an evangelistic team, but he wanted Stacey to know that he was beginning a separate student campus work. Stacey was hopeful that, after this conversation, some kind of cooperation could be worked out and promised Bright that he would bring the matter up at the senior staff council meeting.[5] Following the senior staff council meeting, Charles Troutman wrote to Bright from Campus in the Woods:

Stacey is leaving England today for the student camp at Darmstadt, Germany, and (since I am on an island in Canada) I am unable to find out whether he wrote you or not concerning the decision of the senior staff council. . . . Very briefly, it is our desire to do everything we can to bring university students face to face with the claims of Christ in order that they might accept him as Savior and obey him as Lord. Whether it is better for us as a campus student organization, organized in almost every case under the authority of the Dean of Students, to work openly and aggressively with the Campus Crusade for Christ; or whether it is better to work independently but in harmony with each other, is a matter which we do not feel we have enough data or information to assess. Accordingly the senior staff council has asked me to write you regarding the possibility of working together experimentally during this coming academic year in order that we might determine God's will with assurance. If you will be so kind as to let me know the campuses where you feel God is leading the Crusade to concentrate, I shall get in touch with the groups that exist and discuss the matter with the staff concerned, in order that we might work together for God's glory.[6]

In 1954 Campus Crusade for Christ (CCC) began to spread out across the country. Inter-Varsity chapters were frequently approached by deans of students who inquired about the appropriateness of allowing CCC to operate on campus. Inter-Varsity students expressed hope about working together. The cooperation that marked the first days, however, soon evaporated. Differences in philosophy made practical difficulties. CCC was a staff-generated movement, not a student movement. IVCF staff were spread too thin. Some chapters only saw their staff member a half-dozen times a year, others less often than that. Crusade would come on to campus with a full team of permanent staff, often fifteen or more, each prepared to do the work that IVCF expected students to do. The Crusade view of student work and of the university was different from that of IVCF. Crusade's immediate goal was student converts; IVCF's goal was to establish chapters of Christian students whose goals were evangelism, discipleship and missions. Inter-Varsity's philosophy meant building student initiative and responsibility. Inter-Varsity was a *student* mission; Crusade was a mission to students.

The mature, postwar students had graduated by now, and students who were products of the "good life" of the fifties often knew little about leadership or serious responsibility. The next years had tense moments in working out ways to cooperate and to face the realities of different philosophies of student work and understanding of the university.

The differences in philosophy were largely lost on the general Christian public receiving Crusade's reports of evangelistic success. Crusade went into fraternities and sororities and reported hundreds of students confessing Christ in each place. Inter-Varsity's reticence to count converts or to consider conversions genuine until follow-up had taken place, made its organization seem more prosaic. Discounting Inter-Varsity's evangelism outreach, simplistic explanations began circulating that Crusade was for evangelism and IVCF was for discipleship. Since Inter-Varsity's public relations had always been minimal at best, this kind of publicity caused confusion among the Christian public. Faithful and godly staff members sometimes felt as if someone was "pulling the rug out from under them."

Although sometimes outraged by such lack of discernment, Stacey Woods did one of the things he did best. With his prophetic insight into people and situations, he roared a bit and then, with amazing clarity, again defined the theological stance of Inter-Varsity, the philosophy of the work and the necessity of training responsible leaders to spread the good news of the kingdom of God, and told the staff and students alike to "get on with it!"

5/Student Missionary Conventions

The return of David Adeney to the States, following the eviction of missionaries by the communists in China, was fortuitous for the Fellowship. He joined staff late in 1951, taking responsibility for student work in the Central region. In 1953 he was appointed missionary secretary.[7] He began making plans to direct the 1954 Student Missionary Convention at Urbana, choosing the theme: "Changing World; Changeless Christ." Two thousand students from North America and forty other nations met in Huff Gymnasium at the University of Illinois. Two hundred sixty-three colleges and sixty Christian schools and seminaries were represented. A. W. Tozer gave powerful morning messages on biblical characters—Abraham, Elijah and others. His talks ministered a second time when they were later printed in *HIS* magazine.

William Nagenda spoke from his background of God's work in the revivals in Rwanda. Samuel Moffat and Arthur Glasser helped students interpret what they were experiencing in a world now dominated by communism and change. Alan Redpath of Moody Church gave students new insights into a favorite topic: how to know the will of God. Paul White from Australia, a master storyteller, demonstrated practical helps for going on with God. Two hundred missionaries from seventy mission boards came. Paul Beckwith and Homer Hammontree led the music. News media carried positive reports about the strategic nature of the conference in view of the world situation. A steady flow of missionary volunteers had come out of these postwar conventions and, as always, the delegates' fresh commitment to the lordship of Jesus Christ strengthened the campus chapters.

By the time the fifth International Student Missionary Convention came around in late 1957, David Adeney had gone to Hong Kong to become IFES regional secretary for Asia. Stacey Woods, looking for a new missionary secretary to cover both Canada and the U.S., had heard from a number of staff about Eric Fife, a Britisher who was representing the North Africa Mission in the United States. Both Eric and Stacey Woods were slated to speak at Boston's Park Street Church Missionary Conference. Stacey just "happened" to be sitting across from Eric at the banquet the first night. After the courtesies of meeting each other for the first time were over, in true Stacey style, Woods said, "Eric, I want you to be our missionary secretary." Eric Fife objected, "No way, Stacey. The man you want has got to have two qualifications: he's got to be a field missionary and he has to be a college graduate. I'm neither. So that's that." Stacey left the conference on Monday, but he spoke to Eric about it another three times over the weekend. Stacey said, "Eric, God has used you not merely among students in the last three years, but among our staff. If God can do that through you, then quite frankly, that to me is more important than a college degree."

Eric tells the story:

After Stacey left I was sitting in the meeting and suddenly felt very uncomfortable and wondered why. Suddenly it occurred to me, *You never gave the Lord a chance to speak to you about this position. You just refused it. Could this be the will of God?* So I called Stacey and told him that while I wasn't saying I would take the job, I would consider it. I talked to Dit Fenton of the Latin America Mission one day as we walked down the street together, and told him my misgivings. He stopped dead in his tracks in the middle of the road and said, "Fife, it's time you got over your education. This is obviously the job the Lord wants for you." Eric spoke to another Englishman about the problem, saying, "Just imagine how it would be, me going all over the country speaking to students when I've never been to college myself." The man said, "Awfully good for your pride, awfully good for your pride."

Eric Fife knew that his ministry to students and staff had been significant. When he spoke at numerous student weekends, the feedback was always positive and the stimulus students brought to the meetings gave him a keen sense of usefulness. He thought of the first time he had contact with an IV chapter. The North Africa Mission scheduled him to speak at Penn State soon after he came to the U.S. When he arrived on campus he found he had three meetings in one night. The first was in a fraternity, and no one told him what a fraternity was, so he thought, *Brotherhood, that's another name for Inter-Varsity.* When he found out what the meeting was going to be, he developed one of the worst migraines of his life, with all the accompanying sick-stomach emergencies and visual distortions. Somehow he made it through all three meetings.

Three years later on the train on the way to the '57 Missionary Convention he met a fellow who told him he had become a Christian that night at Penn State. It was another confirmation that he was making the right decision in joining Inter-Varsity staff, a commitment that became official in January 1958.

Soon after Fife made the decision to come with Inter-Varsity he received a telephone call from Charles Hummel, who was serving as national secretary, a post Stacey had created when Charles Troutman left. Hummel asked, "Eric, could you direct the '57 Student Missionary Convention?" Although Eric's speaking schedule would not allow him to do this, he did attend the convention. He also gave the closing address. Charles Hummel directed the '57 conference, and he and Stacey saw to it that Eric got a firsthand look at what was involved. Up until Fife's tenure as missionary secretary, every convention had a new director. Woods and Hummel gave Eric an opportunity to have a little training for the job.

Six main speakers developed the theme: "One Lord—One Church—One World" before some 3,500 students. Donald Grey Barnhouse, the venerable pastor of Tenth Presbyterian Church in Philadelphia, did the morning Bible expositions. The meetings were carried live over Moody Bible Institute's radio station WMBI, but nervous broadcasters pulled the plug on Barnhouse one morning when he began to castigate those who held rigid, narrow-minded views. They were afraid that Barnhouse, known for his dogmatic, powerful declarations, might say more than they wanted their listeners to hear. Billy Graham, Harold J. Ockenga, Masumi Toyotome, Kenneth Strachan and Israel Garcia addressed plenary sessions. Fifteen hundred students indicated a willingness to go overseas and a hundred of these were already committed to go.

It was another quality training event, but Hummel and Fife both agreed that the acoustics at Huff Gymnasium worked against the effectiveness of the convention. An assembly hall for the University of Illinois campus was on the drawing boards, and the consensus was to delay the next convention, scheduled for 1960, until 1961 so that a better facility would be available.

6/New Paths in Prayer and Bible Study

Despite all the furor it caused in conservative circles, the publication of the entire Bible in the Revised Standard Version (RSV) in 1952 was a boon to Inter-Varsity's strong commitment to teach students how to study the Bible. The RSV New Testament had been published in 1946, and Jane Hollingsworth began using it almost immediately to help students in inductive Bible study. The contemporary language made evangelistic Bible studies more effective. God's Word was more understandable to biblically illiterate students. Furthermore, the Bible was published with paragraphs, units of thought which helped students to grasp its content. Application of truth was more obvious.

At Cedar Campus Dorothy Farmer taught students to study inductively; Mary Beaton and Jane Hollingsworth led training sessions at Campus in the Woods. Barbara Boyd opened up the Scripture for students on the West Coast, while Marilyn Kunz and Fred Woodberry taught students in the Northeast. A continuing part of teaching students how to study the Bible was instruction in leading small group studies. Evangelistic Bible studies were key ways to win students for Christ and produced the most lasting conversions.

On the West Coast Paul Byer[8] and Rosalind Rinker were staffing the Northwest's growing student groups in 1955. Rosalind Rinker had already begun a significant contribution to Inter-Varsity's training while serving in New York City. While in China she had learned to pray with a friend named Mildred Rice in a conversational style, praying together on one subject, then moving to another and then another. Visiting students on campus she became aware that she needed to teach students how to pray.

One day in a noon daily prayer meeting (DPM), she heard a woman student pray in a way that almost used the name of God as a punctuation mark. "Dear God, We thank you today, dear God, that you are with us, dear God, . . ." Roz asked God to send that student to her for help. After supper she responded to a knock on the door of the dorm room where she was staying, and there the student stood. In her direct but loving way, Roz talked to her about the way she prayed and found her open to help. Later when they prayed together, the student began to pray very slowly, knowing what she was saying, and praying to the Lord Jesus as One who is really present in the room. That experience began Rosalind's ministry in teaching students how to pray conversationally with a friend or in a group, subject by subject, discussing things with the Lord as a real Person who heard their prayers. Conversational prayer has been a major spiritual enrichment for both students and staff, and has not only become part of Inter-Varsity's ethos, but has enriched the church.[9]

In 1955 Roz and Paul were looking for fresh ways to help students learn how to study the Bible. They began experimenting, giving students mimeographed pages of Scripture, triple-spaced, encouraging them to observe repetitions, contrasts, comparisons, verbs and whatever other connectives they found and to mark them on their sheets with colored pencils. The students loved it. When they finished with one course they came back, asking for more. Paul Byer said, "We got students excited about the Scriptures, studying and using the Bible with their friends." Mark I and Mark II Manuscript Bible Study (also called New Testament Seminars) began this way. The development and refinement of manuscript Bible study has enriched both students and staff over the years. Paul Byer followed Mel Friesen as regional secretary in California until 1968, when he became Inter-Varsity's specialist in biblical manuscript study.

7/Training Chapter Leaders

Increasingly, as chapters grew in size and number, the staff began to see the importance of working with chapter executive committees. On campus visits staff members focused on the chapter leadership, discipling these leaders, making sure they attended the weekend conferences and other training events, and then urging them to commit themselves to a four-week camp at one of IV's training camps. Many of these leaders graduated into campus staff members. The four-week camps were key to producing leaders with a vision. They were heavy in theology, designed to expand the student's view of God and give a foundation for lifelong discipleship. While students instructed each other by sharing campus ideas, only one hour a day in the camp schedule, called the Inter-Varsity Hour, was set aside to give practical helps for leading a chapter.

Early in 1959 Paul Byer sat down with Barbara Boyd and Paul Fromer, who were on staff in southern California, to plan the summer program for Campus by the Sea. Byer said, "We need something to really help the executive committees of our chapters. We need to help train our leaders how to lead." Together they refined what Byer had sketched out for a "chapter camp." The plan was to have at least five chapter executive members attend together, having been commissioned by the chapter to do business for the chapter while at camp. These students were already running their own chapters; with a little help they would run them more effectively. It would be a one-week camp, not meant to replace the four-week training session.

It was an idea whose time had come. In the summer of 1959 the first chapter camp was held at Campus by the Sea. Students could attend only as part of a group. Sixteen chapters responded, some having up to nine members present, working with a staff, graduate or faculty member assigned to the group. Chapter members were encouraged to look at their campus as a mission field and make plans accordingly. Each evening National Secretary Charles Hummel spoke on "The Biblical Basis of a Campus Fellowship." The week proved successful; the concept was adapted and refined, and chapter camp has become one of the most strategic parts of Inter-Varsity's training across the country.

8/Stott's University Missions

John Stott, rector of All Souls Church in London, came to North America as chief missioner in 1956-57, speaking at seven university missions and two lectureships. He, a young rector on his first visit to the United States, records in letters to his parents his experience at the lecture series held December 8-14 at the University of Michigan:

> I reached Ann Arbor in a really thick snowstorm. The University of Michigan campus is right in the middle of the city and its 22,000 students comprise nearly half the population of the city. I have been staying in the Michigan Union, which forms one of the chief social centres of the University, mostly for men. . . . The Michigan Christian Fellowship is the founding member of the American Inter-Varsity Christian Fellowship, and I've developed a high opinion of the students in the steering committee which has organized this week. They have worked immensely hard and very efficiently. Their budget was $1,300, to which the students contributed $1,000. This is remarkable because many American students seen to be having difficulties in making ends meet. Consequently many do a job to help towards fees, and I'm told that a majority do a job during the long summer vacation to pay for their schooling.

I've given the main lectures every evening at 8 p.m. in Rackham Hall, a super university auditorium with plush cinema-type seats, seating about 1,200. Impartial observers say that attendance has been good, as there is tremendous competition in leisure hours. We are encouraged that we began with 350 students and increased every night until last night nearly 600 were there. The attention has also been close, and about two-thirds of the audience have stayed each evening after the main lecture, for the short instruction talk in which I try to explain simply what it means to be a real Christian, and how to receive Christ personally.

The faculty . . . have shown a certain amount of interest. Each evening one of them has introduced me, beginning with Dr. Harlan Hatcher, the President of the University, and continuing with one of the Regents. . . . Apart from the main lecture series, no fewer than 72 small discussion sessions have been arranged during the week for "assistant lecturers" and these have been most profitable. Many students have been asking sincere, direct and personal questions about Christianity. There have been countless personal interviews. I'm impressed by the fine quality of the students on this campus. It has been my privilege to see many of them privately. Many of them are truly seeking after God, and we believe a number have found Him in Christ this week. I could tell many stories—of the Jewish lad who is really beginning secretly to believe in Christ but fears his parents, of the 4th year sociology student who is going into the Methodist ministry but until this week had never committed himself personally to Christ, of the Armenian fellow who is one of the most open-minded seekers I have ever met and many others. This has undoubtedly been the most fruitful of the three missions which have so far been held.

On Saturday morning the Michigan Christian Fellowship organized a 10:30 Brunch (yes, they actually called it that on printed invitations!) for those who have been helped by the mission. I was greatly encouraged by the potential of those who came and by the warmth of their appreciation.[10]

The lectures series was entitled, "What Think Ye of Christ?" More than thirty years later Stott smiles over the title and asks, "Can you imagine anyone today coming to hear a series with a title like that?"

At Harvard the crowds were smaller, about 200 students, but deans and professors chairing the meetings said, "This is very good for Harvard!" Stott recounts,

> I found them very open and warm to the gospel and we know of a number who thoughtfully but definitely committed their lives to Christ. Many students came to the whole series and thought hard during the week and only reached a decision at the end. One fine 4th year biochemist from a wealthy background, who had been wrestling with the problem all week, grasped my hand during a gathering on Sunday and said, "God wins, but it'll cause an earthquake at home."[11]

At Yale, Stott did a series of follow-up meetings after a Billy Graham mission at which 300 students had indicated interest in Christ. He finished his tour at the University of Illinois in March 1957. An average of 500 students came to the meetings, growing to 600 for the last lecture. Again, these were augmented by many personal interviews, forty auxiliary meetings in living units and a sizable number of students in new studies on the claims of Christ. Each night a good group of students stayed behind to hear how to become a Christian. Many were born in God's family during the week. Stott wrote in his journal, "I have found the time exacting, but exciting, strenuous but enriching. We are thankful for many who have a first or a fresh commitment to Christ."

John Stott's ministry continued long after he had returned to England, as students gathered on one campus after another to listen to the tapes of his well-reasoned presentation of the gospel. His messages modeled the simplicity of the gospel message given with the forcefulness of his intellectual commitment to it, and helped students learn to express truth in fresh ways. In March 1958 Stott's book *Basic Christianity* began its phenomenal ministry among American students, a book that has probably helped more students understand the gospel than any other book IVP has ever published. More than thirty years later, in its twenty-fifth printing, the book is still being used by students.

9/Trouble in the Rockies

The second year after Charles Troutman left, Stacey Woods asked Gene Thomas to serve as his assistant, under the title "staff and students secretary." Gene agreed to do this as long as he could continue as regional secretary of the Rocky Mountain region. Gene led the staff training program, kept in communication with the regional secretaries and other projects assigned to him 1954-1955. At the end of the second year, Stacey felt it was imperative that Gene move to Chicago and devote full time to the position of national secretary, overseeing both the headquarters departments and field regions. Gene Thomas declined to do this because of commitment to the Rocky Mountain region and Bear Trap Ranch.

By 1957 the Rocky Mountain region and Bear Trap Ranch were in trouble. Gene Thomas, with his dominant personality, had a strong influence on his regional team. One of his strengths was his emphasis on the person of Jesus, the Gospels and the lordship of Jesus Christ. Although his leadership caused the work in his region to flourish, Gene was inclined to systemize some ideas to the point of overemphasis. He tended to use the ranch as a platform for exploring and sharing new ideas. He drew around him staffworkers who were very responsive to him. Evaluating this from hindsight, some have commented that in contrast to Stacey's attracting strong people and encouraging individual development, Gene tended to develop people who would think like he did. Whether or not this was true, the staff team lacked a corrective voice.

In their quest to understand the freedom of grace, and in reaction to the rigidity of much fundamentalism of the forties and fifties, the pendulum in the region had swung toward a kind of libertarianism with an antichurch bias. The staff complained that they saw plenty of legalism in the churches and not nearly enough joy and freedom in expressing personal faith in the Son of God. They were openly critical of this. Without the balance of Scripture or maturity, they overreacted and some of their conclusions were faulty. They began emphasizing the "law of liberty," openly flouting some of the taboos held by many evangelical churches.[12]

What happened had the marks of classic sectarianism. They began to feel that they had graduated to a new plane of understanding. Indeed, they went beyond the confines of Inter-Varsity's way of thinking. They developed their own in-language, so that staff members from other regions felt uncomfortably shut out in their presence. Their attitudes and perspectives ran counter to the basic commitment of IVCF as a movement. The structure of the Fellowship at this time gave Gene too much freedom to do his own thing. The Senior Staff Council had made unwarranted favorable assumptions about his leadership, partly because they were busy with their own regions and responsibilities. Although he heard complaints about the situation that was developing, Stacey Woods did not seem aware of the seriousness of the situation. He trusted Gene Thomas, and his own deep involvement in the work of the International Fellowship of Evangelical Students distracted him from any close supervision.

Most of the staff in the Rocky Mountain region had resigned by 1957, feeling the strictures of being in Inter-Varsity. But as a result of their teaching emphasis, within a year's time Inter-Varsity lost the support of evangelical churches in that region, and most of the chapters under the influence of this staff team also folded. Gene Thomas left Inter-Varsity in 1958. To the leaders of a movement already under stress because of an absent general secretary, what happened in the Rocky Mountain region seemed like a betrayal of the Fellowship. This was not what Inter-Varsity was about.[13] It was like an open wound on the face of the Fellowship. A whole region had been essentially lost, and it would take years to rebuild student chapters and to regain the trust of those who supported the work.[14]

10/Securing a National Secretary

When Gene Thomas declined the position of national secretary at the end of 1955, Stacey desperately needed someone to help him run the American movement. Otherwise his frequent travels overseas would reopen wounds of controversy over his part-time leadership. Stacey Woods turned to Charles Hummel, regional secretary for the Middle Atlantic area, and asked him to pray about coming to Chicago.[15] Since he was only in his fourth year as a regional secretary, Charlie had no desire for national responsibility. Charlie reported:

The last thing in the world I wanted was to go to Chicago headquarters. Our regional team was working well. Anne and I had bought a house in northern New Jersey only three years earlier; we had two small children and were expecting a third within a few months. My parents had just retired a few hours away and enjoyed being near the grandchildren. I had left an engineering position in industry to work with students at the grassroots level, not to manage an organization beset with problems. On the other hand, the Fellowship was in a leadership crisis. The regional secretaries needed a "field director" for regular visits to provide counsel and encouragement. We had been largely on our own to recruit and train our staff, and work out campus strategy, learning largely by trial and error.

Inter-Varsity could ill afford to lose experienced leaders, especially since two regions were already without resident secretaries. Committed to this strategic work and to following the Lord wherever he might lead us, Anne and I were open to consider the new assignment, even with serious reservations about how it would work out.

In January 1956 the senior staff council approved the appointment of Charlie Hummel as national secretary. Stacey was so concerned about the decision that he made a pilgrimage to New Jersey to persuade Anne of the urgent need, and within a few days the Hummels sent word of their acceptance. Several of Charlie's senior colleagues wondered how long the new arrangement would last. It was a strange organizational chart in which the national secretary reported to a general secretary who was out of the country half the time, supervised both the office departments and the regions while at the same time taking responsibilty for two regions until new secretaries could be found. Charlie, however, felt he was being called by God "to serve the leader of our Fellowship, not to a well-defined organizational task."

11/Organizing Alumni

Over the years, the idea of organizing Inter-Varsity alumni had many fits and starts. It was discussed in the early forties, again in 1947 and probably many times in between. In 1951 Stacey Woods asked California-based Bob Baylis to become the extension secretary. He went up and down the State of California starting alumni prayer groups and holding conferences. Stewardship Secretary W. E. C. "Pete" Petersen held a dim view of this. He did not want staff to have contact with donors; that was his domain. At the end of the first year of Bob's work, Pete produced figures showing income in California hadn't risen a bit as a result of Bob's work. It was hard going with Petersen against the idea. Pete insisted that he be totally in control of the mailing list. Charles Troutman believes, in retrospect, that Pete did not understand the American collegiate situation well enough to realize the potential of graduate groups.[16] Bob Baylis took up Charles Troutman's offer to become staff in Minnesota, thus ending another experiment with alumni.

In 1957 another and more effective attempt was begun. The underpinnings of the Fellowship were strengthened when James Reapsome returned to the staff team, after graduating from seminary, to become information secretary for Inter-Varsity. In this year of the Student Missionary Convention, he took charge of getting out releases to newspapers and magazines, telling Inter-Varsity's story and making the public more aware of IV's ministry. His job included speaking at missions conferences and representing the Fellowship at various functions, but especially the development of alumni groups, then called Graduate Fellowships. Jim held public meetings at which graduates could hear what was happening in Inter-Varsity and learn about conferences where they could meet with professional colleagues and be encouraged in personal growth and witness.

Jim took over responsibility for a quarterly publication called *Inter-Varsity News*, which informed graduates about student work. The list of active graduate groups grew longer. This represented one of the most concentrated efforts to encourage new interest in Inter-Varsity since its beginnings.[17] Nevertheless, this advance in alumni work was short-lived. Jim Reapsome left Inter-Varsity staff in 1961 to edit *The Sunday School Times.*

12/Growing Pains

When W. E. C. Petersen was added to the staff as the stewardship secretary in 1948 he had begun to raise funds for the purchase of the first headquarters facility ever owned by IVCF. Inter-Varsity's first office space had been provided through the kindness of the Christian Workers Foundation on 20 North Wacker Drive in Chicago. In 1944 IVCF had moved to rented space at 64 East Lake Street and two years later had again moved to 64 West Randolph Street. Business Manager Paul Hopkins had a total office staff of five. Under Pete's leadership and the generosity of Harriette Davis Weyerhauser, Inter-Varsity had purchased 1444 North Astor Street, a magnificent mansion just off Lake Shore Drive in Chicago's Gold Coast. Its marble elegance and sheen was the first luxury the Fellowship had enjoyed, and the facility was quickly converted into office space. The building was dedicated as a memorial to Frederick Edward Weyerhauser, an early board member whose words in counseling the board were inscribed on the dedication bronze plate:

> We cannot be too careful, too scrupulous in appointing Inter-Varsity staff members. We must be sure that everyone connected with this work is truly spiritual, evangelical, and fundamental—a Christian who walks with God. The work is too great, too important not to give it our best.

The Inter-Varsity office, with a support staff of twenty, moved into 1444 North Astor in 1950.[18] It was a prestigious address, but, more important, it provided sufficient space for privacy and had a room set aside for prayer and committee meetings. After a decade of campus ministry, the Fellowship now claimed 561 total chapters in IVCF, SFMF and NCF. During the last twelve-month period two thousand students had been won to Christ.[19]

By 1956 the growth of the movement (approximately 800 chapters, including NCF amd SFMF) and a support staff of fifty in the office signaled the need for additional space. Another beautiful home, known as the Colonel McCormick Mansion,[20] then owned by Northwestern University and located a block up the street at 1519 North Astor, came on the market. It had twice the space and a warmer kind of beauty with the use of wood instead of marble. It also had a side garden—a gracious touch to a crowded street—where the staff could eat their lunch or meet for conversations. As property values increased, the first purchase provided for the next, and Mrs. Weyerhauser's gift continues to provide housing for a growing movement to this day.

The ledger for Inter-Varsity's ministry in this year of the move (1956-57) showed nearly a half-million dollars in income. Roy Horsey, a Chicago businessman, was then the president of the board. Students had given approximately $30,000 for IFES work. David Adeney had returned to the Far East as IFES regional secretary; Gwen Wong and Mary Beaton were pioneering the IVCF movement in the Philippines; Bob Young was sent to pioneer IFES work in Argentina; and Wayne Bragg had left to work in the Caribbean.

The pace Stacey Woods kept throughout the fifties is nothing short of remarkable. His resilient secretaries—Muriel Clark, Olga Simpson and, for many years, Esther Pedersen—produced voluminous correspondence. Stories are still told of Stacey beginning his dictation as soon as he reached the top step of his office location,[21] inevitably taking his secretary by surprise. The 1956-57 school-year staff listings show that Stacey Woods was acting regional secretary for the Pacific Southwest, in addition to his other responsibilities.

In 1957-58 Charles Hummel was acting regional secretary in the Southeast, as well as national secretary. In 1958 Burton Harding came on staff in the Southeast and, when he later became the regional secretary, he gave that region the help it needed to expand. In 1957 the South Central states had been taken from the Rocky Mountain region, and Paul Little had been sent to Texas as acting regional secretary, in addition to his post as international student secretary. Jim Nyquist, regional secretary for the West Central region, had been appointed acting regional secretary for the Rocky Mountain region and had taken responsibility for Bear Trap Ranch, working hard to recoup losses in that region. As the decade closed, the movement was in a slippery place. Its management was overextended. Almost everyone was responsible for more than could be done well.

13/Inter-Varsity's Personal Impact

On campus the launch of Sputnik by the Russians in 1957 caused fresh concern about excellence in scholarship, and the media shifted its attention from the hilarity and goldfish-swallowing frolics of college life to the classroom, libraries and laboratories. At the end of the decade the first signs of destruction of the fraternity/sorority system became evident. Thoughtful students took the risk of complaining about "the ritualized childishness and grasping narcissism" within fraternity life. More unsettling were the Little Rock Riots and the growing protests of the Civil Rights Movement.

Frank Stenzel, now a twenty-year veteran staff member in northern California, was an entering freshman at Chico State in California in 1959. He remembers,

> The year before, because of the Sputnik era, Chico State flunked out fifty-seven per cent of its freshman class. I was scared about making it academically. But the first day after I moved into the dorm I saw a poster in the cafeteria announcing the Inter-Varsity meeting at noon in the auditorium lounge. I walked over there and found a line of about seventy students enthusiastically shaking hands, giving their name and welcoming me and others to Inter-Varsity (then called Chico Christian Fellowship). They encouraged us to be involved in the Bible study in our dorm, and I was eager for some kind of fellowship, since I had made a real commitment to Christ the year before. When Boyd Baker, our staff member, came to campus on one of his twice-a-semester visits, he had a Quiet Time with me at 6 A.M. and it was my first experience of a one-to-one discipling relationship.

> I was put on the chapter executive committee and went to chapter camp at Campus by the Sea—all very important input into my life. Meanwhile I was leading a dorm Bible study. It was held in another fellow's room, and the students were stacked in, sitting out in the hall in the doorway—about twenty students in all. Even the dorm mother came to the study. Gradually we realized that what was happening in our dorm was a quiet wave of evangelism taking place—and as some became Christians, the word went out, and that gave us a new enthusiasm and a new belief about the Word of God. It changed my life.

> Along with this, at the spring conference the speaker was pretty heavy. I didn't realize how much there was to know or think about—how big a Christian world/life view was. They plugged a lot of books at the conference, and I started my Christian library.[22]

Frank Stenzel was on his way to becoming a mature disciple of Jesus Christ. His story, with the details and names changed, has a familiar theme in the lives of other students of this decade.

Bill York was a student during the first years of this decade. At the end of his freshman year at North Carolina State he ended up at Campus-in-the-Woods and had his eyes opened to the potential of student work. The next fall he felt certain God was telling him to transfer to the University of North Carolina (UNC) to begin an Inter-Varsity chapter there. He reluctantly left his engineering studies at NC State and became an economics major at UNC. Bill says,

> I always asked for a room on the top floor of the dorm so I wouldn't have people scraping their chairs overhead. At UNC I would look out of the window of my room overlooking the campus, see the students on the move and pray for them. I prayed about getting a Bible study going in each of the dorms. I saw that as the best way to reach all those students.[23]

Within a year they had Bible studies going in twelve dormitories.

Bill is one of many students who captured the philosophy of indigenous student work and threw his life into the movement. He instinctively knew how to do it; he is the kind of person a pioneer movement must have. After a brief stint on staff he pioneered student work in Alabama, Georgia and Mississippi as a volunteer while in seminary and then rejoined the staff team, with his wife Beth. He left staff in 1972 and the Yorks now operate a Logos Bookstore in Richmond, Virginia, still helping student work.

In 1955 George McKinney graduated from a Black college in the South and came to Oberlin College in Ohio to attend the Graduate School of Theology. Oberlin College has a strong nonsegregationist history. It was part of the Underground Railroad during the Civil War, and stories of daring in rescuing slaves were surely told among Blacks in the South. George McKinney knew both its history and its academic reputation when he chose that college. The few Blacks in the Oberlin community lived on the outskirts of town, where their church met irregularly. This isolated George from opportunities for Christian fellowship in a local church.

To earn expense money George McKinney worked in the cafeteria, often washing dishes. A White student named Norm Thoms worked next to him, and as they talked, Norm sensed George's need for Christian fellowship. McKinney recalls, "This young brother seemed anxious for fellowship with me, and invited me to a Bible study and then to the meeting of Inter-Varsity Christian Fellowship." The Oberlin School of Theology had taken a liberal turn since the days when Charles Finney founded the school. As a young, impressionable student George McKinney needed the fellowship and the biblical teaching of the Inter-Varsity chapter. McKinney continues, "There I found a group of students who were hungry for God, who were open for fellowship across racial lines and who were consistent in their Christian witness."

After graduating from Oberlin, Norm Thoms went to medical school (his father was a medical missionary) and he now practices medicine in Kansas City. George McKinney has become an influential, enterprising minister of the gospel as a bishop in the Church of God in Christ. Working from St. Stephens Church in San Diego as a discipler of men and women, he boldly proclaims the Word of God in his church and has reached into the Black community with educational opportunities and social programs. His encouragement and practical help has made it possible for numerous young Blacks from his community to obtain advanced education. When he was invited to serve on the board of Inter-Varsity in 1980, McKinney gladly accepted. He was convinced about its ministry from personal experience. Like many student stories, two lives converge and each makes a difference in the life of the other. Norm Thoms's faithfulness and the fellowship of the Oberlin Inter-Varsity chapter are part of George McKinney's story.[24]

14/Continuing Challenge and Growth

By the late 1950s, Inter-Varsity staff were still spread very thinly across the country. What was happening on most campuses was all out of proportion to the help they were getting. Burton Harding joined the staff in the Southeast because "so much was happening and I wanted to be part of it." Many universities by now had a history of large chapters. Strong leaders had emerged from IV chapters for almost two decades.

During the late fifties, however, it became increasingly evident that the Inter-Varsity organization needed help. No adequate funding or staffing policies were in place to cope with organizational growth. The senior staff council was not empowered to make change, and the general secretary gave only parttime to the U.S. movement. That the board allowed this was due in part to the strong support given to Stacey Woods by H. J. Taylor. While regional secretaries supervised and staffed huge sections of the country, directed and developed training programs and centers, they did so with little communication from the board or general secretary. The fallout from difficulties in the Rocky Mountain region and the arrival of the multi-staffed Campus Crusade for Christ on the campus caused both confusion and pain for already overtaxed staff leadership.

But the story is bigger than that. It defies organizational details. Inter-Varsity records contain moving stories from campus after campus: stories of nineteen-year-old men and women who did valiant deeds throughout the 1950s, who won men and women to Christ, who started chapters, who led campus missions and encouraged the kind of leadership that has enriched the church. Every decade seems to have a national flavor that affects both the church and student work, reminding us that we are in a spiritual warfare.

Any indigenous student-led chapter is always only four years from extinction; the vision needs constant reinforcement. Regional Secretary Jim Nyquist commented, "It strikes one forcefully that God works in and through committed students in and through all that may be happening on the national scene, the campus or organizationally within the Fellowship. It is his story, and nothing will keep him from telling it." Not even the revolution that came in the sixties.

10
Long Hours, Low Pay and Little Applause

If the spirit of sacrifice—including financial sacrifice—is absent from a movement, something of God is absent from that movement. For service to God is a call to sacrifice on every level.[1]

C. Stacey Woods, *general secretary, Inter-Varsity Christian Fellowship*

The early staff were, for the most part, strong individualists bound together by their enthusiasm for a common task.[2] Marked by the Great Depression and World War 2, they were drawn to hard work, thrift and a calling bigger than themselves. They enjoyed "the Fellowship" with a hearty sense of camaraderie in the magnitude of the task they faced. Mary Anne Klein accurately remembers those days, "We laughed a lot; we laughed about everything, and we seemed always to be spontaneously praying together."[3] Hilarity played its part, but it was vision that kept them going. Though they wouldn't have said so, most of them had a sense of destiny, knowing they were shaping the work in a given area.

It wasn't the organization per se that was so important; it was students. They were the reward. It was not a job; it was a high privilege, a matter of obedience to God. How else do you account for people who willingly worked for so little, with the agreement that, if the money didn't come in, their meager salaries would be delayed or canceled?[4] Or, in the case of some staff, a staff salary reduced because the spouse was also employed.[5] Every early staff family has its stories of God's provision and care, and while they all can't be told, they are an important part of Inter-Varsity's history.

Peter Haile recalls one example of God's faithfulness to Inter-Varsity staff. Salaries were delayed for two months in a row. Married staff had received a small living stipend at the beginning of the month, but that was almost gone. Peter was on his way to New Hampshire for a three-day staff visit. He left the few dollars they had for the care of his wife, Jane, and their small son, John. He knew he would be staying in the dorm at the college he was visiting, but he had no food money. He planned to use his credit card to buy gasoline for his car. He pulled up and stopped by a pump at the local station to fill the tank. It had been snowing heavily for two days, and the snow was packed on the drive. When he opened the car door, he saw what looked like a dollar bill half-stuck out in the snow. Peter picked it up. It was a ten-dollar bill. He showed it to the attendant, who shrugged and said, "You found it." That ten-dollar bill paid for his meals.

Not all provisions were as miraculous as that. Many times the parents of staff families supplemented income, or sensitive friends gave sustaining gifts. Sometimes money appeared in the mail either anonymously or from people never heard from before or since. One friend asked a staff member for his car payment book, and regularly made those payments. Many personal miracle stories, not told abroad but pondered in the heart, made it obvious to the staff that a great God was in on the venture.

Hospitality was part of the job. Helen Friesen recalls serving each family member a lone frankfurter at their noon meal one day. Their salary hadn't come yet that month, and the larder was almost empty. Her husband, Mel, answered a knock at the door, and Helen heard him say, "Well, come on in and have lunch with us." Mel's mother was visiting at the time and didn't answer when Helen turned to her and said, "Mom, we only have . . ." She simply cut a bit of meat off each serving but one and filled her plate with the pieces. The guest sat down to a whole frankfurter. Helen learned there would always be room for one more.[6] None of the staff ever starved, but they did know how to make two meals out of a can of tuna. One favorite story is of the spaghetti supper, made from a recipe for forty, served sixty instead. Like the widow's cruse of oil, the cupboard which, logically, should have been empty continued to be miraculously stocked when the need was there.

Ruth Bell (Nyquist), a staff candidate at Campus-in-the-Woods, remembers hearing Joe and Mary Lou Bayly discuss with another married

couple the fact that staff salaries were six weeks in arrears, and she wondered how a family would manage in that situation. What really impressed
her was their matter-of-fact attitude and their outward lack of concern. It
wasn't heroism or naivete; it was part of the package they had agreed to
in their concern for students. Most of them would say that they learned to
love God in fresh ways through their experiences. They did not idealize
either their privations or God's provision; these were simply facts of their
lives.

Not everyone could take this lifestyle. Some staff left for financial reasons; it was simply too stressful. Others thought it was an unfair policy to
let the workers finance the work, which was a glaringly honest way to look
at the situation.[7]

1/And They Gave Up More Than Money

But that was only one job stress. Married staff experienced the loneliness
of husband and father being away for two or three weeks at a time—and
those were the weeks when the children usually got sick! In the case of
single staff, the loneliness of travel, of never having a home base, was
sometimes severe. Walter Liefeld, now a professor of New Testament at
Trinity Evangelical Divinity School, traveled as a single staff in a four-state
area. He reflects:

> The main feeling about the work was that it was dawn to dusk and later.
> I did not have an apartment other than my car. I had a one-drawer filing
> cabinet and one suitcase. I had two pairs of underwear and two pairs
> of socks, and I would wash one set out every night, staying in a dorm
> or a fraternity house, constantly working with students. I was utterly
> dependent and lonely as all get out. I remember driving those long
> roads between campuses sometimes at night, passing homes with warm
> lights inside, and seeing families inside or kids playing on the lawn
> outside, and feeling so lonely.

Always having to take the initiative accounted for part of the loneliness staff
felt. Some student leaders made poor preparations for staff visits. Liefeld
tells of driving from Missouri on a Sunday to make a meeting in Indiana,
checking in at the address given him, only to find it a women's residence
with no one knowing anything about him. The IV chapter president finally
showed up a couple of hours after supper, quite unconcerned that he was
hours late for the appointment. When Liefeld said he hadn't eaten anything
all day (his paycheck had arrived on Saturday, he had no opportunity to
cash it, and he was penniless—no bank machines back then!). The fellow

said, "Well, OK, I'll be back around 10 o'clock," and disappeared. Liefeld waited a few more hours, without food, before he found out where he was staying.

On other campuses more responsible students not only lined up housing and meals, but scheduled appointments with students every half hour all day long, and then expected the staff member to speak at the evening meeting. The agenda was enough to overwhelm the most hardy of pioneers.

Staff visits might be only for five days, but each day was full, perhaps beginning with an early morning Quiet Time with a student and ending the day with a discussion session in someone's dorm room. Often being provided with a place to sleep meant staking out a claim on the floor in a student's room or flipping a coin to see who got the bed. Each campus visit called forth enormous amounts of emotional energy, physical stamina and spiritual intensity. The staff member might not be back for several months; ferreting out as many Christian students as possible in order to encourage leadership and vision was important.

Staff initiative has always involved helping students take their responsibility for Christian witness. Inter-Varsity was pioneering not only a student movement, but an idea of responsibility foreign to most Christian students. The staff would often be the initiators, picking up the ball, but the students had the responsibility to move it down the field and score.

While the board minutes in January of 1945 read, "To do his best work a staff member ought to have no more than five to seven colleges," the average was fifteen or sixteen. Some staff visited over thirty schools, which meant visits only twice a year. Women staff like Alice Kitchen, Anna Mary Williams (Ramer), Mary Beaton and others in the Midwest in the 1950s, worked in two to five states. In 1948 Anne Childs (Hummel) took on the whole Southeast for three years. And like others, she traveled the Greyhound buses a week or two at a time, staying on campus or with IVCF friends in the community.

Ruth Bell (Nyquist) traveled in five central states, working primarily with the women students. She comments,

> I was on a different campus every few nights, often staying with faculty members like Hildegarde Johnson at Iowa State or Katherine Watson at Bradley University, both wonderfully caring volunteers in the work. But most of the time I was in the dormitories, usually in some student's room, but sometimes in the guest room of the dorm (which I loved because of the privacy, with a bath) where I didn't have to interact with

people all the time. Stress wasn't something you talked about back then; it was the job and you did it. Every other staff member—single or married—was in the same boat and you didn't feel this was abnormal or unrealistic. It never dawned on me to question whether this was the right way to do the work. I think because of the quality of Stacey's leadership none of us wanted to get into self-pity. You couldn't afford to be a neurotic after hearing Stacey talk.

Charles Troutman remembers the only prayer meetings he ever dreaded. In 1942 under Paul Beckwith's leadership, ten Christian students at University of Minnesota at Duluth had gone through all the formalities of establishing a chapter and invited Charles to campus for the first official meeting. When he arrived he found that the college president, wary of this evangelical group, had postponed his approval at the last minute. Duluth had heavy snows that year, and the fire department had dug out a circular space around each fire plug, piling the drifts fifteen feet high. Since the students couldn't meet in campus buildings, they decided to have their daily prayer meeting each noon in the snow circle in front of the main entrance. The temperature was thirty below, but since the snow was over their heads, they were protected from the wind. Charles says, "Whenever I think of those prayer meetings I realize that I have not yet completely thawed out."

Jane Hollingsworth, assigned to staff the women's colleges in the Northeast, found no Christian student contact at Radcliffe. She would often drive round and round the college, calling on the Lord to open a door for witness there. Her one possible contact for beginning a group at Radcliffe had responded, "I know what you want with me. You want me to start an Inter-Varsity chapter. But I want to tell you I believe in predestination, not evangelism." More drives around the college and prayers. More times of waiting and trusting God. Then she got a letter from someone that a Jewish girl named Ellen had become a Christian at a sailing camp. Jane went to see her and found her eager to have a Bible study in her room. Jane suggested she invite some of her other friends. Ellen was a persuasive leader, and when Jane arrived for the Bible study she could hardly get into the room. Ellen's growth in biblical understanding is a happy memory for Jane and more than made up for all her times of uncertainty. Ellen led several of those who came to the Bible study to know the Lord, and they formed the nucleus of the Radcliffe Christian Fellowship.

As soon as World War 2 was over, Stacey Woods stopped by Toledo, Ohio, to see Howard Larsen, a founding member of the IV chapter of the

University of Michigan. Howard had been considered necessary personnel during the war in his work as a chemical engineer for Sun Oil Company. Stacey wanted Howard to consider coming with Inter-Varsity to do public relations work. Howard accepted the challenge of an exhausting tour of speaking during 1945, traveling with his clergy discount by railroad and contacting people with an "audacity I can't believe I had." Burned out at the end of the year, he enrolled in law school at the University of Minnesota (UM) the summer of 1946. He offered to combine staff work in that area with his studies. For the next years he did full-time staff work in Minnesota and northern Wisconsin during the fall and spring quarters. During the winter quarter, when snow and cold made travel difficult, and during the summer quarter he was a full-time law student.

IVCF at UM was the largest student religious association on campus, with some 500 attending meetings. That made denominational campus chaplains nervous and the dean finally called Howard in to question his status as a religious campus worker. When he found out that Howard Larsen was essentially volunteering while he was also a law student, and that he also traveled to at least six other campuses, he became one of Howard's chief supporters. Although it meant postponing his law degree, Howard did what many others did: he altered his personal plans to help develop student work.[8]

Most staff did not have cars. Charles Troutman tells of some of the staff hitchhiking between campuses in the early 1940s because they didn't have money to take a bus. Because they were paid so little, Troutman said that most of the Christian public looked on the staff as bright, young volunteers who needed to be helped along the way, but they didn't see the necessity of sending in money to headquarters to insure a better salary. By the 1950s staff used discounted clergy passes and went by bus or train. If a staff member used his car, he was only paid the equivalent of a clergy bus ticket. An August 1951 board-meeting minute states, "Automobile remuneration was increased from five cents to six cents per mile. It is understood that transportation of staff members should be by public transportation except by permission of the general secretary or the associate general secretary." In reading the minutes of the board meetings, one is impressed that board members made decisions that indicated that they too considered the staff short-term volunteers.

Single staff usually kept their unused belongings in the closet of a friend's home where they went to crash after traveling a circuit for a couple of weeks. Dorothy Farmer staffed over thirty-five chapters in New York

State, riding the bus from school to school. As she left each campus she wrote her now-famous postcards, in tiny handwriting that circled the edges, reminding each student she had counseled to be faithful to his or her commitments. She may have only visited each campus two or three times a year, but the students whose lives she influenced still "rise up and call her blessed." She was well-qualified to give the demonstration at New Staff Orientation on "how to pack a suitcase and prepare for the change in seasons!" Her home base was an apartment maintained by NCF graduate Rose Brooks, who not only made room for Dorothy but was her partner in prayer and later joined the NCF staff.

2/Valuable Volunteers

It couldn't have been done without volunteers and people who offered hospitality. Inter-Varsity's story contains a long list of people who had a vision and pitched in to help in whatever way possible—a list accurately recorded only in heaven. The forties and early fifties were times of great growth for the Fellowship. In 1950 Jim Nyquist, with only one year on staff, was senior man and regional secretary in the New England states. He rented a room from Wes and Helen Matthews, who were in graduate studies in electrical engineering. Charles Hummel, traveling in New England and the Maritime Provinces, sublet from Jim two feet of his closet and three feet of his bookcase. He would load up his 1946 Chevrolet with typewriter and traveling booktable and be off for two weeks or more. He would return to Boston to check in with Jim and get rested up, sleeping on the sofa in his sleeping bag. Helen Matthews did his laundry, fed him and helped get "his batteries recharged." Then Charlie would be off again.

Other graduates acted as volunteer staff members, and the growth and health of the work was often related to which schools had these kinds of helpers who poured themselves into the lives of the students. Harish Merchant, a graduate student from India who was converted at Ohio's Case-Western Reserve, had an effective ministry as an associate staff member for the chapters at Bowling Green College and the University of Toledo, using free time from his engineering career in teaching, research and development. Later he took on projects to help InterVarsity Press.

Dick and Connie Castor volunteered on staff in New York City for approximately five years in various capacities. They helped do follow-up on the 1,700 students who responded to the 1957 Billy Graham Crusade, and Dick, an insurance executive, served on the board of IVCF a total of twenty-four years.

Eleanor Flor (Bretall) volunteered to work with NCF and foreign students during her years in graduate school, first at the University of Michigan, then at the University of Washington. When Eleanor heard that someone was needed to help with student work at the University of Arizona, she accepted a position there in the College of Nursing, choosing her employment based on Inter-Varsity's need. She also served on the IVCF Board.

Graduate students took up the challenge of working with international students across the country. News of the Campus carried a typical story: five graduates spent a day skiing with six students from Afghanistan, following the day on the slopes with a Bible study on John 9 that lasted three hours.

The campus of Western Montana College grew up around the house where Fred and Dorothy ("Mom and Pop") Bridenstine lived in Dillon. Out of a natural love for college students they made their home a haven for staff and students for decades. Ten per cent of the students on the small campus of Western Montana College were in the IV group and under the influence of the Bridenstines. Fred Wagner, who supervised student work in the Northwest for well over twenty years, says,

> I don't know where Mom Bridenstine picked up all her Inter-Varsity instincts—inductive Bible study and conversational prayer, among others—but she did these things naturally with the students. She had an Inter-Varsity closet that was essentially an IV booktable. The closet door held a shoe storage bag with pockets filled with small booklets which she was always putting in the hands of students.

Marvin Anderson, former staffworker in Montana and now a pastor in the Detroit area, says, "Their love for us was costly, not just in the daily extra meals they served, but also in all the extra time they poured into us, nurturing us in Bible study, counsel and common sense." The Bridenstines became the backbone of student camping in the Montana region, and encouraged a network of volunteer helpers for student training.[9]

While a visiting professor at Penn State, Ed and Gladys Baldwin became interested in Inter-Varsity. Ed served as faculty advisor for the IV chapter, and Gladys opened their home for social events and counseling. Through a Chinese Bible study at Penn State they began to see the possibilities of ministry to international students. When they moved to Pittsburgh in 1952 because of Ed's engineering job with Westinghouse, they determined to increase the openness and availability of their home for God's use and looked for a large house near the campuses of the Carnegie Institute of

Technology (now Carnegie Mellon University) and the University of Pittsburgh. IVCF staff, missionaries, international students and others stayed with them for varying lengths of time. They initiated a work with international students in Pittsburgh, with monthly suppers and speakers. Gladys Baldwin did the contact work, rounding up the international students and American IV graduates to help. Their son, Nick, says, "Mother never really felt a home was her own until she had knocked out a wall to make a room large enough to feed supper to anywhere up to a hundred people!"

The Baldwins' ministry spans the years. They were transferred to Philadelphia in 1960 as they were approaching retirement age. They worked their interest in internationals into an ongoing program at Tenth Presbyterian Church. After leaving Westinghouse Ed accepted consulting jobs that took him and Gladys all over the world, just so they could visit those who had been part of their student family. In 1975 they finally retired to Durham, North Carolina, to be near the campus of Duke University, where they sparked another ministry to international students.

So many others did similar work for the cause of the kingdom of God and student ministry. Gordon Randall, a business executive in Schnectady, and his wife, Genevieve, offered hospitality to traveling staff and speakers and invested their lives in international students. Student conferences came to depend on the volunteer help of Walter Seigfried, an engineer based in Pittsburgh. He kept a mini-bookstore in his home, supplying books for students and local churches for years. His commitment to Inter-Varsity's ministry came out of his own rich experience in the movement. Norman and Ardyth Frisbey, graduates of Michigan State and the IV chapter there, used their home and time in ministry to international students at Wayne State University and later at Penn State.

People who have prayed have given Inter-Varsity a cherished gift. From the early years, staff members have experienced strong support from those who did battle by praying for specific Inter-Varsity chapters. A group of faithful staff from the forties—Bob and Ellen Cressey, Shirley Stephen, Fran and Mary Elizabeth Steele—now all live in the same retirement center in Pennsylvania and meet regularly to pray for student work and IV staff!

3/Faculty Support

When Inter-Varsity began in 1939, the number of Christian faculty members on the secular university campus who were known as evangelicals could be counted on two hands. As students came out of Inter-Varsity chapters with a vision for reaching the university and went on to graduate school, this situation began to change. By the 1950s Inter-Varsity was in contact with well over one thousand evangelical Christian faculty. Many of these aligned themselves with the ministry of Inter-Varsity, becoming faculty sponsors, catalysts for Christian witness and mature counselors to student leaders.

Gordon VanWylen, a founding member of the IVCF chapter at the University of Michigan, went on to be an active member of the group at Penn State while earning his master's degree. Later, during his doctoral studies at Massachusetts Institute of Technology (MIT), he helped begin the student chapter there.[10] He joined the engineering faculty at the University of Michigan (and later became dean of the College of Engineering) where he not only supported the local Inter-Varsity chapter but held a long-term Bible study for international students in his home. He served as president of the IVCF Board from 1959-62.

Kenneth Pike, world-renowned linguist, professor and member of Wycliffe Bible Translators, was also a member of the first IV chapter at Michigan. He and his wife Evelyn influenced many student generations in the IV chapter both through teaching and hospitality. Dr. Edward "Ted" Groesbeck, director of admissions, strongly supported IVCF in administrative channels within the university. He and his wife Jessica, serving as faculty sponsors, kept an open house for students and their social gatherings, and gave generations of students love and personal support. These three faculty members, integral to the university and serving concurrently, strengthened student and chapter life, and contributed to the chapter's reputation as a stable, growing movement.

James Shaw and his wife Vera continue to serve as the backbone to student work in the Boston area, and particularly as long-term faculty sponsor of the Harvard chapter. They, and others like them, have been tireless in their encouragement of student work. Cleon and Lucille Morrill began a similar ministry, first at the University of Illinois and then at Michigan State. Paul and Doris DeKoning's investment in the lives of students at Michigan State is a story in itself. Sacrificially living in small quarters, they hosted Bethel Manor, a men's student house that was also used as the meeting place for the MSU chapter. Students felt free to drop in for counsel, encouragement and fellowship—a constant open house for the DeKoning family.

Norman and Rose Lofgren, on faculty at Chico State in California sustained the work of the chapter for years. They were on hand to counsel and encourage, filling the long gaps between staff visits.

Elizabeth Carlson, one of the first women professors at the University of Minnesota, was the faculty advisor and spiritual counselor for the IV chapter as soon as it was formed in 1940. Her faithful attendance at the early morning student prayer meeting may well have influenced the students more than anything else she did. On that same campus Robert Cameron, head of the department of mathematics, led students in a mind-expanding study of theology, using the book by T. C. Hammond, *In Understanding Be Men.*[11] Charles Hatfield lent his support to the chapter while doing graduate work at University of Minnesota, later undergirding the chapter at the University of Missouri, Rolla campus, where he was a faculty member. Hatfield served on the IVCF Board for many years.

Frank Cassel was interested in Inter-Varsity from the first because of his friendship with Charles Troutman at Wheaton College. When he arrived at Cornell University for graduate work in 1940 he found a group of Christian students disillusioned with the help they were receiving from the League of Evangelical Students. He suggested they contact Troutman, and in the course of time the Cornell IVCF chapter came into being, "without missing a step or a Bible study." Frank met his wife Elizabeth (Peg) while at Cornell, and after World War 2 they began their faculty life at Colorado State College, where they also helped get an IVCF chapter going. (The first DPM was scheduled for the first day of classes in January 1947 at 6:30 A.M., and seventeen students attended.) In 1950 Frank Cassel became a professor of zoology at North Dakota State University, where Inter-Varsity work had just begun. Through the years the Cassels have helped as faculty advisors and prayer partners, directed alumni camps at Campus in the Woods, given nature lessons at camps, helped with college prep camps, served on the board of IVCF and an assortment of other involvements. After retirement from the faculty at NDSU, Frank served as a part-time regional director for the North Central region from 1982-1984.

Ralph Watts had been taught to tithe and to read his Bible regularly, but, as a young professional working in New York City, he knew something was missing from his life. He was attracted to Inter-Varsity student meetings at Columbia University, and one time heard Ruth Paxson speak in a way that drew him to faith in Christ. He became one of the volunteers for IV work in New York City, hauling around the portable booktable for area meetings. After he married Carolyn Chesley, an NCF staffworker, they moved to Texas where they have had an active ministry to international students. Ralph has served Inter-Varsity in many ways, particularly as a corporation and board member since 1951.

Sam Fuenning, a medical doctor associated with the University of Nebraska at Lincoln, and his wife Lillian have had a long-lived interest in student ministry. Summer after summer during the 1950s they served together on the medical staff at Bear Trap Ranch, and humbly did whatever else needed doing in the busy life of camping. Sam Fuenning served on the Inter-Varsity Board and Corporation for twenty-nine years, where he gave camping strong support.

Hazel Meers (Offner) credits staff member Cleo Buxton with helping her answer the stream of questions she raised about orthodox Christianity when she first came in contact with the Inter-Varsity group on the campus of the University of Illinois in 1946. She also met and married David Offner whom she met in the chapter. Recalling her student days at Illinois, Hazel says, "It was straight out of the book of Acts; so many students were hungry to know God." David, now a professor of mechanical engineering at the University of Illinois, has been faculty advisor for the chapter for thirty-five years, and was also a member of the Inter-Varsity Corporation. Their active support includes raising two sons who serve on IV staff—Kevin in New England and Larry in Ontario with the Canadian IVCF.

Edna Anderson, Virginia Ohlson and Cornelia Knight gave long service on the board and corporation. They represented NCF on the board and shared their concern that the work among nurses be properly cared for. Their own professional involvement modeled what NCF was all about. Stanley Block, professor at Illinois Institute of Technology, Kenneth Gieser, a busy physician, Roscoe Sappenfield, a lawyer, are among those early volunteers who gave generously of their time to help Inter-Varsity get under way.

Clarence Radius, a professor in electronics at California Polytechnic, and his wife Myrtle, spiritual advisors to students for many years, helped get the Cal Poly chapter under way in 1947. Myrtle Radius first heard of Inter-Varsity while riding on a bus, seated next to a vivacious woman student. As they began to talk together, the student asked, "Are you a Christian?" When Myrtle responded positively, the student said, "I thought you might be. I learned in Inter-Varsity Christian Fellowship to ask about this early in a friendship." When Mel Friesen called at Cal Poly to contact Christians interested in starting a chapter, he found the Radius's already convinced.

Jim Nyquist, then regional secretary for the Central region, visited John Alexander at the University of Wisconsin and shared a vision for students with him. As a result, John and Betty Alexander began a regular open house for freshmen where they shared practical helps about being a Christian student at the university. Alexander's ministry to graduate students not only kept many of them active in the faith, but also lifted their horizons to see how God could use them on the campus in the future. His brown-bag-lunch faculty Bible study gave credibility to his influence with undergraduate and graduate students. They recruited faculty people like Archie and Shirley McKinney to help with international student work, a ministry which the McKinneys have continued into the next decades.

Frederick P. Brooks, distinguished professor of computer science, and his wife, Nancy, joined the faculty of the University of North Carolina at Chapel Hill in 1965 when they were still new Christians. They began to help graduate students relate their studies to their Christian faith. That graduate fellowship has been active for over twenty-five years. Faculty Bible studies, begun by keen faculty members, give weight to the vision of confronting the university with the gospel. Brooks is one of many of these who have carried on this kind of witness in the university community.

The involvement of volunteers not only spurred the growth within the Inter-Varsity chapters, but continued a pattern of spiritual growth and fellowship in those involved. Many gave prodigious amounts of time and did first-class work. While staff were responsible for huge geographical areas, they were strongly supported by local volunteers. Their work, their hospitality and their prayers were significant in what happened on the campus. God keeps better records than Inter-Varsity has done and sometimes, because of the press and size of the work to be done—but to our shame—people were not only improperly thanked, but neglected after they had finished serving so nobly.

4/Students

Neither can we properly recognize the faithfulness of individual students, who are the heart of the movement. Fred Woodberry, staffing New York City in the 1950s, tells of the year that every student leader graduated from the chapter at City College of New York (CCNY) except a Chinese student who had a speech impediment. He didn't consider himself much of a leader, but he felt a spiritual burden for a Christian witness at CCNY. Every day at a specified time he would sit on a bench outside of CCNY—summer, winter, spring or fall—praying for the college. Fred would find him there, praying, and sometimes join him. Then the Chinese student graduated, and still no work at CCNY. But that fall the Billy Graham Crusade was held in New York City and hundreds of students came to know Christ, and the CCNY chapter was off and running. Who knows where this faithful student is today?

Steve Holbrook went to Union College in Schenectady, New York, in 1952. While he was unpacking his belongings, he responded to a knock at the door and found a fellow standing there who said, "Is your name Steve Holbrook?" When Steve acknowledged who he was, the fellow said, "Let's pray," and proceeded to thank the Lord "for sending this guy to Union College to start an Inter-Varsity chapter." He was Dudley Woodberry,[12] and he told Steve that he had been praying that the Lord would send someone who was a Christian to Union, that he was directed to Steve's room, and that there was work to do! Within a short time they had a chapter going with about ten to fifteen members. (In 1938 a chapter existed at Union College with Herbert Mekeel, pastor of First Presbyterian Church of Schenectady, as the sponsor, but responsible leadership had not been passed on and evidently the chapter had died out.)

Ray Ortlund, who was in his first pastorate at East Glenville near Union, served as the advisor to the chapter and was a great help to the group. Students from the Union chapter (an all-male college) joined students from Rensselaer Polytechnic Institute (RPI), Skidmore and Russell Sage for weekly inspiration at First Presbyterian Church in Schenectady. Holbrook says, "They had a rip-snorting college class at the church taught by Herbert Mekeel, pastor of the church. He taught a class on Romans that I'll never forget. He made us all buy the Williams translation and taught us to really study the Scripture. He helped all of our Inter-Varsity chapters."

Charles Troutman mentions that Herbert Mekeel gave important support to Inter-Varsity in the Northeast between 1938 and 1946, the years in which the movement was getting started. Mekeel worked as a volunteer and regularly spoke at conferences and chapter meetings. Troutman says, "He went to bat for us a number of times to verify the worthy ministry of IVCF in a suspicious religious climate. I do not think we could have gone ahead as we did without him."

Although Holbrook's introduction to the idea of student witness through Inter-Varsity was a bit unorthodox, he and his wife Elaine (a Skidmore IV member) became volunteer associate staff members in Hawaii, where Steve was stationed in the Navy. They provided the living room for meetings, the cars for transportation, besides bankrolling some of the activities. After Navy days they picked up the same pattern in Toledo, Ohio, where Steve was in business. They built a five-bedroom home so that one bedroom could be for Inter-Varsity staff visitors.

Steve, now president of the consulting firm Princeton Management Associates, became a member of the IVCF corporation in 1968 and subsequently served on the board of Inter-Varsity. As a consultant for many missions, Steve travels all over the world. "I always ask the missionaries I meet, 'Where did you accept Christ?' or 'Where did you accept the call to the mission field?' The overwhelming majority answer *Inter-Varsity*—which is very satisfying for me, because that is where God gave me a vision of what He could do in my life, too." There are many others like Steve Holbrook whose involvement as a volunteer extends from student days.

5/Camp Supporters
Inter-Varsity's camping program could hardly have survived without the help of volunteers and minimally paid staff who kept the camps in operation. At Campus in the Woods, the roster of honor would include people like Fredda Kyro and Arthur Holiday. At Bear Trap Ranch, Ron and Jane Knudtsen, Bill and Carol Galambos, Bob and Ruth Mann, Dick and Ruth Young, and Dave and Diane Swanson gave themselves to keep the ministry going even while the directorship of the camp kept changing. At Campus by the Sea the Friesen family had a first love for the camp; then the Mannes family took up the cause for sixteen years. Paul and Virginia Friesen became full-time directors from 1976 to 1990.

The Cedar Campus table was spread with abundant, tasty food for twenty-four years under the capable management of Frances Gailey, who began as a student and kept on coming to camp long after she became a professor. Don Vinkemulder, Wilma Greening, and Bob and Imogene Schrader were key to the expansion of the ministry at Cedar Campus. The Schraders's ministry to the work crew and their building and accounting skills enabled the camp to develop into a year-round operation. In addition to these, a long list of yearly volunteers saw the cause as more important than the salary. The phrase "unsung heroes" may be trite, but it accurately describes those who entered into the work of the Fellowship.

6/Without Applause
Stacey Woods did not consider his own convenience in doing student ministry. He did not expect that his staff would do otherwise. The kind of obedience and diligence he modeled didn't expect applause or praise. And Stacey voiced very little approval or appreciation to the staff. Neither did the board. Though Stacey never said so, many of the staff unconsciously picked up the idea that it was somewhat "unspiritual" to express too much praise. Inter-Varsity people are stronger in an analytical mode than in an

appreciative mode by their very nature. Often they have been attracted to the Fellowship by the modesty and reserve that characterizes it.

People who have been on Inter-Varsity staff in the forties and fifties are incredibly loyal to the movement and concerned about student work. They have received their sense of approval for the job either from students and alumni or, most often, from a sense of call. Applause has not been the hallmark of the Fellowship. Somehow, and it is hard to research how this came about, a feeling of privilege was attached to being a staffworker—and that took away the necessity of appreciation by the hierarchy. Jim Reapsome, assigned in 1957-61 to expand alumni work and public relations and doing an A-1 job, probably felt an attraction to another ministry because no one urged him to stay. No one said, "We need you; you're doing a super job." It wasn't part of Stacey Woods's management style to express praise, and the lingering effects of this has been one of the hurtful parts of IVCF history.

What caused these people to continue to invest their lives in this ministry? Dick Castor says,

We wanted other students to have the same experience we had. In our Fellowship chapter (Adelphi College, New York), and it is not phony nor sentimental to say this, we really loved Jesus. God had given us a thirst for Himself and a desire to share him. We used to meet in the faculty room on our campus to have our morning prayer meetings. And lots of times members of the faculty would come in and we would be on our knees in prayer. Our feeling of community and love for one another made us feel more secure in our witness, and more sure of the Person we were presenting to our friends. We were not concerned to become part of some kind of super organization. The gut issue was sharing our lives with fellow students.

Charles Troutman comments, "In those early years students had an intense desire for holiness that was not seen in the American evangelical church. Students were seeking God—with a concern for character, to be like Him, not in the sense of attaining perfection, but of pleasing Him. It was a form of mysticism, not so much the typical 'search for God,' but an awareness of God's search for us, and thus a desire to know Him and to be holy."

Perhaps that was applause enough for the staff members and volunteers in Inter-Varsity.

11
When the World Changed: Decade of the 1960s

Students have the least to lose through change. They do not have deep roots in material possessions, in social or economic position, or in their children. Consequently, students are impatient for change when they see injustice or the impairment of liberty. The Christian student is sensitive to the needs of others, the injustices done to them. This may create problems for him. When my oldest son was a student at Swarthmore College, he said to me, "Dad, I feel as if I were in between. At school I'm the arch-conservative because I believe the Bible; at church I'm looked on as the arch-liberal because I believe in equal rights for Blacks."
Joseph T. Bayly, *editor,* HIS *magazine*

No one could have predicted what happened in the sixties. Surveying the late fifties, whatever disturbed the complacent seemed healthy and necessary. *The Organization Man* by William H. Whyte (1956) and Vance Packard's *Status Seekers* (1959) stirred up enough conversation to challenge the safety, and what others called the sterility, of the late fifties. Students began to challenge not just football and fraternities, but the courses that were being forced upon them, and the tenure of some of their professors. This proved to be only the beginning to what turned out to be an explosion of protest against authority and against previously established standards of morality. The 1960 election of the youthful John F. Kennedy to the presidency crowned the decade with a seeming new idealism. He made his announcement of the creation of the Peace Corps to crowds of cheering students as he stood on the steps of the Michigan Union at the University of Michigan. But his assassination in 1963 shattered their view of the future, in spite of scientific advances which led to flights into space and cracking the DNA code. The Cuban Crisis and the Berlin Wall set the world on edge. The cumulative effect of a long string of events in the sixties not only altered the campus, but changed everyone's life.

Irrelevant and *meaningful* became in-words. In the spring of 1960 four Black students made national headlines by staging a sit-in when they were refused the right to buy a cup of coffee in a Greensboro, North Carolina, Woolworth store. The moral legitimacy of the civil rights movement grabbed the student imagination. Racism was outrageous, and formerly unorganized and privileged college students began the first semblance of organizational protest. In 1963 two hundred thousand Freedom Marchers, White and Black, went to Washington to demonstrate. While media coverage exaggerated student involvement, a rebellion slowly began to swell.

Long hair, beards, blue jeans and sometimes bare feet became a way to defy the tidiness of a society that seemed to care more about appearances than reality. College women with long straight hair, no make-up and often shapeless attire, defying traditional stereotypes, discussed with intensity what it meant to be feminine and determined to make a new image of *woman*. Old dating codes disappeared. Modern technology, like the Pill, facilitated new ways of behavior. Promiscuity became a statement, a rejection of tradition. As the decade progressed, drugs edged out alcohol as a mind-altering substance. The scents of "pot" and tear gas were in the air. Nobel-Prize-winning discoverer of vitamin C, Albert Szent-Gyorgi, aged 76, asked, "Is there any point in study and work? Fornicate and take drugs against this terrible strain of idiots who govern the world." Dr. Timothy Leary, Harvard University professor and drug-cult guru, chanted his psychedelic advice to "turn on, tune in and drop out." Sound became a cultural phenomenon in "the democracy of rock music and denim." The Beatles mesmerized a growing youth culture with their musical interpretation of the world.

Kindness was reserved for the down and outers; scorn for anything that smacked of position or power. Love-ins were "where it was at," that very phrase often a synonym for self-indulgence. Bewildered parents no longer knew how to relate to their children.

Negroes became Blacks and, under Martin Luther King's leadership, realized Black is beautiful. They dumped their White champions to lead their own cause: Black Power, Black study programs and Black houses on campus, the militant Black Panthers. Students for a Democratic Society (SDS) aggressively proclaimed their purpose: to wrest control of the entire educational process from the bureaucracy of the administration. A network of campus groups, hostile and flag-burning, defied authority, encouraged sit-ins and duplicated Berkeley's 1964 Free Speech Movement. Graduate students dropped out in order to devote all their energy to organizing the protest. It was a time of anarchy. By the late 1960s student rebels were anti-everything: anti-deodorant, anti-bra, anti-parent.

For the most part, college officials abandoned the rituals of college life, and withdrew oversight of morals and behavior; "in loco parentis" died. Without knowing what they were doing, college students were dehumanizing their living situations and discarding all the unappreciated privacy and order of their lives. While only twenty-eight per cent of college students had participated in any demonstration by 1969-70, the height of the protests,[1] their participation profoundly influenced the way the average student thought. Slowly the boundaries that divided rebels and conservatives softened.

Unrealistic idealism led to "the folly of good intentions." Plans to save the world bore negative fruit. The Great Society, in the end, created institutionalized poverty and systemic inflation. The simple lifestyle became surprisingly complicated.

President Lyndon Johnson became a pariah on the campus as the Vietnam War escalated and, together with the draft, set off even more violent campus protests. Then in May 1970, six students were killed in student protests against the Vietnam War at Kent State and Jackson State College. This terrible and needless violence became a flaming symbol of all repression. Angry protests swept through the campus world. Then suddenly it was all over. President Richard Nixon, elected in 1969, saw the handwriting on the wall; he terminated the draft and began winding down the war. Student rage had spent itself, but many families would never be the same. In fact, the whole world had changed.

The number of students involved in violent protests was never a majority, even though media coverage gave that impression by bringing all the ruckus into the homes of the nation. But then, causes are never led by a majority, and those who participated were deadly serious about changing the system. Other students looked upon the whole performance as a charade and went along with some of the escapades as kind of a lark, a chance to be unorthodox. James S. Kunen, an undergraduate of Columbia University (New York), wrote a witty book called *The Strawberry Statement,* published in 1969, in which he irreverently spoofed the protests, mocking the minority who had taken up the cause célèbre. He participated in sit-ins and demonstrations against the government and the governing, but he was not a true radical. He closed his book by announcing: "I have a statement to make at this time, gentlemen. Since the First Republic of the United States is one hundred ninety-two years old and I am nineteen, I will give it one more chance."[2]

On the religious scene Bishop Robinson's *Honest to God* became a best seller in 1963 and Joseph Fletcher's *Situation Ethics,* published in 1966, introduced readers to the wilderness of humanism and moral flexibility. Some saw this as the beginning of the Great Refusal—American society turning against God. Yet in spite of the outrage of the students against the system, their experimentation with drugs and sex, the sound of rock and angry voices, some students became increasingly aware of their lostness as the decade went on. Nothing seemed true or dependable in the last analysis. They had heard it said that you couldn't trust anyone over thirty; now they wondered if you could trust anybody. Then some of them turned to Jesus.

The Jesus Movement defied explanation for conservative Christians. Young people clearly not in the mainstream of society were excited about knowing Jesus and not afraid to talk about Him to anybody. The simplicity of their faith and their zeal often embarrassed their parents and put traditional Christians to shame. New believers from the counterculture found little acceptance in evangelical churches who were suspicious of facial hair and off-beat clothes. This hypocrisy confirmed the complaint that the church was interested only in exteriors. A variety of cults from Hare Krishna to the Children of God led other students, looking for structure and answers, into what amounted to spiritual bondage. Eastern religions and gurus capitalized on the confusion. The explosion of protest had given birth to an explosion of religious ideas.

Woven throughout the decade, the charismatic movement gained momentum in both Catholic and Protestant communities. In some instances it swept people into the kingdom of God; in others, the spiritual renewal led to an unbalanced focus on signs and wonders and only one member of the Godhead. To say it was a confusing time to be a student is to understate the case.

Generalizations about a decade never capture the whole truth, however. Some students went through the sixties seemingly untouched by the revolution, turning their backs on all its phenomena. It didn't happen all at once; the movement slowly coalesced and built up steam. For a while, at the beginning of the decade, Inter-Varsity chapters hardly felt a ripple.

1/The Early 1960s

Fred Wagner's story is a case in point. In 1957 he was a freshman at Tri-State College in Angola, Indiana. He became an active member in the Inter-Varsity chapter, thanks to the faithfulness of the Christian students who used to visit anybody who hadn't shown up at a meeting for a couple of weeks. In a school of 1,200, the chapter had about thirty members—enough students to infiltrate the whole campus. The Bible studies, the conferences, and the leadership thrust upon him in his sophomore year stimulated Fred's growth as a Christian. Fred said the first person he ever met who "had an agenda" of wanting to help him grow as a Christian was staff member George Westerlund. The chapter president was the second such person. He took Fred with him when he went to call on other fellows in this all-male engineering school.

Staffer George Westerlund (called Uncle George by the Tri-State students) wrote to Fred one spring, announcing his forthcoming visit, and asked him to go to all the fraternities on campus to inquire about their openness to host a speaker for a house meeting. When George arrived on campus, he took Fred with him when he spoke in the fraternities, a potent experience for Fred, especially when George told the fraternity men at one house that "Fred would be a good guy to come in here once a week and lead a Bible study." Eleven men were interested, and with George's help Fred began his biggest growing experience to date.

In 1960 Fred went on to Michigan State University to do graduate work.[3] He said, "It was like dying and going to heaven": Inter-Varsity at MSU had two thriving chapters. The graduate group had strong leadership and, in consultation with staffer Don Vinkemulder, Fred decided he would spend his energies working with the undergraduates, trying to get a Bible study going in every men's residence hall on campus. Grad student Jeanette Sprik would do the same in the women's dorms. Together they cut a wide swath of witness in the dorms. The next fall (1962) new growth in numbers encouraged students to form a third Inter-Varsity chapter at MSU, one of the first attempts at multiple chapters on one campus.

Fred Wagner never did become the engineer he planned to be. His regional director saw his natural gifts for student ministry and urged him to join staff. Fred said, "If Inter-Varsity wants me, then I'm going to get more out of this than the kingdom is. I'm going to receive more than I'm going to be able to give, and if that's okay with Inter-Varsity, then I'm going to go for it." In 1962 he was assigned to work in the Northwest; he married Carol Streeter;[4] they raised a family in Portland, Oregon, and are still there, having made student work a life career.

The Wagners' story has a familiar flavor. With the change of a few details, it could be told again and again; in a sense, it is the Inter-Varsity story. They, and others like them, scarcely missed a beat in their pursuit of God as the 1960s got under way.

"Tonight I saw God's glory," wrote staff member Miriam Lemcke in the spring of 1961. She described what happened at the semi-annual membership meeting of the Inter-Varsity chapter at University of California, Santa Barbara. The chapter president lit a large candle on the table at the front of the room and then read the Basis of Faith and the purposes of IVCF to the group of about thirty-five students. He explained that anyone who wanted to join this group should come to the front, light a candle from the large candle and then give a personal statement about faith in Christ. When he turned out the lights, leaving only the single candle glowing, the room was utterly still. Then a young woman stepped forward and lit her candle. "I want to thank this group for all you've meant to me. I received Christ the week before final exams. I want to help spread the gospel on our campus." She had barely reached her seat when a fellow left his. "I thought I was a Christian when I came to college, then I met some of you in Inter-Varsity. Now I know that Jesus is my personal Savior." A woman stepped forward, lit her candle and said, "Just a little over two months ago I became a Christian. I want to state publicly that I want God to use me in this fellowship."

Students wanting to speak began to form a line. One said, "When I came to the IV meeting last week, I knew the difference between right and wrong, but I couldn't do the right. When the speaker was through, I gave my life to Christ. . . . I came in without hope, but now I have hope. I want to join this fellowship and grow."

A woman lit her candle and said, "I went into a friend's room to ask her what a Christian was, expecting a two-minute answer. Instead she asked me if I would like to read the Bible with her daily. After a month I couldn't go on any longer. I knew I had to commit myself to Christ." Fifteen brand-new Christians added their light to the chapter that night, the result of God's work in using the friendships, Bible studies and prayer of faithful students in IVCF.[5]

2/Early Ministry to Black Students

Since 1958 Black staffworker[6] Ruth Lewis (Bentley) had been staffing the Black colleges in the Southeast. By 1961 Regional Director Burton Harding reported that he saw clear signs of a breakthrough in the work, especially in the encouraging weekend conference for Black students held in Georgia. In North Carolina, a state where this was possible, fifteen Blacks came to a regular Inter-Varsity weekend conference. North Carolina staff member Jim Raines spoke to about twenty fellows who gathered in a dorm in Greensboro, and several responded to the claims of Christ. About forty came to hear Burt Harding at Morris College in Atlanta. Ruth Lewis led two girls to Christ in Black colleges in Atlanta. Half of the students studying in the U.S. from Africa were located in the Southeast, and Harding reported that the staff team made a special effort to reach them by sponsoring a series of evening teas, followed by a discussion. "It is only a beachhead," Harding said, "but it is an encouraging response and a ministry that needs to be expanded."

For years the Inter-Varsity students in Georgia had used the Future Farmers of America (FFA) camp for their weekend retreats. In 1962 Ruth Lewis reported that a group of Black students were planning on coming to the conference. Burt Harding visited the manager of the FFA camp and explained that an integrated group would be using the camp site. The manager, Mr. Dickerson, said, "Burt, I would rather lose any other group than yours. We like your group because you always leave the place in good shape and are fine to work with, but we have a rule which I must follow, and we cannot accept any integrated groups." Burt replied, "Then we'll just have to find another location," and proceeded to do just that. But Dickerson went to his supervisors and said, "I've lost one of my finest groups because of our policy of nonintegration. Times have changed and we need to change." And they did change. Dickerson phoned Burt before the spring conference and asked him to bring the group back to the FFA camp. Whether or not the motivation for change was as high as he might have wished, Harding said, "When you do the thing that is right in principle you become an agent of change in society, even in small ways."

3/Renewed Commitment

In January 1960 the entire staff of the Fellowship gathered at Bear Trap Ranch for a national conference on "Inter-Varsity's Distinctive Mission in the United States Today." General Secretary Stacey Woods, National Secretary Charles Hummel, *HIS* editor Joe Bayly, Missions Secretary Eric Fife and International Students Secretary Paul Little developed the theme in morning sessions in what proved to be a stirring renewal for the staff. The Fellowship was twenty years old, and along with an affirmation of the philosophy of the work of IV, staff hammered out a statement which they called *The Bear Trap Statement of Faith.* Joe Bayly presented the first draft as an expansion of the original Basis of Faith, to clarify the theological position in a day of shifting theological emphases. The staff adopted it as their affirmation of Christian conviction. It did not replace the original, more tersely stated Basis of Faith, but became a significant supplemental document.

We receive the Bible in its entirety, and the Bible alone, as the Word of God written, inspired by God, and therefore the inerrant rule of faith and practice.

We accept the formulations of Biblical doctrine represented by the large areas of agreement in such historic declarations as the Apostles' and Nicene Creeds, the Augsburg, Westminister and New Hampshire Confessions, and the Thirty-Nine Articles of Religion.

We desire to safeguard individual Christian liberty to differ in areas of doctrine not common to these formulations, provided that any interpretation is sincerely believed to arise from and is based upon the Bible.

In view of contemporary theological discussion, we explicitly affirm our belief in the following specific Biblical doctrines, even though they are stated in the historic confessional formulations:

(1) The one true God, existing eternally in unity and in the tri-personality of Father, Son and Holy Spirit.

(2) The unique nature of man as a moral and rational being created in the image of God, and the historic fall of man into sin, bringing all men under divine condemnation.

(3) The full deity and true humanity of Jesus Christ, His personal pre-existence, virgin birth and sinlessness.

(4) The historic death of the Lord Jesus Christ for our sins, a voluntary, substitutionary sacrifice, and His bodily resurrection.

(5) The justification of sinners by the Lord Jesus Christ through faith alone.

(6) The deity and personality of the Holy Spirit, the effective agent both in regeneration and in that holy living which is the necessary evidence of true faith.

(7) The fellowship of Christians in the Church, which embraces Biblical doctrine, worships the true God, obeys the Lord's commands to baptize and to remember Him at the table, exercises discipline, adorns its profession by holiness and love of fellow believers, and proclaims the Christian gospel to the world.

(8) The visible return of the Lord Jesus Christ in glory.

(9) The resurrection of the redeemed to enjoyment of God forever in His presence, and the resurrection of the unredeemed to judgment and everlasting punishment.

4/Growing in the Early 60s

InterVarsity Press moved its editorial offices, formerly located in Havertown, Pennsylvania, to the Chicago area in 1960. That year also marked the appearance of the long-awaited *anywhere Songs* edited by Paul Beckwith, containing hymns, spirituals and camp songs. The first quality paperback (also the lead title in the new IVP series in Contemporary Christian Thought) was published—*Christianity and Philosophy* by Arthur F. Holmes of Wheaton College. Two volumes imported from British Inter-Varsity in the Great Doctrines of the Bible series were printed: *The Return of Jesus Christ* by G. T. Manley and *Spirit of the Living God* by Leon Morris. *Standing Orders,* by the staff of Nurses Christian Fellowship and two Bible study guides, *First Century Christians* and Marilyn Kunz's *Patterns for Living with God,* were published. Elizabeth Leake succeeded Joe Bayly as manager of InterVarsity Press in 1959,[7] and Bayly became the full-time editor of *HIS*. In 1960 the Evangelical Press Association again named *HIS* magazine the "Magazine of the Year," in addition to "Best Youth Magazine" of the year, and bestowed two art awards.

The first national faculty conference took place in Madison, Wisconsin, in August of 1961, with John Alexander as chairman of the conference committee. W. Melville Capper of Bristol University in Great Britain gave four addresses and other faculty members, ministers and staff participated as speakers and small group leaders in considering the theme, "The Christian Professor in the University." Alexander hosted a second conference in the summer of 1962 attended by faculty members from 35 secular colleges in thirteen states and Canada. Leonard Verduin, chaplain of the Christian Reformed Chapel at the University of Michigan spoke on the doctrine of man.

The Inter-Varsity chapters at Harvard and Radcliffe held a mission in February 1961, with Kenneth F. Prior, vicar of St. Paul's, London as the missioner. Charles Hummel spoke at the mission planned by the University of Hawaii in late 1960. An evangelistic thrust at Duke University resulted in an estimated fifty per cent of the entire undergraduate student body hearing the gospel. When the news of the Duke mission spread to Woman's College in Greensboro, North Carolina, students planned a similar event that led to about 300 students hearing the gospel. One hundred and twenty-five asked for booklets explaining how to become a Christian. On one campus after another, staff participated in evangelistic dorm meetings and these became "harvesting" times for students who had been witnessing to their friends. As the sixties began, the staff saw only the beginnings of what would later erupt on campus.

5/Administration

Organizationally, however, Inter-Varsity began to experience its own state of confusion. Although they didn't have an immediate effect on most chapters across the country, the events of the first half of the decade were significant in the lives of those who had made full-time commitments to the Fellowship. The first great loss was in January 1960 when Joseph T. Bayly resigned as the editor of *HIS* to form his own publishing company.[8] It was more than losing a gifted editor; the movement lost an influential senior man whose input into the tone of the Fellowship had been invaluable. His Christian character, commitment to the trustworthiness and authority of Scripture, and theological perception of trends within the church were a gift to the Fellowship. Joe was an independent thinker who was willing to take a lonely stand on principle. His humility and deep personal concern for his colleagues were greatly valued by the senior staff council. He modeled a practical kind of godliness as a friend, a father and a husband that made others seek him out for counsel.

During 1959, under the leadership of IVCF Board President Gordon VanWylen, Stacey Woods was asked to choose an area of leadership in which to serve full time. He chose the international work of the IFES, which meant he would resign as general secretary of IVCF in the U.S. at the end of the academic year. It was a hard decision for Stacey to make, but it was an obvious one, both for the work in the U.S. and the world. As much as the Fellowship would miss his dynamic leadership, the demands of work in the U.S. necessitated a full-time general secretary.

The impressive growth of national movements related to the International Fellowship of Evangelical Students increasingly called for his unique skills. Stacey Woods was a true pioneer, more than a manager of a movement that had expansion potential on all fronts. He resigned from his post in June 1960, and was named general secretary emeritus by the board. He moved the IFES offices to the Philadelphia area until 1962 when he chose to establish the IFES headquarters in Lausanne, Switzerland.

The board's search committee appointed by VanWylen failed to find a suitable candidate by the time of Stacey Woods's departure. In June 1960 the board gave Charles Hummel, who was already supervising the work under Stacey Woods, a one-year appointment as interim general director. They dropped the term *secretary* and substituted for it the more descriptive title (for Americans) of *director*.[9] The term *interim* rather than *acting* was specifically chosen to make it clear that the board had no intention of considering the appointment permanent. Since influential board members viewed Charlie's loyalty to Stacey Woods as a "rubber stamp" relationship through which the latter would try to continue control of IVCF, they wanted an outside director to make a clean sweep. "On the one hand," Hummel said, "they wanted me in one year to 'fix the Fellowship,' to get it ready for the new director; at the same time they wouldn't approve significant creative action that might accomplish this goal."

The board's minimal support, coupled with Stacey's departure, encouraged several department heads to resist the interim director's leadership and make the lame-duck year extraordinarily difficult for him.[10] He faced opposition instead of cooperation. Nevertheless, the willingness of Paul Little to take on interim supervision of the regional directors gave Hummel some administrative relief. Hummel's leadership proved a time of stabilization and transition. On campuses across the country good things were happening. The winter national staff conference at Bear Trap Ranch proved to be an experience of renewal of purpose and unity.

6/Missions Emphasis

Every summer since 1954, students interested in missions had gathered at Cedar Campus for missionary training camp (MTC), led by the missionary secretary, David Adeney. When Eric Fife inherited MTC, he continued the program somewhat reluctantly. But he soon saw the potential of the camp for mission leaders as well as students. He found that the coming together of key mission leaders provided an opportunity for sharpening new ideas. Arthur Glasser, U.S. home director for the Overseas Missionary Fellowship, had been coming to MTC since 1954, investing his creativity into making the camp effective. Now he began to brainstorm with Eric Fife about plans for the missionary convention. These two men experienced "iron sharpening iron" in their friendship, and the Fellowship benefited from it. Fife says that all of the innovations used at the Urbana missionary conventions were field-tested at MTC at Cedar Campus.

Missions interest had trailed off by the late fifties; the postwar boom in missions had ended. As he began to make plans for the 1961 IVCF Missions

Conference in Urbana, Eric Fife tried to diagnose the problem and find ways to bring back into center focus the missionary mandate of the church. By 1961 he had collaborated with Arthur Glasser to write *Missions in Crisis,* a book which explored the unparalleled disorder in world affairs and its significance in missions. The church had been placed on the defensive, they reasoned, by revolutions, nationalism, communism, racism and ecumenism. These would be the issues discussed at the next IVCF Student Missionary Convention.

The missionary convention was still relatively unknown in the early sixties. Comparatively few missionaries saw the strategic importance of attending; mission boards often failed to put the event high on their agenda. It was a public relations battle to get articles about the convention in Christian media, and tight finances plagued the planning operations for the convention.

Eric Fife's gift was preaching and prior to the 1961 convention, he traveled the length and breadth of Canada and the U.S. speaking about the lordship of Christ and the person and work of the Holy Spirit. He stirred up students' Christian commitment wherever he went, which turned out to be effective promotion for the missionary convention. He was also a popular speaker at church missionary conferences. Speaking to a large gathering at Moody Church in Chicago he said, "Inter-Varsity is the only youth movement that spends x amount of dollars a year simply to promote missions. Not our missions, because we don't send out missionaries, but your missions." In the end, the truth of these remarks sank in and turned the tide.

A common phrase used in mission presentations in the forties and fifties was "a missionary passion." Eric believed that almost all missionary appeals in the earlier decades were based on emotion. He felt it was important to reach the will by challenging the mind. Students needed to see that the finest brains could be exercised in pursuit of the missions cause. He went after speakers of that caliber for the 1961 convention, which had been postponed a year in the three-year cycle in the hopes that the University of Illinois Assembly Hall would be finished. But that hope was in vain; construction delays meant that IVCF was forced to use Huff Gymnasium for another convention.

However, the year's delay worked out to the advantage of both Eric and the Fellowship. Stacey Woods insisted that Eric take a trip to Latin America and Asia to expand his knowledge of the mission field. Since Fife's only previous exposure to overseas missions had been in North Africa, the variety of kinds of mission work in urban, jungle and rural settings greatly broadened his horizons and enriched his ministry to students.

Eric Fife planned to make five innovations in the 1961 missionary convention: (1) A plenary panel with key speakers who, under the pressure of time, would pour out information about the realities of mission work that would make the most lethargic student sit up and take notice. (2) A plenary forum, a question-and-answer time on critical issues in missions with key leaders. (3) Elective courses, one of which had to be evangelism, to stimulate students in their specific interests. (4) Missionaries would have their own special sessions. (5) Pastors also would meet in their own group. It was an exciting new agenda.

The plenary forum, as Fife envisioned it, could not be held because of the accoustical problems in Huff Gymnasium. Instead, five smaller forums were held around the campus, handling some of the questions that came out of the plenary sessions. The other innovations were put into place. The theme of this sixth IVCF Student Missionary Convention was "Commission—Conflict—Commitment." *HIS* editor Paul Fromer[11] ran a series of articles on missions throughout the spring and fall of 1960 to get students talking about mission issues. The most striking of these was a series of debates by Kenneth Pike, professor of linguistics and member of Wycliffe Bible Translators, and Arthur Glasser on mission strategy. Pike supported the strategy of reaching into hidden language groups with tribal work; Glasser advocated outreach to major population groups who could then reach into their own tribal areas. Not only were the articles stimulating, but the feedback kept *HIS* readers turning first to the letters-to-the-editor pages in each issue. InterVarsity Press kept *Missions in Crisis* in print and added *Man's Peace: God's Glory*.[12] The momentum for missions was picking up as 5400 students arrived at Urbana, an increase of fifty per cent over the last convention.

Eugene Nida (secretary for translations for the American Bible Society and an accomplished linguist who had been an early member of Michigan Christian Fellowship at the University of Michigan), Clyde Taylor (executive director of the Evangelical Foreign Missions Association) and Arthur Glasser made up the plenary panel. They poured out an absorbing mixture of up-to-date ideas, information and frank challenges. Every morning each man spoke briefly on the topic of the day. One student commented that "It sounds like the morning paper edited by the apostle Paul." Others said, "I've never heard anything like it." It was electric, mind-stretching and demanded the best from the students.

Festo Kivengere, an African church leader and later a Bishop in the Anglican Church in Uganda, gave a call for honesty before God in recounting the story in Genesis of Jacob's deception of his father Isaac. "Do not say you are Esau when you are Jacob," he warned. Paul Lindell of the World Mission Prayer League, spoke on servant leadership, saying, "There will always be a place for a servant." Subodh Sahu, an evangelist and assistant pastor of the Carey Memorial Church in Calcutta, in telling the story of his conversion said, "All that I had He took; all that He had has been given to me in Christ." David Adeney, IFES regional secretary for the Far East, was the closing speaker. He reminded students, "There is one thing worse than falling: failing to get up." The speakers and resource people made an impressive list: Billy Graham, S. Barton Babbage, Raymond Buker, William Nagenda, George Cowan and Norton Sterrett plus many other team members. Students gave an offering for student work of $10,000, and an offering to help make up for convention deficits of $7,000.

Another important leader was present: Charles H. Troutman, the new general director of the Inter-Varsity Christian Fellowship in the U.S. He gave the final Bible exposition and summarized the convention for the students, "The church is in conflict; the days ahead are uncertain; but we have confidence in the Sovereign Lord who said, 'I will build my church.' "

7/Leadership

When the board began to process the choosing of a leader for the Fellowship after Stacey Woods resigned in 1960, the name of Charles H. Troutman came up repeatedly. Many of the staff considered him the classic student worker, a friend whose insights into student work had helped to form the Fellowship in its first years. Troutman, for his part, was seeking God's next appointment for him. He felt he had completed his mission in Australia. On first inquiries about his willingness to come back to lead the IVCF in the States, Charles had been wary. He agreed to come to the States to discuss the matter with the board. He had been candid about the fact that administration was not his strongest asset. He would need help in that area if he were to accept an invitation to be general director. In fact, he made the appointment of a director of business affairs a primary condition of his acceptance.

Letters of reference from Australia confirmed Troutman's concern.

Frankly, I would be sorry both for the IVCF/USA and for Charles if he were to take on the job. . . . Charles is unexcelled as a spiritual counsellor for students and staff leaders. He has a wide general knowledge of affairs and of the intellectual climate, and is very helpful in the way he appreciates current trends and gives guidance. . . . If then you have room for a senior spiritual counsellor who would be responsible to your general director to advise him and stand behind him, Charles Troutman would be ideal—a sort of elder statesman.

Charles is such a generous and loving spirit that I feel it would be a pain and a grief to him if he were to be plunged into any situation where there is lack of definition of responsibility between key people or where senior people are prone to make strong criticisms or bring pressures to bear.[13]

Other recommendations contained essentially the same concerns. The consensus, including that of Troutman himself, was that the board should give Troutman a more student-related post, rather than a purely administrative one. Finally, the board voted to call Charles Troutman as the general director, but they did not provide a structure to support his known weakness. As for Troutman, his love for student work governed his decision; like Stacey Woods, he had a founder's love for the movement.

Charles Hummel was among the staff most enthusiastic over the board's decision to bring Charles Troutman back to the movement. Remembering Troutman's counsel and encouragement to him as a new staff member in 1950, Charlie looked forward to serving as field director under the new leader. In July of 1961 Charlie wrote to Troutman:

While I am convinced that God is bringing you to the kingdom for such a time as this, I do not need to tell you that the next year or two will probably be the greatest challenge to your ability and, in some respects, extremely difficult. You come to the IVCF as it finds itself in a period of transition. On the student level a rethinking of our whole work is under way. . . . In the realm of public relations and stewardship we have largely drifted during the last decade. . . . In some respects this is our most urgent problem—a rethinking of the whole problem of financing the student work at a level of almost half a million dollars.[14]

Inter-Varsity Christian Fellowship was, in many ways, a different organization than the one Charles had left eight years earlier. The numbers of chapters, students and staff made the movement more complex, with new organizational layers of management. The pioneer days were past. The growth potential was impressive, but the organization needed leadership. As soon as Troutman arrived in the States, some in the Christian community gave him an alarming picture of Inter-Varsity and its leadership.[15] Charles Troutman said that some on the board led him to believe that if he did not come, IVCF would not survive. Their reports of the dire straits of the Fellowship would have surprised the senior field staff.

The campus staff would have given a more realistic report. This difference in understanding took some time to discover and blocked communication and unity between the general director and the senior staff council (SSC). It may well have kept Troutman from embracing the leadership team and taking them into his confidence from the first. On October 4, 1961, he wrote, "Needless to say, the work here in the U.S. is baffling and staggering and complicated. The sheer size of it is enough to keep me from being able to grasp the situation with any degree of ease and accuracy. On the other hand, I think there are spasmodic spots throughout the country where the Spirit of God is working in an unusual way."[16]

One of Troutman's first concerns was the restrictive budgetary policies that kept the Fellowship from growing. The financial policy required that each year's budget be no greater than the income of the preceding year. Increased income was often eaten up in increased costs, so that new staff could not be appointed. Growth took second place to maintaining the status quo. Troutman insisted that staff salaries be guaranteed; it was not right to fund the organization by canceling modest staff salaries when income failed to equal expenses. He proposed a policy which stated that at the close of the fiscal year (June 30), all unpaid expenses, including salaries, would be carried over as expenses into the next year's budget. The board approved this change.

The first detailed IVCF Financial Policy Statement containing this change was produced in 1962. Other sections in the policy statement included: responsibility for raising funds was delegated to the general director,

who may be assisted by a public relations director or stewardship secretary. Although the primary function of the regional director and other field staff is the campus work, they shall cooperate in stewardship activities. . . . Student chapters shall not be required to support the national work (although they are encouraged to inform parents, friends and churches of the work). . . . Students may be encouraged to support a specific regional project, but only with the approval of the general director. . . . Student chapters shall not solicit funds from off-campus sources for their campus program, except when approved by their regional director. . . . Student chapters are encouraged to support IFES.[17]

The first modest pension plan for employees was executed in 1963.[18] For the year 1962-63 monthly staff salaries were raised to $200 for single staff and $325 for married staff members. Fifty-eight staff members of IVCF, NCF and FMF visited student chapters on 730 campuses.

From the beginning Charles Troutman was aware of some conflict between his plans for the movement and the board's vision. Some on the board defined Troutman's function as one of "restoring IVCF to the effectiveness of the Old Days as a staff fellowship." Troutman told the board that he and Stacey had often talked of future growth, and that they had agreed that the solution was regional autonomy—a plan he hoped to put into action. At its first meeting in September 1961, however, the executive committee recommended that he not make any major changes in structure or personnel for two years.

Charles Troutman wanted Inter-Varsity to continue to be a national movement with national policies, budget and direction. At the same time he wanted the execution of policy and program to function at the most local levels possible. Philosophically he felt the movement had become too centralized; he wanted more initiative to come from the field; that is, he wanted to *regionalize* the movement. He planned to reduce the number of regions from nine to five, based on geographic and cultural criteria: East, South, Central, Southwest and West. Each regional director was to become a field director, reporting to Charles, but having authority to develop initiative and recruit area directors and staff. Regional directors would then begin to raise money for additional staff. He believed it was important that creative, spiritual staff members have the freedom to find the means to meet the unique situations in their areas of responsibility. That was the style most closely parallel to the academic community and was the way in which universities treated faculty and staff. He began to implement this policy in early 1963.

Troutman had a keen sense of the importance of penetrating the university and wanted to build around chapters a supporting structure of alumni, professional groups, friends, associate staff, speakers and area councils who would help students in the task of penetrating the multiversities. In addition to his *Seven Pillars,* Charles Troutman wrote papers on *Sustained University Evangelism, The University Chapter Goals* and other smaller pieces. Charles Hummel's book *Campus Christian Witness,* first published in 1958, contained valuable information for student chapter leaders. At the May 1962 board meeting, Troutman discussed the preparation of a much-needed training manual for student leaders.[19] Penetrating the university meant, among other things, an emphasis on the original concept of Inter-Varsity as an "evangelizing fellowship."

A diagram circulated during Troutman's leadership clearly outlined the distinctive vision and ministry of Inter-Varsity. The movement was to be "in the university," penetrating it from within. IVCF was a student mission, not a mission to students. The campus was not a fishing pond for converts; IVCF was not a group of people making forays onto the campus; it was an evangelizing fellowship *within* the university.

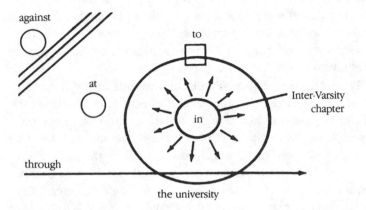

This diagram was published in *HIS* magazine, January 1966, as part of an article written by Warner Hutchinson. In the article, which was written as a letter to a student, he said,

I could be formal and say that each student chapter is autonomous. What that really means is "No one else is going to do it for you." Some people don't think students are mature enough to be responsible for so important a task. . . . *You are mature enough, Bob, to be obedient to God in your present circumstances as a student.* God can win some of your friends to Christ through you. To prepare you for further service in postuniversity days, He will use the experiences learned through having this real (not make-believe) responsibility of university witness. . . . The focus is you on your campus obeying God, as thousands of students have done before you and will do after you.

8/Continuing to Grow

Inter-Varsity on Campus, an informative film showing IVCF's ministry among students, was a first for the Fellowship and widely distributed in the spring of 1962. Filmed at the University of Michigan, the black-and-white documentary was made up of real-life shots of students participating in their weekly meeting and in small group Bible studies. A variety of evangelistic outreach opportunities, including fraternity house discussions, were depicted. Staff from across the country participated, giving a national feel to the production. The film was Inter-Varsity's most extensive attempt since its founding in 1940 to share its ministry with the Christian public.

Paul Little took a team of thirty-five students to the beaches of Ft. Lauderdale in the spring of 1962, the first of many beach evangelism missions since then. The city fathers of Ft. Lauderdale enthusiastically approved IVCF's offer to come and help reach the more than 10,000-plus students expected during Easter week. "Sharp in their memory was last year's Easter vacation debauchery: mobs of students roaming the streets, mocking the hundreds of special police who had been rushed in at a cost of almost $50,000."[20]

Inter-Varsity students set up a large umbrella strategically located between the beach's largest bar and the ocean, which became the site of two brief talks each afternoon on such subjects as "Life: Meaningful or Meaningless." Fifty to seventy-five students usually came to listen to the talk and then participated in a twenty-minute free-for-all discussion with the speaker. Inter-Varsity students moved in to initiate conversations with the listeners who seemed most open. Throughout the day the team fanned out across the beaches in pairs to talk to the "sun-worshipers" on spring break from northern colleges. Each night they showed a Moody science film. The team had worthwhile contacts with about 1,500 students. Some professed newfound faith. Dozens took booklets. A few signed up for a Bible correspondence course. The Inter-Varsity team felt they had learned more than they had given and returned to their campuses to witness with new boldness. In addition, projects began in places like Estes Park, the West Coast beaches and other resort areas.

The IVCF chapter at the University of Chicago sponsored Billy Graham in the spring of 1962, during the Chicago Crusade. Authorities at the university had to be persuaded to permit the student group to invite Graham. Once he was invited, the Divinity School closed the chapel to him and none of the denominational groups would support the meeting. But this negative reaction did not deter the effectiveness of the meeting.

Between fifty and sixty conversions in New England colleges were reported during the 1961-62 school year; of these, twenty students were from Massachusetts Institute of Technology (MIT). "These were not mere decisions, but students who have given evidence of knowing the Lord and going on with him—and this in an area where there has been no full-time regional director."[21] Ten students and an assistant dean became Christians at the University of Wisconsin. Leighton Ford, of the Billy Graham team, conducted a five-day mission for IVCF at the University of Georgia in January of 1963 where 2700 students heard a clear presentation of the gospel.

In addition, the staff team spoke at forty-five small group meetings. The Colorado School of Mines chapter held a three-day mission in January 1963, during which they reached about forty per cent of the campus with the gospel. One hundred students signed cards indicating they were interested in more information. At the University of Pennsylvania an estimated 275 students were faced with the claims of Christ on their lives through presentations in dorms and fraternities. Three students became Christians and thirty-two asked for more information.

The University of Michigan chapter held a campus mission with Billy Graham February 11-13, 1964, to crowds ranging from 3,000 to 4,200. Hundreds of students came forward, and nearly 300 signed cards for follow-up. A team of ninety IV students had the goal of contacting each person who signed a card within forty-eight hours. Two hundred fifty professors came to a faculty luncheon.

On February 18 the first of three meetings was held at Harvard with Billy Graham as the missioner. Attendance rose each evening from 700 to 900 students. The after-meeting was held a block away from the lecture hall, and between 150 to 350 came on successive nights. About seventy-five students made declarations of a personal commitment to Christ. A team of twenty-four students spent the summer in evangelistic outreach at the New York World's Fair in the summer of 1964, headquartering at IVCF's conference center, Hudson House. This recitation of events could go on; they are representative of campus activity in the early 1960s.

9/The Charismatic Movement

The March 29, 1963, issue of *Time* magazine carried a story about the Inter-Varsity chapter at Yale called "Blue Tongues." The story related that twenty students "in the secular, skeptical confines of Yale University report that they can pray in the spontaneous outpouring of syllables that sound like utter babble to most listeners, but has a special meaning to the 'gifted.' The GlossoYalies are far from being Holy Rollers. One is a Roman Catholic, and most of the others are Protestants who belong to the sobersided Inter-Varsity Christian Fellowship. . . . Five have Phi Beta Kappa keys and six plan to enter the ministry after graduation."

News media across the country picked up the story, and members of the Christian public began asking staff about the matter of Inter-Varsity's stand on the issue of tongues. Charles Troutman sent a telegram to *Time* magazine which read:

INTER-VARSITY CHRISTIAN FELLOWSHIP THANKS TIME FOR ITS SO-BERSIDED DESCRIPTION OF GLOSSOLALIA AT YALE. SPEAKING IN TONGUES HAS OCCURRED IN ONLY A FEW OF OUR 300 CHAPTERS. THE EXPERIENCE OF THE YALE MEN APPEARS TO BE A VALID (IF UNUSUAL) EXPRESSION OF CHRISTIAN WORSHIP, AND WE COMMEND THEM FOR THEIR WISDOM IN AVOIDING EMOTIONAL EXCESS. THE CHAPTER'S PRIMARY PURPOSE, HOWEVER, IS TO CONFRONT YALE STUDENTS WITH THE LIVING CHRIST.[22]

Time magazine did not publish this or any of the other hundreds of letters the magazine said it received on the subject.

This charismatic activity on the Yale campus had begun quite unexpectedly in September of 1962 when several students shared their summer discipling experiences in various parts of the country. During the following months similiar charismatic expressions occurred in Inter-Varsity chapters at Penn State, Kent State (Ohio), Indiana University and Purdue (Indiana). Most IVCF leaders had a theological bias against the movement, but did not want to squelch any new work God might be doing. Staff members were caught in the controversy that arose over this issue and felt they needed official guidance since this doctrinal issue was not in the Basis of Faith.

In April 1963 General Director Charles Troutman wrote a memorandum to all IVCF staff. He noted that "increasingly and inevitably Inter-Varsity is being drawn into one of the modern expressions of a healing-tongue-prophecy movement." He emphasized the interdenominational character of IVCF and its primary task of reaching students for Christ. "Over the years our policy has been deliberately to set aside as non-essentials *to our task* such matters as the mode of baptism, the nature of the Lord's Supper, and speaking in tongues." He stated:

If this is a movement of God for all his children—even though it may be abused—then we want to be part of it. If this is not a movement of God, we want to help those of our brethren who have become enmeshed. If there is a misplaced emphasis, we want to bring a balance. We must in no way hinder the Spirit of God from working in individuals as He wills.

He concluded his memorandum with practical suggestions for the field staff. Inter-Varsity's official stance was summarized by the statement, "Require not; forbid not."

The students from Yale registered for chapter camp at Cedar Campus in June of 1963. From the first they were eager to share with other students their experience with tongues and did so around the table at mealtimes and in private conversations. When they asked for a public meeting, Director Keith Hunt asked them to table their request until after Elwyn Davies, the speaker at the camp, had given two optional session Bible studies on the person and work of the Holy Spirit. About ninety per cent of the camp came to these special sessions which included time for questions and discussion. The Yale students were cooperative, earnest and had a winsome eagerness about their lives. It was pointed out several times that the gifts of the Holy Spirit are not shortcuts to spiritual growth and witness, and that the chief purpose of the Holy Spirit is to enable Christians to move into a deeper degree of holiness. The camp was buzzing for the whole week about the subject, and many students were obviously interested in signs and wonders in their lives. This marked the beginning of growing interest in the charismatic movement by students across the country.[23]

10/Administration—Part 2

Many good things were happening among students—conversions, student leadership, campus vision—but organizationally things were slow in coming together for Charles Troutman. His failure to act swiftly (partly mandated by the board's request that he wait two years before making major changes) cost him the confidence of his staff team. From the beginning Charles says he felt his plan to make each region essentially autonomous, met with resistance from people who would lose power by the decentralization. Instead of the encouragement he needed, he felt the resistance of the senior men who were stationed in headquarters.[24] He did not expect this. In the summer of 1962 he wrote to Warner Hutchinson in New Zealand, "A week from tomorrow we begin twelve days at Elburn, Illinois, in staff council meetings. I must confess to a great deal of concern. I am not sure how many of the men are with me. Having talked to me about one another here in the office, I am no exception, and I know some of them have complained to the board about me. We are a long way from a fellowship, yet the habits of ten years are not easily broken."[25]

His relationship with the board was very different than the support he had experienced in Australia. He moved cautiously, trying to come to conclusions that would satisfy everyone, reluctant to move people who had been his friends and loyal to the work. Whether the opposition he sensed stymied communication, or whether his natural abilities failed him, some began to grumble. Troutman's perceptions about the movement did not always match that of the other leaders. He did not communicate clearly with his team; differences were not openly or sufficiently discussed. Correspondence from staff was typified by words such as *confused, misunderstanding, uneasiness.*

In late 1962 he brought back former staff member Warner Hutchinson, who was then general secretary of Inter-Varsity in New Zealand, to be the regional director in the East. That move displaced George Ensworth,[26] who was the Middle Atlantic regional director and long-time staffworker. Because Troutman didn't have all the organizational pieces in place, he did not share his overall plan with the SSC.[27] He appeared indecisive and often seemed to change his mind. That gave his detractors "grist for the mill." His lack of clarity was confusing to the SSC, even though they went on record in March of 1963 stating that there was no lack of confidence in Charles as a person.

The IVCF Board had heard from Charles Troutman himself, as well as from other references, that administrative help would be needed. In the meantime the presidency of the board had changed from an academician (VanWylen) to a businessman (Erickson). Since Troutman wanted administrative help, the executive committee of the board assumed he would take care of that himself. Yet when Troutman had departed from IVCF-USA for Australia in 1952, the board was still appointing staff members and making crucial policy decisions. Troutman was used to the Australian model of top-level leadership in which board members gave encouragement and support to the general secretary, conferring regularly with him about major decisions. Although several offered advice from time to time, the U.S. board members operated on the principle of delegation.[28] They assumed Troutman was doing fine until problems became obvious in 1963.

In May of 1963 Board President Wallace Erickson wrote to Charles, suggesting that he might be helped if he could share the leadership with qualified people within the movement. Charles wrote in reply, "I do feel the need of a body of staff members with whom I can share leadership more closely than the Staff Council provides. Of the department heads, Paul Little (international students) and Tressie Myers (NCF) . . . of the regional directors, Warner Hutchinson, Jim Nyquist and Keith Hunt . . . I realize that this proposal eliminates two men who have expressed themselves strongly against my policies and leadership . . . Jim McLeish (comptroller) and Eric Fife (missions director). They bring a great deal to the SSC, but I am opposed to either man as a member of the staff executive committee." He went on to say that "we must jealously guard the university character of our movement." Troutman felt that experience had proven it unwise to place non-university people in decision-making roles, since the focus of the work of IVCF is centered on the campus.[29]

In July 1963, as they traveled to the board meetings at Cedar Campus, Wallace Erickson, Allen Mathis and Stanley Block came up with a plan to reorganize the movement and presented it to the rest of the board. The new plan was discussed and approved without consulting the senior staff council. Jim Nyquist and Keith Hunt were asked to give up their regional student work and come into headquarters—Jim Nyquist as an administrative assistant and Keith Hunt as director of development. Charlie Hummel would take on Keith Hunt's region (Michigan, Indiana, Ohio and Kentucky) half-time in addition to continuing his work with alumni and faculty as graduate director. Paul Little was assigned special projects and evangelism. Jim McLeish had been made the comptroller following the retirement of W. E. C. Petersen. Understandably the staff involved felt like pawns being moved on a chessboard; nevertheless, they undertook their new roles with vigor for the sake of the work. The senior staff council became the staff advisory committee (SAC) in this new structure.[30] The SAC consisted of Paul Byer, James Nyquist, Keith Hunt, Burton Harding, Charles Hummel, Paul Little, Paul Fromer, Elizabeth Leake (IVP), Eric Fife, Warner Hutchinson, Tressie Myers and James McLeish.

In the end, the administration was not allowed to solve its own problems. In March 1964, before the new plan had opportunity to prove itself,[31] the executive committee of the board agreed to hire an executive assistant and director of InterVarsity Press. Board President Wallace Erickson[32] chose Richard Wolff,[33] a bright, aggressive man whose abrasive manner soon alienated almost every one in the office. In fairness to Wolff, he was given a bleak picture of the state of Inter-Varsity and told by Erickson, who greatly admired his gifts, to go in with a strong hand and take care of the situation.

In the beginning, Charles Troutman welcomed Wolff, believing this was at last the help he had asked for. He expected that Wolff would work with him, rather than against him. In May Erickson wrote a letter to the board saying, "Richard Wolff is doing an excellent job," and that he looked to the future with great enthusiasm because many of "our basic problems are being solved."

It soon became obvious to both Troutman and the members of SAC that Erickson and Wolff were acting independently of the general director, the staff council, and even the board. The board had authorized the sale of the headquarters building at 1519 N. Astor. Troutman got a buyer and had a contract for its sale. He also had a contract which included a gift of two acres of land in the expanding suburb of Oakbrook for a new headquarters for Inter-Varsity.[34] He presented these to Erickson, along with an extensive plan for reorganization of the work, early in the spring of 1964. No action was taken on any of these important documents from the general director, and Troutman did not know whether Erickson showed them to the executive committee.[35] Troutman felt by-passed again and again. Neither he nor the SAC could figure out what was happening and why.

On June 27, 1964, the board executive committee authorized Board President Wallace Erickson to act as chief executive officer (CEO) for IVCF, a move that shocked other board members when they eventually heard the news. It soon became clear to the department heads and regional directors that Wolff and Erickson were taking over the control of IVCF, and that they did not understand student work and held misinformed assumptions about the organization.

In July 1964 Erickson circulated a paper to the board entitled *Basic Concepts in the Organization of IVCF,* in which he stated, "Our staff has been taught that organizationally a fellowship has no hierarchy, no levels of authority, and if its structure were to be drawn, it would be perfectly flat. Each member of this fellowship is on the same level before God. There are varying degrees of training, experience and seniority, but basically the youngest recruit and the most experienced senior are on the same level. . . . There is no chain of command and no line of authority. When problems arise, they are solved by gathering the brethren together in order to seek the will of God for the solution to the problem."[36]

To correct this situation and establish some structure, Erickson suggested that the movement no longer be called *"the Fellowship."* He wanted it called *Inter-Varsity,* which would give it a more corporate flavor. If the regional directors and the staff had seen this paper they would have wondered what organization it was describing. What seems amazing is that some members of the board accepted Erickson's analysis.[37] Margaret Haines was one of those who did not; she sent a strong letter of objection to other board members pleading that board members recognize that a Christian ministry is different from a business corporation.[38]

Wolff was made executive director; all department heads operated under him. His seeming disdain for the staff, as well as the history and the ethos of the Fellowship, threw the movement into disarray. Convinced of his own judgment and expertise, Wolff had plans to fire some of the most experienced and best-loved of the staff team. He went through staff members' files when they were out of the office and threw out papers he thought irrelevant. Morale had never been so low. The senior staff's perception was that Erickson (with approval of the executive committee)[39] and Wolff had moved into the leadership of IVCF, and that Erickson was acting without the approval of the whole board. It became clear to the staff that IVCF would be radically changed if Wolff stayed in control. This was not a struggle between Charles Troutman and Richard Wolff; the basic philosophy of the movement was threatened.

Early in the summer of 1964, soon after he had been named CEO, and without the knowledge of the full board, Wallace Erickson took Charles Troutman out to lunch and "asked him where and in what capacity he thought that, with the gifts God had given him and the experience he had in student work, he could be most useful." While Charles's resignation was not mentioned in this conversation, Charles considered it to be tantamount to an implied request for his resignation, "as general director, but not from the Fellowship." At a tense and confusing July board meeting, Charles Troutman offered to resign from the position of general director, effective after Urbana. "He agreed to stay on in his post until a successor was found. The board instructed its proper officers to seek for a successor."[40]

Every one in leadership knew a misery they had never known before, and those with the most urgent responsibilities were affected the most. Eric Fife was trying to execute plans for Urbana 64, and felt certain it would flop because of the emotional energy expended on relational problems within headquarters. *HIS* had listed the names of the staff teams since its first issue in 1941, but the fall issue in 1964 contained no staff listings because Paul Fromer refused to have Richard Wolff's name in the magazine. Department heads could no longer function responsibly or creatively. The staff held long prayer meetings, asking God for deliverance from continued harassment.

In late September 1964, at the staff advisory committee (SAC) meetings in Elburn, Illinois, Troutman fired Wolff. Wolff, however, said he reported to Erickson, not Troutman. On September 23, the twelve members of SAC wrote to the board and corporation: "Because of your interest, we believe it our duty to inform you that the present situation within IVCF is so grave that the movement as we have known it is jeopardized. The climate is such that most of us who are regional directors and department heads find it difficult to fulfill our ministry. A number are likely to be lost to the Fellowship if the basic character of the movement continues to change. The next few weeks are critical."[41] Troutman prepared a letter to the president of the board, dated October 2, 1964, in which he stated that he was relieving Richard Wolff of his duties in IVCF and suggested the conditions for termination of his employment. Among themselves, SAC members decided to pour their energies into making the '64 Student Missionary Convention a success. They agreed that, if the board did not act on Richard Wolff, they would resign en masse with Charles Troutman following Urbana.

Many of the staff went to trusted friends on the board to share their pain about the situation, wanting desperately to save the movement and not knowing what else to do. In a September 28 letter to board member Roy Horsey, Jim Nyquist stated the conclusions of the members of SAC—that Erickson and Wolff had taken control of IVCF—and objected to (1) Wolff's method of operation (particularly in his relationships), (2) his intent to change some vital aspects of IVCF's philosophy and (3) his hand-in-glove relationship with the president of the board. He lamented "Richard Wolff's inability to trust others, a desire for power, an impatient desire for efficiency which ignores people, and a disregard for proper organizational channels. Richard Wolff has looked for direction to Wallace Erickson, rather than to Charles Troutman."[42]

On September 28 Charles Hummel also wrote a letter to Roy Horsey—eight pages long—in which he analyzed his understanding of what had happened in IVCF and the ensuing tensions between board and staff. He traced the problem back to 1952 when Charles Troutman, along with other staff whose work accounted for over 40 years of experience, left the movement. The problem, said Hummel, went back to a lack of leadership which began when the board allowed Stacey Woods to give only part-time to the work, even though the senior staff council had asked for a full-time leader. He reviewed the powerless nature of his own interim position and the situation which had developed with Charles Troutman. No realistic provisions for effective leadership had been made. Hummel wrote,

One further observation: Sometimes Inter-Varsity has been likened to a business, at other times to a fellowship, and other times to a mission board. May I suggest that a more accurate analogy would be the university. . . . We are a university movement and in many ways our staff function with the freedom an academic person enjoys. Yet universities have found a way to combine academic freedom, the voice of the faculty in university affairs, and sound business management. . . . Nothing quite like academic freedom exists in either mission boards or businesses. While academic freedom can become anarchy and lack of responsibility, it need not necessarily turn out this way. Nor can a university be run completely as a business. Business employees do what they are told or they are fired. But a college president cannot either ignore his faculty or his student body in such a way and hope to survive.[43]

On September 29 James Shaw, a Harvard faculty man and member of the board of IVCF, wrote to fellow board members,

I have become greatly concerned about the clear inadequacy of information made available to the rest of the board and . . . the excessive number of major decisions made by the executive committee without consultation with or ratifications by the board, and the actual administration of substantial areas of responsibility by board members. . . . The oft-repeated statement that the senior staff has lost confidence in the judgment of the board seems to be fully justified. . . . Indeed the events of the past year have shaken my confidence in the board. I prayerfully ask if the time has come when the present board and its officers should resign and give the corporation a free hand to elect a new board and slate of officers in January at the annual meeting. . . . Despite my lack of information of all the problems at administrative and board levels, one thing I do know with complete assurance at the grass-roots level: the philosophy of Inter-Varsity's student-oriented and staff-counselled approach is right. This philosophy has been and will continue to be blessed by God in the United States and around the world.[44]

Charles Troutman said, "I do not have the personality to sustain continued confrontation." Although it was not clear if his July resignation came under duress, the staff advisory committee agreed that it was obvious that too much had happened for him to remain in his position.[45] Troutman had no recourse; at the October board meeting he voluntarily resigned as general director, effective after Urbana.[46] The special ad hoc study committee of the board, chaired by Roy Horsey, then recommended: (1) That the action . . . authorizing the president to act as chief executive officer (CEO) be rescinded; (2) that the board consider John Alexander for the position of general director; (3) that Charles Troutman be made associate general director with assignment to be worked out with the new general director; and (4) that the new general director work out the problems with Richard Wolff.

Troutman had already presented his letter regarding Wolff. After it was moved to approve the dismissal of Richard Wolff, "it was decided to call in the entire SAC to hear as many testimonies (about relationships with Wolff) as time would permit."[47]

At the October 1964 board meeting, Burton Harding, regional director for the Southeast, made the first presentation, followed by Paul Fromer, editor of *HIS*. Jim McLeish, comptroller, had been waiting for an opportunity to tell the board exactly what had been happening during these terrible months. Soon after he began to speak, he uncharacteristically burst into tears. The minutes read: "After three testimonies were heard, it was obvious that the emotional involvement was too great to continue."[48] The board had heard enough, but agreed to table the motion to dismiss Richard Wolff pending a thorough investigation. Troutman requested and received approval to relieve Wolff of all responsibilities, except for InterVarsity Press, until the board came to a decision.

In November the board accepted Richard Wolff's resignation, effective immediately; but with the note that "in appreciation of his fine work he remain on salary for the next three months." Burt Roberts, whom Wolff had brought in as office manager, left with him.

On Monday following that board meeting, Eric Fife, who had been out of town on Urbana business, phoned his assistant, Irene Kemis, to check on registrations for Urbana. When she heard his voice, she said, "Eric, Wolff is gone. Oh, praise the Lord. This whole thing is over."

Wallace Erickson is deeply pained by the memory of what transpired. He considers his decisions a sincere effort, but a great mistake. He intended to bring some structure to the movement; the result was the opposite. Stanley Block resigned from the board, but not from the corporation. The January 1 board minutes record that his resignation was in reality a protest against the board's lack of responsibility.

The details weren't all clear yet, but Inter-Varsity had survived the greatest threat to its ministry since its inception. The turmoil had come in an Urbana year and at the beginning of a decade of student unrest.

11/Meanwhile . . .

Students, unaware of any uncertainty at the national level, kept the movement on a steady course in spite of the confusions of campus life.

Betty Howard had become a Christian through staffworker Jo Rudd in the high-school Inter-School Christian Fellowship in Canada. When she arrived at Ohio University, she naturally looked up the Inter-Varsity chapter and became deeply involved in its ministry. She was taught and began to have a regular Quiet Time. The daily prayer meeting, a vital part of chapter life, was a strong support to her. She organized a discussion meeting in her dorm for IVCF staff member Martha Gray to talk about *The Real Meaning of Christmas*. She read IVP books. Martha Gray taught her how to prepare and lead a Bible study as part of her dorm witness. Betty went to Leadership Camp at Cedar Campus and later to Missionary Training Camp. Urbana 61 got her thinking about missions. After graduating in 1963, she went to Wheaton Graduate School and then in 1970 to Beirut, Lebanon, as a missionary. She said, "I didn't see my staffworker very often, but she had a lasting impact on me. She really modeled what a missionary is. She spent individual time talking with people from every kind of background. She led people to Christ, then taught them how to have a Quiet Time, how to pray, how to do Bible study. She followed through to see them become mature Christians. She did this for me. When I went to Lebanon and later to Jordan (1976) I really only did what I saw Martha Gray (Reapsome) do on my campus at Ohio University."[49]

At Lehigh University in Pennsylvania peer pressure was strong; many voices demanded students' attention; the funky mood on campus held a certain attraction. But in 1963, sophomore Tom Trevethan faced up to the lordship of Christ during a Bible study led by students. His spiritual turning point came as he faced the question: *who is Jesus Christ?* His Christian faith became his own for the first time, not something passed on by his family. The formerly flourishing IV group at Lehigh was in a period of dormancy. Although the group was small, the quality of fellowship met deep needs in Tom. Two professors also left a lasting mark on him: Douglas Feaver, in the classics department, and Al Pense, an engineering professor. Both were first-class Christian thinkers who were not intimidated by the university milieu. The quality of intellectual life in these men gave validity to their statements about the trustworthiness of the Jesus of the New Testament and encouraged Tom to use his mind in pursuit of Christian truth.

Jim Stamoolis[50] became a Christian through the influence of the Inter-Varsity chapter and he joined Tom and Barry Widman[51] and the group who went to chapter camp at Hudson House in the spring of 1964. Stacey Woods was speaking on the life of Moses and how God worked through his humility. During the chapter sessions, the Lehigh group began to think strategically about their campus and laid plans for an outreach to freshmen dorms. But it was the fellowship with Christian brothers that Tom remembers most. After one evening meeting, burdened for the witness at Lehigh, they met together to pray. Time seemed to disappear: for two hours or more they prayed and experienced the reality of Christ's presence in a way that had never before been so tangible. The spirit of oneness, of wanting to know and obey Jesus Christ, of belonging to him together prepared them for witness back on campus.

That fall Tom began his first discussion Bible study on campus. Seven men came; six were not Christians. They continued to meet and the group went with Tom to the IV spring conference. Professor Walter Thorson, a physicist at MIT, gave the talks. When Thorson invited people to receive Christ, one of the guys in Tom's Bible study stood. Tom began to get a taste of seeing folks converted. Professor Doug Feaver suggested the group sponsor a campus mission. Chapter members contacted all the fraternities to ask if they would let a faculty member come in to speak on purpose in life. Professor Al Pense spoke at about eight or nine fraternities. During the campus mission the chapter arranged for a presentation of Christian truth in every living unit on campus, so that every person had an opportunity to hear the gospel.

By his senior year Tom was investing about twenty hours a week in witnessing at Lehigh. Tom feels he encountered a love for learning in Inter-Varsity. When Lehigh students were initiated into both Phi Beta Kappa and Tau Beta Pi (the engineering honorary society), Tom pointed out to one of his professors that most of the students there were from the Inter-Varsity chapter.

Tom credits his involvement in IV with changing his life.[52] He went to Urbana 64 and one night, seated high in the arena of the new Illini Assembly Hall, he watched as Dr. John W. Alexander, head of the geography department at the University of Wisconsin, was introduced as the new general director of Inter-Varsity Christian Fellowship. He knew nothing of the national organization or its recent troubles; his only thought was approval. His experience in Inter-Varsity at Lehigh had shown him the intellectual respectability of the Christian gospel, and it seemed appropriate that a man from the academic world should lead such a movement.

Campus-in-the-Woods on Fairview Island in the Lake of Bays, Canada, was InterVarsity's first student training camp. It held its first session in 1946 and was used by both IVCF—Canada and IVCF—USA. Teaching sessions were often held in an outdoor amphitheater. The lecturer here is Dr. Alan McRae of Faith Theological Seminary.

Plenary session of the first IVCF Missionary Convention, Toronto, 1946. In 1948 the convention moved to Urbana, Illinois, where it has been held ever since.

This bus from Wichita, Kansas, brought students to Urbana, Illinois, for the 1951 IVCF Missionary Convention.

Surveying the statistics of the 1951 IVCF Missionary Convention at Urbana are (l. to r.) General Secretary C. Stacey Woods, Associate General Secretary Charles Troutman and Missionary Secretary/Convention Director Wesley Gustafson.

A Bible study meeting of a local Nurses Christian Fellowship group in the early 1950s.

Tressie Myers (seated), head of Nurses Christian Fellowship, pours tea at a staff gathering following the 1951 missionary convention.

The 1958 Senior Staff Council: (l. to r. standing) James Nyquist, George Ensworth, Gene Thomas, Paul Byer, James Reapsome, Paul Little, Keith Hunt, Peter Haile; (l. to r. sitting) Joseph Bayly, Charles Hummel, C. Stacey Woods and Wilber Sutherland, general secretary of IVCF—Canada.

Paul Little (l.) leads an evangelistic discussion at a fraternity house at the University of Michigan in 1961. The event was filmed for the first public relations movie made by InterVarsity.

Programs at Bear Trap Ranch, located high in the mountains just west of Colorado Springs, Colorado, began to train students in the Rocky Mountain and Plains states in 1953.

In 1952, InterVarsity expanded its camping ministry with the leasing of a site on Catalina Island, off the coast of California. Campus by the Sea has been a center for training students ever since.

1985 aerial view of the five-hundred-acre tract of land on the north shore of Lake Huron in the Upper Peninsula of Michigan known as Cedar Campus, established in 1954 as an IVCF training center.

Hudson House, a beautiful mansion on the Hudson River in Nyack, New York, became an IVCF training center for students from the New York metropolitan area and the East Coast in 1956. It was sold in 1985.

An "umbrella discussion" at the Fort Lauderdale evangelistic beach mission in the mid-1960s. It is now called the Florida Evangelism Project and is held at various sites in the state.

Urbana 70 was a breakthrough for those concerned about racial issues. Pictured here (l. to r.) are John Stott, George Taylor, Myron Augsburger and Tom Skinner.

Students at Cal Christian Fellowship in the 1960s take advantage of the "death of God" debate to attract attention to their book table along the main student walkway on campus.

The national headquarters moved to Madison, Wisconsin, in 1969 and occupied this building at 233 Langdon the next year.

photo credit: Wollin Studios

The National Staff Directors under the leadership of President John Alexander in 1971. Row 1 (l. to r.): Ruth Lichtenberger, Steve Atkinson, John Alexander, Peter Northrup, Grace Wallace, Fred Wagner. Row 2: Neil Rendall, Harold Burkhart, Helen McMurtry, James Nyquist, Bill Sisterson, Yvonne Vinkemulder, Bill McConnell, Bruce Youngquist. Row 3: Pete Hammond, Keith Hunt, Dick Young, James McLeish, Ned Hale, Steve Board, Dave Howard, Don Fields.

The 1987 Board of Trustees of InterVarsity Christian Fellowship. Row 1 (l. to r.): Isaac Canales, Erna Goulding, Doris Burke, Jim Gray, Pat Kissell, Eleanor Edman. Row 2: David Scott, John Irwin, Duane Barney, Robert Hultstrand, Ken Nielsen, Ralph Watts. Row 3: Walter Herbst, Steve Holbrook, Don Powell, Chet Youngberg, Herbert Luxon, James Reapsome, Archie McKinney. Not pictured: Jim Kay, Tom Dunkerton, Allen Mathis, George McKinney, Evan Bogart and Roy Blackwood.

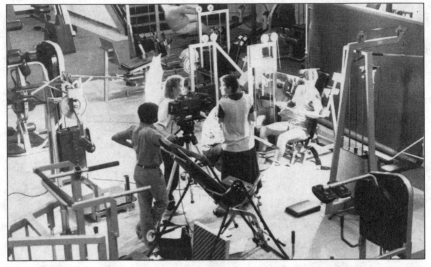

TWENTYONEHUNDRED Productions began its multimedia ministry in 1969 largely with slides set to music and voice. In the 1980s they moved more into video productions. Here a shoot takes place in a health club.

Throughout its five decades, InterVarsity Christian Fellowship has continued to present a witness to Jesus Christ in the midst of a variety of competitors on campus.

InterVarsity's second urban conference, San Francisco '83, drew thirteen hundred delegates from diverse ethnic backgrounds. Here a small group engages in a Bible study related to the theme: City/Church/Career.

The Armory at the 1987 Urbana convention. Here students visit hundreds of mission agencies and purchase books to assist them after the convention.

Tony Campolo addresses the Urbana 87 delegates in the Assembly Hall on the urgency of our call to follow Christ into the world.

Billy Graham, a popular speaker at many IVCF missions conventions, sits on the platform in the Assembly Hall at Urbana 87 to talk with students after a plenary session.

After having spread to three buildings over the years in Madison, Wisconsin, the national offices were able to combine in 1986 at this location on 6400 Schroeder Road.

In 1988 the board announced it had appointed Steve Hayner president of InterVarsity.

12
The Confusion of Order: Decade of the 1960s

God is at work on college campuses where he is building a portion of the body of Jesus Christ. Too often Christians write off the campus as hopelessly detached from God's presence and beyond the reach of his Holy Spirit. We repudiate this defeatist attitude and espouse the belief that even at the most hostile school, the principles in Habakkuk 1:1-5 apply: "Observe and be astounded, be amazed; for I am doing a work in your day which you would not believe even if it were told you." God is the great active agent on these campuses; if he were not thus engaged, there would be little point to our efforts.[1]
John W. Alexander, *president, Inter-Varsity Christian Fellowship*

*H*IS magazine reported the story of one father who gave his son permission to attend the seventh Student Missions Convention in 1964, but added, "Go ahead, but if you decide to become a missionary, don't bother to return home." At Urbana 64 more than 6,300 delegates considered the theme "Change, Witness, Triumph." Each word had a qualifier in this order: unparalleled, unashamed and unquestioned. In the stillness of the half-lit arena, missionary statesman Will Norton led a memorial service for missionaries martyred since 1961—the year of the previous IVCF Student Missions Convention—reading off the names, one after another, and the circumstances of their death. It was a solemn illustration of the theme of the convention, and evidence of the turmoil in the world.

John R. W. Stott, rector of All Souls Church, London, ministered profoundly to students with Bible expositions from 2 Corinthians 3—6 and set the standard for excellence in Bible teaching for years to come.[2] In the plenary forum a student asked Stott, "What is the IVCF position on the inspiration and authority of Scripture?" John Stott smiled and said, "We accept them." He then pointed out that Jesus is the Christian's teacher so that our view of Scripture coincides with his. He then articulated the biblical teaching about the authority of Christ and the Scripture with such clarity and power that his answer has been widely circulated under the title *"Teacher and Lord,"* a classic statement that Inter-Varsity affirms. (See page 384.)

The new University of Illinois Assembly Hall allowed Convention Director Eric Fife to put his plenary panel and question forum plans into operation. *HIS* reported, "During the last period each morning a battery of automatic weapons blazed away at various pre-announced targets. Students sat fascinated by the rapid-fire treatment of topics crucial to contemporary missions." Charles Troutman had urged Eric Fife to have more student participation in the convention, but that change did not come until the seventies. Speakers included Warren Webster (Fife had to ask him if he could help pay his own way from Pakistan because of tight Urbana funds), Clyde Taylor, Ruth Lewis, Ruben Lores (Costa Rica), Arthur Glasser, Charles Troutman, Ben Wati (India), Kenneth Kantzer (Trinity Evangelical Divinity School), P. T. Chandapilla (Union of Evangelical Students of India), Billy Graham and others.

Urbana 64 hadn't been easy to pull off. Paul Little, assisting the convention director, encouraged the team during the difficult days in headquarters by paraphrasing 1 Corinthians 12:26, "Remember, we're in this together. Your ulcer is my ulcer!" Later at the convention, he spoke to students about the growing campus mood, "Most students are convinced that the day of right and wrong has passed and the day of likes and dislikes has come. Students feel that 'if God grades on the curve, I'll make it.' But God doesn't grade on the curve! His standard is perfect righteousness."

Stacey Woods was there to give a report on worldwide student work and added his memorable admonition: "When you graduate, I hope you will avoid that awful state—'settling down.' Venture abroad, literally or figuratively, for Christ's sake." Charles Troutman, speaking on opposition to evangelism, said, "The Christian belief in God, the one God, as the Creator of heaven and earth and the triune Redeemer is bound to put us at odds with the rest of the world, but this is nothing new. We need to remind ourselves that being in this situation must not imply arrogance or tactlessness. Love is still the great demand on Christians." Students from small chapters and small campuses were overwhelmed and inspired to be part of the "big thing God was doing with college students." But John W.

Alexander, who would become the general director of Inter-Varsity on January 1, 1965, opened the convention by reminding the students that numbers didn't impress God; he would meet them one by one. "With him, it makes no difference whether there are seven thousand or seven."

1/The New General Director

John Alexander faced an enormous decision when a special committee of the board asked him to consider becoming the next general director of Inter-Varsity Christian Fellowship. He was a tenured professor at the University of Wisconsin and the chairman of one of the country's leading geography departments. His textbook *Economic Geography* had recently been published. He was in many ways at the peak of his academic career and greatly respected by his colleagues. He also had a heart for God and a desire to obey him whatever the cost. Although he had been a member of the IVCF Board since September 1961, his strong concern for student work on the campus predated that appointment. Influenced by staffworker Jim Nyquist, for twelve years John and his wife Betty had been using their home, energy and time to influence students at the University of Wisconsin in Madison. He was also a frequent speaker at regional Inter-Varsity conferences. As the board committee sought out possible candidates for the general director's post, John W. Alexander was an overwhelming favorite.

John Alexander had been privy to all the board and executive committee discussions during the time of confusion when Richard Wolff was made executive director and knew that the gulf between the board and the senior staff was deep and wide. Charles Hummel had written to board member Roy Horsey, "It will require a period of education to convince some board members that all our troubles don't lie with recalcitrant senior men and to convince some senior staff that our whole problem does not lie in an external board. I think it will take at least two years of working together to mend the broken relationships and restore some of the confidence that has disintegrated."

Alexander submitted stipulations to the board to be met before he would seriously consider accepting the post of general director. The emphasis of the stipulations was on joint staff-board committees, the importance of campus-involved people on the board and corporation, and the necessity for clear communication and understanding of policies.

He asked that fifty per cent of the board and thirty per cent of the corporation nominees meet at least one of the following criteria: (1) the nominee has been an IVCF staff member, (2) the nominee has been an

IVCF chapter leader, and (3) the nominee is now actively involved in some capacity on a particular campus. He asked that four of the seven members of the executive committee meet at least one of the campus involvement criteria, and that two staff members (general director and field director) be on the committee to approve nominees to the board, corporation and executive committee. He insisted that no upper-echelon staff member (including the general director) be hired until each board member had seen his recommendations and a staff committee had interviewed the nominee personally. He would not accept the post without the unanimous approval of the staff advisory council (SAC). He made other stipulations: (1) that the board permit him to have all senior staff with him throughout the board meetings, with the exception of executive sessions, (2) that the board consider paying gym fees to preserve the physical fitness of the staff team and (3) that the headquarters at 1519 N. Astor be sold and a new headquarters established away from downtown Chicago.[3]

The members of the staff advisory committee met with John Alexander and reported to the board, "We have been most impressed with his understanding of IVCF philosophy as expressed in his list of proposals. We are also impressed with his suitability for the position of general director in every avenue we have explored. Since we realize that administrative ability is a crucial requirement for the position, we are awaiting corroboratory information in this area. If this information is also favorable, we will wholeheartedly support a board invitation to John Alexander to become the general director."[4] Charles Hummel and Warner Hutchinson were the only SAC members absent from the signing of the letter.

At the November 1964 board meeting an official invitation, passed unanimously by the board, was given to John Alexander to become the general director of Inter-Varsity Christian Fellowship. He was assured the full backing of the board, all of whom had a strong conviction that God had led them to the right person. Alexander's response combined his thoughts about the tremendous challenge he faced and the apprehension he felt. He said,

> I look upon this as a tremendous challenge, and within me there is a real desire to respond. I am ready to go. I am convinced that God right now is building the body of Christ . . . on the university campus which most Christians have walled off. I am convinced that Inter-Varsity has a peculiar aptitude to be used by the Lord . . . on campus.
>
> There is an inner apprehension that you must know I am facing. Part of that apprehension relates to what I am going to leave. That will be

painful. Part pertains to what I am getting into. I know I have some weaknesses. To counteract my apprehension comes the firm conviction that throughout the entire Scripture God didn't have perfect men to work with. He doesn't have a perfect man for Inter-Varsity. If you realize that, that will counteract my inner apprehension.[5]

John Alexander's appointment as general director took effect on January 1, 1965, coinciding with the national staff conference which followed Urbana 64. He asked Charles Troutman to join him in a question-and-answer session so that all doubts and questions about the change of leadership would be out in the open. Above all, he wanted to restore confidence and rebuild national unity. The changing campus needed full attention and creativity; sixty-eight field staff were eager to get on with their task.

Any feelings of well-being John Alexander had as he began this new adventure were soon dissipated. Shortly after his appointment he received a letter from Eastern Regional Director Warner Hutchinson, who was not present when SAC members signed the letter of approval, pending receipt of corroboratory evidence of his administrative gifts. Hutchinson questioned whether John Alexander had accepted the post of general director too quickly, before the criterion he had specified was met. Alexander had asked for the unqualified approval of the members of SAC. Hutchinson now said that the SAC had been waiting for corroboratory information about his administrative skills before giving final approval. John Alexander read this inquiry as disapproval. Later, when influential people in the East raised questions about his decisions, Alexander wondered if Hutchinson was the source of the queries.

A short time later John Alexander visited William Kiesewetter, a physician at the Children's Hospital in Pittsburgh who had been a corporation and board member from 1951-59, with the hope of encouraging him to consider serving on the board again. To John's surprise, Kiesewetter raised the question of his wisdom in accepting the post of general director of Inter-Varsity. Bill Kiesewetter was disillusioned with the way the organization had been run and thought it might well be a lost cause. He wondered whether John had abandoned his calling to the campus (which had been blessed by God) and asked if there was any possibility that the University of Wisconsin would restore his tenure and his position.

Although John did not share these two messages with anyone until years later, their combined impact, arriving so soon after he took office, did not give him the affirmation he needed. His wife Betty, while supportive of John's leadership in family decision making, had already expressed her conviction that it would be a mistake for John to accept the board's appointment. Now he again had to re-examine his calling. Years later Charles Troutman commented that God must have a large role for IVCF in his kingdom work, considering how frequently its leadership has been under attack.

John Alexander, naturally enough, was wary as he began his task. He appreciated the group of independent and complex entrepreneurs who were now called the national staff directors (NSD, formerly SAC). Their commitment and contributions were great, but they also seemed intimidating, and he found it difficult to be comfortable with the easiness of their relationships and their differing opinions. He was not sure who he could take into his confidence. By training he was more of a linear thinker; their impulsive sweep of ideas made him cautious. How could he best manage such a diverse group? He felt it necessary to standardize and centralize in whatever ways would benefit a national organization. He wanted to begin getting some control over this gangling movement spread across the country.

As often happens, wary feelings beget wary feelings. Alexander tended to act alone, and the team didn't immediately have the sense of unity or leadership everyone longed for. Campus staff members (CSMs), used to being treated as independent professionals, sometimes interpreted his remarks beyond his intent. Some of the more experienced staff became uneasy upon receiving the new series of training papers. Were they going to lose their freedom to minister according to the needs of individual campuses? Something about Alexander's written communications caused unrest.

In October 1965 one of the regional directors wrote to Alexander, "During the course of our discussions I've come to the conclusion that you basically do not trust the regional directors. I don't know why this is, but I sense it strongly and see it in your decisions. . . . I dare say every decision you made this week concerning the authority of the regional directors was to limit it further. . . . I am worried about the root cause of this."[6]

2/Learning the Job

John Alexander said his first priority in leading Inter-Varsity was to become acquainted with its staff. He traveled from one end of the country to the other, meeting with staff teams and student chapters on the campus. He spoke at weekend conferences and summer camps. He was already a firm believer in the training concepts developed by his predecessors and staff over the years. He was eager to experience firsthand the work in the field, what he called "the front lines where you can smell the gunsmoke."

Few national-level training helps existed, apart from the philosophical papers and guidelines by Charles Troutman, and the description of the basics of chapter life in Charles Hummel's *Campus Christian Witness*. As Dr. A (as the staff began to call him) traveled around the country, he found that regional directors and their staff had developed training materials for use in their regions. He wanted to take the best of these and make them available throughout the movement. When he came across the evangelistic tool Burton Harding had developed in training counselors for the World's Fair Project in New York City during the summer of 1964, called "First Steps to God," he realized its potential as a national training tool.

At the July 1965 board meetings, he asked Harding to share the content and use of First Steps to God. A lengthy discussion followed, and "the board agreed that its proper use, allowing for the freedom of the Holy Spirit, could increase Inter-Varsity's evangelistic effectiveness." Board member Edson Peck, a faculty man, "presented several cautions about its use, however, saying that if it became a national tool, it needed to be carefully reviewed in detail. He expressed concern that a staff member who had an effective method might resent having to use this one, and said that if chapter presidents must use this to qualify for the office (as Dr. A had suggested), it would invade the autonomy of the local group."[7]

One of Alexander's top objectives, supported by the NSDs, was a fresh evangelistic thrust by IVCF chapters on campus. He discussed First Steps to God with these senior staff, and they agreed that it could be a helpful tool. John then set down specific goals: (1) all IVCF staff members are expected to have mastered First Steps to God by the next field staff conference in December; (2) by June 1966 chapter leaders should have mastered the document, used it in witness and taught it to one younger Christian; (3) spring conferences for 1966 would be on evangelism; (4) by the end of spring 1966 each chapter should have at least one evangelistic "squash"; (5) Paul Little was assigned to prepare a training manual for staff, giving lesson plans for seminars, workshops, etc.[8]

In September Dr. A sent to the staff a nine-page family letter in which he introduced the outline of First Steps to God, with thoughts about the importance of the staff role as teacher and trainer. Alexander compared the staff to the teaching faculty in a college department offering instruction at three different levels: elementary, advanced and seminars. He expressed his fear that staff were spending most of their time on the advanced or seminar-level courses. He wanted to keep what IVCF had, but also to add more emphasis on the elementary courses for freshmen. In this context he recommended the staff memorize the First Steps (or whatever the presentation would be called—three other titles had been suggested) and plan to teach it to their freshmen to see if it would make a difference in evangelism. He encouraged those who didn't like the outline to prepare their own and compare the two.

Within days Alexander began receiving letters and new outlines from the staff:

> "I do not see how an outline like this can begin to cope with the problem of informal Christian witness. Students cannot witness from an outline. The only witness is a genuine one, not an educated one. Some folks who once tried casting out demons via a formula got into trouble with the demons (Acts 19).
>
> "We must not give students the impression that the universal and timeless dilemma of man can be 'got up' in four steps with subdivisions and proof statements. . . . It invites trouble by asking for an understanding of minimal proportions."[9]

> "As the outline stands, it suffers from a very weak proportion of material devoted to the central figure of the gospel. . . . This outline is in danger of leading to the mechanistic error of making the Lord Jesus one . . . cog in the Plan of Salvation.
>
> "I respectfully request that this outline not be adopted as an official Inter-Varsity Christian Fellowship document."[10]

Others wrote positively and said in essence, "People have become Christians knowing a lot less than this. Let's give it a try."

John Alexander felt the staff needed a time of nurture and morale building and so planned to bring the staff together for fellowship and interaction without the pressure and fatigue that accompanied the Urbana missionary convention. (Traditionally a national staff conference was held immediately following Urbana for economic reasons. However, depleted energy levels hardly made that an ideal time.) A generous offer to use a hotel in Miami, Florida, was accepted for an early December 1965 national staff conference, and staff wives were invited to attend. Nothing so luxurious had ever happened before and expectations were high.

The national staff directors met for five days, and then the field staff joined them for five more days. At John's invitation Stacey Woods, general secretary of the International Fellowship of Evangelical Students, spoke each night on 1 Thessalonians, using the apostle Paul's trust in the new believers at Thessalonica as an example for staff members, "Something is wrong with our ministry if students only function when staff are there clucking like mother hens. We do not want to produce bottle-fed babies, but men and women of God." The staff were divided into small groups for Bible study, discussion and prayer. Much of the week was spent sharing ideas and plans for more effective ministry in producing men and women of God.

This was John Alexander's first opportunity to spend an extended time with the whole staff team and let them hear his thinking. Some tensions were already rising when on Friday afternoon he presented his plan for the First Steps to God outline. When staff began to raise questions, as Inter-Varsity staff are wont to do, John Alexander "dug in his heels." He interpreted their queries as a challenge to his authority. His commitment to the plan made it difficult for him to accept any reluctance on the part of staff members.

Unfortunately, the perception of a few was that he was using the outline as a benchmark for orthodoxy within Inter-Varsity, and they wanted to discuss this openly. Others said that it seemed he was placing minor issues as primary, avoiding the big issues staff were facing on campus. Some who had hoped for a participatory style of leadership believed they were seeing a "dictatorial" one instead. The younger, new staff were bewildered. The merits of the outline fell by the wayside. Alexander calls that day *Black Friday,* one of those days you would like to redo in a different tone of voice and with different responses. He was heartsick that the conference ended with apprehensions still in the air. The year 1965 had not been the best year in John Alexander's life.

Jim McLeish grumbled, "In Inter-Varsity we need a multipaged statement to say *Jesus Saves.*" To which regional director Peter Northrup replied in a letter to Alexander, "That is true. And rightly so, considering our constituency. If we don't have a depth and diversity to match the university situation, we should go to a less complex mission field. . . . We have an amazingly acute staff. They are very sharp in their ability to think, and any pronouncement must be carefully thought through. It seems to me we must maintain diversity throughout the movement so that we keep 'our thinkers' in the movement and fight for creativity."

In the next months, staff discussions continued. How should they interpret Dr. A's words when he said, "This is a floor which is minimal and unchangeable," and then at another time said, "Yes, alter and change it"? In the end, memos went out from regional directors instructing staff that "First Steps is not to be 'the outline for witnessing.' The function of First Steps is to provide for the person to whom we teach it a logical, consistent framework for his own thinking. It is to help him organize his thoughts rather than to have a bunch of loose categories floating around disjointed in his mind. Frequently there may be a similarity, but there is no necessary correlation between what he presents to the non-Christian and First Steps. . . . We must encourage students to pray. People do not become Christians by our activity, but by the Holy Spirit. There needs to be a balance between our activity and our prayer. Are we teaching students to pray?"

3/Growing Pains

Charles Troutman did not stay long in his position as associate general director, partly because he was not given assignments essential to the movement. He resigned from the staff of Inter-Varsity Christian Fellowship on May 31, 1965. He and his wife, Lois, joined the Latin America Mission and moved to Costa Rica, with a special assignment to become a strategist for the burgeoning student work in Latin America. Charles Hummel had accepted an invitation to become the president of Barrington College in Rhode Island before Alexander became the general director and left in July 1965.

In the meantime Inter-Varsity celebrated its twenty-fifth anniversary. *HIS* magazine put out a silver anniversary edition in January 1966. The lead article by John Alexander, entitled "Targets," spelled out his vision for Inter-Varsity. He wrote, "We want IVCF people to become 'men of the Word,' strong in Bible study and love for Scripture. And we must be men and women of prayer, for unless IVCF kneels down, it will not go forward."

The headquarters building at 1519 N. Astor had been sold, and while waiting for a decision about a new location, Inter-Varsity rented space at 130 N. Wells in Chicago's Loop. It was becoming increasingly difficult to find office employees in the center city, and Dr. A had to choose whether to go to a suburb, a university town or another city. Jim Nyquist became director of InterVarsity Press (also interim director of the Central Region and administrative assistant to the general director). When a new headquarters location failed to emerge, Alexander approved a move of the Press to Downers Grove, Illinois, in 1966. The next year the staff and production offices of *HIS* joined the Press.

Troutman had been concerned about training as many students as possible and had suggested to staff that they expand regional training. Since 1961 Cedar Campus had been holding a four-week Student Leadership Camp for students from the eastern third of the country, including the Southeast. (By 1962 the U.S. movement was no longer using Campus-in-the-Woods, partly because it was becoming increasingly difficult for international students to obtain visas and for students to get work permits to serve on the work crew.)

In 1965 Burton Harding and the Southeast staff rented facilities for the first regional four-week training camp in the South. Sixty students, a fifty per cent increase, were able to attend because the camp was geographically closer. Chapter camps were now held in every region and growing in importance. The listing of training sessions across the country became longer and longer.

Early in 1966 Warner Hutchinson wrote to John Alexander about long-range plans for the movement, "What we need is a flexible instrument that breathes a spirit rather than a master plan that dictates the letter. I prefer the way of a thoughtful, helpful plan, flexibly administered by men of varying gifts of high motivation, of influence in the lives of others. . . . Big men will not be attracted to plans that are smaller than themselves. Such men will always be pushing the frontiers of administration, for they are not content merely to wait for direction. . . . If our plan reduces us to be a bureaucracy, we will have a staff of committed bureaucrats—loyal, faithful, responsible, deeply committed to the work and to the Lord, able to meet the expectations of their superiors, but without genius."[11]

"Hutch," and others with him, said he wanted leadership, not simply management.[12] This did not help John Alexander feel more comfortable with Hutchinson. A difference in style was becoming increasingly obvious. He was not surprised when Hutchinson resigned from staff later in 1966. Fred Woodberry, and his wife Jeanne, who had effectively staffed New York City for thirteen years, left the following year, along with New York's acting area director, Stanley Rock.

Southeast Regional Director Burton Harding resigned from Inter-Varsity at the end of the 1966-67 school year. He wrote to Alexander, "My fundamental reason for leaving hangs upon our temperamental difference in the area of leadership. In areas of strategic importance I have felt very unsure of our direction. My difficulty is knowing how to read you, even though I have talked with you at length, I never know your sentiments. If I am to follow you, I have to know you. I am unable to sustain my loyalty and commitment to you in the absence of clarity and decisiveness."[13]

The shortage of regional directors was acute. Because the staff was both small and short on leadership, each resignation echoed like a bell across a canyon. It mattered to everybody. Meanwhile Alexander felt he was getting two different messages: (1) he was giving too much unnecessary management, and (2) he wasn't giving strong enough leadership.

An incident in the late 1960s reflects the differences in the temperament of Dr. A and many staff. "I attempted to make a clear call to commitment. For example, I was carrying in my wallet the IVCF Commitment Card which I had signed in the late 1940s at the University of Wisconsin. The card contained the IVCF purpose statement and the Basis of Faith, and it had a place for me to sign my name if I desired to commit myself. I tried to persuade the staff to reactivate usage of it. They rejected the idea, as one veteran phrased it, 'Today's students are not joiners. We will alienate them if we try to reactivate use of this card.' I chose not to push the issue further."[14] John Alexander's attempt to take a student census met the same fate—the national staff directors did not think it was good timing. It was the late 1960s and the anti-authority mood of the campus was contagious.

Alexander invited Peter Northrup to transfer working as a regional director to becoming his administrative assistant. In the summer of 1966, Keith Hunt expressed a desire to return to the campus ministry and asked to leave his post as director of development.[15] He had been meeting resistance in the matter of necessary funding for the effective operation of the development department. Alexander appointed James McLeish, comptroller, the additional task of director of development. From the first, Alexander had delegated to Jim McLeish, with board approval, the responsibility for financing the organization. This new appointment made McLeish responsible for income and outflow, giving him what proved to be a very powerful position in the movement.

Having been a board member himself, John Alexander assumed the board's support in his new role, even though he was privy to the attacks some had made against staff members. He soon began to feel the crossfire himself as various board members attempted to urge on him their differing views.[16] Dr. A tried to maintain a position of intermediary between the board and the staff, which was sometimes misread as aloofness from both.

At the end of 1966, Peter Northrup urged him in a letter to become one with his staff team. "It is critical to know you stand with us and are one of us—not studying us from the outside. The staff family needs to stand together, and I believe you called for this when you wrote asking for the trust of the staff sometime ago. . . . Trust is a two-way street. If you invite us, we will lay our necks besides yours on the block, but to do so means you will have to open yourself up (to us). You will have to reveal yourself regarding emotional struggle, not just administrative detail, to let us help you withstand some of the pressures you face."[17]

4/Reorganizing

Late in the summer of 1966 John Alexander abolished the posts of field director and regional directors and divided the student work into twenty areas which would be covered by fifteen area staff directors who, along with department heads, would report directly to him. He had a heart for student work, and he felt that this move gave him easier access to the staff teams he needed to know and understand. Alexander was his own field director. The new alignment put Dr. A closer to the campus, but it was an impossible supervisory arrangement and lasted only one year. He then established three regions, with area directors (ADs) again working under regional directors, but the staff chart reveals that many staff were doing double and triple duty, carrying the label of "acting area director." The Eastern region included what was once the East and Southeast region; the Central region included the old Rocky Mountain region. The western region covered the states between Arizona and Washington. A high priority was the development of capable staff leaders who could become area directors, especially since ADs were now beginning to raise funds for the staff in their area.

The organizational charts constantly changed during the years of Dr. A's leadership as he sought for the way IVCF could function at its highest potential.[18] Board member Allen Mathis, Jr., who worked with American Management Association, urged John Alexander to take AMA courses. Alexander also turned to Phillip Armstrong, director of the Far Eastern Gospel Crusade, for management help. As a result of discussions and seminars, Alexander brought into the movement what textbooks call "classical bureaucratic management" principles, a cycle in which planning leads to execution which is followed by review, which in turn feeds new planning. Plans are defined by the purpose, or mission, of the organization. A staff member's role is determined by his job description, and from this he develops his *objectives, goals and standards.* This fit Alexander's penchant for order and a well-articulated philosophy of management. His book *Managing Our Work,* published by InterVarsity Press, details Alexander's philosophy of planning and executing programs.

Staffworkers attending Orientation of New Staff played a thoughtful game developed by Dr. A to define purpose, objectives, goals and standards (POGAS). Producing one's own objectives, goals and standards (OGS) became an annual event for the staff as a tool to measure performance and insure accountability. Increasingly it was clear that John Alexander was a manager in a style not before experienced in Inter-Varsity. Stacey Woods, the pioneer, had cared very little about the specifics; he always saw the end product. Dr. A saw the details and spelled out the procedure he felt necessary to get to the end product. Inter-Varsity was maturing. And as it did so, the Fellowship took on more characteristics of an organization.

Was this good, bad or inevitable? Probably some of each. Some board leaders thought the AMA emphasis was too heavy, that it took away from John Alexander the ability to be who he really was. Others, cut more in the corporate mold, thought Inter-Varsity still had a long way to go to get organized. Still others had hoped for a "collegial model"[19] and were disappointed with the corporate one. Change was inevitable; the pioneering days were over. Yet events are often strangely timed. While hostility to structure and rejection of control became a mark of the youth culture, Inter-Varsity was increasingly structuring its work.

5/Student Growth

Meanwhile on the campus, students were trying old and new ways to confront their peers with the gospel. In the middle of the noisy exchange of ideas and ideals students were often more open to talk about the gospel than they were to commit themselves. Campus turmoil did not silence Christian students, even though it sometimes confused them. During the Berkeley, California, student demonstrations, Inter-Varsity students set up a booktable near Ludwig's Fountain by the student union. They posted an eye-catching sign, which they frequently changed to stir up interest. They began with "If God grades on the curve, I'll make it. But He doesn't. For information on final FINALS, inquire here." The table became the focus of many good discussions, and in that school year about two thousand or more stopped by for significant conversations or to pick up a book. Inter-Varsity chapters on other campuses tried the booktable idea with similar success.

Within the first six weeks of classes in the 1966 school year, twelve students had become Christians at the University of Wyoming. Reports from NCF told of new converts: "Two freshman have come to know the Lord Jesus this fall." "Four new Christians since my last visit here." A

Colorado nursing student who became a Christian through an NCF Bible study said, "I even made an A in medical nursing, and it was for no other reason than that my whole attitude has changed." The year before students at the University of Connecticut had six evangelistic Bible studies. Now they aimed at twelve evangelistic studies in the dorms. About twenty per cent of the hundred students from the University of Hawaii who came to a semester-break retreat were non-Christians. Six made professions of faith before the camp ended. Beach evangelism teams went to Ft. Lauderdale and to California's Laguna Beach.

Bible studies remained a key way to get interested students in touch with truth, as well as a way to mature younger Christians. Students came from all over New England to receive training in leading Bible studies at Boston University and to consider how they might spark new Bible studies on campus when they returned home. Everyone had an opportunity to lead a small investigative Bible study and be evaluated. While some conservative Christian students were afraid of the new mood on campus, others became bold in starting evangelistic studies. No amount of training could prepare them for some of the off-beat discussions that ensued, especially for students who thought of themselves as the final authority for truth. Christian students kept pressing the claims Jesus Christ made about himself and his teaching about what matters in life.

The charismatic movement was spreading on the campus, and in some schools how the Holy Spirit did his work became the number one discussion topic. In some chapters those who claimed to speak in tongues questioned the spiritual experience of those who did not. Some groups split over the issue of the manifestations of the Spirit, who is the Source of unity. Inter-Varsity's official position was "require not; forbid not." A paper by Charles Troutman on the subject of speaking in tongues was circulated again, urging staff "(1) to encourage all students to continue to seek the very highest God has for them in daily study, prayer and obedience, (2) to insist strongly that all of life be brought under the authority of Scripture and that the emphasis must not shift away from Jesus Christ, (3) to be alert to avoid divisions, the use of IVCF for the advancement of this or other nonessential ideas, or the exploitation of students by outsiders."

Two hundred fifty students convened at the University of Chicago in February 1966 for a one-day Inter-Varsity Theological Conference to study in depth the doctrine of the Holy Spirit. Speakers were Vernon Grounds of Conservative Baptist Seminary, Merrill Tenney of Wheaton Graduate School of Theology, Leslie Keylock of St. Norbert College and Walter Liefeld of Trinity Evangelical Divinity School.

Students at the University of Virginia invited members of the Jewish Hillel Foundation to attend a meeting on the subject "Salvation in the Old Testament and the New Testament." The dialogs were so helpful that Jewish students invited the IV students to a meeting where two Jewish students and two students from Inter-Varsity held a panel discussion on the salvation theme.

Black students who used to come to IV meetings dropped out for the most part, pressured to protest white racism through an exclusivism of their own. For international students studying in the States, the 1960s were confusing and even frightening. international student houseparties, more important than ever, were held in a variety of locations across the country. An Indian student at one of these said, "I shall become a Christian, but I shall wait until I leave here, just to make sure I am not acting simply because of the love in this atmosphere."

6/Missions

In the summer of 1964 Evan Adams joined the staff of the missions department with the primary assignment to reknit the tattered structure of the Student Foreign Missions Fellowship within Inter-Varsity.[20] During the early 1960s the missions department had virtually ignored the SFMF chapters, chiefly because of the interests of Eric Fife. Fife served as missions director for both Canada and the U.S. He was a gifted speaker with a heavy schedule, and he tended to place SFMF low on his priority list. In addition, he was in some ways at odds with the leadership in many mission agencies who were cautious about the prophetic nature of the combined Glasser-Fife vision for missions. At both the 1961 and 1964 Urbana conventions, the speakers spoke quite frankly of the mistakes missions had made in the past. Fife and Glasser were pushing missions into the changing world of the 1960s, and this was somewhat of a threat to traditional missions. Part of the alienation that SFMF chapters felt was abetted by disparagement coming from missionary executives who saw IVCF's missions department as a gad-fly movement. The Southeast Region of SFMF had become increasingly independent and created uneasiness in its influence with other regions.

Evan Adams's assignment was to change the stepchild status of SFMF and to act as a mediator between Fife and various groups, while working at a positive task of rebuilding cooperation with SFMF. Adams spent more than a year contacting all the SFMF groups and winning their confidence. In the fall of 1966 a major regional missionary conference was held in the Chicago area, coordinated by the student leadership of the SFMF and Adams. It was well attended by students from the Great Lakes area and showed a fresh spirit of cooperation. From a well-placed booth at Urbana 67, members of SFMF were recruited for a Summer Leadership Training Conference held in Wheaton in June 1968, a kind of SFMF chapter camp that has been repeated over the years. SFMF was again a national movement instead of a regional one, and was on its way to becoming an integral part of the Inter-Varsity Christian Fellowship.

Fife and Adams faced a paradox: students were flocking to missionary conferences, but few were applying to mission boards. One of Evan Adams's assignment was to visit as many campus groups in the U.S. as possible, listen to their thinking and their situations, and then report back to IVCF and the mission boards. This information was also used in preparing missionary personnel for participation in the student interaction at Urbana 67. (The eighth IVCF Student Missionary Convention adopted the "Urbana 67" title for the first time.) Missionary personnel interested in getting closer to student thought had to relate missions and the gospel of Jesus Christ to the more radical sense of mission of the sixties.

As Urbana 67 drew closer it became increasingly obvious that Eric Fife was seriously ill. He had suffered from migraine headaches and colitis through the years, made more acute by the tensions of continual travel and speaking in the university milieu, and he was frequently overmedicated. By late summer he could no longer carry on as convention director. Paul Little, aided by Evan Adams, took over the planning and execution of Urbana 67, with Eric Fife as the figure-head director.

The questions students asked at Urbana 67 told a story of what was happening in the thoughts and lives of contemporary Christian students. In fact, students began sending in questions as soon as they registered. The questions reflected the campus: questions about racial struggle, civil disobedience, Vietnam, violence in the streets. When John Stott began his expositions on 2 Timothy, students were full of questions about suffering, its meaning and whether it is inevitably part of the Christian life. They wanted to know how Stott suffered. They asked questions about the nature and sovereignty of God, and about the Holy Spirit and his power. Their questions revealed a demand for honesty and reality and a willingness to challenge anything inconsistent or smacking of phoniness.

Some of them had messages of their own to proclaim. Although students were unaware of this decision, for the first time staff members guarded the steps to the plenary platform to prevent any student from capturing the microphone to give his message to the convention. The flavor of this eighth missionary convention was captured in a 32-minute sound-color film called *Like It Was,* circulated as a report on the convention and a recruiting tool for the next Urbana.

HIS magazine recorded, "Little escaped student criticism at the convention. They criticized making a distinction between nationals and missionaries, Christians and pentecostals. . . . Anything that seemed to show intolerance came under their indictment, with impatience toward racism leading the list. . . . Many of them focused their most scathing indictment on their home churches."

The speakers spoke the language of 1967 and showed skill in interacting with students. They also revealed their own vulnerability, the most appealing trait of all from the student's vantage point. The missionary greats of the day were on the platform, all male and most of them in their forties. No women, no blacks, few older or younger. The "chauvinistic" flavor of the theme *God's Men—From All Nations to All Nations* was questioned. Grumbling and angry, Black students met to pray and discuss what their role should be in confronting the missionary enterprise. Some things would have to change.

Students did more than ask questions. They laughed, cried, reflected, rebelled, trusted and submitted. "Now the onus to examine his specific guidance is my responsibility," said one student, representing many others like him. "Urbana has brought to my mind the unlimited possibilities for Christian service," said another student. "I don't know yet how God will use me; I only know I want him to do so." "Seldom do we hear such a concentrated presentation of Christian truth. One of the unique things about this conference is the terrific people we are exposed to; we don't run into people like this every day. It sets the sights higher," one student said. It takes time to serve 9,000 people communion, and on that last night of the year "it can be pretty sobering to consider our calling in light of our Lord's death."

Following Urbana 67 Evan Adams left the missions department to return to staff work on the West Coast. Eric Fife was on sick leave all of 1968. After extensive medical examinations the board offered Fife continued Inter-Varsity support if he would agree to be hospitalized. Eric Fife chose instead to resign from staff effective May 1969.

In mid-1968 David Howard came on loan from the Latin America Mission as IVCF's new missions director in time to begin making plans for the next

Urbana. Howard's return was a homecoming, since he had served on the missions staff with SFMF under Christy Wilson. John Alexander was single-minded in his pursuit of David Howard for the post of missions director. David refused the job offer the first time Alexander asked him. He had planned to spend the rest of his life in Latin America, and he felt he no longer understood the college scene of the late sixties.

Alexander asked Howard to pray about it and to stop by to see him before returning to Latin America. He did so and again felt no freedom to take the job offer. John Alexander asked him to pray further. Howard turned it down a third time. Then the details of his missionary responsibilities changed, and Howard began to rethink the offer. He thought that if John Alexander were to ask him again, he might say yes, but he had already given him three refusals and didn't expect to hear from him again. He experienced what he calls "painful inner turmoil." When another letter from Alexander arrived, David Howard accepted the post of missions director for Inter-Varsity Christian Fellowship.

Howard asked Douglas Flood to work as the new SFMF staff member, continuing the work Evan Adams had begun. Doug Flood would be the first staff member in many years to work solely with SFMF chapters. His field responsibilities were for the entire U.S. and Canada. During the first three years on staff, Flood was on the road approximately three hundred days of the year. Many of the SFMF chapters had lost any sense of connectedness to IVCF. When Flood appeared on campus, asking to see student leaders, nobody would know who he was. Yet when he met the students and began talking about basic leadership concepts and goals, the students soaked it up. Consistent training of leaders brought SFMF to the fore again; again many students were heading overseas in the missions enterprise. Lee Howard followed Doug Flood as SFMF staff, along with Dick Crespo, Fred Wilson and others. May Koksma, a key figure and secretary in the missions department, resigned in 1969 after serving seventeen years.

7/Nurses Christian Fellowship

NCF staff doubled in number in 1965 which meant greater contact with nursing students spread across the country. Grace Wallace was appointed the assistant director of NCF. The graduate nurses committee began looking for a Black member as well as a male nurse member to better reflect realities in the profession. Nursing education was undergoing major curriculum changes, and recommendations that diploma (hospital) programs be discontinued began to move nursing education away from a hospital service orientation. NCF staff began working more closely with Inter-Varsity campus staff as more nursing programs moved into university settings. With this change, nursing students no longer lived in separate housing, but were scattered in a variety of dormitories, making it more difficult to identify Christians nurses and arrange for them to meet together. NCF staff faced new challenges with the changing curriculum.

Nursing Director Tressie Myers insisted that NCF work in the heart of professional nursing, not just on the fringes. She encouraged nurses in NCF to become active in professional organizations. She also had a global vision for nursing and inspired dozens of nurses to go overseas as missionaries. Through her influence Christian nursing movements developed in other countries, and she had a special part in encouraging the establishment of the Evangelical Nurses Fellowship of India. In 1967 Lilly Bonner, an NCF leader in India, came to the States to itinerate for the NCF-USA for one year. The NCF groups raised the money for the exchange and profited from this contact. Increased interest in NCF work in other countries culminated in an application to join Nurses Christian Fellowship International (NCFI) in 1969. Tressie Myers retired as director of NCF in 1968, but continued to serve in an advisory capacity and in development until 1971. She was succeeded by Grace Wallace, who had been working as assistant director of NCF since 1965.

Grace Wallace was one of the pioneers of the Christian nursing movement. While a nursing student at University of California School of Nursing in 1939, she and a classmate became concerned that there was no Christian witness of the University of California Medical Center in San Francisco (UCSF). Her friend, a transfer from the Berkeley campus, had been associated with a Christian group known as the Bible League. Together they began to contact Christian medical students and nurses and formed what became known as the Medical Center Bible League. By her senior year, Grace Wallace was in touch with student nurses from different hospitals in the area and within about two years, with the inspiration of Dawson Trotman of the Navigators, began what they called Christian Nurses Fellowship, not knowing that there was a CNF anywhere else in the country. Grace headed up the movement as it grew in the Bay Area, with evangelistic dinner meetings and an outreach to women in the armed services during World War 2.

In 1949 Grace Wallace was recruited by the Red Cross to do nursing work in Texas during a severe outbreak of polio and she ended up teaching at the Texas Children's Medical Center in Dallas. While in Texas she met Glen Zumwalt, the IV staffworker for Texas and Oklahoma. He asked Grace to help him work at the Texas Women's University and help at Inter-Varsity conferences. By now Grace had heard about the Chicago-based CNF through Navy nurses and transfers from the Chicago area and had had some correspondence with leaders there. It was not until 1954, when she went to Teacher's College in New York to study for her master's degree, that she met Nurses Christian Fellowship staffworker Catherine Schell.

During the six years she taught at Cornell Medical Center, Grace became deeply involved in the work of NCF and IVCF. She met staffworkers Harriet Marsh, Jean Metzger, Walt Liefeld, and Paul and Marie Little, and the connection began. She served on the NCF national committee, and in 1964, while on the faculty at the University of Kentucky, was invited to become Tressie Myers's assistant. By this time she had done everything from organizing and helping local groups of nursing students, to cooking at Hudson House for Inter-Varsity conferences, to speaking at student meetings and nursing faculty conferences. She was a natural for the job; she had a heart for the work.

8/Bible Study

Barbara Boyd came back home to the East in 1960, after ten years on staff in Southern California, to take on an assignment for the Eastern women's colleges. Four years later it seemed to her that all the Christians lived on the fourth floors of their dorms—even when they didn't!—she was just plain tired. Charles Troutman suggested that she think about developing a Bible study program for students. In 1964 she began the first Bible study training weekends, teaching students how to lead evangelistic Bible studies. Eight weekend Bible study conferences were held the first year. Seeing the effectiveness of these weekends, Regional Director Warner Hutchinson gave her his old Navy Chaplain's manual which had skeletal teaching plans in it, and said, "Here, write down what you are trying to do so that staff can do what you are doing. Make it simple like this." This was the beginning of what is now called Bible & Life Training courses (B&L).

It was not long before twenty-seven weekend Bible study training events were held each year. The material was refined. If students were going to lead evangelistic studies, they had to be faithful in their own Quiet Times and know what it meant to live under the lordship of Christ. The new curriculum, now called Level I, contained those basics of true discipleship, along with teaching about friendship Bible studies. Students wanted more in-depth study, and Level II was developed to teach the principles and joy of personal inductive Bible study. Level III came later, its emphasis on teaching a student how to help a younger Christian grow.

The program was based on the conviction that the Word of God does the work of God. Bible & Life was designed for a student-led work in which students could become saturated in Scripture, which contains the authority they are looking for. Staff had used the principles of this kind of training since IV's beginnings. The B&L training put them together into graded training to help disciple students.

A friend typed up the materials Barbara wrote. Barbara ran stencils off on a mimeograph machine she purchased; she got cartons and regularly took loads of materials to the post office for staff mailings. She was left on her own to make this a nationwide program until arrangements were made in 1970 for Bible & Life to become part of InterVarsity Press. Then IVP took care of the scheduling and mailing of the materials for the staff, leaving Barbara free to create new studies. The next year there were fifty B&L weekends for students across the country, and thousands of students have been in the program since.

At the end of a four-week student training camp in 1969, Keith Hunt, East Central regional director and director of Cedar Campus, and Barbara Boyd spent some extra days together to plan a new curriculum. The campus ferment was at its peak. If Inter-Varsity was going to get Christian student leaders to camp—the kind of leaders who would build evangelizing fellowships on campus—then the staff needed a well-defined curriculum aimed at leaders. The four-week camp was not for mixed-up drop-outs from campus life. For serious students struggling with the world's problems the idea of "camp" sounded like fun and games. Keith and Barbara wanted something compelling for thoughtful students ready to become disciples.

They designed a wheel diagram, with the Bible as the hub. Surrounding the Bible were the basic numbered curriculum courses: Personal Discipleship (200), Church and Community (300), World View (400), Evangelism and Apologetics (500), and Chapter Leadership (600). The brochure listed the class numbers and the hours given to various subjects. Students were required to get a staff member's signature to attend, based on the intentional nature of the student's discipleship. It became a four-week camp called The School of Discipleship Training.

In the summer of 1970 two four-week sessions of this camp were held at both Cedar Campus and Bear Trap Ranch. In 1971 Regional Director

Harold Burkhart and staff member Jim Hoover came to Cedar Campus to observe the camp curriculum. In 1972 Burkhart began a similar four-week camp (IV East), using Nyack College (New York) as the training site. IV East moved to the facilities of Gordon College in 1974.

9/Refining and Deepening

In 1967 a foundation grant of $55,000 was given to Inter-Varsity for the purpose of compiling a series of handbooks. At a special Handbook Camp at Cedar Campus that summer, resource people from the various facets of ministry worked on specific projects. Peter Northrup directed the session, supplying materials and instructions about the format. By the end of the summer, rough drafts for five handbooks had been completed: staff, associate staff, faculty, chapter leaders and local committees. These augmented other training manuals already in process by John Alexander.

One of the most influential ideas of the conference came from the brainstorming sessions Paul Byer, Keith Hunt, Jim Nyquist and Peter Northrup had with *HIS* editor Paul Fromer. The chaos on the campus seemed to call for a more manageable, caring community than the present chapter structure allowed. These men spent hours recalling characteristics of different-sized chapters. They discussed the quality of relationships, the sense of mission in the chapter, the center of chapter life, the committee and executive structure of the chapter, and its outreach. Weak chapters tended to equate Inter-Varsity with the weekly meeting, not the prayer meetings, Bible studies or outreach. Campus penetration and spiritual growth among peers could be strengthened by a decentralized chapter life. They bounced these ideas off the students in camp to get their reaction. Out of this discussion came a fresh emphasis on the importance of small groups, called action groups to indicate that its members would do more than have fellowship.[21] It was a decision to make the basic unit of chapters the small group, rather than the large group meeting.

The idea went through refinement during the next year, and the November 1968 issue of *HIS* became the handbook of how to make small groups work, including a ten-week curriculum. Paul Byer recalls that this change in the structuring of chapters happened just in time for the snowball of converts that came from the Jesus Movement. Speaking about the University of Redlands, Byer says, "Within a year's time they probably had 250 conversions on that one campus. We would never have been able to disciple that many students under the old structure."

Bill Tiffan, one of the student leaders who helped his chapter of 250-

300 people at the University of Michigan come to terms with the small group concept, was at Cedar Campus the summer of 1967 when small groups was the hot topic of conversation. During the next school year he became a member of an ad hoc committee working on ways to decentralize the chapter at the University of Michigan. Students, concerned about losing the good fellowship of their chapter life, were upset when they heard the chapter was being divided. But other student leaders were convinced not only that the idea could work, but that it would benefit the witness to Christ and the individual student. After a year of communicating together about the idea, the chapter was ready to begin the program in 1968. Tiffan said, "The students grew with the idea," even though it was not without problems.

In August of 1968 John Alexander directed a National Leadership Institute (NLI) at Cedar Campus for key student leaders from across the country. Alexander's goal was to consolidate a student-led movement by giving uniform teaching and vision. Student leaders discussed the idea of action groups as a way to penetrate the campus. How could they present the gospel in a way that would confront the very serious issues on the campus? These students returned to their campuses ready to transfer their vision into reality. Within the next three years many of those who attended NLI became Inter-Varsity staff members.

In 1968 Western Regional Director Paul Byer recommended closing the ministry at Campus by the Sea at the end of the summer. The staff on the West Coast, responsible for physically opening and closing the facility each year, found it was too heavy a load combined with the demands of the student work. A cry of protest went up from those on the West Coast who had come to love the site, and permission was granted for a CBS alumni team (which included Melvin Friesen) to take over the management of the site with the hope that someday Inter-Varsity student camping would return to the site. Bob Mannes, now dean of students at the University of Southern California, became the director, and the camp served alumni families and rental groups.

West Coast student training was held in more accessible rented facilities at Camp Koinonia, eighty miles south of San Francisco, under Jim Berney's leadership. The staff were experimenting with different kinds of training, some of it at the camp and some in the form of on-campus evangelism training.

Paul Byer decided in 1968 that the regional director's job description no longer interested him, and he handed the West Coast Region over to Jim

Berney. When asked what he wanted to do, Byer said, "I want to bring a group of students together to spend a week in the Scripture doing manuscript study." Jim Berney cut him loose to do just that. He began developing an intensive week's program for studying the first half of Mark, called Mark I. Student response asked for more, so he developed Mark II. It got students into the text of the Scripture and excited about meeting Jesus. Byer then taught other staff how to lead by his own example, and manuscript Bible study is now another way to learn to do inductive study.

Each student receives a triple-spaced copy of the biblical text, without verses or chapter divisions, along with a packet of colored pencils. Working alone on the assigned portion of the text, each makes observations about the text: looking especially for verbs, connecting ideas, contrasts, comparisons, etc. After an allotted time small groups share their observations so that they teach each other. After the whole group has shared, the insights of the instructor are added along with a recap of the observations, interpretations and applications of the text. Bible & Life and manuscript study have each demonstrated Inter-Varsity's commitment to take the Scriptures seriously.

For some time Gordon VanWylen, dean of engineering at the University of Michigan in Ann Arbor, had been discussing with Regional Director Keith Hunt the idea of a campus-related Christian bookstore that would serve as a place to disseminate helpful Christian literature and initiate evangelistic conversations. Under VanWylen's leadership an Ann Arbor committee raised the necessary capital ($12,000) and, under the aegis of InterVarsity Press and encouragement of James Nyquist, the first Logos bookstore was opened near the campus of the University of Michigan on July 15, 1968, with James Wilson and James Carlson as bookstore managers.

The timing was right: the confusion of ideas on the campus was at its peak. Within a short time the store was drawing 300-500 students a day and became a solid back-up to campus ministry in the first years of its existence. Discussions about personal faith took place naturally as a prepared bookstore staff were available to dialog about Jesus Christ as well as sell books. Within a few years the idea had spread to other campus-related cities.

In 1968 InterVarsity Press published *The God Who Is There* and *Escape from Reason* by Francis Schaeffer.[22] These two books spoke to the intellectual and spiritual confusion of the counterculture with such insight that they became best sellers within the year. Schaeffer's writings made sense of the sixties; staff and students packed his lectures, listening to Schaeffer for two hours at a time. He modeled for staff and students listening to people who differed from previous social norms, a much-needed lesson in the turbulent days of the late sixties and early seventies. "In a 'touchy-feely generation,' he made people think," IVCF staffer Tom Trevethan commented. "His legacy was the revival of scholastic evangelicalism."

10/The Organization Matures

In 1969 the IVCF headquarters moved from Chicago to Madison, Wisconsin, after four years of discussion about other potential sites. The advantage of being in a university city had been a prime consideration throughout the search for a site. The original move was to Carroll Hall, and a year later to 233 Langdon, a former sorority house. In 1968 an approved change in nomenclature gave the title of *president* to the general director and the title of *chairman* to the board leader. James McLeish became vice president for finance and continued to push for the structure of local committees begun in 1967 to help the area directors raise funds for staff support and to promote interest in the work. This was a strong effort to involve alumni and other supporters to be actively involved in the ministry of Inter-Varsity. Board Chairman Roy Horsey, encouraged by new growth and development, called for twenty-five new staff members by the 1969-70 school year and a budget increase of $250,000.

The new 1969 policy of the board guaranteed staff salaries by a provision giving permission to borrow internally, and also assured that no one would be terminated solely for financial reasons. The policy of requiring new staff to bring one hundred per cent of their support was discussed at length by the NSDs. Funding of staff remained a major hindrance to growth. Yet good people joined the staff during these years and some of them, like Don Fields, John (Pete) Hammond, Jim Berney, Ned Hale, Jim Hoover, Linda Doll, Will Metzger, Bob Fryling, Barney Ford and others have remained in Inter-Varsity over the years, making significant contributions to student work.

Paul Little began teaching evangelism courses at Trinity Evangelical Divinity School in 1967, on loan from Inter-Varsity. Bob Baylis led the first student tour to Europe in connection with IFES, a combination of home stays in various countries, a study of Reformation history and information about student work in Europe. In 1968 Evan Adams led a ten-day student mission to Barbados, a forerunner of many future overseas training events.

Paul Gibson, a Harvard graduate and one of the team members on the Barbados mission, came on Inter-Varsity staff in 1968 as the first Black staffworker since the civil rights movement began. His assignment was Southern California where he worked at six universities. He found himself frequently giving conscience-raising talks on racial issues at the invitation of other staff, trying to sensitize both students and staff about prejudice. After eighteen months, suffering from burnout, Gibson was transferred to student work in New York City.

On his way east, Gibson stopped at Cedar Campus for some rest and refreshment. Camp Director Keith Hunt began discussions with Gibson and William Pannell, an associate of the Tom Skinner Crusades and a speaker at the camp, about what Inter-Varsity could do to reach Black students. Out of the dialog came a detailed proposal, dated August 1969, for a Black Student movement within the Fellowship. The proposal was sent to John Alexander and Tom Skinner with the hope that the two groups could work together to create a strong witness to Black students on campus.

In general it suggested that IVCF pursue a course of action that would propel the movement into redemptive action in the arena of racial strife and that an interdependent fellowship of Black Americans, with the same autonomy as NCF and SFMF, be allowed and encouraged to grow from the already existing Inter-Varsity fellowships on campus. Specific proposals included the recruitment of Black staff who would recruit Black students and begin to disciple them for campus work. John Alexander did not act on the proposal at that time, but it put before the Fellowship the urgent need to take action to bridge the gulf between Whites and Blacks on the campus.

11/Student Initiative

In the spring of 1964 the five Inter-Varsity students who were meeting at California State University at Fullerton were ready to vote themselves out of existence. They couldn't even find a Christian faculty member to act as an advisor to the group. The college was in its beginning days, meeting in an old elementary school building, and morale was not high. Their staffworker asked, "Since when did any Christian body have the right to vote itself out of existence? Who knows what God will do next year?" That caution changed their plans, and when they kicked off their fall term, they found they had five Christian faculty. Within two years their IV chapter was three hundred students strong.

Christian student leaders were taking all sorts of risks: coffee houses with psychedelic lighting, free coffee and lots of conversation; guitars and concerts with loud music and testimonies about the relevance of knowing Jesus Christ; open-air preaching; endless talking about the meaning of life. More than one student, enticed into the mysteries of an LSD trip, ended up scared to death and eager to investigate what Jesus might offer them.

During the summer of 1969 Inter-Varsity students in the Pasadena area met together for what they called a Southern California Leaders Bible study. In August one of the students, Rich Lang, got the idea of having a '69 Kickoff for all the Southern California IVCF students at summer's end so that they would hit the campus all tuned in for fall term. Rich found a big dining room at the top level of the Anaheim stadium that could hold one hundred-fifty students. A week later over two hundred collegians were registered, so Rich set out again to find a bigger place. He went to the Anaheim Convention Center and rented a room that would hold around 1500 people. Staff member Evan Adams gulped when he heard that news. How were they going to pay for that kind of rental? "Don't worry," Rich said, "It will work out all right."

The group began recruiting students as far away as San Francisco and San Diego. They brought in special singing groups, including Randy Stone-hill, a big name singer and guitarist on the West Coast. Things kept rolling. They planned to collect five dollars from everyone at the door, but hadn't planned quite how to do that until Eric Miller, then a Fuller Seminary student, went to Kentucky Fried Chicken and got Colonel Sanders buckets for the money-takers. Eighteen hundred students showed up. "There were these guys holding these chicken buckets and just taking five-dollar bills and stuffing them in—with no inkling of how much money they were taking in or whether it was enough to pay the bill." Four hours of music and student testimonies of what God was doing on campus and in their lives created a "wildly successful" evening. The next day they met to count the money and pay the bills. They had $240 left over.

Enthusiasm was high. Rich Lang, the entrepreneur and originator of the idea, said, "You know, we got something going with this kick-off. This year let's have a traveling evangelistic team in Southern California that will visit all the campuses. Let's use the left-over money for that." Eric Miller said, "Let me tell you about something we did recently in Africa with multimedia." The more he told about what he had seen happen in high schools and in colleges in Tanzania through multi-media presentations of the gospel, the more enthused the group became. They voted that the $240 should go to Eric Miller as seed money to begin a multimedia evangelistic project like that for Southern California. They called the project Multi-Media Communications (MMC). Thus began the ministry of TWENTYONE-HUNDRED—truly grass-roots.

12/Looking Back

Living through the 1960s on campus was like going through a revolution. Some students blew their minds on drugs and would never be whole again. Others became cynical, hanging on to an unrelieved disillusionment. Many cultural Christians fell by the wayside. Yet for many Christian students the years seemed a replay of the trial of faith that the apostle Peter wrote about —where real "faith is proven genuine and results in praise, glory and honor to Jesus Christ." Scores of students came to faith in Jesus Christ on campuses across the country.

For the leadership within Inter-Varsity it was also a trial of faith, with moments of confusion and enormous challenge. Yet even when things looked most muddled, the movement never lost its vision for developing Christlike student leaders whose lives and witness would help build the kingdom of God. As the new president, John Alexander was committed to the same vision and purposes that had marked Inter-Varsity's beginnings under Stacey Woods and Charles Troutman. He and the staff team were carrying on the movement's intent to build strong groups of students whose goals were evangelism, discipleship and missions. The climate of the 1960s would not change the strategy: get students into the Scripture, emphasize daily Quiet Time and the lordship of Christ, urge them to meet together and pray for their outreach on the campus—and then to go and do it.

13
The Challenge of Growth and Stability: Decade of the 1970s

Never mind that the Jesus freaks are scripturally illiterate, that the long-hairs want no part of the organizational church, or that the sandal-clad ones wearing the sign of the fish are insecure in the presence of the short-haired square of the parental generation. They've been motivated by the knowledge . . . that Jesus is the Christ, the Son of God, Savior of men, and the only way out of the amoral, agnostic and atheistic jungle of the 1970s.[1]
Laurence C. Walker, *dean, School of Forestry, Stephen F. Austin State University*

The freshmen class of September 1969 assumed campus protest was normal. Media reports of campus rebellion captured their imagination and some of them arrived on campus primed for battle, already experienced demonstrators from secondary schools. It was a glorious moment of self-confidence and adolescent impatience; they were young, bright and free to express their rage. They discovered protest can be deadly. On May 4, 1970, twenty-eight members of the National Guard, young and frightened, fired sixty-one random bullets into a group of approximately two hundred Kent State students moving toward them in protest on the campus about a hundred yards away. Four students died instantly. It was an unthinkable reality. Four months later antiwar radicals bombed Sterling Hall at the University of Wisconsin, killing Robert Fassnacht, a thirty-two-year-old graduate student. Killing people wasn't part of the radical agenda; angry fires were quickly doused by this stupidity. Undergraduate militancy evaporated. Committed radicals kept on raising political issues, but they could no longer inspire mass student support.[2]

The tragedies sobered everyone. It was as if the government "heard" student protest against the Vietnam War for the first time. The bombing of Cambodia had sent thousands of students to the streets in outrage. President Nixon got the message. He began winding down the war before resigning in August of 1974 as president. The war's end meant a dramatic shift in mood on the campus; students cut back on "conventions in the street." They began to worry about their lives in a new way. Both Vietnam and Watergate left them disillusioned about their ability to bring about change; they didn't matter to the world.

Student grievances were not hard to find—resentment over inadequate Black or Chicano study programs, rent-gouging in private off-campus housing, police harassment of marijuana smokers, hypocrisy in leadership, chauvinism—but none seemed serious enough to warrant days of destructive rioting and the burning of bank buildings or the smashing of plate-glass windows. Plans to bring the "whole establishment to its knees" and the proposal that "guerilla warfare must continue until the university is forced to close" suddenly got little response. A few diehards joined the staff of the student newspaper or political groups on campus, but found that both held little respect. The college rebel was a displaced person.

While students couldn't get many out to a political rally, they could fill a hall if they announced a lecture on Transcendental Meditation. In the middle of an explosion of knowledge (the sheer mass of information to be assimilated was four times greater than that available when their professors were students) the young became increasingly nonrational in their approach to life. Having reacted against authority, some began to buy into authoritative systems that gave them answers to their inward searching. Cults were thriving on the fringes of the campus. In a curious and personally disconcerting way, students found themselves highly sophisticated in the realm of knowledge and yet emotionally empty. The lack of any value structure made decision making difficult, and some students opted for groups that made decisions for them.

The heightened environment in which they lived sensitized young people to human values. Justice, peace, love, tolerance—these were the real virtues to the many who were idealists. Students tended to be more "personal" than the adults they reacted against. Relationships became the new in-word. They had a genuine desire to share their lives, to be known and to enter into the lives of others. At Woodstock (August 15-17, 1969) someone at the mike told the mass of gathered young people, "If we're going to make it, you'd better believe that the fellow sitting next to you is your brother." The small group movement, within IVCF and within society in general, was well-timed; students chose small groups rather than large meetings. "Small is beautiful" became a guiding philosophy for some. Committed believers called their small group experience *fellowship* and put it high on their agenda. They wanted intimacy, not jargon. Yet they sometimes created their own unreality by assuming a closeness that hadn't been cultivated, dumping the file-drawers of their minds on unsuspecting members of their small group, making others responsible for their feelings. Honesty was more important than discretion. They often had warm feelings about each other simply because they shared the same problem. It wasn't so much that they wanted help out of the problem; they just wanted to be understood. They grasped at "least-common-denominator" relationships.

Affluence allowed much of the lifestyle students enjoyed, even while they scoffed at the materialism of their parents. Those who had to worry about tuition and spending money generally stayed out of the revolution, even though they were affected by it. The hedonism that came in with the sixties was entrenched by the seventies. "Seeking a relationship" often meant moving in with your girl or boy friend. Long hair and pony tails for men, and blue jeans and visits to second-hand stores for "role clothes" were part of the simplicity scene, but no one blinked an eye at expensive stereo equipment, guitars or tickets to rock festivals. There was no shortage of people who could pick a tune and sing a thoughtful complaint against the establishment or the pain of loneliness. Students with enough education to make them classroom professors chose instead to be carpenters or farmers—to work with their hands and create something tangible. Career uncertainty became almost epidemic.

Women students entered formerly all-male universities and professional schools made way for them. For all of that, women went through their own crisis. Militant feminists shouted obscene slogans at campus men and raised questions for incoming women freshmen about their sexuality. The popularity of books like *Our Bodies, Ourselves*[3] nudged militant feminism toward lesbianism. For some, lesbianism emerged not only as an alternative possibility but as the correct political choice. College men were sensitized, lest they be labeled "male chauvinist pigs." The women's movement began to have a profound impact on college students.

But that is only half the story. Eventually students forgot that they couldn't trust anyone over thirty and began asking all kinds of questions from people they thought might know the answer, regardless of age. They stood poised with pen and notebook in hand to write down the answers— which they compared with other answers to decide for themselves which they liked best. By the middle of the decade students had rejoined the Establishment and were studying hard to get the job they wanted in the marketplace. Yale University President Kingman Brewster characterized it as "grim professionalism." Students became not only quiet; they were unnaturally quiet.[4] A new reality set in: graduate school assured the best future and they had to place well to get in. The economy soured, unemployment rates soared, jobs were scarce, and parents began to hurry their children toward success, trying to avoid the "downward mobility" that had plagued the lives of their children in the sixties. Selfishness came to the campus with the student; the college did not invent "Me-ism."

In the midsixties several universities had reorganized their calendar year and moved their institutions into the trimester plan. Classes began in late August or early September, allowing students to finish the first trimester by Christmas. The plan was intended to streamline education so that a student could go year-round and finish a college education in three years. It did not work that way.[5] The plan did succeed in getting most students off campus in late April or early May, before weather changes caused their blood to boil over in political demonstrations. A side benefit: these students had an edge in the summer job market. By the early 1970s an increasing number of colleges had adopted the plan. The change brought new pressure on student life and studies. The course material was crammed into a shortened time, making the trimester another policy that "took the fun out of college life."

Sixty-three per cent of freshmen in the late seventies gave "the desire to be prosperous" as their main collegiate objective.[6] That desire changed their clothing. Tattered jeans and faded shirts were replaced by rugby shirts and designer jeans. They wanted the good life. Students were pessimistic about the future, but still wanted to go "first class on the Titanic."[7] One reporter used telling phrases to describe the tone of campus life as "lost civility, a self-centered disregard for others' rights." Rape and thievery were common assaults within the university community. Required books were stolen from the library or mutilated beyond using. The old codes that made the university a safe place had disappeared, partly because college had ceased to be a definable place. A sense of community eroded, fed in part by the wider range of ethnic and socio-economic groups now represented on the campus. Unfortunately ethnic pride often became ethnic isolation.

Drugs, sex and alcohol were college facts of life, increasing as the seventies went on. Some, wanting college life to return to a more carefree tone, thought up some outrageous pranks, and "streaking" or "mooning" seemed a clever diversion. But the old college life was gone. Student governments held elections and no one came. A radical fringe held the student newspaper hostage, but campus conservatives laughed it off. Self-help books rolled off the presses as the decade went on. Humanism, as a philosophy of life, spawned the human potential movement, flooding its ideas everywhere. Health foods, jogging and other ways to improve one's self became obsessions.

Many elements in the counterculture were corrosive to evangelical Christian witness on the campus. The hostility to structure made Christian students reluctant to lay plans. The appeal of emotion over reason led many of these students to be experience-oriented and open to charismatic expressions of faith. History or hard-won comprehension was less satisfying; immediacy and personal feelings of the moment mattered more. Students spiritualized their randomness in planning; it was better just to wait on God. At one university IVCF students held an all-night prayer meeting to determine if they should plan a large group meeting! Christian meetings were prolonged times of informal prayer and praise, singing and expressions of joy, but little teaching. A talk peppered with personal illustrations and, above all, evidence of personal struggle turned more students on than sound teaching from the Scripture. Francis Schaeffer commented that waving "contentless banners was more attractive than wrestling with biblical issues." To be boring was the great crime of the age.

The groups that prospered on campus offered something for students—most often to feed their sense of self. Evangelical Christianity was one of the attractive offerings, but it was scattered shot. On some campuses as many as thirty different Christian groups vied for student attention. While this proliferation of groups could be seen as a positive way to meet a variety of student needs, it also had a down-side. It allowed students to "shop around" and sometimes remain uncommitted to any one group or to evangelizing the campus. Some of the groups pulled Christian students off the campus into the local church, ignoring the campus as a mission field. In contrast to the days when the collegiate YMCA/YWCA confronted the campus with one sizeable and significant voice, campus Christian witness was now diffused among many groups.[8]

Jim Reapsome initiated a monthly four-page newsletter for Inter-Varsity called *Youth Today* in October 1969, highlighting student trends, campus happenings, surveys and other items that might help define what the now generation was doing and why.[9] It was an interesting time to be a student worker on campus. As one staffworker said, "If you work with students you have got to pocket your shock."

1/Campus Life in the Seventies

Life on the secular campus had a hardness to it. Many adults doubted whether Christians could survive in this milieu. A Jewish theologian gave his own analysis:

> The problem of our youth is not youth. The problem is the spirit of our age: denial of transcendence, the vapidity of values, emptiness in the heart, the decreased sensitivity to the imponderable quality of the spirit, the collapse of communication between the realm of tradition and the inner world of the individual. The central problem is that we do not know how to pray, how to cry, how to resist the deceptions of too many persuaders. There is no community of those who worry about integrity.[10]

Inter-Varsity student groups stood in sharp contrast to this analysis. A committed Christian student writing in 1972 from State University of New York at New Paltz describes the tone of college life and how hard it was to be loving toward others:

> Through it all God is teaching us and giving us more stability in him. . . . We are realizing that we are actually New Paltz's missionaries. We're learning how to preach the Good News in the midst of apathy, depression, confusion and even a body of Christians here that has many problems to work out. I've seen so many become Christians since I've been here. From a group of five we are now thirty. For myself, I wouldn't trade the two and a half years I've had here for anything. Lots of time I've wanted to get as far away as possible. But I'm sure God has called me to New Paltz—drugs, free love and all. Living among it is a discipline that I desperately need to become more like him.

The hardness and the confusion sometimes brought an openness to Christian witness that might not have been there in easier days. For example, twenty-four freshmen women responded when four Inter-Varsity students invited them to a Bible study at Agnes Scott College (Georgia) in the fall of 1972. Instead of meeting as one large group, the four originators each led a study for six students. As the year went on they began training each of the freshmen to lead a Bible study, hoping that their witness would be greatly extended in the next year.

The more committed the students, the more they were spiritually tuned to their friends. At Harper College (New York) about twelve to twenty attended the noon prayer meeting during the 1973 school year. They began their meeting by singing a hymn or two, but then got down to the purpose of meeting: they prayed for their friends and specific needs. During one week three Jewish students accepted Jesus as Messiah. One created quite an impact in her dorm with her newfound faith. Another woman student told IVCF staff member Allen Harris, "I became a Christian since you last saw me. I always thought I was one, but I am in Harry's Bible study and came to see I was wrong. Now I've trusted the Lord and what a difference!" Students like these had a kind of spiritual wholesomeness about them, and were not surprised to see their friends come to Christ in answer to their prayers. "Believing God" is what it is all about, one student said.

International students had repeated culture shocks in the moral climate of campus life. Hong-Kong-born Chinese Johnson Lee came to study at Wichita State (Kansas) in 1978. His host family were Christians and through them he became a believer. In the fellowship of the Inter-Varsity chapter his faith continued to grow. When his fellow classmates in the commercial arts department befriended him and offered to drive him to a party the students had planned, he felt he should accept the invitation. At the party most of the people were absorbed in smoking marijuana and paid little attention to him. Johnson felt uneasy and wished he hadn't come. He wondered how he could leave graciously and find a ride home. He noticed a fellow named Rod on the opposite side of the room, sitting alone, occasionally puffing on a marijuana cigarette, but much less involved in the partying. When he approached him, he noticed he was wearing a cross, so he asked him, "What does that mean?"

Rod replied, "It's a cross; you know, where Jesus died for our sins."

Johnson asked, "Do you believe that?"

"I used to," Rod answered. He paused, and then added, "You know, I don't think I belong at this party. Want a ride home?"

Johnson Lee took the ride home and continued to ask questions about Christianity, as though he knew nothing of the faith. They agreed to meet the next day, so that Rod could give Johnson some printed materials about Christianity. After that meeting Johnson was concerned about his deception. He talked it over with faculty member Glen Zumwalt, and they prayed that Rod would not react negatively when Johnson told him that he had only pretended ignorance to get Rod to talk and think through the gospel. As a result of this encounter, Rod and two others who were at the party became Christians.[11]

By the seventies a shift in the background of Inter-Varsity students was noticeable. Previously, chapters had been dominated by students who came from Christian families. Now an increasing number of student leaders had become Christians on the campus. Broken homes and one-parent homes left marks of insecurity on students' lives. The church sent fewer of its students to help in this mission on campus, and some of those who came had little concept of what it meant to live for Christ. The way in which committed student leaders discipled other students during these years kept the grassroots emphasis in Inter-Varsity strong. What happened at UCLA illustrates the way students not only provided leadership, but helped each other grow into mature believers.

Steve Stuckey arrived on campus at UCLA as a freshman in 1966. The Inter-Varsity chapter had fallen on hard times. In the turmoil of the late sixties, for two years in a row the chapter president had resigned. Six women students kept the chapter going and regularly prayed that God would expand their witness and bring men into the chapter. Steve was one of several men who joined the group in answer to their prayers. He describes himself as a shy and immature Christian. Another student, David Sugano, came to the chapter and changed the whole cycle of defeat. As a more mature Christian, Dave decided to invest himself in the life of a younger student each year. During his junior year, Dave chose Steve Stuckey as his "younger student." Steve said, "Dave really matured me as a Christian, sticking with me in his quiet way, discipling me for ministry on campus. He did this each year, pouring himself into individuals, one by one."

Steve became one of the Bible study leaders on campus and, when the November 1968 issue of *HIS* magazine arrived, he and the other students read and believed every word of the article on action groups. The small UCLA chapter heard God's call for a large chapter. Each of the core students in the group became action group leaders. By the end of the year they had thirty students involved in six action groups. The leaders began to disciple others to lead the groups, realizing that they needed to replace themselves. During Steve's senior year, the chapter got its first staff member who could regularly be on the UCLA campus. That staff member, Hank Pott, continued to do what Dave Sugano had done as a student. He chose twelve freshmen and began to disciple them. The chapter executive ran the chapter; Pott discipled twelve freshmen each year. By 1973 the chapter had boomed to two hundred fifty members. Twenty years later Dave Sugano is a Ford Motor Company executive and is actively involved in his church, doing the same thing he did when he was a student at UCLA. Steve Stuckey serves as Inter-Varsity's regional director for the staff teams working with Southern California universities.[12]

2/Student Leadership

The extremes of the charismatic movement brought some Inter-Varsity chapters to the brink of confusion and division—even dissolution—during the late sixties and early seventies. Students with charismatic experiences or yearnings often made the gift of tongues normative for everyone, which led to a hierarchy of spirituality and trouble within the chapter. If "small is beautiful," then outreach is limited, and some groups were content with looking inward, "feeling" their religion in new ways, with a new conscious-ness of the spirit world—both good and evil.

Pete Hammond, regional director in the Southeast, was responsible for 103 chapters, with 97 of them going through agony over "charismatic" disagreements. Staff members found their time on campus consumed with these issues. Often the energy needed for campus outreach was consumed by intense theological discussions about the gifts of the Spirit.

By the late sixties the large and flourishing group at Michigan State University (East Lansing) had dwindled down to a core group of 20-30 students. Others on the fringes observed chapter life but were only occa-sionally involved. The leadership of the chapter was in the hands of gen-uinely sincere students with charismatic persuasions. They longed to ex-perience more of God, but the practical outworkings of this gave the chapter the flavor of an "in-group." The chapter had not been experiencing growth or outreach and had very little staff help.

Three underclassmen who had been concentrating on dorm witness raised the question of the purpose of an Inter-Varsity chapter. In the spring of 1971 when officer-election time came, they decided to present their names as an alternative to the prepared slate of officers, hoping to stimulate chapter members to think of their chapter's mission. It was a risky thing to do. They talked over their concerns with the others already running on the election slate, expressing their support for them as individuals, but were forthright about the difference in their chapter vision. They urged them to join in recruiting the fringe people into the life and direction of the chapter. As a result students began to discuss Inter-Varsity's purpose and vision in a new way. Their youthful commitment to Christ was stretched and a potentially hurtful situation became an occasion for chapter growth. An amiable election brought in the new leadership team.

In the next year through outreach and discipling the group grew to 150. Student leaders asked Elwyn Davies, general director of the Bible Christian Union and one of the most effective speakers at Cedar Campus, to spend a week on campus in the spring. For two years in succession Davies had a powerful week-long ministry to the student chapter. A faculty family gave Davies comfortable housing where he was able to do his own work for the bulk of the day. In the afternoons he went to the campus for private conversations with individual students and spoke each evening on the Christian life and God's call to take the gospel to the ends of the earth. This kind of volunteerism greatly supplemented the work of Inter-Varsity staff who were responsible for many campuses.

In June of 1973, student president Mark Hunt wrote to Missions Director David Howard telling him that the IV chapter was "turned on" to missions.

Elwyn Davies came in January for a week of meetings on missions. . . . Each night before he spoke a student who had been involved with a summer mission project spoke about the experience. During that week one chapter member received a letter from Wycliffe Bible Translators, accepting her as a short term missionary in Ecuador. . . . At an April dinner meeting students talked for two and half hours after the meal where five students made presentations on subjects like "The Biblical Basis for Missions," "What Is a Missionary?" "What Is IFES?" and "On being an M.K. (Missionary Kid)." . . . Since then nine students are planning on going overseas, another dozen are seriously considering a summer's project. Of the seven graduating seniors three are going overseas. God is answering the prayers of the few who prayed for a stirring of concern among his people here.[13]

3/Urbana 70
When David Howard gave the keynote address at Urbana 70 he quoted Clarence Shedd of Yale who said, "In all ages the great creative religious ideas have been the achievement of the intellectual and spiritual insight of . . . young men (and women) under 30 and frequently between 18 and 25. . . . The universities have always been breeding places for such groups."

It was a good reminder as over 12,000 young men and women poured into Urbana, probably the youngest group in the convention's history—young in Christian experience, less well-versed in Scripture, many of them new believers. In dozens of interviews with students conducted by *HIS* staff, students gave as their reason for coming to Urbana: "I needed spiritual help"; "To get together with other Christians"; "My church offered to pay my way." Rarely did a delegate say, "I came to learn about missions and decide if God wants me overseas." Along with the new information about missions, they needed to hear about the excellence of Christ's lordship and gain confidence in the Scripture as the rule for life and faith. They went away with a new concern for prayer, for doing God's will, for understanding Scripture and for campus evangelism.

John R. W. Stott gave morning Bible expositions on John 13—17, giving students a fresh look at Jesus and his teaching, and making applications to students' personal lives. Stott said at one point, "Are you looking for freedom? . . . You will find it in submission to the authority of Christ. This is true of both doctrine and practice." He reminded students of something else they needed to hear: "The Christian life is not just a personal and private relationship to Christ. It also involves mutual love. . . . For we cannot belong to Christ without belonging to his people as well. Are you a conscientious member of a local Christian church? Every Christian should be a church member. Lone-wolf Christianity is not biblical Christianity. If God is our Father, we are brothers and sisters and must express our family life in corporate activities." If you meet rejection in the church instead of acceptance, Stott said, "Do not accept this non-acceptance as an acceptable alternative. Persevere. Claim the membership which is yours by right, if you are Christ's."

Paul Little, convention director, spoke one evening on knowing the will of God. The message targeted student need and was later reprinted as an IVP booklet, *Affirming the Will of God.* He said, "Somehow we have gotten the idea that God is a celestial Scrooge who leans over the balcony of heaven trying to find people who are enjoying themselves and yells down, 'Cut it out!' when he sees us. If he once gets his clammy hands on our lives, happiness is down the tube. This should make us shudder because it is blasphemous." Instead Little urged delegates to affirm the will of God in their lives—affirm that it exists, that it is good, and that God will reveal it in his time.

Speakers explored the convention theme: "Christ the Liberator" in its various dimensions. Tom Skinner, plenary speaker on the second night, described the Black experience historically and his own growing up in the ghetto. He challenged delegates to think about racial prejudice and the gospel. He said, "Blacks are engaged in a revolution of identity in which they are trying to find out who they are. . . . It is also a revolution of community. They are seeking to secure control in their own communities against a White-supported power structure. . . . It is a revolution of power by which they hope to influence the larger society around them." Skinner spoke about a radical Jesus who would not tolerate racism. As he ended his talk, Skinner shouted, "The Liberator has come!" and twelve thousand mostly White young delegates stood to their feet and cheered.

Later that night most of the 600 Black student delegates met for half the night to share newly aroused pain and discuss their own reactions to racism within the Christian church.[14] They asked Whites to leave the gathering; they needed privacy. What was their place in missions, in Inter-Varsity? The next night they met again and invited concerned White delegates to meet with them. A White student from Houston stood and asked for help from the several hundred Blacks around him. He related the racial prejudice he had grown up with in his family. "With my background, how do I know where I'm prejudiced? What kind of mistakes must I avoid?" Others asked similar questions. Whether the frequent laughter and banter indicated a relaxed atmosphere or nervousness is unimportant. They were meeting together and talking. One staff member commented, "Both Blacks and Whites have got to remember that the issue is really the lordship of Christ. Racism is a sin, ultimately, against God, not the Blacks, and it is to God that we must go for forgiveness. . . . This means we will also make amends with our Black brothers and sisters."

The Black delegation requested the thrust of the convention be changed. David Howard recounts,

> They wanted the missions emphasis dropped in the middle of the week. They wanted us to get on "the real issues of the day," the racism issue, the poverty within the inner city. But in *Student Power and World Evangelism* I had traced the history of the Student Volunteer Movement (SVM). SVM began in 1886 and by 1920 it had taken a nosedive. The SVM put missions aside because they wanted to get on with more relevant issues like war, poverty, racism. Now we were faced with the same issue. At Des Moines, Iowa, in 1920 students were saying almost word for word what we were hearing from the Black delegation fifty years later. And the timing was amazing. From 1886 to 1920 is thirty-four years. The Student Foreign Missions Fellowship had begun in 1936, and that was thirty-four years ago in 1970. I was so glad for that recent research in my book which so clearly pointed to the importance of sticking with the purpose of the convention.[15]

Howard held to the planned program in spite of the strong momentum behind the Black cause. The Black students did not feel they had been fully heard, and they were right. But it was a beginning, a rallying point. The necessary communication had only begun.

In many ways Urbana 70 was a high-water mark for the Fife-Glasser kind of convention in which issues were discussed and students thoughtfully responded. The messages of speakers like Samuel Escobar, with IFES in Latin American, and Myron Augsburger, president of Eastern Mennonite College and Seminary, had a prophetic note, powerfully linking evangelism and social action in the gospel. The theology of this Urbana was perhaps the Black student's best hope for being heard. By the late seventies Urbana had steadily moved away from the intellectual issue-oriented programs and, by the eighties, purposefully emphasized more emotional recruitment appeals, following the mood of the student world.

The delegate members of the 113 mission boards had a great time talking missions with students, most of whom knew nothing of the Black confrontation. The convention used the computer services of Inter-Cristo for the first time. Students filled out a questionnaire when they sent in their registration regarding their training and interests. This information was fed into a computer and upon arrival at the convention each student was handed a printout of mission openings that fit his/her background. This meant that during the early afternoons they could look up specific mission agencies for more information. TEAM (The Evangelical Alliance Mission) had the names of 2,000 students by the week's end. A most spectacular match came for the Red Sea Mission team who had been looking for two years for a veterinarian specializing in camels, donkeys and goats. They found someone with that specialization at Urbana.

The large delegation made for some inconveniences. At midnight on the opening night, Paul Little apologized to some 1200 students waiting in Huff gymnasium for late registration. He explained that because of a snafu in university housing, temporary facilities had to be created. Half of these students ended up sleeping on cots in public lounges. Michigan State delegate Tom Bowers said that, to his great surprise, he heard no gripes or complaints. Instead the students sat and sang until 3 A.M. when the final registrations were processed. A police officer on duty was so impressed he volunteered the use of his squad car to go look for coffee and food. Once in their housing, getting the cots assembled and usable caused so much hilarity that Bowers said the men assigned to his room soon forgot their fatigue. Five students—two Canadians, two Americans and one Nigerian—experienced such unifying love for Christ and each other in the process of creating their own Bible study and prayer group that they refused the offer of better housing and stayed together through the convention. Bowers says, "On the last night of the convention the five of us sat together in the Assembly Hall. Someone brandished a camera, and while the other 12,000 stood to sing, we remained seated with our arms around each other and smiled at the camera. A copy of that picture was taped to my desk for a long time, reminding me of the whole event—the fellowship of these men I had come to love in Christ, the post-midnight singing in the gymnasium, the speakers, the Urbana experience."[16]

4/A Decade of Urbanas

Four Urbanas were held during the 1970s. Campus staff members *were* the Urbana staff, along with some volunteers. The missions department consisted of the director and anywhere from two to four others. That meant that all of the staff left their families on Christmas or the day after Christmas. Those responsible for major Urbana functions left earlier. The efficiency of the whole operation of Urbana was impressive, and the staff team gave themselves to make it run so smoothly that no one who attended would be aware of all that went on behind the scenes. During the seventies it seemed to some that Urbana was the tail "wagging the whole dog." It was a huge undertaking that continued to grow: something like registering and operating the entire life experience of a sizeable college for a five-day curriculum. Who can forget the efficient convention manager Kay Barton? Or campus staff members Mark Malan and Fred Neubert organizing all the buses and volunteers for the shuttle service so necessary for the parts of the program work? Or Vice President of Finance Jim McLeish and Area Director Barney Ford supervising the registration floor in Huff Gym? Or NCF staff Marian Hall managing all the pre-registration process, handling all the problems? And the hundreds of others who supervised Bible study leaders early each morning, handled the office, the media, the ushers, the platform, the speakers. It was exhausting, exciting and more worthwhile than staffworkers even knew.

Jim Reapsome, writing about Urbana 73 for *HIS* magazine, described it as "a multicolored, multilingual, international throng worshiping the Lamb." Registration totals were 14,158; 11,288 were students for this 10th triennial missionary convention. Urbana 73 centered on a tightly-knit, carefully developed theme: "Jesus Christ, Lord of the Universe, Hope of the World." Canadian poet Margaret Clarkson[17] wrote a theme hymn that captured student enthusiasm and which has made its way into church hymnals. ("Lord of the Universe" can be found in *Hymns II*, no. 176.) On the closing night, sound as of thunder rolled through the Assembly Hall: "Our Father in heaven . . . the kingdom is yours, and the power and the glory."[18]

On the day before the convention a bus carrying staff and volunteer helpers turned over on an icy Illinois highway and staff members Susan McClure and William Scadding were killed. Susan's ministry had been with students in Boston and Bill's in Toronto. Nine others on the bus were hospitalized. It was a sober beginning, particularly for the staff. What would God do with this convention which had already cost the lives of some?

Student enthusiasm was high as the week progressed. Fourteen hundred small groups met for Bible studies in their residence halls, and again for prayer before retiring. Songleader Bernie Smith led traditional hymns and praise songs, calling for a frequent attitude check, to which the crowd responded "Praise the Lord!"[19] Diverse sounds of praise came from Soul Liberation, a gospel rock group from New York City; from singer and guitarist John Kilner, IVCF chapter president at Yale; from the Mennonite Brethren Bible College in Winnipeg, Manitoba,[20] and from the students themselves. Philip Teng of Hong Kong did the Bible expositions; John Stott spoke on the authority of Scripture; Paul Little gave a talk on the lordship of Christ; Edmund Clowney addressed the lostness of man. Elisabeth Elliot Leitch was the first woman speaker to bring a major address at an Urbana Convention. Christy Wilson, Bill Thomas, Pius Wakatama, Gregorio Landero (who spoke in Spanish with David Howard translating) and two students—Donald Curry, a medical student in Canada, and Russell Weatherspoon, Black leader from Brooklyn College—were among the speakers.

By this time TWENTYONEHUNDRED had become a national resource production department for Inter-Varsity. Their blockbuster eight-screen multimedia presentation called "Family Portraits—the Church in the World" in the huge Urbana arena was a photographic narrative of tensions Christians face in the witness to Christ around the world. It was the first of many educational media productions TWENTYONEHUNDRED would produce to instruct students at Urbana.

There are sacred moments in the Urbana experience that stick in the memory, like jewels in the fabric of the convention. One of these was certainly Edmund Clowney's talk on the lostness of man in which he began with an ancient song from 1300 B.C. and ended with a quote from George Herbert's "The Agonie." Clowney urged students to "go to the very depths of your doubts and gather them all up; take all your unsolved problems, all the whys that come out of the anguish of your hearts, whys that grow out of major tragedies, whys when you do not understand. Just bring your whys, your questions to God. But come there to stay. . . . Come there to listen while Jesus Christ the God-man in his human nature cries out, 'Why?' Then do not say that the Father's wrath against sin is too much."

5/*HIS* magazine and InterVarsity Press

For eleven years Paul Fromer, editor of *HIS* magazine, published thoughtful reading material for a student-led movement, aiming at highly motivated students and grabbing the interest of others by the relevance of its content. He had given the magazine the same timely voice it had during Joe Bayly's editorship. Fromer had been a campus staff member; he knew what students needed. His philosophy in editing reflected the basic values of Inter-Varsity. The underlying principle for *HIS* was the lordship of Jesus Christ. Over the years the message came through repeatedly. A person receives Jesus Christ. Who is he? He is both Lord and Christ. A Christian must consciously live under Christ's lordship. Many of the American fundamentalist churches during the sixties spoke of receiving the Savior and being saved, with Christ's lordship as a subsequent option. "In nonmoral days when people were looking for a fire escape from hell," Fromer said, "*HIS* stressed the lordship of Christ over every part of life." This affected students in their witness and was particularly important as the Jesus Movement began to influence student culture.

HIS presented Christians as the people of God (1 Peter 2:9-10). Every Christian represents God, tying the Christian life to the nature of God which, Fromer believes, leads to a proper world/life view. It avoids the simplistic "to be an obedient Christian you must witness," which is only one part of a larger life lived under the lordship of Christ. The gospel and social concerns must also be linked under his lordship. Fromer's theory was that students would pick up a world/life view by reading the magazine. For this reason he did not ask students what they liked; he gave them what he thought would help them become what God wanted them to *be* like. *HIS* also carried articles heavy on doctrine. When Fromer saw the *New Yorker* publish articles in serial form, he thought *HIS* could do the same. John Stott wrote a series on the Apostles Creed; Fromer found and published a series on the glory of God by A. W. Tozer. Vernon Grounds wrote a scholarly series on Christianity and psychology. Fromer says, "In a nondoctrinal era *HIS* emphasized doctrine. When our teaching is nondoctrinal, it fastens people on elementary terms of Christianity and does not help them grow."

Back in 1959 when Joe Bayly hired Gordon Stromberg as art editor, *HIS* became one of the first Christian magazines to have a full-time graphic designer. Bayly wanted Stromberg to enlarge the reader's understanding of art under the lordship of Christ.[21] It did more than give the magazine a classy look. Stromberg used art to integrate the content of the magazine. He was gifted in typeface selection and used it skillfully. For an important article on *David,* Stromberg did the magazine cover in Hebraic style, including the letters of the magazine's name, *HIS.* Assistant Editor Virginia Krauss (1957-63) had a sense for forceful, precise writing, and she set the standard for high-quality prose in *HIS.* She understood poetry and helped *HIS* publish quality material. These three: Paul Fromer, Gordon Stromberg and Virginia Krauss (Hearn) were a formidable team. Over the years *HIS* received many prizes for excellence from the Evangelical Press Association. Over sixty-five per cent of the magazine's readers were students during the 1960s.

Under Fromer *HIS* increased its coverage of Inter-Varsity happenings (eighteen pages on the 1970 Urbana!) *HIS* published practical how-to articles, instructive for building Inter-Varsity chapters. Joe Bayly had introduced the use of rich "twisted tales" and won wide acclaim with the publication of his own "I Saw Gooley Fly." Fromer continued the use of spoof articles that charmed readers or, at the very least, made them read more carefully. An article on the advantages of living in "Bible City" brought 100 letters, some of protest from those who thought *HIS* was actually promoting the idea. "I Recruited Wally Wakefield" told the story of a man who was always preparing to enter the Navy, studied naval strategy, decorated his house with naval flags, always preparing, but he never joined the navy. Students loved it.

Stacey Woods hired Paul Fromer as editor in 1960. *HIS* had been Stacey's "brain-child" and he reveled in discussions about what to include in the magazine in a way that excited editors. Since the magazine represented Inter-Varsity, any discussion of its content and the freedom of the editor focused on what students needed to hear. But it was always clear; the editor was in charge. *HIS* was for students; it was not a public relations piece. When Charles Hummel became interim general director he told Fromer, "We will not have a committee that approves of what goes into *HIS.* You are the editor." When Charles Troutman succeeded Hummel, he took Fromer for a walk and said, "I want you to know that you have full responsibility for *HIS.* I trust you, and if I don't like what you do, I'll fire you." Fromer said that kind of clear-cut authority produced responsible editorship.

HIS had been central in Inter-Varsity since its beginning. In the early years the magazine was entirely subsidized by the national movement because of the importance of its ministry and its clear statement of the IVCF's ethos. Some said it was really subsidized by the staff, who were paid salaries only after the bills were paid, and *HIS* was one of the bills. By the late 1960s, Fromer found himself competing against the bottom line because of pressure to make *HIS* more self-supporting. He developed the program of sustaining subscribers, asking readers who saw the value of *HIS* in student ministry to underwrite its cost. The subscribers' loyalty to *HIS* made the sustaining subscriber program remarkably effective, and forestalled financial difficulties. However, the editorial staff of *HIS* were picking up signals from Inter-Varsity leadership that indicated that *HIS* no longer had the same priority that it had enjoyed in the past.

Unwittingly other seeds of the demise of *HIS* may have been sown in the changes that took place during this time. Fromer began to feel uneasy about inquiries from the leaders in the movement about what he published in *HIS*. He felt that the credibility of the magazine for student readers rested on editorial freedom. In the February 1967 issue of *HIS*, Fromer wrote an editorial that he admits was intended to chase away his underlying concerns and to speak in a brave voice about editorial freedom. He wrote,

> I should say here that no one in Inter-Varsity, the general director, or anyone else, is ordering me to print any particular thing in *HIS*. I get suggestions from all directions, and welcome them. But in exactly the same way as with the editor of a magazine like *Harpers* or *Atlantic,* I am given the authority and the responsibility by IVCF to veto any item I think should not be in *HIS,* and to include any item I am convinced should be included. Naturally, Inter-Varsity outlines in a very general way the kind of magazine it wants (in terms of statement of faith and purpose, etc.) but within that framework it says, "Go to it." My conscience is not up for sale. Both the general director, John Alexander, and I wholeheartedly support this policy.

Fromer saw editorial freedom as superordinate. He had unusual freedom because of the commitment of IVCF to *HIS* magazine over the years, a situation not always characteristic of other magazines. As editor of *HIS,* Fromer was a member of the senior staff council, which meant that he participated in policy-making shaping student work. What he chose to put in *HIS* magazine was directly related to what was transpiring at the heart of the movement.[22] In 1970 the editor of *HIS* magazine was placed organizationally under Jim Nyquist, the director of IVP. For the first time since it began, the editor did not report to the president (or general director) of Inter-Varsity. This change removed the editor from membership on the staff council, and thus away from ready access to national leaders. Paul Fromer resigned as editor of *HIS* in 1971.

HIS magazine took on a startling contemporary look in the 1970-71 school year, changing to an 8½ x 11 format. The art editor, Mickey Moore, designed an almost psychedelic look.[23] The more crisply written and shorter articles were targeted for a new student generation: "Shattering the Plastic Culture" and "Christian Revolutionaries" by Francis Schaeffer; "Violence" by Paul Fromer; "The Fight to Save Kent State" by Robert Swierenga; "Drugs, Sex and the Good Life" by Paul Byer; "Are You a Practicing Heretic?" by Stacey Woods; "A Christian Homosexual" (name withheld); "The Gospel and Social Justice" by Samuel Escobar; "What Should You Do About Coed Dorms?" by Larry Sibley, and many others. Poetry became a regular feature; everyone was reading and writing poetry in the late sixties and seventies. Student readers continued to respond well to the magazine. Urbana 70 produced 2,000 new subscriptions, and during Fromer's time circulation reached 27,000. (At its peak in 1979 *HIS* magazine came close to 40,000 subscribers; however, that was artificially inflated by the inclusion of a gift subscription for each Urbana delegate.)

Stephen Board edited *HIS* from 1971 until 1975 during some of the most turbulent years of the student revolution. Board had been a staff member in Chicago and was convinced about the philosophy of *HIS* magazine as a pastoral vehicle to teach and encourage highly committed Christian students. He purposed to carry on the Bayly/Fromer tradition. Board said, "It was a most satisfying experience. We often felt that students read every word."[24] Letters from students at Harvard, Yale, UCLA and other major universities indicated that *HIS* was shaping student thought in significant ways. It was written for university students, but alumni found it appealing and often wrote long and persuasive letters to the editor. Their interest in *HIS* is indicated by the 400-600 sustaining subscribers who helped underwrite the magazine, in some years supplying over $100,000. Subscriptions were at 30,000.

In November 1973 Stephen Board was informed that the editors of *HIS* would not be writing the official Urbana 73 report for *HIS* magazine. The president wanted a positive public relations piece to appear in the March 1974 issue, and James Reapsome was asked to write it.[25] Reapsome's article depicted a glorious event with no mention of any problems, in contrast to Fromer's eighteen-page report on Urbana 70. No mention was made of the confrontation between Black delegates and the leadership of the convention who met together in the Assembly Hall after one of the plenary meetings. *HIS* had always done its own reportage on Urbana; forbidding the editor this evaluation was an affront to the editorial freedom of the magazine.

Trouble doubled for Stephen Board with the January 1974 issue of *HIS,* which was supposed to be handed out at Urbana 73. That issue carried two articles objectionable to David Howard, missions director and director of Urbana. "Be Your Own Mission Board" by Miriam Adeney compared the advantages and disadvantages of nonprofessional missions; "Computer Missions: Cause for Caution," by Richard Shumaker, was subtitled "How to Interpret Your Career from the Printout." Howard believed these two articles would be criticized by mission leaders and create too much distraction from the main goals of the convention. The Urbana distribution of this issue was forbidden. Board wrote, "The *HIS* team felt a loss of morale at this action." Steve Board felt the March 1974 issue was "editing by committee" and a poor way to encourage an editor.

Additional discouragement came his way: each year Steve Board received a memo asking him to analyze sales and justify the publication of the magazine. Leadership in headquarters, whether realizing it or not, communicated to the editorial staff that *HIS* magazine was expendable to the movement. About this same time Jim McLeish issued brief memos to Alexander and the staff directors, questioning the place of the literature department in IVCF and whether *HIS* was needed if only thirty per cent of the subscribers were actively involved with IVCF.[26]

In retrospect, Stephen Board says,

Although it implicated principles of editorial freedom, I wonder if what happened during my years as editor of *HIS* does not more clearly indicate the *institutionalization* of IVCF. That is, in the earlier years the movement was on the offensive; at some point in the late sixties and seventies it got on the defensive, as institutions tend to do. This phenomenon marks "maturing" organizations, companies, denominations, and colleges: a concern about external criticism, fluctuations in money flow, competing organizations, numerical growth, conformity and central control.[27]

Linda Doll succeeded Stephen Board as editor of *HIS* in 1975. She purposed to keep the magazine on the tradition established by Bayly, Fromer and Board. She listened carefully to suggestions by staff and students. *HIS* was addressing a student generation affected by the media. By the midseventies how-to books, many of them simplistic, were rolling off the presses; a number of popularized magazines for youth had appeared on the market. Over half the students in tertiary education were in community colleges. The dysfunctionality of family life was showing up, and *HIS* attempted to give solid help for students trying to find their way in relationships. Jim Conway, pastor of Twin City Bible Church located near the University of Illinois, wrote a monthly column called "Free To Be," giving practical wisdom about life based on his contact with students. *HIS* carried articles that reflected "the therapeutic thinking of the seventies."

The *HIS* editorial staff felt the heavy doctrinal articles of Fromer's day were being read by fewer students. Yet when the shocking newly styled *HIS* hit the market, staff members like Tom Trevethan complained that *HIS* was "putting the cookies on the lower shelf," and not giving students the help it formerly did. Others said *HIS* needed to lighten up for the average student. *HIS* faced the problem of being market-driven rather than purpose-driven. Meanwhile the finance department put increasing pressure on *HIS* to be self-supporting, in the same way that was expected of IVCF regions and other departments.

Articles were edited differently, but still handled the basic issues. In 1976-77 issues of *HIS* included "Living under the Lordship of Christ," by Bill Cutler; "Social Science: Friend or Foe," by Miriam Adeney; "The Christian and the Dilemma of Doubt," by Os Guinness; a series by Clark Pinnock on "The Basis of Faith;" "Prayer Makes Evangelism Work" by John Alexander; and other articles of substance. As the decade wore on, Linda Doll was under pressure from her editorial staff and some of the campus staff to do more to lighten the content. The 1979 issues of *HIS* show a new trend of thoughtful articles mixed with more popular subjects: "Listening In on the Christian Music Industry," "Sin and the Christian Lifestyle," "God, Me and My Guitar," "Two Were Sent: A Comparative Study of Jesus and Paul," "Jehovah: The Intimacy of God," "We are Driven: The Success Syndrome."

HIS interviews brought a contemporary touch to information exchange. The magazine still carried articles on controversial subjects. The February 1978 issue focused on homosexuality and caused a good bit of stir. *HIS* was one of the first Christian magazines to deal with this subject in some depth. The response was mixed. The editorial staff received telephone calls of praise; they also received an envelope containing a copy of the magazine torn in shreds.[28]

At the April 1978 board meeting a member reported that he had received several calls from subscribers concerned about the content of *HIS*. When John Alexander was questioned about his views, he said IVCF had always been willing to face a controversial issue and to probe Scripture to see what God says about it. He added that he was not always in agreement with what *HIS* published, but that he had delegated the responsibility of *HIS* to Jim Nyquist, director of InterVarsity Press. Nyquist reported enthusiastic response from the students. "Following further discussion, it was moved by Robah Kellogg, seconded by Virginia Ohlson, that *HIS* magazine continue to face critical life issues and address these within the philosophy of IVCF. Motion carried."[29]

InterVarsity Press had occasional problems with critics. From time to time the editors at IVP found it necessary to defend proposed books. Concern over Inter-Varsity's publications was a recurring pressure during Alexander's presidency, causing him to comment, "I believe there was never a board meeting when I was free of flak on this count." Widely varying opinions surrounded IVP's publication of *Rich Christians in an Age of Hunger* by Ron Sider and John White's *The Golden Cow* because of the view of economics each presented.[30] Students were struggling with the issue of the rich and the poor and the use of resources. Could IVP trust its readers with stimulating ideas propounded by sincere Christians without making their ideas Inter-Varsity's position? Should, in fact, Inter-Varsity in its diversity have a position on such subjects?

InterVarsity Press defended its policy of publishing thought-provoking literature without having to endorse everything in a book.[31] Distribution of the kind of books IVP published deeply influenced the thinking of IVCF staff and the more thoughtful students, educating and stimulating them for more effective ministry.

The 1966 publication of Paul Little's book *How to Give Away Your Faith* put InterVarsity Press (IVP) on the map as a significant publisher. Francis Schaeffer's books followed. The first *HIS* readers (a collection of essays taken from back issues of *HIS* on the subjects of prayer, love and guidance) were also winners that helped give IVP a financial base. In 1968 IVP hired James Sire, its first full-fledged editor. Up until this time the director of IVP was its chief editor. By the midseventies, IVP was publishing between twenty-four and thirty books a year, about a fourth of these coming from IVP in Britain. Little's *Know Why You Believe* (1968); *Your God Is Too White* by Columbus Salley and Ron Behm (1970); *Christ and the Modern Mind* by Robert W. Smith (1972); *Knowing God* by J. I. Packer (1973); *The Dust of Death* by Os Guinness (1973); *The Problem of Wineskins* by

Howard Snyder (1975); *The Universe Next Door* by James Sire (1976); *The Fight* by John White (1976); *Out of the Saltshaker* by Rebecca Manley Pippert (1979) are among the books that chart the development of Inter-Varsity Press during the 1970s. A new Inter-Varsity hymnal, *Hymns II,* edited by Paul Beckwith, Hughes Huffman and Mark Hunt, was introduced at Urbana 76.[32] Sales of IVP books in bookstores were increasing. Students bought $80,000 worth of books at Urbana 70 and $100,000 worth at Urbana 73. Quality paperbacks with distinctive covers became the hallmark of IVP. Douglas Feaver, formerly a professor at Lehigh University and long-time member of the Inter-Varsity Corporation, comments, "If the Press were the only contribution Inter-Varsity has made, it would have been a more than significant contribution to the Christian world."

What began as a part-time assignment for Jim Nyquist in 1964 became full-time by 1968. As director of IVP, Nyquist began with two people and built the team. He said,

> When I became IVP director, I realized that the critical success factor was not money or buildings, but people. I asked God to lead us to those He was calling and equipping for this work. . . . Former staff members like Linda Doll, Nancy Fox, Ralph Gates, Jim Hoover, Andy Le Peau and many others joined the team. From different backgrounds came people like Herb Criley, who gave invaluable help as business manager; Kathy Lay Burrows, whose gift in design made IVP books look inviting and readable; and James Sire, an English professor who had the gift of editing and procuring good manuscripts. Many of those who joined the team in the early years are still contributing their full energies to IVP in 1990. Members of the literature committee of the IVCF Board— Joseph Bayly, Don Powell, Harold Shaw, Allan Bagge and others—provided wise counsel when we needed it.

Meanwhile the Logos bookstore idea (retail book stores in university communities) spread across the country. Five new stores opened soon after the Ann Arbor store began in 1968. By 1975 it was obvious that IVP had a franchise operation on their hands and the venture was out of hand. The Logos Bookstore Association was formed in 1975 with IVCF's Basis of Faith and a similar statement of purpose. Under former staff member Willard ("Butch") Dickerson, this separate organization has prospered. During the seventies more than eighty Logos bookstores were opened.

6/Training Programs
Camping and summer student training programs went to an all-time high

in the seventies. The four-week School of Discipleship Training (SDT) began at Cedar Campus in 1970 and expanded to include two sessions each summer at both Bear Trap Ranch and Cedar Campus. By 1972 a staff member reported, "We turned away many students who didn't qualify in order to enable us to train those with the greatest potential for influencing others." Similar SDT programs were held at IV East (held in rented facilities at Nyack, New York, or Gordon College near Boston) and in the Southern Region at the Southern Biblical Leadership Training (SBLT), at Covenant College on Lookout Mountain, Tennessee. Week-long chapter camps and ten-day Christian life camps were crowded. Across the country in the early seventies, over two thousand students were being trained in summer programs each year. During that same time annual reports show that between 1,700 and 2,300 students became Christian believers each year.

In 1972 a week-long Christian Study Project for graduate students was held at Cedar Campus for about twenty students. Charles Hatfield, professor of mathematics at University of Missouri, Rolla, served as a major resource as staff and graduate students wrestled with relating an intelligent grasp of Christian doctrine to the academic milieu. This camp was continued for three years and then dropped for economic reasons. Its influence in challenging graduate students to think Christianly is seen in the lives of those who came on staff or went on to other careers.

Students gladly drove great distances from all across the Central and Rocky Mountain regions to attend training programs at Bear Trap Ranch. Bear Trap, as was true for other IV camps, became a spiritual home for many students. Its beautiful setting in the mountains and the spirit of the place was only part of its appeal for students. They honed their spiritual life and leadership skills there, and it made a difference back on campus. Inter-Varsity's commitment to student leadership made the kind of training given at camps crucial to the movement. In return, the graduates with the greatest loyalty to Inter-Varsity were those who have been trained in IV's camping programs.

The 1974 IV West's program scheduled students to spend ten days at Koinonia Conference grounds in their choice of a study track, such as Bible study leadership, chapter camp, or Old or New Testament Seminar. One of their assignments was to write an evangelistic letter to a friend. The letters were critiqued in small groups and then mailed. Through those letters and follow up, two people became Christians and others wrote to say they wanted to hear more. Students in the program spent the next five days at Berkeley doing street evangelism with skits, music and testimonies.

The last week of the course was spent at Campus by the Sea. In addition, each year a significant number of students attended the New Testament Seminar (the manuscript study begun by Paul Byer), a training program that was spreading across the country, west to east.

In the Northwest, fifteen hundred students participated in fifty planned training activities throughout the summer of 1974. At IV West, students drafted "A Resolution for Social Action" after studying the book of Amos at camp. A hundred nurses attended the annual leadership camp at Camp Li-Lo-Li.

In the summer of 1970 Missions Director David Howard moved the Missionary Training Camp (held at Cedar Campus since 1954) to Costa Rica, working closely with the Latin America Mission and the Central American Mission. He wanted to get students onto the mission field outside of the U.S.A., to let them experience the tensions and the delights of a crosscultural ministry. This was the first of the Overseas Training Camps (OTC) that were held in the various countries of Central America (Costa Rica, Guatemala, Honduras, Dominican Republic) throughout the seventies. Two former staff members (Charles Troutman, then with the Latin America Mission, and Bill Taylor, with the Central American Mission) along with David Jones, IVCF staff in California who by 1974 was also directing OTC, worked closely with Howard. They helped provide a curriculum and professors for the study of the history and theology of missions as well as crosscultural issues. After studying in the camp setting, students were assigned to work with a missionary on the field for the second half of their time. Howard's plan was to give students a combination of missionary education and real-life mission field experience. He arranged for a sizeable cadre of IVCF staff to share the experience with the students. This was particularly important in the early seventies when some of the younger staff, influenced by the counterculture, had a dim view of missions.

A longer crosscultural missions opportunity began in Michigan in 1971 when Regional/Area Director Keith Hunt and staff member Richard Crespo began the Students in Missions Program (SIMP). The name was changed the next year to Student Training in Missions (STIM). Hunt worked with Ted Ward, Sam Rowan and Norman Bell, professors at Michigan State University, to devise a training curriculum that would prepare students for crosscultural ministry. After appointment to the program, these Michigan students attended six weekend training sessions as preparation for their learning experience. Students were assigned to mission agencies in a number of different countries, working with a specific missionary. They met for debriefing upon their return to the U.S., after an eight- to ten-week stint overseas. Back in their chapters, STIM students significantly influenced fellow students. Missions prayer meetings began to flourish. In most cases, chapter members raised money and sent the student volunteers as their representatives to the STIM program. Mission agencies referred to the STIM training as "the Cadillac of training programs" for short-term missions. Students from other areas wanted to get in on the program, and it became a national program under the missions department in 1976, with Ken Shingledecker heading up the effort.

SFMF chapters on Christian college campuses fed students into the OTC and STIM program throughout the seventies, and many students went out with projects originating from their individual colleges. Regional mission workshops, such as the one in the Northeast led by Lee Howard in February 1975 (attended by forty-five students) were held across the country and directed by the SFMF staff.

Apart from missions programs, attempts at national training programs failed during the seventies. The ministry was increasingly decentralized and training programs outside the regions were unsupported. John Alexander's repeated efforts to schedule national leadership institutes for key students within IVCF lacked the support of the staff directors. Student work in the New York City area had outgrown full use of the facilities of Hudson House, Inter-Varsity's training center in Nyack, New York. In 1975 Keith Hunt, as director of specialized training, introduced the idea of a Discipleship Training Center (DTC) modeled after the program of the Overseas Missionary Fellowship in Singapore. DTC, like Stacey Woods's original dream for the Summer Seminar of Biblical Studies held in the late fifties, was designed for the person planning on witness in a secular career. The curriculum would provide basic theology and courses on Christian disciplines in a Christian community setting. Norton and Eloise Sterrett, returning from over thirty years of ministry with the IFES in India, led the program. However, it was short-lived because of the death of Norton Sterrett in February 1978 and lack of support from national leadership.

After eight years of general camping for alumni and rental use, Campus by the Sea (CBS) was reclaimed for student use by Regional Director Jim Berney in 1976. Concerned alumni had saved CBS for Inter-Varsity by operating the camp during those years. Berney appointed Paul Friesen year-round director of the camp. John Alexander's support in re-establishing CBS as an Inter-Varsity Camp and his support for camping in general was significant. He knew firsthand what a time away at camp could mean to students, not just for the content, but for the out-of-doors experience. He said, "To me, our camping programs are the second heart of our work (the first being student work on campus). If we can get students to camp, especially the four-week leadership training camp, we will markedly reinforce our training of students for campus witness." In his concern that students "witness with works and words" he saw the importance of training in Christian character which camps afforded in providing godly models and discipling in the context of Christian community. He spent weeks of the summer at camp and held the major part of Orientation of New Staff at Cedar Campus.

One of Alexander's very important contributions to Inter-Varsity's training program is the "retreat of silence" which he instituted at ONS and is now part of many student camps nationwide. Once a week students take a sack lunch and find a private spot on the site to spend three hours alone with God. Over the years students have consistently rated that time alone as crucial in their Christian growth. Bob Ewing, who became a campus staff member in Michigan in 1989, went on four such retreats as a student attending the four-week SLT training program. He recounted his experience:

> The first Sunday afternoon on the retreat I finished my business with God in about fifteen minutes and fell asleep for the rest of the three hours. I was appalled that I had so little to say to him. Each week the time became more intimate. On the last retreat the time was gone, and I felt like I had only begun my fellowship with God. The Word of God spoke so powerfully to me; I sensed God's presence in a way I never had known before. I was overwhelmed with his love, that he would want to spend those hours with me. My earthly father never had much time for me. I can't tell you what it means to me to have God, my heavenly Father, want to fellowship with me like this.

7 A/Changing Movement

Inter-Varsity had a solid pattern of growth in the early seventies. The number of chapters (IVCF, NCF, SFMF) peaked in 1973-74 at 882 with one hundred thirty-five staffworkers.[33] John Alexander gave the movement what it needed most: stability. His character was his greatest strength and elicited the respect and admiration of the staff. Tully Fletcher, campus staff member (CSM) in the Southeast, said,

> John Alexander set me free to do my task. I interpreted his directives as: "Here are your guidelines—don't bend them or break them, but

accomplish everything you can within them. Don't feel you've got to go down a narrow brick road. Make yourself a four-lane highway if you want—as long as you're paying for it, as long as you adhere to our Basis of Faith, are not on an ego trip but are a committed, believable Christian." So in Virginia and North Carolina we started making four-lane highways.

Alexander observed that in the formative stages of the movement too little information about student work had been written down. Since he communicated best on paper, the flow of papers from his desk increased the volume of staff mail beyond anything they had known before. The staff began to affectionately refer to the movement as "Inter-Varsity Paper Fellowship," using humor to protest the amount of time it took to read all their mail. Policy and training manuals were regularly updated. Staff members were given helps and instruction in great detail. Manuals for staff director meetings were sometimes over one hundred fifty pages of agenda and backup papers.

In "Guidelines for a Campus Staff Member," Alexander encouraged staff to use a training concept called TDOEE—Teach/Demonstrate/Observe/Evaluate/Encourage. He developed a "House Diagram" in which he demonstrated the development of a healthy chapter. The foundation of the house has two levels: new life in Christ and commitment to Christ. The superstructure of the house is analogous to the life of a visible Christian group and is a triplex. The three sections of the house include (1) one-to-one witness, (2) small groups and (3) large group meetings. The roof of the house is embodied in Colossians 1:18. His teaching on this subject was published as the booklet *Building a Christian Group* in 1983.

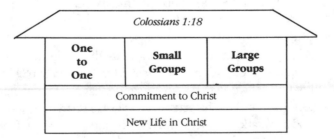

John Alexander's "House Diagram"

Alexander contributed extensively to the curriculum for chapter camps, whose goals he saw as vital to the purpose of the movement: *to establish student groups whose aims are evangelism, Christian growth and missions.*[34] Working papers developing strategy or re-structuring the organization came frequently from his hand. He addressed character and appearance standards in these papers; even such issues as conduct on the volleyball court did not escape his purview. The subject of punctuality came up repeatedly. In the years when dress, hair styles and casual arrangements reflected the culture, Alexander worked on a standard more acceptable for campus staff members (CSMs), who were role models for student leaders. Participation and stewardship in a local church was urged on all student leaders and required of staff members.

Alexander also sent out a weekly family newsletter containing news of his own itinerary, his thoughts, personnel changes, engagements, marriages, illnesses, new addresses—and whatever else he wanted to communicate. This weekly newsletter was widely circulated to current and past staff, members of the IVCF Board, faculty sponsors, interested supporters. Those who received it felt part of the movement. When it stopped in 1981 when the leadership changed, some who had received it said it was "as if a door slammed and we could no longer see inside."

The Staff Policy Manual issued in 1971 contained detailed instructions for staff life, including financial matters. The manual emphasized that a new staff member was not to be appointed until it was evident that his full support would be forthcoming. For the first time, students were encouraged to give toward staff support. "We encourage students to give first to their local chapter's budget, then to IFES and third to IVCF. We believe it important that students be encouraged to give at least something in voluntary support of the staff members who minister to them."

Early termination of staff appointment would take place (after at least thirty days' notice) if income sagged drastically and all economy measures failed to keep expenditures within income. Salary checks would be mailed out by the first of the month. Checks would be smaller in the event of inadequate income, the differential to be mailed as income warranted. Fringe benefits—(1) pension, (2) life insurance and (3) medical insurance—were provided as an additional support expense to the staff member. A staff member was not allowed to hold two jobs for which he received financial remuneration.[35]

For some time the salary structure of Inter-Varsity had been under discussion by the cabinet. On September 13, 1971, Peter B. Northrup submitted a fifteen-page memo regarding "Field Staff Salary Structure." With charts and comparisons to public-school teachers, Northrup showed how far behind IVCF was in salary levels. He set up levels of salary with incremental increases to close the gap between IVCF staff salaries and teacher salaries in eight years, the first serious attempt to get salary levels to a norm that the Christian public could understand. The finance committee of the board endorsed this plan, and staff recruitment was markedly helped.

The staff selection process became more complicated, as tighter criteria for evaluating potential staff members were developed through screening tests and a centralized personnel department. Some joked that Stacey Woods would not have passed the screen. The staff profile changed with the seventies; the evaluation grid left little room for irregulars and could not measure creativity, zeal or spiritual authority. Some became campus staff members who only performed 'according to the manual,' giving satisfactory, if unimaginative leadership, but these did not stay long.

Dick Karppinen, then director of financial services, comments, "I remember how shocked I was the first time I heard a new staff member talk about a forty-hour week. The whole concept of working conditions, terms of employment, and rights and obligations began to be important. This was a long way from the commitment I had learned in Inter-Varsity and seen modeled in leaders like Stacey Woods and John Alexander—that giving of total self to the task." A paradigm shift was taking place. "Nights away from home" and "hours worked each day," while legitimate management concerns, fed into a "job mentality."

However, over the years the campus work was producing the leaders IV needed who saw the work as a high calling, rather than a job. Outstanding long-term staff members who were chapter leaders during the seventies include Jim Worden, Janet Luhrs (Balajthy), Jimmy Long, Pete Sommer, Jim Lundgren, Mark Malan, David Ivaska, Doug Whallon, Jeanette Yep, Beth Goldhor (Domig), Terrell Smith, Conrad Sauer, Paul Tokunaga, Bobby Gross, Becky Manley (Pippert), Bob Hunter, Dan Denk, Terry Erickson, Fred Neubert, Sandy Flanigan (Zull), Nancy Fox, Becky Hendrickson, Judy Johnson, Barbara Benjamin, Doreen Fox (Herron) and many others.

The quality and quantity of staff training had increased over the years. One week of formal staff training was held in 1949 when "potential candidates" were invited to staff training sessions, a practice continued in later years as a part of the selection process. But in the early years, at the end of the camp session, some of the candidates were invited to come on staff and given their assignment, while others were released. The possibility of not being chosen made this an emotionally charged training session. After Charles Troutman returned as general director this policy was changed, so that the training sessions were only for accepted candidates.

John Alexander fine-tuned the training curriculum over the years. He tried various locations, and eventually brought new staff from across the country first into the Madison headquarters for part of the orientation. But he liked the natural camp setting for its informality, its recreational possibilities and its family feel. By the midseventies the bulk of the orientation took place at Cedar Campus. Sessions on individual staff fund raising inevitably brought questions and worry. The organizational details took up more and more time. Eventually the leadership concluded that campus ministry training should be conducted by the regional and area directors on the campuses.

8/Shortage of Leaders

Growth within the movement was not without a struggle. In the early seventies a crisis in leadership continued with temporary assignment of regions to already overextended regional directors. Only three regional directors are listed for the whole country in 1972-73: Jim Berney (West Coast), Ned Hale (Central region) and Keith Hunt (Eastern region). Hale's responsibilities covered what was once the Central region and the Rocky Mountain region. Hunt's supervision covered almost everything east of the Mississippi, including what had once been the East Central region, the Eastern region and the Southeast. Within a two-year period he had the difficult assignment of being the responsible regional director for all student work except the West Coast.

In 1973-74 John "Pete" Hammond was appointed regional director for the Southeast. Peter Northrup was given the Eastern and East Central regions in addition to his other responsibilities. In 1975 Charles Hummel returned to Inter-Varsity as the faculty specialist. Keith Hunt became an assistant to the president, responsible for training programs at Hudson House, Bear Trap Ranch, Cedar Campus and Schloss Mittersill, the Austrian castle affiliated with IFES used as a student training center. The movement was desperately short of top management. Then on July 9, 1975, Inter-Varsity received another blow. Paul Little, who had been on loan to Trinity Evangelical Divinity School to teach evangelism, was killed in an automobile accident while on vacation in Canada.[36]

In 1970 ninety-five field staff ministered to the various Inter-Varsity chapters across the country. Beginning in 1970 *all* staff (not only new staff) were expected to raise twenty-five per cent of their support in order to boost the income of the organization. By 1975 staff numbers had grown to one hundred and eighty-two. Money was still a problem, even though the total budget was over seven million dollars. In 1972 four-page fund-raising letters appeared in the mailboxes of IV's constituency. Local committees of alumni and businessmen worked hard to raise the funds necessary for the work in their areas.

Jim Berney, regional director for the West Coast, began using campus interns as a way to train and screen staff at less expense as well as providing extra staff for the growing work. As campus interns were trained throughout the nation, the position of associate staff member (ASM) was virtually eliminated. ASMs were volunteers who usually lived near a campus and gave time to help staff the campus chapter. Campus interns (CIs) were potential staff who raised their own limited budget, were paid a minimum amount by IVCF and worked on the staff team on a trial basis. Many of these graduated to staff positions the second year.

9/Keeping on Track

In 1975 John Alexander had been president of Inter-Varsity for ten years and showed signs of exhaustion. The board of IVCF granted him a three-month leave for rest and refreshment. The movement had experienced rapid growth. Staffing needs and fund raising produced constant tension. Leadership decisions demanded attention. John Alexander says, "I was most fulfilled when I was in the field with my RDs, ADs and CSMs—colaboring alongside them as they went about the business of fulfilling IVCF's purpose of building groups of students who witness to the Lord Jesus Christ as God incarnate at their schools." For the last ten years he had been both president and field director, keeping close touch with student work. At the midpoint in the decade of the seventies, the organizational chart was still undergoing regular changes. Inter-Varsity needed stability and creativity in second-level management so that leaders could put new ideas to work and follow through on developing well-rounded staff teams.

For all that was happening, what encouraged the Inter-Varsity staff most was the privilege of influencing the quality of student life. A guest speaker at a weekend Inter-Varsity student conference wrote:

Last weekend it was my privilege to speak at an IVCF retreat. I was particularly impressed with the seriousness and dedication of the participants. The froth and silliness which characterizes much of current

American evangelicalism was absent. There was a deep sense of personal commitment and even a sense of destiny concerning the importance of one's Christian witness in the world. It was during the Sunday morning worship that I began to realize that other people my age should be observing and experiencing what was going on. Some of the members of my own congregation would have been deeply impressed by what I was witnessing. The hymns they sang with such thoughtfulness, and the use of Scripture by the students would put many evangelical churches to shame.[37]

The seventies present a picture of a maturing organization, with plans, programs and new policies. Yet on the campus Inter-Varsity staff continued emphasizing the elementary principles at the heart of the movement. The importance of the discipline of meeting God daily in Quiet Time, the critical nature of the daily prayer meeting (DPM) to the health of the chapter, the concept of "an evangelizing fellowship" in which each student shares the good news, and a stress on world missions: these essentials remained constants in the ministry of staff members to students on the campus.

The practical outcome of this training is illustrated in stories such as this: Phil Fields, a music major at Wichita State, moved out of the dorm into private housing so he could practice his clarinet without disturbing other students. He determined not to let his isolation from natural contacts with his friends be an excuse for not sharing his faith. He decided that every morning he would schedule a breakfast appointment with a different friend, usually a non-Christian. Mike Nichols, a fellow music major, was Phil's Thursday morning breakfast companion. Mike became a Christian largely because of Phil's faithfulness in these conversations over breakfast. After growing in his faith through the ministry of the IV chapter, Mike spent four years on Inter-Varsity staff before attending Regent College. He now pastors a church in Vancouver (British Columbia.) Phil went to New England Conservatory following his graduation, then spent two years teaching missionary children in New Guinea. Today he works with Wycliffe Bible Translators in Irian Jaya.

Inter-Varsity's emphasis that believers are responsible for spreading the good news has sent students in many directions: to the ends of the earth in Christian work and into challenging careers where personal faith and integrity are a strong witness to the validity of the gospel.

14

A Maturing Ministry: Decade of the 1970s

The mind submitted to Christ's teaching receives a glorious freedom from prejudice; freedom to explore and enjoy everything he has revealed; freedom from the despair that sees no meaning in existence; freedom from the shifting sands of subjectivity where there is no objective criterion to assess opinions; and freedom from the kaleidoscope of the changing theological fashions of the day.[1]
John R. W. Stott, *rector, All Souls Church—London*

The issues raised by Black students at Urbana 70 made President John Alexander aware that Black ministry in Inter-Varsity needed to be put on the "front burner." He pulled from his file an earlier proposal for developing a Black student work written at Cedar Campus in 1969 by Gibson, Pannell and Hunt, and circulated it to the cabinet for discussion in September 1971. Area Director Neil Rendall and New York City staff-worker Paul Gibson presented a second paper for discussion outlining three practical steps for beginning a Black student work within Inter-Varsity: (1) more intense recruitment of Black staff, (2) a special training program for Black staff and (3) focus on New York City as a Black training center. The cabinet and the staff directors agreed something needed to be done, but doing something proved harder than discussing the proposals.

The Rendall-Gibson proposal was not activated until 1973 when Barbara Brown, a new Black recruit from Detroit, was sent to New York City for special staff training under the leadership of Paul Gibson. The earlier 1969 proposal had asked for the election of a Black leader to the Inter-Varsity Corporation. In 1971 James Earl Massey, a faculty member at Anderson College, was elected to the corporation.[2] While some saw this appointment as tokenism, it was at least a statement and an overdue inclusion. It was a beginning, at the board level, of representation of the ethnic plurality of Inter-Varsity's mission field.

At Urbana 73 Black students again confronted the leadership of Inter-Varsity. In their "Statement from the Afro-American People" Black students said they did not feel "the ministry and message of this convention was sufficiently responsive to the needs of oppressed and poor peoples everywhere, and in particular, the inner bowels of the Black community in the homeland." The paper lamented the lack of response from leadership about the Black situation. "We cried oppression in '67. We cried oppression in '70. We are crying oppression in '73. These cries of oppression are only scratching the surface of rumblings that are deeply embedded in the Black community. If you don't hear those rumblings, ask God to give you ears to hear them before they erupt and a will to obey what he tells you to do."

Other students formed a support group and sent a statement calling for action: "We feel that the structural and institutional manifestations of sin in society have not been adequately dealt with at Urbana 73. We specifically call on those responsible for the planning of Urbana 76 to address the concerns expressed in the 'Statement from the Afro-American People' in plenary session." David Howard, convention director, John Alexander and some members of the cabinet of Inter-Varsity met with about two hundred Black student leaders following the plenary session on Sunday night to hear their complaints. An open mike gave many of the Black delegates an opportunity to air their grievances, and some spoke harsh words against the Blacks who had agreed to be part of the convention programming. The Black delegates' complaint was against the status quo; they had no positive proposal. That would come from within Inter-Varsity as the years passed.

Multi-ethnic ministry was not entirely new to Inter-Varsity. As early as 1947 Eugene Callendar had worked as a Black staff member in New York City. That same year Asian staff member Hong Sit worked with the Chinese of New York City. The appointment of Gwen Wong in 1949 added another gifted woman with an Asian heritage to the staff. In 1952 Ivery Harvey was appointed to minister to "the Negro schools" in the South. Ruth Lewis (Bentley) joined the staff team in 1958 and worked in the Black Southern schools for five years.

The civil rights movement brought new awareness to the issue of Blacks in a White-dominated society. Racism, whether latent or active, needed to be confronted. The Black Power movement began to isolate Blacks who had formerly participated in Inter-Varsity groups in the North. At Urbana 73 a Black woman student said it was not easy to be a member of Inter-Varsity on her campus because she got static from fellow Black Christians for her association with a White group. She said they wanted her to make her Blackness more important than her Christianity. Racial feelings needed to be acknowledged and worked through. In the North, except in colleges that had a major Black enrollment, Black students disappeared from Inter-Varsity chapters and camps. Chapters in New York City were an exception to this, under the leadership of Conrad Sauer, who had become an Inter-Varsity staff member in 1969.

Paul Gibson and Ted Moran were two Black students in the Harvard Inter-Varsity chapter in 1964. Staff member Willard "Butch" Dickerson influenced Gibson in important ways during his student days by showing a consistent interest in his spiritual development and, Gibson would add, "by asking me the inevitable question: How is your Quiet Time going?" Faculty advisor James Shaw provided the encouragement Gibson needed to attend Urbana 67. This put Gibson in touch with about two hundred Black students attending the convention and gave him a new consciousness of the responsibility of being a Black American Christian. Black students had a new connectedness and one night they prayed together all night. Speaker Warren Webster's broad outlook on obeying Jesus Christ captured Gibson. By 1968 Gibson had signed on for IV staff in Southern California.[3]

Between 1963 and 1967 Bill York had encouraged Carl Ellis, Jr., a Black student at Hampton Institute in Virginia to begin a chapter at that college. In North Carolina staff members encouraged a young Black student named Elward Ellis to recruit others and begin a chapter at Shaw University, modeled after what Carl Ellis had done at Hampton Institute. Both of these men later served the ministry of Inter-Varsity. In 1966 Pete Hammond, staffing schools in Mississippi, encouraged Inter-Varsity students at the University of Southern Mississippi in Hattiesburg to actively recruit Black students into the Fellowship. That chapter became one of the few integrated groups, Christian or otherwise, in Mississippi in the sixties. In the early 1970s other Black staff were recruited by Inter-Varsity. Among them were Tony and Veronica Warner, two Black Brooklyn College alumni, who began working with Inter-Varsity at Atlanta University Center in 1973.

In 1976 Thom and Marcia Hopler, both Caucasians, joined Inter-Varsity staff in the Eastern Region after serving as missionaries to Africa for ten years. Hopler gave Inter-Varsity its strongest push toward multi-ethnic ministry by giving it a biblical basis and a practical vision. InterVarsity Press published his ideas in book form, *A World of Difference,* in 1981. A study guide for small groups followed, with exercises and activities to put the principles of his book into practice. In 1978 Hopler, one of the speakers at IV East's summer training program, died suddenly from a heart attack while jogging. At a crucial time his respected ministry was lost to Inter-Varsity.

The following November the staff directors from across the nation met together. Neil Rendall called Peter Northrup to ask if he could address the group about multi-ethnic concerns. It was his first time to be the chief spokesperson for this cause. But Thom was gone and Paul Gibson had left staff. IVP Editor Jim Sire said, "For me it was one of the most impassioned pleas to the movement I had ever heard." Inter-Varsity must not let the importance of this issue fade. Rendall now says it may have been the most significant thing he did to promote interest in racial pluralism within our chapters. On the basis of what he did at that November meeting, John Alexander invited Rendall to New Staff Orientation to give teaching about multi-ethnicity.

The Black staff within Inter-Varsity formed the Black Staff Fellowship in 1977. This led to a conference called "Young, Black and Christian" designed to prepare Black students for leadership. In 1976 staffworkers in Southern California developed "ABC" conferences (Asians, Blacks and Chicanos). John Perkins, founder of Voice of Calvary ministries in Jackson, Mississippi, became a member of the Inter-Varsity Corporation. The next year, 1978, InterVarsity Press published Barbara Benjamin's *The Impossible Community,* the story of the ethnic diversity within the Brooklyn College Inter-Varsity chapter of the late sixties and early seventies. This book helped staff and student leaders to see how they could shape a multi-ethnic chapter. Rudy Hernandez transferred to South Texas in 1973 to pioneer ministry to Hispanic students. Rich Hong, Brenda Wong, Donna Dong, Elward Ellis and Doreen Fox also joined the staff of Inter-Varsity during this era.

A group of both Black and White staff had been attending the meetings of the National Black Evangelical Association (NBEA) since the early seventies, building bridges, learning and sharing IV's vision for students. At the 1978 meeting of the NBEA, John Alexander read from the podium the

General Confession from the Book of Common Prayer (Anglican/Episcopal), symbolizing the need of Whites for forgiveness by Blacks for the continued distance in their relationship. At that meeting Alexander was presented with a special award for being an agent of racial reconciliation. That same year a foundation grant of $125,000 in matching funds gave Inter-Varsity's Black Campus Ministry a new boost.

By the end of the decade, a Black staff executive council was formed with Elward Ellis, Paul Gibson, Tony Warner, Doreen Fox, and two non-Blacks sensitive to their cause—Neil Rendall and Pete Hammond. It was a beginning, but this group was to struggle long and hard before Black ministries would have a secure place within the Inter-Varsity movement. The problem of funding and management of this ministry came under regular discussion. More disillusioning for Black leaders were the questions raised about the necessity of a separate ministry. It was hard going and they were often frustrated. Would the results of their work be enough to favorably impress Inter-Varsity as a movement?

1/Urbana 76 and 79

David Howard felt that the changes in campus mood could almost be charted by the student response to Urbana. In 1970 only six per cent of the 12,000 students present signed the world evangelism decision card.[4] In 1973 twenty-eight per cent out of approximately 15,000 signed the card. In 1976 fifty per cent of 17,000 used the card to indicate their serious intentions regarding world missions. Howard says, "I personally presented the card at all three of those conventions, using exactly the same approach. I am not a high-pressure person, and I don't believe in high-pressure tactics to commitment. The percentages reflect the change in student views toward missions and the establishment."

It may also have reflected the increased conformity among students during the late seventies, as well as a more emotional response to what the students were hearing at the convention. Students were quick to get on the bandwagon, but sometimes opted out of commitments easily. In the next decade, the decision cards were increasingly used as a mark of the success of the convention. Collection boxes were placed at the exits, in contrast to earlier Urbanas where the card was mailed in after consideration and prayer.

Choosing a theme for Urbana 76 had its comic side. Everyone seemed to want to be on the planning committee. Eventually an unwieldy committee of about thirty people were assembled. When they met to discuss a possible theme for the convention, someone came up with the idea of Acts 1:8 as the basis for four-day breakdowns: Jerusalem, Judea, Samaria and the ends of the earth. No one had any problems with the meaning of the first two categories—Jerusalem and Judea—but what Howard called "an incredible four-hour discussion" ensued on *what is Samaria.* Every interest group defined Samaria in their own terms. The Blacks said Samaria was Black America; the French Canadians said it was French Canada; and others championed yet other strong definitions.

A few days later at a luncheon at Fuller Seminary, Howard posed the question to the professors seated near him. "I wish I had used a tape recorder, because it was terribly funny. Everyone had a different view, and for about an hour over lunch these men butted heads on the meaning of Samaria, and they came to absolutely no tangible or helpful conclusions at all." David Howard concluded that as the missions director and director of Urbana 76, he needed to choose a new theme and inform the committee of his choice, without discussion.[5]

The theme for Urbana 76 was "Declare His Glory Among the Nations," and the program fell into place around that theme with amazing ease. Margaret Clarkson wrote another theme hymn for the convention.[6] John Stott gave expositions on the biblical basis for mission and declared, "Our God is a missionary God." Edmund Clowney gave a stellar address on the glory of God, a subject almost too profound for words and almost too glorious for young students to grasp. Elisabeth Elliot stirred students with her talk on the will of God. Helen Roseveare addressed "Declaring His Glory in the Midst of Suffering," and received one of the many standing ovations. Eric Frykenberg, who had served as a missionary to India for forty-seven years, spoke on "The Joy of Declaring His Glory." Seventeen thousand student delegates filled the Assembly Hall, making it impossible for extra people to get in to hear Billy Graham's call for commitment.

One afternoon during the convention President John Alexander chaired a question-and-answer session in the Assembly Hall for people who wanted to know more about Inter-Varsity. After a number of questions had been answered, one young man took the mike and asked, "Sir, who are you? I don't know who you are." To which John Alexander replied, "Your question tells you a lot about Inter-Varsity," and proceeded to introduce himself. He underscored that the focus of Inter-Varsity has never been on personalities, but on the student work on the campus. The way he handled the question also told a lot about John Alexander.

Students skipped a meal and gave $23,000 for the needy in addition to their offering for student work around the world; a daily newsheet called "Get It Together" kept the delegates informed about the extras; red-vested bus guides helped delegates find the right yellow school bus to get to their dining hall or the next meeting. Seventeen hundred small groups met each morning for Bible study and each evening for prayer. TWENTYONE-HUNDRED educated the audience with their multimedia presentations, including one program dedicated to Paul Little who died in 1975, called "The Effective Ambassador," a training tool for evangelism that has had an enduring ministry within Inter-Varsity. Any Urbana student missions convention leaves its participants breathless and full of positive comments. David Howard received many accolades from people who thought Urbana 76 topped them all.

David Howard said John Alexander was exuberant about the convention and immediately asked him to direct Urbana 79. Howard was reluctant to accept; he was exhausted. He had served as missions director with a minimal staff since 1968 and had responsibilities for SFMF as well as Urbana.[7] David Howard said the dual responsibility of Urbana and the missions department was too much for him. He asked Alexander to find another missions director and to let him focus on Urbana. Early in 1977 Reuben Brooks, a professor from Michigan State and a former missionary, was selected as missions director to replace Howard. During his short tenure of less than a year, he brought David Bryant to the missions department as a missions specialist. By this time Alexander had made David Howard an assistant to the president and director of Urbana. However, before Howard made the decision to lead Urbana 79, Leighton Ford invited David Howard to help organize the Lausanne Committee for World Evangelization meetings to be held in Pattaya, Thailand. The invitation appealed to David's international interests, and Inter-Varsity seconded Howard to that task.[8]

John Alexander took on the task of directing Urbana 79, using the theme "That All Nations Might Believe and Obey Jesus Christ." Applause, cheers and uplifted hands were common throughout the convention. Students even cheered themselves for giving more than a half million dollars for student work overseas. The convention was less issue-oriented and less cohesive than those of the previous decade, but Isabelo Magalit got the convention's only standing ovation by raising the problem of American ignorance and insensitivity to other cultures.[9] Daily John Stott prayed that "your written Word be our rule and guide, your Holy Spirit our teacher, and your greater glory our supreme concern," as he began his expositions from Romans. A holy hush came over the whole arena as he expounded Romans 1. It was one of the most memorable Urbana moments.

The effervescent Luis Palau talked about the need for Christ around the globe. Billy Graham, Elwyn Davies, Elisabeth Elliot, Michael Haynes, Ruth Siemens, Gottfried Osei-Mensah, David Adeney and Warren Webster rounded out the impressive team of speakers. During afternoon workshops, eager students stood on boxes at open windows and squeezed into already crowded rooms. Mission booths were packed with students asking questions—good questions, according to missions representatives. TWENTYONEHUNDRED, Inter-Varsity's multimedia team under the leadership of Eric Miller, gave a global perspective on missions with five evening presentations on huge screens hung in the Assembly Hall. The new show "Habakkuk," a comment from the Old Testament on contemporary culture, had special showings each day in the Armory.

Students had been turned away from Urbana 79 because of overregistration. Leaders within the movement discussed two possible alternatives to insure that every student would have an opportunity to attend Urbana. Some urged decentralization, holding missionary conventions in various parts of the country. Some suggested holding Urbana on a two-year cycle. When the convention was over, exhilarated by the event and with the encouragement of Jim McLeish, Alexander announced that the next Urbana would be in 1981, following a two-year cycle instead of the normal three. John Kyle had become the new missions director in the fall of 1978 and made plans for the first "Urbana Onward" conferences scheduled for the early months of 1980. The missionaries who counseled and spoke at these conferences, which were spread across the country, found it a strategic opportunity to influence the 3500 students who came. Some of these were students who had registered too late to come to Urbana 79.

Later when David Howard completed his Lausanne assignment in 1980, he came back to Inter-Varsity. He expected to be given responsibility for Urbana 81; instead John Alexander gave him a new assignment: minister-at-large for Inter-Varsity. While David Howard had been gone, John Kyle had been given responsibility for Urbana as part of his assignment as missions director. Howard stayed with Inter-Varsity for a time, but increasingly felt that he had no challenging role. In 1981 he left to become the international director of the World Evangelical Fellowship.[10]

2/Organizational Changes

The organizational chart for the 1976-77 school year showed five regions:

Eastern, Regional Director (RD) Robert Fryling; Great Lakes, RD Terry Morrison; Southern, RD Pete Hammond; Central, RD Ned Hale; and Western, RD Jim Berney. Peter Northrup was vice president in charge of specialists—NCF Director Grace Wallace, Missions Director Reuben Brooks, Missions Specialist David Howard, Faculty Specialist Charles Hummel and Training Specialist Keith Hunt. Jim Nyquist as literature director reported to Finance Vice President Jim McLeish.

The 1977 reports show Inter-Varsity work at 855 universities and colleges, including IVCF, NCF and SFMF chapters, involving approximately 26,000 students. The movement showed impressive growth in numbers of field staff (200). While pleased at the solid growth of the movement, Alexander warned against multiple staffing at a single school, lest student initiative be destroyed. In 1978 he was concerned that student involvement was plateauing, that Inter-Varsity was employing more staff to reach fewer students.

In 1976 the decision was made to initiate an American version of the Theological Student Fellowship (TSF). TSF had a British heritage. It was designed to provide fellowship and a theological anchor for students studying at a variety of theological institutions, not all of them necessarily evangelical. For years the U.S. Inter-Varsity offered the journal of the British TSF to its theological students. Mark Lau-Branson was asked to head up a U.S. TSF and produce a theological journal. From a wobbly beginning, which required reactivating the idea in 1979, the TSF experiment continued for American theological students. It folded its wings in 1985 for lack of sufficient support.

In 1974, when Alexander heard that Charles Hummel was resigning from the presidency of Barrington College in Rhode Island, he phoned him to ask if he would consider coming back to Inter-Varsity as faculty director. Charles Hummel said, "I highly regarded John's performance as a Christian professor for many years and appreciated his concern to strengthen faculty witness to Jesus Christ within the university. I had just started in that arena the year before I left in July 1965." It seemed an attractive offer, and the Hummels rejoined the staff team in November of 1975.

Hummel attempted to strengthen the faculty in their spheres of influence and provide on-the-job training for field staff in faculty relationships. He also helped faculty plan weekend conferences or seminars, and worked with a team to conduct faculty workshops at the Urbana missionary conventions. One of his objectives was to encourage faculty to start meeting on campus once a week for Bible reading, sharing and prayer. This was not an easy task because of the faculty members' involvement in community and church affairs. Both Hummel and Alexander were eager to see professors become aware of the sacredness of their call to serve Christ in their profession.

3/Student Work

Student work was uneven in the late seventies; it was part of the fallout of the student revolution. Kentucky staff member Bill Christiansen complained, "Leaders are not initiators. The chapter meetings are awful with poor singing. They are singing the same choruses week after week. No one is putting in the time to make the meeting a quality event." Students who talked about being disciples didn't understand what leadership meant—the risk-taking and the planning.

The School of Discipleship Training (SDT), Inter-Varsity's four-week training session, changed its name to School of Leadership Training (SLT) to emphasize the importance of Christian leadership. Students had been so intent on being disciples that they had little sense of call to be leaders. The aftermath of a feeling-oriented mood in the culture, combined with the onslaught of feminism, left many male student leaders passive, rather than assertive.

Staff member Donna Ring, writing about one of her schools in Indiana observed, "Quite a few come as 'church kids,' but have no real desire to live the Christian life on campus. They never think of asking the real questions about God's plan for their time in college. This school seems to draw that kind of student." At these colleges and others, the staff faced the same challenge: to give students a vision of what could happen on the campus.

On other campuses the staff were encouraged by student initiative. At Northwestern University in Evanston, Illinois, staff member Larry Brown reported, "Students here are openly and actively declaring Jesus Christ with a boldness rare in these days of student apathy. One group of students had a vision for reaching every student in the dormitory where they live. They divided up the student directory and prayed for each student by name. Then they went around to each room and invited students to a dorm discussion where one of the Christian students gave a brief talk and answered questions about who Jesus claimed to be. About thirty students showed up for the discussion. Since then one person has become a Christian and many more have heard the gospel.

"Last week students at Northwestern held the first of two 'noontime forums,' an outdoor miniconcert followed by a twenty-minute presentation of the gospel by a student. Many students and faculty heard the message loud and clear as it came over a powerful PA system. Some stopped to listen and asked questions."[11] At Illinois Institute of Technology eleven students became Christians through the witness of members of the chapter—friend to friend. At the University of Washington a thousand students came out for an evangelistic meeting; three thousand attended a similar meeting at Washington State.

Joyce Smith became a Christian at the University of North Carolina in the school year 1977-78. She studied Romans 3 in her first-ever Quiet Time at her first-ever IV conference in the spring of 1978, where the speakers were Ruth Siemens and David Adeney, and she was suddenly overwhelmed by her sinfulness and God's grace. That summer at home she read John White's *The Fight* (IVP) and saw a family revival take place before her eyes. Since then her life has been discipled by summer camps, books, staff members and the fellowship of her local group. She went with STIM to the Philippines for crosscultural missions training the summer of 1979. After graduation she volunteered for two years on IV staff in Oregon, before doing a five-year stint in Paris with IFES.

4/Uncertain Leadership
Over the years Alexander had chosen Jim McLeish as his closest confidant. Commenting on this, Alexander said, "When the board of trustees asked me to take the position in late 1964, they understood that I had no experience in fund raising or finance management. They said they were aware of these shortcomings and were giving me a free hand in locating a dependable person to whom I could delegate those responsibilities. I chose Jim. During ensuing years his commitment to Christ, to Inter-Varsity and to me were priceless resources. His boundless energy, enthusiasm and eagerness to see the work go forward were an optimistic tonic to me, especially during the 1960s when criticism of me was heavy. Jim was vocal in his encouragement. His attitude gave constant emotional support upon which I leaned. His faithful service enabled me to devote more time to my first love: working alongside field staff in their working with students and faculty in fulfilling the purpose of Inter-Varsity."

By the midseventies staff across the country noted that Jim McLeish was making an increasing number of administrative decisions. His control of the finances—income and outgo—had already given him a large measure of organizational clout. John Alexander had written in 1973, "I will not approve any recommendations by any committee—if money is involved—unless Jim McLeish has approved it. This means that—just as on board level the board never makes decisions involving money without the input from their board finance committee—just so in the administration I will not make recommendations without the input from Jim McLeish. I realize this places enormous power in Jim's hands."[12] Staff leaders began to notice signs of uncertainty in John Alexander's leadership. He seemed emotionally preoccupied with the personal problems and illness within his extended family.[13] Cabinet memos reveal introspection, uncertainty and depressed thoughts about the movement and his own leadership. He turned more and more to Jim McLeish, allowing him to play an increasing role in decision making for Inter-Varsity. McLeish raised questions about the placement and contribution of various people and departments within the movement. He used change to manage the movement and it became characteristic of his leadership. John Alexander essentially gave approval to McLeish's decisions, which proved confusing to other leaders within the movement.

The constant changes were hard on staff morale. In 1978 the "cabinet" (the name given the senior management team consisting of the president, department heads and regional directors) was renamed. A new group was formed, called the senior management group (SMG). The middle management group was composed of the area directors. In June 1978 Jim McLeish and Peter Northrup were made senior vice presidents and, to relieve Alexander, were assigned to supervise the regional directors. This proved only a temporary assignment, because it did not work well. Regional boundaries were redefined.

By the late seventies the regional directors felt uncertain about national leadership. In a January 1978 paper for the regional directors' meeting, Alexander commented, "The RDs respect me as a person, but they are not comfortable with the way I am leading the movement." It was not clear to them how the team fit together. Jim McLeish's hand was seen again and again, controlling the movement from his position in finance. When McLeish was temporarily given the responsibility of supervising the campus work west of the Mississippi, while still serving as the finance and stewardship director, he became the most influential person on IVCF staff.[14]

5/Financial Matters

Don Powell, student president of IVCF at Ohio State in 1947-48 and now the president of an automotive contract research and testing company, was chairman of the Inter-Varsity Board from 1969-74. He believes that changes in policy for funding the movement was the most crucial issue on the agenda. Again and again the board discussed the matter of individual staff support as a way to fund the movement. Board member Joe Bayly was adamant in his opposition to the idea. He said that IV seeks to place people who are gifted in working with students, and that doesn't necessarily make them either good at raising funds or comfortable in doing so. He felt it would deflect good people from the movement and be "a terrible mistake." Others felt it would help the movement to expand. The problem was discussed over a period of time at several meetings. Finally the board hammered it out as the only way to take care of the money problem. Powell says, "It released the possibility of growth in the work. I think it was the most significant thing that happened during my tenure."

By 1978-79 all new Inter-Varsity staff were required to raise one hundred per cent of their support. More sophisticated accounting procedures and more detailed record keeping were needed. Staff directors had complained that reports did not get out on time, lacked adequate detail, and the areas never knew in a timely way where they stood financially. As the field workers were now full partners in the finances of the movement, the lack of accurate timely information was a problem. The accounting department became more than record keeping; it processed information vital to the growth of the movement.

Jim McLeish had been looking for someone with financial management skills. Richard Karppinen, working on his Ph.D. in accounting research, fit the need. His addition to the staff team in the early seventies, began a whole new era of accounting systems. Karppinen worked closely with John Liss, who did the day-by-day accounting, and this allowed Karppinen to work more conceptually on accounting systems which would meet the needs of the movement. In the early seventies Inter-Varsity had broken the million-dollar donation mark, and the accounting systems of the fifties and sixties could no longer handle that. Advancement in technology permitted accounting procedures not previously available. David Sironi, knowledgeable about computers and data processing, joined the staff team. Together with Karppinen, they redid the income system completely.

Dick Karppinen,[15] in commenting on the policies in the accounting department, said, "I didn't understand the impact of this when I came to the Fellowship, but Inter-Varsity had insisted on an outside auditor since its beginning. As late as the midsixties many Christian organizations had resisted an outside audit. This voluntary step into what is now seen as essential management control was almost unheard of when Inter-Varsity began."

By this time Vice President Jim McLeish, working with the area directors, had established a strong network of local committees who were helping to raise money for Inter-Varsity's expansion. Growth was running from twenty-five to thirty per cent a year. This meant the accounting department was serving the area committees as well as the employees. Area committees were underwriting significant amounts of the support of local staff. When staff were required to raise one hundred per cent of their support costs, the control moved from the committee to the staff person, who felt under great pressure to make the budget. The local committee often moved too slowly for a staff member whose job depended on raising the budget.

No one during the seventies was terminated from staff purely for lack of support. If one area was behind, another area who had a surplus "shared the wealth" as a permanent gift, not as a loan. Jim McLeish would strategize with area directors and local committee people to prevent proposed termination, if possible. Yet the needs of raising support brought changes within the movement over a period of time. Staff members who were behind in their support spent days away from the campus to do fund raising. New staff received a different assignment. Whereas in the past new staff had been assigned to summer training camps as part of their staff training, now they needed to spend the summer months raising their support. Another subtle thing happened: during the next few years staff reports and prayer requests moved from an emphasis on students to an emphasis on staff needs. Reports of earlier years contain one student or chapter story after another, but staff now became more concerned about their support and defining their role to the public.

Summers became the months for raising staff support. Fund raising preoccupied both staff and area directors. The completion of a staff team depended on the promise of income. Any change has a down-side when it first begins. It is hard to prove the relatedness of events, but recruitment of students for camp slowed down at the same time. Staff reported that students couldn't afford to come. Whether typical or not, one college senior gave a run-down on the scenario at his campus. "A few years ago when a student said he couldn't come to SLT, the staff member said he couldn't afford not to. Now when a student says 'I can't afford it,' our staff member says, 'I know.' " Registration at the four-week camps at Bear Trap

and Cedar Campus nose-dived. In other parts of the country, staff concluded that the day of the four-week camp was past and planned their
training sessions accordingly.

The new support plan had problems, but it worked. The financial dead-
lock was broken, and the funding problems of the organization were
eased. One of the negative effects of the program was the reluctance of
some keen potential staff candidates to put themselves under this kind of
fund-raising pressure. Others completed their staff commitments and left.

6/Training

In 1978 John Alexander made Cedar Campus a national camp, instead of
a regional camp. In addition to the Orientation of New Staff, Alexander
hoped to hold National Leadership Institutes on the site. He wanted to
expand the facility at Cedar Campus. Funds for the project would be raised
by the national development team. Camp Director Hunt was instructed to
begin the development of a second major site at Cedar Campus, including
the building of a new lodge at what would come to be called "Mariners
Cove." New buildings were erected, and architects drew up plans for additional facilities, one of which was a building with meeting space for over
four hundred people so that campers from the two major sites (Old Mill
Point and Mariners Cove) could meet together when programs called for
joint meetings.[16] The missions department had plans to use the site for a
major missionary training camp. The regions using Cedar Campus for student training faced the possibility that regional programs might have to be
held elsewhere, depending on how much time would be used for national
programs. Three major buildings were built, but by 1982 all plans for
national camps at Cedar Campus were canceled, including the Orientation
of New Staff, leaving the camp in a precarious financial position.

The Bible & Life Training Course grew significantly under the leadership
of Barbara Boyd during the seventies. Teacher Training Courses helped
prepare leaders who could present the material to others, thus expanding
the number of B&L courses across the country. The curriculum of Level
I helped students see the importance of Quiet Time and the staff noticed
that those who attended had a deeper regard for the Scriptures. Students
came away from the weekend with enthusiasm for friendship evangelism
and investigative Bible studies. B&L became a key discipling tool during
this decade.

At a Level I B&L conference one weekend, a student named Bill shared
his story of how he came to know Christ. His parents were ardent atheists,

and his father instilled in Bill a distrust for other people. Having friends was a weakness. Bill's first two years in college were painfully lonely. One night he came by Hank's room to pick up some class notes and met Hank's roommate Steve. After chatting together for a while, Steve turned to Bill and asked him what he thought about God. Bill said, "I don't think about God; I'm an atheist." Steve's only reply was, "Oh." But the next day when Steve saw Bill eating breakfast alone, he left his group of friends and ate with Bill. After that Steve frequently ate with Bill, and Steve invited him to go places with him. Steve didn't talk to Bill about God; he cared for him as a friend. Bill did a lot of thinking. He saw Steve's life was joyful and godly.

About a month later, Steve asked Bill what he thought about Jesus Christ. Bill launched into a diatribe about what he didn't believe that went on for six hours. But later in his bed, he couldn't sleep. He was rethinking his case. The next day after classes he went to Steve's room and unloaded all his locked-up feelings. Steve simply listened. The next day Bill went back again to find Steve, and this time when he talked about the hopelessness of life, he gave Steve a chance to respond. For forty minutes Steve explained the gospel. While Bill claimed he couldn't believe, he did agree to let Steve pray. While Steve prayed, Bill felt God's call to him. He could not contain himself. He interrupted Steve and began to pray, addressing the Lord in words of confession and repentance. As Bill prayed, he gave himself over to the Lord Jesus Christ.

Steve began to share the Scriptures with Bill and showed him how to apply God's truth to his life. Bill began his own daily Quiet Time. The Inter-Varsity chapter on campus had been praying for weeks, so when Bill began attending chapter meetings, he was warmly received. Others in the group began to meet regularly with him for Bible study. Going to church seemed a big hurdle to Bill because of all the negative things his father had taught him, but one Sunday Steve and the Bible study group went with Bill to his first worship service. It was a beautiful experience of worship in God's family. Steve took Bill home with him, and Steve's family became his second family. The details of the story change, but this is how one student after another comes into God's family on the campus. Bill's story explains what Inter-Varsity means by "friendship evangelism."

7/NCF in the 1970s

Looking back over a decade of development within Nurses Christian Fellowship, Director Grace Wallace said, "NCF pioneered the 'marketplace' concept as we helped students and nurses work together to integrate biblical principles into their lives and profession. We have a growing concern to see Christians influence the nursing profession for Christ, and this has kept NCF on the cutting edge amid changes in nursing and nursing education." The importance of integrating personal faith into the practice of the nursing profession has become increasingly obvious over the years. NCF has helped students and nurses learn how to daily apply biblical standards to their work, rather than to simply be "a Christian and a nurse."

In reviewing the basic values of NCF, Wallace said, "The movement builds on the solid foundation of love for the Lord and obedience to the Scriptures. NCF began as a result of prayer and in a real sense we have 'moved forward on our knees.' Prayer is also the natural companion of an emphasis on sharing personal faith with classmates and peers."

The ministry of NCF expanded during the 1970s both in numbers of staff, in vision and in outreach programs. As the number of staff increased, the ministry was regionalized, allowing for more effective concentration on discipling students and new graduates. Marian Hall transferred from field staff to headquarters as an assistant to Grace Wallace and to provide continuity for NCF groups in unstaffed areas.

Staff member Mary Thompson discipled a core of new graduates in California and developed workshops and Bible studies with professional application to help students and nurses in the dilemmas they faced. Ruth Lichtenberger, area director in the East, simultaneously developed a discipleship program in Philadelphia in which potential staffworkers were prepared for student ministry or work as associate staff volunteers. Sensing the need among nurses and laity for God's healing, Bonnie Meyer (Miller) put together a four-to-six-week seminar called "Love That Heals." This seminar series helped many nurses in their own need for healing as they ministered to the critically ill and their families. NCF staff served supporting churches by teaching leaders the principles of "Love That Heals" as the seminar extended from coast to coast. The seminar proved so enriching that some volunteer teachers subsequently developed an extended ministry or authored books based on their experience with this seminar.

Humanism became a controlling philosophy as changes in nursing education took place. The vacuum within nursing of spiritual care became markedly evident as the 1970s progressed. Although NCF had spoken to total patient care from its inception, leaders in NCF now found it necessary to give more attention to a curriculum to prepare faculty and nurses to provide spiritual care in education and practice. Helen McMurtry and other advisory committee nurses worked as an ad hoc committee to produce

materials on spiritual care. Ruth Stoll and Jeanne Stallwood (Hess), formerly NCF staff and on faculty respectively at University of Kentucky and Wayne
State University (Detroit), were major contributors to research and publication in this area. After Helen McMurtry joined NCF staff as Central area
director, she led the NCF staff team in developing a ten-year plan which
included goals to refine and increase professional seminars and to produce
a text for students on spiritual care in nursing. The publication of a journal
for nurses with a Christian emphasis was also part of the ten-year plan.

These goals stretched the NCF staff and developed some of their latent
abilities. Sharon Fish and Judith Allen Shelly, NCF staff, authored *Spiritual
Care: The Nurse's Role* in 1978, which was followed by a *Spiritual Care
Workbook*. In the next few years Judy Shelly wrote *Spiritual Needs of
Children, Spiritual Dimensions of Mental Health* and *Dilemma: A Nurse's
Guide for Making Ethical Decisions* (all published by IVP). Grace Wallace
says, "A faculty member recently asked me how one person can write so
authentically on so many topics. I replied that God has gifted Judy Shelly
with ability to take scriptural principles, her own nursing experiences, and
those of pediatric and mental health nurses who served in task forces and
combine them with research to produce these books. Judy has contributed
much to the integration of biblical principles into nursing."

Students as well as nurses welcomed these helps. Two or three students
at the University of Sacramento in California wanted to do an independent
study project on spiritual care. Reluctantly their professor gave permission
and watched with interest what they would do. She was so impressed with
their work and their resources from NCF that she began to ask searching
questions about their faith. Before the semester ended this professor became a Christian.

When NCF became a member of Nurses Christian Fellowship International in 1970, the staff knew little about NCF work in other countries.
Gradually their horizons widened. Grace Wallace was an elected member
of the executive board from 1970-88. She served as president of NCFI from
1976-80. Ruth Lichtenberger had been an NCF staffworker since 1964 and
had an influential ministry in teaching students how to study the Bible. In
1975 Ruth was appointed the general director of NCFI and moved to
London. Many nurses with involvement in NCF have gone overseas as
Christian workers and helped to pioneer and strengthen the NCF movements in other countries by sharing their experiences in the American
movement.

NCF in Australia and NKSS in Norway sent nurses for experience with

NCF-USA, exchanges that were mutually beneficial. NCF student ministries developed within the Norwegian movement following this visit. Grete Scharfe of Denmark and Chieko Fukushima of Japan met NCF while studying or working in the United States. Grete returned to Denmark to introduce NCF concepts of spiritual care to nurses there. Chieko prepared to bring God's Word and the message of Jesus Christ to nurses in Japan and introduce them to NCFI.

When NCF merged with Inter-Varsity in 1948, the identity of NCF was to be retained as a specific ministry to students in nursing with NCF staff who were themselves nurses. Volunteers who served as associate staff and faculty advisors were the backbone of the ministry as they prayed and financed the movement, prepared and presented workshops and helped in a variety of ways. The NCF National Committee worked closely with Tressie Myers and was given representation on the official IVCF Board, according to the stipulations at the time of merger. Over the years, however, the board and the leaders of IVCF have questioned NCF about being a professional society—more than a ministry to students. Grace Wallace said, "Each NCF director has had to defend the ministry, to integrate it into the larger IVCF movement and to keep it from becoming a step-child."

NCF's ministry encourages both student nurses and graduates to apply their Christian faith in their daily work. In the midseventies three NCF graduates met in the hospital parking lot at Los Angeles County Hospital each morning at 6:30 to pray. Work at the county hospital was never easy. They prayed for one another, the staff in their units, patients they cared for, quality nursing care and their own witness. Work relationships were often strained. As these three nurses prayed, they saw a difference in attitude, more openness and greater concern for quality care. An uncooperative orderly began responding to the kindness and love shown him. Nurses have some of the very best opportunities to practice the gospel, and NCF staff and students know this.

8/Strategy at UNC

James Long, or Jimmy, as he is called, became a Christian, went to Florida State University in 1968 and got involved in Inter-Varsity. After graduation he went on to Gordon-Conwell Theological Seminary and came on Inter-Varsity staff in the fall of 1975. He was assigned to staff the chapter at the University of North Carolina (UNC), where two hundred students were involved in chapter witness. It would be a new experience for him. Forty students had been in his undergraduate chapter at Florida State. Long said,

"I came with fear and trepidation. I did not want to be known as a staff-worker who killed a large chapter."

About six months before Jimmy arrived, under the leadership of staff member Don Bryant, the students had made the decision to divide the group into four chapters and leave the graduate student chapter as it was. The students felt they did not have leaders who knew how to lead a chapter of two hundred. That move meant that Long had twenty-eight students in executive responsibilities in four chapters, only one of whom had any leadership experience. The students had a strong commitment to take on responsibilities of leadership which they believed had been given them by God. They cared for the people in their chapters; they had a vision for outreach.

The first two weeks of school were critical in reaching new Christians on the campus and finding others who were willing to investigate the Christian faith. Each chapter was divided into small groups, and new people were immediately put in touch with a small group. As soon as the contact was made, group members were committed to visit each person within the next twenty-four to forty-eight hours, offering help and inviting each one to the large group meeting. Freshman outreach was the key to chapter building.

The history of the chapter at UNC began in 1951 when Bill York transferred from North Carolina State to begin an Inter-Varsity chapter. For nearly twenty years the group had stayed at a steady twenty to forty students. Their consistent prayer was that God would use them at UNC. In 1971 the chapter suddenly dwindled to two students: Roger Anderson and Jeanne Haibach. Instead of folding the chapter, these two decided to make a strong outreach to freshmen in the fall. In answer to their fervent prayers and hard work, forty students came to their first meeting. They began shifting the momentum of the group to small group meetings where relationships could develop and people could more easily be concerned for each other. By the end of the year they had six small groups reaching out to friends in the dorms. By 1975 the strategy of outreach to freshmen and small groups had grown the chapter to over two hundred students. And these two hundred were now divided into four chapters, with new IVCF staff member Jimmy Long.

For the next three years the UNC chapter went through the trauma of regrouping. It wasn't easy; each year the students had to make a fresh commitment to the vision for the chapter. By 1977-78 the four chapters had 430 members. By 1979-80 the combined chapters had mushroomed to 650 members. From the students' point of view, prayer was central to the growth. The staff role of giving training and vision put legs on their prayers. Every exec member had to be committed to going to chapter camp. By the summer of 1977 every small group leader was committed to go to Small Group Leaders Camp or to working on a correspondence course Jimmy Long developed. Student participation in the spring beach missions in Florida at Ft. Lauderdale gave evangelism training. By the end of the decade students were planning for a campus-wide evangelistic outreach.

The strategy used by students at UNC is at work on campuses across the country. Its success is determined by the commitment of the students to pray and to work, and the staff's ability to impart a vision to students. Inter-Varsity continues to ask for high-level commitment on the part of students. It means living under the lordship of Christ in every area of life; it demands a quality spiritual life with Quiet Time and prayer. While the goal of Inter-Varsity is to build groups of students whose aims are evangelism, discipleship and missions, the building of chapters is not focused on the size of the group, but on the quality of personal life and outreach to others.

9/Teamwork at Berkeley

During the first three decades of Inter-Varsity's history, staff members maintained student witness in large geographical areas without the benefit of close teamwork with other staff. The contribution of this long roster of "heroes of the faith" can hardly be overestimated in the ministry of Inter-Varsity. The idea of having a team of people with whom to discuss strategy and problems—not just at official staff meetings—was a luxury they were denied. By the late 1970s numbers of staff had grown sufficiently to allow closer team work and more adequate staffing. This was particularly important as demographics within the U.S. changed and Inter-Varsity groups began to reflect the diversity within the country.

Donna Dong, a third-generation American-born Chinese, grew up in San Francisco. When one of her friends invited her to a Chinese church in Chinatown, Donna found herself open to investigate the Christian faith. She was especially impressed with Gwen Wong,[17] who spoke at a church retreat. Donna Dong says, "I wasn't quite a Christian yet, but I thought, 'I don't know what this woman has, but whatever it is, that's what I want.' And somewhere during this time, through the witness of a Filipino in my high school I became a Christian." She remembered Gwen Wong's words to her, "When you get to college, why don't you look up Inter-Varsity Christian Fellowship?"

Donna did what Gwen suggested, and during her four undergraduate years and year of graduate school, she was deeply involved with the IV chapter at Cal—Berkeley. She was also part of a Chinese-American student group, the Pacific Alliance of Chinese Evangelicals (PACE), which provided her with similar experiences of Christian growth and commitment, as well as Chinese-American role models. At a PACE retreat, Donna was one of the students who made a commitment to full-time ministry.[18] These two groups nurtured her as a young, growing Christian.

The Berkeley IV chapter stayed at about forty members for a number of years. Staff were about to conclude that was Berkeley's pace. The chapter had been producing many strong student leaders who later became staff members for Inter-Varsity. When she graduated in 1972, Donna was one of these and Jim Berney invited her to join the staff of Inter-Varsity to work primarily at Berkeley and continue the vision she had for campus work.

In 1974 Donna Dong took a leave and went to Singapore to study for two years at the Discipleship Training Centre, led by David Adeney. Describing the benefits of her time in Singapore, Donna says, "I spent two years sorting through my identity as an Asian American. There in a Chinese community I suddenly discovered where part of who I am came from. I put the pieces together." When she returned to staff in 1976, she came back with an urban concern. She saw San Francisco in a new way. She also had a concern for Asian-Americans. "I thought of all the benefits I had from my involvement in Inter-Varsity as an Asian-American. I realized I knew all kinds of Asian-Americans who were not getting the training I had. I wanted to get them involved. I wanted to stay in San Francisco and make a difference."

Since 1976 Donna Dong has been working on a team of staff, concentrating at Cal—Berkeley where approximately sixty-five per cent of the chapter is made up of Asian-Americans. The chapter now numbers over three hundred. Donna, who serves as an associate area director, believes this staff team are giving the students in-depth experiences in leadership and discipling. "I would describe what we are doing as the Philippian model of partnership in the gospel —partnership between strong staff and strong student leaders. My vision for Asian-Americans has branched out into a reconciled multi-ethnic fellowship. I really have a concern for Blacks. In a group made up largely of Asians, I'm concerned that the White minority participate effectively. It is what Paul talks about in Ephesians, a breaking down of dividing walls between Christians of many racial backgrounds."

10/A Prospering Work

By the late seventies, Inter-Varsity's student work looked more prosperous than ever. However, John Alexander was ambivalent and took scant comfort from its obvious successes. He wondered if the movement was failing to maintain the thoroughly indigenous concept the founding fathers had established. He comments, "The ideal in the first twenty-five years of Inter-Varsity's history in the U.S. was that each campus witness would be maintained by students and faculty working together on their own campus. The role of the IVCF staff was to visit the campus occasionally, coming alongside the students and faculty to facilitate witness. During the 1970s the proportion of responsibility carried by the staff gradually increased and the proportionate responsibility carried by students—and especially by faculty—slowly shrank."[19]

The work of Inter-Varsity had become increasingly decentralized. Area teams concentrated on fewer campuses. That meant the staff team could do more planning and executing of training programs. It also met some of the challenges of the fragmentation of Christian witness brought by the proliferation of groups. A few chapters (for example, University of North Carolina and University of California at Berkeley) already had one or more staff members assigned to work with them. The positive consequences of a larger staff team was a resurgence of the work across the country. In some ways it was a two-edged sword. At the same time non-itinerating staff began to take the place of faculty advisors or other volunteers who had been giving themselves to student work. With a staffworker on hand, and sometimes more than one, faculty and volunteers no longer felt needed, with a resultant loss of helpful input and fellowship. However, the campus had changed greatly during this decade, and a stronger partnership between staff and students brought an advance to Inter-Varsity's work on campus.

15
Revolving-Door Leadership: Decade of the 1980s

Spiritual leadership possesses inevitably some relationship to an individual's natural powers of leadership. Natural powers of leadership are to be regarded by the Christian as God-given, to be used carefully for His glory.[1]
Derek Prime

Historians like to bundle years in ways that make sense, provide continuity and link past to present, almost as if God had designed the world on the decimal system."[2] A close-up view of the eighties, without the perspective of time, can blur the truly significant cultural trends of the decade. Some big events took place. Mount St. Helens introduced the eighties by blowing 1,377 feet of summit sky-high, perhaps a portent of the decade to come. But for all the disastrous happenings of the decade, the prevailing analysis identified our materialistic lifestyles as the basic cultural problem. The news media did not spare us in highlighting all the ways in which Americans will deservedly suffer for yesterday's pleasures. Greed. People were bent on "having it all" in the affluent eighties.

Living "beyond your means" (over sixty-six per cent of credit card holders pay interest on their monthly bills) meant more than spending money; it also meant frenetic spending of energy to get in on life's goodies. Slim thighs, a nonpolluting environment and child-care rated high on the list of desirables. Women had found their place in the marketplace in ways never realized before, an achievement that changed many people's world. Long lines of students waiting to use the bank's money machines was a new phenomenon, evidence of both affluence and the high cost of living. And no one jogged, biked or kayaked in ordinary clothes; every pleasure demanded its costume. People wore their messages in the 1980s, mostly on the front of T-shirts.

Certainly the culture became more secular than it had ever been. Numerous groups, spearheaded by the American Civil Liberties Union, have seen to that. Children in public schools no longer sang carols or had pageants at Christmas time. The religious roots of the country were deleted from the textbooks. Students arriving on campus had distorted ideas of Christianity, and their biblical illiteracy should have been shocking even to themselves. Separation of church and state called into question the right of Christian student groups to meet on some campuses. The media managed to do its share of "Christian-bashing," portraying adherents as either crazy or crooked. The behavior of a few religious television personalities fed fuel to the fire. Even those committed to the church, who call themselves Christians, became more secular in their thinking. The idea of holiness got short shrift; it didn't fit in with "having it all." A "prosperity gospel" flourished.

At the same time world headlines portrayed the grip of religious passions and the power of ideologies in countries of the world which were once only on the periphery of the average American's interests. "Uncivilized" tales of fanaticism, terrorism and barbarism were matched by "civilized" tales of junk-bond sales, savings-and-loans embezzlements, and corporate take-overs. Under the veneer of our affluence, the world was looking messier than it had before with stories of abused children, "street people" and the starving on the front pages of the newspapers.

In 1981 medical research identified a new plague—Acquired Immune Deficiency Syndrome—and reported that two hundred sixty-nine Americans died from AIDS that year. Homosexuals (who had been coming out of the closet during the seventies) made AIDS a political issue and became a recognized political force. Sexual behavior of all sorts became front-page news.

Never before in our history had there been so intense a discussion about the unborn. Pro-lifers fought pro-choicers in front of abortion clinics and on the media, making the life of the unborn the number one domestic issue of the decade. At the same time, animal-rights groups fought research on animals, vandalized laboratories and spray-painted the fur coats people wore as they walked down the streets.

Other trends and events chronicled changes in America's lifestyle. When the 1980s began, the world's largest corporations, banks and stock markets were all American. As the eighties ended, the Japanese had moved into first place. A paper loss of five hundred billion dollars on the stock market on Black Monday in October 1987 warned Americans that their economy was not inviolate. Other problems were closer to the ordinary person. The nation that inspired freedom in eastern Europe seemed powerless to keep its streets safe and its work force educated. The most advanced technological society in the world became the most violent domestically. Increasingly people struggled with ethical values, which made for a less secure society than Americans had ever known. A cultural climate of alarm took away feelings of well-being. Chemicals in foods, polluted air and water— hardly anything was safe anymore.

Home became less safe as well. Salt-of-the-earth, whole families who provided emotional nurture and took responsibility for each other became fewer. Instead, dysfunctionality increasingly plagued relationships, with mothers and fathers destroying their own lives and breaking the hearts of their children. Counselling and therapy became commonplace. A value-free society had trouble finding a rallying point. New Age books took over the religion section of campus bookstores. A mixture of Eastern religions, tarot cards, crystals and channelling got people looking for the god within themselves, rejecting objective authority. Many college students took a liking to the idea of individual deity and authority. Some even stirred Bible verses into the mix. Yet there was evidence of spiritual hunger, even if it was the do-it-yourself kind.

Around the world it was a decade of causes, of hopes dashed. It was a decade of risk taking and boldness in other parts of the world. For his daring Mikhail Gorbachev, the leader of America's most-feared nation, was declared Man of the Decade by *Time* magazine. When eastern Europe burst out of the prison of Communism in the winter of 1989 and the Berlin Wall fell, the whole world seemed poised on the edge of hope. The events of Tiananmen Square in Beijing, China, however, reminded everyone of the fragility of freedom and hope. The doctrine of salvation through progress, through changing societal structures, was phony. Chinese students on American campuses talked freely about a crisis of faith in China. After June 4, 1989, it became evident that any hope for the perfect society is doomed by the sinfulness of the human race. For all the dazzle of technology and material achievements, some sobering questions remained to haunt the thoughtful.

But the decade wasn't all gloom. A healthy economy meant new houses and new cars. "Yuppies" became a new, young, affluent designation of society. The pluses include a new sobriety regarding sexuality, a decrease in smoking, alcohol consumption and television viewing. Even the drug scene on campus lessened. The handicapped got new rights signed into law; people began to recycle their trash in concern for the environment; and evangelicals like Everett Koop, the surgeon general, came into the public sector. It was a prosperous decade with little inflation and increased production. Compared to other countries with runaway inflation, Americans knew they had the good life. At the decade's end, volunteerism was on the rise through agencies like *Habitat for Humanity,* and giving to charitable causes had increased. On the world mission front, short-term mission volunteers had more than doubled in number during the decade. But some hard choices faced Americans at the end of the eighties. The baby boom was over. Downsizing the government to take care of national debt, downsizing the economy and the universities, and putting limits on an extravagant lifestyle will be necessities in the nineties.

1/The Campus Scene

Whatever happened in the 1980s, the trends of the decade affected the work of Inter-Varsity. Events in other countries brought opportunity and excitement to international student work, and IVCF increased its staff and outreach. With the encouragement of Terry Morrison in the new IFES-Link program, a number of staff began working overseas in IFES movements or with English Language Institutes during the eighties.[3]

The increased breakdown in family life brought students to the campus with deep emotional needs. Students who came from evangelical churches seemed increasingly secular in their attitudes and were often wary of genuine commitment. The affluence of the culture affected the values of students. By the midseventies over seventy per cent of the students gave "being financially well-off" as the chief motivation for attending college. A June 1990 cartoon depicted one graduate wearing gown and mortar board saying to another, "I'm going to devote myself to the betterment of mankind—if the money is decent." The most popular careers were in business and commerce. The least-wanted jobs were homemaking and the clergy. History was one of the least popular courses, along with religion and philosophy.

In interpersonal relationships, tolerance for the beliefs and behavior of others became a major value. It was a tolerance that kept students from telling the good news. "I wouldn't do that, but if he wants to . . ." meant that students did not spontaneously use their influence to bring about change. The nature of sexuality and sexual behavior became even more relevant as homosexuals grabbed power positions on the campus and crusaded against discrimination on the basis of sexual choice. Parading under the banner of equal opportunity, sexuality was often the battle ground of the late eighties.

2/Focus on Leadership

In the mix of this climate in the eighties, the Inter-Varsity Board faced many challenges in its attempt to provide stable leadership for the movement. Over the years members of the board of trustees had given generously of their time and energy, serving sacrificially and making complex decisions. Their decisions involved people, vulnerable human beings who are charged with the combination of maintaining a vision, doing a spiritual work, and running a diverse "business." One of the important threads in any history chronicles the story of its leaders and the results of their leadership.

Leadership is a fragile commodity, often criticized, often lonely, carrying heavy loads others cannot share. Leaders make things happen and what they make happen eventually bends the organization and the people being led. This is true on the national political level and true in organizations like Inter-Varsity Christian Fellowship. It is also true for campus chapters. Biblical leadership cares about how things happen, not just that they happen. Leadership is a serious business.

Within Inter-Varsity the decade of the 1980s could be labeled "Turbulence at the Top." In this ten-year span Inter-Varsity had five different presidents. Each change of leadership left marks of gain and pain on the movement. Yet the genius of Inter-Varsity is that it is not based on a single leader. It is based on a biblical idea: the priesthood of the believer, the necessity of living under the lordship of Christ, the importance of the authority of Scripture in personal life and student responsibility. Most Inter-Varsity students do not know who their regional director is, let alone who the president of Inter-Varsity is. They know their staff worker, their student leaders and the responsibility they have as members of the group. That is enough. Inter-Varsity works to build the people of God on campus, providing training in godliness to student leaders. The focus is students, not the organization. As a result, student work on the campus scarcely felt the turbulence that marked organizational management during the eighties. Much of the credit for this goes to a faithful team of staff whose keen vision for the movement kept student work on target. Staff, for the most part, have the values of the movement "in their bones" because they are products of it.

The closing two chapters on the eighties will chronicle the two stories that run through the history of Inter-Varsity: (1) its work in building strong groups of students who will be faithful to Jesus Christ on the campus, and (2) the management of its mission by its leadership. This chapter will focus on the management of Inter-Varsity during the 1980s.

3/A Surprising Decision

At its November 1979 meeting the Inter-Varsity Board voted to extend John Alexander's fifteen-year contract as president of Inter-Varsity for another five-year term. The board wanted to prepare for an orderly transfer of leadership in choosing a new president at the end of this five-year term. They asked Alexander to prepare and submit a report for the April board meeting on criteria that would constitute a screen for the next president. The second phase would be to procure a list of names as a starting point to find a successor for the presidency who would take over at the end of the five-year appointment in 1984. At that same November 1979 board meeting Allen Mathis, Jr., was elected as chairman of the board, succeeding Chester Youngberg.

Five months later, on the first day of the April 1980 board meeting, Mathis invited Chester Youngberg and Don Powell, former board chairmen, to a breakfast meeting with John Alexander. Alexander said later that he assumed they would discuss his report on the criteria for a successor. Instead, Mathis said the three of them were an ad hoc committee within the board executive committee appointed to confer with Alexander about administrative alignment for the next five years. The discussion turned to the possibility of looking internally for a successor for John Alexander. Mathis asked who, in Alexander's opinion, they should consider within the movement. Alexander said, "Well, I suppose you would turn first to the senior vice president, Jim McLeish." The three men agreed with this idea, and Mathis suggested Alexander appoint Jim McLeish as chief operating officer (COO).[4] McLeish would be given a trial of two years to see if he could run the movement. Alexander would remain the chief executive office (CEO) and president, but all regional directors and department heads would report to Jim McLeish.[5] The arrangement could be terminated at any time if it was not working out. Mathis encouraged Alexander to proceed with the plan by suggesting that this would free him up to do the things he most liked doing.[6] In a May 12, 1980, letter to the executive ad hoc committee, Alexander asked permission to put this plan into operation beginning July 1, 1980. The possibility of McLeish becoming the COO was not reported to the board at its April meeting.[7]

4/The Role of the Corporation

A major discussion took place at that April board meeting, growing out of the executive committee minutes of the March 8, 1980, meeting: Should the IVCF Corporation be restructured? Mathis felt the board had trouble acting as the board. It was too large and the task of the corporation was poorly defined. The existing procedure provided for the members of a larger corporation, often as many as eighty-five or more men and women who were committed to the Fellowship, to meet at an annual corporation meeting to elect the board and hear reports about Inter-Varsity's ministry. It was not deemed cost-effective to have so many involved, since the elected board of twenty-four members plus officers conducted the business of IVCF. The by-laws had not been updated for seventeen years and Chairman Allen Mathis proposed "the appointment of a by-laws committee to consider a number of matters."[8] Mathis was keen on "streamlining the operation" of the board, and the pros and cons of downsizing the corporation were discussed for the next two years. At the April 30, 1982, meeting, the board concluded that the various working committees of the board should be eliminated in favor of a committee of the whole.[9]

At the November 12, 1983, board meeting, the by-laws were amended with a vote of 17-5, making the corporation and the board coextensive, thus eliminating a corporation larger than the board. While this made the organization more manageable from a business point of view, the efficiency of "streamlining" meant that fifty-eight loyal supporters were disenfranchised from official input into Inter-Varsity. Many corporation members represented the academic community and had long-term involvement with student work as volunteers and faculty advisors. The change in corporation membership left some of these disillusioned about the course the Inter-Varsity Board was taking.[10] Although a smaller board had been under consideration, the board still consisted of twenty-four members.

5/Alexander Resigns

In January of 1981 John and Betty Alexander were given a month-long trip to Africa to visit the IFES movements and later to visit England. As they traveled they were frequently asked about the presidency of the American movement and told that rumors had come from the States that McLeish was really the president. Alexander began to feel increasingly uneasy. Jim McLeish had been pushing to expand the number of campus staff members beyond what Alexander felt was wise. Later that summer a severe kidney infection put Alexander in bed, a malady the doctor said was caused by internal stress. His son-in-law was battling for his life with a brain tumor. John Alexander questioned whether he had the board support to resolve the situation in the Fellowship. It was too much.

On November 7, 1981, the board met in executive session to handle a serious matter. They had received a letter of resignation from President John Alexander. Alexander's subsequent explanation for his action was that the sixteen-month trial with McLeish as COO had not been successful. He said he was being blamed for decisions that had been made because the staff had not been told that Jim McLeish had been made Chief Operating Officer (COO).[11] Members of the staff said they did not know who was really in charge. Barry McLeish became the director of development and began aggressive direct mail fund raising. Both the content and style of fund raising letters caused increasing criticism from the staff, alumni and other donors. Alexander felt he had lost his clout to resolve the problem and felt drained emotionally from the constant flow of complaining letters he received. He did not know what else to do; he gave his letter of resignation and opted not to attend the board meeting.

Under Chairman Allen Mathis, Jr., the board accepted Alexander's letter of resignation. They appointed Jim McLeish president and chief executive officer (CEO) of IVCF, both decisions effective November 7, 1981.[12] John W. Alexander was made president emeritus with full pay for the duration of his appointment. He was asked to stay on and chair the Urbana 81 convention at the year's end and thus make a smooth transition for the new leadership. John Alexander's presidency was over, and the pain and remorse that followed hit him hard. He had served as Inter-Varsity's president for seventeen years.

6/The McLeish Presidency

Jim McLeish had been tireless in his concern for Inter-Varsity. In the last years, during Alexander's presidency, he had spent most of his waking moments planning changes that he thought would make Inter-Varsity more progressive. He believed change meant progress and proposed many changes that Alexander agreed to. When he became the COO in April 1980 he reorganized the management group, eventually calling it "the alpha group." It consisted of COO McLeish; Peter Northrup, vice president; Bob Fryling,[13] whom he had appointed director of campus ministries; Jim Nyquist, director of InterVarsity Press; Grace Wallace, director of Nurses Christian Fellowship; Pete Hammond,[14] director of evangelism; Comptroller Dick Karppinen; and John Kyle, director of missions. The regional directors (Jim Berney, Ned Hale, Terry Morrison, Ed Good, Jim Worden, Fred Wagner) reported to Bob Fryling.[15] When Jim McLeish was asked to take the presidency, he said he wanted to check with the alpha group to ask if they would back him as president. McLeish says, "Every one of them said, 'Yes.' They knew I was sixty-two, and it was just a matter of time [before my retirement]." McLeish also requested that a search committee be appointed by the board to find his successor.

Jim McLeish accepted the presidency, stating that he felt it a great honor. He said, "I appreciate your confidence in me and trust I can be used of God."[16] Jim had done a good job with the finances of Inter-Varsity and had won the confidence of Allen Mathis, Jr., who had been chairman of the finance committee for the past years. He became McLeish's advisor in the years ahead in the running of the movement. Many of the staff leaders, aware of Jim's influence in administration under Alexander, took McLeish's appointment in stride. They were used to working with him.

During his time as COO, Jim McLeish wanted to capitalize on the success of Urbana and schedule more national conferences in the non-Urbana years. After the 1979 Urbana Convention, John Alexander, John Kyle and Jim McLeish had discussed the overcrowding of Urbana and made the observation that a conference that did not focus only on the foreign field could ignite a new concern for ministry to the ghettos and other ethnic or non-professional mission outreach. Under McLeish's encouragement Elward Ellis and Pete Hammond codirected a conference called Washington '80. About eleven hundred attended Washington '80, with thirty-five per cent of the attendance consisting of racial minorities—"people of color." While the conference did not draw the expected number of delegates, Inter-Varsity learned some important lessons about ministries to ethnic minorities. The debriefing that followed the convention became the seed-bed for the development of the Asian-American ministry under the leadership of Jeanette Yep and Nina Lau-Branson. A Spanish student ministry called La Fe began with Ruth Lewis as coordinator in the summer of 1981. With the encouragement of Area Director Rudy Hernandez and others they recruited approximately two hundred Hispanics for Urbana 81.

A second urban conference, San Francisco '83, directed by Pete Hammond with Geri Rodman as associate director, built on the first experience.[17] The conference focus: City/Church/Career. For the first time the brochure promoting the conference was multilingual. Thirteen hundred attended from diverse ethnic background. Those interested in Hispanic ministry met again, and Isaac Canales emerged as the spokesman for this group. Creative programming and the use of "mentors" (not yet so called) set the stage for the future Marketplace ministry and gave a needed boost to ethnic ministries.

McLeish was a restless leader who often made decisions based on his "hunches." He wanted to make Inter-Varsity grow into a bigger organization. He multiplied the number of regions to seventeen, restructuring to provide management for the much larger field staff team he envisioned, even though he did not always have people to fill all the slots. He pushed for recruitment of new staff in larger numbers than before. During this time Janet Luhrs (Balajthy)[18] was appointed the first woman regional director in 1983, and several women were made area directors.[19]

McLeish was not comfortable on the campus or at Inter-Varsity camps and generally distanced himself from students. The university was not his milieu. He delegated the campus work to Bob Fryling, the director of campus ministries. Barney Ford[20] and Roger Anderson,[21] Ron Nicholas[22] and Bill Tiffan,[23] all regional directors, became associate campus directors under Bob Fryling's leadership. Field people were moved to headquarters to direct special ministries. Ned Hale was moved to international student ministries in 1981 and also made associate director for Student Foreign Missions Fellowship (SFMF) under John Kyle. Eric Miller, the initiator and director of TWENTYONEHUNDRED, was replaced by Scott Wilson. Miller was freed to work with member movements of the IFES in media productions. Jim Berney left his post as regional director for the West Coast to become general director of IVCF in Canada. Terry Morrison left a regional director post to direct IFES-Link, a new plan to tie in IVCF people resources with needs of the international movement.

In 1983 Jim Nyquist was made administrative vice president for Inter-Varsity, and Linda Doll became the director of InterVarsity Press.[24] Bob Fryling's position was changed to the director of human resources. Bill Tiffan was brought in from southern California and made director of campus ministries. Ron Nicholas became director of planning. The name of the management group was changed from the "alpha group" to the "national leadership team" (NLT), a group of seventeen people. Non-field support staff numbered two hundred sixty at the beginning of 1984 (which included IVP and TWENTYONEHUNDRED). The number of field staff jumped to three hundred eighty-nine, and the annual budget was twenty million dollars.

The McLeish presidency was marked by change and expansion of headquarter personnel. However, the increase in headquarters personnel required growth in the size of budget. The department of development (including the foundation department which was begun in the seventies) was pushing hard to locate needed funds.[25] Barry McLeish's development team used the latest direct mail techniques, but while the department could show some positive donor figures, the content and style of the letters continued to irritate the staff and alumni of Inter-Varsity. Staff members said that they were deluged with requests to "get off the mailing list."

Unrest began to grow as McLeish's presidential term in office lengthened. Most of the staff had presumed his appointment was "interim," until such time as the board could initiate a formal search process. As time went on without any move in that direction, a number of the staff expressed surprise that the board's intent was to continue with McLeish as president.[26] Serious morale problems existed among some staff leaders in the field, particularly in the Midwest and on the East Coast.[27] Interviews indicate that discouragement and distrust became widespread. The conflict orientation of McLeish's leadership became a burden to some of the regional directors. With an accountant's background, Jim McLeish tended to quantify the task, making expansion a premier value. The staff felt the rift between Madison and the field widen.

Board Chairman Mathis emphasized a policy that prohibited staff members from contacting board members directly, without going through the IVCF line of authority. When a group of regional directors brought their complaints directly to McLeish, members of the national leadership team were later confronted by Mathis who asked if they opposed McLeish on any moral grounds. When they answered negatively, he asked them to sign a statement of loyalty to McLeish. Still the unrest grew. Meetings scheduled to discuss differences failed to solve issues which were largely philosophical.

By 1984 alumni picked up the scent of trouble and began writing to some of the board members. Disturbed staff members who could not get a hearing from the president put their jobs in jeopardy by writing directly to the board. No communication came from the board to alleviate the unsettled feelings of the staff. No mention was made of a search for a replacement for McLeish. Allen Mathis addressed the Urbana 84 convention, the first board chairman to do so. Hoping to encourage the staff, he spoke at the staff conference following Urbana, but made no mention of the concerns of the staff. It seemed doubtful to some of the staff that all the board members were adequately informed about what was happening within the movement.

Over the months Jim Nyquist, the administrative vice president, had listened to complaints about low morale from staffworkers in the office and in the field. Some resignations had followed personal disillusionment with central leadership. Jim Nyquist and Peter Northrup, the two vice presidents, had gone together to speak to McLeish about the problem. Later both put their thoughts in writing. McLeish was unresponsive to their concerns. Nyquist says that from that point on he felt that both he and Northrup were "persona non grata" in terms of relationship to McLeish. Peter Northrup quietly submitted his resignation letter on November 1, 1984.[28]

At Urbana 84 discouraged groups of staff, unaware that a search committee was looking for a new president, met to pray and share their grief and grievances. Although they helped make the convention effective, the morale of many was very low. Jim Nyquist felt he must do what he could to alert the board to the seriousness of the problem. Since the president had ignored his several requests for a meeting with the board chairman and the president during the preceeding months, at the end of Urbana Nyquist distributed a letter describing his evaluation of the situation to all board members. This was in violation to the directive about the chain of command.[29]

The tensions within the movement were philosophical, not personal. From its inception, Inter-Varsity had been task-driven, a fellowship directed by an understood ethos or set of values.[30] The values began to shift as financial pressures and the demands of growth altered previous ministry patterns. Each department or unit within the Fellowship was expected to raise adequate income to meet expenses. Informally these were referred to as "profit centers," or "separate ministry" centers. If a department or region could raise the money, its growth potential was unlimited. The "bottom line" began to determine the direction of the movement.

No one questioned Jim McLeish's love for the Lord and his deep loyalty and concern for the Inter-Varsity movement nor his intentions. No one could fault his hard work and his ingenuity. Yet some who worked closely with him said "the presidency was not a good job fit."[31] In interviews staff members commented that he was not articulate nor did he understand the campus; he failed to interact with those whose opinion differed from his; he made impulsive changes. The university student part of the job and inspiring "the troops"—that was not his strength. He was more pragmatic than philosophical.

The staff conference following Urbana 84 was both tense and discouraging to many who feared for the future. After three difficult weeks, the board met in Atlanta on January 25 and 26, 1985, and made several decisions. They gave Jim McLeish[32] retirement, effective January 25. They confirmed McLeish's decision to retire Jim Nyquist for insubordination.[33] Jim McLeish had served Inter-Varsity thirty-two years, and Nyquist had served for thirty-five years. The important and sacrificial contributions both men had made to the movement were scarcely mentioned publicly at their departure, although both were given generous retirements.

Gordon MacDonald was elected the new president and chief executive officer of Inter-Varsity, effective January 25, 1985.[34] At its next meeting Chester Youngberg was elected to complete the remaining months of Allen Mathis's term as chairman. He served as chairman until September 1986 when Jim Kay was elected to chair the board.

A group of shaken, heartbroken administrators and board members left Atlanta after the January board meeting, still more concerned about the future of student work than their own hurts. Later in 1986 Gordon MacDonald wrote in a staff letter: "Gail and I have learned over and over that the ministry to which we are called is indeed a fight. It draws wounds and involves fatigue. Sometimes the shots come from behind our own lines, so confused is the warfare."

7/MacDonald Becomes President
Gordon MacDonald had been at Urbana 84 as one of the speakers, leading the special session for pastors. MacDonald, a gifted and popular conference speaker, had recently left his pastorate at Grace Chapel in Lexington, Massachusetts, and had accepted the post of minister-at-large for World Vision. He was one of the most sought-after speakers for Christian groups in the States, and his book *Ordering Your Private World* further catapulted him into the public eye. He had earlier been approached about taking the presidency of Inter-Varsity Christian Fellowship at some future date, following the retirement of Jim McLeish. At Urbana 84 some board members realized that an immediate change of leadership was needed and the search committee approached MacDonald with greater urgency. By mid-January

MacDonald had agreed to join Inter-Varsity as its new president.

Gordon MacDonald was Inter-Varsity's first "outside" president. He had observed the work, but did not have experience with its philosophy and way of working. Some staff felt that his use of the phrase "reinventing Inter-Varsity" was his way of getting a handle on the organization he was charged to lead. Gordon and Gail MacDonald came as a team. They crisscrossed the country to get to know the staff, the philosophy of the work and the problems peculiar to each region of the country. MacDonald identified his three tasks to the board shortly after he accepted the position: (1) the healing of the organization, (2) running the organization and (3) getting the right kind of control of the movement psychically, spiritually and structurally. The latter he expected would take four years.[35]

MacDonald quickly made a decision to keep the headquarters in Madison, Wisconsin. During McLeish's presidency, ideas for relocating the headquarters in Atlanta, Dallas or Chicago had been tossed about. MacDonald saw this as a cause for unrest. He brought Peter Northrup back into the organization to implement the decision to stay in Madison. After examining several options, property on Schroeder Road seemed the best choice, even though it was away from the university and in an area of small businesses. This property was purchased and remodeled, and the move made in 1986. The larger facility brought all departments located in Madison under one roof.

MacDonald made other changes: he saw that the power had been placed in headquarters, instead of in the field. He moved to make the field work central in the organization, replacing the term "headquarters" with "National Service Center (NSC)," stressing that the NSC existed to serve the field, not to run the movement. The work of a design team, earlier appointed to produce a new logo, was approved and the new designation became "InterVarsity, dropping the hyphen."[36]

MacDonald reduced the size of the senior management team and made the organizational structure more hierarchical. He continued the appointment of Bob Fryling as director of campus ministries with Roger Anderson and Barney Ford as associate directors of campus ministries. Ron Nicholas and Peter Northrup became special assistants to the president. Appointments made in 1986 further solidifed the structure: Barney Ford became vice president and chief administrative officer; Bob Fryling, vice president and director of campus ministries. With the regional directors, MacDonald hammered out a *Vision Statement*—an expanded expression of the purposes of InterVarsity. The key words are in boldface type. The vision of

InterVarsity Christian Fellowship is to

BUILD collegiate fellowships which

ENGAGE their colleges in all of their ethnic diversity with the gospel of Jesus Christ and

DEVELOP disciples who embody these Biblical values:

Evangelism We believe that every person ought to have an opportunity to respond to Jesus Christ as Lord and Savior and to accept His invitation to follow Him into a life of Christian discipleship.

Spiritual Formation We will teach and practice spiritual discipline (i.e., personal Bible study, prayer, reliance upon the Holy Spirit, worship) so that men and women can learn to grow in Christian obedience and Christlike maturity.

The Church We will serve the church by helping each person to appreciate its purpose and by encouraging their activity as lifelong worshipers and participating members.

Human Relationships We will teach and demonstrate by example the command of Christ that we love one another, and that healthy human relationships are a mark of true discipleship and eventuate in fruitful friendships, marriages, and working partnerships.

Righteousness Aware of the reality of evil as it exists in the human heart and in the social structures and systems of the global community, we will teach and demonstrate repentance and humility and the importance of personal integrity, compassion, and prophetic renunciation and confrontation.

Vocational Stewardship We will challenge Christians to acknowledge the stewardship of personal skills and vocational opportunity so as to bring honor to God through our work in the college community, in the home, or in the marketplace.

World Evangelization Believing that God has called all Christians to involvement in the world evangelization, we will seek to help each person know how to hear that call and discover their place of maximum participation.

Gordon and Gail MacDonald's pastoral ministry to the staff brought significant healing within the movement. They affirmed the staff team by their personal friendship and encouragement and, for many of the younger staff, they became parental models. Each of them sent monthly letters to the staff team, encouraging their family life, stretching their reading habits and reestablishing a family feeling within the movement. The staff were pleased to have MacDonald represent InterVarsity at churches and other Christian gatherings.

Gordon kept a frenetic pace, continuing a speaking ministry outside of InterVarsity, as well as traveling across the country to visit staff teams. Some of the board began to feel that he was becoming an absentee president, that his schedule distracted him from running the movement.[37] While planning an evaluation meeting with him at the regular June 1987 meeting of the IVCF Board, the members of the board were not prepared for what took place. Gordon MacDonald requested an executive session and submitted his resignation from the presidency of InterVarsity. A news release was issued, approved by both the board and Gordon and Gail MacDonald:

James Kay, Chairman of the Board of Trustees of Inter-Varsity Christian Fellowship announced the resignation, effective immediately, of Gordon MacDonald as president of Inter-Varsity Christian Fellowship. After a meeting of the Board where MacDonald tendered his resignation, Kay said, "Gordon has resigned for personal reasons, having been involved in an adulterous relationship in latter 1984 and early 1985." MacDonald told the Board he had done his best to handle the situation in a biblical fashion by requesting and receiving discipline from a council of evangelical church leaders. Nevertheless, he felt it necessary to remove himself from the presidency of InterVarsity.

MacDonald had been with the movement for slightly over two years; he was only beginning to know InterVarsity. The shock and pain was felt by both the board and the staff within the InterVarsity movement. "You could hear board members sobbing as they prayed together, following Gordon's announcement," reported one member of the board. The news release was flashed across the country because of the prominence of the MacDonalds.[38] Both Gordon and Gail took it on the chin. It was important to both of them that they handle this sorrow in a biblical way.[39]

Many of the staff had come to regard the MacDonalds as surrogate parents and experienced genuine grief and some anger at this turn of events. Later that summer at the four-week School of Leadership Training, Regional Director Jim Lundgren made the announcement of MacDonald's resignation to student leaders.[40] He used it as a time to give instruction about the biblical way to handle personal sin and the destructive nature of sin to the whole body of Christ.

8/Dunkerton Takes Over

Board member Tom Dunkerton was elected president of InterVarsity at the June 1987 board meeting. Dunkerton was free to take this immediate and temporary assignment because he had recently retired as senior vice president of the Saatchi and Saatchi Compton advertising agency in New York City. The board members, under Chairman Jim Kay[41] were eager to have someone immediately in place as president and Dunkerton was free to do the job and had the necessary experience. Dunkerton brought a fresh openness to the task and a firm commitment to keep things moving until such time as a new president could be appointed.

Dunkerton was a small boy when Stacey Woods used to come and speak at the assembly (Plymouth Brethren) that his family attended. He says, "I can still see Stacey sitting in the rocking chair, rocking back and forth, talking to my dad. And I was a nine-year-old kid listening to him talk. He was very impressive." When Tom went to New York University (NYU) in 1946, he ran into Jane Hollingsworth, and she suggested he work with a couple of other students to get an InterVarsity chapter going there. They met three times a week for prayer meetings and once every two weeks for a chapter meeting. In contrast to the eight or ten students meeting at NYU, the monthly area meetings had about three hundred people present, with Joe Bayly and Walt Liefeld and others as speakers. This gave students a sense of being in on something significant. Over the years people like Paul Little, Joe Bayly and others kept in touch with Tom, but it wasn't until Regional Director Janet Luhrs contacted him that he became actively involved again. He became one of InterVarsity's committee leaders —an advisor and fund raiser for the work in the New York area.

It took some adjustment to the academic world after having been in the New York City business world, Dunkerton says when speaking about his first days as InterVarsity's president. Coming from an ad agency where "it's bang, bang, shoot from the hip and go, I could hardly understand the process and consensus approach of the folk in InterVarsity. But I got used to it, and grew to love the job." His philosophy was "If it's not broken, don't fix it," because he saw InterVarsity running on an even keel. He humorously described it as "twelve or more regional directors who act as franchise holders, somewhat like the Jeep Dealers Association, who are pleased to be part of InterVarsity and who follow the guidelines. It's a pretty independent operation." While calling this conglomerate a strange management structure that would "drive a businessman up the wall," he also observed that it was working. He said, "If we ever take our eyes off the goal—which is student work—then we are not going to be InterVarsity anymore."

Dunkerton was good for InterVarsity because he brought stability with him. He knew he was temporary and had no personal agenda; he had nothing to prove, and he talked straight. He also made some important appointments. He supported the appointment of Dan Harrison as missions director, recruited by John Kyle who left after Urbana 87. He appointed Sheldon Nix the second director of the Black Campus Ministry (BCM), after Elward Ellis resigned in December 1987, following nearly eight years of leadership in the BCM. Sam Barkat was made director of multi-ethnic ministries just before Dunkerton left office.[42]

The search committee of the board had been working hard on their task of finding a new president for InterVarsity, someone who could serve long term and someone who was already experienced in student work. They hired a professional consultant to aid in the process. A group of three staff members acted as staff advisors to the search committee. In the spring of 1988 the board announced that Steve Hayner had been elected the new president of InterVarsity.

9/Hayner Appointed President

Steve Hayner was a student at Whitman College in 1966, and became part of a newly formed Christian fellowship on campus. The group steadily grew until about ten per cent of that small student body participated in the fellowship. IVCF staff member Steve Smith came to campus periodically; so did staff members of Campus Crusade for Christ and the Navigators. During the summer of 1969 the staff of IVCF, Campus Crusade and the Navigators met together and decided to divide up the small schools in Washington, instead of all visiting the same group.

In that meeting Whitman College was given to InterVarsity. (It was hardly the indigenous principle at work, and the students were rightfully annoyed!) Steve Hayner returned to campus in the fall of 1969 to find that he was president of an InterVarsity chapter.

By the time Steve was ready to graduate, Regional Director Jim Berney was recruiting him for InterVarsity staff. Steve Hayner had his sights set on graduate school, however, and declined. While at Harvard he was active in Park Street Church's student work, which included many InterVarsity students. Following his master's degree at Harvard, and his training at Gordon-Conwell Theological Seminary, Hayner did college ministry for eleven years at University Presbyterian Church in Seattle, Washington, again working closely with InterVarsity in the context of the church. He completed a Ph.D. in Old Testament from the University of St. Andrews in Scotland in 1984. From 1984-1988 he served as vice president for student affairs at Seattle Pacific University.

Hayner was pursued as a prime candidate for the presidency of InterVarsity. Although he was more interested in the church than in parachurch organization, he had always loved InterVarsity. When his wife, Sharol, read the profile for the position given him by the search committee, she said, "That's you, Steve." The profile said InterVarsity wanted someone who loved students, who had done student work, and who looked forward to a lifetime vocation with students. Steve Hayner read the profile again with new interest. The more he prayed and investigated the details of the ministry, the more convinced he was that this job was for him.

When asked what he saw as InterVarsity's essentials, Steve had a ready reply. (1) The lordship of Christ over all of life; (2) indigeneity, that is, the people in the situation are responsible for witness; (3) the authority of the Scripture in personal life; (4) contextual evangelism, a deep sense of getting alongside people and making genuine friendships in which the gospel can be shared. "InterVarsity wants authentic, transparent lives reflecting Jesus Christ within the university world. It is focused on the university world," says Hayner. "The university is not just a fishing pond to take fish out; InterVarsity is concerned about the nutrients and the pollutants in the pond as well."

Hayner's statement about InterVarsity's concern for the "nutrients and pollutants in the pond" represents a renewed commitment by InterVarsity to influence the thought-life of the university. The first leaders of InterVarsity felt strongly about being in the university; the community of the university was important. The university was not simply a job-training opportunity. During the confusion of the sixties and seventies this focus became somewhat blurred. During the last half of the eighties, a renewed concern to confront the university as a system with God's truth again became a primary value.

After Hayner became president he subdivided InterVarsity's Vision Statement into two parts. The first part is the vision statement, and is the interpretation of InterVarsity's stated corporate purpose. The key words are *building collegiate fellowships, engaging the university, and developing disciples*. The second part of the Vision Statement defines IVCF's ministry values. "Engaging the university in all its cultural diversity" is the banner for the nineties.

In the annual report from the president's department in 1988-89, Hayner gave tribute to the staff and board for the way they had adjusted to the changes that have accompanied five presidencies in nine years. He outlined his observations on the progress made in the transition needs of the organization.

> The energy, personal vision, and morale of a movement are influenced significantly by the tone, values, corporate ethos, and style of management which is modeled by its leadership. "Movements of God's Spirit" must be served by sound management and organization, but can very quickly be diminished by authoritarian patterns and an overemphasis on bureaucratic technique. I have found more than a little discouragement, anger and fear among our staff—symptoms which are indicative of a lack of empowerment, support, and encouragement. These we are attempting to address through an emphasis on servant leadership and spiritual formation, a diminishing of the symbols and inappropriate use of power, and the establishment of a matrix management system which highlights relational integrity in our interaction. We want to honor people who do right things—and who do things right. We want to have the internal reputation at every level that we care about people before programs and that we are committed to helping each other be all that we can be in Christ.

In the three years since Hayner has become president, he has made important administrative decisions. He has charged Sam Barkat with the task of helping InterVarsity becomes a truly multi-ethnic movement. He appointed Robert Peitscher as director of marketing, communication and development. Glandion Carney will lead the Student Foreign Missions Fellowship (now called InterVarsity Missions Fellowship) into the 1990s. He established a president's council to coordinate national activities and stimulate strategic thinking. He has encouraged renewed team work between the missions department and student work in the field.

Hayner leads a movement that has developed multiple projects and programs and a diverse staff team, many more of whom are making student work their life calling than ever before. Will they be content to keep the focus on what Charles Troutman called "the unending kindergarten" that makes up student ministry? As InterVarsity enters the next decade under the leadership of Steve Hayner, it enters its sixth decade of campus witness, and Hayner's job will be to see that the movement stays on course.

16
At the Crossroads: Decade of the 1980s

The main thing is to keep the main thing the main thing.
Anonymous

When InterVarsity staff member John Roeckeman arrived back on the campus of his alma mater—the University of Illinois in Champaign Urbana—in 1980, it was like coming home. He had been a student on this campus in 1970, active in the InterVarsity chapter, on the executive committee, involved in small group Bible study, making sense of his Christian commitment in the climate of student revolution. Glenn Deckert had been his staff member. Since Roeckeman's time as a student leader he had completed seminary and served on InterVarsity staff in Maryland and Washington D.C. Reassigned in 1980 to staff work at the University of Illinois, John and his wife Nancy found a lively chapter of one hundred and thirty-five undergraduates and about forty graduate students. The chapter has sustained a continuous witness since 1940, and a long line of IVCF staff had come from its ranks—as well as professors, college presidents, business executives, teachers, engineers and scientists—who trace the beginnings of a strong spiritual life to the fellowship of this Illinois chapter.

The size of the InterVarsity chapter had varied greatly over the years. In the fifties it grew from two hundred to almost four hundred; in the late sixties it fell down to thirty, then climbed back up to well over two hundred. Its history was typical of many large campus chapters. Roeckeman and the student leaders began to pray for a breakthrough to greater penetration of the campus. Roeckeman continued what David Ivaska, his predecessor, had begun.

Throughout the spring and summer, diligent prayer and preparation by staff and students focused on new student outreach during the university-sponsored New Student Week in the fall. The chapter planned a series of activities to capture the attention of students arriving on campus for the first time. Popcorn parties followed by a square dance in the Illini Union, a watermelon bash and other social events were woven together with a large-group meeting to introduce new students to InterVarsity. IV students saturated the campus with fluorescent publicity flyers, wore brightly colored InterVarsity T-shirts and made themselves helpful and conspicuous. They sent each new resident a mailing from the InterVarsity chapter. The secret to their effective outreach was the follow-up after each event during New Student Week. Within twenty-four hours chapter members contacted the newcomers personally, inviting them to join small groups and attend other activities. One freshman said, "Everywhere I went I recognized someone from Inter-Varsity. It felt good to be welcomed to the campus like that."

As a result of consistent follow-up and outreach over the next ten years, the InterVarsity chapter had 520 members by the end of the 1980s—440 undergraduates and 80 graduate students.The chapter was able to accommodate this kind of growth by splitting the undergraduate group into the Champaign and Urbana chapters. With leadership doubled, more students could be cared for. An evangelism workshop, a five-week course offered each semester, helped keep the focus on reaching out. A discipleship program kept students growing as Christians. Evangelist Cliffe Knechtle's open-air preaching on the campus in the fall of 1989 drew hundreds of interested students, and resulted in a dozen professions of faith and the start of five new investigative Bible studies. By the end of the eighties, five staff were serving the InterVarsity chapter as trainers, with ninety-seven per cent of the leadership of the chapter coming from the students, according to veteran staffworker John Roeckeman.

Since 1985 a chapter missions team, composed of eight to ten juniors and seniors, has met biweekly to prepare to go overseas for summer mis sion work. They have gone principally to the Philippines to partner with the national church by leading Bible studies and helping train lay leaders. Some of those who have participated are now preparing for the mission field. Members of the missions team help lead the chapter's World Christian action group which provides prayer support and missions information and works with international students on campus.

About one hundred Asian-Americans were a part of the Illini InterVarsity chapter. Pastor Masaya Hibino, who has served the Church of Christ, Presbyterian, in Chicago for twenty-four years, encouraged high-school graduates to consider attending the University of Illinois and to become active in the InterVarsity chapter. His encouragement and the training these students have received prepare them for roles in chapter leadership and a natural outreach into the Asian-American community on campus. Four Japanese-American chapter presidents have come from this church. It has been a reciprocal ministry. In 1990 four men and one woman out of the ten members of the session of the Chicago church had been active in InterVarsity as students. Pastor Hibino says, "We are the ones who most benefit from our students' involvement in InterVarsity. We send our students to IV; they are trained and return to the church to serve. Some key leaders were converted during college and came back to our church to become active members."[1]

Todd Okamoto is one of these. He says he was not a Christian when he came to the University of Illinois in 1979, but in his sophomore year he found himself playing racquetball and basketball with a group of Christians and feeling welcomed into their group. He didn't know it then, but he was the subject of prayer at the DPM on campus. One day, when the time was right, a student from the Navigators group who lived on his floor helped him to personally trust Christ. He immediately got into a Bible study. "The InterVarsity students nurtured me and gave me a good example for living the Christian life," Todd says. He took advantage of the chapter opportunities for fellowship and growing as a Christian. Ten years later he works in Chicago as a program analyst and is active in the Church of Christ, Presbyterian, in the Japanese-American community. He serves on the church missions committee and is teaching English to international students in the Chicago area, doing his own friendship evangelism.

John Roeckeman credits the consistent concern for evangelism as key to building the chapter at the University of Illinois. It begins with the daily prayer meeting (DPM) and prayer partnerships. Almost every member in the Champaign chapter is involved in the "two plus" program, praying for two friends who are not yet Christians. Friendship evangelism and investigative Bible studies have been the most effective ways for students to bring their friends to faith in Christ.[2]

For the past twenty years students from the University of Illinois have trekked to Cedar Campus in upper Michigan each spring for participation in chapter camp, and many have returned later in the summer for the four week School of Leadership Training (SLT) camp. This training, along with staff training on the campus, has given members of the University of Illinois chapter in-depth discipling.

Mark Malan, area director for downstate Illinois, says of the chapter at the University of Illinois,

> One of the major reasons that the chapter has grown so significantly in the past ten years is the long tenure of David Ivaska, followed by John Roeckeman. There has been a solid, consistent level of training with only two primary staff in the past twenty years. It is not erratic growth, but a solid ten to twenty per cent each year. The consistent quality of staff leaders has been wonderful to work with and helps in maintaining relationships with alumni and Christian faculty. Alumni have been willing to support InterVarsity work because of their close ties to the staff team and commitment to the campus.

Long-term staff have made a significant difference in the Great Lakes West region (Indiana, Illinois, Wisconsin), according to Jim Lundgren, regional director.

> Don and JoAnne Fields have been in Indiana for over twenty years. Mark and Judy Malan have been committed to southern Illinois since graduation in 1969, Mark serving for three years as a volunteer staff member before becoming a paid staff member. Jeanette Yep, Sandy Beelen, John Hochevar, Rick Richardson, Cameron Anderson, Ann Beyerlein and, of course, David Ivaska and John Roeckeman have given long-term leadership in the Great Lakes West region. They have given the region the kind of stability that keeps the movement solidly moving forward.

Long-term staff represent only a part of staffing needs, however. Staff directors like Don Fields believe that young recent grads have a special authenticity in relating to students because of their recent campus involvement, and he keeps a sharp eye out for recent graduates who can give two or three years on campus as InterVarsity staff. Fields feels it is a matter of balance. Effective campus work needs a solid cadre of older staff who can give the training and oversight necessary for the development of younger staff.

1/Diverse Strategies

Not all chapters have flourished numerically like the University of Illinois chapter, but across the country InterVarsity chapters have been steadily producing quality student leadership. These students become the graduates who influence their churches, their professions and their communities. Over the years a continual stream of InterVarsity graduates have headed for the mission field overseas, from Robert Foster, a student host at the Toronto missionary convention in 1946 who went to Africa as a surgeon, to Dennis and Sue Brogan, who left InterVarsity staff in early 1990 to go to the Philippines for a church-planting ministry. It is not the size of the chapter that produces the discipleship but the personal commitment of the students in it.

The campus ministries department, under Bob Fryling, has a more diverse strategy for staffing student groups than was used in the early days of InterVarsity. For the first three decades of IVCF's history, staff members stretched themselves to cover every school where a fledgling witness was possible. Each region now develops its own strategy, so that there is no longer a single national philosophy of ministry. Fryling says, "I want staff workers to wrestle with what is most effective for the students they are working with. So we've adapted different philosophies of ministry, based on Scripture, to what is most helpful to the students that staff are working with. There are different philosophies for different types of schools and for different parts of the country."[3] Some regions have chosen not to staff smaller schools where little student initiative and concern exist, consolidating instead to give quality staff care to colleges that have significant potential. Other regional directors assign multiple schools to their staff team, but give guidelines about the ratio of time spent at each school.

This has created much discussion about the nature of student initiative in chapter life. The northern California staff team exerts strong influence in chapter life. Staff members lead and speak at large group meetings; they also take care of some of the details of chapter life. This frees the students, according to Pete Sommer, to do what they do best.[4] The students are taught how to lead small groups, how to witness, how to lead Bible studies, and other facets of personal outreach and growth. Strong commitment is required of a central core of student leadership, and many of them give as many as forty hours a week to the work of the chapter.

In 1978-88, under the leadership of Greg Read, the staff at Stanford gave strong direction to chapter life. Entering freshmen students had to meet a series of requirements in order to become chapter leaders, which left little room for late bloomers or people whose time schedule did not permit them to participate in the requirements. Their DPM, led by a staff member, had about fifty students attending each noon hour. The chapter was large and flourishing, but it was a staff-managed chapter. A team of staff with a variety of gifts, concentrating on one campus, provided what they called "mentor model" leadership. Each staff discipled eight to twelve small group leaders. This approach led to many joining staff, but did not result in hoped-for evangelistic fruit. While staff leadership in California was still more intense than in other areas of the country, by 1990 the Stanford staff team had modified its input and developed more of a "partnership" model.

At Cal—Berkeley, a large, multi-ethnic, residential university, the chapter is built on small groups led by students under the supervision of a multiple staff team. Each staff member supervises a number of small groups, spending three hours a week with key student leaders for leadership training and preparation of the Bible study they will lead that week in their small groups. An exposition of the passage being studied is given at the large group meeting by one of the staff.[5]

While increased regional autonomy has developed creative approaches to campus ministry, it also risks the possibility of theological emphases that may need tempering. During the eighties, for example, a number of northern California staff were greatly influenced by the writing of John Piper, adapting his book *Desiring God: The Meditations of a Christian Hedonist* into a philosophy of ministry. This became the subject of discussion among the staff leaders.

As director of campus ministries, Bob Fryling's response was to appoint a task force to come up with a resolution to this debate, a process which he says has resulted in a greater unity in philosophy of ministry across the country. Fryling's strategy was to "build partnership and form a new coalition of commitment among regional directors based on relational commitment to each other." He says, "The lordship of Christ and the authority of Scripture remain the final arbiter in the ministry of InterVarsity."

Staff leaders like Dan Denk (Great Lakes East region), Cameron Anderson (Wisconsin), Jimmy Long (North Carolina), Doug Whallon (New England), Jeanette Yep (Chicago), Don Fields (Indiana), Steve Stuckey (Southern California) and many others across the country intentionally place leadership on the shoulder of the students. In some areas lighter staffing is necessitated by funding. Each region and area have freedom to create their own staffing policies, depending on their fund raising. (Monies are no longer shared as gifts across regional boundaries according to need, as they were in the seventies, but are held in escrow according to areas.)

The large chapter at the University of North Carolina, for example, has four geographic subchapters with over a hundred members in each chapter. That necessitates multiple student leadership, with a staff member assigned to each chapter. Staff in New York City, where students commute to classes, necessarily play a large role in keeping the "evangelizing fellowships" on track. Staff at the University of Michigan work one-to-one with the leaders, but expect the students to do the leadership decision making.

2/Creative Strategy for New York City

Creativity in planning for the needs of a given area is one of the strengths of InterVarsity. One example of this has been a reach-out program called "Audio to Go," which provides a cassette ministry for the commuter students on the twenty-five campuses in fast-paced Metro New York. Observing the number of students using Walkman-style cassette players, Marc Andre, an IV alumnus, began brainstorming with staffworker Mackenzie Pier to produce quality Christian cassettes as a way to redeem time lost commuting to and from classes. The staff plan to produce cassettes ranging from basic evangelism to discipleship in order to establish a university booktable or prepare a campus for a university mission.

Mackenzie Pier has served on staff in New York City as an area director, supervising two White staff and three Asian-Americans for the past six years. After he had been on staff in South Dakota for three years, he and his wife, Marya, felt God calling them to work with students in New York City. They have since had an intense and satisfying crosscultural experience. Mac Pier has built a strong volunteer team to help the staff working in the five boroughs of New York, where he supervises student work on fifteen state and private campuses. "Eighty per cent of our students are non-White," says Pier, who has also helped mobilize believers in the city for Concerts of Prayer in a way never dreamed of previously. More than four hundred churches participate on a regular basis in prayer for New York City.

Area Director Bill Sweeting, who oversees the student work at nine other City University of New York (CUNY) colleges, says, "Many of our students may not have the option of being a part of a small group or attending a large-group meeting regularly because they work or have other ties at church or in their families. We have to find other ways to be involved in their lives. We take the initiative to have one-to-one time with students, or grab one or two for an informal lunch—or use other ways to have an opportunity to sit down and talk and share a vision." Bill's staff team is even more diverse: White, Black and Hispanic. About ninety students make up the InterVarsity chapter at Columbia University, and about eighty to ninety per cent of these members are Asian, mostly Korean. Chapter members feel an urgency to reach out to Black students on the campus.[6]

3/Regional Differences

Douglas Whallon, regional director for New England, believes that staff have to work harder to develop student leaders now than in the past. "I do think the culture has changed—that students are not as willing to accept leadership on campus. Staff must give strong leadership, but the leadership must be exerted to *produce student leadership*. I have every intention of praying and making student leadership work," Whallon says. Doug believes that the concept of an effective ministry by passive staff is a myth and has no basis in history. InterVarsity staff have always taken initiative to encourage student leadership.

Doug believes evangelism is crucial; it is a litmus test of InterVarsity's viability for ministry on campus. He is convinced that students can only be discipled in the context of ministry, following Christ's example. When a student takes the risk of beginning an evangelistic Bible study, for example, the staff member has opportunity to disciple on many levels in a way not possible if the student is passive. Doug wants staff to help students get moving, to keep a balanced view of the Christian life, and to experience joyful obedience.

Schools in New England are staffed in a way that encourages the use of graduate and faculty supporters. Whallon finds volunteers work very efficiently in non-urban settings, in contrast to an urban center in which the pace of life and financial pressures seem to mitigate against volunteerism. Faculty witness suffered a setback in 1990 in his region when three active Christian professors were not given tenure. As a result all three have left the teaching field.[7]

Other regions have experienced similar problems with faculty witness. Although it cannot be proved, some evidence suggests that in some departments on some campuses, untenured faculty members who are too open about their Christian commitment may have difficulty securing professional academic status. Charles Hummel, InterVarsity's faculty specialist for the past fifteen years, has tried to encourage Christian faculty to form support groups, meeting together for prayer and Bible study. He concludes that many Christian faculty are finding off-campus resources for their Christian life and do not see the importance of a support group on the campus that will help them function as Christian academics in a hostile society. At the same time untenured faculty often put in sixty- to ninety-hour work weeks, which leave little time to meet personal or group needs. Wherever faculty see their profession as a sacred calling, they have unique opportunities for a Christian influence that permeates the entire university, Hummel concludes.

John Bower, a California staff member since 1975, agrees with observations others have made about the changes in students' family backgrounds and abilities:

I see these people in our chapter who come from broken homes with real problems, but God's Spirit has touched them, and they have bought into the truth. They are being transformed, and are living changed lives. I've watched students pass on the vision for witness and responsibility year after year at University of California—Santa Barbara—one student to another.

Along about the seventies, the students' thinking and comprehension skills plummeted, but we got them into Bible & Life and New Testament manuscript studies and taught them how to think, how to observe. I've had students go to one of our Bible & Life Level II weekends and come back and get an A on an English paper. A student told me she had never had an A on an English paper, and the professor asked her how she did it. She said she typed up the Milton poem and studied it the way she had learned to study the Bible in InterVarsity. The Mark manuscript studies help students the same way; they learn to make observations and connections. It helps them think. I believe InterVarsity offers students a way out of the cultural trap.

The small group leaders' track in our camping program teaches students how to relate, how to express feelings, how to communicate. The students come with more problems today, but the goal of the gospel is "lose yourself in order to find yourself." And I believe we are helping students do this.

Bower staffs the two hundred twenty member InterVarsity chapter at University of California—Santa Barbara, a chapter with an unbroken history of campus witness since 1947. As a student on this same campus in 1968-72, Bower's own life was affected by his time in InterVarsity. A long list of outstanding InterVarsity staff have come from the leadership of this chapter.[8]

Regional differences temper evaluations of the student population.

Norm Swett, regional director for the North Central region, wrote in his 1989 report,

> I have been encouraged by the stronger students that God seems to be bringing to campus. They are committed students and have an understanding of the lordship of Christ. I have discovered anew that when God grabs hold of someone in the eighteen to twenty-two age range, all kinds of special things can happen. It has been tremendous to have a front-row seat in this kind of process. It has been both a concern and a pleasure to see the high level of ownership these students have as they gently demand that InterVarsity provide the staff they need to carry out the work on campus. That poses somewhat of a problem for me. Our staff recruitment process is really hurting because we have not had a management structure in place in this region long term.[9]

Some regions of the country have suffered from neglect. In 1989 Terry Erickson was made regional director for the Central Region (Iowa, Kansas, Nebraska and Missouri, Arkansas—all states that have had vital InterVarsity chapters in the past) after about six years without a full-time person in that role. In the early eighties during the big push for growth, Iowa had eleven staff working in colleges, but they did not have a long-term ministry. Erickson arrived to find one staff member (Tony Hershey) working the whole state, tending twelve groups. Len Andyshak and Ron Semmelbeck, area directors in Kansas and Missouri respectively, each had four staff working with them in a total of eleven chapters. Arkansas had no InterVarsity staff. The lack of leadership had left the region somewhat demoralized.

Since taking over leadership in the region, Erickson has found people eager to help. In Des Moines, Iowa, ten people began giving $200 a month to start a fund for a staff member for that area. People called Erickson on the phone, volunteering to help on staff. Through encouragement and prayer, within the first year of his arrival, Terry saw things began to happen. "Most of what has been happening in Iowa," Erickson says, "is the result of student initiative." The chapter at Drake University came alive in 1988-89 with sixty members and sent twenty students to the spring conference in the spring of 1990. By the year's end Erickson saw a fifty per cent increase in attendance at chapter camp.[10]

In April 1983 Jim Worden, regional director for the Southwest, on his way home from an InterVarsity gathering in Texas, was killed in a head-on collision with a drunk driver.[11] Along with the serious loss of Worden as part of the InterVarsity family, his death caused a leadership vacuum in the region for the next seven years. No long-term replacement could be found.

Roger Anderson, associate director of campus ministries, took on the Southwest regional directorship. Staffing an area like Texas where distances between schools are significant requires a certain kind of pioneer staff. The South is different from the North; rural states offer a different challenge than a high-population center. How the work is done may differ, but the goal of helping students come to grips with the lordship of Christ, the authority of Scripture in personal life, and the responsibility of witness remain the same everywhere.

4/Working Toward Multi-Ethnic Ministry

Alex Anderson is part of a Black staff team working in Georgia and Alabama, staffing about fifteen campuses. Anderson says that InterVarsity is not perceived as a White student movement on his campuses. "In fact," he smiles, "our students are often shocked when they come to a statewide regional conference and see White students there." One day a student at West Georgia College walked past an all-White sorority house and wondered how she, as a Black woman student, could ever reach out to share the gospel in that house. She brought her concern to her InterVarsity chapter. As a result of discussions which followed, students from the Black chapter at West Georgia and the White chapter at the University of Tennessee paired up as teams to witness on the West Georgia campus. The response was so positive that the University of Tennessee chapter invited the West Georgia students to do a reciprocal witness project on their campus. Modeling reconciliation, they talked with others about being reconciled to God through Christ.[12]

Discussing how to staff colleges in the Southeast Paul Tokunaga, regional director, points out the need for steady input and perseverance. He says that Anderson's ministry in south Georgia didn't "break loose" until his tenth year on staff. Tokunaga also feels that the Southern culture is more difficult for non-Southerners to penetrate, and sees an urgent need to recruit more staff from the Southeast. In 1988 only about a quarter of their staff team came from the Southeast. He and the staff team are making a concerted effort to mobilize alumni to help with the work on campus.

In 1981 two staff members—Bobby Gross and Janice Thom—went to southern Florida to begin work at three colleges in the Miami area. Whatever witness had existed at the University of Miami had died out, and this school became a prime target in this pioneering effort. Janice represented diversity; she was from Guyana, a Black woman fluent in Spanish. Together they developed the beginnings of a multi-ethnic chapter. White students were clearly a minority, with a large part of the chapter composed of international students. When Janice left staff, she was replaced by Joy Goss in 1985. "Joy has a gift of strategy," said Area Director Bobby Gross.[13] Very deliberately she began to work on new student outreach. The chapter soon numbered over a hundred students from diverse racial backgrounds: a third are Black, a third are White, a third are International students. The chapter life of the University of Miami has become a model for other campuses.

Multi-ethnic student ministry became a central thrust of InterVarsity in the late eighties. With appointment of Sam Barkat as vice president and director of multi-ethnic ministries, InterVarsity made a strong statement about its importance. The resurgence of racism on the campus also made staff newly aware of InterVarsity's role in offering hope, change and reconciliation. Barkat hopes to develop within InterVarsity an attitude of partnership, not patronage, as it encourages church and community leaders to work with them on the campus to produce the kind of Christian leadership the community needs. He is convinced that everybody in InterVarsity needs to think about multi-ethnic ministry. InterVarsity managers took a whole day during the 1989 management meetings to learn more about racial sensitivity and ways to minister to the campus in all its diversity. A national statistic indicates that approximately eighteen per cent of all students on campuses across the country are from minority groups. Twenty-four per cent of InterVarsity students are non-White or non-American, if international students are included.[14]

Multi-ethnic ministry affects the way InterVarsity works on campus. For example, it has already affected InterVarsity's styles of worship. Jim Lundgren, regional director for the Great Lakes Region, says, "It is one thing to bring students of diverse ethnicity together in our chapters. It is quite another to find ways to worship together that honor their various ethnic and church styles of worship."[15] Lundgren, along with other staff leaders, would like to expand the worship experience of all InterVarsity students so that their spiritual lives will be deepened by thoughtful singing of great truths and strong biblical exposition.

5/Funding the Work

Financing the movement was uneven in the eighties. Some areas were wealthier than others, allowing the potential for easier fund raising. Other area teams struggled year after year to make their budget, with staff accepting partial salaries to do campus work. Some projects captured the imagination of business executives and generated large amounts of money; in contrast, a young staff member—who became a Christian on campus without a Christian family or church heritage—had trouble raising funds to do work on a campus, especially if his or her assigned chapter did not look like a model of success.

InterVarsity's policy requiring staff to raise one hundred per cent of their support meant that funding for the general fund has suffered. An overhead percentage added to the support package of each staff member funds the general work, as well as the ethnic work. The burden for funding campus work is placed on staffworkers, and ultimately on the area and regional directors who manage the budget. As many as fifty-five per cent of staff in the middle of the decade were working below salary level. In 1989 this percentage was lowered to thirteen per cent. Throughout the years, regional reports show the funding of the movement as the biggest problem the field staff faced.

The areas with the least funding problems have worked hard to maintain ties with their alumni. Over the years and across the country, contact with the alumni of InterVarsity has been uneven, largely because of overextended field staff and the turnover of personnel. Steve Hayner, InterVarsity's president, plans to make alumni work one of the goals of the 1990s.

6/Recruiting for Missions

When John Kyle[16] became the director of the missions department in 1979 he found three people in the department: Ken Shingledecker (working with Student Training in Missions), David Bryant and his assistant. Every other missions director before him had been essentially a campus staffworker specializing in missions, speaking and influencing students across the country, in addition to directing the Urbana missionary conventions. John Kyle wanted to build a missions department; he was a visionary, an expansionist. He had numerous specific projects he wanted to see implemented. One of those involved a missionary placement service. Kyle had been a missions recruiter and knew how hard it was for mission agencies to get connections with students on the campus. He began to work closely with them, trying not to get ahead of their needs and their ability to place people.

At Urbana 84 Kyle planned to hit the issue of unreached peoples; at Urbana 87 he would focus on urban missions. At Urbana 84 he pushed the idea of short-term missions and asked all the agencies to list their short-term openings. Reports indicate that as many as 21,200 people from a variety of backgrounds, including IVCF students, did a short stint on the mission field during 1985.[17]

Kyle was interested in people getting to the field, not just signing a card indicating the intent to be a missionary. The Urbana conventions during the eighties aimed at recruitment, not the discussion of missionary issues that had marked the Urbanas under Eric Fife's leadership. Kyle wanted to motivate people to respond, and thus the conventions perceptibly shifted away from the controversial and theological.

Kyle had large-sized dreams. When Jim McLeish was planning a major fund-raising project in 1980, John Kyle outlined his goals for the missions department in InterVarsity as his part of the fund-raising project. A major objective was to challenge and assist five thousand students to serve as full-time overseas missionaries by the end of 1984. To accomplish this he planned to have a staff of three hundred working with the Student Missions Fellowship, including two hundred seventy-two furloughing missionaries serving part-time. By the end of 1984 he projected a separate Urbana Missions Convention department which would sponsor Urbanas on a two-year cycle, increasing the size of the conventions to 32,000 delegates by 1985. He spelled out plans for three missionary training camps on three sites with six hundred students enrolled annually.

The Student Missions Fellowship was to be the central core of the IVCF missions emphasis, and would include all Christian colleges and three hundred secular campuses, with a staff of three hundred who would conduct four leadership training camps each year. The STIM program would be expanded to send six hundred students overseas on summer assignments, and another two hundred graduate students for one-year assignments. He projected five Overseas Training Camps with five hundred students involved. He wanted a Chinese department to reach Chinese students in the United States, and planned for two hundred twenty-five groups with a national staff of six. Also on the drawing board was an overseas counseling service, a non-professional overseas work program, an international missions institute with fifteen hundred enrolled for college credit, and hopes to increase the international student outreach with forty staff members.[18] Although he missed his deadlines, and the fund raising was not successful, Kyle adjusted his goals and continued on.

John Kyle was not only a good recruiter, but a successful fund raiser, capturing the imagination of others with his dreams. However, Kyle did not always have the support of InterVarsity staff. His dreams were largely announced to the staff, rather than coming from dialog with them. A number of his plans were stymied because he did not have an enthusiastic group of staff involved in recruitment.

Kyle took seriously his responsibility to the Student Foreign Missions Fellowship (SFMF) and used his influence to strengthen its ministry by providing key staff and conferences for its advancement. SFMF groups experienced phenomenal growth on some campuses, with as many as six hundred students coming to meetings in some of the larger Christian colleges. Teams of young graduates traveled from campus to campus to stir up interest in missions. Student teams went to nearby campuses to present the call of God to world missions. SFMF chapters held "Concerts of Prayer," as a new movement of prayer took place on campus. Numerous regional missions conferences and workshops were announced in the new *Campus Missions News,* a six-page quarterly bulletin going to members of SFMF chapters.

Both Jim McLeish and John Kyle saw the Urbana missionary convention as bigger than InterVarsity. McLeish talked about the possibility of spinning off the convention as an entity apart from InterVarsity. Kyle said, "Urbana alone has become a five-million-dollar operation. It serves the church and the world, not just InterVarsity." Both men considered it InterVarsity's best public relations effort. At the same time some of the staff were asking if bigger was necessarily better. They expressed concern "that the Urbana Convention ought not to be an event, but rather more of a training experience which has its roots inside of InterVarsity as a movement."[19]

Kyle was under pressure from outside the movement to make the conventions more appealing to the "average young person," to bring in more musical groups which would resonate with the youth culture. He resisted that. He had been in attendance at the missions conferences in Europe and had observed that large blocks of time had been assigned to musicians. That was not his plan for Urbana. He said, "In essence Urbana is a lordship conference and touches all areas of life. We want Christ to be Lord in the area of mission involvement in a student's life."[20]

7/Urbana and the 1980s

The striking publicity poster for Urbana 81, reproduced on the front cover of the Urbana 81 compendium, was an artful illustration of the convention theme: "Let Every Tongue Confess That Jesus Christ Is Lord." More than any other publicity piece, students displayed this graphic illustration of the world mission of the church on the walls and doors of their dorm rooms.

Ed Beach, a student at Urbana 70 and now a Wycliffe Bible translator in

Guatemala, grabbed student attention with a plenary address that made the Urbana 81 experience relevant to student delegates. In ten years' time any student in the audience could be standing where he was. His winsome conclusion made that a desirable choice: "It dawned on me that there was nothing else in all the world that I would rather be doing than sitting right there in that tiny, thatch-roofed hut, talking about Jesus to a friend with an aching soul and helping him to understand the Word of Life in the language of his heart."

Fourteen thousand attended Urbana 81. Eric Alexander, from St. George's Tron Parish Church in Glasgow, Scotland, gave stirring Bible expositions from the book of Acts. Gordon MacDonald spoke on "The Sending Church," and Isabelo Magalit responded as a member of "The Receiving Church." Magalit said, "My brothers and sisters in Christ, please don't make us into little brown Americans. We want to be, we need to be, genuinely Filipino Christians for the sake of the gospel." Marilyn Laszlo, Bible translator in Papua New Guinea, won the students' hearts with her description of pioneering the gospel with her coworker among the Sepik Iwam people who had never seen White women before. Billy Graham gave a call for commitment; George McKinney spoke about the needs of the city, Rebecca Manley Pippert witnessed about being a witness for Christ, and Eva den Hartog gave a glimpse of the suffering world. At the end of the convention, a public transfer of the presidency of InterVarsity was made from John W. Alexander, who had chaired the convention, to James McLeish.

At Urbana 84 the daily newspaper published by the convention media team heralded the first time the convention had exceeded eighteen thousand delegates. The convention theme was "Faithful in Christ Jesus," and Eric Alexander returned to give the morning Bible expositions on the book of Ephesians. Giving the same first-class expository preaching that had marked earlier conventions, Eric Alexander emphasized the importance of prayer. "We're not to wait until we get a tingle in our spine. It's a matter of moral obedience and duty. It is not a glandular condition where one does not pray until he feels like it." Morning by morning he allowed the Scripture to hammer home the message of what it meant to be "in Christ." In the months ahead, his teaching profoundly changed the prayer life of many chapters.

Forty French-speaking delegates came from Quebec, Haiti, Madagascar, Mali and Zaire. Claude and Anne-Marie Decrevel did simultaneous translation. TWENTYONEHUNDRED showed *Complete the Task* about unreached peoples and *To Every People,* which offered in-depth information about tribal, Chinese, Hindu and Muslim peoples. Delegates also had an opportunity to view a newly completed campus evangelistic tool called *M.A.R.K.* and give evaluations as to its effectiveness. Nearly five thousand indicated on the World Evangelization Card their willingness to become overseas missionaries. Students also gave $360,000 in offerings—$240,000 to student work around the world through IFES and $120,000 to hunger relief.[21]

The theme for Urbana 87 was taken from the last line of the book of Jonah where God questions Jonah about Nineveh: "Should I not be concerned for this great city?" While the names of cities were different, the focus of the convention was on the great urban centers of the world. Ajith Fernando, the national director for Youth for Christ in Sri Lanka, followed the pattern of careful and relevant Bible expositions from the book of Jonah. Ray Bakke, Floyd McClung and Harvie Conn hit hard on the need of the cities of this world. "We're going to have to incarnate the gospel; wrap it up and deliver it in person in the streets," Bakke said. Three women—Helen Roseveare, Roberta Hestenes and Rebecca Pippert—gave outstanding plenary addresses to challenge the minds of the delegates.

More than 18,000 delegates filled the Assembly Hall.[22] The workshops and seminars were packed out, missionaries meeting delegates at their booths in the Armory grew hoarse from talking to so many students, and the students sang their hearts out under the leadership of Bernie Smith, songleader. Mentors in dozens of mission-related specialities fielded questions from students. TWENTYONEHUNDRED productions backed up the plenary speakers with a multimedia look at the cities of the world. David Bryant led the students to pray in small groups, each evening praying for a specific city. Nearly 6,000 delegates made written decisions, indicating that they believed God was calling them to serve overseas.

John Kyle resigned from his post to return to *Mission to the World,* the mission arm of the Presbyterian Church of America, following Urbana 87. When he came to IVCF he found three people in the missions department; he left behind forty employees in the missions department. David Bryant also left InterVarsity to continue "Concerts of Prayer" as an independent ministry.

8/Harrison Plans for the 1990s

Dan Harrison, who succeeded Kyle, inherited not only a large staff, but great funding needs.[23] Harrison set about to consolidate some of the programs and personnel, and began to expand in other directions. He was challenged to pull a burgeoning missions department back into the center of InterVarsity's student work. He took some bold steps. He formed a new department called InterVarsity Global Partnerships, combining IFES-Link (formerly called InterVarsity Link, which serves as the structure for placing staff and students with IFES-related movements around the world) with two crosscultural training programs: Global Preparation, formerly called Student Training in Missions (STIM), and Global Projects, formerly called Overseas Training Camp (OTC).

Harrison also changed the name of the Student Foreign Missions Fellowship (SFMF) to InterVarsity Missions Fellowship (IVMF) and appointed Glandion Carney as director. Harrison said, "SFMF has been motivating and equipping Christian college and seminary students to take part in world evangelization for fifty-five years. We want to help these students in missions chapters to realize they are part of something that is national, as well as international in scope. The basic structure of the organization, with its emphasis on student leadership and initiative, will not change." The six-page news bulletin called *Campus Mission News* became *InterVarsity Missions Update*, a vehicle of information for the new IVMF.

Much of Harrison's creative energy in his first years went into planning for Urbana 90, which took place December 27-31, 1990. Harrison says, "The convention theme, "Jesus Christ: Lord of the Universe, Hope of the World," was chosen to deliver a message of hope to this generation." Working with the InterVarsity Missions staff and the Urbana advisory council, Harrison planned, as one of his primary goals, for "the plenary platform to reflect the multi-ethnic realities of the church, the role of both genders in mission, and the increasing role of the two-thirds world in the global mission of the church."

Harrison said, "We wanted to avoid the suggestion that Urbana is an issues conference, because it is not. The issue of Urbana is the issue of world missions. God is a global God and we want students to have a global vision." A Global Issues Conference, planned for approximately four hundred preselected students, took place within Urbana 90 during the afternoons and focused on ten complex contemporary world concerns.

Students studied the book of Colossians in their Quiet Time and in small groups each morning. As an Urbana first, Harrison chose four people from different ethnic groups to do the morning Bible expositions from Colossians: Luis Bush from Argentina, Ajith Fernando from Sri Lanka, Philemon Choi from Taiwan, and Isaac Canales, an Hispanic pastor from California.

An eleven-person band (with multi-ethnic musicians) called "Full Armour" provided music and lead the singing, with the words projected on the screen. Approximately fifty songs were chosen, among them thirteen hymns, with the "words only" placed in the student handbook. The Full Armour worship band, with leader John Wood, and Randy Stonehill, a contemporary musician from California, gave a late evening concert. Singer Steve Green sang at the closing service on New Year's Eve.

Plenary speakers were encouraged to use a narrative style in speaking to the delegates. Mary Fisher, the keynote speaker, spoke on "Jesus Christ: Hope of the World," introducing the strong theme of hope that marked the convention. Keren Everett spoke about the joy and cost of living out the gospel in another culture. Dan Harrison addressed the brokenness in students' lives by telling his own story. About 1500 students responded to a special prayer time to deal with the dysfunctionality in their personal backgrounds. George Otis and Anita Dyneka both spoke about getting the gospel to "creative access" countries.

Paul Tokunaga's talk on hope for the student world rang bells in the lives of the students present at the convention. Videos of his talk were taken back to the campus to inspire classmates to learn to love their college or university for Jesus' sake. A moving expression of racial reconciliation took place on Sunday morning when South African Caesar Molebatsi spoke. Ada Lum, Peter Kuzmic (Yugoslavia), and Glandion Carney also addressed plenary sessions.

For visually-oriented delegates, TWENTYONEHUNDRED productions put together nine videos, giving facts about missions, challenging students to obedience and service. These accounted for about an hour and a half of plenary time. As a first, the convention plenary speakers met for a prayer and sharing retreat late in 1989 at Harrison's request. That same spirit of prayer was part of the convention, as Mary Anne Voelkel, of the Latin America Mission, led the plenary prayer sessions and worked with a team of intercessors who prayed around the clock.

Over five hundred thousand dollars was raised for Urbana to keep down registration costs for delegates. One hundred seventy- five thousand dollars provided Urbana scholarships, some of which helped delegates from other IFES movements attend the convention.

9/Nurses Christian Fellowship in the 1980s
A report of the Commission on Nursing in the Department of Health and Human Services stated in December 1988: "The need for knowledgeable,

sophisticated, caring nurses is greater now than at any time in the profession's history. Yet a critical nurse shortage currently exists and is expected to grow worse in the future. . . . As American values change, the values influencing nursing are also changing." Speakers at a nursing conference in March 1990 identified the need for moral and spiritual values if nursing is to move forward. The theme of caring is emerging in professional literature. Secular professional leaders in nursing are identifying a need that NCF has been speaking to for over fifty years.

Responding to needs in the nursing profession, Mary Thompson, who became director of NCF in 1984, wants to make the concept of "recapturing nursing for Jesus Christ" more and more a reality.[24] She made arrangements for NCF to sponsor a worship service on Sunday morning during the American Nurses Association convention in Boston in June 1990. She planned a church bulletin insert to help mobilize Christians to pray for nurses on National Nurses Day, May 7, 1990. NCF coordinated a North American Nurses Conference sponsored by nine Christian nursing networks on the theme "Jesus Christ: The Hope for Nursing" scheduled for June 15-19, 1991, in Minneapolis/St. Paul. "Workshops, conferences, written and video resources are aimed at bringing God's agenda to people in nursing in the decade of the 1990s," Thompson said. "We want to influence the thought life of nursing."

The first issue of the *Journal of Christian Nursing (JCN)* came out in the spring of 1984. Grace Wallace recruited Ramona Cass to edit *JCN* and it has become a key tool for NCF to influence the nursing profession. The magazine has since won awards of excellence from the Evangelical Press Association. Cass had prepared as an English teacher, a nurse, an ordained minister and a hospital chaplain. She is largely responsible for the Journal's fine reputation and reception in the nursing profession. *JCN* has proven an effective vehicle in which to address the problems facing nurses today. Subscriptions were twelve thousand in 1990, and a program of sustaining subscribers has begun. When Cass resigned in August 1990, Judy Shelly was appointed senior editor.

Judy Shelly's books, *Spiritual Care: The Nurse's Role* (cowritten with Sharon Fish), *Not Just a Job, Spiritual Dimensions of Mental Health* and others, offer resources for those concerned about contemporary trends. In July 1985 two task forces began to put together NCF resources on spiritual care and ethics. One of the results was a book describing basic concepts foundational to nursing, *Concepts in Nursing—A Christian Perspective*. Judy Shelly and Arlene Miller collaborated on a book about Christian values in nursing, released in 1991 as *Values in Conflict.* Videos workshops on "Spiritual Distress" and "Ethics" have given Christian nursing students, as well as professional nurses, valuable resources. The materials and workshops coming out of NCF serve as instructional antidotes to contemporary feelings of hopelessness within nursing. Mary Thompson reflects that "God has given us a unique Christian education role in nursing, teaching his agenda in the midst of secular and New Age influences."

Although NCF work has been more difficult than in previous decades, students who catch a vision for their profession can make a strong statement about purpose in this secularized field. When some nurses encouraged NCF students at the University of Minnesota to "get out of nursing while you can," the students made plans to sponsor a series of forums where Christian nurses spoke of Christ's resources and the meaning of nursing as a Christian ministry. NCF nurses in places like Topeka, Kansas, and Lorain, Ohio, have been involved in staffing health-care clinics for the poor. "When nurses pray and have a sense of hope that God is involved in what they do, their actions speak volumes to the disillusionment and loss of morale within the nursing program," Thompson said.

NCF no longer itinerates its staff over huge areas, but is building teams of staff and volunteers in strategic centers to enable more intensive discipling. Professional nurses are encouraged to volunteer as staff in areas where NCF groups have no staff help.

10/Under New Leadership

By the late eighties the InterVarsity movement had been stabilized by the unassuming and nonthreatened leadership of Steve Hayner. His open, fair way of interfacing with his staff built confidence in his leadership. "No longer are the real decisions made during the coffee break," Barney Ford said. "There is more unity on the focus of the ministry than ever before."[25] Bob Fryling adds, "We have made a commitment to each other that we would not allow anything to create a separation or division. Following a difficult time within the leadership of InterVarsity and prior to Hayner's arrival, those of us in national leadership, along with the staff teams, had times of prayer and confession. There is a spirit of reconciliation among us. I see a movement of people with integrity and a real dedication to serve the Lord among students."

Hayner is a pastor/administrator/student worker turned president, whose decisions are based on understanding the needs of the student work. He wants InterVarsity to be a student movement; at the same time he wants strong and committed staff members. InterVarsity has become a complex organization with many departments and programs that have the potential to diffuse InterVarsity's focus. Hayner is steering a ship on a steady course, with many different cargoes in the hold.

The field work was restructured at the top with the 1990 appointment of five associate directors of campus ministries (ADCM)—Doug Whallon, Jimmy Long, Jim Lundgren, Pete Sommer and Roger Anderson. Each ADCM will supervise one other regional director, while keeping his own regional post. This provides a leadership team to supervise the work under director Bob Fryling. The appointment is reminiscent of the five regional directors who supervised the work on the campus during the previous decades. In contrast to those earlier years when a single layer, the regional director, was between the president and the staff, four layers of management now lie between the president and the campus staffworker. Those at the top of the organizational charts are increasingly removed from natural student contact. However, the staff numbers have grown from fifty-six field staff at the end of the fifties to over five hundred at the end of the eighties, demanding such a reorganization. (See Timeline beginning page 385.)

11/Diversity in Programs

The historical news briefs of the eighties give a picture of the creativity and intensity of the growth within InterVarsity. The brief descriptions that follow give only a glimpse of the direction InterVarsity is taking with its areas of specialization, outreach and special events.

National Leadership Institutes (NLI). In 1981 John Alexander directed an NLI at Cedar Campus; another was held at Bear Trap Ranch in 1982, with Ned Hale as program director. After a seven-year hiatus, another NLI was held in 1989 at Bear Trap Ranch with Bob Fryling as program director. The NLI enables InterVarsity to give in-depth training to its key student leaders from across the country and to pass on InterVarsity's values in a more direct way. Fryling says students who attended went away with a new vision for "engaging the campus." This group of students become prime candidates for InterVarsity staff with a vision for reaching students clearly in place.

Nurses Christian Fellowship (NCF). NCF/USA hosted the NCF International Conference at Eastern College near Philadelphia in July 1988. Four hundred forty people from fifty countries gathered to learn about being God's people in the profession of nursing.

InterVarsity Missions Fellowship (IVMF). Campus Missions '90 provided three U.S. leadership training workshops designed to equip students and faculty responsible for the missions emphasis on their campus or in their chapter. About a hundred students attended from seventeen colleges, according to Frank Gorsline, field staff director for IVMF. Dan Harrison also began to develop a team of regional missions counselors, seconding the service of experienced missionaries, to contact and offer help to students who plan on full-time missions careers.

Overseas Training Camp (OTC). In 1989 a team of students from the InterVarsity chapter at the University of North Carolina—Chapel Hill went to Kiev State University in the Soviet Union under the leadership of staff member Rich Henderson in a cultural exchange program. A similar group of students went to Kiev Pedagogical Institute with IVMF Associate Director David Jones as leader. Both programs succeeded beyond expectations, with a warmth and openness to friendship on the part of both Americans and Soviets. One Soviet participant commented at the close of the summer: "It was terrible when we bid farewell to them. I never cry, but yesterday was miserable for me because our Americans left. And I'm awfully sorry that they left. They changed something in my soul."

These two USSR programs were repeated in 1990, along with two others: David Jones pioneered a program at the University of Rostov in the Soviet state of Russia, and a reciprocal exchange between the Pedagogical Institute and Warner Pacific College in Portland, Oregon, involved about fifteen students and staff spending a month in Kiev and a month in Portland.

Other OTCs in the 1980s were held in Hong Kong, Africa, Europe, China, the Philippines, the Middle East, Malta, Latin America, Kenya, India, Brazil, Poland, China. Eleven OTCs took place in 1990, involving two hundred forty-nine staff and students. The designation OTC has been changed to Global Projects beginning in 1991.

Student Training in Missions (STIM). STIM died temporarily in 1984 because of excessive national overhead costs and the difficulty of placing large numbers of students with missionary agencies. It was revived by staff teams who took on the leadership of the training and the recruiting. In some places student teams went from a single school, an area or a region, working closely with mission agencies. Staff who lead STIM go through a national training program to assure consistent and high-quality training. In the 1990s STIM will become the training vehicle for all students in IV Missions Global Projects and will be called Global Preparation.

Faculty specialist Charles Hummel retired in June 1990 after thirty years of service in InterVarsity. Hummel, one of the early pioneers of the movement, had focused on faculty ministry for the last fifteen years of his time on the staff of InterVarsity. Terry Morrison succeeds him as faculty specialist and will continue to work with faculty groups to encourage an effective witness on the campus.

Bible & Life Training (B&L) founder Barbara Boyd retired in June 1990, following a joint retirement celebration with faculty specialist Charles Hummel at management meetings in Madison. Barbara joined the staff of InterVarsity in 1950 as a campus staff member in California. For the last twenty-five years she has focused on Bible & Life Training, developing curriculum and conducting teacher training courses.[26] Bob Grahmann returned from working with IFES in Austria to become the director of Bible & Life in June 1990.[27] Over fifty thousand students have participated in one or more of the three levels of training offered in the program by 1990.

National Institute for Staff Education and Training (NISET). This program, developed to provide specific training and educational resources for the professional development of IVCF personnel, was launched in 1984 with twenty-one courses offerings. The three-week program included the Orientation of New Staff held the first two weeks. Week two had numerous courses running concurrently, and week three had two-and-a-half-day sessions, allowing a person to choose two different programs during the last week. With minor changes, this program has been held every year since. Numerous courses are designed to equip the staff for campus ministry. Of vital importance has been the campus strategy track, where new student outreach has become a major and successful strategy. Judy Johnson is the director of training and education.[28] In 1990 one of the courses was for volunteer graduates, and Johnson senses a new interest in the use of more volunteers.

HIS magazine. In January 1987 *HIS* magazine changed its name to *U* magazine in an effort to reach a larger general student audience. Since about 1980 *HIS* had been losing the strong support of staff members who formerly were the magazine's chief boosters. Subscription numbers began to decline. The effort to make it a collegiate magazine, rather than a magazine that represented InterVarsity, failed. When *HIS* editor Linda Doll was moved to the post of director of InterVarsity Press in 1983, she was succeeded as editor by David Neff (1983-85) and Verne Becker (1985-88), neither of whom had IV staff experience. In June 1988 *U* merged with *World Christian* magazine, and the last vestige of what was once an important ministry in InterVarsity was gone.

Student Leadership Journal (SLJ). At Urbana 87, chapter presidents brainstormed with Bob Fryling and asked for a networking resource that would help them in leadership responsibilities on campus. Out of this grew the idea for a journal for student leaders, conceptually replacing the resource *HIS* had once been to student leaders. The first issue of *Student Leadership Journal* was introduced in the fall of 1988 with Robert Kachur as editor for the first two years. In the fall of 1990 Jeff Yourison became the editor. Approximately ten thousand copies per issue are distributed free of charge to student leaders and staff. Funding has come from foundation money and a major donor. *SLJ* has received positive student response and has become an important tool from the campus ministries department.

The summer 1990 issue of *SLJ* focused on student witness in sororities and fraternities. One student wrote,

> The summer issue on Greek outreach was literally an answer to prayer. When I came to college I got involved with InterVarsity immediately, and in the spring I took over as our chapter's treasurer. I also pledged Kappa Alpha Theta sorority. Recently I had been wondering why I ever joined Theta. But after reading this issue I realized my whole attitude was wrong. The Lord showed me the main purpose to my being in a sorority is to be a witness, not just to make some friends. I now have a new vision for my sorority, and am excited about all that the Lord is going to do. I am going to give the article to all the girls in my group.

Graduate Christian Fellowship. With the 1988 appointment of Randy Bare as graduate student coordinator, InterVarsity made a fresh commitment to help graduate students from the beginning of their studies to integrate their faith into their discipline. Full-time graduate staffworkers have been appointed to help establish graduate groups. The window of opportunity for graduate students over the next ten years comes from the estimate that two hundred fifty thousand faculty positions will be vacated as professors retire. Twenty-five top graduate schools produce seventy-five per cent of the faculty for these positions. InterVarsity will begin by targeting some of these key schools, with a goal of encouraging graduates to consider a teaching career a sacred calling and a way to influence the thought-life of the university. In 1989 six hundred thirty-three InterVarsity graduates were studying at the top thirty-five graduate schools in the country. That number is expected to increase.

Evangelism. The "two plus" program encourages students to pray for at least two of their friends to become Christians. Almost a third of InterVarsity students have committed themselves to this outreach, which is intentional friendship evangelism in action. Many of the larger chapters report fifty to seventy conversions each year. Approximately 1,600 to 2,500 students become Christians each school year through the ministry of Inter-Varsity.

Cliffe Knechtle's aggressive open-air preaching and public debates encourages student evangelism on the campuses he visits. Investigative Bible studies begin as a result of the interest his presentations stir up in individuals. Characteristic of some student response Cliffe receives is the comment of a student at University of California—San Diego: "I enjoy creating my own purpose in life. Why should I give up that thrill and allow Christ to dictate my purpose in life?" Cliffe says, "In a time when 'tolerant' people are intolerant of truth, it is a challenge to present the authority of Jesus Christ." After an open-air dialog, a professor told Cliffe, "The students keep pressing you for more evidence for the existence of God and the reliability of Jesus after you have given more evidence than I give in articles for scientific journals. Their demands for exhaustive evidence are unrealistic."

Jim Sire, senior editor for IVP, began traveling to various campuses during the 1980s to speak at campus-wide evangelism and apologetic lectures sponsored by IVCF chapters. The intellectual challenge of his topics, ranging from New Age beliefs to "Why Believe Anything At All?" have given students opportunities to penetrate segments of university life not easily available to them.

In 1988-89 the Great Lakes East Region, under director Dan Denk, tried a pilot program called Student Witness Action Team (SWAT), composed of five recent grads who took a year off to itinerate among chapters within the region to encourage evangelism. The program stirred up evangelism outreach on the twenty-five campuses, resulted in conversions and was effective in maturing those who participated. The program developed into a new category of staff called campus trainee—a recent graduate committed to give one year, with minimal fund raising, who will work alongside a staff member at one school. When a group of trainees travel from campus to campus to do evangelism, they will still be called by the SWAT designation.

FLEP, the Florida Evangelism Project, goes where the students congregate during spring break on the Florida beaches and each year provides evangelism training for a large cadre of students.[29] Some who came to sun on the beaches also came to Christian faith. Other regional programs are held at beaches off the coast of California and Texas. The regions also carry on summer outreach in the inner cities and at resort areas with teams of students.

When the Mackinac Island evangelism project was closed down by the

Great Lakes Region in 1988 after twenty years of continuous operation, five IVCF students from University of Wisconsin at Platteville, including the president of the chapter, decided to come to the island as a group during the summer of 1990. They found employment and established their own witness to the college students who work on the island. "Their dedication was impressive," says David Armour, deputy director of the Mackinac Island State Park Commission and original initiator of the project. "They reached about thirty students on Sunday evenings and about fifteen for a week-night Bible study. I was impressed that these students were following the early InterVarsity model of student initiative."

Intervarsity magazine, begun in 1982, has become a primary tool to share the ministry of InterVarsity and campus concerns with the friends and donors of InterVarsity. Approximately forty-five thousand people receive this quarterly publication.

Spiritual formation became the new in-word to describe InterVarsity's goal for personal obedience and piety in the individual student's life. Students began to pray more in the 1980s, with increased attendance at DPMs. A new surge began after Eric Alexander's exposition at Urbana 84. David Bryant's teaching about "concerts of prayer" took hold, and on many campuses two- to three-hour prayer meetings are held regularly.[30] Bible & Life training and the New Testament Seminars (manuscript study) have been widely used, and students continue to grab hold of the inductive method of studying the Scripture, as well as the authority of the Bible in their personal lives.

TWENTYONEHUNDRED. Under Scott Wilson's leadership the 2100 team has continued to produce media pieces that give visual expression to the basic message of each Urbana.[31] *Habakkuk* was an effective campus evangelism tool in the early eighties, but the team is in transition to focus on video productions, away from films and slides. Since students are using videos as books, the team is producing more issue-oriented videos (such as "Ripped Down the Middle," "Stained Image" and "Quantum Connection") and other evangelism pieces. *M.A.R.K., Making A Response to the King* and basic Christian discipleship pieces are being prepared for use on campus. Nine new productions were completed in 1989, and TWENTYONEHUNDRED had a major input in missionary information at Urbana 90. Videos are now available for personal and church use as quality educational tools.

InterVarsity Press. Linda Doll resigned as director of InterVarsity Press and in March 1990 Ken DeRuiter was named the new director.[32] In 1991 the Press increased its publication program from about fifty-four titles per year to an average of sixty titles. A total of 450 InterVarsity Press titles are in print.

IVP's recent fortunes have reflected those of the entire Christian publishing industry. Its sales dramatically increased in the early eighties, but slowed down as the decade ended. To meet changing market trends, IVP added a line of popular books in the late eighties. At the same time it has continued to produce the style of books that established its reputation— books for people who take their Christianity seriously, written by biblically and culturally literate authors. The Press specializes in publishing books on cultural issues and theology, and in recent years has become an innovative leader in the areas of Bible studies and reference works.

By publishing books intended for college students, IVP continues an important focus of its earliest years. Building on the cadre of IVCF alumni, it has broadened its market to include the general Christian reading public. IVP anticipates steady growth and is experimenting with Christian fiction, humor, children's books and gift books.

The campus division of IVP continues to cooperate with staff in encouraging students to begin building a Christian library as part of their academic training, particularly in the area of biblical reference tools. Students need continual encouragement to use books in evangelism and Christian growth—their own and that of those they are discipling.

InterVarsity Marketplace. Pete Hammond, director of Marketplace ministries, comments that this new movement is InterVarsity's historic world/ life view in a new set of clothes. Marketplace '86 grew out of San Francisco '83, where the "mentor concept" was first used and the need to nurture witness in the work-world became obvious. When eight hundred students and three hundred seventy young alumni turned out for the five-day conference, Pete Hammond knew he had "a tiger by the tail." Delegates spent forty per cent of their time on job sites. All the teaching was done by people in the marketplace. One hundred eighty-three mentors became enthusiastic supporters of the Marketplace concept. The conference was a strong statement about the option of secular vocation under the lordship of Christ.

When it was over Pete Hammond knew he wanted to give himself full-time to "the Christian in the work world." Tom Dunkerton, then IV's president, made the decision in October 1987 to make this ministry a part of InterVarsity's program. Since then the Marketplace team has produced "Marketplace Networks," a quarterly information piece. "Marketplace

Voices" is a daily five-minute interview broadcast on fifty mid-size city stations. A "Marketplace Bible" is in process. By 1990 the Marketplace team had sponsored or designed about eighty events, with approximately twelve thousand in attendance.

Camp programs took a beating in the early 1980s from lack of focus on the role of camping in training. Registrations fell when word went out to staff that they did not need to use existing InterVarsity camps, confusing staff about the value of camping. Camps far from population centers took a financial nose-dive. John Kyle's plan to use Cedar Campus as a major missions training center failed for lack of recruits, and it took time for new programs to gain ground.

The tide turned in the later eighties for both Cedar Campus and Campus by the Sea, when staff teams rediscovered the value of wider training programs and began recruiting large numbers of students to camp. Family camps built new loyalties, and soon the camps were again full. Laura "Cookie" Walden became director of Bear Trap Ranch and Mike Vaal the director of Cedar Campus in the last half of the eighties. Paul Friesen, who has led the ministry of Campus by the Sea since 1976, resigned as CBS director in 1990, but remains as the national camp coordinator.

Multitrack training has become an important part of camping programs and weekend conferences. Chapter camps, which used to involve only the executive members, now have multitrack training, and chapter members are urged to come as a group to camp. This gives a wide range of training to chapter members: exec sessions, small group leaders, evangelism, New Testament Seminar, discipling, understanding the gospel, confronting the culture—and other tracks that the staff feel are helpful to students.

Chapter camps generally take place immediately before summer (or just before college classes begin in the fall) and have become sizeable training events. In addition to fall or spring weekend conferences, some areas hold weekend statewide conferences at a hotel during the school year, captioned as "Genesis" or "Breakaway" or other appealing titles, with five to seven hundred students in attendance. These are also multitrack events.

Legal counsel. Yvonne Vinkemulder returned from law school in 1983 as general counsel for InterVarsity.[33] Her job is multifaceted, but includes sorting out legal issues involving student witness on secular campuses. Issues involving the rights of students continue to emerge in the form of "the right to meet on campus" or freedom of speech rights: Can a chapter be prohibited from evangelizing? Discrimination issues became common in the last half of the eighties: Does IVCF have the right to require student leadership to affirm a statement of faith? Can IVCF refuse leadership to practicing homosexuals and still remain an approved campus organization? Tax laws, nonprofit status, increased liability issues and government regulations—all matters for the general counsel to investigate—reveal the complexity of InterVarsity's operation in the last decade.

International student work flourishes across the country. Director Ned Hale has a team of international specialists spread across the country, implementing ministry to students from overseas. Long-term staffworkers like Fred Wagner in Portland, Oregon, and Joe Lorencz in Detroit, Michigan, coordinate hospitality within the church community, organize Bible studies and coffee houses. International houseparties and summer conferences get help from graduates who are involved in this ministry. The unique opportunity to share the Christian message with students from "closed" countries makes this an important and exciting part of the mission outreach of InterVarsity, Hale said.

The International Fellowship of Evangelical Students (IFES). The growing number of staff who have left the U.S. movement to work with IFES have brought the fellowship of other member movements nearer to IVCF students. Each student generation needs encouragement from staff leaders to give financial support to IFES and to share in the pioneering of indigenous evangelical student work around the world. In 1991 the World Assembly of IFES convened at Wheaton College in Illinois. The American movement welcomed delegates from approximately one hundred different IFES movements. Approximately one hundred thirty countries have indigenous student groups in fellowship with the IFES.

This quadrenniel gathering is hosted by various member movements. The last time IVCF-USA hosted the quadrenniel meeting was in 1963, at Nyack College in New York. Ninety delegates came from the twenty-six national movements that formed the IFES. A stirring account of the event was given in the December 1963 issues of *HIS* magazine, keeping students abreast of student work in other countries.

12/A Prototype

Most InterVarsity staff have a prototype for their ministry. Staff members have the end product in mind as they work in their "never-ending kindergarten" for the glory of God. Color may differ; the details will vary. Everybody's story is unique; but give or take a few variants, the elements of the InterVarsity experience are much the same in the life of any student who responds to God. The classic end product will doubtless resemble Doug

Goetz, who comes from the University of Illinois chapter where this section of the history began.

Doug Goetz arrived on campus at the University of Illinois in 1976, never having heard of InterVarsity. A poster on the wall in his dorm grabbed his attention. It announced that "Inter-Varsity Christian Fellowship is proclaiming Jesus Christ: Lord of the Universe, Hope of the World."[34] The poster also listed the activities the InterVarsity chapter was sponsoring during New Student Week. Doug attended some of the activities and kept running into the students he had met, all wearing colorful IVCF T-shirts. He not only felt connected, he got connected and found himself in a small group Bible study in the dorm where he lived. By second semester he was coleading the study.

InterVarsity students got Doug to sign up for Urbana 76, held at the end of his first semester on the Illini campus. The theme was "Declare His Glory Among the Nations." Although he had become a Christian in high school, at Urbana 76 Doug heard for the first time about God's concern for the world. It was also his first exposure to high-quality Bible exposition. Doug said, "It changed my life and my way of thinking about the Bible and even my studies." He attended Level I of Bible & Life training and began to have a regular Quiet Time. In the spring of his freshman year, TWENTYONEHUNDRED brought an evangelistic production to campus at the chapter's invitation. The experience of planning, praying, bringing friends to the show—all of this expanded Doug's world view.

The next summer he worked as a roofer to earn extra money, but was laid off in early July. He remembered staff member Peggy Lowry telling him, "You really ought to think about going to SDT, the four-week School of Discipleship Training camp at Cedar Campus." He counted his money; he had enough to attend. InterVarsity founder Stacey Woods and Michael Baughen, rector of All Souls, London, were the speakers. Doug says, "It was a milestone in my life. I still go back to my notes. And I began to understand InterVarsity on the national scene and got a sense of history about being part of a movement of students. I knew I was into something Big. But it was mostly having time and being exposed to intense Bible teaching, to be able to spend time being serious with God that influenced my life."

In 1976 when Doug entered the University of Illinois, the chapter's DPM had eight to ten people in attendance. By the time he graduated in 1980, forty-five to fifty met daily to pray. The chapter began to grow as the result. Doug is sold on Bible & Life training and feels the most important tool he got from InterVarsity was a love for inductive Bible study. He has since helped staff B&L training weekends as a graduate.

Doug went on to graduate school at the University of Illinois, met and married staff member Lori Lahti, who was active in InterVarsity at Harvard and came on InterVarsity staff at the University of Illinois. Since then Doug has become an engineer with Minnesota Mining Manufacturing Corporation, an active churchman and a father. His wife, Lori, serves as a part-time volunteer, helping with student work at Carleton College in Minnesota.

The shaping of a life for the glory of God is what InterVarsity is about. It has been happening for fifty years.

/13 A Fifty-Year Record

For fifty years InterVarsity staff members have been meeting with students to teach them how to have a Quiet Time, how to study the Bible in a way that changes their character and guides their lives. For fifty years staff members have been handing out books for students to read, helping to stretch their world and life view, urging them to build their personal library. For fifty years staff have insisted on the lordship of Christ in the whole of life—in vocation, in dating, in studies. For fifty years staff have been working with students to build strong Christian fellowship chapters that contribute to the nurture of their classmates and reach out into the campus. For fifty years students have responded to these disciplines.

For fifty years students have been meeting for daily prayer meetings on campus, daring to start evangelistic Bible studies, witnessing to their friends, struggling with their Quiet Times and growing in the climate of Christian fellowship. For fifty years, in one cultural climate or another, Christian students have taken the risk to believe God is absolutely trustworthy. They have stood in the classrooms to speak out for God; they have befriended lonely classmates and shared the gospel. They have stood at Urbana conventions to indicate their willingness to go wherever God wants to send them; they have gone by the hundreds to the mission fields of the world.

Some have gone on to places of great influence in the business world, in medicine, in education. Others have ordinary lives in ordinary communities where they are continuing the lifestyle they began on campus—serving in the church, leading Bible studies, encouraging prayer, trusting God. Many have reproduced themselves over and over by investing in the lives of others. They find ways to build the kingdom wherever they go. Their children have followed in their footsteps, becoming members of InterVarsity chapters and influencing the campus for Christ. Some families are into the third generation of InterVarsity affiliation. The torch has been passed on, and a goodly number of chapters have fifty-year histories of witness.

For fifty years faithful people have cared about the work of InterVarsity. Donors have remained loyal, alumni have kept on praying and supporting the ministry wherever there was a need. These are people of vision who see what can happen on the campus. Without them the work of InterVarsity could not have prospered.

The success of the movement has not been without a battle, without personal wounds or cost and casualties. Spiritual work always has spiritual opposition; the history written in the Bible affirms that principle. The history of InterVarsity is not the story of continuous glorious triumph, with no mistakes or struggles. It is mostly a story of many unsung heroes and heroines (many of them spouses), of people convinced of the call of God, convinced about the way to do the ministry, people who hung on in the hard places and did the job that largely went unnoticed in the chronicles of time. Titles and places of honor are few in this sort of organization, and they are not what count to the staff and students who are doing the kind of work that will stand the test of fire. They have been attracted to serve with InterVarsity largely because of its uncompromising spirituality and the breadth of its vision of what constitutes the Christian life. The first general secretary, Stacey Woods, called InterVarsity "a work of God," and those involved in its current ministry are content to let it be God's work, not theirs.

Fifty years beyond its beginnings, InterVarsity is no longer the guerrilla movement it once was, where a handful of staff inspired hundreds of students to create a student movement. The national climate has changed; the movement has grown; the number of evangelical campus groups have multiplied. The campus, never a simple place to witness, has grown more complex and diverse. The student deans who once gave permission for religious groups to exist on campus and carefully watched their influence, hardly recognize their existence today. But InterVarsity is still there—on the campus, doing essentially the same thing it did fifty years ago, doing a spiritual work to build students into mature believers who can make an impact on the campus, the church and the world.

Afterword

Having completed our writing of the history of its first fifty years, we are optimistic about the future ministry of InterVarsity Christian Fellowship. On every campus we visited we found students meeting together for daily prayer meetings, studying the Bible in small groups, encouraging each other in matters of faith and practice, wrestling with their daily Quiet Times, planning campus outreach, witnessing to their friends. Although the culture has changed since the forties, God's solution to the human problem has not, and neither has the basic thrust of InterVarsity. Staff members are still honing in on the elements that build mature Christians and "evangelizing fellowships." What we have seen happen on the campus is far more exciting and encouraging than we have been able to portray.

The stories have a biblical pattern to them. We've heard them repeatedly in forty years of ministry, but each one has its own ring of reality and wonder. We listened at a 1990 summer training camp to a senior engineering student give public praise to God for changing his life. He said, "When I look back on my life three years ago, I can hardly recognize myself; I have changed more than I can tell you. And it has happened on campus, through studying the Bible in the fellowship of my friends in the InterVarsity group. I have learned something of how great God is, how much he loves me, how much he has forgiven me, and how much I need to trust him each day. And I have some inkling of what he wants to do with my life." The miracle behind his words has been repeated thousands of time in students' lives in these last fifty years and is still going on.

The commitment of students like these challenges the average church member. We regularly met students who give unstintingly of their time to further Christian witness. Jenny is a typical example: she is a junior, a member of her chapter's leadership team. She meets with four different women students each week in a one-to-one relationship, encouraging their Christian faith through Bible study together. In addition she leads her own small group, attends a daily prayer meeting, meets with the leadership team, attends the weekly meeting and is a full-time student. She has a vision for reaching the campus with God's good news and an infectious way of sharing her vision with others.

These students represent the principle of "the remnant" mentioned in the "Seven Pillars" document in chapter four. Dedicated Christian students will likely always be a minority in a hostile environment. They face the opposition of a thoroughly secular culture. The "value-less values" on campus infect those who have only good intentions. Christian commitment must be intentional, not half-hearted. In the 1940s students faced the hostility of the science-faith debate. What about evolution and the reliability of the New Testament documents? Today these questions are almost irrelevant. Contemporary students must come to terms with the lordship of Christ in a relativistic climate where ethnic and gender diversity, multiculturalism and pluralism often blunt their presentation of the gospel, where sexuality is flaunted and secular thought patterns are firmly entrenched. Out of such a hostile environment as this come "jewels, tried in the fire," students who have wrestled with Truth, loving and praying their friends into the kingdom.

Life doesn't end with the university, however. Over the years students from InterVarsity chapters have gone into careers and ministries as broad as those offered in the university. They have become the professors, the nurses, the schoolteachers, the ministers, the lawyers, the business men and women, the research scientists, the church members and the parents whose integrity and lifestyle give evidence of their Christian commitment. Stacey Woods used to tell staff that the effectiveness of IV's student work is measured by the way our students use the rest of their lives.The Christian church increasingly seems to avoid the secular campus, both in the matter of sending students who are prepared to stand for truth and in encouraging graduates to invest in academic careers. In his book *Confessions of a Theologian,* Carl F. H. Henry tells of a meeting with evangelical Christian leaders in Montreux, Switzerland, in 1962 where he listened to plans for future evangelization of the world. He writes, "I saw little emphasis on the war of ideas, little concern for the university world, for doctrinally powerful literature or for the world of work. Stacey Woods and I walked the streets of Montreux late into the night speaking of the neglected campuses and the forfeited world of modern learning."

Thirty years later, evangelical scholarship and witness on the university campus still has not captured the imagination of most Christian leaders. The church must see the campus as significant, not only because the academic community influences the thought-life of America, but because God owns truth. The university campus is a battleground for truth; the need for Christian faculty and students who see the campus as a place where God is at work has never been greater.

Looking Ahead for InterVarsity

Whenever a mature movement looks ahead, it needs to ask questions about its direction. Roy Swanstrom, in his book *History in the Making* (IVP), writes,

We can see cycles in all kinds of human endeavor, including Christian movements. These movements are born in a great burst of enthusiasm to change the world, attracting people wholly committed to the cause. Such devoted effort brings rapid growth. Growth necessitates greater attention to organization, while success attracts new adherents lacking the self-sacrificing zeal of the founders. Eventually the movement is institutionalized and takes its comfortable place alongside others in respectable society, and the stage is set for a new movement, born in a great burst of enthusiasm to change the world. (p. 56)

The pattern is one we recognize. Yet this cycle is not a historical necessity. Revival and renewal, or what Swanstrom calls a "baptism of fire," can break the chain of cause and effect. As InterVarsity enters the second fifty years of its history, renewal will be critical to keep it a movement rather than an organization.

One of InterVarsity's area directors saw the quote that begins chapter sixteen: *The main thing is to keep the main thing the main thing.* He turned to another staff member, asking, "What is the main thing?" They felt the "main thing" sometimes can get lost in the shuffle of ideas, and that the "main thing" needs to be regularly articulated. The possibility exists for ancillary groups or emphases within the movement to become primary. Even something as fine as our emphasis on ethnic diversity has the potential to divert us from the essentials of our calling. The crisp and clear goals of the original purpose statement of InterVarsity—to establish groups of students whose aims are evangelism, Christian growth and missions—or the newly stated vision statement of the eighties—building collegiate fellowships, engaging the university and developing disciples—captures InterVarsity's raison d'etre.

The matter of student initiative and student leadership will continue to be critical to the movement. The multiplication of Christian groups on the campus has confused the issue of student initiative. Charles Troutman, one of IVCF's founders, recently commented, "The proliferation of student groups, along with numbers of fulltime staff, has almost choked out the initiative of students. I have been disappointed wherever I have gone to see what this has done to the attitude of staff, students and faculty." Throughout the history of InterVarsity, students rarely arrived on campus with well-developed vision or leadership skills. The job of the staff member has always been to plant a vision for the work of God on campus and then encourage students to do it.

Our interest and concern for the sociological factors that affect students' lives, legitimate as these may be, must not keep staff members from calling students to their highest level of obedience to God. While sympathetic and sensitive to human need, the movement needs campus staff members who call students beyond their circumstances. If the work is to flourish in the next decades, students in this generation need to trust in the God of grace and power no less than in earlier generations. That means a continued emphasis on the development of Christian character and stability in IVCF's training that goes beyond the how-tos of leadership.

A second challenge continues to dog the operation of InterVarsity as a middle-aged movement. It is that age-old problem of financing campus work in an even-handed way so that one area does not experience famine while another flourishes. Money cannot be allowed to determine the philosophy of the movement. The development of closer alumni ties for ministry money—so difficult and yet essential to the movement—stands the best chance for more stable income patterns, along with increasing ties with supporting churches. The capable campus leaders within the movement will be discussing strategy and philosophy of support for years to come.

A third consideration is the decentralization of the work which has allowed the student movement to grow and prosper. Regionalization is a great strength as long as the leaders within the movement remain a team united by the same goals under strong leadership. Without that, regionalization could blow the movement apart. With autonomy come opportunities for restless or independent staff to try to "create a better way" and to develop emphases which move the work imperceptibly in other directions. A tension between consensus thinking and prophetic leadership will test the movement in the days ahead.

The Most Serious Challenge

InterVarsity needs to pay attention to its theological roots. Many organizations go off-track by the time they reach their fiftieth anniversary. Doctrinal statements are not enough; they need to be constantly checked and their finer points taught and emphasized. It is easy to "get on with the mission" and belatedly discover that the faith that began the movement has eroded away. If history tells us anything, it's that theological drift occurs almost imperceptibly over long periods of time. One little change here, another there. The IVCF statement of faith was intentionally brief, responding to the theological ferment at the time it was written. Later, facing the problems of another generation, the 1960 staff members unanimously accepted an expanded theological statement known as the Bear Trap statement. As a member of the International Fellowship of Evangelical Students (IFES), IVCF-USA supports that group's more detailed theological statement (see page 382). Perhaps the climate is right today for InterVarsity Christian Fellowship to adopt a more complete statement as its official Basis of Faith, thus placing fresh emphasis on the importance of our theological roots.

A Valuable Legacy

Christian witness in the world's universities has always been a very difficult and strenuous activity. The nature of representing biblical revelation and offering an unwanted Redeemer makes this inevitable.

We do well to remember that this is InterVarsity's calling. We do not expect that it will become easier with the passing years.

Historically, the teaching of InterVarsity has cut across the grain of much of the Christian subculture by insisting that expressions of personal faith be rooted in a proper view of God and a careful handling of Scripture. It has linked the heart and the mind in a way that combines awe and joy in the worship and service of God. Alumni are wistful in remembering the quality of fellowship this brought to their lives as students. An emphasis on excellence in thought-life, in singing, in careful Bible exposition, on the wholeness of life before God and the importance of the Quiet Time have kept generations of students exposed to life-giving truth.

Stacey Woods would disagree with those who suggest our distinctives come from our "British influence"; he insisted that what we were teaching students came from a theology about God and the Scripture. Out of this have come patterns that have enriched generations of students. These factors constitute "the golden thread that has provided continuity and consistency" in InterVarsity. All of them have at center great loyalty and submission to the Word of God, written and living.

No objective, written statement of faith alone can keep the heart or protect the fellowship. The future ministry of InterVarsity Christian Fellowship is dependent on God's gracious work in us and among us. The psalmist has said it well:

Unless the LORD builds the house,
　　its builders labor in vain.
Unless the LORD watches over the city,
　　the watchmen stand guard in vain. (Psalm 127:1)

Basis of Faith, IVCF-USA

The Statement of Basis of Faith of the Inter-Varsity Christian Fellowship of the USA is taken from the Articles of Incorporation, Article IV

Each member of the Corporation, Board of Directors, Staff and Council of Reference, as a qualification of membership or office, as the case may be, shall subscribe ex animo, at the time of election or before taking office and yearly thereafter, to his belief in the Doctrinal Basis of the Fellowship, which shall be the basic Biblical truths of Christianity, including:

a. The unique, divine inspiration, entire trustworthiness and authority of the Bible.

b. The deity of our Lord Jesus Christ.

c. The necessity and efficacy of the substitutionary death of Jesus Christ for the redemption of the world, and the historic fact of His bodily resurrection.

d. The presence and power of the Holy Spirit in the work of regeneration.

e. The consummation of the kingdom in the "glorious appearing of the great God and our Savior Jesus Christ."

Bear Trap Statement

This Statement of Faith was adopted at Bear Trap Ranch, Colorado, in January 1960, and unanimously accepted at the National Staff Conference of IVCF. Though not our official statement, it proved to be a useful supplement to the IVCF Basis of Faith.

We receive the Bible in its entirety, and the Bible alone, as the Word of God written, inspired of God, and therefore the inerrant rule of faith and practice.

We accept the formulations of Biblical doctrine represented by the large areas of agreement in such historic declarations as the Apostles' and Nicene Creeds, the Augsburg, Westminster and New Hampshire Confessions, and the Thirty-Nine Articles of Religion.

We desire to safeguard individual Christian liberty to differ in areas of doctrine not common to these formulations, provided that any interpretation is sincerely believed to arise from and is based upon the Bible.

In view of contemporary theological discussion, we explicitly affirm our belief in the following specific Biblical doctrines, even though they are stated in the historic confessional formulations:

1 The one true God, existing eternally in unity and in the tri-personality of Father, Son and Holy Spirit.

2 The unique nature of man as a moral and rational being created in the image of God, and the historic fall of man into sin, bringing all men under divine condemnation.

3 The full deity and true humanity of Jesus Christ, His personal pre-existence, virgin birth and sinlessness.

4 The historic death of the Lord Jesus Christ for our sins, a voluntary, substitutionary sacrifice, and His bodily resurrection.

5 The justification of sinners by the Lord Jesus Christ through faith alone.

6 The deity and personality of the Holy Spirit, the effective agent both in regeneration and in that holy living which is the necessary evidence of true faith.

7 The fellowship of Christians in the Church, which embraces Biblical doctrine, worships the true God, obeys the Lord's commands to baptize and to remember Him at the table, exercises discipline, adorns its profession by holiness and love of fellow believers, and proclaims the Christian gospel to the world.

8 The visible return of the Lord Jesus Christ in glory.

9 The resurrection of the redeemed to enjoyment of God forever in His presence, and the resurrection of the unredeemed to judgment and everlasting punishment.

IFES Statement of Faith

The doctrinal basis of the International Fellowship of Evangelical Students is the fundamental truths of Christianity, including:

a. The unity of the Father, Son and Holy Spirit in the Godhead.

b. The sovereignty of God in creation, revelation, redemption and final judgment.

c. The divine inspiration and entire trustworthiness of Holy Scripture, as originally given, and its supreme authority in all matters of faith and conduct.

d. The universal sinfulness and guilt of all men since the fall, rendering them subject to God's wrath and condemnation.

e. Redemption from the guilt, penalty, dominion and pollution of sin, solely through the sacrificial death (as our Representative and Substitute) of the Lord Jesus Christ, the incarnate Son of God.

f. The bodily resurrection of the Lord Jesus Christ from the dead and His ascension to the right hand of God the Father.

g. The presence and power of the Holy Spirit in the work of regeneration.

h. The justification of the sinner by the grace of God through faith alone.

i. The indwelling and work of the Holy Spirit in the believer.

j. The one Holy Universal Church which is the Body of Christ and to which all true believers belong.

k. The expectation of the personal return of the Lord Jesus Christ.

Teacher and Lord

John R. W. Stott's widely circulated statement on the authority of Christ and the Scriptures, was given at 1964 IVCF Missionary Convention, Urbana, Illinois. (For background see pp. 236-237.)

"You call me Teacher and Lord, and you are right; that is what I am." John 13:13.

The Christian is under both instruction and authority. He looks to Jesus as his Teacher to instruct him, and as his Lord to command him. He believes what he believes because Jesus taught it, and he does what he does because Jesus said to do it.

He is our Teacher to instruct us, and we learn to submit and to subordinate our minds to his mind. We do not presume to have views or ideas or opinions which are in contradiction to the views and ideas of Jesus Christ. Our view of Scripture is derived from Christ's view of Scripture, just as our view of discipleship, of heaven and hell, of the Christian life and of everything else is derived from Jesus Christ. Any question about the inspiration of Scripture and its authority therefore resolves itself to: What did Jesus Christ teach about these points?

We would say, without any doubt, that he gave reverent assent to the authority and inspiration of the Old Testament. There is no indication anywhere in his teachings that he disagreed with the Old Testament writers. He regarded the words of the Old Testament writings as being the words of God. He submitted to them in his own life, he believed them, he accepted their statements, and sought to apply their principles. He regarded Scripture as the great arbiter in dispute. He said to his contemporaries, 'You make many mistakes, because you don't know the Scriptures.' We find in the New Testament that he invested the apostles with authority to teach in his Name. He said that the Holy Spirit would lead them into all truth, would bring to their remembrance what he had spoken to them, and would show them things to come. He evidently expected that in the providence of God there would be others to interpret, expound, and bear witness to the revelation given in himself, just as there were prophets raised up by God and inspired to bear witness to what he did in Old Testament days.

To sum up, the authority of Scripture is due to the inspiration of Scripture. The Old and New Testaments are authoritative in our lives, because they are in fact inspired. And therefore, since Jesus Christ is our Teacher as well as our Lord, the authority of Christ and the authority of Scripture stand or fall together.

Timeline

YEAR:	up to 1920-21	1922-23	1924-25	1926-27
Christian Student Activities Overseas:	In 1877 Cambridge Inter-Collegiate Christian Union (CICCU) formed; first conf. of Chr. Unions in U.K. held in 1919; student work begun in Denmark in 1920.	In 1923 Inter-Varsity Fellowship formed in England, with strong leadership of CICCU; student work begun in Norway.		Isolated Christian Union formed at Vancouver, B.C., Canada.
Christian Student Activities U.S.A.:	Student Volunteer Movement (SVM) convenes in Des Moines, Iowa in 1921 with 6,890 delegates.		SVM Conf. Indianapolis, Ind. (1924); in 1925, first League of Evangelical Students (LES) conference held at Calvin College (Mich.), Gen. Sec. E. VanDeusen.	
World and U.S. History:	Prohibition (1919); start of League of Nations; radio licensed; Warren Harding elected pres. of U.S.; Hitler's storm troops terrorize political opponents in Germany.	KKK revival; first sound movies; Mussolini forms Fascist government in Italy; Soviet states form USSR.	Calvin Coolidge elected pres. of U.S.; J. Edgar Hoover appointed director of FBI; comedian Will Rogers at height of career; Scopes Trial (1925).	Hirohito becomes emperor of Japan; Gene Tunney wins heavyweight boxing title from Jack Dempsey.

YEAR:	1928-29	1930-31	1932-33	1934-35
Christian Student Activities Overseas:	Norman Grubb, from England, tours Canada, April '28; Howard Guinness from England to Canada Nov. '28; IVCF-Canada formed, 1929.	Arthur Hill, president of IVCF-Canada; Pioneer Camps of Canada started.	Howard Guinness tours Canada again.	C. Stacey Woods recruited as General Secretary of IVCF of Canada (1934); conf. of Evangelical Students, 1935, in Stockholm.
Christian Student Activities U.S.A.:	SVM convenes in Detroit, Mich. 3,375 attend. Milo Jamieson at UCLA; Horton Hall at U. of Calif., Berkeley; Student House at U. Wash.		Student Volunteer Movement convention at Buffalo, N.Y. 2,260 attend.	Scripture tracts given by students through Scripture Distribution Society to U. Chicago, Northwestern, U. Wis., U. Minn.
World and U.S. History:	Herbert Hoover elected president of U.S.; first scheduled TV broadcasts (in N.Y. State). Stock market crash and start of worldwide depression (1929).	Charles Evans Hughes is appointed chief justice of U.S. Supreme Court; congress creates Veterans Administration; Federal Bureau of Narcotics is organized.	Franklin D. Roosevelt elected pres. of U.S. over Hoover; Karl Barth publishes *Church Dogmatics* vol.1; Hitler is appointed German chancellor and establishes the first concentration camps (1933).	USSR admitted to League of Nations; Hitler and Mussolini meet in Venice, Italy; Evangeline Booth elected General of the Salvation Army; Italy invades Abyssinia; FBI shoots John Dillinger.

YEAR:	1936-37	1938/39
Number of IVCF Chapters/ Groups:		
Total Number of Field Staff:		
Total Support Personnel:	Out of Canadian IVCF office.	Out of Canadian IVCF office.
IVCF National Leadership:	(Canadian Gen. Sec. C. Stacey Woods; Charles Troutman joins staff of IVCF Canada.)	(Canadian Gen. Sec. C. Stacey Woods; Charles Troutman on staff of IVCF Canada.)
Corporate/ Legal Leadership:	IVCF of Canada prays about expansion to U.S.A.; Donald Fleming, Chairman.	Beginning of U.S.A. work out of Canadian IVCF Board.
Total Expense:		$1,113
IVCF Headquarters and Training Locations:	Out of IVCF-Canada.	Out of IVCF-Canada.
IVCF National Events:		Woods and Troutman visit U.S.A.
Administrative Structure and Expansion:		IVCF chapter formed at U. of Mich., Ann Arbor; additional groups join: Drexel U.; Michigan State College; Wayne U.; U. of Wash.
Christian Student Activities Overseas:		4th International Conference of Evangelical Students held at Cambridge, England, summer '39, attended by 800 delegates from 33 countries.
Christian Student Activities U.S.A.:	Student Foreign Missions Fellowship (SFMF) starts in Christian schools, Wil Norton, Sec; Chicago Christian Nurses Fellowship begun (1937); 12th quadrennial of SVM at Indianapolis attended by 2,769.	League of Evangelical Students continues. SFMF grows.
World and U.S. History	Franklin D. Roosevelt re-elected pres.of U.S.; Social Security begins.	Japan invades China; N.Y.C. has 20,000 TV sets.

YEAR:	1939/40	1940/41
Number of IVCF Chapters/ Groups:	22	31
Total Number of Field Staff:	4	4 (+ 4 p.t.)
Total Support Personnel:	Out of Canadian IVCF office.	1 (in Chicago)
IVCF National Leadership:	C. Stacey Woods, Gen. Sec.; Charles Troutman, Grace Koch, Herb Butt appointed by IVCF Canada to serve in the U.S.A.	C. Stacey Woods, Gen. Sec; Chas. Troutman; Herb Butt; Grace Koch; Paul Beckwith. (All appointments made by IVCF-Canada, pending U.S. incorporation.)
Corporate/ Legal Leadership:	Continues to operate out of Canada, adding U.S. Board members: H. J. Taylor, J. F. Strombeck, T. Edward Ross.	H. J. Taylor, Chrmn. of Board; E. Ross; M. Haines; C. D. Weyerhaeuser; J. F. Strombeck; C. Troutman, Sr. plus Canadians: Donald Fleming; John Howitt.
Total Expense:	$4,100	$9,000
IVCF Headquarters and Training Locations:	Out of IVCF-Canada.	20 N. Wacker Dr., Chicago (with Christian Workers Foundation, H. J. Taylor, Trustee).
IVCF National Events:	Campus visits by Woods, Troutman, Koch, Butt.	Details of U.S. incorporation begun.
Administrative Structure and Expansion:	Groups formed at Johns Hopkins, Swarthmore College, Univ. of Maryland, U. of Chicago, U. of Wis., U. of Ill., State Teacher's College (Duluth), Wash. State College, Wash. College of Education (Eastern, Central and Western); Oreg. State College.	
Christian Student Activities Overseas:		
Christian Student Activities U.S.A.:		With limited attendance requirements, 465 attend the Toronto SVM meetings.
World and U.S. History	Germany invades neighbors; Italy to Albania.	FDR re-elected over Wendell Wilkie; in Europe, WW2 starts.

YEAR:	1941/42	1942/43
Number of IVCF Chapters/ Groups:	46	
Total Number of Field Staff:	8 (+3 p.t.)	11
Total Support Personnel:	2	2
IVCF National Leadership:	C. Stacey Woods (CSW), Gen. Sec.; Chas. Troutman, Jr.; Herb Butt; David Adeney, Missions; Ken Taylor; Neil Nellis; Bob Oerter; Grace Koch.	CSW; Lois Troutman; Jane Hollingsworth; Irene Webster-Smith; Ann Chapman; Shockley Few; Herb Butt; David Adeney. (Many male staff go to war.)
Corporate/ Legal Leadership:	H. J. Taylor, Chrmn. of Board; Edw. Ross, VC; Paul Westburg, Treas.; Margaret Haines; J. F. Strombeck; C. Davis Weyerhaeuser; Chas. Troutman, Sr.	H. J. Taylor, Chrmn. of Bd.; Edw. Ross, VC; Paul Westburg, Treas.; Margaret Haines; J. F. Strombeck; C. Davis Weyerhaeuser; Chas. Troutman, Sr.; plus Mrs. F. Cliffe Johnston; Cameron Peck; F. E. Weyerhaeuser.
Total Expense:	$18,000	$25,000
IVCF Headquarters and Training Locations:	20 N.Wacker Dr., Chicago	20 N.Wacker Dr., Chicago
IVCF National Events:	Constitution of IVCF-USA adopted 9/2/41; IVCF incorporated Nov. '41; tax exempt status granted Dec. '41.	Many chapters started by service men assigned to Army/Navy training programs.
Administrative Structure and Expansion:	Paul Beckwith, Extension.	
IVCF Literature and Media Resources:	HIS magazine Editor: Robert Walker. Produced in 5½" X 8" size.	HIS magazine Editor: Robert Walker.
IVCF Missions Work:	David Adeney, Missions.	David Adeney, Missions.
IVCF Overseas Activity:		
Christian Student Activities U.S.: (not IVCF/ IFES)	SFMF: 2,628 in 36 chapters in Christian colleges; CNF in Schools of Nursing.	
World and U.S. History:	Pearl Harbor attacked; U.S. enters WW2.	WW2: Bataan death march; 100,000 Japanese on West Coast relocated; MacArthur appointed Far East commander-in-chief.

YEAR:	1943/44	1944/45
Number of IVCF Chapters/ Groups:		"20 new chapters"
Total Number of Field Staff:	14	19
Total Support Personnel:	3	4
IVCF National Leadership:	CSW; Lois Troutman; Jane Hollingsworth; Catherine Alexander; Ann Chapman; Alice Reid; Herb Butt; Christy Wilson; Constance Johnston; Paul Beckwith.	CSW; Lois Troutman; Jane Hollingsworth; Catherine Alexander; Ann Chapman; Alice Reid; Herb Butt; Christy Wilson; Constance Johnston; plus Paul Beckwith, Alumni Sec.; Joe Bayly.
Corporate/ Legal Leadership:	H. J. Taylor, Chrmn. of Board; Edw. Ross, VC; Paul Westburg, Treas; Margaret Haines; J. F. Strombeck; C. Davis Weyerhaeuser; Chas. Troutman, Sr.; Mrs. F. Cliffe Johnston; Cameron Peck; F. E. Weyerhaeuser. (NOTE: hereafter, only Executive Committee of Board is listed.)	H. J. Taylor, Chrmn; Paul Westburg, VC; Cameron Peck, Treas; J. F. Strombeck, Mrs. Philip Armour.
Total Expense:	$36,000	$50,000
IVCF Headquarters and Training Locations:	64 E. Lake St., Chicago.	64 E. Lake St., Chicago.
IVCF National Events:		National Day of Prayer for U.S.A. and Canada IVCF.
Administrative Structure and Expansion:		Bob Finley, Evangelist.
IVCF Literature and Media Resources:	*HIS* magazine Editor: Ken Taylor; Bible study on Mark produced; *Hymns* edited by Paul Beckwith; *Intercessor* begun.	*HIS* Editor: Ken Taylor. Booklet *Taboo* published.
IVCF Missions Work:	Raymond Joyce, Missions.	J. Christy Wilson, Missions.
IVCF Overseas Activity:	CSW makes exploratory trip to Latin America 4/20-5/23. A "world movement of evangelical students" proposed.	Edward Pentecost sent to Mexico; Mr. and Mrs. Leon Headington to Costa Rica.
Christian Student Activities U.S.: (not IVCF/ IFES)	CNF plans to go National; Theological Students Fellowship and Teachers Christian Fellowship begun in U.S.	
World and U.S. History:	WW2: Russia stops Hitler; Eisenhower appointed European commander-in-chief; Italy surrenders. Rationing begins in U.S.; invasion of Europe (D-day) 6/6/44.	Franklin D. Roosevelt re-elected; V-2 rockets on Britain; battle of the Bulge; victory in Europe (V-E Day) 5/8/45.

YEAR:	1945/46	1946/47
Number of IVCF Chapters/ Groups:		"277 campuses on which IVCF was operating." In touch with 10,000 students.
Total Number of Field Staff:	14	18
Total Support Personnel:	4	6 (est.)
IVCF National Leadership:	C. Stacey Woods, Gen. Sec.; Chas. Troutman, Jr., Assoc. Gen. Sec. (back from the army); Herb Butt; Joe Bayly; Jane Hollingsworth; Mary Anne Klein, Office Mgr.; Paul Beckwith, Extension; Howard Larson, Pub. Rel.	C. Stacey Woods, Gen. Sec.; Chas. Troutman, Assoc. Gen. Sec. Midwest; Herb Butt, Assoc. Gen. Sec. West Coast; Joe Bayly, Assoc. Gen. Sec. Eastern; Paul Hopkins, Bus. Mgr.; Chas. Miller, Publications.
Corporate/ Legal Leadership:	H. J. Taylor, Chrmn. of the Board; Paul Westburg, VC; Cameron Peck, Treas. plus J. F. Strombeck, Mrs. Armour.	H. J. Taylor, Chrmn. of the Board; Paul Westburg, VC; Cameron Peck, Treas. plus J. F. Strombeck, Mrs. Armour plus exec addition of Wm. Culbertson.
Total Expense:	$74,000	$94,000
IVCF Headquarters and Training Locations:	64 E. Lake, Chicago; Campus-in-the-Woods begun (in Canada); 85 attend.	64 W. Randolph, Chicago; Campus-in-the-Woods.
IVCF National Events:	SFMF merges with IVCF.	1st IVCF Missionary Conf. (Toronto) C. Wilson, Dir.; 575 attend.
Administrative Structure and Expansion:	Evangelist Bob Finley; Teachers Christian Fellowship (TCF): Shirley Stephen.	Evangelist Bob Finley; TCF: Shirley Stephen.
IVCF Literature and Media Resources:	*HIS* Editor: Ken Taylor (circ: 4,000); "This Morning With God" in *HIS* starts Jan. '46.	*HIS* Editor: Ken Taylor Assoc. Ed.: Virginia Lowell.
SFMF/IVCF Missions Work:	J. Christy Wilson, Missionary Secretary and Assoc. Gen. Sec.	J. Christy Wilson, Missionary Secretary; *Missionary Mandate* begun, M. A. Klein, Editor.
IFES/IVCF Activities Overseas:	C. Stacey Woods on Latin American trip.	IFES formed (at Oxford, England), Co-Secs.: D. J. Johnson and C. S. Woods; Ed Pentecost to Mexico.
Other Student Organizations (Not IVCF/ IFES)	David Adeney to China with China Inland Mission (CIM) to assist China/IVCF.	KGK (IVCF in Japan) started in Tokyo, aided by Chas. Hummel.
World and U.S. History:	Invasion of Japan planned; atomic bombs dropped on Japan; Aug. 14, 1945, Japan surrenders.	United Nations formed; Jackie Robinson, first black in baseball; RSV New Testament translation printed.

YEAR:	1947/48	1948/49
Number of IVCF Chapters/ Groups:	295 (IVCF 249; FMF 46)	494 (IVCF 321; FMF 64; CNF 109)
Total Number of Field Staff:	19	25
Total Support Personnel:	8 (est.)	10 (est.)
IVCF National Leadership:	C. Stacey Woods, Gen. Sec.; Chas. Troutman, Assoc. Gen. Sec. Midwest; Herb Butt, Assoc. Gen. Sec. West Coast; Joe Bayly, Assoc. Gen. Sec. Eastern; Paul Hopkins, Bus. Mgr.; Chas. Miller, Publications; plus Paul Hopkins, Bus. Mgr.; Paul Beckwith, Extension; Bob Finley, Evangelist.	C. Stacey Woods, Gen. Sec.; Chas. Troutman, Assoc. Gen. Sec. Midwest; Herb Butt, Assoc. Gen. Sec. West Coast; Joe Bayly, Assoc. Gen Sec. Eastern; Paul Hopkins, Bus. Mgr.; Chas. Miller, Publications; Paul Beckwith, Extension; Bob Finley, Evangelist; plus Wm. E. C. Petersen, Stewardship Sec.; Carl Thomas and Cleo "Buck" Buxton, regional secretaries.
Corporate/ Legal Leadership:	H. J. Taylor, Chrmn. of the Board; Paul Westburg, VC; Cameron Peck, Treas.; J. F. Strombeck; Mrs. Armour; Robert McQuilkin.	H. J. Taylor, Chrmn. of the Board; Paul Westburg, VC; Cameron Peck, Treas.; J. F. Strombeck; Mrs. Armour; Robert McQuilkin.
Total Expense:	$108,000	$131,000
IVCF Headquarters and Training Locations:	64 W. Randolph, Chicago; Campus-in-the-Woods.	64 W. Randolph, Chicago; Campus-in-the-Woods.
IVCF National Events:	First edition of *Hymns* published, edited by Paul Beckwith.	2nd IVCF Missionary Conference[1] (or Urbana 48), Norton Sterrett, Dir.; 1,294 attend.
Administrative Structure and Expansion:	Evangelist Bob Finley.	Board affirms policy that IVCF be "color-blind." CNF organized nationally and merges with IVCF.
IVCF Literature and Media Resources:	*HIS* Editor: V. Lowell; IV Press formalized. Distribution to bookstores handled by Fleming H. Revell Co.	*HIS* Editors: V. Lowell and Wilbur Smith; with Jan '48 issue, *HIS* goes bigger (7″ X 10″).
SFMF/IVCF Missions Work:	T. Norton Sterrett, Secretary FMF.	T. Norton Sterrett, Secretary FMF.
IFES/IVCF Activities Overseas:	IFES formalized (at Harvard U.) Gen. Sec.: C. Stacey Woods.	CSW tours France; Gwen Wong to Hawaii.
Other Student Organizations (Not IVCF/ IFES)	Christian Nurses Fellowship local groups meeting in eight metropolitan areas in U.S.A.	
World and U.S. History:	India made independent amd partitioned into India and Pakistan; more than 1 million war vets enroll in colleges in U.S.A.	Gandhi assassinated; Harry Truman elected president of U.S.

[1]Note: This timeline will use the current system of "Urbana Year" for consistency, although until the 8th (which was held in 1967) the IVCF Missionary Conferences were titled as Inter-Varsity's 2nd or 3rd etc.

YEAR:	1949/50	1950/51
Number of IVCF chapters/ groups:	499 (IVCF 229, CNF 210, FMF 60)	561
Total Number of Field Staff:	28	35
Total Support Personnel:	15 (est.)	20 (est.)
IVCF National Leadership:	C. Stacey Woods (CSW), Gen. Sec.; Chas. Troutman, Jr., Assoc. Gen. Sec.; W. E. C. Petersen, Joe Bayly, Alvera Anderson, CNF.	CSW; Chas. Troutman, Jr.; W. E. C. Petersen; Carl Thomas; Melvin Friesen; Eugene Thomas; Cleo Buxton; Jim Nyquist; Joe Bayly; Alvera Anderson; Keith Hunt, Office Mgr.
Corporate/ Legal Leadership:	H. J. Taylor, Chrmn.; Paul Westburg, VC; Cameron Peck, Treas.; plus J. F. Strombeck; Robt. McQuilkin; Ken Gieser.	Cameron Peck, Chrmn.; Paul Westburg, VC; Mortimer B. Lane, Treas.; plus H. J. Taylor; J. F. Strombeck; Ken Gieser; Mrs. Armour, Jr.
Total Expense:	$166,000	$199,000
IVCF Headquarters and Training Locations:	64 W. Randolph, Chicago; Campus-in-the-Woods; work camp at Cedar Campus, "Buck" Buxton, Leader.	1444 N. Astor, Chicago; Campus-in-the-Woods; work camp at Cedar Campus (repeated).
IVCF National Events:		Year of Evangelism. Missions held at 58 campuses. Speakers include Leith Samuel, Karlis Leyasmeyer, John Gerstner, J. Edwin Orr.
Administrative Structure and Expansion:		British team arranged to travel New England in 1951/52: Peter Haile, John Holmes, Dane Gordon, John Weston.
IVCF Literature and Media Resources:	HIS Editors: Virginia Lowell and C. Stacey Woods; HIS circulation: 7,469.	C. Stacey Woods and Virginia Lowell, HIS Editors; Lois Thiessen, Asst. Editor; HIS circulation: 7,909.
SFMF/IVCF Missions Work:	Wes Gustafson, Sec. FMF; David Howard, Field Sec.	Wes Gustafson, Sec. FMF.
CNF/IVCF Nurses Work:	Alvera Anderson, Sec. CNF.	Alvera Anderson, Sec. CNF.
IFES/IVCF Activities Overseas:	Ed Pentecost to Mexico; Norton Sterrett to India.	
Other Student Organizations (Not IVCF/ IFES)		
World and U.S. History:	Berlin Blockade ended; Chiang Kai-shek flees to Formosa; communist People's Republic of China founded; Israel enters UN.	McCarthy begins Communist hunt; Alger Hiss sentenced; Korean War starts; U.S. sends advisors to Vietnam.

YEAR:	1951/52	1952/53
Number of IVCF chapters/ groups:	578 (IVCF 371, FMF 77, CNF 130)	584 (IVCF 296; FMF 77; NCF 211)
Total Number of Field Staff:	40	41
Total Support Personnel:	26	30
IVCF National Leadership:	CSW; Chas. Troutman, Jr.; W. E. C. Petersen; Keith Hunt; Paul Beckwith; Robt. Baylis; Jim Nyquist; Joe Bayly; David Adeney; Gene Thomas; Mel Friesen; Tressie Myers, CNF.	CSW; Chas. Troutman, Jr.; W. E. C. Petersen; Keith Hunt; Jim McLeish; David Adeney; Jim Nyquist; Joe Bayly; David Adeney; Gene Thomas; Mel Friesen; Tressie Myers, CNF.
Corporate/ Legal Leadership:	Cameron Peck, Chrmn.; Paul Westburg, VC; E. A. Gordon, Treas.; plus H. J. Taylor, J. F. Strombeck.	Paul Westburg, Chrmn.; J. F. Strombeck, VC; Roy Horsey, Treas.; plus H. J. Taylor, James Barnes. End of fiscal year changed from 8/31 to 6/30.
Total Expense:	$245,000	$208,000
IVCF Headquarters and Training Locations:	1444 N. Astor, Chicago; Campus-in-the-Woods; Cedar Campus. Overflow Camp from Campus-in-the-Woods with Chas. Troutman, PD; opened Campus by the Sea with Mel Friesen, Dir.	1444 N. Astor, Chicago; Campus-in-the-Woods; Campus by the Sea.
IVCF National Events:	Urbana '51 directed by Wes Gustafson; 1,646 attend.	CSW vacates Canadian IVCF Gen. Sec. office. In Mar. '53 Cameron Peck resigns. In June '53 Charles Troutman resigns.
Administrative Structure and Expansion:	Senior Staff Council formed: CSW, Chrmn.; Chas. Troutman, Jr.; W. E. C. Petersen; Joe Bayly; Wes Gustafson; Gene M. Thomas; Jim Nyquist; David Adeney; Mel Friesen. David Adeney appointed to head up international student work.	Ivery Harvey appointed to cover "Negro schools," IVCF's second full-time Black staff member.
IVCF Literature and Media Resources:	Joe Bayly, Editorial Sec.; CSW, HIS Editor; Gertrud DeGroot, Editorial Asst.	Joe Bayly, Editorial Sec. and HIS Editor; Gertrud DeGroot, Asst. Editor.
SFMF/IVCF Missions Work:	Wes Gustafson, Sec. FMF.	Wes Gustafson, Sec. FMF.
CNF/IVCF Nurses Work:	Tressie Myers, CNF Sec.; July '51 first issue of CNF Bulletin. In Oct. name changed to The Lamp.	Name changed to NCF; Tressie Myers, NCF Sec.
IFES/IVCF Activities Overseas:		Gwen Wong to Philippines to pioneer an IVCF movement.
Other Student Organizations (Not IVCF/ IFES)	Bill Bright starts Campus Crusade for Christ (CCC) at UCLA; Cleo Buxton leaves IVCF to be first full-time leader of Officers Christian Union.	Bob Finley starts International Students Inc. (ISI).
World and U.S. History:	Gen. Douglas MacArthur relieved of command by Pres. Truman; Korean peace plan fails.	Dwight Eisenhower elected pres. of U.S.; RSV version of entire Bible published.

YEAR:	1953/54	1954/55
Number of IVCF Chapters/ Groups:	708 (IVCF 366; NCF 254; FMF 88)	736 (IVCF 384; NCF 261; FMF 91)
Total Number of Field Staff:	47 1/2	56
Total Support Personnel:	28	33
IVCF National Leadership:	C. Stacey Woods (CSW), Gen. Sec.; Joe Bayly, Publications/HIS; W. E. C. Petersen, Bus. Mgr./ Stewardship; James McLeish, Ofc. Mgr.; plus Senior Staff Council.	CSW, Gen. Sec.; Gene Thomas, Asst. to Gen. Sec.; W. E. C. Petersen, Stewardship Sec.; Jim McLeish, Comptroller; plus Senior Staff Council.
Corporate/ Legal Leadership:	Paul Westburg, Chrmn.; Ken Gieser, VC; Roy Horsey, Treas. and Sec.; plus H. J. Taylor; Roscoe Sappenfield, James Barnes.	Roy Horsey, President; James Barnes, VP; Roscoe Sappenfield, Treas.; plus H. J. Taylor, Ken Gieser, Paul Westburg.
Total Expense:	$265,000	$361,000
IVCF Headquarters and Training Locations:	1444 N. Astor, Chicago; Campus-in-the-Woods; Campus by the Sea; opened Bear Trap Ranch (Gene Thomas, Dir.).	1444 N. Astor, Chicago; Campus-in-the-Woods; Campus by the Sea; Bear Trap Ranch; reopened Cedar Campus (Keith Hunt, Dir.) with Missionary Training Camp, David Adeney, Prog. Dir.
IVCF National Events:	Death of staff member Ralph Willoughby on 8/27/53.	Urbana '54 directed by D. Adeney; 2,141 attended; faculty conference held.
Administrative Structure and Expansion:		U.S. Evangelistic team appointed: Bill Young, Swede Christensen, Bud Murray, Frank VanAalst.
IVCF Literature and Media Resources:	Joe Bayly, Lit. Sec. and HIS Editor.	Joe Bayly, Lit. Sec. and HIS Editor.
SFMF/IVCF Missions Work:	David Adeney, Director.	David Adeney, Director.
NCF/IVCF Nurses Work:	Tressie Myers, NCF Sec.	Tressie Myers, NCF Sec.
IFES/IVCF Activities Overseas:	Troutman to IVF in Australia. IFES Journal begun.	
Other Student Organizations (Not IVCF/ IFES)		Campus Crusade for Christ goes national.
World and U.S. History:	Korean armistice signed; all price controls in U.S. removed; Stalin dies; Supreme Court rules segregation in public schools is unconstitutional.	Witch-hunting activities of Sen. McCarthy censured by Senate.

YEAR:	1955/56	1956/57
Number of IVCF Chapters/ Groups:		836 (IVCF 419; NCF 322; FMF 95)
Total Number of Field Staff:	52	46
Total Support Personnel:	31	28
IVCF National Leadership:	CSW, Gen. Sec.; Eugene (Gene) Thomas, Staff and Student Sec.; W. E. C. Petersen, Stewardship Sec.; Jim McLeish, Comptroller plus Senior Staff Council.	CSW, Gen. Sec.; Chas. Hummel, Natl. Sec.; W. E. C. Petersen; Jim McLeish plus Senior Staff Council.
Corporate/ Legal Leadership:	Roy Horsey, President; James Barnes, VP; Roscoe Sappenfield, Treas.; plus H. J. Taylor, Ken Gieser, Paul Westburg.	Roy Horsey, President; James Barnes, VP; Roscoe Sappenfield, Treas.; plus H. J. Taylor, Ken Gieser, Ralph Watts.
Total Expense:	$420,000	$491,000
IVCF Headquarters and Training Locations:	1444 N. Astor, Chicago; Campus-in-the-Woods, Campus by the Sea, Bear Trap Ranch, Cedar Campus; obtained Hudson House.	1519 N. Astor, Chicago; Campus-in-the-Woods, Campus by the Sea, Bear Trap Ranch, Cedar Campus; Hudson House.
IVCF National Events:	Paul Little, International Student Sec.; Manuscript Bible studies with Ros Rinker, Paul Byer.	John Stott speaks at series of campus evangelistic "missions."
Administrative Structure and Expansion:	Senior Staff Council: CSW, W. E. C. Petersen, David Adeney, Joe Bayly, Peter Haile, John Hermanson, Chas. Hummel, Tressie Myers, Jim Nyquist, Eugene Thomas, and Wilber Sutherland (Canada).	50% support required for all new staff members.
IVCF Literature and Media Resources:	Joe Bayly, Lit. Sec. and *HIS* Editor.	Joe Bayly, Lit. Sec. and *HIS* Editor.
SFMF/IVCF Missions Work:	David Adeney, Director.	*Missionary Mandate* speaks out on South Africa and race.
NCF/IVCF Nurses Work:	Tressie Myers, NCF Sec.	Tressie Myers, NCF Sec.
IFES/IVCF Activities Overseas:	Ruth Siemens to Peru; Mary Beaton joins Gwen Wong in Philippines.	Adeney with IFES to Far East; Gwen Wong to SE Asia; Bob Young to South America.
Other Student Organizations (Not IVCF/ IFES)		Fellowship of Christian Athletes begins.
World and U.S. History:	Blacks in Montgomery boycott bus lines; U.S. Air Force academy opens in Colo.; Albert Einstein dies.	Nasser seizes Suez Canal; Soviet troops march into Hungary; D. Eisenhower is re-elected pres. of U.S.; Martin Luther King leads bus boycott.

YEAR:	1957/58	1958/59
Number of IVCF Chapters/ Groups:	844 (IVCF 451; NCF 306; FMF 87)	829 (IVCF 412; NCF 338; FMF 79)
Total Number of Field Staff:	52	56
Total Support Personnel:	36	42
IVCF National Leadership:	C. Stacey Woods, Gen. Sec.; Chas. Hummel, Nat. Sec.; W. E. C. Petersen, Stewardship Sec.; James McLeish, Comptroller; James Reapsome, Information Sec.; plus Senior Staff Council.	C. Stacey Woods, Gen. Sec.; Chas. Hummel, Nat. Sec.; W. E. C. Petersen, Stewardship Sec.; James McLeish, Comptroller; James Reapsome, Information Sec.; plus Senior Staff Council.
Corporate/ Legal Leadership:	Ken Geiser, Pres. and Chrmn.; Gordon VanWylen, VP; Roscoe Sappenfield, Treas.; plus H. J. Taylor; Ralph Watts.	Ken Geiser, Pres. and Chrmn.; Gordon VanWylen, VP; Roscoe Sappenfield, Treas; plus H. J. Taylor; Ralph Watts; Sam Fuenning; Wallace Erickson.
Total Expense:	$660,000	$663,000
IVCF Headquarters and Training Locations:	1519 N. Astor, Chicago; Campus by the Sea; Bear Trap Ranch; Cedar Campus; Campus-in-the-Woods; Hudson House.	1519 N. Astor, Chicago; Campus by the Sea; Bear Trap Ranch; Cedar Campus; Campus-in-the-Woods; Hudson House.
IVCF National Events:	Urbana '57 C. Hummel, Dir.; 3,486 attend.	*Campus Christian Witness* by Chas. Hummel published.
Administrative Structure and Expansion:	Paul Little heads student work with Billy Graham N.Y.C. Crusade; Ruth Lewis becomes third Black staff worker in South.	Members of Senior Staff Council: Stacey Woods, Joe Bayly, Paul Byer, Eric Fife, Peter Haile, Keith Hunt, Paul Little, Tressie Myers, Jim Nyquist, and W. E. C. Petersen.
IVCF Literature and Media Resources:	Joe Bayly, Lit. Sec. and *HIS* Editor.	Joe Bayly, Lit. Sec. and *HIS* Editor.
SFMF/IVCF Missions Work:	Eric Fife, SFMF Missionary Sec. (as of Jan 1, 1958)	Eric Fife, SFMF Missionary Sec.
NCF/IVCF Nurses Work:	Tressie Myers, NCF Sec.	Tressie Myers, NCF Sec. *The Lamp* retitled *The Nurses Lamp*.
IFES/IVCF Activities Overseas:	Wayne Bragg to Caribbean; Tressie Myers (NCF) visits nurses around the world.	As Regional Director for IFES, David Adeney visits Vietnam.
Other Student Organizations (Not IVCF/ IFES)	Campus Crusade for Christ lists a total field staff of 76.	
World and U.S. History:	First earth satellites from USSR., Sputnik I and II; Rome treaty begins Common Market; Michigan's Big Mac bridge opens; Little Rock riots.	Alaska is 49th State; Gov. Faubus closes Little Rock schools as anti-integration protest; first U.S. satellite launched; stereo recordings come into use.

YEAR:	1959/60	1960/61
Number of IVCF Chapters/ Groups:	831 (IVCF 451; NCF 298, FMF 82)	747 (IVCF 368; NCF 293; FMF 86)
Total Number of Field Staff:	56	60
Total Support Personnel:	45	38
IVCF National Leadership:	C. Stacey Woods, Gen. Sec.; Chas. Hummel, Nat. Sec.; W. E. C. Petersen, Stewardship Sec.; James McLeish, Comptroller; James Reapsome, Information Sec.; plus Senior Staff Council.	Chas. Hummel, Interim Gen. Director; Paul Little, Interim Field Dir.; W. E. C. Petersen, Stewardship Sec.; Jim McLeish, Comptroller; CSW, Gen. Sec., Emeritus; Jim Reapsome, Public Relations; plus Senior Staff Council.
Corporate/ Legal Leadership:	Gordon VanWylen, Pres.; Ken Gieser, VP; Stan Block, Treas; plus exec: H. J. Taylor; Ralph Watts; Wallace Erickson; Sam Fuenning	Gordon VanWylen, Pres; Ralph Watts, VP; Stan Block, Treas.; Wallace Erickson, Sec.; plus H. J. Taylor; Sam Fuenning.
Total Expense:	$728,000	$717,000
IVCF Headquarters and Training Locations:	1519 N. Astor, Chicago; Campus by the Sea; Bear Trap Ranch; Cedar Campus; Campus-in-the-Woods; Hudson House.	1519 N. Astor, Chicago; Campus by the Sea; Bear Trap Ranch; Cedar Campus; Campus-in-the-Woods; Hudson House.
IVCF National Events:	Joe Bayly resigns Jan. '60.	C. Stacey Woods full-time in IFES; moves to Philadelphia.
Administrative Structure and Expansion:	Stacey Woods resigns as Gen. Sec. to give full time to IFES; Board designates him General Secretary Emeritus; *HIS* editoral office moves from Philadelphia to Chicago.	Senior Staff Council: Chas. Hummel; Paul Byer; Geo. Ensworth; Eric Fife; Peter Haile; Burton Harding; Keith Hunt; Paul Little; James McLeish; Tressie Myers; James Nyquist; James Reapsome.
IVCF Literature and Media Resources:	Betty Leake, Publ. Sec.; Joe Bayly, *HIS* Editor.	Betty Leake, Mgr., IV Press; Paul Fromer, *HIS* Editor.
SFMF/IVCF Missions Work:	Eric Fife, SFMF Missionary Sec.	Eric Fife, SFMF Missionary Director.
NCF/IVCF Nurses Work:	Tressie Myers, NCF Sec.	Tressie Myers, NCF Director.
IFES/IVCF Activities Overseas:	CSW Latin America trip. John White to Latin America; Gwen Wong to Korea.	Al Fairbanks to Africa.
World and U.S. History:	Fidel Castro takes over Cuba; Hawaii is 50th State; DeGaulle is pres. of France; first U.S. nuclear-powered merchant vessel.	John Kennedy elected pres. of U.S. over Nixon; U-2 plane shot down by USSR; lunch counter sit-ins at Greensboro; U.S. TV sets total 85 million.

YEAR:	1961/62	1962/63
Number of IVCF Chapters/ Groups:	722 (IVCF 398; NCF 237; FMF 87)	749 (IVCF 414; NCF 248; FMF 87)
Total Number of Field Staff:	56	58
Total Support Personnel:	49	50
IVCF National Leadership:	Chas. Troutman, Jr., Gen. Dir.; Chas. Hummel, Field Dir; Paul Little, International Students; W. E. C. Petersen, Stewardship Sec.; Jim McLeish, Comptroller; plus Staff Council.	Chas. Troutman, Jr. Gen. Dir.; Chas. Hummel, Field Dir; Paul Little, International Students; W. E. C. Petersen, Stewardship Sec.; Jim McLeish, Comptroller; plus Staff Council.
Corporate/ Legal Leadership:	Gordon VanWylen, Pres.; Ralph Watts, VP; Stan Block, Treas.; Wallace Erickson, Sec.	Wallace Erickson, Pres; Gordon VanWylen, VP; Sam Fuenning, Sec.; Stan Block, Treas.; plus John W. Alexander, Allen Mathis, Jr. and Ralph Watts.
Total Expense:	$873,000	$648,000
IVCF Headquarters and Training Locations:	1519 N. Astor, Chicago; Campus by the Sea, Bear Trap Ranch, Cedar Campus, Hudson House; (Campus-in-the-Woods over to Canada).	1519 N. Astor, Chicago; Campus by the Sea, Bear Trap Ranch, Cedar Campus, Hudson House.
IVCF National Events:	Urbana '61 (6th IVCF Missionary Conference), Eric Fife, Dir.; 5,027 attend.	
Administrative Structure and Expansion:	Membership Senior Staff Council: C. Troutman, C. Hummel, P. Byer, G. Ensworth, E. Fife, P. Haile; B. Harding, K. Hunt, P. Little, J. McLeish, Tressie Myers, J. Reapsome, J. Nyquist. Ft. Lauderdale Evangelism Project instituted by Paul Little.	Membership Senior Staff Council: C. Troutman; C. Hummel; P. Byer; G. Ensworth; E. Fife; P. Haile; B. Harding; K. Hunt; P. Little; J. McLeish; Tressie Myers; J. Nyquist; W. Hutchinson.
IVCF Literature and Media Resources:	Paul Fromer, HIS Editor; Elizabeth Leake, IVP Mgr.	Paul Fromer, HIS Editor; Elizabeth Leake, IVP Mgr.
SFMF/IVCF Missions Work:	Eric Fife, SFMF Missionary Director.	Eric Fife, SFMF Missionary Director.
NCF/IVCF Nurses Work:	Tressie Myers, NCF Director.	Tressie Myers, NCF Director.
IFES/IVCF Activities Overseas:	Summer Training Abroad with Bob Baylis.	IFES Gen. Sec. Stacey Woods leaves U.S.A. for Switzerland 7/5; Mel Friesen appointed North America IFES Representative.
World and U.S. History:	Bay of Pigs invasion of Cuba fails; President Kennedy establishes Peace Corps; Shepherd makes first U.S. space flight; "Freedom Riders" attacked in Birmingham, Ala.	USSR installs missile base in Cuba; Kennedy blockades until removal, then blockade lifted; start of N.Y.C. paper strike; U. Thant elected United Nations Secretary-General.

YEAR:	1963/64	1964/65
Number of IVCF Chapters/ Groups:		772 (w/ 9,053 students) (IVCF 415; NCF 264; FMF 93)
Total Number of Field Staff:	52	68
Total Support Personnel:	42	42 (est)
IVCF National Leadership:	Chas. Troutman, Gen. Dir.; Jim Nyquist, Adm Asst; Chas. Hummel, Faculty Dir.; Keith Hunt, Devel. Dir; Paul Little, Evangelism; Jim McLeish, Comptroller; plus Staff Advisory Council (See [1] below).	Chas. Troutman, Gen. Dir. to Jan '65; then J. W. Alexander, Gen. Dir.; J. Nyquist, Adm. Asst. and IVP Dir.; K. Hunt, Devel. Dir; P. Little, Evangelism; J. McLeish, Comptroller; plus Staff Advisory Council (See [2] below).
Corporate/ Legal Leadership:	Wallace Erickson, Pres.; Gordon VanWylen, VP; Sam Fuenning, Sec.; Stan Block, Treas.; plus John Alexander, Allen Mathis, Jr., and Ralph Watts.	Wallace Erickson, Pres.; Stan Block, VP; Sam Fuenning, Sec.; John Alexander, Treas.
Total Expense:	$851,000	$1,137,000
IVCF Headquarters and Training Locations:	1519 N. Astor, Chicago; Campus by the Sea, Bear Trap Ranch, Cedar Campus, Hudson House.	1519 N. Astor, Chicago; Campus by the Sea, Bear Trap Ranch, Cedar Campus, Hudson House.
IVCF National Events:	Depts. of Evangelism and Int'l. Students eliminated; appointment of Paul Little as Evangelist; Keith Hunt as Dir. of Development; Jim Nyquist as Adm. Asst.	Urbana '64; Eric Fife, Dir.; 6,264 attend; Bible and Life begun by Barbara Boyd; Chas. Troutman resigns 5/31/65, goes with Latin American Mission to Costa Rica; World's Fair Evangelism Project at N.Y.C.
Administrative Structure and Expansion:	Senior Staff Council name changed to to Staff Advisory Committee (SAC); Add March '64: Richard Wolff, Exec. Dir.; Burt Roberts, Ofc. Mgr.; See [1] below for listing of SAC.	Billy Graham at U. of Mich.; Burt Harding leads Ft. Lauderdale Evangelism Project. Nov '64, departure of Richard Wolff and Burt Roberts; See [2] below for listing of SAC.
IVCF Literature and Media Resources:	Paul Fromer, *HIS* Editor; Elizabeth Leake, IVP Mgr.	Paul Fromer, *HIS* Editor; James Nyquist, IVP Dir.
SFMF/IVCF Missions Work:	Eric Fife, SFMF Missionary Director.	Eric Fife, SFMF Missionary Director.
NCF/IVCF Nurses Work:	Tressie Myers, NCF Director.	Tressie Myers, NCF Director.
World and U.S. History:	Riots, beatings in Birmingham, Ala.; arrest of Martin Luther King; 200,000 "Freedom Marchers" go to D.C.; Kennedy assassinated in Dallas 11/22; C. S. Lewis and A. Huxley die same date.	World's Fair in N.Y.C.; 24th Amendment abolishes poll tax; U.S. ship attacked in Vietnam; war escalates; Lyndon B. Johnson elected U.S. president and signs Civil Rights Act.
	[1] SAC: C. Troutman, P. Byer, E. Fife, P. Fromer, B. Harding, C. Hummel, K. Hunt, W. Hutchinson, B. Leake, P. Little, J. McLeish, T. Myers, J. Nyquist.	[2] SAC: J. Alexander P. Byer, E. Fife, P. Fromer, B. Harding, C. Hummel, K. Hunt, W. Hutchinson, B. Leake, P. Little, J. McLeish, T. Myers, J. Nyquist.

YEAR:	1965/66	1966/67
Number of IVCF Chapters/ Groups:		
Total Number of Field Staff:	76	74
Total Support Personnel:	42	52
IVCF National Leadership:	John W. Alexander, Gen. Dir.; Jim Nyquist, Adm. Asst.; Keith Hunt, Dev. Dir.; James McLeish, Comptroller; Paul Little, Evangelism; plus Staff Advisory Council.	John W. Alexander, Gen. Dir.; Peter Northrup, Field Asst.; James McLeish, Comptroller; Herb Criley, Ofc. Mgr.; Paul Little, Evangelism; plus NSD.
Corporate/ Legal Leadership:	Roy Horsey, Pres.; Gordon VanWylen, VP; Sam Fuenning, Sec.; Wil Norton, Treas.; Virginia Ohlson, Richard Castor, Wallace Erickson.	Roy Horsey, Pres.; Gordon VanWylen, VP; Sam Fuenning, Sec.; Wil Norton, Treas.; Virginia Ohlson, Richard Castor, Wallace Erickson.
Total Expense:	$1,366,000	$1,288,000
IVCF Headquarters and Training Locations:	130 N. Wells, Chicago; Cedar Campus; Campus by the Sea; Bear Trap Ranch; Hudson House.	130 N. Wells, Chicago; Cedar Campus; Campus by the Sea; Bear Trap Ranch; Hudson House.
IVCF National Events:	National IVCF Staff Conference held at Miami, Fla., Dec. 6-14; Staff Advisory Committee (SAC) changed to National Staff Directors (NSD).	Regional Director position eliminated; NSD changed to Staff Directors (SD).
Administrative Structure and Expansion:	*First Steps to God* by Harding; Proposed that new staff come to IVCF with 100% support; Chas. Hummel resigns, becoming president of Barrington College; Warner Hutchinson resigns.	Objectives/Goals/Standards materials circulated to Staff Directors; Keith Hunt returns to field as Mich. Area Director; Burt Harding resigns.
IVCF Literature and Media Resources:	Jim Nyquist, IVP Director; Paul Fromer, *HIS* Editor.	Jim Nyquist, IVP Director; Paul Fromer, *HIS* Editor. IVP to Downers Grove, Ill.
SFMF/IVCF Missions Work:	Eric Fife, Missions Director.	Eric Fife, Missions Director.
NCF/IVCF Nurses Work:	Tressie Myers, NCF Director; Grace Wallace, Asst. Dir.	Tressie Myers, NCF Director; Grace Wallace, Asst. Dir.
World and U.S. History:	Electric power blackout in NE U.S.; tornados strike Midwest; race riots in Selma, Ala. and Watts, Calif.; students demonstrate against Vietnam war.	DeGaulle is pres. of France; Mrs. Gandhi, prime minister in India; Red Guard (China) demonstrate; Days of Protest against U.S. Vietnam policy; Medicare starts.

YEAR:	1967/68	1968/69
Number of IVCF Chapters/ Groups:		
Total Number of Field Staff:	71	71
Total Support Personnel:	44	73
IVCF National Leadership:	John W. Alexander, Gen. Dir.; Peter Northrup, Field Asst.; James McLeish, Comptroller; Herb Criley, Ofc. Mgr.; Paul Little, Evangelism; plus SD.	John W. Alexander, Pres.; Jim McLeish, VP/Dev. and Comptroller; Peter Northrup, Asst. to Pres.; Paul Little, Asst. to Pres.; plus SD.
Corporate/ Legal Leadership:	Roy Horsey, Pres.; Gordon VanWylen, VP; Sam Fuenning, Sec.; Wil Norton, Treas.; Virginia Ohlson, Richard Castor, Wallace Erickson.	Roy Horsey, Chrmn., Sam Fuenning, Sec.; Don Powell, Treas.; Dick Castor, Virginia Ohlson, Stan Block.
Total Expense:	$1,474,000	$1,790,000
IVCF Headquarters and Training Locations:	130 N. Wells, Chicago; Cedar Campus; Campus by the Sea; Bear Trap Ranch; Hudson House.	130 N. Wells, Chicago; Cedar Campus; Campus by the Sea; Bear Trap Ranch; Hudson House.
IVCF National Events:	Regional Director position reinstalled; Urbana '67, Eric Fife, Dir.; Paul Little, Asst. Dir.; 9,200 attend; National Handbook Camp held at Cedar Campus.	National Leadership Insitiute (NLI) held at Cedar Campus 8/3-24; Last listing of staff in *HIS* Magazine.
Administrative Structure and Expansion:	Ft. Lauderdale Evangelistic Project with Pete Hammond; Jim McLeish pushes for Local Committees. Paul Little goes to Trinity Evangelical Divinity School to teach.	A committee begins the Ann Arbor, Mich. Logos Bookstore with Jim Carlson and Jim Wilson; Black campus work with Paul Gibson and Neil Rendall.
IVCF Literature and Media Resources:	Jim Nyquist, IVP Director; Paul Fromer, *HIS* Editor.	Jim Nyquist, IVP Director; Paul Fromer, *HIS* Editor.
SFMF/IVCF Missions Work:	Eric Fife, Missions Director.	David Howard, Dir. of Missions.
NCF/IVCF Nurses Work:	Tressie Myers, NCF Director; Grace Wallace, Asst. Dir.	Grace Wallace, NCF Director.
World and U.S. History:	Six Day War between Israel and Arabs; Vietnam protests continue; race riots in Cleveland, Newark, and Detroit; Expo '67 opens in Montreal.	Martin Luther King assassinated; also Robert Kennedy; riots at Chicago Democratic Convention; Nixon elected over Hubert Humphrey as president of U.S.

YEAR:	1969/70	1970/71
Number of IVCF Chapters/ Groups:	400 (7,822 students) (IVCF 400; NCF ?; FMF ?)	689 (10,713 students) (IVCF 394; NCF 164; FMF 131)
Total Number of Field Staff:	88	95
Total Support Personnel:	138	137
IVCF National Leadership:	John W. Alexander, President; Peter Northrup, Asst. to Pres.; Jim McLeish, VP Finance; plus RDs: Jim Berney, Harold Burkhart, Keith Hunt plus NCF, IVM as Staff Directors (SD).	John W. Alexander, President; Peter Northrup, Asst. to Pres.; Jim McLeish, VP Finance; plus RDs: Jim Berney, Harold Burkhart, Keith Hunt plus NCF, IVM as Staff Directors (SD).
Corporate/ Legal Leadership:	Don Powell, Chrmn.; Roy Horsey, Vice-Chrmn.; Joe Bayly, Sec.; David Scott, Treas.; plus Sam Fuenning, Virginia Ohlson, Gordon VanWylen.	Don Powell, Chrmn.; Roy Horsey, Vice-Chrmn.; Joe Bayly, Sec.; David Scott, Treas.; plus Sam Fuenning, Virginia Ohlson, Melvin Kalb.
Total Expense:	$2,211,000	$2,548,000
IVCF Headquarters and Training Locations:	Carroll Hall, Madison, Wis.; Bear Trap Ranch, Cedar Campus, Campus by the Sea.	233 Langdon, Madison, Wis.; Bear Trap Ranch, Cedar Campus, Campus by the Sea; School of Discipleship Training (SDT) begun at Cedar Campus.
IVCF National Events:	IVCF Headquarters moves to Madison, Wis.	Urbana '70, Paul Little, Dir.; David Howard, Asst. Dir.; 12,300 attend.
Administrative Structure and Expansion:	2100 Productions start in Pasadena, Calif. with Eric Miller.	Staff expected to raise 25% of support.
IVCF Literature and Media Resources:	Jim Nyquist, IVP Director; Paul Fromer, *HIS* Editor.	Jim Nyquist, IVP Director; Paul Fromer, *HIS* Editor; (*HIS* size increased to 8½″ X 11″).
SFMF/IVCF Missions Work:	David Howard, Director of Missions.	David Howard, Director of Missions.
NCF/IVCF Nurses Work:	Grace Wallace, NCF Director.	Grace Wallace, NCF Director.
IFES/IVCF Activities Overseas:	IFES North America Representative: Bill Sisterson; Overseas Training Camp (OTC) held in Costa Rica.	NCF-USA joins NCF-International; OTC in Costa Rica.
World and U.S. History:	Vietnam anti-war protests continue; Edward Kennedy in incident at Chappaquiddick; Apollo 10, 11, 12: moon walk by N. Armstrong; death of Eisenhower; students protest at Kent State U. on 5/4/70, four killed.	U.S. troop strength falls in Vietnam to less than 400,000; price of gold on free market falls below $35/oz.

YEAR:	1971/72	1972/73
Number of IVCF Chapters/ Groups:	672 (12,949 students) (IVCF 433; NCF 100; FMF 139)	769 (16,256 students) (IVCF 494; NCF 123; FMF 152)
Total Number of Field Staff:	114	116
Total Support Personnel:	139	142
IVCF National Leadership:	John W. Alexander, President; Peter Northrup, Asst. to Pres. Jim McLeish, VP Finance; plus RDs: Jim Berney, Harold Burkhart, Keith Hunt, Ned Hale, David Howard and Grace Wallace as Cabinet.	John W. Alexander, President; Peter Northrup, Asst. to Pres. Jim McLeish, VP Finance; plus RDs: Keith Hunt (Eastern), Ned Hale (Central), Jim Berney (Western), Grace Wallace (Nurses), David Howard (Missions).
Corporate/ Legal Leadership:	Don Powell, Chrmn.; Sam Fuenning, Vice-Chrmn.; Joe Bayly, Sec.; David Scott, Treas.; plus Roy Blackwood, Melvin Kalb, Robah Kellogg.	Don Powell, Chrmn.; Chet Youngberg, Vice-Chrmn.; Joe Bayly, Sec.; Herb Luxon, Treas.; plus Allen Mathis, Robah Kellogg, Roy Blackwood.
Total Expense:	$2,929,000	$3,413,000
IVCF Headquarters and Training Locations:	233 Langdon, Madison, Wis.; Bear Trap Ranch, Cedar Campus, Campus by the Sea.	233 Langdon, Madison, Wis.; Bear Trap Ranch, Cedar Campus, Campus by the Sea.
IVCF National Events:	David Sironi moves IVCF toward computers.	First Local Committee Conference at Bear Trap Ranch.
Administrative Structure and Expansion:	Students In Missions Program (SIMP) initiated in Mich. by Keith Hunt and Richard Crespo; Logos bookstore concept spreads; 2100 goes national.	NCF continues Love That Heals and Persons In Crisis Seminars; SIMP renamed Students Training in Missions (STIM).
IVCF Literature and Media Resources:	Jim Nyquist, IVP Director; Steve Board, *HIS* Editor;. Eric Miller, 2100 Director.	Jim Nyquist, IVP Director; Steve Board, *HIS* Editor; Eric Miller, 2100 Director.
SFMF/IVCF Missions Work:	David Howard, Director of Missions.	David Howard, Director of Missions.
NCF/IVCF Nurses Work:	Grace Wallace, NCF Director. Persons In Crisis Workshop begun; also Love That Heals.	Grace Wallace, NCF Director.
IFES/IVCF Activities Overseas:	OTC in Costa Rica.	Stacey Woods retires from IFES, Chua Wee Hian appointed General Secetary of IFES; OTC in Guatemala.
World and U.S. History:	26th Amendment to U.S. Constitution permits vote for 18 year olds; Jesus Movement is much publicized; 10,000 die in Bengal in cyclone and tidal wave; Manson guilty of Tate murder.	Nixon reelected pres. in landslide; space shots of Apollo 16, 17; Watergate Affair; Gov. Wallace (Ala.) shot, partially paralyzed.

YEAR:	1973/74	1974/75
Number of IVCF Chapters/ Groups:	882 (20,301 students) (IVCF 544; NCF 181;FMF 157)	797 (22,578 students) (IVCF 510; NCF 185; FMF 102)
Total Number of Field Staff:	135	152
Total Support Personnel:	153	176
IVCF National Leadership:	John W. Alexander, Pres.; Jim McLeish, VP, Finance; Peter Northrup, Asst. to Pres; Grace Wallace, NCF; David Howard, Missions; plus RD's: Jim Berney, Keith Hunt, Ned Hale, Pete Hammond; as Cabinet.	John W. Alexander, Pres.; Jim McLeish, VP Finance; Peter Northrup, Asst. to Pres; Keith Hunt, Dir. of Specialized Training; Grace Wallace, NCF; David Howard, Missions; Plus RD's: Jim Berney, Ned Hale, Pete Hammond as Cabinet.
Corporate/ Legal Leadership:	Don Powell, Chrmn.; Chet Youngberg, VC; Joe Bayly, Sec.; Herb Luxon, Treas.; plus Roy Blackwood, Robah Kellogg, Allen Mathis.	Chet Youngberg, Chrmn.; Allen Mathis, VC; Joe Bayly, Sec.; Herb Luxon, Treas.; plus Roy Blackwood, Robah Kellogg, James Reapsome.
Total Expense:	$5,552,000	$5,802,000
IVCF Headquarters and Training Locations:	233 Langdon St., Madison, Wis.; Campus by the Sea; Bear Trap Ranch; Cedar Campus; Hudson House.	233 Langdon St., Madison, Wis.; Campus by the Sea; Bear Trap Ranch; Cedar Campus; Hudson House.
IVCF National Events:	Urbana '73, directed by David Howard; 14,158 attend.	Report by Dr. Ted Ward "Effects of SLT Training."
Administrative Structure and Expansion:	Dept. of Specialized Training formed with Keith Hunt, Director. Minneapolis Logos Bookstore begun under IVP.	Faculty Department formed with Chas. Hummel, Director; Dept. of Specialized Training eliminated in Sept.
IVCF Literature and Media Resources:	Jim Nyquist, Director IVP; Steve Board, Editor *HIS*; Eric Miller, Director 2100.	Jim Nyquist, Director IVP; Steve Board, Editor *HIS*; Eric Miller, Director 2100.
SFMF/IVCF Missions Work:	David Howard, Director of Missions.	David Howard, Director of Missions.
NCF/IVCF Nurses Work:	Grace Wallace, NCF Director.	Grace Wallace, NCF Director; Marian Hall, Asst. Dir. NCF.
IFES/IVCF Activities Overseas:	OTC in Guatemala.	OTC in Guatemala.
Other Student Organizations (Not IVCF/ IFES)		Keith Hunt directs Schloss Mittersill (part time).
World and U.S. History:	Watergate hearings; U.S. VP Spiro Agnew resigns, replaced by Gerald Ford; Arab oil embargo leads to energy crisis; abortion legalized; successive cease-fire accords broken in Vietnam.	Worldwide inflation fuels cost-of-living increase; fad of "streaking"; on 8/9 Nixon resigns, Ford made President; world population is 3.782 billion.

YEAR:	1975/76	1976/77
Number of IVCF Chapters/ Groups:	760 (24,798 students) (IVCF 532; NCF 142; FMF 86)	620 (26,248 students) (IVCF 620; NCF ?; FMF ?)
Total Number of Field Staff:	182	195
Total Support Personnel:	145	187
IVCF National Leadership:	John W. Alexander, Pres.; Jim McLeish, VP; Peter Northrup, and Keith Hunt, Asst. to Pres.; Grace Wallace, NCF; David Howard, Missions; plus RDs: Jim Berney, Pete Hammond, Ned Hale, Terry Morrison, Bob Fryling; as Cabinet.	John W. Alexander, Pres.; Jim McLeish, VP; Peter Northrup, VP; Keith Hunt, Asst. to Pres.; Grace Wallace, NCF; David Howard, Missions; plus RDs: Jim Berney, Ned Hale, Terry Morrison, Pete Hammond, Bob Fryling, as Cabinet.
Corporate/ Legal Leadership:	Chet Youngberg, Chrmn.; Allen Mathis, VC; Joe Bayly, Sec.; Herb Luxon, Treas.; plus Roy Blackwood, Robah Kellogg, James Reapsome.	Chet Youngberg, Chrmn.; Allen Mathis, VC; Roy Blackwood, Sec.; Herb Luxon, Treas.; plus Ken Nielsen, Virginia Ohlson, James Reapsome; and John W. Alexander, Pres.
Total Expense:	$7,093,000	$8,956,000
IVCF Headquarters and Training Locations:	233 Langdon St, Madison, Wis. expanded to Women's Building; Campus by the Sea; Bear Trap Ranch; Cedar Campus; Hudson House.	233 Langdon St, Madison, Wis, plus Women's Bldg; Campus by the Sea; Bear Trap Ranch; Cedar Campus; Hudson House.
IVCF National Events:	John W. Alexander on 3 month study leave; Paul Little dies 7/9/75 in accident.	Urbana '76 directed by David Howard; 17,112 attend.
Administrative Structure and Expansion:	Black Staff Fellowship begun. 2100 moves to Madison.	Theological Students Fellowship, M. Branson; Discipleship Training Center at Hudson House, Norton Sterrett, Dir.
IVCF Literature and Media Resources:	Jim Nyquist, Director IVP; Steve Board, Editor *HIS*; Eric Miller, Director 2100. Logos Service Center sold to Jim Carlson.	Jim Nyquist, Dir. IVP; Linda Doll, Editor *HIS*; Eric Miller, Dir. 2100.
SFMF/IVCF Missions Work:	David Howard, Director of Missions.	Reuben Brooks, Dir. of Missions; David Howard, Asst. to Pres.; STIM moved from Mich. to Madison, Wis.
NCF/IVCF Nurses Work:	Grace Wallace, NCF Director; Marian Hall, Asst. Dir. NCF.	Grace Wallace, NCF Director; Marian Hall, Asst. Dir. NCF.
IFES/IVCF Activities Overseas:	OTC in Guatemala; Ruth Lichtenberger becomes Gen. Dir. of NCFI.	OTC in Guatemala; Grace Wallace becomes Pres. of NCFI.
Other Student Organizations (Not IVCF/ IFES)	Keith Hunt directs Schloss Mittersill (part time) with Mel Friesen (full time) Resident Mgr.	
World and U.S. History:	U.S. ends involvement in the Vietnam war; disappearance of James Hoffa; Patricia Hearst caught by FBI; heavy fighting in Beirut; sentencing in the Watergate cover-up.	Jimmy Carter elected pres. of U.S.; celebration of U.S. Bicentennial; North and South Vietnam re-united, with Hanoi as capital.

YEAR:	1977/78	1978/79
Number of IVCF Chapters/ Groups:	640 (24,816 students) (IVCF 640; NCF ?; FMF ?)	664 (26,067 students) (IVCF 664; NCF ?; FMF ?)
Total Number of Field Staff:	215	270
Total Support Personnel:	187	168
IVCF National Leadership:	John W. Alexander, Pres.; Jim McLeish, VP; Peter Northrup, VP; Keith Hunt, Asst. to Pres.; plus RDs: Jim Berney, Ned Hale, Terry Morrison, Pete Hammond, Bob Fryling. "Cabinet" disbanded.	John W. Alexander, Pres.; Jim McLeish, VP; Peter Northrup, VP; Keith Hunt, Asst. to Pres.; plus RDs: Jim Berney, Ned Hale, Terry Morrison, Pete Hammond, Bob Fryling; plus Nyquist, Wallace, Kyle; Above now Senior Management Group (SMG).
Corporate/ Legal Leadership:	Chet Youngberg, Chrmn.; Allen Mathis, VC; Roy Blackwood, Sec.; Herb Luxon, Treas.; John W. Alexander, Pres.; Ken Nielsen, Virginia Ohlson, Duane Barney.	Chet Youngberg, Chrmn.; Allen Mathis, VC; Ken Nielsen, Sec.; Bill Stewart, Treas.; John Alexander, Pres.; Duane Barney.
Total Expense:	$8,501,000	$9,877,000
IVCF Headquarters and Training Locations:	233 Langdon St. Madison, Wis. plus Women's Bldg; Campus by the Sea; Bear Trap Ranch; Cedar Campus; Hudson House.	233 Langdon St. Madison, Wis. plus Women's Bldg; Campus by the Sea; Bear Trap Ranch; Cedar Campus; Hudson House.
IVCF National Events:	Norton Sterrett dies 2/9/78; H. J. Taylor dies 5/1/78; Thom Hopler dies 6/12/78.	Board discusses going to required 100% staff support 11/4/78.
Administrative Structure and Expansion:	"Discipleship Community" at Hudson House with Norton Sterrett, Director, through January.	Dr. Alexander's "house diagram" is widely used; RDs now report to either McLeish or Northrup.
IVCF Literature and Media Resources:	Jim Nyquist, Director IVP; Linda Doll, Editor *HIS*; 2100, Eric Miller, Director.	Jim Nyquist, Director IVP; Linda Doll, Editor *HIS*; 2100, Eric Miller, Director.
SFMF/IVCF Missions Work:	Reuben Brooks, Missions Director, resigns; Peter Northrup fills in; David Howard, Asst. to Pres., seconded to Lausanne Committee.	John Kyle, Director of Missions.
NCF/IVCF Nurses Work:	Grace Wallace, NCF Director.	Grace Wallace, NCF Director.
IFES/IVCF Activities Overseas:	OTC in Guatemala.	OTC in Guatemala.
Other Student Organizations (Not IVCF/ IFES)		Rudie Matheuszik appointed Schloss Mittersill Director.
World and U.S. History:	President Carter pardons most American draft evaders of Vietnam; pushes human rights; Elvis Presley dies; oil flows through Alaska pipeline.	Senate ratifies new Panama Canal treaties; diplomatic relations restored between U.S. and People's Republic of China; Israeli Begin and Egyptian Sadat meet at Camp David, hosted by President Carter; Bakke case upheld.

YEAR:	1979/80	1980/81
Number of IVCF Chapters/ Groups:	658 (27,317 students) (IVCF 658; NCF ?; FMF ?)	629 (28,559 students) (IVCF 629; NCF ?; FMF ?)
Total Number of Field Staff:	324	340
Total Support Personnel:	186	208
IVCF National Leadership:	John W. Alexander, Pres.; Jim McLeish, VP; Peter Northrup, VP; Jim Nyquist, IVP; John Kyle, Missions; Grace Wallace, NCF; plus RDs: Jim Berney, Ned Hale, Terry Morrison, Ed Good, Bob Fryling: as Senior Management Group (SMG).	John W. Alexander, Pres; Jim McLeish, Sr. VP and COO; Peter Northrup, VP; Jim Nyquist; John Kyle; Grace Wallace; plus RDs: Jim Berney, Ned Hale, Terry Morrison, Ed Good, Bob Fryling; as SMG.
Corporate/ Legal Leadership:	Allen Mathis, Chrmn.; Ken Nielsen, VC; Rose Pinneo, Sec.; Bill Stewart, Treas.; John W. Alexander, Pres., plus Duane Barney, Dick Hart, Ruth Stoll.	Allen Mathis, Chrmn.; Ken Nielsen, VC; Rose Pinneo, Sec.; Bill Stewart, Treas.; John W. Alexander, Pres.; Don Powell, Dick Hart, Chet Youngberg.
Total Expense:	$14,771,000	$15,316,000
IVCF Headquarters and Training Locations:	233 Langdon St. Madison, Wis. plus Women's Bldg; Campus by the Sea; Bear Trap Ranch; Cedar Campus; Hudson House.	233 Langdon St. Madison, Wis. plus Women's Bldg; Campus by the Sea; Bear Trap Ranch; Cedar Campus; Hudson House.
IVCF National Events:	Urbana '79, directed by John Alexander; 16,624 attend.	Washington '80 directed by Pete Hammond; 1,100 attend.
Administrative Structure and Expansion:	Urbana Onward attended by 3,500 students; Theological Student Fellowship (TSF) reactivated.	
IVCF Literature and Media Resources:	Jim Nyquist, Director IVP; Linda Doll, Editor *HIS*; 2100, Eric Miller, Director; plus Barbara Boyd, Director, Bible and Life.	Jim Nyquist, Director IVP; Linda Doll, Editor *HIS*; 2100, Eric Miller, Director; plus Barbara Boyd, Director, Bible and Life.
SFMF/IVCF Missions Work:	John Kyle, Director of Missions.	John Kyle, Director of Missions.
NCF/IVCF Nurses Work:	Grace Wallace, NCF Director.	Grace Wallace, NCF Director.
IFES/IVCF Activities Overseas:	OTC in Honduras; increasing numbers of IVCF staff seconded to IFES: Hank Pott, Dave Ivaska, Jim Stamoolis, etc.	OTC in Honduras.
Other Student Organizations (Not IVCF/ IFES)		
World and U.S. History:	Three Mile Island nuclear crisis; world population at 4.5 billion; Shah of Iran overthrown by Khomeini and Islamic fanatics; Chinese troops invade Vietnam; Israel and Egypt sign peace treaty; Mount St. Helens erupts on 5/18/80.	U.S. Supreme Court decision: universities are not to discriminate against religious groups; Ronald Reagan elected pres.; USSR invasion of Afghanistan condemned by UN; Islamic militants hold U.S. embassy staff hostage; price of gold exceeds $800/oz.

YEAR:	1981/82	1982/83
Number of IVCF Chapters/ Groups:	859 (32,126 students) (IVCF 728; NCF 111; FMF: ?)	875 (29,371 students) (IVCF 680; NCF 115; FMF 80)
Total Number of Field Staff:	388	382
Total Support Personnel:	246	243
IVCF National Leadership:	John Alexander, Pres. to 11/7; then James McLeish. Pres. Peter Northrup, Sr. VP; Bob Fryling, Dir. Campus Minsitries; Jim Nyquist, Dir. of Literature; Grace Wallace, NCF; Pete Hammond, Evangelism Dir.; Dick Karppinen, Dir. of Finance; John Kyle, Dir. of Missions; as "Alpha Group."	James McLeish, Pres.; plus Alpha Group, as listed in '81/'82.
Corporate/ Legal Leadership:	Allen Mathis, Chrmn.; Roy Blackwood, VC; Rose Pinneo, Sec.; William Stewart, Treas.; James McLeish, Pres.; Don Powell, Ken Nielsen, Chet Youngberg.	Allen Mathis, Chrmn.; Roy Blackwood, VC; Rose Pinneo, Sec.; William Stewart, Treas.; James McLeish, Pres.; Don Powell, Chet Youngberg, Clark Breeding.
Total Expense:	$19,664,000	$18,602,000
IVCF Headquarters and Training Locations:	233 Langdon St., Madison, Wis. plus Women's Bldg. plus Park Street offices; Campus by the Sea; Bear Trap Ranch; Cedar Campus; Hudson House.	233 Langdon St., Madison, Wis. plus Women's Bldg. plus Park Street offices; Campus by the Sea; Bear Trap Ranch; Cedar Campus; Hudson House.
IVCF National Events:	John Alexander directs Nationsl Leadership Institute at Cedar Campus; John Alexander appointed President Emeritus 11/7/81; Urbana '81: JWA directs, 13,714 attend; U-Onward held.	Jim Berney to Gen. Dir., IVCF-Canada; National Leadership Institute at Bear Trap Ranch, Ned Hale, Dir.; death of C. Stacey Woods and Mel Friesen; auto crash kills RD Jim Worden 4/29/83.
Administrative Structure and Expansion:	The national leadership team now called "Alpha Group"; Elward Ellis pioneers Black Campus Ministries (BCM); Ruth Lewis, LaFe; Nina Lau-Branson, Asian-American Ministries Fellowship; Mark Lau-Branson, TSF; Ned Hale, International Student Ministries.	Billy Graham at Chapel Hill, N.C.; in August, IVCF policy implemented that 100% of a new staff support must be raised prior to going on campus.
IVCF Literature and Media Resources:	Jim Nyquist, Dir., Lit. Div.; Linda Doll, Editor HIS; Scott Wilson, Dir., 2100; B. Boyd, Dir., Bible and Life.	Jim Nyquist, Dir., Lit. Div.; Linda Doll, Editor HIS; Scott Wilson, Dir., 2100; B. Boyd, Dir., Bible and Life.
SFMF/IVCF Missions Work:	John Kyle, Missions Dir.; Ned Hale, Assoc. Dir. for SFMF.	John Kyle, Missions Director.
NCF/IVCF Nurses Work:	Grace Wallace, Dir. NCF.	Grace Wallace, Dir. NCF.
IFES/IVCF Activities Overseas:	Eric Miller brings multi-media to IFES; OTC in Honduras.	OTC in Honduras and Dominican Republic; IFES-Link begun by Terry Morrison.
World and U.S. History:	Worldwide terrorism; Anwar Sadat gunned down; assassination attempts on Pope John Paul II and U.S. Pres. Reagan; fifty-two American hostages freed in Iran.	Iran-Iraq war remains deadlocked; Argentina ousted from Falkland Islands by Britain; Equal Rights Amendment is defeated; Polish people support Solidarity.

YEAR:	1983/84	1984/85
Number of IVCF Chapters/ Groups:	919 (27,577 students) (IVCF 734; NCF 93; FMF 92)	753 (24,746 students) (IVCF 689; NCF 64; FMF ?)
Total Number of Field Staff:	384	389
Total Support Personnel:	255	260
IVCF National Leadership:	James McLeish, Pres.; Peter Northrup, Sr. VP; Jim Nyquist, VP; Bob Fryling, Dir. Human Resources; Bill Tiffan, Dir. Campus Ministries; John Kyle; Grace Wallace; Pete Hammond; Ron Nicholas, Dir. of Planning, as the National Leadership Team.	James McLeish, Pres.; Peter Northrup, Sr. VP; Jim Nyquist, VP Adm.; Bob Fryling, Natl. Field Adm.; Barney Ford; Roger Anderson; Barry McLeish; John Kyle; Pete Hammond; Linda Doll; Ron Nicholas; as the National Leadership Team, until Jan. when Gordon MacDonald appointed president and CEO.
Corporate/ Legal Leadership:	Allen Mathis, Chrmn.; Ken Nielson, VC; Rose Pinneo, Sec.; William Stewart, Treas.; James McLeish, Pres.; Don Powell, Erna Goulding, Chet Youngberg.	Allen Mathis, Chrmn.; Ken Nielson, VC; James McLeish, Pres. (Jul.–Jan.); Gordon MacDonald, Pres. (Feb.–Jun.); Yvonne Vinkemulder, Sec.; Dick Karppinen, Treas.
Total Expense:	$20,432,000	$26,087,000
IVCF Headquarters and Training Locations:	233 Langdon St., Madison, Wis. plus Women's Bldg. plus Park Street offices; Campus by the Sea; Bear Trap Ranch; Cedar Campus; Hudson House.	233 Langdon St., Madison, Wis. plus Women's Bldg. plus Park Street offices; Campus by the Sea; Bear Trap Ranch; Cedar Campus. Hudson House sold.
IVCF National Events:	San Francisco '83, 1,300 attend; IVCF Board votes to make Corporation to have same membership as Board.	Urbana '84, John Kyle, Dir., 18,144 attend; National Institute for Staff Education and Training (NISET) begun.
Administrative Structure and Expansion:	Legal Dept. of IVCF opens, Yvonne Vinkemulder, Counsel. Multi-ethnic task force formed with Jeanette Yep as Chair. All campus staff required to have 100% support by 8/31/83.	Peter Northrup resigns 11/1; in Jan '85, Jim McLeish and Jim Nyquist are retired; Gordon MacDonald made pres. and CEO; Peter Northrup returns as consultant to help in relocation of Madison headquarters.
IVCF Literature and Media Resources:	Linda Doll, Dir. IVP; David Neff, Editor *HIS*; Scott Wilson, Dir., 2100; Barbara Boyd, Dir., Bible and Life.	Linda Doll, Dir. IVP; David Neff, Editor *HIS*; Scott Wilson, Dir., 2100; Barbara Boyd, Dir., Bible and Life.
SFMF/IVCF Missions Work:	John Kyle, Missions Director.	John Kyle, Missions Director.
NCF/IVCF Nurses Work:	Grace Wallace, Dir. NCF. *The Journal of Christian Nurses* replaces *The Nurses Lamp.*	Mary Thompson, Dir. NCF.
IFES/IVCF Activities Overseas:	OTC held in the Philippines, Dominican Republic, Hong Kong/China.	OTC held in Africa, Europe, Philippines, Hong Kong/China.
World and U.S. History:	Terrorist blows up U.S. Marine Headquarters at Beirut International Airport; Chicago elects first black mayor; Israeli Prime Minister Begin resigns; U.S. Interior Sec. James Watt resigns.	Ronald Reagan re-elected as pres. of U.S.; U.S. invades Grenada; India's Prime Minister Indira Gandhi shot; Iran-Iraq war continues; ships in Gulf attacked.

YEAR:	1985/86	1986/87
Number of IVCF Chapters/ Groups:	773 (24,802 students) (IVCF 695; NCF 78; FMF ?)	750 (24,682 students) (IVCF 667; NCF 83; FMF ?)
Total Number of Field Staff:	505	503
Total Support Personnel:	259	265
IVCF National Leadership:	Gordon MacDonald, Pres.; Bob Fryling, Dir. Campus Ministries; Barney Ford and Roger Anderson, Assoc. Dirs. Campus Ministries; Ron Nicholas, Peter Northrup, Special Assistants.	Gordon MacDonald, Pres.; Barney Ford, VP and Chief Adm. Officer; Bob Fryling, VP and Dir. of Campus Ministries.
Corporate/ Legal Leadership:	Chet Youngberg, Chrmn.; James Kay, VC; Gordon MacDonald, Pres.; Yvonne Vinkemulder, Sec.; Dick Karppinen, Treas.	James Kay, Chrmn.; Tom Dunkerton, Vice-Chrm; Gordon MacDonald, Pres.; Yvonne Vinkemulder, Sec.; Dick Karppinen, Treas.
Total Expense:	$22,758,000	$25,337,000
IVCF National Service Center and Training Locations:	233 Langdon St, Madison, Wis. plus Women's Bldg and Park St.; Campus by the Sea; Bear Trap Ranch; Cedar Campus.	6400 Schroeder Rd, Madison, Wis.; Campus by the Sea; Bear Trap Ranch; Cedar Campus.
IVCF National Events:	"Headquarters" term replaced by "National Service Center" or NSC.	Marketplace '86; Gordon MacDonald resigns in June '87; Tom Dunkerton appointed pres.
Administrative Structure and Expansion:	Theological Students Fellowship dissolved.	
IVCF Literature and Media Resources:	Linda Doll, Dir. IVP; Verne Becker, Editor *HIS*; Scott Wilson, Dir. 2100; Barbara Boyd, Dir. Bible and Life.	Linda Doll, Dir. IVP; Verne Becker, Editor *HIS*; Scott Wilson, Dir. 2100; Barbara Boyd, Dir. Bible and Life.
SFMF/IVCF Missions Work:	John Kyle, Missions Dir.	John Kyle, Missions Dir.
NCF/IVCF Nurses Work:	Mary Thompson, Dir. NCF.	Mary Thompson, Dir. NCF.
IFES/IVCF Activities Overseas:	OTC expands to Latin America, Middle East, Africa, Malta. Student Training in Missions (STIM) continues.	Peter Northrup moves to IFES London in March '87.
Other Student Organizations (Not IVCF/ IFES)	Schloss Mittersill is re-organized and incorporated.	
World and U.S. History:	Growing international pressure on South Africa for apartheid policy; 2,000 die in gas leak in Bhopal, India; Gorbachev becomes new USSR leader; Challenger explodes at launch killing all seven aboard.	Major nuclear accident at Chernobyl, Russia; Aquino named pres. of Philippines; new tax law passed in U.S.

YEAR:	1987/88	1988/89
Number of IVCF Chapters/ Groups:	776 (23,603 students) (IVCF 624; NCF 70; FMF 82)	740 (23,273 students) (IVCF 571; NCF 69; FMF 100)
Total Number of Field Staff:	474	463
Total Support Personnel:	275	266
IVCF National Leadership:	Tom Dunkerton, Pres.; Barney Ford, Exec. VP; Bob Fryling, Exec. VP; John Kyle, VP and Dir. of Missions.	Steve Hayner, Pres; Barney Ford, VP and CAO; Bob Fryling, VP and Director of Campus Ministries; Sam Barkat, VP Multi-Ethnic Ministries; Robert Peitscher, Chief Development Officer.
Corporate/ Legal Leadership:	James Kay, Chrmn.; Robert Hultstrand, VC; Tom Dunkerton, Pres.; Bob Fryling and Barney Ford, Exec. VPs; Yvonne Vinkemulder, Sec.; Tom Witte, Treas.	James Kay, Chrmn.; Robert Hultstrand, VC; Steve Hayner, Pres.; Bob Fryling and Barney Ford, VPs; Yvonne Vinkemulder, Sec.; Tom Witte, Treas.; Sam Barkat, VP, Multi-Ethnic Min.
Total Expense:	$30,392,000	$26,812,000
IVCF National Service Center and Training Locations:	6400 Schroeder Rd, Madison, Wis.; Campus by the Sea; Bear Trap Ranch; Cedar Campus.	6400 Schroeder Rd, Madison, Wis.; Campus by the Sea; Bear Trap Ranch; Cedar Campus.
IVCF National Events:	Urbana '87, John Kyle, Dir.; 18,702 attended; Kyle resigns from IVCF; Dan Harrison appointed Missions Dir.; Steve Hayner selected as pres.	*Student Leadership Journal* begun, Robt. Kachur, Editor; Graduate Student Dept formed; National Leadership Inst. held at BTR, Bob Fryling, Dir.
Administrative Structure and Expansion:	Sam Barkat appointed Multi-Ethnic Dir.; Sheldon Nix appointed Black Campus Ministries Dir.; Marketplace becomes IVCF Dept., Pete Hammond, Dir.	Multi-Ethnic Ministries Div. formed; South Padre Island (Tex.) Evangelism Project assumes national scope.
IVCF Literature and Media Resources:	Linda Doll, Dir. IVP; Verne Becker, Editor *U*; *HIS* renamed *U*. *U* discontinued and merged with *World Christian*. Scott Wilson, Dir. 2100; Barbara Boyd, Dir. Bible and Life.	Linda Doll, Dir. IVP; Scott Wilson, Dir. 2100; Barbara Boyd, Dir. Bible and Life.
SFMF/IVCF Missions Work:	John Kyle, Missions Dir. through Jan. when Dan Harrison appointed Dir.	Dan Harrison, Missions Dir.
NCF/IVCF Nurses Work:	Mary Thompson, Dir. NCF.	Mary Thompson, Dir. NCF.
IFES/IVCF Activities Overseas:		OTC includes Brazil,China/Hong Kong, India, Liberia, Malta, Middle East, USSR, Kenya; STIM continues.
Other Student Organizations (Not IVCF/ IFES)	Destiny '87, first black "Urbana," planned.	
World and U.S. History:	10/19/87 worst day in history of stock market; Gorbachev's "glasnost" policy brings new era in USSR; sex scandal for Jim Bakker, TV evangelist.	Fourth summit held in Moscow with Gorbachev and Reagan; Iranian aircraft shot down by U.S. ship; George Bush elected pres.; USSR departs Afghanistan; Chinese student protest crushed.

YEAR:	1989/90
Number of IVCF chapters/ groups:	727 (23,273 students) (IVCF 553; NCF 75; FMF 99)
Total Number of Field Staff:	476
Total Support Personnel:	268
IVCF National Leadership:	Steve Hayner, Pres.; Barney Ford, VP and CAO; Bob Fryling, VP and Campus Ministries Director; Sam Barkat, VP Multi-Ethnic Ministries; Dan Harrison, VP Missions; Robert Peitscher, VP Marketing/Communications/Development.
Corporate/ Legal Leadership:	James Kay, Chrmn.; Robert Hultstrand, VC; Steve Hayner, Pres.; Barney Ford, Bob Fryling, Sam Barkat, Dan Harrison, Robert Peitscher, VPs; Yvonne Vinkemulder, Sec.; Tom Witte, Treas.
Total Expense:	$27,070,851
IVCF Headquarters and Training Locations:	6400 Schroeder Rd, Madison, Wis.; Campus by the Sea; Bear Trap Ranch; Cedar Campus.
IVCF National Events:	
IVCF New Ministries	Global Issues Congress planned for Urbana 90. "IV-Overseas" formed to combine IFES-LINK, STIM and OTC, with William McConnell as Dir.
IVCF Literature and Media Resources:	Linda Doll, Dir. IVP (through Mar.); Ken DeRuiter, Dir. IVP (starting Mar.); Scott Wilson, Dir. 2100; R. Kachur, Editor, *Student Leadership Journal*.
SFMF/IVCF Missions Work:	Dan Harrison, Missions Dir.
NCF/IVCF Nurses Work:	Mary Thompson, Dir. NCF.
Multi-Ethnic Ministries Work:	Sam Barkat, Dir.
IFES/IVCF Activities Overseas:	STIM continues; OTC planned for Brazil, Europe, Hong Kong/China, India, Kenya, Liberia, Malta, Middle East, Philippines, USSR, Ghana, Hungary, Nigeria, Poland, South Africa, Tanzania, Vietnam, Yugoslavia.
World and U.S. History:	Chinese leaders deny extent of student protest last June; Hurricane Hugo slams into Caribbean and U.S. SE coast; Gorbachev allows thaw in Europe; Berlin Wall comes down; Eastern Europe en masse rejects Communism; Nicaragua votes out Sandinistas; AIDS continues to spread; war on drugs heats up.

Urbana Statistics

Year	Theme	Directed by	Speakers included:	Song Leader	Attendance
1946	Complete Christ's Commission	Christy Wilson	Harold Ockenga, J.G. Holdcroft, Bakht Singh, Robt. McQuilkin, L. E. Maxwell	Homer Hammontree	575
1948	From Every Campus to Every Country	Norton Sterrett Wes Gustafson, asst.	Frank Houghton, Raymond Edman, Allen Fleece, Frank Torrey, W. Robt. Smith	Homer Hammontree	1,294
1951	By All Means— Proclaim Christ	Wes Gustafson	Eugene Nida, Northcote Deck, Stanley Soltau, W. Robt. Smith	Homer Hammontree	1,646
1954	Changing World—Unchanging Christ	David Adeney	A. W. Tozer, Sam Moffett, Art Glasser, Paul White, Alan Redpath, J. Oswald Sanders, William Nagenda	Homer Hammontree	2,131
1957	One Lord/ One Church/ One World	Charles Hummel	Donald Grey Barnhouse, Billy Graham, Ken Strachan, Masumi Toyotome, Harold Ockenga, Israel Garcia, Eric Fife	Ray McAfee	3,486
1961	Commission/ Conflict/ Commitment	Eric Fife	Larry Love, Subodh Sahu, Billy Graham, Eugene Nida, Arthur Glasser, Clyde Taylor, Festo Kivengere, Paul Lindell, David Adeney, Charles Troutman	Paul Beckwith	5,027
1964	Change/ Witness/ Triumph	Eric Fife	John Stott, Horace Fenton, Ben Wati, P.T. Chandapilla, Warren Webster, Billy Graham, Ruben Lores, C. Stacey Woods	Kerchal Armstrong	6,264
1967	God's Men—From All Nations to All Nations	Eric Fife Paul Little, asst.	John Stott, Michael Griffiths, Stacey Woods, Akira Hatori, George Verwer, David Adeney, David Howard, Francis Steele, Warren Webster	Ray McAfee	9,200
1970	World Evangelism: Why? How? Who?	Paul Little David Howard, asst.	John Stott, Myron Augsburger, Dennis Clark, Tom Skinner, Leighton Ford, C. Peter Wagner, Samuel Escobar, George Taylor, Ted Ward, Warren Webster, Samuel Kamaleson, Byang Kato, Paul Little, John Alexander	Bernie Smith	12,304
1973	Jesus Christ: Lord of the Universe. Hope of the World	David Howard	John Stott, Philip Teng, Samuel Escobar, Gregorio Landero, Elisabeth Leitch, Edmund Clowney, Paul Little, Samuel Moffett, J. Christy Wilson, Bill Thomas, Pius Wakatama, Don Curry, Russell Weatherspoon	Bernie Smith	14,158

Year	Theme	Directed by	Speakers included:	Song Leader	Attendance
1976	Declare His Glory Among the Nations	David Howard	John Stott, Festo Kivengere, Elisabeth Leitch, Isabelo Magalit, Luis Palau, Edmund Clowney, Samuel Kamaleson, Billy Graham, Lemuel Tucker, John Perkins, Helen Roseveare, Eric Frykenberg	Bernie Smith	17,112
1979	That All Nations Might Believe And Obey Jesus Christ	John Alexander	John Stott, Michael Haynes, Luis Palau, Elwyn Davies, Isabelo Magalit, Elisabeth Leitch, Chua Wee Hian, David Adeney, Billy Graham, Gottfried Osei-Mensah, Gregorio Landero, Warren Webster, Ruth Siemens, Ronald Mitchell, John Kyle	Bernie Smith	16,625
1981	Let Every Tongue Confess That Jesus Christ Is Lord	John Alexander John Kyle, asst.	Eric Alexander, Robert Munger, Gordon MacDonald, Eva denHartog, Billy Graham, Helen Roseveare, Samuel Escobar, Becky Pippert, Isabelo Magalit, Marilyn Laszlo, Ed Beach, Simon Ibrahim, David Howard, George McKinney, Chua Wee Hian	Bernie Smith	13,714
1984	Faithful in Christ Jesus	John Kyle	Eric Alexander, George McKinney, Ray Bakke, Joanne Shetler, Luis Palau, Ada Lum, Mariano Di Gangi, Billy Graham, David Bryant, Tokunboh Adeyemo	Bernie Smith	18,144
1987	Should I Not Be Concerned?	John Kyle Dan Harrison, asst.	Ajith Fernando, Billy Graham, Helen Roseveare, Tony Campolo, Floyd McClung, Roberta Hestenes, George Verwer, Harvie Conn, Becky Pippert	Bernie Smith	18,702
1990	Jesus Christ: Lord of the Universe. Hope of the World	Dan Harrison Mary Fisher, asst. Karon Black Morton, asst.	Ajith Fernando, Luis Bush, Philemon Choi, Mary Fisher, Glandion Carney, Paul Tokunaga, Caesar Molebatsi, Joni Eareckson Tada, Isaac Canales, Ada Lum, Peter Kuzmic, George Otis, Keren Everett, Anita Deyneka, Mary Anne Voelkel	"Full Armour" band	19,262

Notes

Chapter 1/A Long Look at Student Witness

[1]Charles H. Troutman, *The Universities and the Christian Faith,* unpublished papers, section I (1981), p. 20.

[2]During the Dark Ages monks at some 1,500 monasteries must be credited with saving Scripture, as well as art and science. These monasteries were the precursors of the modern university. Over the centuries renewal movements among young monks similar to those we recount in this chapter led to the conversion of many. We must take seriously the repetitive role of corruption, a tendency for fires to go out. The history of the church in the Dark Ages is significant but calls for another study.

[3]C. S. Lewis, "The Weight of Glory," *Transposition and Other Addresses* (London: Geoffrey Bles, 1949), p. 30.

[4]Hastings Rashdall, *The Universities in the Middle Ages, Vol. 1* (Oxford: At the Clarendon Press, 1936), pp. 50-59.

[5]John Foxe (1516-1587) wrote down the testimony of martyrs, which has been published as *Foxe's Book of Martyrs.* His work has made a deep impression on English-speaking Christianity.

[6]Rashdall, vol. 3, p. 271.

[7]Ibid., p. 233.

[8]The tradition for such rules for the devotional life of believers may well have come from "the pattern of monastic life set down by Benedict (c. 500) in the Rule for his community at Monte Cassino. In time the Benedictine Rule became the norm throughout western monasticism, and reforms centered on a return to strict observance of the Rule, which was of extraordinary importance throughout the monastic centuries of European Christianity" (*New Dictionary of Theology* [Downers Grove, Ill.: InterVarsity Press, 1988], p. 85). Scougal's rules later became important in the Praying Societies of Scotland and in Methodism. Similar principles were used at Halle in Germany in the *Order of the Grain of Mustard Seed.*

[9]Douglas Johnson (*Contending for the Faith* [London: Inter-Varsity Press, 1979], p. 43) notes that other nicknames were the Godly Company, the Bible Moths, The Enthusiasts and the Methodists.

[10]Although John Wesley was a moral, religious person while at Oxford and later in 1735 as

a missionary in the American colony of Georgia, his own account of his religious pilgrimage cites his Aldergate experience on May 24, 1738, as a turning point in his life. He speaks of his heart "being strangely warmed" as he listened to a reading from the preface to Luther's exposition on Romans and understood salvation by faith alone. Prior to this time he had preached and tried to practice a salvation by works, which left him depressed and powerless.

It was after Aldersgate that he began to preach powerfully, often in the fields because he had been ousted from the church, calling men and women from all stations in life to faith in Jesus Christ. He did not intend to begin a new denomination; it was simply the unavoidable outcome of having the Church of England closed against him, another example of the repetitive role of corruption within organizations.

[11]Nikolaus L. von Zinzendorf (1700-1760) is also the author of the hymn "Jesus, Thy Blood and Righteousness," translated into English by John Wesley.

[12]"Conversions that Count," *HIS* magazine, Inter-Varsity Christian Fellowship, spring issue 1942.

[13]*The Dictionary of National Biography,* vol. 15, p. 756.

[14]Johnson, p. 33.

[15]Among those deeply influenced by Simeon was the Cambridge student Henry Martyn (1781-1812), the well-known missionary to India, who translated the New Testament into Urdu and supervised translations into Persian and Arabic. Interestingly, David Brainerd and Jonathan Edwards also had a profound spiritual impact on Martyn's life.

[16]Johnson, p. 39-40.

[17]Clarence P. Shedd, *Two Centuries of Student Christian Movements* (New York: Association Press, 1934), p. 6.

[18]Shedd, p. 2.

[19]Timothy Dwight was the grandson of Jonathan Edwards. The Edwards family had eleven children and an impressive list of offspring who made significant contributions to early America.

[20]*The Haystack Centennial* (Boston: American Board of Commissioners for Foreign Missions, 1907), p. 216.

[21]Shedd, p. 113.

[22]The contemporary term "evangelical" equals the earlier "conservative" or "Bible-believing Christian" in our usage.

[23]Shedd, pp. xvii-xxi.

Chapter 2/The Rise and Fall of the Student Christian Movement

[1]Douglas Johnson, *Contending for the Faith: A History of the Evangelical Movement in the Universities and Colleges* (Leicester, England: Inter-Varsity Press, 1979), pp. 42-44.

[2]Oliver R. Barclay, *Whatever Happened to the Jesus Lane Lot?* (Leicester, England: Inter-Varsity Press, 1977), p. 2. A more detailed account of the Moody meetings is well worth reading. The Cambridge Seven included C. T. Studd—twenty-three years old and one of the most brilliant all-round members of England's cricket team—William Cassels, Stanley Smith, Dixon Hoste, Montague Beauchamp, Cecil and Arthur Polhill. C. T. Studd later founded the Worldwide Evangelization Crusade. They purposed to set off for China and their dedication and zeal shook the student world. Thirty-one CICCU members offered themselves for missionary work in 1886 and 140 in 1893. Bishop Handley Moule pled with students not to forget entirely the needs of their own country.

[3]Clarence P. Shedd, *Two Centuries of Student Christian Movements,* p. 295.

[4]Robert P. Wilder, *The Student Volunteer Movement: Its Origin and Early History* (New York: The Student Volunteer Movement, 1953), pp. 9-13.

[5]Luther D. Wishard, "The Beginning of the Students' Era in Christian History [unpublished manuscript]" TMs, pp. 99-100, Historical Library of National Council, New York Young Men's Christian Association.

[6]Shedd, p. 247.

[7]Ibid., p. 250.

[8]Ibid., p. 260, quoting letter from John Mott.

[9]Wilder, p. 21.

[10]Ibid., p. 7.

[11]From a manuscript written by David Howard on the occasion of the fiftieth anniversary of Student Foreign Missions Fellowship in 1986.

[12]The International Fellowship of Evangelical Students, officially organized in 1947, is a federation of indigenous evangelical student movements around the world.

[13]Charles H. Troutman, *The Universities and the Christian Faith,* unpublished papers, section 4 (1981), p. 8.

[14]Wilder, p. 42.

[15]Risto Lehtonen, *The Story of a Storm: An Ecumenical Case Study* (WSCF, 1972), p. 5.

[16]Shedd, p. 287.

[17]*Apologetics:* concerned with the defense of Christian doctrine.

[18]One who stood for the *fundamentals* was called a fundamentalist. Inter-Varsity identified itself as fundamentalist.

[19]Shedd, p. 422.

[20]Looking back at this tendency of mature staff to lose sight of what students really need, C. Stacey Woods, first general secretary of the American IVCF, sought to avoid this problem by adopting a policy of short-term staff who had proven their mettle during their student days and who had not forgotten what it was like to be a freshman. In the early days of Inter-Varsity most of the staff were single and only the exceptional campus staff member stayed more than a three-year term.

[21]Shedd, p. 399.

[22]Ibid., p. 419.

[23]C. Howard Hopkins, *John R. Mott: A Biography* (Grand Rapids, Mich.: Eerdmans, 1979), p. 567.

[24]Cindy Smith and Joe Cumming, *Rebuilding the Mission Movement* (National Student Coalition, 1982), p. 487.

[25]Tissington Tatlow, *The Story of the Student Christian Movement* (London: SCM Press, 1933), p. 272.

[26]*The Christian Century,* January 7, 1976, pp.19-20.

[27]Howard Nemerov, *War Stories,* quoted by Melvin Maddocks in *World Monitor,* December 1989, p. 17.

Chapter 3/The Resurgence of Evangelical Student Witness

[1]Douglas Johnson, *Contending for the Faith: A History of the Evangelical Movement in the Universities and Colleges* (Leicester, England: Inter-Varsity Press, 1979), p. 216.

[2]C. S. Lewis, *The Screwtape Letters* (New York: Macmillan, 1961), p. 56, description of the road to hell.

[3]Johnson, p. 92.

[4]Ibid., p. 97.

[5]Ibid., p. 98.

[6]Interview with Douglas Johnson, October 25, 1986.

[7]Ibid.

[8]Brochure of the League of Evangelical Students, circa 1940.

[9]"In some places attempts to reach students locally met with some success, but there was no thought of a national fellowship of students. The Plymouth Brethren had monthly Saturday Night Rallies in many cities, often with over a thousand in attendance. Youth for Christ eventually took over these rallies, but by 1940 there were few college students attending.

"In 1919 R. A. Torrey became the president of the Bible Institute of Los Angeles and set in motion a number of networks within the Presbyterian churches on the west coast to reach students. Torrey had been the missioner at CICCU in 1910 just after CICCU broke from the SCM and he had never forgotten the vitality of that group. From his efforts the Hollywood Presbyterian Church student department formed The Fellowship of the Burning Heart for students. (Richard Halverson, Bill Bright and Eugene Nida were some of its members.)

"Later that same church established Christian fraternities at UCLA which were effective until they became ingrown. Through Torrey's influence a student house (Horton Hall) was founded on Berkeley's campus as a witnessing center. (Mary Beaton, Carl Thomas and Wes Gustafson were active in its last days.) The university later appropriated Horton Hall. First Presbyterian Church in Seattle had a similar ministry. All of these groups were tied to a house and a full-time professional staff and exclusive to their campus, not intercollegiate. This is why Stacey and I were never too enthusiastic about residential staff and Christian Houses" (From a letter to the authors from Charles H. Troutman, September 23, 1989).

[10]Douglas Johnson interview, October 25, 1986.

[11]Johnson, *Contending for the Faith,* p. 144.

[12]Ibid.

[13]Howard Guinness, *Journey Among Students* (Sydney, Australia: Anglican Information Office, 1978), p. 19.

[14]Geraint Fielder, *Lord of the Years* (Leicester, England: Inter-Varsity Press, 1988), p. 40.

[15]The private diary of Howard Guinness, Archives of IVCF, Toronto, Canada.

[16]Arthur Hill, speaking at the 40th anniversary of the Canadian IVCF in 1969, quoted by Mel Donald in the unpublished history of IVCF of Canada.

[17]The only record of this announcement is in the IVFEU magazine in England, Michaelmas, 1929, p.26.

[18]Howard Guinness, interviewed by Charles Troutman, 1955.

[19]Arthur Hill at 40th anniversary of IVCF, Canada.

[20]The above information taken from an unpublished manuscript by Mel Donald, "A Spreading Tree: The History of the Canadian Inter-Varsity," 1987.

[21]In his book *Growth of a Work of God,* Stacey Woods writes that the first letter of invitation to be the general secretary of the Canadian Inter-Varsity offered him a salary of one hundred dollars a month, but that the second letter offered only fifty a month. This proves a mental merger of two different offers to Stacey Woods. He had received an offer to a different work in western Canada from a man who promised the first salary. Arthur Hill affirms that with the financial condition of the Canadian IVCF, there was no way they could have offered him more than fifty dollars (C. Stacey Woods, *Growth of a Work of God* [Downers Grove, Ill.: InterVarsity Press, 1975]).

[22]Woods, p. 16.

[23]From a conversation with Grace Koch Belden on November 11, 1989, in San Diego, California.

[24]Correspondence of C. Stacey Woods, Box 33, Collection 88-89, Archives of the Billy Graham Center, Wheaton, Illinois.

[25]Woods, p. 18.

[26]It would be a mistake to think that IVCF was not interested in apologetics. It was simply that the emphasis was on evangelism and extension of the gospel witness. For the first twenty years IVCF staffworkers were not only strong themselves in apologetic presentations, but also trained students to understand these issues. It was a necessary part of witnessing.

[27]Interview with Edmund Clowney at Cedar Campus, July 17, 1986.

[28]The University Christian Union at the University of Washington had been in existence for some time as a chapter of LES. They were closely associated with the IVCF chapter at the University British Columbia in Vancouver and participated with them in conferences and had close ties with IVCF before their actual affiliation. In the spring of 1939 Stacey Woods wrote, "We have received word from the U.C.U. at the University of Washington that they are going to officially affiliate with IVCF" (File 34, Box 2, Collection 11, Archives of the Billy Graham Center, Wheaton, Illinois).

[29]Grace Koch Belden helped start an unofficial Inter-Varsity chapter at Swarthmore College during her senior year in 1937-38. Stacey Woods had been speaking in the area about student work and planted the idea. Apart from a visit by Charles Troutman in the spring of 1938, they were on their own and principally met for prayer and fellowship. Following graduation Grace, wanting a better background in Bible, enrolled at Moody Bible Institute. One day when Stacey was speaking on radio station WMBI, Grace saw him sitting in the lounge as she walked past and went in to introduce herself. She told Stacey about the group that continued to meet at Swarthmore and asked if he could send any help to them. He

in turn asked Grace if she would ever think of coming on Inter-Varsity staff and developing work in the eastern United States. She spent the next summer at Pioneer Camp getting to know some of the other people involved in the work and came on staff in September 1939, working primarily in schools in Philadelphia and the surrounding area.

Earlier in her student life at Swarthmore, a representative of the League of Evangelical Students came to call on her. He had just been visiting the dean, whose liberal theological beliefs were well known, and was sufficiently discouraged to say to Grace, "You don't think you can do anything here, do you?" Her answer was no, of course. Grace said she made up her mind she would never ask any student that question in that way. In 1941 Stacey asked her to move to Boston to extend student work in New England. In 1942 she left to marry Lorin Belden, a classmate and close friend of Stacey Woods at Dallas Theological Seminary.

[30]Herbert Butt enrolled at the University of Washington in the fall of 1935. Sometime during his freshman year he heard someone remark, "If you want to be educated you must read the Bible"—a comment that stuck in his mind. He took his noonday meals at a cafeteria run by a Christian woman and washed dishes in exchange for his food. Over the sink hung a Christian calendar. One day hiking in the Olympic Mountains with a group of friends, Herb became overwhelmed with a sense of majesty and awe. Deeply moved, he prayed, "God if you are real, make yourself known to me." God did and sometime during Herb's sophomore year he became a Christian.

He became active in the University Christian Union at UW, then a League of Evangelical Student chapter (likely in name only, since the school was so far from the center of LES movement in Philadelphia). He became the chapter president and a keen influence on others. Because of the close fellowship of the UCU with the student group in Vancouver, Herb was well known in Inter-Varsity circles. When he graduated in 1939 Stacey asked him to help pioneer Inter-Varsity in the northwestern states.

Chapter 4/The Making of an Ethos

[1]John White, *Excellence in Leadership* (1986, IVP, Downers Grove), pp.47-48.

[2]Charles Troutman in a tape to the authors, November 1989.

[3]Tom Howard, a Wheaton graduate who served on SFMF staff before going on to get his doctorate, used to keep bits of paper with Stacey-isms on them. "At staff training at Cedar Campus one summer, Stacey was trying to explain how IVCF is entirely orthodox, but not brittle. Speaking of the importance of our Basis of Faith, he said, with appropriate grimaces, his voice getting lower and lower into a growl of mock-scorn which he affected, 'We don't hoist them (the dogmas) to the height of a flagpole and salute them with a couple of muted huzzahs. Instead, they are foundational.' " Another time when he and Tom were treading water in the surf at a beach, Tom mentioned the name of an interesting Christian leader. Stacey seized his nose with his right hand, raised his left arm straight into the air, and sank below the waves without a word (from a private letter to the authors, November 12, 1988).

Stacey Woods's letters often had unorthodox tidbits in them, almost as if he was weary of dictation and needed to amuse himself. He was full of surprises. A letter to Polly Barkhuff in March of 1950 asked her to make plans for a dinner gathering for an important leader from overseas. After a serious description of dinner plans, he closed the letter with, "Yours for bigger and better banquets and more hot air and less eternal value. C. S. Woods" (Correspondence of C. S. Woods, Box 33, Collection 88-89, Archives of the Billy Graham Center, Wheaton, Illinois).

[4]C. Stacey Woods in "Graduately Speaking," published in *Inter-Varsity News* (March 1957), p. 3.

[5]Ibid.

[6]Ibid.

[7]Gladys Hunt, in interview: This fits my own experience. When Prudie Todd, my staffworker, came to visit me in one of the resident halls at Michigan State in 1945, she inquired into my own spiritual life. Then she asked me a surprising question: "Have you seen any evidence that the Holy Spirit is working in any of the women in your hall?" I hadn't bothered to collect any evidence. I thought the goal was survival—go in a Christian; come out a Christian. She told me I might be the only Christian some of them would ever meet. I asked

her what she thought I ought to do. "Why not invite all of them to a Bible study in your room!" That was a mind-blowing suggestion, but doing it was a life-changing experience. I found out how to let the gospel loose.

[8]C. Stacey Woods, *Some Ways of God* (Downers Grove, Ill.: InterVarsity Press, 1975), p. 56.

[9]Charles Troutman, Jr., "Student Work Papers, 1985," Unpublished papers, personal collection.

[10]Also found in *Some Ways of God,* p. 33.

[11]C. Stacey Woods in *HIS* magazine, December 1945, p. 28.

[12]Charles H. Troutman, *The Seven Pillars,* Distinctives of Evangelical Student Witness (IVP, 1962).

[13]Charles H. Troutman, tape to authors, November 1989.

Chapter 5/A Whirlwind of New Beginnings: Decade of the 1940s

[1]Staff reports, Box 37, Collection 88-89, Archives of the Billy Graham Center, Wheaton, Illinois.

[2]Gordon Addington, staff member in the Philadelphia area in 1948, tells of Margaret Haines's ministry to him when she invited him to stay on the third floor of her home for a few weeks when staff salaries were in arrears. "I remember one time when she went to Chicago for an Inter-Varsity board meeting, she said, 'Now Gordie, I've made arrangements with the cook and I want you to take your meals here.' I would sit down in her big dining room at her huge table and be served by the cook. It was incredibly kind. So many people came through her home, I had the opportunity to meet people I would not otherwise have known, like Canon T. C. Hammond, who wrote *In Understanding Be Men.* When people came she would always invite me in. 'Gordie, I want you to be here.' "

[3]Herbert Taylor put Scripture to work in his life in practical ways. He memorized the Sermon on the Mount and repeated it aloud every day. He also took the truths of those passages and wrote a "Four Way Test for Truth," which was adopted by Rotary International as a check on business ethics. His ethical conduct in business, his common sense and business acumen, as well as his devotion to Jesus Christ gave him an important ministry to many parachurch organizations over a period of forty years.

[4]Howard Kelly, a prominent medical doctor at Johns Hopkins, had urged Inter-Varsity to come to the United States ever since he heard of Howard Guinness's tour of Canada. He backed up his enthusiasm with his support and became a mentor to Stacey Woods. His own simplicity in witness inspired everyone who knew him. Woods writes of Kelly's decision to take a taxi instead of driving his own car so that he could speak to the driver about Jesus Christ.

Grace Koch Belden, staff member in the East, knew him when he was in his eighties. On one occasion, when she was staying at the Kelly home, he returned to Baltimore from a lengthy train ride to see his sister in Bryn Mawr who had not been at home. He wasn't in the least irked with the waste of time. Instead he said, "I had the most wonderful time. I read from my New Testament all the way up and all the way back. I don't have time for anything else anymore."

Grace says, "One of my greatest privileges was to know a man like this who was world famous and yet such a humble, dedicated Christian." Dr. Kelly was responsible for founding an IVCF chapter at Johns Hopkins University and the NCF chapter at Johns Hopkins Hospital.

[5]Interview with Charles Troutman, January 24, 1990.

[6]Ibid.

[7]Correspondence with Charles Troutman, File 3, Box 2, Collection 111, Archives of the Billy Graham Center, Wheaton, Illinois.

[8]William F. Buckley, *God and Man at Yale* (Chicago: Regnery Press, 1951).

[9]*HIS* editorial (Winter 1942), p. 1.

[10]*HIS* was one of the first Christian publications to use photographs illustrating current activities. It attracted attention for that reason alone. Editor Bob Walker tells of a man coming into the office holding a copy of the magazine. He had picked it up in a Chicago Loop hotel and had been so intrigued by it that he wanted to meet those who had produced it. He turned out to be an executive of a Chicago brokerage house who, although admittedly not

a Christian believer, was nonetheless excited by the possibility of a Christian magazine with stories of people and evidences of God's dealing with them.

[11]Interview with David H. Adeney, January 17, 1987.

[12]Interview with Jane Hollingsworth Haile, June 5, 1989.

[13]The Biblical Seminary in subsequent years changed its name to The New York Seminary and modified its curriculum substantially, with the Bible considerably less central than previously. Dr. Robert Traina went to teach at Asbury Theological Seminary in Wilmore, Kentucky, retiring in 1988.

[14]In an interview with Barbara Boyd in Summit, New Jersey, July 7, 1988.

[15]Interview with Glen Zumwalt, now Distinguished Professor of Aeronautical Engineering at Wichita State University, July 3, 1990. Zumwalt has been an active participant in Inter-Varsity since his V-12 days. While serving a brief stint on staff (1949-1952), he helped the IV chapter at Texas A & M go into its boom stage. The chapter had forty-five Bible studies that met twice a week with about four hundred men involved. Later, after earning advanced degrees, he was one of a group of men (Ralph Watts, Ed Headington, Cub Culbertsen, Larry Walker and Bob Adams were the others) who formed what would later be called "a local committee" and underwrote the salary of Steve Atkinson so that the work in Texas could be revived after its near demise in the late 1950s. He was also active in the local committee in 1968 when he joined the faculty at Wichita State. That local committee guaranteed a portion of the staff support to bring Maria Grulla and Allen Busenitz to Kansas to build student work there in 1968. He presently works with international students and has served on the corporation of Inter-Varsity.

[16]These figures are hard to verify because exact records do not exist. Stacey Woods in his book *The Growth of a Work of God* (Downers Grove, Ill.: InterVarsity Press, 1975) gives the number at the close of the war as "approximately two hundred." Woods gives the figure of forty-one officially accepted chapters in September 1941 with an additional pioneering work at nine other schools (p. 30). In other places he reports that staff were working on ninety campuses. The variation in number may reflect poor memory and the large number of groups with which the staff had contacts but who may not have yet become official groups.

[17]Ibid., p. 34. In *Some Ways of God* (Downers Grove, Ill.: InterVarsity Press, 1975), Woods writes of this venture: "First, students in Canada, to be followed by students in the young Inter-Varsity Christian Fellowship, USA, caught the vision of student work in Latin America. Quickly they raised money for travelling expenses and urged me, then General Secretary of the movements in both countries, to make an exploratory trip."

[18]Woods, *The Growth of a Work of God,* p. 81.

[19]Cornelius Van Til was a scholarly theologian from Westminster Theological Seminary who stretched students in their capacity to think about God, truth and redemption. Northcote Deck had been a missionary doctor to the Solomon Islands for over twenty years and was a good Bible teacher. J. F. Strombeck was a keen layman who authored a number of books and spoke on practical Christian living. Irene Webster-Smith had been a missionary in Japan and during the war years served on our staff in the Southwest. Her emphasis was warmly devotional. Jane Hollingsworth Haile had a generous portion of *joie de vivre* and taught students how to study the Bible for themselves.

[20]Interview with Barbara Boyd, July 7, 1988.

[21]Woods, *The Growth of a Work of God,* p. 27.

Chapter 6/Growing the Movement: Decade of the 1940s

[1]Charles H. Troutman, *Seven Pillars* (Downers Grove, Ill.: InterVarsity Press, 1962), pp. 16, 18.

[2]In November 1949 Stacey Woods wrote to Lois Thiessen, assistant editor of *HIS,* "I think you know that I was responsible really for initiating a campaign against choruses in the IVCF, the chief reason being that hymns were not used and choruses were sung exclusively. This has had an effect upon the staff and some students, and the fiction has grown that Inter-Varsity almost considers it a sin to sing choruses, or that I do, and I'm sort of the big bad wolf responsible for this desolating position." He suggested Lois write for a copy of a chorus

written by an IVCF alumnus in Canada, and if she liked it, she could run it in *HIS* to counterbalance his emphasis on hymns.

Lois Thiessen wrote back: "Your sudden concern about our position on choruses amuses me, Mr. Woods! Yes, I think it is probably quite true that many think that 'Inter-Varsity almost considers it a sin to sing choruses' and that you are the responsible 'big bad wolf.' But when people really learn our *Hymns,* I think they agree with our position. Most choruses today just don't measure up to 'Unto the Hills' or 'Speak, Lord, in the Stillness.' I'll send for the Canadian chorus, teach it to the office staff, and then we'll see what we think!"

[3]From a letter from Robert Warburton, alumnus of University of Michigan, March 1989. Bob tells another story which gives insights into Stacey's relationship with students: "I was at Campus-in-the-Woods for the one-month camp in 1948. In our assigned work-time we were hauling wheelbarrows and bags of sand from the beach to various locations on the island. Hard, sweaty work. The night before Stacey had spoken so clearly, so insightfully on John 6 about discipleship, about those who ate his flesh and drank his blood, and about those who murmured and 'fell away.' Paul Little and I were sweating and lugging and disagreeing with some of Stacey's exegesis. We had our heads down in the dirt and sand and sweat. I remember looking up at one point to see somebody else sweating along with us and realized the sinewy arms belonged to someone older, and in the middle of some Great Point I was making in opposition to Stacey's talk, I looked smack into the twinkling, smiling eyes of Stacey Woods. Paul kept right on grumbling, never seeing Stacey. Stacey kept on smiling and working. And I never realized until then how much I loved him."

[4]David Miller, an IVCF alumnus and son of IVCF alumni, announced his approaching marriage with a note, "My future wife Joy is from the Philippine IVCF. We find we have a lot in common. What more is there than the Lord and *Hymns II?"* Congregational singing of at least two hymns from *Hymns II* seems an important part of many Inter-Varsity student weddings.

[5]Interview with Burton Harding, July 20, 1988.

[6]Inter-Varsity owes much to those early graduates of Wheaton College who came on the staff and helped pioneer student work. Woods and Troutman were students together at Wheaton. Many of the early staff came from contacts made at the college or through former classmates.

[7]Rosalind Rinker had been a missionary with the Oriental Missionary Society. Two Canadian friends took her to visit Campus-in-the-Woods in 1948 to meet Stacey Woods. She sat at the Woods's table along with eight other people, but did not converse with Stacey. However, the next morning he asked to speak with her on the dock, and in between greeting everyone who came by, invited her to come on staff and work in New York City. In 1951 she was assigned to Oregon, remaining on staff until 1958. This kind of hiring was typical of Stacey. He seemed intuitively to recognize strong people, and always seemed remarkably well-informed about them.

[8]Mary Beaton exemplified the strong kind of woman who came on staff in the early days of Inter-Varsity and lasted—a true pioneer. She was soft-spoken and commanding at the same time. Students had a feeling she saw right through their shabby excuses, and loved her for it. She made an invaluable contribution to student work during her years on the staff of IVCF in the U.S., serving from 1949 until 1955, when she left to help Gwen Wong pioneer student work in the Philippines.

[9]Interview with Eugene Thomas, Denver, Colo., April 24, 1989.

[10]Wilbur Smith was only a part-time editor, and while his contributions were always significant, the arrangement may also have been to assure the public that a Christian scholar was watching over this periodical that listed a woman editor.

[11]Staff members had a basic list of books they urged student leaders to read that included *Quiet Time, Henceforth, Sacrifice, Therefore Go, Hudson Taylor's Spiritual Secret, If We Believe, Missionary Methods, St. Paul's or Ours?, The Spontaneous Expansion of the Church* and *The New Testament Documents: Are They Reliable?* Along with small booklets, staff members urged the reading of missionary biographies, such as *Behind the Ranges* (the life of J. O. Fraser) and *William Carey.* It was part of a student's basic training.

[12]In the early 1940s, at a student conference held at Keswick, New Jersey, Stacey Woods was taken to task by the management over women students who were wearing two-piece

bathing suits. The rule was one-piece suits! Stacey listened and with feigned seriousness asked, "Which part do you want them to take off?"

[13]IVCF would not give in to the separatist movement by making the taboos part of the gospel. This often put IVCF at odds with pastors of churches where the taboos were packaged as part of the message of salvation. Theologically they were in agreement, but culturally they were at odds. IVCF believed Christ was the issue. The Fellowship considered itself "fundamentalist," but the separatists often questioned even the validity of its call since they considered the university sold out to the "enemy."

[14]Interview with Mary Anne Klein, April 29, 1988.

[15]While this encounter did not completely change Mrs. Johnston's mind on racial issues, it does show her heart in spiritual matters. Over the years she was a keen supporter of Inter-Varsity, showing concern for students and staff. She served on the board from 1942 until 1961 when she was made board member emeritus. Her daughter, Connie Johnston, served on the staff of Inter-Varsity in NYC during 1943-44, and her other daughters also have supported the movement over the years. Cliffe Knechtle, evangelist to students and Mrs. Johnston's grandson, carries on the family tradition of effective ministry through Inter-Varsity.

[16]Correspondence shows that Hong Sit received forty dollars for fifty hours of work each month, a generous eighty cents an hour. He worked in colleges through the eastern region.

[17]Under the GI Bill of Rights, the federal government paid the tuition of veterans. GIs came in great numbers, some 2,230,000 in all, swelling enrollments, especially at the institutions with highest prestige. In 1948 at the University of Michigan, the undergraduate student body reached 20,000, of whom 11,000 were veterans (Keith W. Olson, *The G.I. Bill, the Veterans, and the Colleges* [Lexington: The University Press of Kentucky, 1974], pp. 43-44).

[18]Melvin Friesen was decisive and forthright in manner. He brooked no sham or weakness of character, which inspired both respect and affection for him. An IVCF student at Cal Poly once told Mel, "When I hear you are coming to campus I always started reading my Bible." Mel went on to explain that if anything this was a sign of failure. Another girl in IVCF later told Mel, "You make me so mad, and you are so right!" (Patrick Wall, "A Brief History of Inter-Varsity at Cal Poly" [1981], TMs.).

[19]"Big, broad Cleo Buxton," as Stacey Woods referred to him, had been an active student in Spartan Christian Fellowship (IVCF at Michigan State), and later as an infantry captain he had led his company in the invasion of Italy during World War 2, awarded the Purple Heart several times. He served as a regional secretary in the Midwest until he left to begin The Officers Christian Union (now Fellowship) in the USA and later ACCTS, an equivalent of IFES for Officers Christian Fellowship, in many countries.

Cleo "Buck" Buxton was a natural leader, not afraid of confrontation, and a good discipler. He led two work camps at a rustic site on Prentiss Bay in Michigan during the summers of 1949 and 1950, prior to the development of Cedar Campus and enjoyed taking a group of men on stress camping trips. He was once assigned to a women's dorm at a conference, which is one reason he went by the name Buck. Among other details of his life with the Fellowship was a reduction of his pay check because his wife Louisa was employed, a policy in the early days.

[20]Carl Thomas became a regional secretary for the West Coast and a strong leader in the Fellowship. Bob Young, who pioneered student work in Latin America, first met him on the Stanford campus in the spring of 1947. Bob had dropped in on the weekly meeting of the Stanford Christian Fellowship and, unimpressed with the thirteen students gathered there, was heading for the door. He was stopped by a burly guy who blocked the door. Bob recounts: "He looked me straight in the eye and asked, 'Are you a Christian?' I thought this was a poor approach, but I said, 'Yes, I think so.' His response was, 'Well if you are, this is a very weak group and I am sure you can help them.' That was the first of many conversations. He became my model for the Christian life—fervent, devoted, aggressive."

After he left IVCF staff, Carl became a pastor of a Presbyterian church. Years later he lost his confidence in the authority of Scripture and left the Christian faith. Bob comments, "It was heartbreaking to those of us who had been taught the Scriptures by him."

[21]Minutes of the IVCF Board, January 25, 1947, p. 143.

²²Paul Hopkins joined Inter-Varsity in 1946 and remained its business manager for four years. He had an important role in setting procedures in order for an organization that had "grown like topsy." He left IVCF to become business manager for The Evangelical Foundation, begun by Dr. Donald G. Barnhouse.

²³Corrie ten Boom, scheduled to speak at Campus-in-the-Woods, arrived at the dock on Lake of Bays a day earlier than she was expected, so that no one came to take her to the island. Hearing of her situation, a man who lived near the boat dock offered to take her across the lake. He piled her luggage in what turned out to be a canoe-like craft, and Corrie ten Boom, who was not a small woman, settled herself in the boat. A short way off from shore the wind came up and the water became very rough, lapping over the sides of the boat. Corrie was certain she was on the way to meet her Maker. They managed to make it back to shore, where the man and his wife offered over-night hospitality to Corrie. That night, sitting at their dinner table, Corrie ten Boom asked them "if they knew the Savior." The man and his wife heard the gospel for the first time and believed. The next afternoon a boat came across to transport Miss ten Boom to Campus-in-the-Woods.

²⁴Married women were sometimes treated differently. Jane Hollingsworth, who was given great freedom to teach the Bible as an unmarried woman, says, "When I married Peter Haile, it was if I had died. I was never asked to do another thing for students." Interview, June 5, 1989.

²⁵Correspondence with C. Stacey Woods, Box 32, Collection 88-89, Archives of the Billy Graham Center, Wheaton, Illinois.

²⁶C. S. Woods letter to staff, November 5, 1949. Box 32, Collection 88-89, Archives of the Billy Graham Center, Wheaton, Illinois.

Chapter 7/Two Important Mergers and Worldwide Fellowship

¹C. Stacey Woods, *The Growth of a Work of God* (Downers Grove, Ill.: InterVarsity Press, 1975), p. 121.

²H. Wilbert Norton, *To Stir The Church: A Brief History of the Student Foreign Missions Fellowships* 1936-1986 (Madison, Wis.: SFMF, l986), pp. 7-12.

³Norton, p. 19. A second Constitutional Convention of the SFMF was held in December 1938 at the Keswick conference grounds, officially ratifying the constitution and spelling out the nature and policies of SFMF.

⁴Ibid., p. 16.

⁵The general secretaries of the SFMF prior to its merger with IVCF were Joe McCullough, Will Norton, Kenneth Hood, Neill Hawkins, Peter Stam III and Herb Anderson (Norton, p. 19).

⁶Raymond Joyce, a missionary to the Muslim world, had followed David Adeney in 1943 to visit the campuses on behalf of missions.

⁷Interview with Christy Wilson, Urbana, Illinois, December 31, l987.

⁸Ibid.

⁹With the experience of a long series of IVCF missions conferences at Urbana, it is easy to forget that the 1946 missions convention in Toronto was an historic first in a new student witness. The last influential student missionary convention took place in 1920, twenty-six years before, and the most effective SVM conventions were much earlier than that. The average student and church were totally unaware that there had been a great student missionary movement in the past. Probably only the leaders knew they were building on the past.

¹⁰"Urbana Report," *HIS* 7 (March 1947):11.

¹¹Interview with Christy Wilson, December 31, 1987.

¹²From interview with Christy Wilson.

¹³Woods, p. 129. Burgon Bickersteth may well have left the conservative faith of his ancestors. One of his forbears, Edward Henry Bickersteth, wrote the hymn, "For My Sake and the Gospel's Go to Tell Salvation's Story," which was in IV's *Hymns*.

¹⁴Stacey Woods, writing about this event in *The Growth of a Work of God*, conveys the drama of the moment in his own colorful prose. "Scrapping his prepared speech, Ockenga, at his magnificent best, launched into an off-the-cuff defense of the importance and necessity of a biblical witness on campus. Smiting hip and thigh, he flayed liberalism and accommo-

dation theology. He insisted on the right and necessity of Inter-Varsity to exist as an independent society. Here was reformation preaching at its best. The atmosphere was electric" (p. 129).

[15]To understand the generous giving of these 576 delegates in 1946, $3,500 in 1990 dollars would be $22,200. To equal that, if 17,000 students come to Urbana in 1990 they would have to give an offering of about $655,208.

[16]Norton and Eloise Sterrett began working for IFES as staffworkers for the Union of Evangelical Students of India (UESI) in 1953. Three Christian unions begun by students existed on three different campuses. The Sterretts, along with David Watson, began to encourage the formation of other CUs, working as the first official traveling secretaries. The constitution and the formal beginning of UESI dates to 1953.

[17]Stacey Woods always had his antenna out for people who would make a contribution to student work. He began talking to David Howard during his undergraduate days, telling him about student work and inviting his interest. At Urbana 1948 Stacey found David and asked him if he would come on the missionary staff to work with Wes Gustafson, saying Wes would be presented to the convention as the new missionary secretary and he would like to announce David's appointment at the same time. David says, "He really put the bee on me to make a decision while at the convention. I kept telling him that I was planning on going to the mission field, and he kept saying that was just the kind of person he wanted in this job. So I gave my commitment and Wes Gustafson and I were presented on the platform the final night of Urbana 1948. I graduated in June and spent the next year travelling full-time for the missions department."

[18]Annual Report of the missionary secretary, 1948-49, p. 16.

[19]See chapter four.

[20]The name was changed to Nurses Christian Fellowship in 1952.

[21]Joseph Butwell, "The Cross and the Scalpel," *HIS* (April 1947). Christian Medical Society (CMS) was organized in 1942 as the result of two students praying together in 1931 at Northwestern University Medical School and beginning a witness similar to CNF in the Chicago area. They also had offices at 64 Lake Street in 1947. CMS and IVCF had drawn up a Basis for Cooperation which the board of IVCF and the voting members of CMS had ratified agreeing to "mutual support in the respective fields of endeavor wherever feasible and for consultation on mutual problems." A similar agreement was made with CNF. CMS chose to be a professional society and never became part of IVCF.

[22]Pete Lowman, *The Day of His Power* (Leicester, England: Inter-Varsity Press, 1983), p. 48.

[23]Carl-Frederick Wisloff was the IFES chairman 1959-67 and then president of IFES 1967-69.

[24]Lowman, p. 67.

[25]Ibid., pp. 66-69.

[26]From the advertising brochure "Cambridge 1939" furnished by Dr. Douglas Johnson, IVF England.

[27]Personal letter to Keith and Gladys Hunt from Dr. Douglas Johnson, December 5, 1989.

[28]*HIS* 7 (October 1947):18. That headline was incongruous with the philosophy of the American movement; namely, that we would not export the American Inter-Varsity in our involvement in the IFES movement. The U.S. movement has constantly monitored itself and has a record of restraint and partnership in helping indigenous movements.

Chapter 8/Gains and Losses: Decade of the 1950s

[1]The terms "insider" and "outsider" are used by Helen Lefkowitz Horowitz in *Campus Life* (New York: Alfred A. Knopf, 1987), as characterizing two distinctive subcultures within university life over the decades. Her third subculture of "rebels" becomes increasingly powerful in the 1960s.

[2]William G. McLoughlin in *Revivals, Awakenings and Reform* (Chicago: Univ. of Chicago Press, 1978) argues that the evangelical resurgence led by Billy Graham (and these parachurch organizations) was the "Fourth Great Awakening" in America (pp. 1-12, 212-16).

[3]Interview with Bonnie Addington, March 22, 1988.

[4]Seventeen staffworkers did a survey of the questions students most often asked during the Year of Evangelism. The most often repeated questions in order: (1) How do you know

the Bible is true and authoritative? (2) What about the heathen? (3) How can I effectively witness to my family and friends? (4) How can I know God's will? (5) How can my Quiet Time and prayer be more effective? (6) Why does Christianity claim to be exclusive? (7) Why do I need to believe in Christ? (8) How can you assert that Christianity is the only way? Only five people asked questions about God permitting suffering or the existence of hell.

[5]Paul Little came to the University of Pennsylvania with a sound biblical background. His father was a Bible teacher, and Paul had been immersed in truth since childhood. What he lacked was a way to put it to work and a feeling of ease with non-Christians. Gordon Addington, the staff member who first suggested Paul come on IV staff, remembers taking a reluctant Paul knocking on doors in his dormitory to invite fellows to a Bible study. Gordon said, "Just come along and watch me do it."

The fellow who answered the door said, "Well, thanks, I might be there."

Paul said, "That blew me away!"

Then Gordon said, "OK, Paul, now it's your turn."

Gordon evaluated Paul after he finished his turn, "Look the person in the eye, Paul. Always look the person in the eye. You were looking at the ceiling."

Paul joined the staff team in 1950 and led his first fraternity discussion at the Univ. of Kansas during this Year of Evangelism. He was scared and after it was over he judged it a disaster. But the next day a fellow from that frat phoned him and said he wanted to talk. Paul helped him become a Christian that day. Twenty years later that man's son came up to Paul at Urbana 70 and said, "You led my father to the Lord in 1950 following a fraternity meeting at the University of Kansas."

[6]Wesley Pippert has gone on to become a UPI reporter, with assignments to the White House (during the administration of Jimmy Carter) and Israel. He is presently a professor with the University of Missouri School of Journalism, based in Washington, D.C.

[7]Christian Emphasis Week or Religious Emphasis Week ("RE Week"), common during the 1950s on many campuses, was an attempt by the university or college to encourage students to think about truth and ethics, and offered Inter-Varsity chapters an opportunity to give a strong Christian witness by supplying one of the speakers for the event. Some of the content was bland do-goodism, but it was not without merit as a way for Christian students to "fly the flag."

[8]John Paterson became an influential professor of geography in Great Britain, but has kept close ties with the IVCF work in the States. International Student Specialist Al Fairbanks is one of many students John discipled. Some of Paterson's reminiscences illuminate life in the 1950s. "In the course of a few weeks of my own travels in the spring of 1950, I encountered Jane Hollingsworth in Estes Park (Colorado), Portland (Oregon), and Pasadena (California)—and IV staff travelled by train or bus, not by plane. The sedentary staff worker of today bears no resemblance to the back-packing traveller of old. Patterns of work had not become fixed; the territory was open, and the staff improvised as they rode the buses from campus to campus. Charles Troutman was once snow-bound on a train somewhere in the west. So he bought up the entire local stock of stamped postcards and sat out the storm writing prayer reminders to all the students he knew. In those days, if you were a student, you still spoke Stacey Woods's name with awe. Students feared Stacey and loved Charles, and the fact that they were almost certainly wrong in their estimations did not alter their opinions. Soft-spoken Charles could be firm and severe when occasion demanded. And Stacey could be soft and loving. Stacey was feared because he had a disconcerting way of making you account for yourself with questions that began with, 'Why do you say that?' or 'In what respect?' "

[9]Harry Truman was the president at the time. As they traveled in the States the British team were horrified to hear Americans tell the popular Harry Truman jokes, jokes which would never touch the lips of a Britisher about the queen.

[10]Inductive Bible study, now used around the world in member movements of the IFES, was shaped by the American IVCF. The early adoption of this method of study by the IVCF has similarly influenced its use in the church.

[11]The reverse side of this kind of training had already taken place. In 1948 Jane Hollingsworth

had some important staff training in Britain. (In fact, she declares it to be the only staff training she ever had.) She stayed on in Britain after an IFES meeting on the Continent and went up to Swanwick in Derbyshire for a British student conference. Her opportunity to participate and learn from student work in Britain depended on whether individual student groups would invite her to come to their university or college. The policy of the British IV was to send a traveling secretary by student-invitation only. General Secretary Douglas Johnson hoped some groups would invite Jane, but he couldn't do anything about initiating it. Taken by surprise at the conference, Jane was asked to bring greetings from America, and in her winsome way and with the charm of a southern drawl, she said, "I bring you greetings from America. I have been sent to England to learn from you, because the British are always right. We know they are right because they have always been right." She brought the house down, and suddenly she was overwhelmed with attention and invitations, which pleased Douglas Johnson.

¹²John Holmes married staff member Paula Cliffe, who came on staff in 1949 after being an active member in the chapter at Michigan State College. Together they taught in Ghana, West Africa, and pioneered a student movement there before returning to teach at Stony Brook School in New York.

¹³George "Bud" Murray was a very young Christian catapulted into situations he was not ready to handle, which was extremely stressful for him. This added to other physical problems that necessitated his leaving the team. Within a few years team members heard that he had died from some illness.

¹⁴Interview with Austin Christensen, January 1990.

¹⁵Following his time in the U.S. Army, James F. Nyquist became an active member of the IV chapter of the University of Minnesota (UM) in 1946. He knew about IVCF because a cousin had given him a subscription to *HIS*. The chapter grew enormously during his years at UM, necessitating their move from a hall that held 225 to the museum of Natural History auditorium that seated 500. A weekly newsletter called "Almost Confidential" was produced on an ancient mimeograph in Jim's room. Jeanne Axelson (on NCF staff and later married to Fred Woodberry, staffing chapters in New York City) armed with the mailing list of eight hundred, would stuff them in student mail boxes. By 1948 Jim was the chapter president, "majoring in Inter-Varsity." He had plans to go to India as a missionary, and both his undergraduate and graduate studies were preparing him for that. Just before graduation, staff member Mary Beaton said, "Why don't you think about coming on IV staff?" Jim thought he could give IV one year; he ended up making it a career. He was made regional secretary for New England his second year on staff, which was only the beginning of many important assignments with IVCF.

¹⁶H. Wilbert Norton, p. 37.

¹⁷As early as 1951 Carl McIntire, editor of *The Christian Beacon,* attacked *HIS* for an article on "The Christian and Social Reform," written by Samuel H. Moffat, a Presbyterian. McIntire indicated that Moffat's affiliation made IVCF liberal by association. McIntire continued his attacks in 1957 over the Billy Graham Crusade in New York City:

> When IVCF announced its cooperation in the Crusade and loaned Paul Little to the Billy Graham team for the student section of the planning, the reaction of these critics was immediate and sharp and in some instances bitter. Some people withdrew their support of IVCF.

Again in 1957 Joe Bayly was attacked by McIntire, both in *The Beacon* and on his radio program, for publishing communist propaganda:

> But the point of issue between us right now is that *HIS* has published its communist propaganda . . . and the material is so attractive and disarming as . . . communists would want it to appear when it is read by American youth. What has happened to Inter-Varsity Christian Fellowship that such a thing should occur?

The three articles in question were "The Church in Russia" by John L. Cowan, "Of Salt and Society" by Ferenc Kiss and a lengthy editorial by Bayly.

Stacey Woods was very supportive of Bayly. A letter from Woods to Bayly following the above events gives insights into Woods as a leader:

December 5, 1957

Dear Joe,

You have written an excellent and a moving letter, a far better letter than I could have written and I thank you for it. I believe you have done the right thing, and God will justify you and us.

I should like your permission by return mail [the phone was rarely used for financial reasons], please, to have your letter mimeographed. . . . I want to send the letter to a number of my friends, including McIntire's satraps in Italy who are now attacking us, our student movement and the Brethren.

Cordially yours,

C. Stacey Woods

P.S. I enclose a November 28 issue of The Christian Beacon and suggest you look it over carefully. . . . Joe, we must be very careful, in our reaction to McIntire's reaction, not to react too far the other way. Please understand, I have not changed my judgments or evaluations. . . . You know how I react to this and how revolting I find McIntire's mention of myself and IVCF. On the other hand, I must be fair, and if what McIntire says is true. . . he has made his point. The difficulty in the whole situation, Joe is this. If McIntire is 80% wrong and 20% right in his general ministry, we must not reject the 20% of rightness in our revulsion against the 80% of falsehood. Likewise, if Billy Graham is 80% right and 20% wrong in compromising, we cannot accept that 20% of wrongness. How difficult it is these days! CSW

[18]One of the southern board members insisted that Ivery Harvey be called the "Negro staff worker." The senior staff men, led by Cleo Buxton, stood with Stacey Woods and said Ivery should be called an Inter-Varsity staff member. They felt so strongly they communicated that they would resign as a body if he were to have any other designation.

[19]Interview with Ivery Harvey, June 18, 1988.

[20]Ivery Harvey became an educator in the City of Detroit, and has good insights into what he has seen take place in the years of the civil rights movement and subsequent history. Stacey Woods had a significant impact on his life, and he, like everyone else who worked with Stacey, enjoys telling stories about him. Ivery tells of the time a distressed student approached Stacey with the problem of a roommate who smoked. "Mr. Woods, what shall I do?"

Stacey replied, "Give him an ashtray."

[21]Interview with Betty Cole Richter, May 1989.

[22]C. Stacey Woods, *The Growth of a Work of God* (Downers Grove, Ill.: InterVarsity Press, 1975), p. 79. Leadership by conflict was part of Woods's style. He often set people up against each other, whether consciously or not, something that often caught his colleagues unaware, even though they knew he did this.

[23]Memo from Charles Troutman to C. S. Woods, June, 1951, Campus-in-the-Woods, File 3, Box 2, Collection 111, Archives of the Billy Graham Center, Wheaton, Illinois.

[24]Until this time the sole communication to the board about the work of the Fellowship came from Stacey Woods. Stacey was, in many ways, as jealous of his relationship to the board as W. E. C. Petersen was of the mailing list.

[25]Official minute book of senior staff council of Inter-Varsity Christian Fellowship—USA, April 14, 1953, pp. 27-30.

[26]Ibid.

[27]IVCF board minutes, January 23, 1954, p. 6.

[28]Herbert J. Taylor, long-time board member who had significant input in the founding of IVCF in the U.S., was a strong supporter of Stacey Woods. Board member Russell Hitt said, "I was annoyed when Taylor would say, 'IVCF is Stacey Woods and Stacey is IVCF.' It was demeaning to the staff." When the board discussed the recommendations of the SSC, Taylor was adamant that he would rather have half of Stacey Woods's time than all of someone else's time. Wallace Erickson relates that the board later learned that Taylor had supplemented Stacey Woods's salary through the years, and this caused some difficulty among its members.

[29]Charles Troutman, with his wife, Lois, and their children—Charles, Jr., Miriam and David—

accepted an invitation to work with the Australian Inter-Varsity. Two years later he was appointed acting general secretary for the Australian IVF. A few months after their arrival in Australia, Lois and two of the children, Charles Jr. and Miriam, were hospitalized with polio. Lois was the hardest hit and has courageously coped with braces, crutches and other ailments. Many echo the words of Archbishop Mowll, primate of Australia's Church of England, "The whole Troutman family has been a blessing to Australia."

Chapter 9/The Expansion of Student Training: Decade of the 1950s

[1]Interview with Eugene Thomas, April 24, 1989, Denver, Colorado.

[2]In 1953 Ralph Willoughby, an outstanding young man who had served briefly on staff in New York State and part-time in California while a seminary student, was given responsibility to develop the Cedar Campus site after his graduation from Fuller Seminary. That summer he contracted a polio-related disease at Pioneer Camp in Canada and died within three days, at the age of twenty-nine. The lodge on Cedar Campus's Old Mill Point is named after him.

[3]At this time Keith Hunt was the campus staff member for all the colleges and universities in downstate Illinois, Missouri and Iowa. Following his time in service during World War 2, Keith met his wife, Gladys Schriemer, while they were leaders in the Inter-Varsity chapter at Michigan State. The Hunts served as volunteer staff following their marriage, helping at conferences and using their Detroit-area home as an Inter-Varsity "hotel." On one occasion when Stacey Woods was their house guest, he asked Keith if he would consider leaving his engineering career to help organize the growing movement by developing business procedures and staff for the headquarters. The Hunts came with Inter-Varsity in May of 1951. Subsequently, Keith became a campus staff member and a regional secretary, among other assignments, and was responsible for developing new student training programs.

[4]Mr. Taylor added the $10,000 honorarium he received as president of Rotary International, which paid for the two huge fireplaces in the lodge. Later he also gave a $10,000 foundation gift that enabled the work crew under the supervision of Bob Schrader to build the swimming pool at Cedar Campus. The foundation also built Deck Cabin for family housing.

[5]Letter to Charles Troutman from C. Stacey Woods, April 29, 1952, File 41, Box 1, Collection 111, Archives of the Billy Graham Center, Wheaton, Illinois.

[6]Ibid.

[7]May Koksma joined the staff in June of 1952 as David Adeney's administrative assistant. Along with Lois Thiessen, she played a key role in stabilizing the missions department with her skills and quiet efficiency through the next decade and a half. Lois Thiessen continued editing *Missionary Mandate* and served as assistant missionary secretary. Frank Tichy, Tom Howard and Ross Lyon traveled across the U.S. and Canada as staff for SFMF during the 1950s, succeeding each other. The missions department never consisted of more than four people.

[8]In May 1946, after Paul Byer returned from World War 2, he heard about Inter-Varsity from some students from University of Southern California (USC) who gave their testimony at a Youth for Christ meeting in Los Angeles. Paul looked up the group when he enrolled at USC the next fall. In the middle of the year he met Stacey Woods, who spoke at a student conference and mentioned the IVCF heritage at Cambridge and spoke about the daily prayer meeting (DPM). The USC students talked about the idea after Sunday lunch and decided that their campus chapter ought to have a DPM. They began Monday morning.

That year Paul became vice president, and the next year the president of the chapter. He was a sophomore and knew he needed training, so he went to Campus in the Woods in July of 1947. By the end of the second year this fledgling chapter had grown to two hundred students. Paul comments that one of the biggest obstacles to effective campus witness during his college days on the West Coast was competition from large student groups associated with churches, because Christian students were siphoned off to activities away from the campus. Paul and Marilyn Byer came on staff in 1951 and were sent to the Northwest to replace James Reapsome, who had been drafted into the army for the Korean conflict.

[9]Rosalind Rinker's book *Prayer: Conversing with God* (Grand Rapids, Mich.: Zondervan,

1959) probably has changed contemporary prayer meetings more than any other thing written before or since.

[10]Quoted from the journal of John R. W. Stott, written during his time in the States during 1958 to inform his parents about the details of the mission.

[11]Ibid.

[12]The taboos included drinking, smoking, movies, dancing, etc.

[13]Inter-Varsity has always had a positive view of the church, and its leaders took an active role in the local body of believers. Over and over again leaders in the Fellowship would emphasize that IVCF was not the church, that it was an arm of the church, and both staff and chapter members should belong to a local church.

[14]Gene Thomas and his staff moved to Boulder, Colorado, where they began what they believed to be the ideal New Testament church. It was an experiment that failed within a short time. Gene Thomas subsequently refers to those years as "my black years." He now says, "It was a crazy idea. We thought we had arrived; we lacked humility. The New Testament Church is the Corinthian church, and all the churches of the book of Acts." It was a costly sidetrack.

[15]Stacey Woods first met Charlie Hummel when he was an undergraduate at Yale. Hummel had carried the Inter-Varsity idea to Japan after the war. Although deferred because of his chemical engineering major, after graduation Charlie was eventually drafted and sent to Japan in October 1945 for occupation duty following World War 2. Toward the end of his year of military service, he met Japanese Christians and American soldiers who had started the G.I. Gospel Hour in Tokyo. He began leading Bible studies for Japanese and saw the potential for student work in universities.

Instead of going home at the end of 1946, he took a civilian job with GHQ for another year and in his free time got acquainted with Japanese university students. By spring 1947 he had four student groups going on nearby campuses. Irene Webster-Smith, a missionary to Japan who had served on the American IVCF staff during the war, returned to her former mission in Kyoto. Charlie looked her up and asked her if she would come to Tokyo to help with the student work. Their ministry helped the Japanese students start the intercollegiate Kirisutosha Gakusei Kai (KGK—that is, "Christian Student Fellowship"), a sister organization to the American IVCF.

Charlie Hummel had grasped the idea of indigenous student witness. At a critical time in history God used him in the beginning of a new student movement. (At the fortieth anniversary of the KGK, the Hummels were invited to Japan for the celebration.) After returning home Charlie served on staff in northern New England and the Maritime Provinces, married Anne Childs, and after a year of biblical studies at Wheaton College Graduate School, became Middle Atlantic regional secretary in 1952.

[16]W. E. C. Petersen was a Danish immigrant. He learned to speak English and went to work in the men's department of Carson Pirie Scott in Chicago. One of his customers, James Gray, invited him to work in the stewardship department of the Moody Bible Institute. "Pete" defied his lack of a college education with his intelligent grasp of fund raising for Moody. With this background he had come to IVCF, and because his beginning fund raising proved effective and help was desperately needed, he was given considerable latitude. Shortly after he came with Inter-Varsity the staff gave him the names of 6,000 graduates to put on the mailing list. According to Troutman, not until after Petersen left in the sixties was it discovered that he had disposed of the names.

[17]It was timely, because in June 1957 the board began requiring *new* staff to raise half of their own support. The policy could only be adhered to very loosely, partly because of unsophisticated accounting procedures. The work could not grow without more income, and the Fellowship was financially hard-pressed by the late fifties. The idea of new staff bringing partial or full support was discussed by C. Stacey Woods at a board meeting in June of 1955. It was agreed that such a major change in policy would need time for promotion. The minutes of the senior staff council, January 10, 1957, read, "The SSC expresses itself as agreeing in principle with the recommendation of the executive committee that new staff members shall have at least 50% of their support pledged, and the SSC further requests that while implementation of this policy be made this year, discretionary powers be granted for

exceptions." The May 1957 *Inter-Varsity News* announced this new policy to IV supporters.

[18]Some neighbors on North Astor Street objected to the zoning board's decision to sell 1444 to Inter-Varsity and took the city to court, trying to get a reversal. The city attorney asked, "What will you use that large room on the second floor for?" Peterson replied that the board would meet there several times each year and "every day we'll have an office prayer meeting."

"How can you pray there?" the lawyer asked. "Will you have a crucifix or some other kind of worship center? I'm Jewish." Pete replied, "We don't need a worship center. As Christians we believe we can pray anywhere." The lawyer asked, "Even in this courtroom?" Petersen replied in the affirmative and added "I've been praying here all morning."

"Your Honor," the city attorney said, turning to the judge, "that's the sort of religion I'd like to have—where you don't need to go anywhere to pray, but can come to God right where you are." The court approved the zoning board's decision. (Told by Joe Bayly in his column "Out of My Mind," *Eternity* magazine, December 1985, p. 12.)

[19]Statistics from annual report for year ending August 31, 1950.

[20]Colonel Robert McCormick was the owner and publisher of *The Chicago Tribune*.

[21]The hastily written and illegible signature of C. Stacey Woods became the subject of many jokes. One man wrote to him as "Mr. C. Macey Worms." Another story is told of Stacey calling out to Olga Simpson, his secretary, "Olga, Olga, where are you? I've already dictated three letters to you!"

[22]Interview with Frank Stenzel at Chico State College, Chico, California, January 21, 1988.

[23]Interview with Bill York in Richmond, Virginia, January 14, 1989.

[24]Interview with George McKinney in San Diego, California, June 14, 1988.

Chapter 10/Long Hours, Low Pay and Little Applause

[1]Woods, *The Growth of a Work of God,* 69.

[2]Helen Friesen recounts an incident that occurred shortly after she and Melvin joined the staff of the Fellowship. She was with Mel at a staff meeting in the Chicago office, the first she had ever attended. In the discussion each of the leaders voiced a different opinion with such forcefulness that Helen felt fearful about their decision to join an organization in which people disagreed so strongly. After lengthy discussion, Stacey Woods suggested the group spend some time in prayer, seeking God's direction. When they got up from their knees after praying, the group had one mind about what they should do. Helen says, "I never saw anything like it. I knew then it was the organization I *did* want to be part of." For these early leaders the freedom to speak their mind and be taken seriously was appealing and a part of the creative shaping of the movement.

[3]An amusing interruption to an office prayer meeting: One day a group of firemen exited from an emergency vehicle, stormed into the Chicago office on Lake Street and broke up one of these spontaneous gatherings for prayer. Someone in the building across the street could see into the room and had called the fire department to report "that a whole room full of people who had been active suddenly seemed to pass out, everyone sitting with their heads hanging down or kneeling on the floor in front of a chair."

[4]A distinction is made between delayed salaries and cancelled salaries. Salaries were often delayed because of insufficient funds (one time as long as three months), but provision was made for an "advance," and full salaries were paid as soon as funds became available. At the end of the fiscal year any salaries in arrears were canceled in order to start the new year without debt. Salaries were cancelled twice during the 1950s, totalling five weeks of earnings never paid.

[5]The board minutes of January 1948 record one of these instances of a salary reduction because of a working wife: "It was moved by Mr. Peck and seconded by Mr. Barnes that Mrs. Herbert Netsch be appointed to the staff of the Fellowship at a salary of $90 a month, and that the salary of Mr. Herbert Netsch be reduced from $185 a month to $135 a month." Cleo Buxton's salary was also reduced because his wife was employed as a nurse.

[6]On the West Coast they tell the story of the time young Carol Friesen answered the doorbell to see a man at the door with a suitcase. She did what she saw her parents do; she invited him in and said he could have the first room on the left down the hall. The bewildered

man identified himself as a Fuller Brush salesman! Hospitality has always been a big part of Inter-Varsity life.

[7]A November 3, 1949, letter from Joe Bayly to his staff reads in part:

The 1/4 salary checks which we have just received impress upon us several things: (1) The necessity for daily dependence upon God, looking to him to provide. Our trust must be in Him, not in the Fellowship. (2) The necessity for a close walk with God. Such times of God's withholding should bring us up short for a personal spiritual inventory. . . . (3) The necessity of thrift, personally and in the work. Vegetable plates are as nourishing as steaks. A postcard (1¢) may do the work of a letter (3¢). Planning ahead may save the cost of a telegram. (4) The necessity of making the Day of Prayer, November 15, a time of asking and receiving from God.

With warm personal greetings,
Sincerely in Christ,
Joseph T. Bayly

P.S. If the 1/4 salary check has left anyone of you in straits, will you please let me know. (Further advances were available in case of need.)

[8]The cover of the July 1946 issue of *HIS* showed a map of Afghanistan, and on its inside pages Margaret Haines had written about opportunities for teachers and technicians to enter that country which was closed to ordinary missionaries. After obtaining his law degree Howard Larsen married Weips Rozelaar, who was a staff member in New York City, and left for Afghanistan to work with UNESCO.

[9]It's not too surprising that Jan (Bridenstine) and Boyd Keefer would follow in the Bridenstine tradition. The Keefers once served on the staff of Inter-Varsity. Now as an Albuquerque realtor, Boyd and Jan live near the University of New Mexico campus. Their large den—converted from the original garage—is often filled with laughter, discussions, prayer and people crowding in for a potluck supper. After eating together, the group settles down for a manuscript Bible study. The Keefers, like their parents, have had their own share of "five loaves and two fishes miracles" in sharing their home and working as volunteers with students. Their children are following their lead.

[10]Charles Hummel was also at MIT working on a master's degree in 1948-49. With VanWylen, he and Wylie Childs, a postdoctoral fellow, had started the IVCF chapter at Rensselaer Polytech. They helped plan and lead student conferences assisting the staff as volunteers. They also got monthly meetings going for students in the Boston area.

[11]*In Understanding Be Men* was an important book in the 1940s and early 1950s. Cameron at the University of Minnesota, DeKoning at Michigan State, and other faithful professors across the country used this book to give theological training to students whose beliefs were under attack by professors on the campus.

[12]Dudley Woodberry is now a professor of Islamics at the School of World Missions, Fuller Theological Seminary, following mission experience in the Middle East.

Chapter 11/When the World Changed: Decade of the 1960s

[1]Horowitz, p. 223.

[2]James Simon Kunen, *The Strawberry Statement —Notes of a College Revolutionary* (New York: Random House, 1969), p. 151.

[3]Fred Wagner is somewhat of a legend among his peers at MSU. As the oldest of ten children, he felt responsible to make it through school on his summer earnings. He became a model of frugality, spending $2.37 a week for food during his time in grad school. Oatmeal was his basic diet, but he also made applesauce by filling his pockets with apples found in the fields on surveying trips. All the cooks knew what to do with leftover food from weekend IV conferences!

[4]In 1959 Carol Streeter, Fred Wagner's childhood sweetheart, enrolled at the new Oakland University in Rochester, Michigan. She helped initiate the first Inter-Varsity chapter there, led Bible studies, went to Campus-in-the-Woods and helped students grow. One of her memories of student days: "I am awed by the wonderful, godly speakers who accepted our invitation to address our chapter. They often drove a long distance. We never reimbursed them adequately, and yet they poured what they knew about God into that group of eager

students. Thinking back at what this must have meant to them to do this, my heart fills with gratitude at their willingness to be used by God."

[5]Miriam Lemcke, *Inter-Varsity News,* July 1961, p.1.

[6]The word *Negro* was used from the 1940s through the early 1960s when the more acceptable phrase was *Afro-Americans,* and then *African-Americans.* The use of *Black(s)* did not come until later in the 1960s. However, former Inter-Varsity staffworker Ivery Harvey, who first staffed Black schools in the South, states that Blacks have called themselves Blacks since slave times. The White community used *Negro* and *Colored.*

[7]The publishing arrangements with the British Inter-Varsity Press were uneven. The American InterVarsity Press, with a slim budget, was interested in publishing largely for students, while much of what the British IVP offered was for the general Christian public. Understandably the British IVP wanted an American outlet for their publishing and had such arrangements with both Fleming H. Revell and Eerdmans publishers, as well as the American IVP. The British IVP gave IVP—U.S.A. first chance for publishing, but financially the U.S. movement could not always take advantage of the offer. Elizabeth Leake, who came from McGraw-Hill to InterVarsity Press, realized the same problem Bayly had faced and set about to increase sales. InterVarsity Press lacked capitalization to develop a full-fledged publishing arm. It was not until Jim Nyquist became the director of the Press in the mid-1960s that InterVarsity Press had sufficient sales to begin an aggressive publishing schedule.

[8]Joe Bayly began Windward Press, which published a few of his own books and a Bible study guide by the founders of Neighborhood Bible Studies—former staffers Catherine Schell and Marilyn Kunz. Joe then joined the editorial staff of David C. Cook Publishing House in Elgin, Illinois, and later was named president. He became a member of the IVCF Board and served the Fellowship in that post until he resigned in 1982.

[9]Stacey Woods preferred the term *secretary* to *director.* The early workers in the collegiate YMCA movement had been called secretaries and the term was also used in Britain. *Director* smacked of American business to Stacey, and he had determined that Inter-Varsity should function as a fellowship, not as a corporation. By 1960 the term *secretary* was confusing to the American public.

[10]Stewardship Secretary W. E. C. Petersen, Business Manager James McLeish and Missions Director Eric Fife had not accepted Hummel's authority from the onset of his appointment as national secretary. They considered his position an encroachment on their respective domains. Several years later, after he had retired in 1962, Mr. Petersen returned to the office one day to ask Hummel's forgiveness for having resisted his leadership. The older man's humility was deeply appreciated on what proved to be their last meeting. (Conversation with Charles Hummel, April, 1990.)

[11]Paul Fromer, a student at Cal Tech, came on staff in the 1954-55 school year, working in southern California and Arizona. He inherited the mantle of editorship of *HIS* in the summer of 1960. Although Paul was a chemistry major, he was a creative "idea" man and with the encouragement of Virginia Krauss (Hearn), his capable and experienced assistant editor, and Gordon Stromberg, the art editor, this team continued to make *HIS* one of the most-read Christian magazines, the winner of repeated awards.

[12]Eric Fife, *Man's Peace, God's Glory* (Downers Grove, Ill.: InterVarsity Press, 1961).

[13]Letter from Colin Becroft to Gordon VanWylen, November 11, 1960, Herbert J. Taylor files, Folder 31, Box 61, Collection 20, Archives of the Billy Graham Center, Wheaton, Illinois.

[14]Letter from Charles Hummel to Charles Troutman, July 11, 1961, Box 36, Collection 8-9, Archives of the Billy Graham Center, Wheaton, Illinois.

[15]The complex reasons for this excessively negative report needs to be explored. Stacey Woods and some of the men in headquarters who had board contacts were known to have made discrediting remarks about Fellowship senior leaders. Second, the loss of many chapters in the Rocky Mountain region in the late fifties due to what the staff called "Rocky Mountain Fever," was, undoubtedly, hard for Stacey Woods to accept. A third difficulty for IVCF was Campus Crusade's strategy of placing numerous staff on a single campus, often where IV already had a chapter, and CCC's public relations output which claimed impressive results. These reports may have embarrassed some of the board members concerned about IV's image, and convinced others who were impressed by reports of CCC success that IVCF

was in its death throes, particularly if they knew of a chapter that was not flourishing or no longer existed.

Inter-Varsity chapters have always had ups and downs, depending on student leadership. Whatever brought it about, the facts do not support the diagnosis that was being circulated. What *is* true is that the board had allowed Stacey Woods to be out of the country for weeks at a time, giving only a portion of his time to the U.S. movement. Those in second-level leadership had responsibilities almost impossible to handle. They gave sacrificial and diligent oversight to the work, often filling multiple roles because the movement was financially hard-pressed. These senior staff sustained an effective witness at great personal cost. They deserved support and even acclaim. Charles Hummel wrote to Roy Horsey, then board president, refuting claims that the movement was in disarray.

Charles Troutman was surprised to realize so many good things were happening on the campus and that the staff was so competent. John Alexander had been a board member; when he became general director in 1965, he had the same negative impressions about the late fifties and early sixties. Stacey Woods, who was essentially an absentee leader during those years, kept the rumor alive when he echoed this same negative note about the state of IVCF in his book *The Growth of a Work of God.* Pete Lowman, writing *The Day of His Power—the History of IFES,* quoted from Stacey's writing.

None of the senior staff leaders who worked on the campuses agree with that negative analysis of IV work in the late 1950s and early 1960s. Paul Byer says, "We accomplished a maximum with the amount of money and staff we had. I was not discouraged." Burton Harding said that he had joined the staff in 1958 because he wanted to be a part of the fine work he saw on the campus. Other regional secretaries—George Ensworth, Jim Nyquist and Keith Hunt—gave similar positive reports of evangelistic outreach, with students taking responsibility for chapters, many of which had between a hundred and two hundred members. Tressie Myers, with her small NCF staff, felt the work was sufficiently well cared for so that during 1957-58 she took a six-month tour of other countries to encourage them to begin NCF work. Statistics show that in 1960, 56 field staff were visiting 831 organized groups (IVCF/NCF/FMF).

[16]C. H. Troutman letter to a friend, October 4, 1961, Folder 17, Box 61, Collection 20, Archives of the Billy Graham Center, Wheaton, Illinois.

[17]*Manual of Financial Policies and Procedures* of Inter-Varsity Christian Fellowship of the USA, September 1962, Collection 88-89, Archives of the Billy Graham Center, Wheaton, Illinois.

[18]Minutes of the executive session of the board of directors, September 29, 1962.

[19]Following Charles Troutman's report on the Student Manual, board member and faculty man Dr. Edson Peck interjected a word of caution—that care be taken to avoid methodology which would result in systematizing procedures, lest Inter-Varsity's pattern of autonomy and student initiative would be destroyed. Troutman assured the board that the manual would instruct in basic steps only and beyond that would deal with principles rather than methods. (Board minutes, May 4-5, 1962, p.4.)

[20]"Inter-Varsity at Fort Lauderdale," *HIS* magazine report, June 1962, p. 14.

[21]Board minutes, May 4-5, 1962, p. 5.

[22]Troutman's use of the figure of 300 chapters needs explaining. Other records indicate that there were 400 IV chapters, 240 NCF groups and 90 SFMF chapters. These figures represent "chapters and organized groups," so the number of 300 was doubtless referring only to officially chartered IVCF chapters.

[23]Letter to Charles Troutman from Keith Hunt, June 1963, Box 46, Collection 88-89, Archives of the Billy Graham Center, Wheaton, Illinois. Additional information about the history of tongues-speaking at Yale can be found in Charles Hummel, *Fire in the Fireplace* (Downers Grove, Ill.: InterVarsity Press, 1978), pp. 19ff.

[24]Troutman worked with the board to mandate retirement at sixty-five. This meant that W. E. C. Petersen, who had controlled the financial income and outgo, was forced to retire in 1963. The board agreed with this policy, solving one difficult problem. The policy has since been rescinded.

[25]Letter from C. H. Troutman to Warner Hutchinson, August 1962, Folder 17, Box 61, Collec-

tion 20, Archives of the Billy Graham Center, Wheaton, Illinois.

[26]During his student days George Ensworth had been president and a key leader in the Inter-Varsity chapter at Michigan State University. While attending Fuller Seminary he served as a part-time staffworker in southern California. He and his wife, Kathy, attended staff training at Campus-in-the-Woods in 1953 and were assigned to staff schools in eastern Pennsylvania. He became the regional secretary for the Middle Atlantic region in 1957. He left IVCF in 1963 to do doctoral studies in psychology. Ensworth had intended to make Inter-Varsity his life work, but now says, "I was becoming more uncomfortable in the role of regional director because I knew that what I liked best was talking with students and other staff, not administrative work. At the time I felt I was being shifted around in IVCF, and maybe even forced out, although that was not the intention. Now I think it was the best thing in the world for me because it got me into the field where God could best use me." He was on the faculty in pastoral counseling at Gordon-Conwell Theological Seminary until his retirement and has an extensive practice as a therapist north of Boston.

[27]Troutman's plan to make every regional director a field director who reported to him took Charles Hummel by surprise, since he did not hear about it until early in 1963. The plan had been presented to the board soon after Troutman came, but Hummel had not heard that his position of field director was in jeopardy. Although Troutman wanted to make Hummel a regional director, Hummel requested that he be appointed to work among faculty and alumni instead.

[28]Gordon VanWylen, founding member of the University of Michigan chapter, engineering faculty, dean of engineering at the University of Michigan, board president of IVCF 1959-1962, and president of Hope College until his retirement, talks about his experience in leadership: "The worst thing you can do is to present a problem to the board without a solution. Now, if you've got a solution, then the board can react to it, and if it's not the right one, they can give some good feedback. But if the board tries to solve problems, they just can't do it. First of all, they don't have the time commitment, and they don't have the perspective. But if you have the right board members, they do have enough wisdom to know whether members of the administration are on the right track." This was a different philosophy than the one under which Troutman had been operating.

[29]Verified in telephone conversation with Charles Troutman, May 20, 1990. He felt even more strongly that university people need to hold decision-making positions. When Troutman spoke of guarding the "university nature of our work" he meant taking the university seriously in every respect. Much of his point of view was mirrored in contributions made by faculty member Edson Peck in board meetings during his tenure on the board. Troutman saw Inter-Varsity as collegial in mindset, not corporate. Many believe that Troutman has the clearest philosophical grasp of the nature of Christian university work of anyone who has been part of IVCF.

[30]*Inter-Varsity News,* December 1963.

[31]Sabbatical leaves had been approved for Keith Hunt and Charles Hummel prior to the reorganization, which meant that two key people were missing during the first half of 1964.

[32]Wallace Erickson is the president of Chicago-based Wallace A. Erickson and Company, manufacturers of cosmetics. He has been an active Christian businessman, as well as a member of the board of the Evangelical Foundation and Young Life.

[33]Richard Wolff, a gifted multilingual man, was a German-Jew who went into hiding in Belgium during World War 2 and came to the U.S. following the war. An effective writer and speaker, he came to Inter-Varsity from the *Back to the Bible* ministry in Lincoln, Nebraska, where he directed the French radio programs released throughout the French-speaking world. His primary acquaintance with the university campus came from invitations to speak at Bear Trap Ranch.

[34]The Butler Corporation, developers of Oak Brook, offered a tract of land to Northern Baptist Seminary and later an additional tract to Inter-Varsity Christian Fellowship, feeling that these two organizations would bring a good tone into the new development. Northern Baptist Seminary accepted the gift and moved to the location. Inter-Varsity never acted on the offer, according to Charles Troutman. Phone conversation, May 20, 1990.

[35]Conversation with Charles Troutman, May 20, 1990.

[36]Files 31, Box 61, Collection 20, Archives of the Billy Graham Center, Wheaton, Illinois.

[37]The Fellowship *had* been operating under a "hierarchical structure" since the appointment of regional secretaries in 1948. Charles Hummel suggested in May 1961 that area directors should be appointed to work under regional directors, and two men were appointed on a trial basis. Every staff member knew who he reported to and what organizational chart they operated under. However, Erickson's definition of a *fellowship* continued to circulate among board members, depicting "every man doing what was right in his own eyes."

[38]Margaret Haines wrote, "We need to distinguish between a business corporation which is for profit, constructed on secular lines, and a Christian organization which is missionary in character. The Christian fellowship aspect is what has blessed and made the movement strong under God. We do recognize lines of authority, but authority should be shown with love and consideration of differences of opinion and conviction in carrying on student work. A form of dictatorial hierarchy is contrary to the spirit of the movement and hinders the full working of the Holy Spirit. The whole name Inter-Varsity Christian Fellowship needs to be emphasized. The words *Inter-Varsity* could very quickly become secularized. The phrase could be used as Inter-Varsity football, or debating team, or what have you." Miss Haines also commented, "The present executive director (Richard Wolff) should be removed from that position as soon as possible." (File 31, Box 61, Collection 20, Archives of the Billy Graham Center, Wheaton, Illinois.)

[39]The executive committee members included Stan Block, vice president; Sam Fuenning, secretary; John Alexander, treasurer; Alan Mathis, Jr., and Ralph Watts.

[40]From the board minutes, October 2-3, 1964, p. 2.

[41]Members of SAC who signed the statement were Paul Byer, Eric Fife, Paul Fromer, Burt Harding, Charles Hummel, Keith Hunt, Warner Hutchinson, Paul Little, James McLeish, Tressie Myers, Peter Northrup and James Nyquist.

[42]File 31, Box 61, Collection 20, Archives of the Billy Graham Center, Wheaton, Illinois.

[43]Ibid.

[44]Ibid.

[45]In response to action already taken by the board, on September 30, 1964, the members of the staff advisory committee (in consultation with Charles Troutman) sent a letter to Roy Horsey, chairman of a special ad hoc study committee, affirming the board's decision that Charles Troutman could best serve Inter-Varsity in a capacity other than general director. He had already given a second official resignation statement to the study committee for the board meetings October 2-3.

[46]Shortly after that board meeting, Roy Horsey telephoned Charles Hummel to ask if he wanted to be considered for appointment as the new general director. Charlie was reluctant to accept since he had experienced too many other leadership controversies in recent years. He believed the new leader needed to have a mandate from the staff advisory committee (SAC) as well as the board—a clean slate that, at that point, only an outsider could have. He said, however, that he would be open to guidance from the SAC. A straw vote at its meeting a few weeks later confirmed his evaluation; only two-thirds of the members indicated their support. Hummel preached at the spiritual life week at Barrington College in early November; the college subsequently invited him to become its president.

[47]Minutes of the October 2-3, 1964, meeting of the board of directors.

[48]Board minutes, October 2-3, p. 5.

[49]Betty Howard has had an effective ministry. Since 1976 she has worked in Jordan, in a largely Muslim culture among women who have few leadership opportunities within the church. She begins with evangelistic Bible studies, and after conversion, teaches the women the importance of prayer and how to have a Quiet Time. Then she instructs them in preparing and leading Bible studies. They invite their friends and take the same kind of leadership they have seen Betty take in their lives. Betty does not do their work for them; she comes alongside to help, just as her staff member did when she was a student.

[50]James Stamoolis became a Christian at Lehigh and eventually served as the IFES theological secretary. He is now dean of Wheaton Graduate School, Wheaton, Illinois.

[51]Barry Widman, an engineer with General Electric, says of his student days, "We learned what was important in those years of fellowship in our IV chapter."

[52]Following his graduation from Lehigh University, Thomas Trevethan spent a year at Trinity Evangelical Divinity School, and did a study term abroad. He then worked as campus staff for two years under Ned Hale, serving five colleges in downstate Illinois. (Glenn Deckert staffed the University of Illinois and eastern Illinois colleges.) Ed Bradley, John Hochevar and Mark Malan were students during Tom's early staff days, and later joined the staff of Inter-Varsity. The integrity in the lives of faculty members like Katherine Watson and Tom Cummings at Bradley University lent support to the student ministry in this area for over two decades. Tom Trevethan staffed the University of Wisconsin during the turbulent years of student revolution, taking a chapter that had almost disappeared and turning the situation around so that culturally relevant evangelism could take place in Madison. He married Barbara Miller, an IV student from Bowling Green University (Ohio), who was an IVCF staff member in Michigan. They have served over twenty years, first in Pittsburgh, Pennsylvania, and later in Ann Arbor, Michigan, where Tom is currently an area director.

Chapter 12/The Confusion of Order: Decade of the 1960s

[1]John W. Alexander, *Student Handbook,* Inter-Varsity, 1973, Part One, I-A-I (2).

[2]John R. W. Stott's ministry at successive Inter-Varsity Student Missionary Conventions has been one of IVCF's gifts to the American church. His preaching has given a new appreciation and a new standard for biblical exposition, influencing the many ministers attending Urbana. Arthur Glasser tells of sitting next to a minister during the 1964 Bible expositions. When Stott finished, the pastor turned to Glasser and said, "God helping me, I am never going to enter the pulpit unprepared again and, God helping me, I am going to do biblical exposition. I want to let people hear the Word of God like Stott did this morning. I never realized how fascinating and instructive that kind of preaching is."

John Alexander says that when he invited Stott to return and speak at subsequent Urbanas, he demurred, saying that being the Bible expositor at Urbana was such a privilege that no man should enjoy it twice when others had not experienced it. Alexander wanted him back for two reasons: (1) to model to American Christians what IVCF meant by *Bible exposition* and (2) to keep Bible exposition at the forefront of our ministry.

[3]Inter-Varsity Christian Fellowship minutes of the board of directors, October 2-3, 1964, pp. 15-16. Wallace Erickson evidently had not acted on the contract Charles Troutman had for the sale of the building.

[4]Ibid, p. 15.

[5]Ibid, November 6-7, 1964, p. 4.

[6]Personal letter from Peter Northrup, dated October 22, 1965.

[7]Board minutes, July 30-31, 1965, p. 4.

[8]Minutes of the staff advisory council, July 26-29, 1965, Hudson House, Upper Nyack, N.Y., pp. 2-3.

[9]Excerpt from letter, Fred Woodberry, September 7, 1965.

[10]Excerpt from letter, Paul D. Steeves, August 24, 1965.

[11]Letter from Warner Hutchinson to John W. Alexander, Box 6, Collection 88-89, Archives of the Billy Graham Center, Wheaton, Illinois.

[12]This fit well with Stacey Woods's view of leadership: "Don't try to manage creative people in the usual sense of management. They need good sensible systems and someone who sets very high standards. Talented people take pride in their work and respond by reaching beyond the obvious. A friction-free fellowship can't be very creative. Discuss ideas; argue; the key element is respect. As long as respect is in place, it's productive." In that sense Woods felt it was more satisfying to have "all chiefs and no Indians" because it insured quality.

[13]Letter from Burton Harding to John W. Alexander, Box 6, Collection 88-89, Archives of the Billy Graham Center, Wheaton, Illinois.

[14]From a personal letter to the authors from John W. Alexander, June 8, 1990.

[15]Yvonne Vinkemulder had been working as secretary and administrative assistant for Keith Hunt in the East Central Region and moved with him to the development department in the headquarters in 1963. When Hunt chose to go back to the field, Yvonne Vinkemulder remained in the development department. She later became the director of development.

[16]John Alexander admits he is thin-skinned about criticism. It was something that plagued him during his tenure as president. The criticism he perceived coming from board members was so distressful to Alexander that, he says, "I developed a Pavlovian reflex of dread as I anticipated any kind of board meeting." Alexander speaks highly of his relationship with Board Chairman Roy Horsey, whose personal interest and encouragement he found very supportive.

[17]Letter from Peter Northrup to John Alexander, dated January 5, 1966, Box 33, Collection 88-89, Archives of the Billy Graham Center, Wheaton, Illinois.

[18]John Alexander knew how to laugh at himself. He once posted a cartoon in which the chairman of the board (labeled Allen Mathis) is handing a gift package to a senior employee (labeled Dr. A). The caption reads, ". . . and as a memento of your 40 years with personnel, eight leather-bound volumes of revised organizational charts."

[19]In response to this John Alexander felt that it was impossible to press the university or collegial model onto IVCF. "No university has a mission statement like ours. We are an evangelizing fellowship, in business to penetrate the university and take every thought into captivity for Christ. . . . The university rejects and ridicules such a concept. IVCF is, in this instance, more like an army in which every member is admonished to put on the whole armor of faith. . . . My point is that it would be foolish to follow the 'university model' when it comes to our purpose and strategy." Those who recommended the "collegial model" refer, not to the mission of the university, but to the free flow of ideas and the autonomy and trust given to professors.

[20]Will Norton in his book *To Stir the Church* writes that Eric Fife in 1960 announced there would be no SFMF staff member and that he would try to visit a Christian school with an SFMF chapter once every three years. From 1960-66 the missionary committee, a board committee, did not meet. Those who had initiated SFMF and had been key in the merger with IVCF were not happy with this hiatus in relationship.

[21]Other IFES movements in Asia had been implementing the small group concept for some years, calling them "cell groups." IVCF leaders decided to use the term "action groups" to indicate that the small groups were not to be ingrown, but to have an outreach.

[22]InterVarsity Press, under the leadership of Director Jim Nyquist, received the rights for *Escape from Reason* from Inter-Varsity Press in Britain and purchased the rights for *The God Who Is There* from Hodder & Stoughton in England. Nyquist firmly believed these books would meet a great need in the student world.

Chapter 13/The Challenge of Growth and Stability: Decade of the 1970s

[1]Laurence C. Walker, "The Layman and His Church," *The Presbyterian Journal,* December, 1972, p. 13. Walker, a long-time friend of Inter-Varsity, was influenced by its ministry in his student days. He worked as a volunteer, opened his home to students and staff as well as serving on local committees for IVCF and the corporation.

[2]Horowitz, p. 244.

[3]The Boston Women's Health Book Collective Staff, *Our Bodies, Ourselves,* 2d ed. (New York: Simon & Schuster, 1976).

[4]Horowitz, p. 245.

[5]By the 1980s only fifteen per cent of university students finished college in four years, and fewer than half made it to a bachelor's degree after six years.

[6]Cooperative Institutional Research Program, *The American Freshman National Norms* (December 1984).

[7]Arthur Levine, *When Dreams and Heroes Died: A Portrait of Today's College Student* (San Francisco: Jossey-Bass, 1980), p. 103. Levine surveyed the despair of students about the world and all its problems and their desire to "have it all" in face of uncertainty about the future. He called their attitude "going first class on the Titanic."

[8]From time to time campus Christian groups cooperate on outreach projects and special events. Students soon learn to identify the focus of each group and make choices accordingly. The groups feel comfortable with each other, and there is no longer a spirit of competition, such as existed in the 1950s. The leaders of the major evangelical parachurch student organizations meet regularly together to pray and encourage each other.

[9]By 1972 a funding problem caused the cancellation of Inter-Varsity's sponsorship of *Youth Today*. Jim Reapsome carried on its publication on his own for the next year. The publication then became part of *Eternity* magazine. Reapsome also edited a four-page monthly newsletter for parents, called "Hotline to Parents," given away as a public relations piece by the development department of IVCF during 1971-72.

[10]Abraham Joshua Heschel, *The Insecurity of Freedom* (New York: Farrar, Straus & Giroux, 1966), p. 39.

[11]Story told in interview with Glen Zumwalt, July 3, 1990. Johnson Lee is now pastor of a Chinese Church in Long Beach, Calif.

[12]Interview with Steve Stuckey, June 16, 1988.

[13]Letter from student president Mark Hunt to David Howard, June 7, 1973. Correspondence of David Howard, Collection 88-89, Archives of the Billy Graham Center, Wheaton, Illinois.

[14]As a result of a promotional film designed by Elward Ellis and Carl Ellis, about 600 Black students participated in Urbana 70, considered a watershed by many in Inter-Varsity.

[15]Interview with David Howard, New Brunswick, New Jersey, May 7, 1988. Every student received a copy of Howard's book *Student Power and World Evangelism* (IVP, 1970) in their packet at Urbana, and the book title was the topic of Howard's keynote address. The Black delegation responded negatively to his keynoter because no mention was made of any Black student in recounting the history of what students had done in missions. All Howard could say was that he did not find a record of any Blacks in his research. John Alexander had been in the SVM at the University of Illinois during his student days and remembered seeing exactly what Howard described—the demise of the SVM as a result of the change of focus. He said, "As long as I am president of Inter-Varsity we will never allow this to happen to the missions emphasis of our movement."

[16]*HIS* magazine, March 1971, p. 12.

[17]Margaret Clarkson also wrote "We Come, O Christ to Thee" (p. 22, *Hymns II*) at the request of Stacey Woods, and it was a theme hymn at the first missionary convention in Toronto in 1946.

[18]From James Reapsome (editor of the *Evangelical Missions Quarterly* and *Youth Today*), "Perspective on Urbana 73: A Report on the Feeding of the 14,000," *HIS* magazine, March 1974.

[19]Bernie Smith was an IV graduate from Kent State (Ohio) who served on the staff of Inter-Varsity in Canada. He led the singing at seven consecutive Urbanas, beginning in 1970, and was greatly loved by the students.

[20]Staff members later evaluated the use of musical performers during convention and strongly recommended that student participation in singing made a stronger experience for the delegates and was more in keeping with IVCF's emphasis on student involvement.

[21]Gordon Stromberg was attracted to *HIS* magazine before he knew its connection to Inter-Varsity. When he saw a copy of *HIS* at a meeting, he thought he had never seen a Christian magazine as beautiful and as well-designed. Because *HIS* carried no ads, as the graphic designer he had carte blanche to design the total product.

[22]Perhaps the best example of the way *HIS* spoke to what was happening within the movement is the November 1968 issue of *HIS* in which Fromer gave a lengthy explanation of the "action group" concept. He had helped develop the idea and gave practical suggestions of how to make action groups work within a chapter. Students read every word in that issue and put the ideas to work.

[23]Gordon Stromberg resigned as art editor of *HIS* at the end of 1968. He was followed by Grant Smith in 1969. Kathy Lay (Burrows) served as interim art director prior to Mickey Moore's arrival. Moore did not have an Inter-Varsity background, and Fromer felt his world/life view did not represent IV's, making it difficult to integrate the contents of the magazine artistically in the way that had been done before.

[24]Interview with Stephen Board, June 20, 1990.

[25]James Reapsome had left Inter-Varsity staff in 1961 to edit *The Sunday School Times* in Philadelphia. He subsequently served two years (1967-69) as chaplain of Malone College (Ohio) and in the early 1970s was a free-lance writer, editing the *Evangelical Missions Quarterly, Youth Letter, The International Uniform Sunday School Lesson Commentary*, etc.

He also served as a board member, and succeeded Will Norton as chairman of the missions committee.

[26]Box 3, Collection 88-89, Archives of the Billy Graham Center, Wheaton, Illinois. The figure thirty per cent was only a guess because *HIS* had not taken an accurate poll. Nevertheless, assuming the statistic was accurate, one IVCF staffer responded, "But what if those 30% are members of the chapter's executive?"

[27]Ibid.

[28]A gallant troupe of gifted and creative people worked as assistant editors for *HIS* during the sixties and seventies. Doris Roethlisberger, Linda Sellevaag, Barbara Sroka, Verne Becker, Noel Becchetti and Joan Wulff. Kathy Lay (Burrows) was the art director for *HIS* as well as InterVarsity Press during some of those years. Wynema Marlatte served as business manager for the magazine for over a decade.

[29]Minutes of the board meeting, April 1978, p. 6.

[30]As a policy, IVP asks knowledgeable people (according to the subject of the book) for evaluation of manuscripts whenever in-house editors lack expertise in the subject. In the beginning days of publishing in IVCF, a literature committee helped choose books for publication. A book is chosen for its merit in stimulating Christians to think, not for its public relations value.

[31]The only book ever removed from publication was *Brave New People* by D. Gareth Jones. James McLeish, then president of IVCF, took this action in the summer of 1984 because he believed the controversy was divisive and harmful to Inter-Varsity's relationship to the public.

[32]Paul Beckwith, the editor of Inter-Varsity's *Hymns* who had done so much in the Fellowship to encourage students to sing thoughtfully and biblically, developed a brain tumor shortly after his first and only meeting with the *Hymns II* editors. He died in November 1975.

[33]In 1974-75 the number of chapters had dropped to 797, with 22,578 students seriously involved in IVCF. Statistics show 152 field staff and 176 non-field support staff. By the close of the decade, IVCF had 381 field staff who were reaching 820 chapters with 30,000 students. John Alexander expressed concern repeatedly that IV was giving more staff help to fewer students as the years progressed.

[34]This basic purpose of Inter-Varsity is emphasized in the Revised By-Laws of the IVCF-USA constitution (November 14, 1970). Article XVI delineates how a group becomes a chapter: "Chapters of the Corporation: Each established group, when qualified, shall be chartered by the Fellowship and shall thereupon become a chapter of the Fellowship. To qualify, a group shall subscribe to the Doctrinal Basis of the Fellowship, and its purposes. Each group shall be self-sustaining, self-governing, and self-propagating, and shall have the right to choose its own name." This by-law reiterates the policy in effect since the beginning of the movement in 1940.

[35]Staff Policy Manual, 1971, pages 65 ff.

[36]Charles Smith, a medical doctor in Indianapolis, long a faithful friend and supporter of IVCF, along with his wife Lee, wrote, on April 15, 1988, "Paul Little spoke at college night at our house the Friday night before he died. It may have been his last ministry to students. We had 275 students at our home that night in a pouring rain. I had noticed that his light was still on at 2 A.M. Saturday morning, so when we got up to go to the airport at 6 A.M. I asked him if he had trouble sleeping. He excitedly answered, 'No, I was reading Packer's *Knowing God!'* The next Wednesday he was killed in a car accident in Canada and knew God better than Packer." (The Smiths designed their home for college student ministry. Each summer on Friday nights they have a college night program for students home from university.)

[37]Box 6. Collection 88-89, Archives of the Billy Graham Center, Wheaton, Illinois.

Chapter 14/A Maturing Ministry: Decade of the 1970s
[1]John R. W. Stott, "Christ, Lord and Liberator," *HIS* magazine, June 1971.
[2]James E. Massey, a gifted speaker, writer and preacher, continues to be a strong influencer in the Black community. He is presently Dean of the School of Theology, Anderson University, Anderson, Indiana.
[3]Interview with Paul Gibson, June 18, 1988, Pasadena, Calif.

[4]The World Evangelism Decision Card was an important part of every student missions conference, beginning in Toronto in 1946. The card was designed to help a student make a commitment regarding foreign missions on three levels: (1) to say yes to the call of God to go overseas, (2) if uncertain, to pray about God's will regarding foreign missions and (3) a sense of God's call to stay at home with a commitment to participate by generous giving and prayer. Under David Howard's leadership, students were encouraged to think and pray about personal commitment, fill out the card, mail one-half of it in to the office (or place in receptacles at the convention) and keep the other half as a reminder of personal commitment. This enabled the missions department to send further encouragement and counsel by mail.

[5]Interview with David Howard, July 5, 1988.

[6]Margaret Clarkson, "Declare His Glory," Hymns II, #178.

[7]Will Norton, in his book To Stir the Church, writes, "Throughout the years IVCF . . . had difficulty understanding the place of SFMF. With such an overwhelming number of new staff coming from university campuses where the SFMF did not relate, the support and empathy needed to accept the SFMF often was lacking. . . . With the coming of David Howard as missions director to the campus scene in the late 1960s, the issue of missions was directly addressed. . . . Howard presented the Biblical basis of missions so clearly that his tenure may be regarded as the watershed of Inter-Varsity's mission outreach." (Student Foreign Missions Fellowship, 1986, p. 57.)

[8]The seconding of David Howard to this task was not unusual. Inter-Varsity had previously seconded Paul Little to Lausanne I to direct the world-wide gathering in Switzerland in 1974, and he was later seconded to teach evangelism at Trinity Evangelical Divinity School.

[9]Isabelo Magalit was then the associate general secretary for IFES in Southeast Asia. He is now the first Asian president of the Asian Theological Seminary in the Philippines. He has also pastored the Diliman Bible Church in Manila. He spoke at Urbana 76, 79 and 81.

[10]Details about David Howard from an interview, July 8, 1988, New Brunswick, N.J.

[11]Staff report of Larry Brown, campus staff member (CSM) in the Chicago area from 1973-78.

[12]Letter from John Alexander to Jim Nyquist, January 23, 1973, Box 6, Collection 88-89, Archives of the Billy Graham Center, Wheaton, Illinois.

[13]John Alexander had a strong commitment to his family. His son-in-law Terry Finigan, father of two small children, suffered prolonged deterioration from a brain tumor before he died. One of John's brothers died, and another had a serious problem. These events caused Alexander deep distress and may have affected his ability to concentrate on organizational events.

[14]Letter from James Berney, West Coast regional director until 1981, dated July 20, 1990.

[15]Interview with Richard Karppinen, now professor in the business school at Calvin College, Grand Rapids, Mich., on April 26, 1989. Dick Karppinen was a student in Pittsburgh, active in Inter-Varsity, and attended Campus-in-the-Woods and Urbana. While in graduate school at the University of Pittsburgh during the early sixties, he helped staff the Inter-Varsity chapters in western Pennsylvania, along with several other graduates. Western Pennsylvania was without a staff member during those years, until Neil Rendall arrived in 1965. Dick went to Nigeria with the Peace Corps in the fall of 1967. When he returned to get his doctorate in accounting, he heard about the opening with Inter-Varsity. He was torn about what to do. He said, "I sort of set up this deal with God that if my very orthodox Jewish faculty advisor would approve of my doing a thesis on the way a Christian organization sets up its accounting, then I would accept the offer from Inter-Varsity. So I put together a proposal for my thesis and submitted it. The faculty advisor came running down the hall and said, "This is tremendous. It's right on the edge of where accounting research is going. By all means, go!" The contribution of those who have taken responsibilities in the business procedures of Inter-Varsity has given the movement not only efficient procedures, but integrity.

[16]The development of Mariners Cove began with an all-purpose building, named after Susan McClure who was fatally injured in the Urbana 73 bus accident, and the H. J. Taylor lodge, honoring the man who had done so much for Inter-Varsity as a board member and friend, plus additional housing space. The C. S. Woods Memorial Meeting Hall, designed for large

groups, was not built. Before completion of the site, John Alexander left the presidency and those in charge of programming in the national office canceled all national programs at Cedar Campus.

[17]Gwen Wong became an Inter-Varsity staffworker in 1949 in Hawaii and subsequently pioneered student work in the Philippines.

[18]Ellie Lau, now working with IFES in Hong Kong, and Greg Owyang also made commitments at this retreat. Greg Owyang was serving as pastor for the First Chinese Baptist Church in Los Angeles when a demented church member rushed into a worship service and killed Owyang and another member.

[19]Letter to the authors from John Alexander, December 26, 1988.

Chapter 15/Revolving-Door Leadership: Decade of the 1980s

[1]Derek Prime, *A Christian's Guide to Leadership* (London: Hodder & Stoughton, 1964) p. 17.

[2]Daniel J. Boorstin, "The Luxury of Retrospect," *Life* magazine, Special Issue: The 80s (Fall 1989), p. 37.

[3]David and Sally Ivaska spent seven years in Kenya where David was Bible study training secretary for FOCUS (the unbrella organization for African student movements) and are now back in the States where David is on staff at Northwestern University (Illinois); Tom and Nancy Balma left in 1981 to serve IFES in Italy; Fred and Gwyneth Bailey went to Vienna, Austria; Terrell and Mary Smith began a ministry to international students in Germany. Gordon and Marilyn Woolard went to Belgium; Andrea Sterk went to Yugoslavia; Ann Bennighof (Maouya) went to French-speaking Africa with a Fulbright scholarship, and has since served as the Bible study secretary for that area. Many other staff were seconded to national movements like Zambia, Brazil, France, Italy, Switzerland, Spain.

[4]John Alexander later related his perceptions about that breakfast conversation. He had expected a discussion about criteria and instead was asked who should be considered internally as his successor. He said, "I was so stunned by this turn of events that, without thinking, I numbly suggested the name of the senior vice president. I did not say what I was thinking, that Jim McLeish would not pass the critera screen I had prepared. I felt that the decision to make this appointment had been made before the breakfast began." (Interview with John Alexander, November 11, 1987.)

[5]Allen Mathis believed John's health was failing. "The last four or five years of Alexander's administration, McLeish was really running the operation. Alexander wanted to put McLeish between him and anything that might develop confrontation." (Interview with Allen Mathis, January 25, 1989.)

[6]Knowing Alexander's love for Cedar Campus, in 1980 the national office made funds available to build a cabin on the camp site for the president's department, and Alexander was encouraged to use Cedar Campus for his training programs. The Alexanders were also sent to Africa in January of 1981 to visit IFES movements, since John Alexander was chairman of the IFES Executive Committee at that time. (Interview with John Alexander, February 1988.)

[7]At the next board meeting on November 1, 1980, board member Stanley Block expressed surprise when the president's report mentioned Jim McLeish as "primary executive officer." The explanation was given that this was a misnomer; the correct title being "primary operating officer," and that the step was taken by the president and discussed with the executive committee. (Minutes of the board meeting, November 1, 1980, p. 3.)

[8]Official minutes of the board, April 26, 1980, p. 3.

[9]Board minutes, April 30, 1982, p. 3. "The board would function as a committee of the whole, thus eliminating committees other than the nominating committee." Board committees eliminated included committees which made reports and recommendations about missions, literature, camping, nurses, development committee, faculty and finance. Subsequently in 1990 four committees became operative: human resources, employee benefits, nominating and audit.

[10]Joseph T. Bayly, president of David C. Cook Company and former InterVarsity staff member, resigned from the board September 7, 1982, protesting the board's decisions on several issues and the concentration of power in the chairman. (Box 46, Collection 88-89, Archives

of the Billy Graham Center, Wheaton, Illinois.)

[11]Alexander relates, "During the summer of 1981 at Cedar Campus, every day as I sat on the deck of our cabin, another staff member would stop by to describe the agony he or she was going through, the confusion about why things were happening and why I wasn't doing something about it. I didn't feel I could tell them what was happening. It was like seeing an orchestra where you've worked with your first chair people, your second chair people and you've recruited good new musicians—and then you see the orchestra taken over by a new conductor, a new producer and see manuscripts replaced with different scores and see musicians handicapped—that was a painful year." Interview with John Alexander, February 1987.

[12]Regarding the decision to make Jim McLeish president and CEO, Mathis said, "McLeish was Alexander's first and only choice to succeed him. He wrote me a number of memos to that effect." (Interview with Mathis, January 25, 1989.) The authors found no written evidence to indicate that Alexander protested the appointment of McLeish as COO, which if successful would probably result in his presidency.

However, in a letter dated September 14, 1990, Alexander writes, "I know of no memos indicating that Jim was my first and only choice to succeed me—except the two letters written seventeen months after that historic April 30 breakfast when the [ad hoc committee within the] board executive committee tabbed Jim to succeed me. Prior to that breakfast Jim had always said, 'When John walks out the door, I'm going with him.'" Alexander clearly felt the decision to make McLeish COO (and eventually CEO, if he proved capable) in July 1980 was a board committee decision, one that defeated him. The two letters to which Alexander refers were the two letters he wrote (October 27 and November 2) resigning as president in which he said, "He (McLeish) has led the movement with commitment, creativity, enthusiasm and zeal. He has earned his spurs." In an interview on November 11, 1987, he mentioned his concern that he respond in a way that would not split the movement. Of further interest, in a letter addressed to the Inter-Varsity family, dated November 10, 1981, Alexander told of his resignation and said, "I first entertained private thoughts of resignation in the autumn of 1980. In the summer of 1981 I sketched in pencil a letter of resignation. And tore it up. In August of 1981 I typed a letter of resignation. And tore it up also. But on October 27 I sent Board Chairman Allen Mathis a note saying I thought I should resign. Reason: fatigue." (Letter to IVCF staff, November 10, 1981.)

[13]Bob Fryling began as a staffworker in the Eastern region in 1969 after graduating from Drexel University, where he had been an active student leader. In 1975 he was appointed regional director for the Eastern region. He became director of campus ministries in 1981 and again in 1984, serving as director of human resources in 1983.

[14]John "Pete" Hammond became Southeast regional director in 1973, after serving as a campus staff member. In 1979 he left with his family for a year in the Philippines, teaching at the Asian Theological Seminary, expecting to return to his regional post the next year. However, the Southeast Region was given to Ed Good in his absence, and Pete returned to be moved to the Madison office where he was assigned to special projects. Jim McLeish appointed him director of evangelism in 1981.

[15]In the alpha group composed of eight people, two (Fryling and Wallace) were the only ones with direct supervision of field staff members. The regional directors had been included in all previous management teams.

[16]Minutes of the board, November 7, 1981, p. 2.

[17]Geri Rodman graduated from the University of Toronto in 1972 and joined InterVarsity staff in 1979. She was the first woman to be made an area director in 1981.

[18]Janet Luhrs (Balajthy) was an undergraduate student at Wagner College (New York), later studying for a master of counseling degree at Hofstra University (New York) and a master of biblical studies at Wheaton College. She began staff work in 1975 in Metro New York and became area director for northern New Jersey in 1981. She was appointed a regional director for New York and New Jersey in 1982.

[19]Jeanette Yep (Chicago), Janet Luhrs (New York), Geri Rodman (San Francisco), Susie Veon (Northern California), Sandy Beelen (Northern Illinois) and Donna Dong have held area director posts.

[20]Barney Ford graduated from University of Evansville (Indiana) in 1969 after active student participation in IVCF. Area Director Don Fields invited him to come on staff in 1969. He became an area director in 1974 in Ohio and subsequently in Michigan. Under McLeish's presidency he became an associate director of campus ministries, and in 1986 he became the chief administrative officer for InterVarsity.

[21]Roger Anderson played a strategic role in maintaining a witness at University of North Carolina as a graduate student in 1970-72. During his undergraduate days he had served as president of the IV chapter at the University of Delaware. He joined the staff of IVCF in 1973 and became an area director in 1975 and a regional director in 1979. In 1983 he was appointed an associate director of campus ministries.

[22]Ron Nicholas graduated from the University of Minnesota at Duluth in 1969, served on staff in Iowa in 1971, and became an area director for Minnesota in 1974 and a regional director for the North Central Region in 1978. In 1981 he was appointed an associate director of campus ministries. In 1983 he was made director of strategic planning and put together the *Small Group Leaders' Handbook* used by IV chapters. Nicholas has since been seconded to Educational Services Exchange International where he serves as vice president.

[23]Bill Tiffan graduated from the University of Michigan in December 1968. He attended leadership camp at Cedar Campus the summer of 1967 and caught a vision for the small group emphasis in IV that summer. After graduation he attended Columbia Bible College where he worked with the IVCF chapter at the University of South Carolina. He came on staff in 1971, assigned as a CSM to staff about seven colleges in the San Diego (California) area. In 1975 he became area director of half of southern California, became a divisional director in 1983, and then became an associate director of campus ministries. In 1983 he moved to Madison, Wisconsin, to become the director of campus ministries for a year and a half. He left InterVarsity in 1987.

[24]Linda Doll graduated from the University of Massachusetts after active participation in the IV chapter there. She had become a Christian through a Bible study group that later turned into an IVCF chapter. While teaching for four years in the East, she served as an associate staff member helping at Smith and Mt. Holyoke. She joined the staff in New England in 1961 and, along with Stan Rock and later others, staffed all of New England until 1966. After a year at London Bible College she returned to staff New Hampshire and Vermont. She moved to InterVarsity Press in 1968 and became *HIS* editor in 1975.

[25]The foundation department included businessmen who took early retirement to help raise money for InterVarsity. Among them were men like Will Townsend, Bill Bonfield, Curt Kenney, Fred Woolard and others who served IVCF well. In the late eighties other younger men, who are making financial development their life's work, joined the development team.

[26]The minutes of the November 1982 board meetings confirm that Jim McLeish agreed to serve until retirement in December 1986, but that information was not widely known outside the board. Chester Youngberg and Donald Powell, former board chairmen, agreed to serve as a committee to look for a successor, but they were not pressing their search since 1986 was four years away. Although there had been some in-house interviews and a few contacts with prominent Christian leaders regarding the presidency in early 1982, after the November 1982 board meeting the search was not given high priority.

[27]The staff leaders on the West Coast felt isolated from much of what was happening in headquarters, and since Jim McLeish had supported them emotionally and financially, they wanted to maintain distance from the Madison crisis situation. (Interview with Pete Sommer, January 20, 1988.)

[28]Interview with Peter and Martha B. Northrup, August 16, 1989. Peter Northrup served three presidents as a faithful administrative assistant: John Alexander, Jim McLeish and, briefly, Gordon MacDonald. He was honest, fair, insightful and forthright in communicating on difficult issues.

[29]Interview with Jim Nyquist, March 22, 1989.

[30]Roger Harrison, "Understanding Your Organization's Character," *Harvard Business Review on Management* (New York: Harper & Row, 1975), p. 39, gives four organizational ideologies: (1) power orientation, (2) role orientation, (3) task orientation and (4) person orientation. He argues that failure to understand these differences often causes conflict

within organizations. "In a task-oriented organization members have come together because of a shared value or goal and the highest value is the achievement of this goal. . . . Authority is considered legitimate only if it is based on appropriate knowledge and competence; it is not legitimate if it is based solely on power or position."

[31]Bill Tiffan describes McLeish's leadership style as "innovative, risk-taking and conflict-oriented. He was a political person. The political aspects of Jim's administration meant that people were more divided. Tension surrounded his leadership. He had a good heart; his intentions were good. He loved InterVarsity."

[32]Discussions among board members about Jim McLeish's departure were confusing. At first he was asked to stay on for six months. Then the suggestion was made that he stay on for two months. After further discussion the board voted on immediate retirement. Commenting on this later, McLeish said that he never thought so much trouble would come for the sake of five months, his having planned to retire that June, although this was never made public information. Recounting his contribution to InterVarsity, Jim said, "When I came, they had about forty people and half of them were paying their own way. The budget went from that small amount to what it was when I left—twenty-six million dollars, with about seven hundred employees. This is a great thing that God has done." (Interview with Jim McLeish, December 27, 1987.)

[33]Jim Nyquist said he felt that he was seeing the movement to which he had given his life fall apart before his eyes. Peter Northrup's resignation had been accepted without much apparent concern on the board's part. Nyquist said he knew that vice presidents are expendable, but he was concerned about the widespread distress in the field and especially when he heard a rumor that two regional leaders might be fired for their opposition to McLeish's leadership. He felt that the concentration of power in the hands of Mathis, Youngberg and McLeish was harmful to the movement and had shut off communication between the board and staff of InterVarsity. He distributed his letter directly to the members of the board as an appeal for informed action. Following Nyquist's letter to the entire board, Jim McLeish informed Nyquist he could no longer work for InterVarsity and offered him retirement. This was reviewed at the January 25, 1985, board meeting in Atlanta and Nyquist, who had come on staff in 1949, was officially retired. (Interview with Jim Nyquist, March 22, 1989.)

After Nyquist's release from Inter-Varsity, Chua Wee Hian, general secretary of the International Fellowship of Evangelical Students, asked him to serve as literature secretary to help young movements with their literature programs, a post Nyquist had previously held in an honorary capacity. In 1986 he began editing a regular information sheet called *Administry,* designed to help leaders of national movements with matters of administration. He has traveled widely for the IFES.

[34]Minutes of the board, January 25-26, 1985, p. 3.

[35]Minutes of the board, June 6-7, 1986, p. 5.

[36]*Inter-Varsity Christian Fellowship of the United States of America* is still the legal name for the movement. *InterVarsity* (without the hyphen) is a useful logo for public relations purposes.

[37]Interview with Allen Mathis, Jr., January 25, 1989.

[38]Gordon MacDonald's voluntary resignation and up-front admission of a past wrongdoing was trumpeted across the country. The Madison, Wisconsin, paper gave the story prominent display, but chronicled MacDonald's behavior as unusually straightforward and honest. Here was someone who "expressed sorrow and asked forgiveness. He acknowledged that he had made a mistake and did not try to shift the blame to anyone else." Instead of blasting another fundamentalist as a religious failure, this newspaper in a liberal town, contained an editorial entitled, "Candor, Contrition a Welcome Change."

[39]Gordon MacDonald was formally restored to public ministry of the gospel at a recommissioning service at Grace Chapel in Lexington, Massachusetts, in May of 1988. He has since pastored Trinity Church (Baptist General Conference) in east-side Manhattan, with a growing ministry among young professionals. He also continues an extensive writing and speaking ministry.

[40]Jim Lundgren was active in IVCF as a student at the University of Illinois, joining the staff in 1973 in central Wisconsin. In 1975 he was made an area director for the state of Wis-

consin. Later he moved to the area director post for Metro-Chicago and northern Illinois. He became a regional director in 1982, a divisional director in 1983 and an associate director of campus ministries in 1990.

[41]Jim Kay was a key man at a key time in InterVarsity's history. He enabled the board to act swiftly to put Dunkerton in the presidency. He also made an effort to interact with staff following the resignation of MacDonald to find out what they were thinking and to elicit new trust in the board of trustees.

[42]Sam Barkat, InterVarsity vice president and director of multi-ethnic ministries, was vice president for academic affairs at The King's College (New York) before joining the staff of IVCF. He has had twenty-eight years in higher education as a professor of psychology and various administrative posts.

Chapter 16/At the Crossroads: Decade of the 1980s

[1]Telephone interview on August 21, 1990, with Masaya Hibino, pastor of the Church of Christ, Presbyterian, in Chicago for twenty-four years, now pastor of the Wintersburg Presbyterian Church, Garden Grove, California.

[2]Information taken from Nancy Sanborn's article, "InterVarsity's Other 'Urbana,' " *InterVarsity* magazine, Winter 1989-90, p. 12, and an interview with John Roeckeman, July 21, 1990.

[3]Interview with Bob Fryling, November 20, 1987.

[4]Pete Sommer left his regional director post in 1990 to become a national trainer, helping field staff raise the support for their ministry.

[5]In the early days of IVCF, the itineration of staff would have made it impossible to have a staff member speak at every chapter meeting. Even so, Stacey Woods was concerned about chapters and regions becoming ingrown and told staff, "Get your students in touch with great men and women of God from outside InterVarsity circles."

[6]Information taken from interview with Regional Director Bobby Gross on August 26, 1990, and from Georgia Beaverson, "In All Its Diversity," *InterVarsity* magazine, p. 11.

[7]Interview with Doug Whallon, August 24, 1990.

[8]Interview with John Bower, June 16, 1988.

[9]Interview with Norm Swett, March 22, 1988.

[10]Interview with Terry Erickson, August 20, 1990.

[11]Pete Wilson, a Texas staff member, was driving the car. He suffered critical multiple injuries, but escaped with his life.

[12]"Setting the Stage for Evangelism," Annual Report 1986, p. 4.

[13]Bobby Gross was active in InterVarsity at University of North Carolina, coming on staff after his graduation in 1977. He served as a staffworker in Gainesville, Florida, for four years. In 1981 he was sent as Team Leader to southern Florida to open up work there, becoming an area director in 1983. He moved to Manhattan the summer of 1990 to become the regional director for New York, succeeding Janet Luhrs Balajthy.

[14]Bob Fryling, Annual Report of Campus Ministries Division, 1989.

[15]Jim Lundgren, Great Lakes West Regional Report, 1989-90.

[16]John Kyle and his wife Lois served with Wycliffe Bible Translators in the Philippines for two terms, doing administrative work for the mission before returning to the States in the late 1960s to begin Mission to the World for his denomination. He had many contacts with InterVarsity prior to joining the staff as a speaker and counselor to students. Kyle has a zeal for reaching the world for Christ and is eager to see students reach the mission field as career missionaries. He left InterVarsity following Urbana 87 to return to the Presbyterian Church of America's Mission to the World program.

[17]*Missions Handbook,* 14th edition (Grand Rapids: MARC/Zondervan, 1989), p. 51, reports 21,200 short-term missionaries in 1985. In 1988 the report indicates 30,748 short-term missionaries.

[18]Taken from an interview with John Kyle, October 15, 1988, and *Case for Support,* written July 23, 1980, prepared by Mayes International, Dallas, Texas.

[19]Letter from Barney Ford to Terry Morrison, dated April 3, 1979.

[20]Interview with John Kyle, October 18, 1988.

[21]Offerings for IFES have been affected by the inclusion of offerings for hunger relief. At

Urbana 79, $322,000 was given to IFES, with no hunger relief. Offerings at Urbana 84 were $240,000 for IFES, $120,000 for hunger relief. In 1987, $270,000 was given to IFES, with $200,000 for world hunger. The analysis of these figures must take into consideration increasing attendance at Urbanas.

[22]An overflow of about fifteen hundred to two thousand met in another auditorium for the evening meetings, seeing the convention by video screen. Most often these were InterVarsity personnel and missionaries.

[23]Dan Harrison was born in Tibet of missionary parents. He became familiar with InterVarsity through Student Foreign Missions Fellowship at Bryan College (Tennessee). Later when he studied at Cornell University (New York) he was involved in the IV chapter there. From 1966 to 1974 he taught high school in Papua New Guinea under Wycliffe Bible Translators. He also served as area director and vice president for Wycliffe. Before coming to InterVarsity Harrison was executive vice president of the English Language Institute/China.

[24]Interview and correspondence with Mary Thompson, June 1990. Mary Thompson's father was a Lutheran pastor, and she was a committed Christian when she went to the University of Minnesota for her bachelor of science degree in the early sixties. She went on to California State University in Los Angeles for her master's degree and joined NCF staff in 1968. Mary has played a strategic role in the development of NCF across the country.

[25]Interview with Barney Ford, October 25, 1989.

[26]Nancy Fox and later Carolyn Boyes served as B & L Coordinators, carrying the organizational responsibility for the training program during the last fifteen years.

[27]Bob Grahmann is also coordinator of discipleship resources.

[28]Judy Johnson was involved in InterVarsity as an undergraduate student, and as an alumna did volunteer work with students. She joined IV staff in 1976 as a campus staff member in Minnesota. In 1980 she became a team leader and in 1982 was made associate regional director for training in the Central Region. She has held her current post as NISET director since 1986.

[29]This spring-vacation evangelism project was formerly called the Ft. Lauderdale Evangelism Project. When the popular place for students to gather changed, the evangelism project moved with them and changed its name.

[30]David Bryant joined the missions department staff in 1977 as a missions specialist. His book *In The Gap*, published by IV Missons, and his organization of concerts of prayer made significant contributions to student chapters where such prayer meetings are often regular events. He left InterVarsity in 1987 to begin a separate Concerts of Prayer organization which ministers in churches and other Christian gatherings.

[31]Scott Wilson did his undergraduate work at Westminster College (Pennsylvania) and went on to Gordon-Conwell Theological Seminary for an M.Div. degree before joining InterVarsity's TWENTYONEHUNDRED team in 1974.

[32]Ken DeRuiter left a long-term military career to begin a Christian literature ministry by establishing four Christian bookstores in New Jersey in 1981. Reading Francis Schaeffer's *Death in the City* (IVP) was a turning point for Ken and his wife, Jacqueline, and they pursued a vision of getting thoughtful Christian literature into the hands of others. DeRuiter's twenty-one years of active military service gave him experience in management and business. He has an M.B.A. in financial management from George Washington University.

[33]Yvonne Vinkemulder has been on the staff of IVCF since August 1961, when she became secretary for Regional Director Keith Hunt. She served as the director of development from 1975 to 1980 when, under the encouragement of IVCF management, she went to law school at the University of Miami. She returned in September 1983 as legal counsel for InterVarsity. The next year she was elected Secretary of the IVCF Board and appointed General Counsel.

[34]"Lord of the Universe, Hope of the World" had been the theme of Urbana 73, which the University of Illinois InterVarsity students were using, utilizing old posters—or at least the theme—for their publicity.

Bibliography

Barclay, Oliver. *Whatever Happened to the Jesus Lane Lot?* Leicester, England: Inter-Varsity Press, 1977.

Beahm, William H. "Factors in the Development of the Student Volunteer Movement for Foreign Missions." Dissertation, University of Chicago, 1941.

Benjamin, Barbara. *The Impossible Community.* Downers Grove, Ill.: InterVarsity Press, 1978.

Buckley, William F., Jr. *God and Man at Yale.* Washington, D.C.: Henry Regnery Co., 1951.

Donald, Mel. "A Spreading Tree." An unpublished history of Inter-Varsity Christian Fellowship of Canada, 1928-88.

Grun, Bernard. *The Timetables of History.* New York: Simon & Schuster, 1979.

Guinness, Howard. *Journey Among Students.* Sydney, Australia: Anglican Information Office, 1978.

Hopkins, C. Howard. *A History of the Y.M.C.A. in North America.* New York: Association Press, 1951.

_____ . *John R. Mott.* Grand Rapids, Mich.: Eerdmans 1979.

Horowitz, Helen Lefkowitz. *Campus Life.* New York: Alred A. Knopf, 1987.

Howard, David M. *Student Power in World Evangelism.* Downers Grove, Ill.: Inter-Varsity Press, 1970.

Hummel, Charles E. *Campus Christian Witness.* Downers Grove, Ill.: InterVarsity Press, 1958.

Johnson, Douglas. *Contending for the Faith.* Leicester, England: Inter-Varsity Press, 1979.

Latourette, Kenneth Scott. *A History of the Expansion of Christianity.* Vol. 5. Grand Rapids, Mich.: Zondervan, 1943.

Levine, Arthur. *When Dreams and Heroes Died.* San Francisco: Jossey-Bass, 1981.

Little, Paul E. "A History of Inter-Varsity Christian Fellowship and its Affiliated Movements in the United States." Unfinished Ph.D. dissertation. Papers given to us by the kindness of his widow, Marie H. Little.

Lowman, Pete. *The Day of His Power.* Leicester, England: Inter-Varsity Press, 1983.

Marsden, George. *Reforming Fundamentalism.* Grand Rapids, Mich.: Eerdmans, 1987.

Norton, H. Wilbert. *To Stir the Church.* Madison, Wis.: SFMF, 1986.

Pollock, John. *A Cambridge Movement.* London: John Murray, 1953.

_____ . *Moody.* Grand Rapids, Mich.: Zondervan, 1967.

Rashdall, Hastings. *The Universities of Europe in the Middle Ages.* 3 vols. Oxford: Clarendon Press, 1936.

Rouse, Ruth. *The World's Student Christian Federation.* London: SCM Press, 1948.

Shedd, Clarence P. *Two Centuries of Student Christian Movements.* New York: Association Press, 1934.

Tatlow, Tissington. *The Story of the Student Christian Movement.* London: SCM Press, 1948.

Troutman, Charles H. "The Universities and the Christian Faith." Unpublished papers, 1981.

Wilder, Robert P. *The Student Volunteer Movement for Foreign Missions: Some Personal Reminiscences of Its Origin and Early History.* New York: Student Volunteer Movement, 1935.

Woods, C. Stacey. *Some Ways of God.* Downers Grove, Ill.: InterVarsity Press, 1975.

_____ . *The Growth of a Work of God.* Downers Grove, Ill.: InterVarsity Press, 1978.

INDEX OF NAMES

SUBJECT INDEX

Subjects listed in the Timeline and Urbana Statistics are not included in this index.